Mind/Body Integration
Essential Readings
in Biofeedback

Mind/Body Integration
Essential Readings
in Biofeedback

Edited by
Erik Peper
San Francisco State University
San Francisco, California

Sonia Ancoli
University of California
San Francisco, California

and

Michele Quinn
Psychophysiological Treatment Center
Oxnard, California

PLENUM PRESS • **NEW YORK AND LONDON**

Library of Congress Cataloging in Publication Data

Main entry under title:

Mind/body integration.

Bibliography: p.
Includes index.
1. Biofeedback training. 2. Psychotherapy. 3. Medicine, Psychosomatic. I. Peper,
Erik. II. Ancoli, Sonia. III. Quinn, Michele, [DNLM: 1. Biofeedback (psychology)
2. Electroencephalography. 3. Electromyography. WL103 M663]
BF319.5.B5M55   615.851   78-27224
ISBN 0-306-40102-9

First Printing – June 1979
Second Printing – October 1981

© 1979 Plenum Press, New York
A Division of Plenum Publishing Corporation
227 West 17th Street, New York, N.Y. 10011

Printed in the United States of America

Acknowledgments

The editors would like to thank the following copyright holders for permission to reprint previously published articles in this volume.

American Association for the Advancement of Science
Control and training of individual motor units, *by* J. V. Basmajian [pp. 371–375], originally published in *Science*, 1963, *141*, 440–441.

American Medical Association
Clinical applications of biofeedback training: A review of evidence, *by* E. B. Blanchard and L. D. Young [pp. 77–110], originally published in *Archives of General Psychiatry*, 1974, *30*, 573–589.

Control of states of consciousness. II. Attainment through external feedback augmenting control of psychophysiological variables, *by* K. Gaarder [pp. 47–56], originally published in *Archives of General Psychiatry*, 1971, *25*, 436–441.

Behavioral Engineering
Belief in biofeedback for the control of short-term stress, *by* J. D. Gibb, E. Stephan, and C. E. T. Rohm [pp. 223–227], originally published in *Behavioral Engineering*, 1975, *2*(3), 80–83.

Behavioral Science
Dysponesis: A neurophysiological factor in functional disorders, *by* G. B. Whatmore and D. R. Kohli [pp. 379–410], originally published in *Behavioral Science*, 1968, *13*(2), 102–124.

Biofeedback and Self-Regulation
Detection of EEG abnormalities with feedback stimulation, *by* T. Mulholland and F. Benson [pp 299–312], originally published in 1976, *1*(1), 47–61.

Facts vs. myths in EMG biofeedback, *by* J. V. Basmajian [pp. 377–378], originally published in 1976, *1*(4), 369–371.

Feedback-aided self-regulation of skin temperature with a single feedback locus, *by* E. Taub and C. S. Emurian [pp. 469–487], originally published in 1976, *1*(2), 147–168.

Biofeedback Society of California
Standard specifications for the description of biofeedback instruments, *by* H. Toomim, S. L. Schandler, T. H. Spiegel, J. A. Freeman, and W. Elder [pp. 261–267], originally published in *Handbook of the Biofeedback Society of California*. San Francisco: Biofeedback Society of California, 1976. Pp. 105–111.

A bioelectric glossary, *by* H. Toomim, S. L. Schandler, T. H. Spiegel, J. A. Freeman, and W. Elder [pp. 269–273], originally published in *Handbook of the Biofeedback Society of California*. San Francisco: Biofeedback Society of California, 1976. Pp. 112–116.

Biofeedback Technology Inc.
The possible uses of biofeedback in education, *by* E. Peper [pp. 111–117], originally published in *Journal of Biofeedback*, 1976, *3*(2). 13–19.

BioMonitoring Applications
EMG biofeedback in physical therapy, *by* C. K. Fernando [pp. 453–464], originally published in C. K. Fernando, *How to use EMG biofeedback in physical therapy*. New York: BMA Audio Cassette #T32, 1976.

Brain Information Service, UCLA
Autoregulation of the EEG alpha rhythm: A program for the study of consciousness, *by* J. Kamiya [pp. 289–297], originally published in M. H. Chase (Ed.), *Operant control of brain activity* (*Perspectives in the brain sciences*, Vol. 2). Berkeley, California: Brain Information Service, UCLA, 1974. Pp. 227–236.

California Dental Association
The use of biofeedback devices in the treatement of bruxism, *by* W. K. Solberg and J. Rugh [pp. 553–556], originally published in *Journal of the Southern California Dental Association*, 1972, *40*, 852–853.

Division of Psychotherapy, American Psychological Association
GSR biofeedback in psychotherapy: Some clinical observations, *by* M. K. Toomim and H. Toomim [pp. 513–521], originally published in *Psychotherapy: Theory, research and practice*, 1975, *12*(1), 33–38.

Epilepsia
Effects of central cortical EEG feedback training on incidence of poorly controlled seizures, *by* M. B. Sterman and L. R. Macdonald [pp. 347–362], originally published in *Epilepsia*, 1978, *19*, 207–222.

Grune & Stratton, Inc.
Biofeedback treatment in medicine and psychiatry: An ultimate placebo?, *by* C. F. Strebel and B. C. Glueck [pp. 207–222], originally published in *Seminars in Psychiatry*, 1973, *5*(4), 379–392.

Psychosomatic self-regulation of migraine headaches, *by* J. Sargent, E. D. Walters, and E. E. Green [pp. 493–506], originally published in *Seminars in Psychiatry*, 1973, *5*(4), 415–428.

Harper & Row
Autogenic training, *by* W. Luthe [pp. 167–186], taken in part from About the methods of autogenic therapy, *by* W. Luthe and S. R. Blumberger, originally published in E. D. Willkower and H. Warnes (Eds.), *The psychosomatic approach in medical practice*. New York: Harper & Row, 1977. Pp. 146–163.

The Lancet
12-Month follow-up of yoga and biofeedback in the management of hypertension, *by* C. Patel [pp. 529–533], originally published in *Lancet*, 1975, *1*, 62–65.

Randomized controlled trial of yoga and biofeedback in management of hypertension, *by* C. Patel and W. North [pp. 535–540], originally published in *Lancet*, 1973. *2*, 93–95.

The New England Journal of Medicine
Operant conditioning of rectosphincteric responses in the treatment of fecal incontinence, *by* B. T. Engel, P. Nikoomanesh, and M. M. Schuster [pp. 545–551], originally published in *The New England Journal of Medicine*, 1974, *290*, 646–649.

Plenum Publishing Corporation
Biofeedback and physiological patterning in human emotion and consciousness, *by* G. Schwartz [pp. 57–67], originally published in J. Beatty and H. Legewie (Eds.), *Biofeedback and behavior*. New York: Plenum, 1977. Pp. 293–306.

Cultivated low arousal—an antistress response?, *by* J. Stoyva and T. Budzynski [pp. 411–433], originally published in L. V. DiCara (Ed.), *Limbic system and autonomic nervous system research*. New York: Plenum, 1974. Pp. 369–394.

Prentice-Hall, Inc.
Learned control of physiological function and disease, *by* D. Shapiro and R. S. Surwit [pp. 7–46], originally published in H. Leitenberg (Ed.), *Handbook of behavior modification and behavior therapy*. Englewood Cliffs, New Jersey: Prentice-Hall, Inc., 1976. Pp. 74–123.

Scott, Foresman & Co.
Passive attention: The gateway to consciousness and autonomic control, *by* E. Peper [pp. 119–124], originally published in P. G. Zimbardo and F. L. Ruch (Eds.), *Psychology and life*. Glenview, Illinois: Scott, Foresman & Co., 1977. Pp. 7A–7D.

Springer-Verlag
Feedback regulation of the alpha electroencephalogram activity through control of the internal and external parameters, *by* E. Peper [pp. 313–324], originally published in *Kybernetik*, 1970, *7*, 107–112.

Tektronix, Inc.
Blood pressure, *by* P. Strong [pp. 527–528], originally published in P. Strong, *Biophysical measurements*. Beaverton, Oregon: Tektronix, Inc., 1971. Pp. 100–101.

Electrodes, *by* P. Strong [pp. 253–259], originally published in P. Strong, *Biophysical measurements*. Beaverton, Oregon: Tektronix, Inc., 1971. Pp. 219–227.

Electroencephalography, *by* P. Strong [pp. 283–287], originally published in P. Strong, *Biophysical measurements*. Beaverton, Oregon: Tektronix, Inc., 1971. Pp. 131–137.

Galvanic skin reflex, *by* P. Strong [pp. 509–512], originally published in P. Strong, *Biophysical measurements*. Beaverton, Oregon: Tektronix, Inc., 1971. Pp. 197–199.

Muscle action and the sensory system, *by* P. Strong [pp. 367–370], originally published in P. Strong, *Biophysical measurements*. Beaverton, Oregon: Tektronix, Inc., 1971. Pp. 31–35.

The University of Chicago
Problems in biofeedback training: An experiential analogy–urination, *by* E. Peper [pp. 69–75], originally published in *Perspectives in biology and medicine*, 1976, *19*(3), 404–412.

The Williams & Wilkins Company
Biofeedback equipment (Chapter 12), *by* K. Gaarder and P. Montgomery [pp. 241–251], originally published in K. Gaarder and P. Montgomery, *Clinical biofeedback: A procedural manual*. Baltimore, Maryland: Williams & Wilkins Co., 1977. Pp. 193–204.

On the mechanisms of the feedback control of human brain wave activity, *by* J. J. Lynch and D. A. Paskewitz [pp. 325–340], originally published in *Journal of Nervous and Mental Disease*, 1971, *153*, 205–217.

Contributors

Sonia Ancoli, Langley Porter Neuropsychiatric Institute, University of California, San Francisco, California 94143

John V. Basmajian, Department of Medicine, McMaster University, and Chedoke Hospitals, Hamilton, Ontario, Canada.

René Beck, Department of Psychology, San Francisco State University, San Francisco, California 94134

Frank Benson, Neurobehavior Center, Veterans Administration Medical Center, Boston, Massachusetts 02130

Edward B. Blanchard, Department of Psychology, State University of New York at Albany, Albany, New York 12222

Charles Burgar, Department of Psychiatry, University of Texas Health Science Center, San Antonio, Texas 78284

Thomas Budzynski, Biofeedback Institute of Denver, Englewood, Colorado 80111

Dona Culver, Biofeedback Clinic, Student Health Service, University of Colorado, Boulder, Colorado 80309

W. Elder, Biofeedback Research Institute, Los Angeles, California 90048

Cleeve S. Emurian, Department of Psychiatry and Behavioral Sciences, The Johns Hopkins School of Medicine, Baltimore, Maryland 21205

Bernard T. Engel, Laboratory of Behavioral Sciences, National Institute on Aging, Baltimore City Hospitals, Baltimore, Maryland 21224, and Johns Hopkins University School of Medicine, Baltimore, Maryland 21205

C. K. Fernando, Physical Therapy Department, Schwab Rehabilitation Hospital, and Mount Sinai Medical Center, Chicago, Illinois 60608

J. A. Freeman, Autogenic Systems Inc., Berkeley, California 94710

Kenneth Gaarder, Gerontology Research Center, National Institute of Aging, Baltimore City Hospitals, Baltimore, Maryland 21224

J. Douglas Gibb, Department of Speech and Dramatic Arts, Brigham Young University, Provo, Utah 84602

Bernard C. Glueck, Institute of Living, Hartford, Connecticut 06106

Alyce M. Green, Biofeedback Center, Research Department, The Menninger Foundation, Topeka, Kansas 66601

Elmer E. Green, Biofeedback Center, Research Department, The Menninger Foundation, Topeka, Kansas 66601

Judith Green, Biofeedback Consultant, Aims Biofeedback Institute, Aims Community College, Greeley, Colorado 80631

Elmer Grossman, Private Practice, Berkeley Pediatric Medical Group, Berkeley, California 94709

Joe Kamiya, Langley Porter Neuropsychiatric Institute, University of California, San Francisco, California 94143

Daniel R. Kohli, Pacific Northwest Research Foundation, and Private Practice (Internal Medicine and Functional Disorders), Medical–Dental Building, Seattle, Washington 98101

David Low, Stanford Research Institute, Menlo Park, California 94025

Wolfgang Luthe, Medical Centre, Montreal, Canada

James J. Lynch, Department of Psychiatry, University of Maryland School of Medicine, Baltimore, Maryland 21201

L. R. Macdonald, Veterans Administration Hospital, Sepulveda, California 91343, and Departments of Anatomy and Psychiatry, University of California, Los Angeles, California 90024

Penny Montgomery, Department of Psychiatry/Division of Psychology, University of Texas Health Science Center, San Antonio, Texas 78284

Thomas Mulholland, Veterans Administration Hospital, Bedford, Massachusetts

Parviz Nikoomanesh, Baltimore City Hospitals, Baltimore, Maryland 21224, and Johns Hopkins University School of Medicine, Baltimore, Maryland 21205

W. R. S. North, MRC Department of Epidemiology, Northwick Park Hospital, Harrow, Middlesex, England

Leon S. Otis, Departments of Psychobiology and Physiology, Stanford Research Institute, Menlo Park, California 94025

David A. Paskewitz, Department of Psychiatry, University of Maryland School of Medicine, Baltimore, Maryland 21201

Chandra Patel, General Practitioner, Croyden, Surrey, England. Present affiliation: Senior Research Fellow, Department of Epidemiology and Medical Statistics, London School of Hygiene and Tropical Medicine, University of London, London WC1, England

Dale M. Patterson, Center for Self-Regulation and Biofeedback, Carrier Clinic Foundation, Belle Mead, New Jersey 08502

Kenneth R. Pelletier, Department of Psychiatry, University of California School of Medicine, San Francisco, California 94143

Erik Peper, Center for Interdisciplinary Science, San Francisco State University, San Francisco, California 94134

Michele Quinn, Psychophysiological Treatment Center, Oxnard, California 93030

C. E. Tapie Rohm, Jr., College of Osteopathic Medicine, Ohio State University, Athens, Ohio 45701

John D. Rugh, Department of Restorative Dentistry, University of Texas Health Science Center, San Antonio, Texas 78284

Joseph D. Sargent, Department of Neurology, Neurosurgery and Internal Medicine, The Menninger Foundation, Topeka, Kansas 66601

S. L. Schandler, Department of Psychology, Chapman College, Orange, California 92666, and Human Physiology Research, Veterans Administration Medical Center, Sepulveda, California 91343

Carol Schneider, Biofeedback Clinic, Student Health Service, University of Colorado, Boulder, Colorado 80309

Marvin M. Schuster, Division of Digestive Diseases, Baltimore City Hospitals, Baltimore, Maryland 21224, and Departments of Medicine and Psychiatry, Johns Hopkins University School of Medicine, Baltimore, Maryland 21205

Gary E. Schwartz, Department of Psychology, Yale University, and Department of Psychiatry, Yale University School of Medicine, New Haven, Connecticut 06520

Stephen Shambaugh, Human Development and Aging Program, University of California, San Francisco, Berkeley, California 94143

David Shapiro, Department of Psychiatry, University of California, Los Angeles, California 90024

Barbara Silverberg, Autogenic Systems, Inc., Berkeley, California 94710

William K. Solberg, School of Dentistry, University of California, Los Angeles, California 90024

T. H. Spiegel, Biofeedback Program, Ross–Loos Group, Los Angeles, California 90026

Eric Stephan, Communications Department, Interpersonal and Organizational Division, Brigham Young University, Provo, Utah 84602

M. B. Sterman, Departments of Anatomy and Psychiatry, University of California, Los Angeles, California 90024, and Neuropsychology Research, Veterans Administration Medical Center, Sepulveda, California 91343

Johann Stoyva, Department of Psychiatry, University of Colorado Medical Center, Denver, Colorado 80262

Charles F. Stroebel, Psychophysiology Clinic and Laboratories, Institute of Living, Hartford, Connecticut 06106, and Department of Psychiatry, University of Connecticut Health Center and Medical School, Storrs, Connecticut 06268

P. Strong, Tektronix, Inc., Beaverton, Oregon 97077

Richard S. Surwit, Department of Psychiatry, Duke University Medical Center, Durham, North Carolina 27710

Barbara Tandy, Institute for Research in Social Behavior, Oakland, California 94612

Edward Taub, Institute for Behavioral Research, Silver Spring, Maryland 20910

Marjorie K. Toomim, Biofeedback Institute of Los Angeles, Los Angeles, California 90048

Hershel Toomim, Biofeedback Research Institute, Los Angeles, California 90048

Ann Turner, Psychiatrist, Palo Alto, California 94301

E. Dale Walters, Biofeedback Center, Research Department, The Menninger Foundation, Topeka, Kansas 66601

George B. Whatmore, Pacific Northwest Research Foundation, and Private Practice (Internal Medicine and Functional Disorders), Medical–Dental Building, Seattle, Washington 98101

Larry D. Young, Department of Psychology, University of Mississippi, University, Mississippi 38677

I hear, and I forget;
I see, and I remember;
I do, and I understand.

—Chinese proverb

This book would have remained a dream without the support of our many teachers. For their faith and encouragement in our growth and exploration, we thank Lester Fehmi, Joe Kamiya, Gay Luce, and Thomas B. Mulholland, and our parents, Nissan and Esther Ancoli, Philip and Gonda Peper, and Grace and Don Quinn.

We would also like to thank the following people, who, in their many ways, helped us in this endeavor: Susan Axelrod, Margaret Bomar, Adele Dybdahl, Reggie Eisenberg, Don Gerrard, Andrew G. Israel, J. Michael James, Casi Kushel, Elvira McKean, John McKean, Kenneth Russ, Sheelah Sigel, Charles Stroebel, Richard Surwit, Helena Weil, and David Sweet. We would especially like to thank Barbara Tandy, whose editorial help made our work so much easier, and our many students, experimental subjects, and clients, who unknowingly contributed so much to our growth.

Contents

Introduction

Biofeedback training is a research methodology and training procedure through which people can learn voluntary control over their internal physiological systems. It is a merger of multiple disciplines with interest deriving from many sources—from basic understanding of psychophysiology to a desire for enhanced self-awareness. The goals of biofeedback are to develop an increased awareness of relevant internal physiological functions, to establish control over these functions, to generalize control from an experimental or clinical setting to everyday life, and to focus attention on mind/body integration.

Biofeedback is explored in many different settings. In the university, biofeedback equipment and applications can be found in the departments of experimental and clinical psychology, counseling, physiology, biology, education, and the theater arts, as well as in the health service (student infirmary). Outside the university, biofeedback may be found in different departments of hospitals (such as physical medicine), private clinics, education and self-awareness groups, psychotherapy practices, and elsewhere. Its growth is still expanding, and excitement is still rising as a result of biofeedback's demonstration that autonomic functions can be brought under voluntary control and that the long-standing artificial separation between mind, body, and consciousness can be disproven.

This separation has been deeply rooted in modern Western thought since before the time of Descartes. Cartesian dualism (the separation of mind and body) strongly influenced the development of modern medical and psychological approaches to health. Society progressively delegated to the physician authority over the body below the neck, to the psychiatrist and psychologist the body above the neck, and to the clergy anything outside the body. Biofeedback can serve to reconnect the mind, body, and spirit. With the development of psychophysiological instrumentation, the correlation between mental and emotional events and the neurological processes is being elucidated. Through the further development of biofeedback instrumentation, this mind/body integration can be brought into the trainee's awareness. (The word *trainee* is used instead of *client* or *subject*, since we see biofeedback as a learning process.) Even more important is the implicit role of biofeedback in making individuals aware that they alone must take responsibility for the maintenance and control of their own health.

The philosophy of biofeedback training is based on the psychophysiological principle that Elmer Green and his associates, the early biofeedback investigators at the Menninger Foundation in Kansas, describe in Chapter 8. It proposes that every change that occurs in a physiological state is accompanied by a change in the mental and emotional state, whether conscious or unconscious, and vice versa. Understanding this philosophy of biofeedback is just a beginning to understanding biofeedback. In addition, the practitioner must also be able to discriminate true signals from noise (i.e., artifacts) and have a basic understanding of psychophysiology and the biofeedback equipment. In both cases, one needs to know what is going on inside the black boxes—the human being and the machine.

The instrumentation used in biofeedback continuously monitors the psychophysiological changes within the individual. Used as a tool, it becomes a psychophysiological mirror that reflects a physiological process back to the person. A neutral physiological signal from the body is amplified by biofeedback instruments and "fed back" to the subject through a sensory modality. In order for training to be successful, the physiological function to be controlled must be continuously monitored, the signal immediately fed back, and the subject motivated sufficiently to utilize the information. By practicing and using this procedure, the trainees may become aware of and adept at recognizing their own subtle physiological process and internal states, thus reflecting a mind/body integration.

As a training procedure, biofeedback can be used in the clinic, in the school, and/or for self-development. As a research tool, it can be used to test hypotheses, to investigate autonomic self-regulation, and to explore cybernetic patterned interactions (for an elaboration of cybernetic theory, see p. 275). When used in these fashions, biofeedback can be in the fore- or background of many other disciplines, used by itself, or immersed in other approaches. While at times it is used literally to reeducate a physiological system (e.g., neuromuscular reeducation), at other times it is used to illustrate a principle (e.g., different emotional states correspond to different body reactions). As a merging point for interdisciplinary science, its potential has not yet been realized.

Implicit in the paradigm of biofeedback is that it is *experiential;* it must be experienced. Regardless of how much one reads, it is impossible to describe how it feels or what a person does during the training to effect autonomic change. For example, anyone who has attempted to teach a child to ride a bicycle has experienced the frustration associated with the inability of words to describe the experience. Yet it is precisely in this experiential boundary that biofeedback has become one of the new and exciting tools and approaches of science. It integrates mind and body. In order to understand its potential and applied use, researchers, practitioners, and students must do it themselves. Only with the actual experience that autonomic self-regulation is possible does biofeedback begin to make sense.

This important concept is well illustrated by Peper (Chapters 4 and 6), who suggests that without the practitioners' knowingness (which means having *experienced* something that was previously believed) one would most likely terminate training prematurely. This suggests that a prerequisite for teaching biofeedback is that the researchers, practitioners, or teachers must have learned biofeedback autonomic control themselves before attempting to teach others. The cues that transmit this belief structure of knowingness are usually nonverbal, and they permeate the whole atmosphere.

The moment one attempts self-regulation, the critical questions arise: *what* to control and *why* to control. Is it healthy to have control over previously unconscious physiological functions? Is such control harmful? With these questions, biofeedback opens up new areas of exploration for the parameters of optimum and ideal human functioning, and raises the question, "What is health?"

Before attempting to answer these questions, it is important to consider the machinery of regulation and physiological equilibrium. The autonomic nervous system's primary function is to maintain a stable internal environment by mediating visceral activities (e.g., digestion, temperature, blood pressure) and emotional expressions (e.g., palpitations of the heart, clammy hands, blushing).

The autonomic nervous system is also represented in the central and peripheral nervous systems. These conceptual divisions of the nervous system are by no means mutually exclusive. Due to corticalization, higher conscious processes also influence autonomic regulation via neocortical, limbic, and thalamic projections,* along with emotional states and constant negative feedback from the internal milieu. So the effects of cognitions, emotions, and external and internal changes on vital visceral functions necessitate compensatory mechanisms (reflex arcs) that must act continuously to regulate and to prevent excessive fluctuations of visceral activities. These mechanisms, however, have biological limits, time/age restrictions, and efficiency boundaries.

Homeostasis is the concept expressing this maintenance—negative feedback that operates to stabilize the level of activity. All disease, illness, or injury represents a disruption of the equilibrium level of homeostasis; death is an expression of its ultimate failure.

When reconsidering the question (is it healthy to have control over physiological functions that are normally mediated below the level of waking consciousness or only vaguely recognized by the mind?), it is important to ask: Is the control applied toward a healthy state? If learning facilitates regulation of a function or behavior that operates to minimize extreme levels of activity in intensity, frequency, and/or duration, then it is of unquestionable value in the maintenance or reestablishment of a healthy state. The degree to which one can and does regulate, adjust, and coordinate one's mental/emotional and physical activities to harmonize with physiological needs, abilities, and limitations will ultimately allow us to define the parameters of optimal functioning—or health in the human organism.

While the boundaries of illness are known, many parameters of optimum functioning have not been explored. Research and clinical studies that have focused on autonomic self-regulation have discovered a number of parameters of autonomic control that are related to pathology. Consequently, it is important for people using biofeedback to be familiar with these. This is discussed in more detail in Section II.

ORGANIZATION OF THE BOOK

This book is an outgrowth of our own need to have a collection of articles on biofeedback readily available for teaching and learning, rather than scattered

---

* Perhaps it is time to adopt the synonym *trophotropic* system in preference to *autonomic* or *involuntary* nervous system.

through many journals. We chose articles from different frameworks, thus balancing the pure and applied areas. In this fashion, we hope to transmit the excitement and flavor of biofeedback practice. By using this collection of basic articles, the reader can alternate among overviews, generalizations, critical analyses, and research studies within a matrix of knowledge of psychophysiology and instrumentation.

Biofeedback is a tool through which the organism has conscious control over visceral responses; hence this book does not include animal studies or nonvoluntary conditioning paradigms (i.e., operant conditioning), although they can be a special case of biofeedback. Our focus is on the use of biofeedback to enhance the harmonious function of the individual by teaching self-awareness through self-regulation.

This collection of readings is crucial for the student who takes a class in biofeedback and needs a critical textbook and list of additional readings, for the professional who is currently applying or contemplating the inclusion of biofeedback into a professional practice, and for the interested reader and researcher who may sort through these articles (some of which have not been previously published) to expand their horizons.

The book is organized into 10 sections. The introduction of each section covers the salient points of the articles and those concepts that underlie the practice of biofeedback. Obviously this book is not exhaustive; for each article included, a number had to be discarded. Each section therefore has some suggested additional readings.

Section I is a general introduction to the different applications and concepts as well as the philosophies expounded within biofeedback. Sections II and III focus upon information critical to biofeedback, i.e., the use of adjunctive relaxation and homeostatic balancing techniques, the importance of belief structure and placebo, and the basic feedback equipment—electronics and instrumentation.

In each of the next five sections (IV–VIII: EEG, EMG, temperature, GSR, blood pressure) we have attempted to describe some physiology and some recording techniques, and have included, when available, a research study, a clinical application study, and a suggestive idea paper.

The book integrates applied, experimental, and pure theoretical areas, covering both analytical and speculative articles. Section IX introduces special devices and less common applications of biofeedback. The appendices contain additional sources of reading in biofeedback and related areas, information on biofeedback societies, and a list of biofeedback manufacturers. Our hope is that through all these articles, the reader will attain an overview—a gestalt—for the richness of biofeedback.

We hope that this collection is comprehensive enough to familiarize the reader with biofeedback's expanding breadth. It is our hope and wish that by delving into these articles, the reader can share with us the richness and excitement of biofeedback as an interdisciplinary process.

Erik Peper, Sonia Ancoli, and Michele Quinn

Berkeley

GENERAL OVERVIEW OF BIOFEEDBACK: AN INTRODUCTION

In his introduction to the 1973 *Biofeedback and Self-Regulation Annual*, Neal Miller, one of today's outstanding psychologists, stated, "This is a new area in which investigators should be bold in what they try but cautious in what they claim" (p. xviii). The area of biofeedback is no longer new. Many new investigators, practitioners, and students have joined the field; many have been bold in what they have tried. Through a sampling of the different theories, applied areas, and research, the chapters in this section provide an overview of the work done in biofeedback.

Shapiro and Surwit (Chapter 1) give an excellent introduction and review of recent clinical applications of biofeedback training with special emphasis on hypertension and cardiovascular control. Gaarder's article (Chapter 2), though written 6 years ago, still provides relevant information on the history of biofeedback. He also compares operant conditioning and biofeedback, thereby providing a good introduction to the beginner in this field.

Schwartz's article (Chapter 3) is more advanced but with careful reading will provide a stimulating approach to biofeedback. Schwartz takes us away from the idea of biofeedback as a single modality treatment to the idea of patterned self-regulation; since the body is controlled by the brain, no system acts independently. Only by considering patterned biofeedback training will we be able to further understand our physiology and its relation to emotion and consciousness, and thus find more efficient ways for learning control.

In Chapter 4, Peper clearly explores some of the more fundamental (and too often ignored) problems of biofeedback training and offers an analogy that all readers can relate to, i.e., urination. The basic postulates and questions raised here are crucial to the understanding of biofeedback and the reader is advised to keep them in mind while reading the remainder of this book.

The rest of the chapters in this section represent the wide range of possible applications of biofeedback training. Blanchard and Young (Chapter 5) offer a good critical review of clinical applications. Research done since that article was first written has improved and some of the problems and criticisms no longer apply. However, only by being aware of past problems can we avoid repeating them. Peper (Chapters 6 and 7) refers to educational use, Green, Green, and Walters (Chapter 8) refer to healing and creativity, Peper and Ancoli (Chapter 9) refer to the study of adepts and meditation, while Peper, Pelletier, and Tandy (Chapter 10) integrate the frontiers and concepts of biofeedback. These are just a few examples of how biofeedback training can be used, and it is hoped that they will stimulate the readers' imaginations to expand the range of traditional as well as nontraditional applications.

In summary, there are some central issues and questions that continuously arise. As the readers read these articles and those in the following sections, the following concepts should be kept in mind:

1. Biofeedback training is broad in that it ranges from clinical applications to the study of altered states.
2. Biofeedback training is an approach that deals with processes once seen as automatic and uncontrollable.
3. Biofeedback training is limited by the equipment (technology) used.

The following questions should also be kept in mind:

1. How is biofeedback training being used as a research tool?
2. Can one body system truly reflect the whole person or does one need to record multiple systems?
3. Is learned control over these autonomic systems healthy?
4. How does one achieve control?

For further overviews, the reader is referred to the following books: Beatty and Legewie (1977), Birk (1973), Brown (1974, 1977), Green and Green (1977), Hume (1976), Schwartz and Beatty (1977), Stern and Ray (1977), and the *Biofeedback and Self-Regulation Annuals* (1971–1976). In addition, Butler (1978) has compiled an exhaustive bibliography arranged by topics, and McCrady and McCrady (1975) have edited a useful annotated bibliography.

REFERENCES

Beatty, J., & Legewie, H. *Biofeedback and behavior*. New York: Plenum, 1977.
Biofeedback and self-regulation annuals. Chicago: Aldine, 1971–1976.
Birk, L. (Ed.). *Biofeedback: Behavioral medicine*. New York: Grune and Stratton, 1973.
Brown, B. *New mind, new body*. New York: Harper & Row, 1974.
Brown, B. *Stress and the art of biofeedback*. New York: Harper & Row, 1977.
Butler, F. *Biofeedback and self-regulation: A guide to the literature*. New York: Plenum, 1978.
Green, E. E., & Green, A. M. *Beyond biofeedback*. New York: Delacorte, 1977.
Hume, W. I. *Biofeedback: Research and therapy*. Montreal: Eden Press, 1976.
McCrady, R. E., & McCrady, J. *Biofeedback: An annotated bibliography of published research with human subjects since 1960*. Pomona, California: Behavioral Instrument Co., 1975.
Miller, N. E. Introduction: Current issues and key problems. In N. Miller, T. X. Barber, L. V. DiCara, J. Kamiya, D. Shapiro, and J. Stoyva. (Eds.), *Biofeedback and self-control 1973*. Chicago: Aldine, 1974.
Schwartz, G., & Beatty, J. *Biofeedback theory and research*. New York: Academic Press, 1977.
Stern, R., & Ray, W. J. *Biofeedback*. Homewood, Illinois: Dow Jones-Irwin, 1977.

Learned Control of Physiological Function and Disease

David Shapiro and Richard S. Surwit

This chapter concerns itself with the application of learning techniques to the remediation of disease. Although the idea of teaching people to control their physiology can be traced back to antiquity, learned control of visceral responses and other involuntary functions has only recently come under systematic investigation by psychologists. This research has developed techniques that, for the first time, have enabled therapists to place the physiological activity of the body under the control of environmental contingencies, in much the same way as has been done with other types of behavior. In essence, it now seems feasible to extend the scope of behavior modification into the domain of medicine.

Traditionally, the area of overlap between medicine and psychology involving the psychological treatment of physical diseases is known as *psychosomatic medicine* (Dunbar, 1943). This field has generally concerned itself with the relationship between emotion and illness, and has relied mainly on the *personality* of the patient as both the prognosticator and the focus of therapy (Alexander & Flagg, 1965). The psychosomatic approach to disease is essentially the same as psychodynamic methods of dealing with behavioral disorders and falls prey to the numerous criticisms that have been leveled at the latter (e.g., Bandura, 1969). In brief, such formulations invoke unnecessary hypothetical constructs between the stimuli confronting the patient and the behavior in question. This results in a treatment plan aimed more at a *hypothetical cause* than at the presenting problem itself. Therapy may therefore be slow and inefficient with the presenting symptoms largely neglected. In contrast to the approach of psychosomatic medicine, a behavioral model employing learning techniques would see as its target for therapy the environment of the individual rather than his or her personality. For this reason, Birk (1973) has proposed calling this new area of research and treatment *behavioral medicine*.

Although the application of learning techniques to behavioral disorders followed nearly half a century of animal and human laboratory experimentation,

David Shapiro • Department of Psychiatry, University of California, Los Angeles, California 90024. Richard S. Surwit • Department of Psychiatry, Duke University Medical Center, Durham, North Carolina 27710. Sections of the original article have been deleted so as not to repeat information in other sections of this book. The reference list, however, has remained intact. For the entire article the reader is referred to the original reference.

the clinical applications of biofeedback and autonomic instrumental conditioning have been dovetailed in less than 10 years of basic research. In many areas, clinical application has preceded systematic research and is therefore hard to evaluate. Consequently, this chapter has been organized to provide the reader with a grasp of the experimental background upon which each treatment application is based. The following section presents an overview of the evaluation of the basic research on instrumental autonomic learning in animals and man. Further sections are ordered with respect to the amount of research done in each area. Each contains a brief review of the physiology of the disorder, the documented ability of the relevant systems to be brought under learned control, and clinical experiments and/or case studies exploring the effectiveness of biofeedback and instrumental learning techniques in the treatment of the disorder. The final sections of the chapter are devoted to a discussion of theoretical, methodological, and clinical issues in the learned control of physiological functions and its application to disease.

REVIEW OF EXPERIMENTAL FOUNDATIONS

The earliest research on the instrumental modification of autonomically mediated behaviors was carried out in human subjects. Although this research involved numerous complications of subject cooperation and motivation, individual differences, and reward definition, it is of historical interest that much of it preceded the more systematic and highly controlled animal work to follow.

One of the most promising functions from the standpoint of instrumental conditioning was electrodermal activity, which is under sympathetic nervous system innervation. Early in the 1960s, a number of laboratories independently reported that the human electrodermal response, measured as either a skin resistance or a skin potential change, could be relatively increased or decreased in frequency by contingent reinforcement (Fowler & Kimmel, 1962; Johnson, 1963; Shapiro, Crider, & Tursky, 1964). The electrodermal response is typically considered a reflexive, automatic, or "involuntary" response, and there is an enormous body of research showing how it relates to attentional, emotional, and motivational variables (see Edelberg, 1972). The electrodermal response also occurs spontaneously, without being correlated with external stimuli, and it can thus be classified as an unelicited or emitted response. The spontaneous electrodermal response is relatively discrete in nature, and it occurs intermittently. Unlike continuously varying biological functions such as heart rate or skin temperature, the fact that the electrodermal response is discrete lends it still further to operant analysis and experimentation. It is akin to a simple response of the skeletal muscles and can be analyzed by the traditional methods of operant conditioning.

One study in this series (Shapiro et al., 1964) is highlighted because it contains within it many of the critical issues that have preoccupied basic researchers in the field. In this study, a spontaneous fluctuation of palmar skin potential of a given amplitude was selected as the response to be brought under

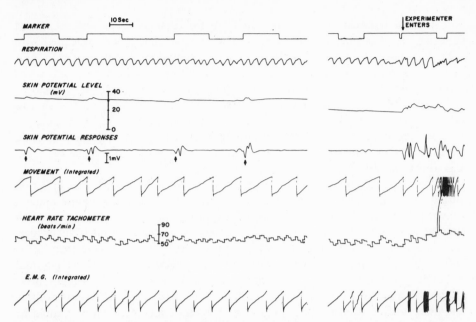

Figure 1. Portion of a typical record of a subject reinforced for criterion spontaneous skin potential responses (panel on left). Arrows indicate reinforced responses. Marker indicates onset of a 1.5-second tone followed by a "time-out" period. Tone is cue to subject of a monetary bonus. Note that polarity of "skin potential responses" channel (AC recording with 1-second time constant) is opposite from polarity of "skin potential level" channel (DC recording). Panel on right indicates reaction of subject to experimenter opening subject room door and talking with subject (Crider, Shapiro, & Tursky, 1966. Copyright 1966 by the American Psychological Association. Reprinted by permission).

control by means of operant conditioning (Figure 1). One group of subjects was given a reward each time the response occurred, and a second group was given the same number of rewards but at times when the response was absent. All subjects were given the same instructions, that the purpose of the experiment was to study the effectiveness of various devices for measuring thought processes and that their task was to think actively about emotional experiences. The subjects were instructed that each time the apparatus detected an "emotional thought" they would hear a tone and earn a 5¢ bonus. As a result of the reinforcement contingency, the first group showed increases in response rate relative to the second group, which showed a decrement in response rate over time. That the same reward could be used either to enhance *or* to diminish the autonomic behavior eliminated the explanation that the eliciting effect of the reinforcer itself could account for the observed differences. In subsequent research, even aversive stimuli such as very loud tones were found to have differential effects on electrodermal responding depending on their relation in time to the occurrence of the response (Crider, Schwartz, & Shapiro, 1970; Johnson & Schwartz, 1967). That is, the contingent presentation of a punishing stimulus suppressed the electrodermal response, while pairing the aversive stimulus with the absence of or randomly with the response resulted in sustained electrodermal activity, as would be expected.

A more significant result emerged from the Shapiro et al. study. Learned variations in electrodermal response rate were found not to be associated with such physiologically related functions as skin potential level and heart rate. Nor were the variations obviously associated with differences in breathing rate or breathing irregularities. Moreover, cognitive factors, to the extent they could be detected by blind ratings of recorded postsession interviews, were not relevant to the observed effects. Response contingent and nonresponse contingent subjects reported the same moderate relationship between the reinforcer (tone indicating bonus) and their thoughts or ideation; the level of involvement in the task was also about the same for the two groups.

The apparent capability of an operant procedure to have a selective effect on an autonomically mediated behavior such as the skin potential response made a convincing argument for the value of exploring autonomic regulation with operant conditioning methods. The methods also provided a means of investigating the extent to which an autonomic response can be differentiated from other autonomic and somatic behaviors. The association between learned electrodermal responding and somatomotor responses was explored in further research (Birk, Crider, Shapiro, & Tursky, 1966; Crider, Shapiro, & Tursky, 1966). From these and other related studies (Rice, 1966; Van Twyver & Kimmel, 1966), it could be seen that the role of somatomotor activity was not entirely consistent. As Birk et al. concluded, "Whether these variables [somatomotor] are to be classified as 'mediating' phenomena cannot be decided until such questions are phrased in terms of known physiological mechanisms or testable hypotheses" (p. 166). Critical experiments on these mechanisms could best be carried out in animal subjects using drugs and surgical procedures.

The fact that a given autonomic function could be increased or decreased while other presumably related functions (somatomotor, autonomic, cortical) did not covary was to be given a more comprehensive interpretation in later research. It was reasoned that if the other concurrent functions were in reality *independent* of or only slightly interrelated with the function to be learned, under natural or nonexperimental conditions, then the dissociation of one from the others through conditioning would not be surprising. This line of reasoning was followed closely in research on the operant control of human blood pressure and its association with heart rate. It had been reported that subjects rewarded for increases or decreases in systolic blood pressure showed relative pressure changes in the appropriate direction without differential changes in heart rate (Shapiro, Tursky, Gershon, & Stern, 1969; Shapiro, Tursky, & Schwartz, 1970b). Similarly, subjects could learn to increase or decrease their heart rate without corresponding changes in systolic blood pressure (Shapiro et al., 1970b). Starting with these reports, Schwartz (1972) developed a model for research and theory on the control of "multiautonomic" functions, a model that explained specificity of learning in the autonomic nervous sytem. He hypothesized that if two functions such as heart rate and blood pressure are very highly correlated, then when one is reinforced and shows learning, the other should do the same. If they are not correlated, however, then reinforcing one should result in learned changes in that function but not in the other. As a further implication, if you give feedback and reward for a given function and it shows learning, the degree to which other concurrent functions also show learning is informative about the natural interrelations of the functions to begin with. This model of autonomic learning is based on the measurement and analysis of the commonality of responses comprising a complex set of functions. In an empirical test of the model, Schwartz developed an on-line procedure for assessing the simultaneous pattern of systolic blood pressure and heart rate at each beat of the heart. Thus, when subjects were reinforced for a *pattern* of simultaneous change in *both* heart rate and blood pressure, these two functions could be either deliberately associated (both going in the *same* direction) or deliberately dissociated (going in *opposite* directions). The degree of association or dissociation was further limited by certain biological and adaptive constraints. The relative independence of heart rate and systolic blood pressure, established in the context of autonomic learning, was also confirmed by their relative independence under preconditioning resting conditions.

In a further test, it was observed that under resting conditions diastolic blood pressure and heart rate tended to covary in large measure. In this case, conditioning one system (diastolic pressure) resulted in associated changes in the other (heart rate), a finding that was clearly predictable on the basis of the commonality model (Shapiro, Schwartz, & Tursky, 1972b). Furthermore, it was found difficult, if not impossible, to make these two highly integrated functions go in opposite directions by reinforcing differential patterns (Schwartz, Shapiro, & Tursky, 1972).

These basic data obtained in systematic human experiments provide a framework for extending the principles of instrumental learning to visceral and glandular responses and for examining the associated mechanisms involved in the learning process. Through the analysis of concurrent changes in multiple response systems and the study of autonomic pattern learning, a simple predictive model of concurrent changes during visceral learning can be stated. The degree of commonality of the separate responses occurring in contiguity with the feedback and reinforcement determines the degree to which the responses remain associated or become dissociated as a result of the conditioning procedure. With this model, the study of "mediational" processes in visceral learning can be given further precision.

While emphasis above has been given to heart rate, blood pressure, and electrodermal activity, the phenomenon of learned physiological self-regulation in man has also been demonstrated for electrical activity of the brain (Beatty, 1971; Kamiya, 1969; Nowlis & Kamiya, 1970; Rosenfeld, Rudell, & Fox, 1969), peripheral vasomotor activity (Lisina, 1958/1965; Snyder & Noble, 1968), single motor unit activity (Basmajian, 1963; Hefferline & Keenan, 1961), skin temperature (Roberts, Kewman, & Macdonald, 1973), and muscle tone (Budzynski, Stoyva, & Adler, 1970). Specific therapeutic applications of biofeedback techniques to abnormal response processes and additional basic studies will be reviewed in later sections of this chapter.

So far, we have focused entirely on research with human subjects. A great deal of systematic research has been published indicating that a wide variety of functions can be modified in a number of other species. Examples of physiological responses studied in nonparalyzed animals are: salivation in dogs (Miller & Carmona, 1967), heart rate in monkeys (Engel & Gottlieb, 1970), blood pressure in monkeys (Benson, Herd, Morse, & Kelleher, 1969), blood pressure in baboons (Harris, Gilliam, Findley, & Brady, 1973), and the cortical sensorimotor rhythm in cats (Sterman, Howe, & Macdonald, 1970; Wyrwicka & Sterman, 1968).

A large number of studies have also been carried out in rats paralyzed by curare in which the reward is either electrical brain stimulation or shock escape and avoidance; for example, heart rate (DiCara & Miller, 1968a; Trowill, 1967), blood pressure (DiCara & Miller, 1968b), intestinal contractions (Miller & Banuazizi, 1968), peripheral vasomotor activity (DiCara & Miller, 1968c), amount of blood in the stomach wall (Carmona, Miller, & Demierre, 1974), and kidney urine formation (Miller & DiCara, 1968). Black, Young, and Batenchuck (1970) found that dogs paralyzed by Flaxidil could learn to control their hippocampal theta waves. The point of these experiments on paralyzed animals is that they rule out the effects of purely peripheral aspects of respiratory changes and skeletal muscle activity. That rather large changes could be achieved in relatively short periods of time without the aid of peripheral muscular activity suggested that paralysis might even *facilitate* visceral learning (Miller, 1969). Moreover, a high degree of specificity of learning was often observed. For example, rewarding differential vasomotor responses in the two ears of the rat, vasodilation was observed in one ear and either no change or vasoconstriction in the other (DiCara & Miller, 1968c).

Recently, however, the significance of the curare research has been called into question by the reported difficulties in reproducing results of experiments on heart rate control (Brener, Eissenberg, & Middaugh, 1974; Miller & Dworkin, 1974). This failure to replicate has been discussed in terms of certain undesired peripheral autonomic and central nervous system effects of curare and of difficulties in maintaining a stable animal preparation with artificial respiration (Hahn, 1974; Roberts, 1974). Moreover, curare does not affect the central nervous system linkage between cardiovascular or other autonomically mediated behaviors and somatomotor behaviors. That is, central somatomotor activity may initiate peripheral autonomic and skeletal motor activity, but the latter cannot be observed because the muscles are paralyzed. With respect to this central linkage, therefore, the use of curare cannot provide a *critical* experimental test of the role of central somatomotor processes in learned visceral control (Obrist, Howard, Lawler, Galosy, Meyers, & Gaebelein, 1974). Nevertheless, experiments with animals in both paralyzed and nonparalyzed states provide data on some of the limiting conditions of visceral learning. Basic research in animals along these lines using surgical lesions, as well as paralytic and various biochemical agents should help further elucidate physiological mechanisms of visceral learning.

This review of experimental evidence has touched on some of the major studies and trends in an area of research that has grown rapidly over the past 10 to 15 years. Hundreds of studies have been published, and many are reprinted in a series of annuals and a reader (Barber, DiCara, Kamiya, Miller, Shapiro, & Stoyva, 1971; Kamiya, Barber, DiCara, Miller, Shapiro, & Stoyva, 1971; Miller,

Barber, DiCara, Kamiya, Shapiro & Stoyva, 1974; Shapiro, Barber, DiCara, Kamiya, Miller, & Stoyva, 1973; Stoyva, Barber, DiCara, Kamiya, Miller, & Shapiro, 1972). A number of major reviews and position papers have also recently been published (Blanchard & Young, 1973; Brener, 1974; Miller, 1975; Schwartz, 1973).

CLINICAL APPLICATIONS

Hypertension

Hypertension is a disorder that has interested researchers concerned with behavioral physiology. It is an illness that poses a major public health problem in the United States, and methods that can augment those already in common medical practice are obviously important. The prevalence of hypertension is estimated to be about 5 to 10% of the general population, and high levels of arterial blood pressure increase the risk of other life-threatening disorders such as coronary artery disease, atherosclerosis, and nephrosclerosis (Kannel, Gordon, & Schwartz, 1971). Even occasional large increases in resting levels of pulse and blood pressure are thought to be associated with a shortening of the life-span (Merrill, 1966).

A vast proportion of all cases of hypertension is classified as "essential." These are cases in which a specific endocrine or renal disorder cannot be found. With no known physical etiology, essential hypertension is defined solely by the presence of a chronic elevation in blood pressure. While medical investigators are not in agreement about the significance of psychological factors in hypertension, there is evidence that the disorder is related to and can be aggravated by behavioral, social, and environmental conditions (Gutmann & Benson, 1971). Hyperreactivity of the sympathetic nervous sytem may be a major factor in the elevation of blood pressure, particularly in the early stages of the illness, as evidenced by increased heart rate, high cardiac output, and increased cardiac contractility. This hyperreactivity may occur in individuals who are particularly susceptible by reason of genetic, constitutional, and other factors such as obesity, smoking, or particular personality and emotional patterns.

In view of the assumed environmental, personality, and autonomic nervous system components of essential hypertension, a method of psychophysiological relearning such as biofeedback could offer a nonsurgical, nonpharmacologic means of lowering pressure. It is important to point out that current medical practice advocates drug treatment, especially where there is any reason to suspect that the illness is becoming more severe. "Since various effective hypotensive agents exist, it is now justifiable to utilize mild forms of therapy (including reassurance) for mild forms of hypertension, . ." (Merrill, 1966, p. 711).

Although the measurement of blood pressure posed many technical problems, particularly for purposes of providing continuous feedback, the relation between blood pressure and the illness itself seemed simple and direct to researchers. The course of action was clear. By obtaining a continuous measure of blood pressure, providing feedback to subjects, and rewarding the appropriate decreases, blood pressure could presumably be lowered, and the illness thereby brought under control. Furthermore, basic research on blood pressure regulation in normal human and animal subjects using operant conditioning techniques provided ample evidence for the extension of the techniques into a therapeutic setting. In the curarized rat, instrumental conditioning of systolic blood pressure was demonstrated using a shock escape and avoidance procedure (DiCara & Miller, 1968b). The learned changes were about 20% of baseline in both increase and decrease directions, and they were not associated with heart rate or rectal temperature. In a subsequent study in noncurarized rats, the changes obtained were much smaller—about 5%—and the learning was found not to transfer to the curarized state (Pappas, DiCara, & Miller, 1970). Elevations in diastolic pressure of large magnitude were obtained in the rhesus monkey using a shock avoidance procedure in which the elevations functioned as the avoidance response (Plumlee, 1969). Benson et al. (1969) reported more modest elevations of mean arterial pressure in the squirrel monkey using similar procedures. In the dog-faced baboon, substantial elevations in blood pressure were established by an operant conditioning procedure that provided for food delivery and shock avoidance contingent upon increases in diastrolic pressure (Harris, Findley, & Brady, 1971; Harris et al., 1973). In their recent work, these investigators produced sustained increases of about 20 mmHg in both systolic and diastolic blood pressure with the additional significant finding that the increases in blood pressure were associated with elevated but progressively decreasing heart rates.

An experimental animal with behaviorally induced hypertension is of great significance, particularly if the high blood pressure can be maintained for long periods of time. It suggests that the illness can in fact be learned in this fashion, and it provides a means of applying and exploring the value of different relearning procedures. Benson et al. (1969) put squirrel monkeys on a work schedule in which they were required to press a key in order to avoid electric shock, and the schedule resulted in increases in mean arterial blood pressure. The shock avoidance keys were then removed, and an increase in blood pressure was the instrumental response required to avoid shock. Prolonged elevations in pressure were maintained in this way. When the schedule was reversed, and decreases in pressure became the criterion for shock avoidance, pressures were shown to decline 10 to 20 mm Hg. However, there is no certainty that in this experiment stable elevations in pressure were achieved. The capacity to reduce blood pressure using an operant procedure may be related to the length of time that the high level is present (Teplitz, 1971).

Turning to research in normotensive humans, Brener and Kleinman (1970) used a finger cuff method of following systolic pressure. In an experimental group, subjects were instructed to decrease their blood pressure with the aid of pressure feedback. In a control group, subjects were instructed to observe the feedback, but they were not informed about its meaning. Differences of about 20 to 30 mm Hg were obtained between the two groups after about 30 minutes of training, and the differences were not associated with heart rate. Inasmuch as blood pressure values obtained with a finger cuff are different from those obtained with an arm cuff, it is difficult to compare these results with the smaller effects (4 mm Hg) reported earlier by Shapiro et al. (1969) using a constant cuff technique (see below). The differences may be greater in the Brener and Kleinman study as a result of giving the experimental subjects specific instructions to lower pressure. No blood pressure instructions were employed in the Shapiro et al. experiment. Subjects were merely informed to increase the feedback, which signified some undefined physiological response.

Inasmuch as most of the normal human data on blood pressure control follow the procedures first described by Shapiro et al. (1969), a brief description of the measuring technique will exemplify the development of a feedback technology. A method had to be devised to obtain a measure of blood pressure on each beat of the heart so as to be able to provide as complete information as possible to the subject. Intermittent measurements (once or twice a minute) using an ordinary pressure cuff provide information on only 2 to 3% of the changes. They are also inadequate because of the inherent variability of blood pressure. A single determination of systolic or diastolic pressure every half minute can be as much as 20 to 30 mm Hg off from the average measurement. For example, in a single minute's direct recording of pressure via a catheter in a given patient, two successive cuff blood pressure measurements in that period would have yielded 124/90 and 144/60 mm Hg, while the median value for the 50-odd pressure waves was actually 128/68 mm Hg (Tursky, Shapiro, & Schwartz, 1972). Direct arterial catheterization is not feasible for routine repetitive training.

The automatic procedure designated the "constant cuff" method is as follows. A blood pressure cuff is wrapped around the upper arm and a crystal microphone is placed over the brachial artery under the distal end of the cuff. If the cuff is inflated to about the average systolic pressure and held constant at that level, whenever systolic pressure rises and exceeds the occluding cuff pressure, a Korotkoff sound can be detected from the microphone. When the systolic level is less than the occluding pressure, no Korotkoff sound is detected. Using a regulated low-pressure source, logic and programming apparatus, it is possible to find the constant cuff pressure at which 50% of the heartbeats yield Korotkoff sounds. This pressure level is by definition *median* systolic pressure. Inasmuch as the time between the R-wave in the electrocardiogram and the occurrence of the Korotkoff sound is approximately 300 msec, it is also possible to detect either the presence of the Korotkoff sound (high pressure relative to the median) *or* its absence (low pressure relative to the median). In this way, the system provides information about directional changes in pressure relative to the median on each successive heartbeat. Typically, the cuff is inflated for 50 heartbeats and deflated for about 30 seconds to allow recirculation of the blood. Depending on the percentage of Korotkoff sounds in a single 50-beat trial, the constant pressure in the next trial can be changed by a small amount (±2 mm Hg) to return to the subject's median. Thus the system can provide blood pressure feedback on each heartbeat and can also track median pressure from trial to trial. This system has been evaluated against simultaneous data obtained using a direct arterial recording, and close correspondence has been obtained for all of its essential features (Tursky et al., 1972). Comparable procedures can be used to determine the diastolic values.

Typically, subjects are provided with binary (yes–no) feedback of either relatively high or low pressure on each heartbeat. After a prescribed number of feedback stimuli, rewarding slides are presented. Figures 2 and 3 illustrate the procedures.

The initial studies attempted to determine whether normal volunteer subjects could learn to modify their systolic or diastolic blood pressure. Complete details may be found in Schwartz (1972), Schwartz, Shapiro, & Tursky (1971), Shapiro et al. (1969), Shapiro, Tursky, & Schwartz (1970a), Shapiro et al. (1970b), and Shapiro et al. (1972b). In these studies, subjects were simply told to make the feedback occur as much as possible and to earn as many rewards as possible. They were not told that the feedback was being given for changes in blood pressure; nor were they told in what direction it was to change. This controlled for any complications due to the natural ability of subjects to control pressure "voluntarily," and tested the pure effects of feedback and reward contingency. Current research in this area is concerned with the ability of subjects to modify their blood pressure with instructions only and with the effects of combining feedback with instructions (Shapiro, 1973; see also Brener, 1974). "Pure" voluntary control of blood pressure and other changes in circulation has been reported in unusual individual cases (Ogden & Shock, 1939) and may be more widespread than previously believed.

Using the above procedures, subjects could learn to modify their blood pressure with feedback and reward. Average differences in systolic pressure between increase and decrease conditions for groups of subjects at the end of a single session of training varied from 3 to 10% of baseline. The best results were obtained for diastolic pressure (Shapiro et al., 1972b) with individual subjects showing increases up to 25% and decreases up to 15% of baseline values. Heart rate was found to be clearly independent of the learned changes in systolic but not of the changes in diastolic pressure. In a related study, systolic pressure was not associated with the learned changes in heart rate.

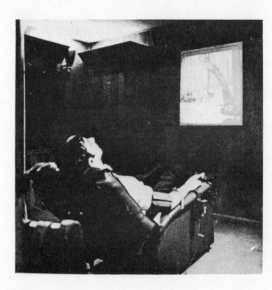

Figure 2. Subject in blood pressure study. Light at right is turned on with cuff inflation and cues subject that trial period has begun. Light at left flashes for 100 msec with correct pressure change (feedback). Simultaneously, brief tone is presented. Slides (correlated with monetary bonus) are projected either for criterion number of feedback stimuli or predetermined change in median pressure.

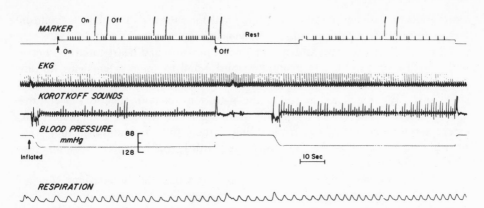

Figure 3. Segment of polygraph record of a subject in a *decrease* systolic blood pressure condition in which subject is reinforced for lowering his pressure. Two trials are shown. Marker channel indicates onset of trial with presentation of blue light as cue (first arrow), feedback (small marks), and slide presentations (large spikes). Rest period begins when blue light is turned off. For this subject in a decrease condition, feedback was administered when Korotkoff sounds were below critical amplitude. Blood pressure channel shows cuff inflation and deflation. Applied pressure was 116 mm Hg on first trial shown. During this trial there was 76% success. On second trial shown, applied pressure was changed to 114, making task more difficult. Note reduction in success rate to 37% on this trial (Shapiro, Tursky, Gershon, & Stern, 1969. Copyright 1969 by the American Association for the Advancement of Science.)

Although the average curves indicated that it was easier to obtain reductions rather than increases in pressure (in a single session), further data under conditions of random reinforcement suggested a tendency for baseline values to adapt over time. Increases in pressure over baseline values are probably more likely (Shapiro et al., 1970a). This is a common interpretation of findings in heart rate and other autonomic biofeedback studies (see Engel, 1972). Moreover, as in the case of heart rate, the processes involved in increasing blood pressure may be completely different from those involved in decreasing pressure (see Lang & Twentyman, 1974). In normal subjects, typical resting pressures are close to minimal values, but there is a potential for large increases above baseline, depending upon motor activity, emotionality, and so on. For individuals who already have significantly elevated pressure levels, significant decreases are more likely.

By and large, normal subjects could not report whether they were in fact learning to raise or lower their pressure; nor did they reveal the consistent use of specific thoughts, images, or physical strategies such as respiratory maneuvers, as far as could be detected.

To explain the conditions under which specificity of conditioning would occur, Schwartz (1972) hypothesized that when feedback is given for one response, simultaneous learning of other responses will depend on the degree to which these other responses are directly associated with the response for which feedback is given as well as on other homeostatic mechanisms. Schwartz developed an on-line procedure for tracking both phasic and tonic patterns of blood pressure and heart rate in real time and for showing that subjects could in fact learn to control patterns of simultaneous changes in *both* functions. Subjects could readily learn to integrate systolic blood pressure and heart rate (i.e., make both increase or both decrease simultaneously) and to some extent learn to differentiate both functions (i.e., make one increase and the other decrease simultaneously). Further analysis of the patterning of both functions over time and of natural tonic reactivity in this situation made it possible to predict the extent and time course of pattern learning in the different conditions. Subjective reports of a "relaxed" state were associated with learned reduction in *both* systolic pressure and heart rate.

These basic data in animals and man provided the foundations for the clinical use of biofeedback techniques in hypertension. Using the constant cuff method, Benson, Shapiro, Tursky, and Schwartz (1971) investigated the application of operant feedback techniques to the lowering of systolic blood pressure in seven hypertensive patients, five of whom had essential hypertension. Of the other two, one did not have elevated systolic pressure and the other had renal artery stenosis. The latter patients showed little or no decrease in systolic pressure as a results of the conditioning procedure. The five patients responding positively showed decreases of 34, 29, 16, 16, and 17 mm Hg with 33, 22, 34, 31, and 12 sessions of training, respectively. No reliable pressure readings were taken outside the laboratory so the general effectiveness of the training could not be determined.

The average amount of in-session decrease in systolic pressure for the patients was about 5 mm Hg, about the same as in normal studies. In resting control conditions, no such reductions were observed in the patients. Although the lowered pressure tended to carry over from one session to the next, the trends were not always consistent. The individual curves suggested a pattern of successive cycles of decreasing pressure, followed by an increase, and then a new lowering trend. Apparently, certain events in the life of the patient, or other factors not now understood, disturbed the decremental process and the pressure bounced back, although not necessarily to the original level. The data suggested a possible process of successive habituation interrupted by periods of dehabituation. It may be hypothesized that the feedback reward technique facilitates the process of habituation. It is not known whether random feedback, attempts at voluntary control without feedback, muscular relaxation, or simply sitting in the laboratory would achieve the same results. The latter possibility seems remote, inasmuch as little or no reduction in pressure was observed after as many as 15 control sessions under resting conditions with no feedback or rewards. Nonspecific placebo effects have to be considered, in addition to simple adaptation to the laboratory situation, as an alternative explanation of the observed reductions. The patients studied had been in treatment for hypertension for long periods of time, and no changes in their drug treatment were made. However, the innovation of "biofeedback" as a new technique involving unusual instrumentation, feedback displays, and the idea of self-control may have served a placebo function.

Using essentially the same feedback procedure, Kleinman and Goldman (1974) recently reported maximum decreases of 18% in systolic and diastolic pressure in seven patients with average baseline values of 167/109 mm Hg. Those patients showing the greatest maximum decreases in both systolic and diastolic pressure during biofeedback training also showed the greatest improvement on a Category Test of the Reitan Neuropsychological Test Battery for Adults. As this test is related to cognitive dysfunctioning, the results of the study imply that biofeedback may be useful not only in lowering pressure but also in overcoming a cognitive impairment associated with hypertension. Neither Benson et al. (1971) nor Kleinman and Goldman (1974) has provided data on the persistence of training effects outside the laboratory. The cognitive improvement reported by Kleinman and Goldman, however, suggests that the training may not be entirely laboratory-specific.

Miller (1975) reported on unpublished research in his laboratory in which he attempted to train 28 patients with essential hypertension to reduce their diastolic blood pressure. A few patients appeared to reduce their blood pressure, but after reaching a plateau the pressure drifted up again. One patient showed excellent results and was trained to alternate in increasing and decreasing her pressure. Over a period of 3 months, this patient acquired the ability to change pressure over a range of 30 mm Hg. Her baseline pressure decreased from 97 to 76 mm Hg, and similar decreases were observed on the ward. Later on, she lost voluntary control and was put back on drugs as a result of emotional stresses. Miller reported that this patient came back to training 2½ years later and rapidly regained a large measure of control.

An instructive quote from Miller's paper underscores the role of environmental events in controlling a function such as blood pressure. "The question raised sharply by this patient, however, is whether she is merely using her voluntary control to produce a spuriously low measure in clinical tests while failing to transfer it to crucial parts of her daily life and thus conceivably misleading her physician about her need for antihypertensive medication." The need for continuous recording of blood pressure in daily life situations is apparent, and techniques are now being developed to make this possible.

The above clinical trials attempted direct control of blood pressure with biofeedback. An alternative indirect approach has been employed by Moeller and Love (personal communication). In their view, by teaching subjects to relax their muscles, it may be possible to reduce blood pressure that they assume to be associated with muscle tension. According to these investigators, this procedure has an added advantage in that patients are more likely to be able to "sense" and control their muscles and thereby possibly develop a means of self-control of blood pressure outside the laboratory. A sample of six patients with average baseline pressures of 153/100 mm Hg was given exercises that included muscle feedback and autogenic training as a means of facilitating general bodily relaxation. The training covered a period of 17 weeks. Moeller and Love reported that both systolic and diastolic pressure were reduced by 13% in this program.

A number of other indirect behavioral methods of lowering blood pressure, not involving the use of feedback, need to be mentioned in this context. These include progressive relaxation (Jacobson, 1938), meditation (Benson, Rosner, Marzetta, & Klemchuk, 1974), yoga practices (Datey, Deshmukh, Dalvi, &

Vinekar, 1969), and autogenic training (Luthe & Schultz, 1969). An innovative approach to relaxation training was utilized with some success in lowering pressure in patients with essential hypertension, as discussed in a recent preliminary report by Brady, Luborsky, and Kron (1974). It is called "metronome-conditioned relaxation" (see Brady, 1973) and requires that the patient lie down for ½ hour with eyes closed and listen to a tape recording. The recording consists of instructions to relax the muscles, and it includes suggestions to "let-go" and "re-lax" the muscles, paced with rhythmic beats of an auditory metronome set at 60 beats per minute. With repeated training, several patients showed significant reductions in pressure. Two patients who used the tape recording at home for a protracted period showed further reductions in pressure.

These indirect behavioral procedures have all been shown to be effective in reducing high blood pressure to some degree. Comparative studies are needed to determine their relative effectiveness. It would appear from the studies reported so far that the various procedures discussed, including biofeedback, have more or less similar effects. This suggests that a relaxation or low-arousal state may be a common factor (see Benson, Beary, & Carol, 1974; Stoyva & Budzynski, 1974). This state may well be facilitated if the patient is confident that he is able in fact to exert control over his own blood pressure. While the different behavioral procedures do not seem to affect blood pressure to different degrees, it is reasonable to expect that detailed analysis of the results of extended training will show differences in extent, degree, and persistence of achieved self-control and in the physiological patterns associated with this control.

The problem of transfer of training outside the laboratory may be illustrated by observation of a single case studied in our laboratories at the Massachusetts Mental Health Center. The patient was a 35-year-old mental health worker who was highly motivated and cooperative. He was diagnosed as having essential hypertension with a pressure of 160/110 mm Hg taken during a routine medical examination. The patient was given feedback for reductions in diastolic pressure after six resting control sessions in which he fluctuated from 80 to 105 mm Hg diastolic. Over nine training sessions, he steadily reduced his pressure from over 100 to about 85 mm Hg. A variety of other procedures were then tried, including autogenic phrases and progressive relaxation in addition to feedback, and the patient began oscillating in diastolic pressure between 85 and 95 mm Hg. His systolic pressure, recorded in a final session, ranged from 135 to 130 mm Hg over a 35-minute period. Following these sessions, he returned to his physician for a second examination, and he was recorded again at 160/110 mm Hg (see Shapiro, 1974).

Although it is hazardous to draw any conclusions, this patient, in the laboratory, seemed to show reduction in pressure with the aid of feedback, although nonspecific factors cannot be ruled out. Was he unable to transfer this learning to other relevant situations, or was his hyperreactivity confined to the medical examination? The latter could be a classically conditioned response unique to the physician taking his pressure. It seems likely, however, that other stressors in the patient's environment would have also yielded abnormal responses.

Several approaches to the problem of transfer of training in the case of hypertension are suggested: (1) More extensive long-term training may be needed. Then, periods of training without feedback could be instituted as a means of enhancing self-control and effecting permanent reductions. (2) In cases exhibiting hyperreactivity that appears to be situation-specific, some combination of a desensitization procedure and biofeedback could be used to facilitate adaptation to real-life situations (see Sirota, Schwartz, & Shapiro, 1974). (3) Feedback training could be instituted in a stimulating or a mildly stressful environment (produced by noise or distracting tasks) as a means of possibly building up resistance to and reducing abnormal physiological responses to stress in general, and possibly to specific stressful events. (4) Other behavioral procedures (meditation, relaxation, autogenic training, yoga exercises) could also be combined with feedback procedures to facilitate more effective behavioral control.

Finally, diastolic pressure is thought to be more critical in certain later stages of hypertension because of its closer relationship to peripheral resistance (Merrill, 1966). Initial studies at the Thorndike Memorial and Channing Laboratories of the Boston City Hospital in collaboration with Dr. Herbert Benson indicated that it is difficult to reduce abnormally high diastolic levels. Part of the problem may be related to some unreliability in obtaining consistent diastolic values over repeated sessions. Learned control of diastolic pressure was observed in a single-session study of normal subjects with consistent changes occurring in most subjects (Shapiro et al., 1972b). However, systolic pressure by itself may be a meaningful prognostic index of future disease. Comprehensive data have been obtained in the Framingham Study on the contribution of various indices of blood pressure to the risk of coronary heart disease (Kannel et al., 1971). It was concluded that "the association between antecedent blood pressure and the incidence of coronary heart disease is actually stronger for systolic than for diastolic pressure" (p. 340). For these reasons, one possible strategy is to work with early cases of illness and to concentrate on reductions in the systolic level, which is most reliably measured and easiest to work with. Additional case material and further discussion of the clinical data and the problems of clinical management in hypertension may be found in Schwartz (1973), Schwartz and Shapiro (1973), and Shapiro (1974).

In conclusion, the major trends in this research on hypertension may be summarized as follows.

1. Biofeedback techniques are effective in controlling normal blood pressure levels in a laboratory situation, and further research is needed to determine whether larger changes can be achieved with more refined feedback and reward techniques, relevant instructions, and long-term training. The degree to which the training persists over time and carries over to other situations needs to be investigated.

2. Both direct and indirect feedback methods appear to be useful as a means of reducing blood pressure in patients with essential hypertension. By and large, the clinical studies have not employed adequate controls for placebo and other nonspecific effects. Such controls are needed to distinguish between those effects

that are unique to the use of feedback itself and those that are related to the novelty of this method of treatment, enthusiasm of the clinician, or attitudes of the patient.

3. The simplifed notion of direct symptom treatment (blood pressure training per se) may be inadequate, and alternative biofeedback strategies should be considered, e.g., giving feedback for a pattern of reduced pressure and heart rate, giving feedback for reductions in overall sympathetic activity or cardiac output as general functions of importance in the lowering of pressure (particularly in early or labile phase of hypertension), or giving feedback for combined decreases in muscle tension and blood pressure. The choice of feedback strategy depends upon an understanding of the dynamics of the cardiovascular system (see below) and of the mechanisms of hypertension. These are complex issues under extensive investigation by scientists in physiology, medicine, and other disciplines. Moreover, the physiological processes in hypertension are probably not uniform from case to case and may depend upon many factors. In our view, further interdisciplinary research on the part of behavioral, physiological, and medical scientists will enhance the potential of biofeedback and other behavioral methods in research and treatment of hypertension.

Cardiac Arrhythmias

"A cardiac arrhythmia is defined as any abnormality in the site of impulse formation, in the spread of impulses through the conduction system, in the rate at which the heart beats, or in the rhythm with which the heart beats" (Engel & Bleecker, 1974, p. 457). Certain arrhythmias occur in the absence of structural disease of the heart, e.g., sinus arrhythmias, bradycardia or tachycardia of sinus origin, atrial and ventricular premature beats, milder forms of first degree heart block, and paroxysmal atrial tachycardia. Disorders of these rhythms may be associated with specific eliciting factors such as tobacco or coffee, but they generally occur in the absence of structural heart disease. Other arrhythmias occur in persons with organic heart disease. These arrhythmias include fibrillation and tachycardia of the ventricles, atrial flutter and fibrillation, and advanced degrees of atrioventricular block (Eddleman, Resnik, & Harrison, 1966).

A rationale for the use of operant conditioning and biofeedback techniques in bringing cardiac arrhythmias under control is summarized by Engel:

> By the time we began our experiments, we already had carried out three cardiac conditioning studies with normal subjects (Engel & Chism, 1967; Engel & Hansen, 1966; Levene, Engel, & Pearson, 1968), and Miller and his colleagues had shown that it was possible to operantly condition heart rate in the rat (Miller, 1969). Furthermore, there was extensive literature that showed that the nervous system could play a major role in modulating the prevalence of cardiac arrhythmias (Scherf & Schott, 1953), and that showed that temperamental variables affected the prevalence of many arrhythmias (Stevenson, Duncan, Wolf, Ripley, & Wolff, 1949). These data indicated that the nervous system exercised a significant role in cardiac function, and that at least some aspects of this nervous control were associated with volitional behavior. (1973, p. 433)

Engel and his associates applied operant training procedures in a number of different arrhythmias—premature ventricular contractions (Weiss & Engel, 1971), atrial fibrillation (Bleecker & Engel, 1973b), and Wolff-Parkinson-White syndrome (Bleecker & Engel, 1973a). In the most up-to-date summary, results with other arrhythmias are cited (Engel & Bleecker, 1974). These included sinus tachycardia, supraventricular tachycardia, paroxysmal atrial tachycardia, and third-degree heart block.

A variety of training procedures were employed in these studies. In most cases, the patients were trained both to increase and to decrease their heart rate, and the training procedures were found to be coupled with variations in the prevalence of their arrhythmias. Typically, the patient was provided with a display consisting of lights and a meter. A green light was a cue to the patient to speed up his heart rate, and a red light was a cue to slow it down. Whenever the patient met the heart rate performance criterion, a yellow light was turned on indicating success in the task. A meter ran whenever the patient was performing successfully and indicated the percentage of time he was successful during the session. One important training innovation involved the use of a kind of intermittent reinforcement, in this case variable periods of practice without feedback but with specific instructions to continue attempting control.

In the most extensive clinical study in this series (Weiss & Engel, 1971), eight patients with premature ventricular contractions were trained to increase, decrease, alternately increase and decrease, or maintain their heart rate within a certain range. Variations in the heart rate training procedure were associated with different frequencies of this arrhythmia. Five patients showed significant decreases in frequency of the premature contractions, and four of them persisted in this control for periods up to 21 months. One patient has since been followed over a 5-year period, and her arrhythmia continued at a very low rate (Engel & Bleecker, 1974).

During the 21-month period, one of the patients had no reported myocardial infarctions as compared with three in the 11 months prior to training. Weiss and Engel (1971) conjectured that this consequence may be related to the diminished prevalence of the arrhythmia. Premature ventricular contractions are associated with diminished coronary artery and cerebral blood flow (Corday, Gold, DeVera, Williams, & Fields, 1959; Corday & Irving, 1960) and with an increased probability of sudden death (Chiang, Perlman, Ostander, & Epstein, 1969; Lown & Wolf, 1971). Biofeedback and reward techniques provide a specific behavioral means of direct symptom control in cardiac arrhythmias and an indirect influence on related cardiovascular disorders.

Using autonomic nervous system drugs, Weiss and Engel (1971) were able to distinguish at least two different physiological mechanisms involved in the diminution of premature ventricular beats. In one patient, drug-induced diminished sympathetic tone resulted in fewer premature beats; and, in another, the mechanism involved an increase in vagal tone. In both these cases, a decrease in heart rate could be associated with *either* physiological process. In other patients, increases in heart rate, reflecting different underlying physiological processes, could also be associated with a reduced frequency of premature beats. Weiss and Engel argue that it is not the heart rate per se that determines the presence or absence of premature beats, but rather the degree to which such a change reflects the critical underlying physiological process. For example, in the patient for whom reduced sympathetic tone to the heart was responsible for the decreased incidence of premature beats, increases in heart rate induced by isoproterenol were associated with premature beats, whereas similar heart rate increases induced by atropine were not. If this patient were to reduce heart rate by means of an increase in vagal tone, no reduction in the symptom would be observed.

It is apparent in this research that the relations between feedback training procedure, actual heart rate change, symptom frequency, and the critical underlying physiological mechanisms are not unambiguous. Although Weiss and Engel concluded that operant conditioning can be used to alter pathologic conditions mediated by different physiological mechanisms, the choice of an appropriate feedback strategy is also not clear. If sympathetic nervous function is critical in the particular case, there may be other responses aside from heart rate that, if altered, could serve to alter the function in the required direction. That is, other indices of sympathetic function could be equally effective for feedback training purposes. As in other disorders, the issues in this research are quite complex. There is no question that wisdom and judgment have to be exercised in the choice of a feedback training method. In the final analysis, the clinical value of the method must be empirically tested to determine its efficacy. As Weiss and Engel suggest, extensive, short-term experimental drug studies are useful in clarifying the mechanisms of the cardiac symptoms in different patients and, therefore, in suggesting a feedback strategy.

Miller (1975) reported on attempts to replicate Engel's research on premature ventricular contractions. In Miller's laboratory, T. Pickering succeeded in training two patients to control their arrhythmia with data supporting Engel's findings that patients can voluntarily suppress or control the responses. The lasting therapeutic value of this more recent work has not been determined.

Weiss and Engel (1971) proposed six factors that are important in learning to control frequency of premature ventricular contractions: (1) Peripheral receptors are stimulated by the arrhythmia and provide the possibility of the patient learning to recognize and control the abnormal response. This process is facilitated by external feedback in the early stages of training. (2) Afferent nerves carry the information to the central nervous system. (3) Central nervous system processes enable the patient to recognize information about the arrhythmia and provide the necessary motivation to facilitate learning and sustained change in performance. (4) Efferent nerves bring about the desired change in cardiac functioning. (5) The heart must be able to beat more regularly, that is, not be too diseased. (6) The patient's homeostatic system must be able to tolerate a more normal heart function.

All together, the findings of Engel and his associates are among the most remarkable of the clinical applications of biofeedback and operant conditioning techniques to date. Some reasons for this success may be isolated. First, cardiac arrhythmias are circumscribed disorders in which the symptom is quite specific and the physiological rationale for the specific training procedure more or less straightforward. Second, the training sessions were extensive and comprehensive in design. As many as 50 to 60 sessions of different contingencies were conducted in individual cases. Third, patients were trained *both* to increase and to decrease the frequency of the abnormal rhythm, and it was thought that this experience enhanced self-control. Fourth, Engel used periods of self-control without feedback, the goal of which is summed up as follows:

> Our purpose in including this procedure was to wean the patient from the gadgetry, because the clinical value of the conditioning depended on the subject being able to perform successfully in nonlaboratory environments. Apparently this technique was successful, since the patients report that their ability to perform without feedback is strong evidence *to them* that they have developed their own intrinsic cues, and that they "know" when their hearts are beating normally *and* abnormally, and that they "know" how to change the rhythm in either direction. (Engel & Bleecker, 1974 p. 473)

Raynaud's Disease

Raynaud's *disease*, like essential hypertension, is a functional disorder of the cardiovascular system involving no observable organic pathology in its early stages. Its symptoms consist of intermittent, bilateral vasospasms of the hands, feet, and rarely, the face, which can be elicited by cold stimulation and/or emotional stress. During an attack, the affected area usually goes through a three-stage color change, first blanching, then turning cyanotic blue, and finally becoming bright red as the spasm is relieved and reactive hyperemia sets in. When this syndrome results secondarily from an identifiable pathological process, it is known as Raynaud's *phenomenon* (Fairbairn, Juergens, & Spittell, 1972).

The first modern-day report of voluntary vasomotor control came from the USSR, where Lisina (1958/1965) was able to demonstrate that subjects could learn to increase the blood flow in their arms if allowed to watch their plethysmographic record. Snyder and Noble (1968), using a dichtomous feedback procedure, were able to train subjects in vasoconstriction of the fingers independent of changes in heart rate, finger movement, muscle tension, or respiration. Volow and Hein (1972), using analogue and discrete feedback, trained subjects both to increase and to decrease blood flow in their fingers. They reported, however, that constriction seemed to be easier to learn than dilation. Taub and Emurian (1972) trained subjects to increase or decrease the skin temperature of their hands by an analogue feedback method, while Roberts, Schuler, Bacon, and Zimmerman (1974) have been able to train subjects to differentially raise and lower skin temperature in the two hands. Despite these encouraging data, there have been some recent unpublished reports of negative results. Surwit and Shapiro (1974) did not find significant skin temperature learning both with and without autogenic-like instruction in a one-session study, while Lynch, Hama, Kohn, and Miller (1974) have been unable to replicate the work of either Roberts or Taub and Emurian. Lynch, however, has found reason to believe that skin temperature learning is possible in some subjects but points out that the exact variables necessary to reliably reproduce this phenomenon are not known.

Surwit (1973) recently reviewed four cases in which biofeedback was successfully employed as the major mode of treatment of Raynaud's disease or Raynaud's phenomenon. Although these four reports involve the implementation of somewhat different methods and are probably not all dealing with Raynaud's disease per se, they have in common one essential point; in each case, patients reported achieving control of a Raynaud's symptom they previously thought to be involuntary. The first of these cases involved a patient treated for over a year at the Allen Memorial Institute of McGill University. Upon referral, the patient, a 21-year-old female, had been suffering from Raynaud's disease for about 5 years and had both cervical and lumbar sympathectomies. Training consisted of a temperature feedback procedure. A sensitive thermistor was mounted on the patient's left hand. If there was a net increase in temperature in excess of .1° C, the patient was given feedback. This consisted of a bell, a flashing light, and an increment in a cumulative graph displayed on a videoscope. The therapist would then verbally reinforce the patient for her success. Each session consisted of three 10-minute trials separated by 5- or 10-minute rest periods. Fourteen sessions were administered over a 3-week period, after which time the patient stopped treatment for 1 month to go on vacation. Upon her return, sessions were administered twice a week and consisted of two 10-minute trials for each hand. This mode of therapy lasted for 4 months and was supplemented by counseling and assertive training (Wolpe, 1958) for family problems. All therapy was then discontinued for 1 month, after which feedback training was resumed at weekly intervals for the next 6 months. Since the beginning of training, this patient managed to increase her basal hand temperature (both hands) from an average of 23° C to 26.6° C. She no longer required elaborate protective garments for the Montreal winter and markedly decreased the number of Raynaud's attacks she experienced.

Two other investigators employed temperature feedback in the treatment of Raynaud's phenomenon or Raynaud's disease. Peper (personal communication) reported treating a 50-year-old woman who suffered from what appeared to be Raynaud's disease for about 30 years. As in the previous case report, this patient was first instructed in relaxation and autogenic techniques before the onset of biofeedback training. Biofeedback training, however, followed a different procedure. Thermistors were placed on both the temporal artery and the finger of one hand. The net difference between the readings of these two thermistors was used to drive an analogue auditory feedback system. That is, the patient received an auditory signal that varied directly with the temperature difference between the reference thermistor placed on the temporal artery and the thermistor on her finger. The patient was instructed in the use of the auditory feedback device and was told to practice with it twice a day for 10 minutes. After a month of training, the patient's basal skin temperature, as measured on the fingertip, increased from 75° to 85° F. In addition, she reported that for the first time in 30 years she could hold onto the cold steering wheel of her car without gloves. No systematic follow-up data are available.

Working with a similar technique, Jacobson, Hackett, Surman, and Silverberg (1973) have reported success in the alleviation of Raynaud's-like symptoms
in a 31-year-old male. The patient experienced these symptoms for 4 years and
claimed they were increasing in severity during the year preceding treatment. The
patient was first trained in autohypnosis for relaxation and then given four
sessions of differential temperature feedback like that employed by Peper. After
this brief treatment, the patient was able to voluntarily produce increases in skin
temperature of up to 4.2° C, even outside the feedback situation. Corresponding
color changes, suggesting increased blood flow, were also observed. As in the case
reported by Peper, the patient reported that for the first time in years he was able
to grasp very cold objects without triggering a vasospasmodic attack. Seven and a
half months after treatment, the patient reported continued relief from Raynaud's
symptoms.

Finally, Shapiro and Schwartz (1972) reported the successful application of
biofeedback for a related circulatory problem. Their patient was a 60-year-old
man who complained of chronic sensations of cold in his hands and feet for 2
years. Although no signs of vascular disease or specific reaction to cold were
found by the examining physician, this patient did complain of increased difficulty in winter months as found in Raynaud's disease. A treatment procedure was
devised by using a measure of digital blood volume, the DC component of a
photoplethysmograph, for feedback. A photoplethysmograph transducer was
attached to the patient's large toe of each foot. Feedback training was conducted
for 30-minute sessions four times a week for 3 weeks. At first, feedback was given
for increases in blood volume in the left toe (where he experienced the most severe
discomfort), and later training was done for increases in blood volume in the right
toe. One month later, five additional sessions were administered following the
same procedure. Although the patient was given no direct autogenic instructions,
he reported that he experienced the most success in increasing his blood flow
while imagining experiencing warmth. Through the surreptitiously arrived-at
strategy, this patient obtained much relief and showed control of his symptoms
for approximately a year. Recently he has requested some further training
because he felt he was losing the control he experienced earlier. Unfortunately,
the same procedure failed to produce positive results with a second patient. This
woman had more severe manifestations of vasospasms and was very ambivalent
about this mode of treatment. Upon mutual agreement, treatment was terminated
after approximately 10 sessions because of lack of progress and sufficient motivation. More recently, Taub, Emurian, and Howell (1974) reported that several
Raynaud's patients have been able to demonstrate the same amount of skin
temperature control as is found in normals.

Persuasive though these reports are, it would be premature to conclude that
biofeedback was the sole therapeutic agent responsible for improvement. In each
case, relaxation and/or autogenic imagery were used by or suggested to the subject in the process of training. In addition, the large amount of attention given to
each patient coupled with the enthusiasm of the therapists for this new treatment
may have given these procedures considerable placebo value. It is noteworthy,
however, that in two cases (Jacobson et al., 1973; Surwit, 1973) patients specifi-

cally reported that they first had to abandon relaxation and autogenic strategies in order to control the feedback. As in many biofeedback studies of physiological systems, these patients could not verbalize what, if any, strategy they used to control blood flow. Nevertheless, it is clear that carefully controlled investigations must precede any conclusion about the exact contribution biofeedback can provide in the treatment of Raynaud's disease and other peripheral vascular disorders.

The optimal physiological measures to use in a biofeedback treatment for Raynaud's disease would, of course, depend upon the precise physiological mechanism involved in the disorder. Unfortunately, Raynaud's disease, like essential hypertension, is by definition of unknown etiology. Though it is known that during a spasm blood is initially absent in the capillaries (Lewis, 1949), it is not known whether the spasm occurs at the arterial, arteriolar, or capillary level (Willerson, Thompson, Hookman, Herdt, & Decker, 1970). Langer and Croccel (1960) have suggested that arteriovenous anastomoses might play a central role in Raynaud's disease, shunting the blood away from the outermost layers of the skin during an attack. If indeed this is true, then skin temperature would not be the measure of choice in a biofeedback treatment procedure. Rapid flow through the arteriovenous anastomoses might heat the finger but leave the affected layers deprived of blood. Indeed, one of the patients discussed in Surwit (1973) reported persistent pain even after her temperature had risen to normal ranges, confirming the earlier observations of Mittlemann and Wolff (1939). If arteriovenous shunting is involved in the production of Raynaud's disease, then a photoplethysmographic measure of surface blood volume might be a better response for feedback than skin temperature in the treatment of this vascular problem.

In evaluating the place of biofeedback in the treatment of Raynaud's disease, one must consider the record of conventional treatments now available. Medical-pharmacological remedies have not been particularly effective in relieving this disorder (Fairbairn et al., 1972). Sympathectomy seems to have been equally unreliable, having the added disadvantage of permanent side effects (Ruch, Patton, Woodbury, & Towe, 1965). It might therefore be preferable to attempt biofeedback in lieu of surgery when more conservative techniques have failed.

Asthma

Asthma is a disorder in which the mucous membranes of the trachea and/or bronchi swell up and restrict the flow of air to the lungs. This response can come in reaction to a variety of allergens and can be exacerbated by emotional and physical stress. Using an allergen as an unconditioned stimulus, it has been demonstrated that the asthmatic reaction can be conditioned to occur to once-neutral stimuli following a simple classical conditioning procedure (Ottenberg, Stein, Lewis, & Hamilton, 1958). In light of this ability of the reaction to be learned, there is good reason to assume the possibility of behavioral components in the development of some asthmatic conditions. Nevertheless, as in the case of other disorders, a behavioral etiology is not necessary in devising a successful behavioral treatment.

Perhaps because asthmatic attacks are commonly thought to be emotion-related (Dunbar, 1943) and can be objectively measured, the behavioral literature contains a variety of conventional behavior therapy approaches to this problem as well as more recent methods employing biofeedback. The first report of a successful behavioral treatment of an asthmatic was by Walton (1960). Working empirically, Walton successfully used assertive training (Wolpe, 1958) for a patient whose asthmatic reactions seemed to occur most frequently when the patient had difficulty expressing aggression. Moore (1965) carried out a controlled study in which she compared systematic desensitization (Wolpe, 1958) with relaxation and suggestion and relaxation alone using subjects as their own controls. She found that while all methods produced subjective reports of improvement, only systematic desensitization produced objective improvement in respiratory function. Sargeant and Yorkston (1969) also reported the successful application of systematic desensitization in the treatment of bronchial asthma.

More recent evidence seems to suggest that, contrary to Moore's findings, relaxation training alone is effective in treating asthma. Alexander, Miklich and Hershkoff (1972) demonstrated that peak expiratory flow rates were increased in children trained in progressive relaxation as compared to children who were asked to sit quietly for a comparable period of time. In a second study, Alexander (1972) replicated the results of Alexander et al., and through the use of a questionnaire technique concluded that anxiety changes were not mediating the therapeutic effect. It was found, however, that subjects whose asthmatic attacks tended to be emotionally related benefited more from relaxation training than other treated children. Although the overall treatment effect was about a 10% increase in peak expiratory flow rate, the effect reached about 35% in the top third of the sample. Alexander concluded that relaxation could therefore be a clinically useful technique if patients were carefully screened by an interview for emotional asthma-precipitating factors. Sirota and Mahoney (1974) also found relaxation training to be of benefit in the treatment of asthma. They described a case in which a patient was taught to abort her asthma attacks and decrease her use of a portable nebulizer by relaxing on cue.

In addition to the promising results obtained with conventional behavioral techniques, there are some indications that direct biofeedback for respiratory resistance can also be used to control asthma. Levenson, Manuck, Strupp, Blackwood, and Snell (1974) devised a technique in which respiratory resistance is measured on each breath, quantified, and fed back to the subject via a digital display. Preliminary data indicate that learned control of airway resistance established in this manner can be of therapeutic benefit in the treatment of asthma.

Pain

Pain is an extremely complex and interesting sensory phenomenon. It can occur in the absence of apparent stimulation, and it can fail to occur even after extensive tissue damage (Melzack, 1973). In that pain seems to be extremely susceptible to attentional shifts and expectancies (Barber, 1970), it seems reasonable that any technique that could influence attention might be beneficial for people experiencing severe pain.

Gannon and Sternbach (1971) reasoned that since meditative states have been shown to coincide with increased EEG alpha activity, and that since alpha activity could be increased with feedback (Kamiya, 1969), feedback training for alpha enhancement might be useful in the treatment of pain. They reported treating one patient who suffered from headaches resulting from an injury. After he was taught to increase occipital alpha activity with eyes open and closed, the patient reported that he was able to prevent some headache from occurring by inducing alpha but was not able to abort pain once the headache began.

Melzack and Perry (personal communication) explored the use of alpha feedback training more systematically. Patients suffering from severe clinical pain received one of three treatments: alpha feedback training, hypnotic suggestion, and alpha feedback and hypnosis in combination. Only the group receiving both alpha feedback and hypnosis together showed a significant reduction in pain as measured by the McGill pain questionnaire. These authors concluded that suggestion plays a major role in determining whether or not alpha training will have an ameliorative effect on pain.

Control of EEG is not the only method in which biofeedback has been shown to be useful in affecting the perception of pain. Sirota et al. (1974) attempted to control directly the visceral components of emotional reactions to pain by manipulating heart rate through feedback. These investigators hypothesized that since heart rate control seems to affect fear in animals (DiCara & Weiss, 1969) and heart rate is closely associated with human fear (Lang, Rice, & Sternbach, 1972), learned control of heart rate should affect human performance in an experimental fear situation. Twenty female subjects were given feedback and reward for either heart rate increases or decreases. Half of the 72 15-second training trials were followed by an electric shock. Warning lights allowed the subjects to differentiate shock from nonshock trials. Voluntary reduction of heart rate was found to lead to a relative reduction in the perceived aversiveness of the shock, particularly for those subjects who reported experiencing cardiac reactions to fear situations in daily life. This novel application of biofeedback has provided a mechanism through which the old James–Lange (James, 1890) theory of emotion might be employed for therapeutic benefit.

Male Sexual Response

Penile tumescence is normally thought to be a reflexive spinal response produced by innervation of the parasympathetic vasodilator fibers emanating from the sacral cord (Weiss, 1972). However, as has been the case with the other autonomic responses discussed so far, recent evidence has suggested that penile tumescence can be brought under the control of both external contingencies and the "volition" of the subject. Laws and Rubin (1969) demonstrated that subjects could voluntarily partially suppress erections to an erotic film and produce partial erections on demand without external stimulation or manipulation. Henson and Rubin (1971) replicated the suppression results using taped verbal erotic stimuli, which minimized the possibility that subjects were using antagonistic cognitive strategies to suppress erections.

More recently, Rosen (1973) has demonstrated that direct feedback for penile tumescence was more effective than instructions alone in suppressing erections elicited by tape-recorded erotic stimuli. It is therefore apparent that aversion therapy techniques (e.g., Bancroft, 1966; Bancroft, 1971; Rachman & Teasdale, 1969) are not necessary in erection suppression paradigms for the treatment of deviant sexual responses.

Feedback and reinforcement have also been found to be useful in the production of erection. Quinn, Harbison, and McAllister (1970) used iced lime to reinforce heterosexually stimulated penile tumescence in a patient who had been water-deprived for 18 hours. Although this patient had been given prior aversion training for homosexual arousal, he showed no response to female stimuli before training. Interestingly, increases in penile tumescence in response to female nude pictures were accompanied by verbal expression of increased heterosexual interest. A controlled study on feedback-induced tumescence was carried out by Rosen, Shapiro, and Schwartz (1974). These investigators gave normal subjects instructions to develop erections without external stimulation during cued periods. A variable-intensity light provided half of the subjects with analogue feedback of tumescence while the other half received no feedback. All subjects received monetary bonuses for increase in tumescence. While all subjects showed substantial ability to increase tumescence, analogue feedback seemed to increase performance. Despite these promising results, Rosen (1974) cautions against therapists using biofeedback in lieu of couples counseling for treatment of sexual dysfunctions because most cases of erectile failure seem to involve crucial relationship factors.

Contraception

French, Leeb, and Fahrion (1974) have explored a novel method of contraception using biofeedback. Several male subjects, first trained in hand temperature control, were then trained in producing scrotal hyperthermia utilizing temperature feedback from the scrotal sac. Regular training sessions were found to produce a marked reduction in viable sperm production, which was reversible when training was discontinued. Scrotal hyperthermia training without prior hand temperature training, however, was not found to be effective in reducing sperm output. While this application of biofeedback technology is dramatic, the data available to date are preliminary and cannot be used as a basis for application as a means of contraception. Data need to be collected on the long-term effect of such training in order to assure that the procedure is both safe and practical.

LIMITATIONS AND PITFALLS OF CLINICAL APPLICATION

The preceding review has suggested that it now seems possible to consider using behavioral techniques in the treatment of a wide variety of physiological disorders. Specifically, there is tentative evidence that direct biofeedback can help in the remediation of physical problems once treatable only by somatic therapy. Much research needs to be done before biofeedback can be advocated as a viable treatment for any disorder. In addition to the question of efficacy there are a host of practical issues that need to be dealt with in evaluating the possible place of biofeedback in the treatment of disease.

The first and perhaps most obvious question of practical concern in the evaluation of biofeedback as a clinical tool is the question of economy. How much time and effort, on the part of both the patient and the practitioner, is needed to obtain a clinically useful result? Even if biofeedback techniques can be shown to be therapeutically effective, what patient would opt for a costly, time-consuming training course if equal therapeutic benefit could be obtained from a pill? It is true that there are no medications that are completely effective for Raynaud's disease, tension headache, and cardiac arrhythmias. However, in many cases medication can be a simple, effective, and painless way to remedy hypertension, epilepsy, and migraine headaches. Unless the side effects of the medication are serious or the efficacy of biofeedback is shown to be superior to that of medication, it seems unlikely that biofeedback will be considered as a treatment of choice.

A related issue has to do with patient motivation. Several articles (e.g., Schwartz, 1973; Schwartz & Shapiro, 1973; Shapiro & Schwartz, 1972; Surwit, 1973) have commented on the importance of patient motivation in any biofeedback treatment program. It is not sufficient to assume that feedback indicating therapeutic improvement will, in and of itself, act as reinforcer and maintain the presistent practice required to gain therapeutic benefit. Indeed, those who have used biofeedback clinically have noted this problem. In one case, Surwit (1973) reported that a patient who had made a long trip to receive biofeedback training complained of being bored during the training sessions and made no progress.

One of the reasons for this problem has been elaborated by Shapiro and Schwartz (1972). Many of the disorders to which biofeedback might be applied have no short-term aversive consequences. Hypertension works its insidious destruction within the cardiovascular system without causing any serious discomfort to the patient. By the time a painful heart attack occurs it is often too late to correct the damage. It is only the knowledge that the patient has hypertension in conjunction with the knowledge that this disorder is not good for him that provides motivation to undergo treatment. However, in light of the fact that most hypertensive patients will not even take their medication regularly, it becomes rather doubtful if biofeedback training requiring long periods of practice will prove useful for most patients. Similar problems can be seen for any disorder in which the practice of biofeedback is not immediately reinforcing. Conversely, one might expect biofeedback treatments to be most appropriate for disorders such as tension headaches where training can lead to immediate relief from pain. Unfortunately, no data exist on the comparative effectiveness of biofeedback in treating disorders such as hypertension as opposed to tension headache.

A second motivational problem encountered in the clinical application of biofeedback is that the symptom itself may be reinforcing for the patient. In other words, the disorder may have secondary gain. A striking example of this was reported by Surwit (1973). A patient who was involved in intensive biofeedback treatment for Raynaud's disease spontaneously expressed her ambivalence of "giving up" her illness because she did not known how to relate to people without it. She was aware of using her Raynaud's disease as an excuse for a poor social life and dependent relationship with her mother. In this case social training was carried out to attempt to remedy the problem. Patients suffering from psychosomatic illnesses often use their well-known sensitivity to emotional situations to manipulate others (Lachman, 1972). A therapy based on "voluntary control" would tend to undermine their manipulations and consequently might not be seen as desirable by the patient. Although early models of behavior therapy tended to ignore the more subtle contingencies implicit in some behavioral problems, more recent writers are taking them into account (e.g., Kraft, 1972; Lazarus, 1971). In that some of these contingencies might not be known to the patient explicitly, they may be considered unconscious. A behavioral therapy designed to treat a disorder supported by secondary gain would therefore have to include techniques aimed at making up any social deficit left by the removal of the symptom. These might include setting up family contingencies and/or working on alternative means of social interaction. When the patient himself does not see the need for such additional procedures, an insight-oriented approach may be called for as a first step.

A third possible area of motivational difficulty may arise from other behaviors strongly entrenched in the patient's repertoire which are in conflict with the aim of therapy. This is best illustrated in a case discussed by Schwartz (1973). A patient was treated for essential hypertension and a week of treatment would lower his blood pressure by as much as 20 mm Hg. Over the weekend his pressure would become elevated again. The difficulty turned out to be that the patient liked to gamble at the race track on weekends and persisted in doing so despite the fact that such activities were countertherapeutic. This last point is extremely important. There is good evidence that certain schedules of reinforcement can induce ulcers and hypertension in normal animals (Benson et al., 1969; Benson, Herd, Morse, & Kelleher, 1970; Brady, 1958; Harris et al., 1973). It would seem futile to attempt to treat a disorder by biofeedback unless work were also done on analyzing and correcting contingencies that might be aggravating the problem.

An issue closely related to motivation and equally important in the successful application of biofeedback techniques is transfer of training. It is often all too easy to forget, even for psychologists, that learning techniques cannot be administered the way most medical treatments can. There is no reason to believe that biofeedback, like radiation therapy and diathermy, can be expected to produce sustained effects outside the treatment session. It is completely logical that a patient may show perfect control over his problem during a feedback session and no control at home. In basic research in normal subjects, some investigators have explored the use of intermittent reinforcement schedules as an aid to generalization (Greene, 1966; Shapiro & Crider, 1967; Shapiro & Watanabe, 1971), but the evidence is too scanty to conclude that partial reinforcement increases resistance to extinction in the case of visceral responses. Weiss and

Engel (1971) in their study of the control of premature ventricular contractions phased the feedback out gradually, making it available all the time at first, then 1 minute on and 1 minute off, then 1 on and 3 off, and finally 1 on and 7 off. The purpose of the procedure was to wean the patient from the feedback and also enable the patient to become more aware of his arrhythmia through his own sensations rather than through the feedback. Hefferline and Bruno (1971) described a similar technique of slowly fading out the feedback as a means of transferring external to internal control. There is also evidence for the short-term maintenance of learned control of diastolic pressure (Shapiro et al., 1972b), but the need is great for comprehensive research on extinction processes and on self-control without feedback in autonomic learning.

A related but more complex issue concerns the need of patients to control their reactivity to stressful stimuli or situations. In most cases, biofeedback procedures are applied in resting, nonstimulating laboratory settings. Will the patient be able to transfer this training to the relevant situations in everyday life? Sirota et al. (1974) attempted to explore the effects of feedback-assisted voluntary control of heart rate to facilitate adaptation to noxious events. An earlier study (Shapiro, Schwartz, Nelson, Shnidman, & Silverman, 1972a) combined skin resistance feedback and reinforcement with a variant of desensitization procedure in attempting to facilitate adaptation of phobic subjects to the feared stimuli (snakes). The methodology of this research follows from several studies indicating that discrete electrodermal responses to stimuli in human subjects can be relatively increased or decreased by means of reinforcement for the appropriate response, and that these changes may have consequences for performance related to these stimuli (Kimmel, Pendergrass, & Kimmel, 1967; Shnidman, 1969, 1970; Shnidman & Shapiro, 1971).

In the Sirota study, in anticipation of receiving noxious electrical stimulation, subjects learned to control their heart rate when provided with external heart rate feedback and reward for appropriate changes. In this study, subjects were also informed about the actual physiological response required for reward. The results showed that voluntary slowing of heart rate led to a relative reduction in the perceived aversiveness of the noxious stimuli, particularly for those subjects who reported experiencing cardiac reactions to fear situations in their daily life. Sirota et al. concluded:

> Taken together, the results support the general conclusion that direct feedback control of autonomic functions which are appropriate for given subjects in terms of their normal fear responding and/or whose relevance for fear has been instructionally induced may possibly be used in systematic desensitization to inhibit anxiety from occurring in response to phobic stimuli and as an adjunct to other therapeutic techniques for the prevention and reduction of anxiety and fear reactions. (1974, p. 266)

Procedures such as these should be studied to increase the potential of transfer of learned control to relevant situations for the individual. In the case of different psychosomatic disorders, to the extent that they involve behavioral and physiological reaction patterns specific to certain types of eliciting stimuli or situations, a physiological desensitization procedure can be designed accordingly.

In addition to motivation, Shapiro and Schwartz (1972) have pointed out that patient characteristics must also be considered in determining the feasibility of biofeedback as a treatment. Because most clinical and experimental work on biofeedback has been done with highly educated, motivated individuals, it is at present unclear how the variables of intelligence, socioeconomic status, and overall adjustment are related to treatment outcome. Until more data shed light on these questions, therapists should be cognizant of the particular characteristics of the population from which successful behavior therapy patients have been drawn.

Because biofeedback involves the treatment of disease, it is one area of psychological practice where the medical model of illness cannot be dismissed. Although many physical disorders can be exacerbated by emotional and environmental variables, most of them have a distinct physical etiology and may represent the "symptom" of a more profound physiological dysfunction. Also, certain disorders that have resulted in permanent destruction and/or alteration of tissue may not be amenable to a behavioral treatment. In many cases, it is conceivable that medication should be used as a valuable concomitant to biofeedback. Engel and Bleecker (1974) have recently argued that one can treat cardiac arrhythmias as isolated symptoms. However, it is probably wise to employ an eclectic strategy in determining the treatment of any physiological disorder. As Pinkerton (1973) aptly remarked, ". . . no single factor is of overriding importance in symptom production [in psychosomatic illness]. The clinical outcome is always determined by a composite etiological sequence, so that the key to successful management lies in correctly evaluating each factor's importance in any given case" (p. 462).

In any event it is clearly not up to the psychologist alone to decide how biofeedback will contribute to the treatment of a physical problem. Consequently, biofeedback should be used clinically only after a competent medical diagnosis has been made and the examining physician has decided that biofeedback may be valuable. Patients coming directly to psychologists for biofeedback or other behavioral treatments of a physical disorder should be referred first to a medical specialist for a thorough examination and work-up. The need for medical participation in any biofeedback case is both an ethical and a legal responsibility of the psychological practitioner. Conversely, it is also the ethical responsibility of a physician who wishes to employ biofeedback in treatment to consult with a psychologist for the behavioral aspects of the proposed therapy. Medical training usually does not provide the in-depth knowledge of behavioral variables of which the practitioner must be cognizant in order for training to be successful. Therefore, the use of biofeedback in therapy for various physiological disorders should be a collaborative endeavor involving both medical and behavioral specialists.

CONCLUSION

This chapter has reviewed research on the behavioral regulation of visceral, somatomotor, and neural processes by means of biofeedback and operant conditioning techniques. Considering the newness of the field and that its major push came such a short time ago with Neal Miller's review in *Science* (1969) on the powerful effects obtained in curarized animals, it is surprising that scores of basic empirical studies have been published. This attests to the recognition by behavioral scientists and psychophysiologists that the approach represents the most significant advance since Pavlov in systematic theory and method for the study of learned modifications of visceral and neural activities. The studies have largely been demonstrative in nature—to show that a wide variety of responses in different species can be altered and to evaluate to some degree concurrent changes in related physiological processes. Although there have been difficulties in reproducing the findings in curarized rats, the human experiments have yielded relatively consistent and convincing data. Experiments on the control of electrodermal activity, heart rate, blood pressure, and brain waves have been repeated successfully in the same and independent laboratories.

Now investigators are turning their attention to more incisive questions of a theoretical and practical nature: (1) What are some of the biological, behavioral and environmental mechanisms of learned physiological control? How is the learning constrained by other forces within and outside the individual? (2) What can be said about the extent and persistence of learning brought about by the techniques? Can they bring about a *true* "altered" state of physiology? Of consciousness? (3) How do the effects achieved by these techniques compare with other factors, perhaps less well defined, known to influence physiological functioning, e.g., stress, anxiety, emotion, and attitudinal dispositions of the individual? (4) What is the practical value of this new development in research? Can the techniques and concepts be used to enhance potentialities for human growth and development? Can abnormal physiological processes be altered significantly? What are the possibilities for nonmedical use of the techniques, e.g., in education or recreation?

We have focused our attention on clinical application, reflecting the wide interest and enthusiasm for biofeedback as a corrective therapy, as evidenced by its extensive coverage in the media, the founding of "biofeedback clinics," and the advertising, sometimes misleading or distorted, of feedback devices for individual use. In a short period of time, the Biofeedback Research Society has grown to a membership of more than 400, and many members are in the hot pursuit of clinical goals. Yet, while the clinical work we have reported is extensive, its scientific quality is not up to par. The stage has been one, for both scientists and clinicians, of finding therapeutic effects as rapidly as possible. This has meant the short-circuiting of time, effort, and money involved in long-term, controlled clinical trials. This has also meant that there is *not one* well-controlled scientific study of the effectiveness of biofeedback and operant conditioning in treating a particular physiological disorder. The clinical data and case studies described are convincing in some instances, not at all in others. The most substantial work has been done where medical and physiological factors in the illness are given precise definition, where symptoms are shown to vary as the treatment conditions are varied, and where long-term and follow-up data are reported. As yet, the lack of controls for placebo and other nonspecific effects leaves open the question of what is unique to biofeedback training methods and what is not. Carefully controlled and evaluated clinical trials are obviously difficult, but they are vital before biofeedback methods will take their place alongside other established practices in medicine.

In his 1973 overview, Schwartz introduced a note of pessimism about the application of biofeedback techniques to chronic physical disease, particularly in the absence of other therapeutic procedures. He opposed the simplistic use of the feedback method without regard for a thorough appraisal of the interaction of biological and environmental factors in any particular disorder or patient. He advocated a combined "behavioral-biological" approach that stresses three broad factors: (1) the natural interrelations of responses (pattern of interaction among various concurrent physiological responses), (2) the exact manner in which the feedback and reward is presented, and (3) the role of biological, cognitive, and environmental constraints. This is a tall order, yet an important acknowledgement that biofeedback is neither panacea nor magic pill, that most symptoms do not exist in a vacuum, that a *comprehensive* approach to treatment is required utilizing as many positive forces within and outside the individual as necessary. The mindless application of biofeedback training is no more sensible than the mindless taking of pills or patent medicines.

The power of the biofeedback concept and method, it seems to us, lies in its preciseness. Unlike other disciplines such as various forms of yoga and meditation practice, which are only recently beginning to be defined in terms of specific associated physiological and behavioral processes (see Benson et al., 1974), the focus of biofeedback is on specific responses or patterns of responses and its potential to bring these under specific control. In disorders with circumscribed, isolated, or well-defined symptoms, this precision is of enormous significance from a behavioral standpoint. In disorders in which the symptomatology is less well defined or the critical responses or response patterns are not readily accessible to peripheral measurement or available feedback techniques, the precision of biofeedback is to less avail, although feedback for global patterns of response such as in total relaxation has its place. As research on the physiological and behavioral concomitants of the different disorders progresses, the potential value of biofeedback as a treatment will improve.

We must also highlight the apparent split focus that exists in this area of research and clinical application. The feedback concept appears to emphasize internal processes, internal regulation and awareness and self-control. The operant or instrumental concept appears to emphasize external forces, reinforcers in the environment that shape behavior *and* physiology. While feedback and reinforcement may be seen as separate but interdependent processes, the techniques themselves are essentially the same. However, when viewed as separate techniques, the implications for their effective application in therapy may be sufficiently different to call attention to them. In some respects, the feedback concept, ignoring reinforcement and motivation, would seem to put the onus on the individual—on *his* turning off his maladaptive responses and on *his* developing a general attitude toward the environment (for example, a passive unreactive stance). The instrumental concept would seem to give greater emphasis to external events or reinforcers, to environmental contingencies acting in relation to the individual's behavior and physiological responses. In this perspective, the onus is not on the individual per se but on the interaction of his behavior with environmental events, usually social reinforcers. It is the link between behavior and reinforcement that needs to be altered. Of course, what is external becomes internal; both forces come together, and both must be recognized and accounted for in any effective application. Both the individual *and* the environment must be involved in any corrective therapy.

Finally, the translation of biofeedback into a form of "behavioral medicine" (Birk, 1973) calls attention to the importance of man's adaptive and coping mechanisms, both internal and external, in illness and in health. With this, we see an important renewed emphasis in medicine on *behavioral* approaches, not only in treatment but also in prevention of illness and maintenance of good health. We hope that the clinical and research potentials of biofeedback and instrumental learning will provide further means of integrating behavioral sciences, biology, and medicine.

ACKNOWLEDGMENTS. This work was supported by National Institute of Mental Health Grants K5-MH-20,476, MH-08853, and MH-08934; Office of Naval Research Contract N00014-67-A-0298-0024, NR 101-052. We thank J. Alan Herd for his advice.

REFERENCES

Ádám, G. *Interoception and behavior.* Budapest: Akademiai Kiado, 1967.

Adams, R. D. Recurrent convulsions. In J. V. Harrison, R. D. Adams, I. L. Bennett, W. H. Resnik, G. W. Thorn, & M. M. Wintrobe (Eds.), *Principles of internal medicine.* New York: McGraw-Hill, 1966.

Alexander, A. B. Systematic relaxation and flow rates in asthmatic children: Relationship to emotional precipitants and anxiety. *Journal of Psychosomatic Research,* 1972, *16,* 405–410.

Alexander, A. B., Miklich, D. R., & Hershkoff, H. The immediate effects of systematic relaxation training on peak expiratory flow rates in asthmatic children. *Psychosomatic Medicine,* 1972, *34,* 388–394.

Alexander, F., & Flagg, G. W. The psychosomatic approach. In B. B. Wolman (Ed.), *Handbook of clinical psychology.* New York: McGraw-Hill, 1965.

Amato, A., Hermsmeyer, C. A., & Kleinman, K. M. Use of electromyographic feedback to increase inhibitory control of spastic muscles. *Physical Therapy,* 1973, *53,* 1063–1066.

Annett, J. *Feedback and human behavior.* Baltimore: Penguin Books, 1969.

Anthony, M., Hinterberger, H., & Lance, J. W. Plasma serotonin in migraine and stress. *Archives of Neurology,* 1967, *16,* 544–552.

Bahrick, H. P., Fitts, P. M., & Rankin, R. E. Effect of incentives upon reaction to peripheral stimuli. *Journal of Experimental Psychology,* 1952, *44,* 400–406.

Bair, J. H. Development of voluntary control. *Psychological Review,* 1901, *8,* 474–510.

Bancroft, J. The application of psychophysiological measures to the assessment and modification of sexual behavior. *Behaviour Research and Therapy,* 1971, *9,* 119–130.

Bancroft, J. H. J. *Aversion therapy.* Unpublished dissertation for Diploma, Psychological Medicine, University of London, 1966. (Reported in S. Rachman & J. Teasdale, 1969.)

Bandura, A. *Principles of behavior modification.* New York: Holt, Rinehart & Winston, 1969.

Barber, T. X. *LSD, marihuana, yoga, and hypnosis.* Chicago: Aldine, 1970.

Barber, T. X., DiCara, L. V., Kamiya, J., Miller, N. E., Shapiro, D., & Stoyva, J. (Eds.). *Biofeedback and self-control 1970: An Aldine Annual on the regulation of bodily processes and consciousness.* Chicago: Aldine-Atherton, 1971.

Baron, J. An EEG correlate of autonomic discrimination. *Psychonomic Science*, 1966, *4*, 255–256.

Basmajian, J. V. Control and training of individual motor units. *Science*, 1963, *141*, 440–441.

Basmajian, J. V. Electromyography comes of age. *Science*, 1972, *176*, 603–609.

Beatty, J. Effects of initial alpha wave abundance and operant training procedures on occipital alpha and beta wave activity. *Psychonomic Science*, 1971, *23*, 197–199.

Beatty, J., Greenberg, A., Deibler, W. P., & O'Hanlon, J. F. Operant control of occipital theta rhythm affects performance in a radar monitoring task. *Science*, 1974, *183*, 871–873.

Beatty, J., & Kornfeld, C. Relative independence of conditioned EEG changes from cardiac and respiratory activity. *Physiology and Behavior*, 1972, *9*, 733–736.

Beeson, P. B., & McDermott, W. (Eds.). *Cecil-Loeb textbook of medicine* (12th ed.). Philadelphia: W. B. Saunders, 1967.

Benson, H., Beary, J. F., & Carol, M. P. The relaxation response. *Psychiatry*, 1974, *37*, 37–46.

Benson, H., Herd, J. A., Morse, W. H., & Kelleher, R. T. Behavioral induction of arterial hypertension and its reversal. *American Journal of Physiology*, 1969, *217*, 30–34.

Benson, H., Herd, J. A., Morse, W. H., & Kelleher, R. T. Behaviorally induced hypertension in the squirrel monkey. *Circulation Research* (Suppl. 1), 1970, *26–27*, 21–26.

Benson, H., Rosner, B. A., Marzetta, B. R., & Klemchuk, H. M. Decreased blood-pressure in pharmacologically treated hypertensive patients who regularly elicited the relaxation response. *Lancet*, 1974, *7852*, 289–291.

Benson, H., Shapiro, D., Tursky, B., & Schwartz, G. E. Decreased systolic blood pressure through operant conditioning techniques in patients with essential hypertension. *Science*, 1971, *173*, 740–742.

Bergman, J. S., & Johnson, H. J. Sources of information which affect training and raising of heart rate. *Psychophysiology*, 1972, *9*, 30–39.

Bernard, J., & Gilbert, R. W. The specificity of the effect of shock per error in a maze learning experiment with human subjects. *Journal of Experimental Psychology*, 1941, *28*, 178–186.

Bilodeau, I. McD. Information feedback. In E. A. Bilodeau & I. McD. Bilodeau (Eds.), *Principles of skill acquisition.* New York: Academic Press, 1969.

Birk, L. (Ed.). *Biofeedback: Behavioral medicine.* New York: Grune and Stratton, 1973.

Birk, L., Crider, A., Shapiro, D., & Tursky, B. Operant electrodermal conditioning under partial curarization. *Journal of Comparative and Physiological Psychology*, 1966, *62*, 165–166.

Black, A. H. The operant conditioning of central nervous system electrical activity. In G. H. Bower (Ed.), *The psychology of learning and motivation: Advances in research and theory.* New York: Academic Press, 1972.

Black, A. H., Young, G. A., & Batenchuck, C. Avoidance training of hippocampal theta waves in Flaxedilized dogs and its relation to skeletal movement. *Journal of Comparative and Physiological Psychology*, 1970, *70*, 15–24.

Blanchard, E. B., & Young, L. D. Self-control of cardiac functioning: A promise as yet unfulfilled. *Psychological Bulletin*, 1973, *79*, 145–163.

Blanchard, E. B., Young, L. D., & McLeod, P. G. Awareness of heart activity and self-control of heart rate. *Psychophysiology*, 1972, *9*, 63–68.

Bleecker, E. R., & Engel, B. T. Learned control of cardiac rate and cardiac conduction in the Wolff-Parkinson-White syndrome. *New England Journal of Medicine*, 1973, *288*, 560–562. (a)

Bleecker, E. R., & Engel, B. T. Learned control of ventricular rate in patients with atrial fibrillation. *Psychosomatic Medicine*, 1973, *35*, 161–175. (b)

Brady, J. P. Metronome-conditioned relaxation: A new behavioral procedure. *British Journal of Psychiatry*, 1973, *122*, 729–730.

Brady, J. P., Luborsky, L., & Kron, R. E. Blood pressure reduction in patients with essential hypertension through metronome-conditioned relaxation: A preliminary report. *Behavior Therapy*, 1974, *5*, 203–209.

Brady, J. V. Ulcers in "executive" monkeys. *Scientific American*, 1958, *199*, 95–103.

Brener, J. A general model of voluntary control applied to the phenomena of learned cardiovascular change. In P. A. Obrist, A. H. Black, J. Brener, & L. V. DiCara (Eds.), *Cardiovascular psychophysiology*. Chicago: Aldine, 1974.

Brener, J., Eissenberg, E., & Middaugh, S. Respiratory and somatomotor factors associated with operant conditioning of cardiovascular responses in curarized rats. In P. A. Obrist, A. H. Black, J. Brener, & L. V. DiCara (Eds.), *Cardiovascular psychophysiology*. Chicago: Aldine, 1974.

Brener, J., & Kleinman, R. A. Learned control of decreases in systolic blood pressure. *Nature*, 1970, *226*, 1063–1064.

Brener, J., Kleinman, R. A., & Goesling, W. J. The effects of different exposures to augmented sensory feedback on the self-control of heart rate. *Psychophysiology*, 1969, *5*, 510–516.

Brown, B. B. Recognition of aspects of consciousness through association with EEG alpha activity represented by a light signal. *Psychophysiology*, 1970, *6*, 442–452.

Brudny, J., Grynbaum, B. B., & Korein, J. Spasmodic torticollis: Treatment by feedback display of the EMG. *Archives of Physical Medicine and Rehabiliation*, 1974, *55*, 403–408.

Budzynski, T. H. Biofeedback procedures in the clinic. *Seminars in Psychiatry*, 1973, *5*, 537–547.

Budzynski, T. A systems approach to some clinical applications of biofeedback. *Proceedings of the Biofeedback Research Society*, 1974, p. 105. (Abstract)

Budzynski, T., Stoyva, J., & Adler, C. Feedback induced muscle relaxation: Application to tension headache. *Journal of Behavior Therapy and Experimental Psychiatry*, 1970, *1*, 205–211.

Budzynski, T. H., Stoyva, J. M., Adler, C. S., & Mullaney, D. J. EMG biofeedback and tension headache: A controlled outcome study. *Psychosomatic Medicine*, 1973, *35*, 484–496.

Bunch, M. E. The effect of electric shock as punishment in human maze learning. *Journal of Comparative Psychology*, 1928, *8*, 343–359.

Bykov, K. M. *The cerebral cortex and the internal organs*. W. H. Gantt (Ed. and trans.). New York: Chemical Publishing Co., 1957.

Carmona, A., Miller, N. E., & Demierre, T. Instrumental learning of gastric tonicity responses. *Psychosomatic Medicine*, 1974, *36*, 156–163.

Chiang, B. N., Perlman, L. V., Ostander, L. D., Jr., & Epstein, F. H. Relationship of premature systoles to coronary heart disease and sudden death in the Tecumseh epidemiologic study. *Annals of Internal Medicine*, 1969, *70*, 1159–1166.

Corday, E., Gold, H., DeVera, L. B., Williams, J. H., & Fields, J. Effect of the cardiac arrhythmias on the coronary circulation. *Annals of Internal Medicine*, 1959, *50*, 535–553.

Corday, E., & Irving, D. W. Effect of cardiac arrhythmias on the cerebral circulation. *American Journal of Cardiology*, 1960, *6*, 803–807.

Crider, A., Schwartz, G. E., & Shapiro, D. Operant suppression of electrodermal response rate as a function of punishment schedule. *Journal of Experimental Psychology*, 1970, *83*, 333–334.

Crider, A., Shapiro, D., & Tursky, B. Reinforcement of spontaneous electrodermal activity. *Journal of Comparative and Physiological Psychology*, 1966, *61*, 20–27.

Datey, K. K., Deshmukh, S. N., Dalvi, C. P., & Vinekar, S. L. "Shavasan": A yogic exercise in the management of hypertension. *Angiology*, 1969, *20*, 325–333.

DiCara, L. V., & Miller, N. E. Changes in heart rate instrumentally learned by curarized rats as avoidance responses. *Journal of Comparative and Physiological Psychology*, 1968, *65*, 8–12. (a)

DiCara, L. V., & Miller, N. E. Instrumental learning of systolic blood pressure responses by curarized rats: Dissociation of cardiac and vascular changes. *Psychosomatic Medicine*, 1968, *30*, 489–494. (b)

DiCara, L. V., & Miller, N. E. Instrumental learning of vasomotor responses by rats: Learning to respond differentially in the two ears. *Science*, 1968, *159*, 1485–1486. (c)

DiCara, L. V., & Weiss, J. M. Effect of heart-rate learning under curare on subsequent noncurarized avoidance learning. *Journal of Comparative and Physiological Psychology*, 1969, *69*, 368–374.

Dunbar, F. *Psychosomatic diagnosis*. New York: Paul B. Hoeber, 1943.

Eddleman, E. E., Jr., Resnik, W. H., & Harrison, T. R. Disorders of rate, rhythm, and conduction. In J. V. Harrison, R. D. Adams, I. L. Bennett, W. H. Resnik, G. W. Thorn, & M. M. Wintrobe (Eds.), *Principles of internal medicine*. New York: McGraw-Hill, 1966.

Edelberg, R. Electrical activity of the skin: Its measurement and uses in psychophysiology. In N. S.

Greenfield & R. A. Sternbach (Eds.), *Handbook of psychophysiology*. New York: Holt, Rinehart & Winston, 1972.

Engel, B. T. Operant conditioning of cardiac function: A status report. *Psychophysiology*, 1972, *9*, 161–177.

Engel, B. T. Clinical applications of operant conditioning techniques in the control of the cardiac arrhythmias. *Seminars in Psychiatry*, 1973, *5*, 433–438.

Engel, B. T., & Bleecker, E. R. Application of operant conditioning techniques to the control of the cardiac arrhythmias. In P. A. Obrist, A. H. Black, J. Brener, & L. V. DiCara (Eds.), *Cardiovascular psychophysiology*. Chicago: Aldine, 1974.

Engel, B. T., & Chism, R. A. Operant conditioning of heart rate speeding. *Psychophysiology*, 1967, *3*, 418–426.

Engel, B. T., & Gottlieb, S. H. Differential operant conditioning of heart rate in the restrained monkey. *Journal of Comparative and Physiological Psychology*, 1970, *73*, 217–225.

Engel, B. T., & Hansen, S. P. Operant conditioning of heart rate slowing. *Psychophysiology*, 1966, *3*, 176–187.

Fairbairn, J. F., Juergens, J. L., & Spittell, J. A., Jr. (Eds.). *Allen-Barker-Hines, peripheral vascular diseases* (4th ed.). Philadelphia: W. B. Saunders, 1972.

Fowler, R. L., & Kimmel, H. D. Operant conditioning of the GSR. *Journal of Experimental Psychology*, 1962, *63*, 563–567.

French, D., Leeb, C., & Fahrion, S. Self-induced scrotal hyperthermia: An extension. *Proceedings of the Biofeedback Research Society*, 1974, p. 62. (Abstract)

Gannon, L., & Sternbach, R. A. Alpha enhancement as a treatment for pain: A case study. *Behavior Therapy and Experimental Psychiatry*, 1971, *2*, 209–213.

Green, E. E., Green, A. M., & Walters, E. D. Voluntary control of internal states: Psychological and physiological. In T. X. Barber, L. V. DiCara, J. Kamiya, N. E. Miller, D. Shapiro, & J. Stoyva (Eds.), *Biofeedback and self-control 1970: An Aldine Annual on the regulation of bodily processes and consciousness*. Chicago: Aldine-Atherton, 1971.

Greene, W. A. Operant conditioning of the GSR using partial reinforcement. *Psychological Reports*, 1966, *19*, 571–578.

Gutmann, M. C., & Benson, H. Interaction of environmental factors and systemic arterial blood pressure: A review. *Medicine*, 1971, *50*, 543–553.

Hahn, W. W. A look at the recent history and current developments in laboratory studies of autonomic conditioning. *Proceedings of the Biofeedback Research Society*, 1974, p. 94. (Abstract)

Harris, A. H., Findley, J. D., & Brady J. V. Instrumental conditioning of blood pressure elevations in the baboon. *Conditional Reflex*, 1971, *6*, 215–226.

Harris, A. H., Gilliam, W. J., Findley, J. D., & Brady, J. V. Instrumental conditioning of large magnitude, daily, 12-hour blood pressure elevations in the baboon. *Science*, 1973, *182*, 175–177.

Hefferline, R. F. Learning theory and clinical psychology—an eventual symbiosis. In A. J. Bacharach (Ed.), *Experimental foundations of clinical psychology*. New York: Basic Books. 1962.

Hefferline, R. F., & Bruno, L. J. J. The psychophysiology of private events. In A. Jacobs & L. B. Sachs (Eds.), *The psychology of private events*. New York: Academic Press, 1971.

Hefferline, R. F., & Keenan, B. Amplitude-induction gradient of a small human operant in an escape-avoidance situation. *Journal of the Experimental Analysis of Behavior*, 1961, *4*, 41–43.

Henson, D. E., & Rubin, H. B. Voluntary control of eroticism. *Journal of Applied Behavior Analysis*, 1971, *4*, 37–44.

Herburg, L. J. The hypothalamus and the aetiology of migraine. In R. Smith (Ed.), *Background to migraine*. London: Heinemann, 1967.

Hull, C. L. *Essentials of behavior*. New Haven: Yale University Press, 1951.

Jacobs, A., & Felton, G. S. Visual feedback of myoelectric output to facilitate muscle relaxation in normal persons and patients with neck injuries. *Archives of Physical Medicine and Rehabilitation*, 1969, *50*, 34–39.

Jacobson, A. M., Hackett, T. P., Surman, O. S., & Silverberg, E. L. Raynaud phenomenon. Treatment with hypnotic and operant technique. *Journal of the American Medical Association*, 1973, *225*, 739–740.

Jacobson, E. *Progressive relaxation* (2nd ed.). Chicago: University of Chicago Press, 1938.

Jacobson, E. *Anxiety and tension control. A physiological approach*. Philadelphia: Lippincott, 1964.

James, W. *The principles of psychology*. New York: Holt, Rinehart & Winston, 1890.

Johnson, H. J., & Schwartz, G. E. Suppression of GSR activity through operant reinforcement. *Journal of Experimental Psychology*, 1967, *75*, 307–312.

Johnson, R. J. Operant reinforcement of an autonomic response. *Dissertation Abstracts*, 1963, *24*, 1255–1256. (Abstract)

Kamiya, J. Operant control of the EEG alpha rhythm and some of its reported effects on consciousness. In C. Tart (Ed.), *Altered states of consciousness*. New York: Wiley, 1969.

Kamiya, J., Barber, T. X., DiCara, L. V., Miller, N. E., Shapiro, D., & Stoyva, J. (Eds.). *Biofeedback and self-control: An Aldine Reader on the regulation of bodily processes and consciousness*. Chicago: Aldine-Atherton, 1971.

Kannel, W. B., Gordon, T., & Schwartz, M. J. Systolic versus diastolic blood pressure and risk of coronary heart disease. *American Journal of Cardiology*, 1971, *27*, 335–343.

Kaplan, B., *EEG biofeedback and epilepsy*. Paper presented at the meeting of the American Psychological Association, Montreal, August 1973.

Khachaturian, Z., Kerr, J., Kruger, R., & Schachter, J. A methodological note: Comparison between period and rate data in studies of cardiac function. *Psychophysiology*, 1972, *9*, 539–545.

Kimble, G. A., & Perlmuter, L. C. The problem of volition. *Psychological Review*, 1970, *77*, 361–384.

Kimmel, H. D., Pendergrass, V. E., & Kimmel, E. B. Modifying children's orienting reactions instrumentally. *Conditional Reflex*, 1967, *2*, 227–235.

Kleinman, K. M., & Goldman, H. Effects of biofeedback on the physiological and cognitive consequences of essential hypertension. *Proceedings of the Biofeedback Research Society*, 1974, p. 37. (Abstract)

Kraft, T. The use of behavior therapy in a psychotherapeutic context. In A. A. Lazarus (Ed.), *Clinical behavior therapy*. New York: Brunner/Mazel, 1972.

Lachman, S. J. *Psychosomatic disorders: A behavioristic interpretation*. New York: Wiley, 1972.

Lance, J. W., & Anthony, M. Thermographic studies in vascular headache. *Medical Journal of Australia*, 1971, *1*, 240–243.

Lang, P. J. Learned control of human heart rate in a computer directed environmnt. In P. A. Obrist, A. H. Black, J. Brener, & L. V. DiCara (Eds.), *Cardiovascular psychophysiology*. Chicago: Aldine, 1974.

Lang, P. J., Rice, D. G., & Sternbach, R. A. The psychophysiology of emotion. In N. S. Greenfield & R. A. Sternbach (Eds.), *Handbook of psychophysiology*. New York: Holt, Rinehart & Winston, 1972.

Lang, P. J., & Twentyman, C. T. Learning to control heart rate: Binary versus analogue feedback. *Psychophysiology*, 1974, *11*, 616–629.

Langer, P., & Croccel, L. *Le phénomène de Raynaud: Aspects cliniques, étiopathogeniques et thérapeutiques*. Paris: L'Expansion Scientifique Française, 1960.

Laws, D. R., & Rubin, H. B. Instructional control of an autonomic sexual response. *Journal of Applied Behavior Analysis*, 1969, *2*, 93–99.

Lazarus, A. *Behavior therapy and beyond*. New York: McGraw-Hill, 1971.

Levene, H. T., Engel, B. T., & Pearson, J. A. Differential operant conditioning of heart rate. *Psychosomatic Medicine*, 1968, *30*, 837–845.

Levenson, R. W., Manuck, S. B., Strupp, H. H., Blackwood, G. L., & Snell, J. D. A biofeedback technique for bronchial asthma. *Proceedings of the Biofeedback Research Society*, 1974, p. 11. (Abstract)

Lewis, T. *Vascular disorders of the limbs: Described for practitioners and students*. London: Macmillan, 1949.

Lisina, M. I. The role of orientation in the transformation of involuntary into voluntary reactions. In L. G. Voronin, A. N. Leontiev, A. R. Luria, E. N. Sokolov, & O. S. Vinogradova (Eds.), *Orienting reflex and exploratory behavior*. Moscow: Akad. Pedag. Nauk RSFSR, 1958 (in Russian); Washington, D.C.: American Psychological Association, 1965 (in English).

Lown, B., & Wolf, M. Approaches to sudden death. *Circulation*, 1971, *44*, 130–142.

Luthe, W., & Schultz, J. H. *Autogenic therapy, medical applications* (Vol. 2). New York: Grune and Stratton, 1969.

Lynch, J. J., & Paskewitz, D. A. On the mechanisms of the feedback control of human brain wave activity. *Journal of Nervous and Mental Disease*, 1971, *153*, 205–217.

Lynch, W. C., Hama, H., Kohn, S., & Miller, N. E. Instrumental learning of vasomotor responses: A progress report. *Proceedings of the Biofeedback Research Society*, 1974, p. 68. (Abstract)

Marinacci, A. A. *Clinical electromyography*. Los Angeles: San Lucas Press, 1955.

Marinacci, A. A. The basic principles underlying neuromuscular re-education. In D. Shapiro, T. X. Barber, L. V. DiCara, J. Kamiya, N. E. Miller, & J. Stoyva (Eds.), *Biofeedback and self-control 1972: An Aldine Annual on the regulation of bodily processes and consciousness*. Chicago: Aldine, 1973.

Marinacci, A. A., & Horande, M. Electromyogram in neuromuscular re-education. *Bulletin of the Los Angeles Neurological Society*, 1960, *25*, 57–71.

Melzack, R. *The puzzle of pain*. New York: Basic Books, 1973.

Merrill, J. P. Hypertensive vascular disease. In J. V. Harrison, R. D. Adams, I. L. Bennett, W. H. Resnik, G. W. Thorn, & M. M. Wintrobe (Eds.), *Principles of internal medicine*. New York: McGraw-Hill, 1966.

Miller, N. E. Learning of visceral and glandular responses. *Science*, 1969, *163*, 434–445.

Miller, N. E. Applications of learning and biofeedback to psychiatry and medicine. In A. M. Freedman, H. I. Kaplan, & B. J. Sadock (Eds.), *Comprehensive textbook of psychiatry—II*. Baltimore: Williams & Wilkins, 1975.

Miller, N. E., & Banuazizi, A. Instrumental learning by curarized rats of a specific visceral response, intestinal or cardiac. *Journal of Comparative and Physiological Psychology*, 1968, *65*, 1–7.

Miller, N. E., Barber, T. X., DiCara, L. V., Kamiya, J., Shapiro, D., & Stoyva, J. (Eds.). *Biofeedback and self-control 1973: An Aldine Annual on the regulation of bodily processes and consciousness*. Chicago: Aldine, 1974.

Miller, N. E., & Carmona, A. Modification of a visceral response, salivation in thirsty dogs, by instrumental training with water reward. *Journal of Comparative and Physiological Psychology*, 1967, *63*, 1–6.

Miller, N. E., & DiCara, L. V. Instrumental learning of urine formation by rats; changes in renal blood flow. *American Journal of Physiology*, 1968, *215*, 677–683.

Miller, N. E., & Dworkin, B. R. Visceral learning: Recent difficulties with curarized rats and significant problems for human research. In P. A. Obrist, A. H. Black, J. Brener, & L. V. DiCara (Eds.), *Cardiovascular psychophysiology*. Chicago: Aldine, 1974.

Mittlemann, B. & Wolff, H. G. Affective states and skin temperature: Experimental study of subjects with "cold hands" and Raynaud's syndrome. *Psychosomatic Medicine*, 1939, *1*, 271–292.

Moore, N. Behavior therapy in bronchial asthma: A controlled study. *Journal of Psychosomatic Research*, 1965, *9*, 257–276.

Mulholland, T. Feedback electroencephalography. *Activitas Nervosa Superior*, 1968, *10*, 410–438.

Nowlis, D. P., & Kamiya, J. The control of electroencephalographic alpha rhythms through auditory feedback and the associated mental activity. *Psychophysiology*, 1970, *6*, 476–484.

Obrist, P. A., Howard, J. L., Lawler, J. E., Galosy, R. A., Meyers, K. A., & Gaebelein, C. J. The cardiac-somatic interaction. In P. A. Obrist, A. H. Black, J. Brener, & L. V. DiCara (Eds.), *Cardiovascular psychophysiology*. Chicago: Aldine, 1974.

Ogden, E., & Shock, N. W. Voluntary hypercirculation. *American Journal of Medical Sciences*, 1939, *198*, 329–342.

Ostfeld, A. M. *The common headache syndromes: Biochemistry, pathophysiology, therapy*. Springfield, Illinois: Charles C. Thomas, 1962.

Ottenberg, P., Stein, M., Lewis, J., Hamilton, C. Learned asthma in the guinea pig. *Psychosomatic Medicine*, 1958, *20*, 395–400.

Pappas, B. A., DiCara, L. V., & Miller, N. E. Learning of blood pressure responses in the non-curarized rat: Transfer to the curarized state. *Physiological Behavior*, 1970, *5*, 1029–1032.

Parry, P. *Effect of reward on performance of hyperactive children*. Unpublished doctoral dissertation, McGill Unversity, 1973.

Paskewitz, D. A., & Orne, M. T. Visual effects on alpha feedback training. *Science*, 1973, *181*, 360-363.

Patterson, G. R. *Families: Applications of social learning to family life*. Champaign, Illinois: Research Press, 1971.

Pinkerton, P. The enigma of asthma. *Psychosomatic Medicine*, 1973, *35*, 461-462.

Plumlee, L. A. Operant conditioning of increases in blood pressure. *Psychophysiology*, 1969, *6*, 283-290.

Quinn, J. T., Harbison, J. J. M., & McAllister, H. An attempt to shape human penile responses. *Behaviour Research and Therapy*, 1970, *8*, 213-216.

Rachman, S., & Teasdale, J. *Aversion therapy and behavior disorders: An analysis*. Coral Gables, Florida: University of Miami Press, 1969.

Raskin, M., Johnson, G., & Rondestvedt, J. W. Chronic anxiety treated by feedback-induced muscle relaxation. *Archives of General Psychiatry*, 1973, *28*, 263-267.

Razran, G. The observable unconscious and the inferable conscious in current Soviet psychophysiology: Interoceptive conditioning, semantic conditioning, and the orienting reflex. *Psychological Review*, 1961, *68*, 81-147.

Rice, D. G. Operant GSR conditioning and associated electromyogram responses. *Journal of Experimental Psychology*, 1966, *71*, 908-912.

Roberts, A., Kewman, D. G., & Macdonald, H. Voluntary control of skin temperature: Unilateral changes using hypnosis and feedback. *Journal of Abnormal Psychology*, 1973, *82*, 163-168.

Roberts, A. H., Schuler, J., Bacon, J., & Zimmerman, R. L. Individual differences and autonomic control: Absorption, hypnotic susceptibility and the unilateral control of skin temperature. *Proceedings of the Biofeedback Research Society*, 1974, p. 67. (Abstract)

Roberts, L. E. Operant autonomic conditioning in paralyzed rats. *Proceedings of the Biofeedback Research Society*, 1974, p. 94. (Abstract)

Rosen, R. C. Suppression of penile tumescence by instrumental conditioning. *Psychosomatic Medicine*, 1973, *35*, 509-514.

Rosen, R. C. Implications of biofeedback for sexual dysfunction. *Proceedings of the Biofeedback Research Society*, 1974, p. 12. (Abstract)

Rosen, R. C., Shapiro, D., & Schwartz, G. E. Voluntary control of penile tumescence. *Psychophysiology*, 1974, *11*, 230-231. (Abstract)

Rosenfeld, J. P., Rudell, A. P., & Fox, S. S. Operant control of neural events in humans. *Science*, 1969, *165*, 821-823.

Ruch, T. C., Patton, H. D., Woodbury, J. W. & Towe, A. H. (Eds.). *Neurophysiology* (2nd ed.). Philadelphia: W. B. Saunders, 1965.

Rugh, C. D., & Solberg, W. K. The identification of stressful stimuli in natural environments using a portable biofeedback unit. *Proceedings of the Biofeedback Research Society*, 1974, p. 54. (Abstract)

Sainsbury, P., & Gibson, J. F. Symptoms of anxiety and tension and accompanying physiological changes in the muscular system. *Journal of Neurology, Neurosurgery, and Psychiatry*, 1954, *17*, 216-224.

Sargeant, H. G. S., & Yorkston, N. J. Verbal desensitisation in the treatment of bronchial asthma. *Lancet*, 1969, *7634*, 1321-1323.

Sargent, J. D., Walters, E. D., & Green, E. E. Psychosomatic self-regulation of migraine headache. *Seminars in Psychiatry*, 1973, *5*, 415-428.

Scherf, D., & Schott, A. *Extra systoles and allied arrhythmias*. New York: Grune and Stratton, 1953.

Schultz, J. H., & Luthe, W. *Autogenic therapy*, Vol. 1. New York: Grune and Stratton, 1969.

Schumacher, G. A., & Wolff, H. G. Experimental studies of headache. *Archives of Neurological Psychiatry*, 1941, *45*, 199-214.

Schwartz, G. E. Voluntary control of human cardiovascular integration and differentiation through feedback and reward. *Science*, 1972, *175*, 90-93.

Schwartz, G. E. Biofeedback as therapy: Some theoretical and practical issues. *American Psychologist*, 1973, *28*, 666-673.

Schwartz, G. E., & Shapiro, D. Biofeedback and essential hypertension: Current findings and theoretical concerns. *Seminars in Psychiatry*, 1973, *5*, 493-503.

Schwartz, G. E., Shapiro, D., & Tursky, B. Learned control of cardiovascular integration in man through operant conditioning. *Psychosomatic Medicine*, 1971, *33*, 57–62.

Schwartz, G. E., Shapiro, D., & Tursky, B. Self-control of patterns of human diastolic blood pressure and heart rate through feedback and reward. *Psychophysiology*, 1972, *9*, 270. (Abstract)

Shapiro, D. Role of feedback and instructions in the voluntary control of human blood pressure. *Japanese Journal of Biofeedback Research*, 1973, *1*, 2–9. (in Japanese)

Shapiro, D. Operant-feedback control of human blood pressure: Some clinical issues. In P. A. Obrist, A. H. Black, J. Brener, & L. V. DiCara (Eds.), *Cardiovascular psychophysiology*. Chicago: Aldine, 1974.

Shapiro, D., Barber, T. X., DiCara, L. V., Kamiya, J., Miller, N. E., & Stoyva, J. (Eds.). *Biofeedback and self-control 1972: An Aldine Annual on the regulation of bodily processes and consciousness*. Chicago: Aldine 1973.

Shapiro, D., & Crider, A. Operant electrodermal conditioning under multiple schedules of reinforcement. *Psychophysiology*, 1967, *4*, 168–175.

Shapiro, D., Crider, A. B., & Tursky, B. Differentiation of an autonomic response through operant reinforcement. *Psychonomic Science*, 1964, *1*, 147–148.

Shapiro, D., & Schwartz, G. E., Biofeedback and visceral learning: Clinical applications. *Seminars in Psychiatry*, 1972, *4*, 171–184.

Shapiro, D., Schwartz, G. E., Nelson, S., Shnidman, S., & Silverman, S. Operant control of fear-related electrodermal responses in snake-phobic subjects. *Psychophysiology*, 1972, *9*, 271. (Abstract) (a)

Shapiro, D., Schwartz, G. E., & Tursky, B. Control of diastolic blood pressure in man by feedback and reinforcement. *Psychophysiology*, 1972, *9*, 296–304. (b)

Shapiro, D., Tursky, B., Gershon, E., & Stern, M. Effects of feedback and reinforcement on the control of human systolic blood pressure. *Science*, 1969, *163*, 588–590.

Shapiro, D., Tursky, B., & Schwartz, G. E. Control of blood pressure in man by operant conditioning. *Circulation Research* (Suppl. I), 1970, *26–27*, 27–32. (a)

Shapiro, D., Tursky, B., & Schwartz, G. E. Differentiation of heart rate and systolic blood pressure in man by operant conditioning. *Psychosomatic Medicine*, 1970, *32*, 417–423. (b)

Shapiro, D., & Watanabe, T. Timing characteristics of operant electrodermal modification: Fixed interval effects. *Japanese Psychological Research*, 1971, *13*, 123–130.

Shnidman, S. R. Avoidance conditioning of skin potential responses. *Psychophysiology*, 1969, *6*, 38–44.

Shnidman, S. R. Instrumental conditioning of orienting responses using positive reinforcement. *Journal of Experimental Psychology*, 1970, *83*, 491–494.

Shnidman, S., & Shapiro, D. Instrumental modification of elicited autonomic responses. *Psychophysiology*, 1971, *7*, 395–401.

Sirota, A. D., & Mahoney, M. J. Relaxing on cue: The self-regulation of asthma. *Journal of Behavior Therapy and Experimental Psychiatry*, 1974, *5*, 65–66.

Sirota, A. D., Schwartz, G. E., & Shapiro, D. Voluntary control of human heart rate: Effect on reaction to aversive stimulation. *Journal of Abnormal Psychology*, 1974, *83*, 261–267.

Slucki, H., Ádám, G., & Porter, R. W. Operant discrimination of an interoceptive stimulus in rhesus monkey. *Journal of the Experimental Analysis of Behavior*, 1965, *8*, 405–414.

Snyder, C., & Noble., M. E. Operant conditioning of vasoconstriction. *Journal of Experimental Psychology*, 1968, *77*, 263–268.

Solberg, W. K., & Rugh, J. D. The use of biofeedback devices in the treatment of bruxism. *Journal of the Southern California Dental Association*, 1972, *40*, 852–853.

Sterman, M. B. Neurophysiologic and clinical studies of sensorimotor EEG biofeedback training: Some effects on epilepsy. *Seminars in Psychiatry*, 1973, *5*, 507–525.

Sterman, M. B., Howe, R. C., & Macdonald, L. R. Facilitation of spindle-burst sleep by conditioning of electroencephalographic activity while awake. *Science*, 1970, *167*, 1146–1148.

Stevens, S. S. Matching functions between loudness and ten other continua. *Perception and Psychophysics*, 1966, *1*, 5–8.

Stevenson, I. P., Duncan, C. H., Wolf, S., Ripley, H. S., & Wolff, H. G. Life situations, emotions, and extra systoles. *Psychosomatic Medicine*, 1949, *11*, 257–272.

Stoyva, J., Barber, T. X., DiCara, L. V., Kamiya, J., Miller, N. E., & Shapiro, D. (Eds.). *Biofeedback and self-control 1971: An Aldine Annual on the regulation of bodily processes and consciousness.* Chicago: Aldine-Atherton, 1972.

Stoyva, J., & Budzynski, T. Cultivated low-arousal—an anti-stress response? In L. V. DiCara (Ed.), *Recent advances in limbic and autonomic nervous system research.* New York: Plenum, 1974.

Stroebel, C. F., & Glueck, B. C. Biofeedback treatment in medicine and psychiatry: An ultimate placebo? *Seminars in Psychiatry,* 1973, *5,* 379–393.

Stuart, R. B., & Davis, B. *Slim chance in a fat world: Behavioral control of obesity.* Champaign, Illinois: Research Press, 1972.

Surwit, R. S. Biofeedback: A possible treatment for Raynaud's disease. *Seminars in Psychiatry,* 1973, *5,* 483–490.

Surwit, R. S., & Shapiro, D. Skin temperature feedback and concomitant cardiovascular changes. *Proceedings of the Biofeedback Research Society,* 1974, p. 69. (Abstract)

Taub, E., & Emurian, C. Autoregulation of skin temperature using a variable intensity feedback light. Paper presented at the second annual meeting of the Biofeedback Research Society, 1972.

Taub, E., Emurian, C., & Howell, P. Further progress in training self-regulation of skin temperature. *Proceedings of the Biofeedback Research Society,* 1974, p. 70. (Abstract)

Teplitz, T. A. Operant conditioning of blood pressure: A critical review and some psychosomatic considerations. *Communications in Behavioral Biology,* 1971, *6,* 197–202.

Thomas, L. J., Tiber, N., & Schireson, S. The effects of anxiety and frustration on muscular tension related to the temporomandibular joint syndrome. *Dental Research,* 1973, *36,* 763–768.

Thorndike, E. L. *An experimental study of rewards.* New York: Columbia University Teacher's College, 1933, publication no. 580.

Trowill, J. A. Instrumental conditioning of the heart rate in the curarized rat. *Journal of Comparative and Physiological Psychology,* 1967, *63,* 7–11.

Tursky, B., Shapiro, D., & Schwartz, G. E. Automated constant cuff-pressure system to measure average systolic and diastolic blood pressure in man. *IEEE Transactions on Biomedical Engineering,* 1972, *19,* 271–276.

Van Twyver, H. B., & Kimmel, H. D. Operant conditioning of the GSR with concomitant measurement of two somatic variables. *Journal of Experimental Psychology,* 1966, *72,* 841–846.

Volow, M. R., & Hein, P. L. Bi-directional operant conditioning of peripheral vasomotor responses with augmented feedback and prolonged training. *Psychophysiology,* 1972, *9,* 271. (Abstract)

Walton, D. The application of learning theory to the treatment of a case of bronchial asthma. In H. J. Eysenck (Ed.), *Behavior therapy and the neuroses.* New York: Pergamon Press, 1960.

Weiss, H. D. The physiology of human penile erection. *Annals of Internal Medicine,* 1972, *76,* 793–799.

Weiss, T., & Engel, B. T. Operant conditioning of heart rate in patients with premature ventricular contractions. *Psychosomatic Medicine,* 1971, *33,* 301–321.

Wickramasekera, I. Electromyographic feedback training and tension headache: Preliminary observations. *American Journal of Clinical Hypnosis,* 1972, *15,* 83–85.

Willerson, J. T., Thompson, R. H., Hookman, P., Herdt, J., & Decker, J. L. Reserpine in Raynaud's disease and phenomenon: Short-term response to intra-arterial injection. *Annals of Internal Medicine,* 1970, *72,* 17–27.

Wolff, H. G. *Headache and other head pain* (2nd ed.). New York: Oxford University Press, 1963.

Wolpe, J. *Psychotherapy by reciprocal inhibition.* Stanford, California: Stanford University Press, 1958.

Wolpe, J., & Lazarus, A. A. *Behavior therapy techniques.* Oxford: Pergamon Press, 1966.

Wyrwicka, W., & Sterman, M. B. Instrumental conditioning of sensorimotor cortex EEG spindles in the waking cat. *Physiology and Behavior,* 1968, *3,* 703–707.

Yemm, R. Masseter muscle activity in stress. *Archives of Oral Biology,* 1969, *14,* 1437–1439. (a)

Yemm, R. Variations in the electrical activity of the human masseter muscle occurring in association with emotional stress. *Archives of Oral Biology,* 1969, *14,* 873–878. (b)

2

Control of States of Consciousness

Attainment through External Feedback Augmenting Control of Psychophysiological Variables

Kenneth Gaarder

By electronically feeding back to a subject information about his psychophysiological variables of which he would ordinarily be unaware, it is possible for the subject to learn to control these variables. Thus, electroencephalographic alpha states can be produced at will, complete muscle relaxation can be achieved, and control of skin temperature can be exercised when the appropriately recorded variable is fed back to the subject. Implications of this for psychiatric treatment are discussed, especially in the treatment of specific psychosomatic diseases and in the treatment of anxiety states associated with muscle tension.

This chapter is entirely concerned with the use of external feedback as a means of controlling psychophysiological variables. The basic idea behind this technique is that by artifically (usually electronically) measuring some psychophysiological variable (thereby making it an "output") and then feeding it back to the subject producing it through a sensory channel (thereby making it an "input"), the subject has available the possibility of gaining control of the variable. For example, if the electroencephalogram (EEG) is measured in the usual way with skin surface electrodes and electronic amplifiers and if the EEG signal is then processed to cause a signal to be given whenever alpha rhythm is present, the subject learns to be able to cause alpha rhythm to be present or absent when he wishes. The principle of external feedback may be understood concretely by referring to Figure 1. Here is shown the homeostatic adaptive control system[1] of the body with the crucial addition (designated by the heavy arrows) of feedback loops completed between an internal process and the sensory input system. Thus channel 1 completes the loop between the central nervous system and sensory input by means of EEG as just described, while channels 2 and 3 complete feedback loops with the muscular and autonomic systems, respectively, as described later.

THE GREAT TRUISM OF INFORMATION THEORY

The essential principle upon which this technique rests can best be stated as *a variable cannot be controlled unless information about the variable is available to*

Kenneth Gaarder • Gerontology Research Center, National Institute of Aging, Baltimore City Hospitals, Baltimore, Maryland 21224.

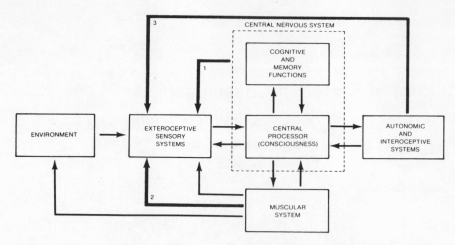

Figure 1. Psychophysiological feedback. Three examples of closing feedback loops are shown by the heavy arrows superimposed upon the homeostatic adaptive control system diagram. In each instance it is assumed that the heavy arrow represents a unit consisting of physiological transducer, amplifier, signal-reducing element, and signal display. Channel 1, feedback of the EEG; channel 2, feedback of the EMG; channel 3, autonomic feedback, such as heart rate or skin temperature feedback.

the controller. This is a truism because it is a self-evident statement within the context of cybernetic principles. It is an important truism, however, because unrecognized the world has one shape and recognized another. When the variable to be controlled belongs to the controller and when information about the variable is presented to the controller, this completes a feedback loop. An elementary understanding of this truism can be gained by study of the error-controlled regulator in Ashby's *Introduction to Cybernetics.*[2] Although some beginnings have been made at providing a more rigorous analysis of psychophysiological feedback than the elementary one just given,[3] there is not yet a great deal more known about the matter.

EARLY HISTORY OF EXTERNAL FEEDBACK

Such an easily achieved goal as the artificial closing of an external feedback loop has occurred many times without the formal logic of its occurrence being necessarily appreciated. One such early example is Narcissus seeing himself mirrored in the pond and becoming self-absorbed. The feedback provided by a mirror is used daily when men shave and women apply makeup and is used by a school of German physiotherapists to train self-awareness. Another hoary example of closing a feedback loop is provided by masturbation, in which a motor output is used to stimulate a sensory input channel to achieve a sought for psychophysiological state.

Completing an external feedback loop electronically has been practical for about 50 years and it is of interest that one of the first things Adrian did with the EEG was to observe his own alpha rhythm and how it was affected by eye movements.[3] Likewise, Jacobson[4] reports closing a feedback loop verbally by telling his subjects how they were doing while he observed their electromyograph (EMG).

Another example of early use of feedback was by Margolin and Kubie,[5] who placed a microphone to pick up a patient's respiration and heartbeat and used the amplified playback to induce a hypnoid state. In all of these instances the use of feedback was incidental to other concerns of the investigator.

CURRENT HISTORY OF EXTERNAL FEEDBACK RESEARCH

It is not easy in reporting the current use of external feedback to do justice to all the investigation involved. One reason is that most current knowledge of the field has not yet been published. Another is that new facets of the early work keep turning up. A third reason is because current feedback work has emerged from different scientific disciplines. Finally, most of us are now fully aware that history, as well as beauty, is in the eye of the beholder and it is necessary to acknowledge the limitations to the scope of one's vision of a scene in which one stands. In making a best effort, however, it seems valid to divide the current history of external feedback into two phases. In the first phase, several investigators used the principles of external feedback without an explicit recognition that a new principle has been discovered, while in the second phase it began to become clear to these investigators and to others that new principles did indeed exist and the explicit recognition of the principles became an end in itself. One of the earliest uses of feedback was in the work of Whatmore and Kohli,[6] who used the EMG as a means to feed back information to patients in teaching muscle relaxation in the early 1950's (G. Whatmore, oral communication, October 21, 1969). Another early worker was Kamiya,[7] who found in the late 1950's while studying alpha rhythm that his subjects were able to control a signal he was providing them of the presence of their alpha rhythm. Although his work was not published in definitive form, Kamiya's findings became widely known and he is now credited by many with founding the study of feedback. Hefferline[8] was another of the earliest workers who used feedback in an experiment where the subject was not aware that he was controlling his muscle tension. During the early part of the decade of 1960 a number of other people became interested in the study of feedback and each may be credited with having had creative insight into feedback and the recognition of a new principle. Among these people were Brown,[9] Green, Green, and Walters,[1] Mulholland,[3] Murphy,[11] and Stoyva.[12] It appears valid to see feedback as another instance of simultaneous discovery of an idea whose time had come.

In the latter part of the decade of 1960 many more people began to study external feedback and there are now over a hundred investigators in this country so involved. In 1969 a scientific meeting was held in Santa Monica, California, at which a Bio-Feedback Research Society was formed to bring together people doing research in the area. Meetings are expected to be held yearly in connection with the Society for Psychophysiological Research.

FEEDBACK FRAMEWORK VERSUS OPERANT FRAMEWORK

The above history of external feedback reflecting the work of people who explicitly recognize feedback has not included a parallel development in another field. That is the evolution of operant conditioning, which can be viewed as a form of feedback. Upon careful reflection, it becomes evident that operant conditioning meets the requirements of a feedback. For example, if it is desired to train a pigeon to tap a key, he is gradually "shaped" into tapping the key by rewarding any activity that brings him closer to the key or to tapping the key. This is a feedback because doing the thing that is desired (i.e., internally initiating an activity) produces external information (in the form of a reward) that is different from the information produced by not doing the desired thing (i.e., from alternative internal states). The fact, however, that operant conditioning is a form of feedback is often not recognized and for the most part there has not yet been much cross-fertilization between the field of operant conditioning and the field of feedback, nor is there yet rigorous and comprehensive analysis of operant conditioning in terms of cybernetics.

The most relevant work in operant conditioning has been from Neal Miller's group.[13] Parallel to the development of external feedback referred to above. Miller and his co-workers have done extensive work in animals showing that psychophysiological variables that had been thought by some to be uncontrollable can in fact be controlled. The essence of the technique is as described above: A variable is measured and if it moves in the desired direction reward is given and information is thereby fed back (naturally, punishment for the variable moving in the undesired direction may also be used). Using this technique Miller's group has found it possible to control many autonomic variables. Thus heart rate, intestinal motility, blood pressure, and skin temperature of selected body regions have been controlled.

One major factor appears to differentiate the feedback of operant conditioning from other feedback. That factor is what might best be called the *valence* of the feedback. Whereas in other techniques (which are used mainly with humans) the information is usually fed back in "neutral" form on a dial or other display, in operant conditioning (which is usually with animals) the information is fed back in the form of a compelling reward or punishment and thereby given a motivating value to the subject. While it is true that the human subject in an ordinary feedback experiment is influenced by his own motivation to succeed at the task or by the social reinforcement of approval from the experimenter or therapist, these influences lack the compelling quality of food to a starved animal or electric shocks. At such point as we understand how to provide the kind of compelling valence to feedback information that is achieved in conditioning experiments without treating the subject in a demeaning manner, some important advances in the use of feedback might be expected.

METHOD

General

The method of external feedback can best be summarized by saying that it is deceptively simple and in that simplicity lies its success or its failure. When a particular psychophysiological variable is continuously measured, usually the resultant measurement is a farily complex signal containing a great deal of information. Most often simply presenting the raw signal to the subject as a feed-back would overwhelm him with irrelevant information. Thus, in EEG feedback control, progress was begun by filtering the raw signal for alpha rhythm to feed back to the subject the information of whether alpha rhythm was present or not. Here again, however, the method is not as simple as it would appear since alpha rhythm is not just present or absent. Instead, one must have recourse to an elementary classification of signals to designate them as continuous (analogue) or discontinuous (digital). Then, among the alternatives are feedback signals that (1) merely say whether an immediate criterion level of alpha is present or not, (2) show both the presence of alpha and its amplitude, (3) show the amount of alpha in a recent short epoch, or (4) show the percent of time a criterion level of alpha was present in a recent short epoch. When it is further recognized that the signal may be fed back in one of several sense modalities such as sight or hearing and that the signal may be scaled into one of several dimensions of that modality, such as pitch or volume, it can be seen that the problem of choosing a feedback is not simple at all. At the present time almost every investigator has chosen a slightly different method of feedback and comparative studies have only begun to be undertaken,[14] so that there is only a small basis for comparing one investigator's work with another.

Another problem has been mentioned above—for the most part the feedback information in human experiments has been relatively neutral or lacking in valence, so as to lack a compelling quality. Also, it is necessary to prescribe a context within which feedback is used—whether in timed sessions or ad lib; whether with other techniques or alone; whether alternating feedback trials with no feedback trials will accelerate learning, etc.

EEG Feedback

The most extensively studied area of feedback is in the EEG. Here it is found that subjects are quite readily able to learn to produce large amounts of alpha in their occipitoparietal or occipitotemporal EEGs.[7,9] They quite uniformly associate alpha with a pleasant state of mind, which is relaxed, quiet, slow, and tranquil, as contrasted to the state with beta (low voltage fast) activity, which is more alert, fast, aroused, and restless.

Among the fascinating problems raised that are beginning to be studied are those of (1) comparing feedback-induced high alpha states with those induced by yogic or zen meditative techniques[15]; (2) comparing occipital alpha with alpha from other parts of the brain, which is more difficult to control (L Fehmi, oral communication, October 21, 1969); (3) seeing how far alpha frequency can be slowed and speeded and the effect of so doing; (4) seeing the degree to which high alpha and high beta states are mutually antagonistic versus the degree to which they can coexist (B. Brown, oral communication, October 22, 1969); and (5) seeing if other brain activity such as theta or 40-Hz waves can be controlled (L. Fehmi & B. Brown). Finally, work has yet to be reported showing what effect learning to control alpha states might have upon long-term anxiety syndromes and what aspects of defensive states are compatible and incompatible with high alpha states.

EMG Feedback

The predominant reason for pursuing the study of EMG feedback has been the finding that complete muscle relaxation is incompatible with anxiety.[4,6,16,17] The issue is to see whether deep muscle relaxation can be learned more readily with EMG feedback than without, and so far several studies have pointed in that direction.[6,14,18,19] The technique is simpler than in EEG feedback because so far only a single dimension of muscle activity—the short-term averaged EMG—has been used. Even here, however, choices must be made between binary, digital, and continuous signal processing; between linear and logarithmic scales; and between auditory and visual displays. Likewise, electrode sites must be chosen from which to measure muscle activity, with alternatives of ranging widely over many muscle groups as done by Whatmore and Kohli[6] versus settling to a few sites as has been done by Cleaves,[14] Budzynski, Stoyva, and Adler,[18] Jacobs and Fenton,[19] and myself. There is also the alternative of measuring postural muscles, which reflect postural tone, versus facial muscles, which reflect a "psychosocial tone." Contrary to former belief, Basmajian[20] and others have shown it possible for muscles to have no nervous tone, so that there is no EMG activity to be recorded. Complete absence of activity is most readily achieved in postural muscles. On the other hand, facial muscles, such as the frontalis (forehead) muscle, do not go below 2 μV of integrated muscle activity and most subjects do not reach less than about 4 μV to 6 μV of activity. It is not yet clear whether this is residual muscle activity or if the EMG is picking up other activities such as electrooculogram and EEG.

Although it appears likely that almost anyone would learn to relax muscle tension better with EMG feedback than without and that everyone could learn to relax more than they do at present, it has not been shown that it would be so much easier to obtain the results Jacobson[4] and Whatmore and Kohli[6] claim because of feedback as to be worth the trouble, nor has it yet been shown unequivocally that muscle tension release is of great value. Rather limited work suggests that most people who achieve fairly deep relaxation do not enter a radically altered state of consciousness, but that a few subjects who have previously experienced altered states of consciousness from drugs or meditation may show facility for relaxing even more deeply and achieving an altered state similar to the alpha state from this still deeper relaxation (C. M. Cleaves, oral communication, March 13, 1970). It is not yet known whether alpha states and low EMG states are equivalent since EEG measurement has not been reported in subjects during deep relaxation.

Autonomic Feedback

A large number of studies, mostly employing operant techniques, have shown that it is possible to use feedback to gain self-control over various aspects of the autonomic nervous system, especially the cardiovascular system. Heart rate has been studied extensively, with many studies showing that it is possible for subjects to raise and lower their rates.[13,21,22] Blood pressure has been lowered in other experiments.[23] Specific changes in the peripheral vascular system are also possible. Since local skin temperature is largely controlled by the state of the peripheral vasculature this is a convenient measure of the vascular system. Miller[13] has found that rats can be conditioned to raise the temperature of one of their ears while Green et al.[10] have found subjects readily learning to control skin temperature when feedback is available.

The galvanic skin response (GSR) is another autonomic variable that can be fed back to the subject, and has been found to add a useful dimension to psychotherapy[24] (see below).

COMMENT

Treatment of Specific Disease

From what has been said about feedback so far, it has some obvious potential uses in the treatment of disease. One simply considers a disease in which the pathological alteration of a physiological variable is an integral part of the condition and then uses feedback as a means of learning to return the variable to normal limits. Among the stark possibilities that immediately come to mind are the treatment of hypertension by feedback control of blood pressure, the treatment of vasoconstrictive peripheral vascular disease by the feedback learning of vasodilation, the treatment of anxiety by learning deep muscle relaxation through feedback EMG, and the treatment of epilepsy by feedback EEG teaching the suppression of spike activity. So far, the major therapeutic use of feedback has been in the treatment of muscle tension, with reports by Jacobs and Fenton,[19] Budzynski et al.,[18] and Whatmore and Kohli[6] showing usefulness.

Feedback in Psychotherapy

Where a patient's disease is not clearly related to a specific derangement of psychophysiological variables, there are several approaches that can be used. One would be to use feedback to teach the achievement of psychophysiological states

'ered desirable in themselves. This might be done either as a treat-
as an adjunct to another treatment procedure. According to the
ᴜacobson,[4] Shultz and Luthe,[25] Whatmore and Kohli,[6] and the
ᴜᴄnts of Yoga and Zen,[15] there is an intrinsic hygienic value in being able to achieve deep muscle relaxation and altered states of consciousness associated with alpha rhythm. Feedback electromyography and feedback electroencephalography both show great promise as ready means of achieving these goals and no doubt investigators will pursue the question of these procedures having intrinsic merit by themselves. On the other hand, it appears likely that feedback techniques might supplement and facilitate other treatment techniques. One instance that readily comes to mind is the use of feedback to objectify and facilitate the deep muscle relaxation considered necessary for systematic desensitization in behavioral therapy.[16] In psychoanalytic psychotherapies many patients are too anxious to be able to cooperate usefully in the necessary intellectual work who might perhaps be helped by relaxation with EEG and EMG feedback. Thus feedback might help patients to achieve the psychophysiological state accompanying free association.[1]

Another use of feedback in psychotherapy is as a source of objective information about the body state that would otherwise go unnoticed. This is possible because most of us are generally unaware of our bodily reactions as we are involved in an interpersonal transaction. Ephron[24] found that the occurrence of GSR was related to rapidly passing mental states, which occurred while defensive operations were put into effect, and that the noticing of this by both the patients and the therapist had a useful role in the treatment.

Limitations of Feedback Techniques

All of the suggested uses of feedback are based on the very promising research reported. It must be clearly recognized, however, that there are as yet no definite studies unequivocally proving the value of feedback, and it is quite possible that feedback will be found to have no great usefulness in the treatment of disease. This must await further study and replication by different investigators.

When studies are done, it is clear the investigator must be aware of a number of issues in order to design useful experiments. One of these is the design of apparatus that optimally achieves the particular use of feedback desired. For example, if one wishes to use feedback to learn control of a particular variable, the best signal to extract from the data is probably a fairly complex continuous one upon which the subject would concentrate. On the other hand, when feedback is used in psychotherapy to indicate a change of emotional state, it is desirable to have a very simple signal that will be obvious when it occurs but will allow the patient to pay attention to other things such as the discourse between himself and the therapist.

From these simple instances of design of apparatus one progresses into the issues mentioned earlier of the specific property of the signal from which the subject can most easily achieve the desired result. This leaves the multiple choices of picking the desired variable, picking the specific property to be displayed, picking the sensory modality for the display, and picking the quality within the modality to express the signal. In addition, there is the problem of whether one can combine simple feedback techniques with operant techniques so as to give a suitable valence to the information without at the same time introducing undesirable elements into the procedure.

A number of important issues in research strategy have been raised implicitly in the above discussion. One of these has to do with the questions that are asked. It is a good deal easier to pick a specific disease, such as Raynaud's disease, and ask whether the condition is helped by using feedback to increase peripheral circulation than it is to ask whether it is adaptive for Western man in an urban culture to be able to produce a tranquil alpha state at will. It seems highly desirable that both sorts of question should be studied. Another issue has to do with how one discovers the best way to use feedback. Here the choice is between designing controlled experiments versus casting about with pilot studies. Because of the large number of variables to be considered in experimenting, it seems desirable to use pilot studies to determine the most promising directions in which to proceed and then do controlled experiments to validate hints from pilot work.

NOTE. This chapter was originally read before the Adult Psychiatry Branch, National Institute of Mental Health, Bethesda, Maryland, February 27, 1970, and the Washington Psychiatric Society, Washington, D.C., March 23, 1970.

REFERENCES

1. Gaarder, K. Control of states of consciousness: I. Attainment through control of psychophysiological variables. *Archives of General Psychiatry*, 1971, *25*, 429–435
2. Ashby, WR. *An introduction to cybernetics*. New York: Wiley, 1963.
3. Mulholland, T. Feedback electroencephalography. *Activitas Nervosa Superior*, 1968, *10*, 410–438.
4. Jacobson, E. *Progressive relaxation*. Chicago: University of Chicago Press, 1938.
5. Margolin, S, & Kubie, L. An apparatus for the use of breath sounds as a hypnogogic stimulus. *American Journal of Psychiatry*, 1944, *100*, 610.
6. Whatmore, G. B, & Kohli, D. R. Dysponesis: A neurophysiological factor in functional disorders. *Behavioral Science*, 1968, *13*, 102–124.
7. Kamiya, J. Operant control of the EEG alpha rhythm and some of its reported effects on consciousness. In C. T. Tart (Ed), *Altered states of consciousness*. New York: Wiley, 1969.
8. Hefferline, R. F. The role of proprioception in the control of behavior. *Transactions of the New York Academy of Sciences*, 1958, *20*, 739–764.
9. Brown, B. Recognition of aspects of consciousness through association with EEG alpha activity represented by a light signal. *Psychophysiology*, *6*, 442–452.
10. Green, E., Green, A. M., & Walters, E. D. Self regulation of internal states. In *Proceedings of the International Congress of Cybernetics, London, 1969*.
11. Murphy, G. Psychology in the year 2000. *American Psychologist*, 1969, *24*, 523–530.
12. Stoyva, J. The public (scientific) study of private events, in E. Hartman (Ed), *Sleep and dreaming*. New York, Little, Brown, 1970. Pp. 355–368.
13. Miller, N. Learning of visceral and glandular responses. *Science*, 1969, *163*, 434–445.
14. Cleaves, C. M. *The control of muscle tension through psychophysiological information feedback*. Master's thesis, George Washington University, 1970.
15. Tart, C. T. *Altered states of consciousness*. New York: Wiley, 1969.

16. Wolpe, J. *The practice of behavior therapy*. New York: Pergamon Press, 1969.
17. Malmo, R. B. Emotions and muscle tension. *Psychology Today*, 1970, *3*, 64–83.
18. Budzynski, T., Stoyva, J., & Adler, C. Feedback-induced muscle relaxation: Application to tension headache. *Journal of Behavior Therapy and Experimental Psychiatry*, 1970, *1*, 205–211.
19. Jacobs, A., & Fenton, G. S. Visual feedback of myoelectric output to facilitate muscle relaxation in normal persons and patients with neck injuries. *Archives of Physical Medicine*, 1969, *50*, 34–39.
20. Basmajian, J. V. *Muscles alive*. Baltimore: Williams & Wilkins, 1967.
21. Frazier, T. W. Avoidance conditioning of heart rate in humans. *Psychophysiology*, 1966, *3*, 188–202.
22. Brener, J., & Hothersall, D. Heart rate control under conditions of augmented sensory feedback. *Psychophysiology*, 1966, *3*, 23–28.
23. Shapiro, D., Tursky, B., Gershon, E., et al. Effects of feedback and reinforcement on the control of human systolic blood pressure. *Science*, 1969, *163*, 588–590.
24. Ephron, L. R. *Physiological feedback in psychotherapy*. Master's thesis, Harvard University, 1968.
25. Schultz, J. H., & Luthe, W. *Autogenic training*. New York: Grune and Stratton, 1959.

3

Biofeedback and Physiological Patterning in Human Emotion and Consciousness

Gary E. Schwartz

INTRODUCTION TO PATTERN SELF-REGULATION

Although we do not usually think about it, we are continually self-regulating complex patterns of neurophysiological processes in our dynamic commerce with the external environment (Schwartz, 1975). Until very recently this fact was virtually ignored by scientists and laymen alike. A major reason for the failure to recognize and appreciate the self-regulation of patterns of brain processes is that the very brain processes involved in patterned neural self-regulation are normally unobservable and not available to direct conscious experience (Schwartz, 1977a). The development of biofeedback procedures for patterns of electrocortical activity serves the important function of bringing these unconscious neural processes, albeit indirectly, into human awareness. Furthermore, pattern biofeedback procedures make it possible for researchers to now manipulate patterns of brain processes differentially as a method for exploring their functional relationship to human experience and behavior.

To the extent that emotion and consciousness are emergent properties of neural patterning in the central nervous system (Schwartz, 1975; John, 1976), it becomes an intriguing paradox when we recognize that the brain is ultimately responsible for its own regulation (and that of the body), yet it has no conscious awareness that it is responsible, or even involved, in its self-regulation. Space precludes a more detailed discussion of neural patterning and the brain self-regulation paradox (see Schwartz, 1977a). However, the more general issue relating biofeedback, physiological patterning, and emergent property to human emotion and consciousness is considered.

BIOFEEDBACK, PATTERNING, AND EMERGENT PROPERTY

A thesis slowly emerging from biofeedback research is that patterns of physiological responses can be both self-generated and processed by the brain,

Gary E. Schwartz • Department of Psychology, Yale University, and Department of Psychiatry, Yale University School of Medicine, New Haven, Connecticut 06520.

producing unique cross-system interactions and perceptual gestalts that make up a significant component of human behavior and subjective experience (Schwartz, 1975). The concept of pattern here does not simply refer to viewing, in isolation, combinations of processes, but rather goes beyond the individual components making up the pattern to recognize the novel, interactive, or emergent property that patterns can acquire. Simply stated, the whole can have properties that are qualitatively and/or quantitatively different from the sum of its parts and yet be dependent upon the organization of its parts for its unique properties. This phenomenon is seen at all levels of physics and chemistry, and extends through biology and neuropsychology (Weiss, 1969). The term *synergism* is also used to describe patterning and emergent property, as recently elucidated in the comprehensive volume by Fuller (1975).

The concept of emergent property or synergism needs to be considered in patterning. Although it is not a new concept, with few exceptions it is still ignored. In the area of consciousness, neuropsychologists concerned with this problem employ a similar idea when they speak of cell assemblies (Hebb, 1974), hyperneurons (John, 1976), holograms (Pribram, 1971), dynamic neural patterns (Sperry, 1969), or functional systems in the brain (Luria, 1973). In the area of emotion, the concept relating physiological patterning to emergent property has a long history, beginning with William James (1890), who described emotion as the brain's perception of patterns of visceral consequences of its action. More recent investigators such as Schachter and Singer (1962), have added biocognitive processes to the visceral activity as an integral part of this pattern. Modern comprehensive theorists like Tomkins (1962) and Izard (1971) stress the interaction of combinations of neurophysiological systems, including the processing of discrete patterns of postural and facial muscle activity, as the neural mechanisms underlying the emergent experience of emotion.

Evidence for patterning of central nervous system activity, and consequently peripheral nervous system activity, in human emotion and consciousness is evolving from two major research directions. The first is an extension of traditional psychophysiology, where differential patterns of electrocortical and peripheral physiological responses are monitored while subjects engage in complex cognitive/affective tasks. For example, recent data from our laboratory have documented that complex cognitive/affective tasks can be meaningfully dissected into their underlying neuropsychological subcomponents that have predictable effects on patterning of hemispheric activity (Schwartz, Davidson, & Maer, 1975). The data indicate that in right-handed subjects, verbal versus spatial cognitive processess differentially involve the left and right hemisphere, respectively. In addition, the right hemisphere seems to play a special role in the nonverbal components of emotion. Consequently, questions involving both verbal (left hemisphere) and emotional (right hemisphere) processes (e.g., "What is the primary difference in the meanings of the words *anger* and *hate*?") accordingly elicit evidence of dual hemispheric activation. Questions that involve both spatial (right hemisphere) and emotional (right hemisphere) processes (e.g., "Picture your father's face—what emotion first strikes you?") elicit evidence of accentuated right hemispheric involvement.

The second research direction is more recent in origin and involves the use of biofeedback. At the simplest level, it has been pointed out that the self-regulation of patterns of responses using pattern biofeedback procedures can have different emergent consequences from those observed when controlling individual functions alone (Schwartz, 1976). This basic observation provides the foundation for the hypothesis that by training subjects to voluntarily control patterns of visceral and motor responses, it is possible to assess central and peripheral linkages between physiological responses and their relationship to human behavior and consciousness (Schwartz, 1975). The development of this hypothesis is interesting in that it emerged somewhat unexpectedly in basic cardiovascular research concerned with the self-regulation of patterns of systolic blood pressure and heart rate. Details regarding the theory, development, measurement, and interpretation of patterning in biofeedback are comprehensively discussed in a recent review (Schwartz, 1977b) and will only briefly be described here.

RELAXATION AND THE SELF-REGULATION OF PATTERNS OF SYSTOLIC BLOOD PRESSURE AND HEART RATE

In an experiment designed to determine the ease with which subjects could regulate the relationship between their systolic blood pressure and heart rate, a procedure was developed for administering binary (yes/no) feedback and reward for patterns of blood pressure (BP) and heart rate (HR): $BP^{up}HR^{up}$, BP_{down}-HR_{down}, $BP^{up}HR_{down}$, $BP_{down}HR^{up}$ (Schwartz, 1972). In order to evaluate the specific effects of the binary feedback and reward itself, minimal instructions were given to subjects. They were not told what functions were to be controlled, nor were they told what direction(s) the functions were to change.

The results indicated that subjects rapidly learn to regulate both functions in the same direction ($BP^{up}HR^{up}$ or $BP_{down}HR_{down}$), and to a lesser degree, to regulate the functions in the opposite direction ($BP^{up}HR_{down}$ or $BP_{down}HR^{up}$). These findings are contrasted with those obtained in the earlier studies which also used minimal instructions but provided feedback and reward for BP itself (Shapiro, Tursky, Gershon, & Stern, 1969; Shapiro, Tursky, & Schwartz, 1970a) or HR itself (Shapiro, Tursky, & Schwartz, 1970b). With BP feedback (BP^{up} or BP_{down}), changes in BP were obtained independently of HR, while with HR feedback (HR^{up} or HR_{down}), changes in HR were obtained independently of BP.

In postexperimental interviews conducted with the subjects given feedback for BP or HR alone, no differences between the up and down conditions could be gleaned in terms of subjective report. However, when reports were obtained from subjects given BP-HR pattern feedback, the subjects trained to decrease both their BP and HR ($BP_{down}HR_{down}$) spontaneously reported feelings of relaxation, floating sensations, and calmness, a subjective gestalt that could be predicted to be associated with a more integrated decrease in multiphysiological systems (Benson, 1975; Davidson & Schwartz, 1976) (see Table 1, cited in Schwartz, 1976).

This accidental observation represents the first instance of a subjective report emerging with pattern biofeedback that did not spontaneously appear when the

Table 1

*Mean Values in Response to the Question: "Rate from 1 (very little) to 5
(very much) how well relaxation/calm helped you to control your
physiological responses" (from Schwartz, 1976)*

$BP^{up}HR^{up}$	$BP^{up}HR_{down}$	$BP_{down}HR^{up}$	$BP_{down}HR_{down}{}^{a}$
.8	.9	.8	3.2

[a] $F (3, 36) = 5.069, p < .01.$

single responses constituting the pattern were independently regulated. It stimulated our recent research on the regulation of patterns of EEG and heart rate and
subjective relaxation (Hassett & Schwartz, 1975), voluntary control of patterns of
facial muscle activity and heart rate and the experience of anxiety (Schwartz,
Davidson, Weinberger, & Lenson, in preparation), and the voluntary control of
patterns of EEG asymmetry and asymmetry and cognitive processes (Schwartz,
Davidson, & Pugash, 1976).

RELAXATION AND THE SELF-REGULATION OF PATTERNS OF OCCIPITAL ALPHA AND HEART RATE

A second procedure for training patterns of physiological responses is
derived from a motor skills model (Schwartz, Young, & Vogler, 1976) and
involves coordination training (Hassett & Schwartz, 1975). Rather than quantify-
ing patterns of physiological responses in real time and providing feedback for the
presence or absence of a specific pattern, the coordination training procedure
involves single-system feedback for the individual responses making up the patterns, followed by multiple feedback for coordinating the combinations of
responses.

Applying this approach to the regulation of patterns of occipital alpha (OA)
and heart rate, Hassett and Schwartz (1975) conducted an experiment in which
subjects were first given single-system feedback training for OA control as well as
HR control in one session. Then, in a second session, subjects were given practice
periods with dual feedback for OA and HR simultaneously. Subjects were
instructed to practice voluntary coordination of the two responses at their own
pace, making them change separately or together, in the same or opposite direction. The results were quite striking, demonstrating that subjects could rapidly
learn to generate, during test trials, all eight possible combinations of OA and
HR: OA^{off} or OA_{on}; HR^{up} or HR_{down}; $OA^{off} HR^{up}$ or $OA_{on}HR_{down}$; or
$OA^{off} HR_{down}$ or $OA_{on}HR^{up}$.

Analysis of postexperimental subjective reports replicated and extended the
Schwartz (1972) findings. Of the four self-regulated patterns of OA and HR,
decreases in multisystem activity ($OA_{on}HR_{down}$) were more closely associated
with subjective reports of relaxation. Interestingly, one female subject given eight
sessions of coordination training reported spontaneously that she found the

$OA_{on}HR_{down}$ pattern so relaxing that she began to practice it on her own outside of the laboratory.

These data highlight the general issue of pattern self-regulation and have important implications for theories comparing different self-regulation procedures. For example, a hypothesis that received popular notoriety stated that since (1) during passive relaxation procedures such as transcendental meditation, increases in occipital alpha (OA_{on}) are often observed (Davidson & Schwartz, 1976), and (2) with the aid of biofeedback, subjects can learn to self-regulate increases in occipital alpha (Hardt & Kamiya, 1976), then (3) occipital alpha biofeedback can be used to produce a rapid, electronic meditator! The fallacy of this line of reasoning is that single-system biofeedback, as described above, tends to result in specificity of learning, whereas biocognitive procedures such as transcendental meditation tend to involve the natural, albeit unconscious, self-regulation of complex patterns of responses (e.g., increases in alpha and theta frequencies over much of the cortex, which is expressed via the peripheral nervous system as decreases in heart rate, blood pressure, sweat gland activity, oxygen consumption, respiration, rate, etc.).

To the extent that the cognitive and behavioral concomitants of transcendental meditation and other complex self-regulation procedures reflect emergent properties of the unique patterns of the underlying neurophysiological systems, then the probability of replicating these patterns using simple biofeedback procedures would seem small. Questions that need to be raised are (1) Is it possible, using biofeedback procedures, to fully replicate the psychophysiological pattern constituting meditation? (2) What combination of responses and biofeedback procedures would be necessary to match the pattern of physiological changes that naturally occur during meditation? (3) If it is possible, is it worth the effort?

My own response to these questions is divided according to the different needs of basic research versus clinical application (Schwartz, 1975, 1976). The pattern-biofeedback approach provides a new research paradigm for investigating how different physiological systems combine to produce unique subjective gestalts and behavioral correlates; at this level, the approach promises to be fruitful. However, if the physiological patterns produced during meditation or other relaxation techniques are themselves of therapeutic value, then they should be induced and practiced using the nonelectronic, easily portable and generalizable machinery of our own biocognitive systems.

ANXIETY AND THE SELF-REGULATION OF PATTERNS OF FACIAL MUSCLE ACTIVITY AND HEART RATE

Patterning theories of emotion (Tomkins, 1962; Izard, 1971) posit that the emergent experience of different emotions involves the differential patterning of skeletal and visceral responses by the brain. Within the skeletal system itself, patterning of facial muscle activity (by the brain) as expressed overtly in facial expression is considered to be a key factor. Recent research from our laboratory has demonstrated that when subjects are simply instructed to self-generate different classes of affective imagery (i.e., happy, sad, and angry imagery; in Schwartz, Fair, Salt, Mandel, & Klerman, 1976), different patterns of facial muscle activity are generated which can be measured electromyographically. Interestingly, these subtle muscle patterns are typically not apparent in the overt face. Further, predictable differences in the underlying covert facial expressions are found between subjects differing in specific mood states such as in patients suffering from depression (Schwartz, Fair, Salt, Mandel, & Klerman, 1976).

One extension of this research is to combine the self-regulation of facial activity with visceral activity as a means of assessing how patterns across these two major systems interact in the emergent experience of emotion. In a recent experiment (Schwartz et al., in preparation), subjects were specifically instructed to increase and decrease their heart rate using biofeedback (1) under normal resting conditions and (2) while simultaneously tensing the muscles in their forehead (FT) region.

Since previous research indicates that (1) unlike minimally instructed subjects, subjects deliberately instructed to increase their heart rate with biofeedback immediately draw on complex cognitive/affective strategies involving negative emotions such as anxiety (Bell & Schwartz, 1975), and (2) forehead muscle tension (loosely referring to tension in the frontalis, corrugator, and related muscles) is observed in the overt frightened and anxious face (Ekman & Friesen, 1975), we predicted that self-regulation of the pattern of high heart rate and forehead tension ($HR^{up} FH^{up}$) would result in a more intense experience of anxiety than the regulation of either component alone (HR^{up} or FT^{up}).

Forty-two subjects were run in a 3×2 within-subject design with HR biofeedback (rest, HR_{down} and HR^{up}) crossed with forehead facial tension (rest and FH^{up}). The means for heart rate, integrated forehead muscle tension (EMG), and anxiety scores, using Izard's differential emotions scale (Izard, 1972) administered after each trial, are shown in Table 2.

The results can be briefly summarized as follows: (1) Self-regulation of heart rate with biofeedback is not affected by the simultaneous tensing of the forehead region, though during HR resting conditions subjects show slightly elevated heart rate when tensing the forehead. (2) Subjects can readily tense their forehead while regulating their heart rate with biofeedback. Interestingly, however, forehead muscle tension covaries with heart rate control during FT rest as well as FT^{up} conditions. (3) Increased heart rate regulation itself (HR^{up} during FT rest) and forehead tension itself (FT^{up} during HR rest) are each accompanied by reported increases in the subjective experience of anxiety (relative to the basic resting condition). Finally, and most importantly, the highest rating of subjective anxiety occurs during $HR^{up} FT^{up}$ pattern regulation.

These data indicate that self-regulated facial forehead tension and self-regulated heart rate increases each contribute to subjective anxiety. When they are regulated as a pattern, moreover, they combine in an additive sense to contribute to the total emergent experience of anxiety. Using this particular pattern of facial muscle tensing and heart rate, the additive effect of FT and HR appears relatively specific to anxiety. On ratings of anger, for example, the subjective reports vary with heart rate control but they are minimally influenced by the tensing of the

Table 2

Mean Scores for Heart Rate, Forehead EMG, and Anxiety Ratings during the Regulation of Heart Rate with Biofeedback (Rest, HR_{down} and HR^{up}) and Forehead Facial Tension (Rest and FT^{up}) (from Schwartz, Davidson, Weinberger, & Lenson, in preparation)

	Condition		
	Rest	HR_{down}	HR^{up}
Heart rate (in bpm)			
Rest	66.8	67.4	74.6
FT^{up}	68.4	67.9	75.2
Forehead EMG (in integrated units)			
Rest	17.1	18.0	28.1
FT^{up}	45.3	39.7	56.5
Anxiety (from 1 to 14)			
Rest	4.47	5.24	8.84
FT^{up}	6.75	6.89	9.75

forehead region itself. Future research can more explicitly manipulate different patterns of facial muscle activity in combination with visceral activity. It might be predicted that generating the muscle pattern of an angry face, coupled with HR^{up}, could lead to a greater subjective experience of anger; generating the muscle pattern of a happy face, coupled with HR^{up}, could lead to a greater subjective experience of happiness.

The point at this stage of research is to illustrate how patterns of skeletal and visceral responses can interact and contribute to the emergent experience of unique emotions, or blends of emotions. This provides a possible rapprochement between "arousal" and "pattern" theories of emotion, and helps to delineate new questions for basic as well as clinical psychophysiological research regarding the regulation and behavioral treatment of affective disorders.

COGNITIVE PROCESSES AND THE SELF-REGULATION OF PATTERNS OF EEG SYMMETRY AND ASYMMETRY

One of the most challenging frontiers in biofeedback research is to specify what patterns of brain processes underlie the self-regulation of visceral and skeletal effectors, and to determine how these patterns of brain processes ultimately generate the emergent experience of emotion and consciousness. Research on the former question has been recently reviewed elsewhere (Schwartz, 1977b). One example of research on the latter question involves the assessment and regulation of patterns of specific EEG changes and their relationship to subjective experience.

Schwartz, Davidson, and Pugash (1976) conducted an experiment addressing two question: (1) Is training for EEG parietal asymmetry using pattern biofeedback accompanied by predictable cognitive concomitants? (2) Are the cognitive concomitants of training for simultaneous bilateral activation of the hemispheres a simple additive combination of the two asymmetry patterns, or do they represent a unique cognitive gestalt not readily predicted from the two asymmetry training conditions?

Bilateral parietal EEG was recorded from 20 right-handed subjects and filtered for 8- to 13-Hz activity. Using a procedure adapted from the Schwartz (1972) blood pressure–heart rate pattern study, patterns of alpha (A) presence and absence across the left (L) and right (R) hemispheres were assessed 10 times per second and automatically counted. All subjects received binary feedback for EEG symmetry training ($LA^{off} RA^{off}$ —Integration) and EEG asymmetry training ($LA^{off} RA_{on}$ and $LA_{on} RA^{off}$ —Differentiation).

Evidence for significant regulation in all three feedback conditions was obtained. As shown in Table 3, analyses of the postfeedback questionnaires revealed that the $LA^{off} RA_{on}$ pattern was associated with significantly more verbal cognitions, while the $LA_{on} RA^{off}$ pattern was associated with more visual cognitions.

Importantly, the cognitive findings from the symmetry training pattern ($LA^{off} RA^{off}$) suggest that the generation of this EEG pattern is not simply the sum of the two differentiation patterns; such a model would predict increases in both visual and verbal cognitions during EEG integration. It is important to recognize that the production of bilateral parietal activation may be accomplished in a myriad of ways, few of which naturally involve the simultaneous generation of verbal and visual thought. Rather, the activation of both hemispheres may typically involve the generation of complementary behavior and cognition. For example, a number of subjects in the experiment reported visualizing an image and holding the image in awareness. Interestingly, this strategy is similar to some meditation techniques that require the generation and maintenance of an image in

Table 3

Mean Self-Reported Cognitive Mode on a 1-7 Scale for Each of Six Thought Categories during Each Biofeedback Treatment, and Difference Scores for Each of the Three Comparisons and Significance Levels (Based upon 2-Tailed t Tests for Correlated Means) (from Schwartz, Davidson, & Pugash, 1976)

Thought category	Condition			Difference score		
	$LA^{off}RA_{on}$ (D1)	$LA_{on}RA^{off}$ (D2)	$LA^{off}RA^{off}$ (I)	D1–D2	D1–I	D2–I
Verbal	3.92	2.40	2.35	1.52[a]	1.57[b]	.05
Visual	3.55	4.65	5.10	−1.10[a]	−1.55[a]	−.45
Numerical	2.80	1.85	2.55	.95	.25	−.70
Musical	2.85	2.25	2.05	.60	.80	.20
Nothing	2.45	2.40	4.35	.05	−1.90[b]	−1.95[a]
Emotional	4.00	4.00	2.60	.00	1.40[a]	1.40[c]

[a] $p < .05$.
[b] $p < .02$.
[c] $p < .10$.

consciousness. Banquet (1973) has reported that such a technique, at certain points during the meditation, is associated with bilateral activation in the EEG (i.e., increments in beta activity in both hemispheres).

These data highlight the use of pattern biofeedback procedures to explore the relationship between neurophysiological patterning and subjective experience. The challenge of recording and training more complex central nervous system EEG patterns as a means of assessing brain/consciousness relationships may reflect one of the most significant contributions to be made by future biofeedback research.

SUMMARY AND CONCLUSIONS

This chapter has developed the thesis that a fundamental theoretical question underlying emotion and consciousness concerns the emergent property of patterning of neurophysiological processes and their expression via the peripheral nervous system as patterns of skeletal and visceral activity. It is suggested that research on biofeedback and the regulation of combinations of responses extends the concept of emergent property by providing a new paradigm for systematically investigating physiological relationships in the intact human. Self-regulation as a general research strategy can be useful to the extent that it enables researchers to isolate component parts of neural/humoral systems and then examine how they combine to produce unique physiological and associated subjective states.

Research indicates that the regulation of patterns of responses can produce effects that are qualitatively and/or quantitatively different from the regulation of single components. Systematic comparison of the emergent properties of different self-regulated patterns of responses then becomes an important research direction. Although this principle has basic as well as clinical implications (Schwartz, 1974, 1975, 1976, 1977b), there are limitations to the use of pattern-regulation procedures that need to be considered. For example, it is not inconceivable that the act of regulating a particular pattern of responses will have emergent consequences that are somewhat different from those found when a similar pattern is generated by other means. If future research should document this to be true, it will restrict the general applicability of the approach accordingly. On the other hand, such a finding could provide a further key to the unique characteristics of self-regulation processes themselves.

NOTE. This research was supported in part by an award from the Stress Grants Program of the Roche Psychiatric Institute and by the Advanced Research Projects Agency of the Department of Defense and monitored by the Office of Naval Research under contract N00014-70-C-0350 to the San Diego State College Foundation. This chapter was completed while the author was on leave from Harvard University as a visiting associate professor of psychology at the Department of Psychiatry, University of California, San Francisco.

REFERENCES

Banquet, J. P. Spectral analysis of EEG in meditation. *Electroencephalography and Clinical Neurophysiology*, 1973, *35*, 143–151.

Bell, I. R., & Schwartz, G. E. Voluntary control and reactivity of human heart rate. *Psychophysiology*, 1975, *12*, 339–348.

Benson, H. *The relaxation response*. New York: William Morrow, 1975.

Davidson, R. J., & Schwartz, G. E. The psychobiology of relaxation and related states: A multiprocess theory. In D. I. Mostofsky (Ed.), *Behavior modification and control of physiological activity*. Englewood Cliffs, New Jersey: Prentice-Hall, 1976.

Ekman, P., & Friesen, W. V. *Unmasking the face*. Englewood Cliffs, New Jersey: Prentice-Hall, 1975.

Fuller, R. B. *Synergetics*. New York: Macmillan, 1975.

Hardt, J. V., & Kamiya, J. Conflicting results in EEG alpha feedback studies: Why amplitude integration should replace percent time. *Biofeedback and Self-Regulation*, 1976, *1*, 63–76.

Hassett, J., & Schwartz, G. E. Relationships between heart rate and occipital alpha: A biofeedback approach. *Psychophysiology*, 1975, *12*, 228. (Abstract)

Hebb, D. O. What psychology is about. *American Psychologist*, 1974, *29*, 71–79.

Izard, C. *The face of emotion*. New York: Appleton-Century-Crofts, 1971.

Izard, C. *Patterns of emotions*. New York: Academic Press, 1972.

James, W. *Principles of psychology*. New York: Holt, 1890.

John, E. R. A model of consciousness. In G. E. Schwartz & D. Shapiro (Eds.), *Consciousness and self-regulation: Advances in research* (Vol. 1). New York: Plenum, 1976.

Luria, A. R. *The working brain*. New York: Basic Books, 1973.

Pribram, K. H. *Languages of the brain*. Englewood Cliffs, New Jersey: Prentice-Hall, 1971.

Schachter, S., & Singer, J. E. Cognitive, social and physiological determinants of emotional state. *Psychological Review*, 1962, *69*, 379–399.

Schwartz, G. E. Voluntary control of human cardiovascular integration and differentiation through feedback and reward. *Science*, 1972, *175*, 90–93.

Schwartz, G. E. Toward a theory of voluntary control of response pattern in the cardiovascular system. In P. A. Obrist, A. H. Black, J. Brener, & L. V. DiCara (Eds.), *Cardiovascular psychophysiology*. Chicago: Aldine, 1974.

Schwartz, G. E. Biofeedback, self-regulation and the patterning of physiological processes. *American Scientist*, 1975, *63*, 314–324.

Schwartz, G. E. Self-regulation of response patterning: Implications for psychophysiological research and therapy. *Biofeedback and Self-Regulation*, 1976, *1*, 7–30.

Schwartz, G. E. Psychosomatic disorders and biofeedback: A psychobiological model of disregulation. In J. D. Maser & M. E. P. Seligman (Eds.), *Psychopathology: Experimental models*. San Francisco: Freeman, 1977. (a)

Schwartz, G. E. Biofeedback and patterning of autonomic and central processes: CNS-cardiovascular interactions. In G. E. Schwartz & J. Beatty (Eds.), *Biofeedback: Theory and research*. New York: Academic Press, 1977. (b)

Schwartz, G. E., Davidson, R. J., & Maer, F. Right hemisphere lateralization for emotion in the human brain: Interaction with cognition. *Science*, 1975, *190*, 286–288.

Schwartz, G. E., Davidson, R. J., & Pugash, E. Voluntary control of patterns of EEG parietal asymmetry: Cognitive concomitants. *Psychophysiology*, 1976, *13*, 498–504.

Schwartz, G. E., Davidson, R. J., Weinberger, D. A., & Lenson, R. Voluntary control of patterns of facial muscle activity and heart rate: Effects on anxiety. In preparation.

Schwartz, G. E., Fair, P. L., Salt, P., Mandel, M. R., & Klerman, G. L. Facial muscle patterning to affective imagery in depressed and nondepressed subjects. *Science*, 1976, *192*, 489–491.

Schwartz, G. E., Fair, P. L., Salt, P., Mandel, M. R., & Klerman, G. L. Facial expression and imagery in depression: An electromyographic study. *Psychosomatic Medicine*, 1976, *38*, 337–347.

Schwartz, G. E., Young, L. D., & Vogler, J. Heart rate regulation as skill learning: Strength-endurance versus cardiac reaction time. *Psychophysiology*, 1976, *13*, 472–478.

Shapiro, D., Tursky, B., Gershon, E., & Stern, M. Effects of feedback and reinforcement on the control of human systolic blood pressure. *Science*, 1969, *163*, 588–589.

Shapiro, D., Tursky, B., & Schwartz, G. E. Control of blood pressure in man by operant conditioning. *Circulation Research*, 1970, *27* (Suppl. 1), 27–32. (a)

Shapiro, D., Tursky, B., & Schwartz, G. E. Differentiation of heart rate and blood pressure in man by operant conditioning. *Psychosomatic Medicine*, 1970, *32*, 417–423. (b)

Sperry, R. W. A modified concept of consciousness. *Psychological Review*, 1969, *76*, 532–536.

Tomkins, S. S. *Affect, imagery, consciousness* (2 vols.). New York: Springer, 1962.

Weiss, P. A. The living system: Determinism stratified. In A. Koestler & J. R. Smythies (Eds.), *Beyond reductionism*. Boston: Beacon Press, 1969.

4

Problems in Biofeedback Training: An Experiential Analogy—Urination

Erik Peper

The research literature on biofeedback training is filled with contradictions. Certain researchers and experimental settings appear to enhance learning in trainees, whereas other combinations appear to inhibit learning. Further, some researchers, educators, and clinicians suggest that biofeedback can be a useful tool for preventive medicine, since a person who can sense his body response can learn to change or modulate the patterns of his behavior.[1] Other researchers, especially those who have been unsuccessful in teaching voluntary control, believe that claims of any usefulness should be made extremely cautiously.

Two examples of the many studies that could be cited are those of Love, Montgomery, and Moeller[2] and Sterman,[3] who report that biofeedback training can be used to ameliorate a number of disorders such as hypertension and epilepsy. Conversely, other researchers report that biofeedback training does not ameliorate these conditions. An even more confused picture of visceral learning is presented in an article describing research on curarized rats,[4] in which the same researchers could not successfully replicate their own studies.

Researchers often discuss in detail the technical problems encountered in biofeedback research, such as the correct physiological feedback or unique combinations of lengths of training-trial periods. However, they usually ignore the subtle qualities of the experimental setting, such as smiles, smells, attitudes, and the comforts of the trainee's chair. The idiosyncratic behavior of the subject, trainer, or both is not well understood, and little attention is given to it. Usually, in experimental psychology, group behaviors are measured (mean, average); however, biofeedback learning is not group behavior but learning unique to an individual. The term *statistical average* in biofeedback training is as meaningless as the term *normal person* in clinical assessment.

In discussing biofeedback learning, sometimes known as visceral learning or autonomic learning, no distinction is generally made between autonomic learning and striate muscle learning. Yet a number of research programs are focused precisely around the question of to what extent those learning processes are the same or different.[5,6] In many cases the major difference seems to be the type of

Erik Peper • Center for Interdisciplinary Science, San Francisco State University, San Francisco, California 94134.

reinforcer or the number of "conscious" learning trials. In muscular striate learning, the learning time involved and the necessity for attentiveness to the task are often underestimated.

The intense practice necessary is easily demonstrated in the training of musicians or athletes. As a more ordinary example, consider the complicated process of learning to type. The fine finger movement and discrimination involved in typing takes an adult weeks to learn. However, this is only a variation of the child's process of learning to tie shoelaces, which takes months to learn. Tying shoes in turn is only a small advance over learning to hold a spoon to eat, which is a small advance over the grasping reflex present at birth.

Whether or not the process in autonomic learning and striate muscle learning is different, both require a large number of learning trials.

Many complicated striate muscular learning tasks are as unconscious as visceral learning in coordination, and often include autonomic processes. For example, in skiing there is a total coordination of balance, breath, blood flow, and timing of muscle movements, which allows the successful skier to experience the sensation of "floating over the slopes." It is no wonder that autonomic learning may take a long time. In trying to make this process conscious, we are having to make ourselves aware of sensations we have not noticed since infancy and have long learned to suppress. Moreover, some of the learning possible for a baby may no longer be possible for an adult; the adult slowly constricts his learning capabilities by the internal physical structure he creates in the process of development.

Biofeedback learning cannot be described accurately, just as we cannot describe the process of getting out of a chair. Although language exists to describe our internal processes or our emotions (words like *angry*, *afraid*, *friendly*), the actual experience behind these words is uniquely different for each person. Each verbal label used to describe an emotion actually describes many components—think of the many meanings of "love," or "anxiety." The biofeedback process used to teach autonomic control is not analytical, logical, or verbal, but poetic. Thus the clearest description is through analogy.

This chapter uses an introspective analysis of urination as an editorial device to encourage research experimenters to become more responsive to the subtleties of autonomic control that affect subjects in biofeedback experiments. By using the analogy of voluntary control over urination as a figure-ground, the conflicting results of biofeedback experiments may become obvious.

The one autonomic process that each of us has learned is voluntary control of urination, which involves a mixture of smooth and striate muscles. Urination occurs under different conditions with immediate knowledge of results and is encouraged by strong motivation and plenty of reinforcement.

Urinary control definitely is executed by autonomic smooth muscles, as Lapides, Sweet, and Lewis[7] demonstrated when they used curare or succinylcholine to paralyze the skeletal muscles of 15 human subjects maintained on artificial respiration. While paralyzed, these subjects were able to initiate and stop urination on command. Urination is neither more nor less subtle than the processes involved in biofeedback learning, such as developing peripheral warmth, cardiac control, or EEG or EMG control.

Analysis of the biofeedback training paradigms of visceral learning in terms of the process involved in urination (especially voluntary onset) reveals many of the reasons for the conflicting results in the literature. For example, many laboratories reporting that learning is difficult or impossible have focused on performance and critical analysis of all the parameters involved and have not allowed the animal or human subject to perform at his own rate.

The research paradigms that analyze "scientifically" all the dimensions of performance are analogous to a doctor's asking you to urinate "now" while he is measuring the penis size. A few people may be able to urinate at that instant, but most, even if they tolerate the doctor's cold fingers holding their genitals, find it impossible to perform on command. But the "results" of such a study would "demonstrate" that humans cannot learn to control urination.

How can one describe experimentally the qualities involved in biofeedback learning? One way is to go to the bathroom and urinate before continuing to read the rest of this paper, and note carefully the following sensations: (1) Feel how you initiate urination. Where does your attention wander? Is part of you feeling the urine flow? Is that the same part that is analyzing the process or looking at the graffiti? (2) Analyze where you hold tensions in your body. Why? Are these tensions necessary? Are you pressing down to enhance the flow?

After completion, reflect on how the urination process felt. Did you notice the warmth? Under what conditions is it more easy or more difficult to urinate? Is there an effect from social pressure or even sexual arousal? Reflect on how you originally learned urination control. Look at some young children and note when they have and do not have bladder control. Is there a difference in control during excitement or passivity?

These obvious and subtle factors make each individual urination unique each time one urinates, and unique for each individual. Similar factors operate during biofeedback training of any visceral function. This means that each trainee needs a slightly different condition for optimum expression of learning. Yet, ironically, most research laboratories emphasize that trainees are trained under *identical conditions* regardless of individual requirements that may be too subtle to be described verbally and regardless of the fact that each individual has different fears and motivations that are brought to the experimental setting.

Some of these fears are "primal." For example, during the process of urination, especially in public, fear reactions are common and often inhibit urination. This is a natural reaction since during urination and defecation the organism is vulnerable and defenseless (observe a defecating dog), and the fight–flight triggers are readily activated. Often the experimenter unknowingly inhibits biofeedback learning by activating these primitive fight–flight responses (personal antagonism, sexual attractions, authority). Also, stress and social constraint affect urination (and biofeedback learning): When one must urinate or hurry the flow, urination becomes more difficult because one is actively striving. Ordinarily, one forgets about the process and just allows it to occur through passive attention.

Teaching passive attention is as nonverbal as teaching control over urination. When trainees are asked to attend passively during feedback training (that is, in the same mode in which they attend to urination), how does one know that they are doing it? A major problem in autonomic learning is defining or explaining *attention*—especially attention to the body. There are no verbal descriptions for the actual process. Even when the trainee reports that he is attending to the biofeedback signal, he may in fact not be. Moreover, how does the researcher know that, when two people report they are "attending," that they are using the same process?

Some subjects appear to be able to learn some physiological gymnastics without learning passive attention. They strive to perform, instead of allowing the process to occur. For example, one of my hypertensive trainees reported that whenever he did his homework exercises in his office he recapitulated the low EMG activity and did some autogenic training exercises. However, he did not appear to benefit from the exercises. When I asked him specifically and in detail what he was doing, he reported that, while doing his exercises, he always listened to the opening or closing of the doors to his office to see if his business partner was entering. He believed his partner would consider him foolish for doing the exercises. Clearly, he was doing the exercises incorrectly, because he should have been listening to his body with the same gentle attentiveness that he gave the door.

"How do you teach biofeedback learning?" This question is the same as, "How do you explain to someone else how to urinate?" Looking for linguistic labels is analogous to trying to teach someone to play the violin by describing how to move the bow and hold the fingers on the strings. It is far easier with the *experience* supplied by the violin instructor. However, these instruction qualities are usually missing from biofeedback experimenters, trainers, and technicians. The problems involved in biofeedback learning are nonverbal and poetic. They can be experienced directly or illustrated through analogy, but even instructions may be inherently contradictory. They demand "relax now," which is as paradoxical as "be creative now" or "be passionate and loving now."

Most experimental biofeedback researchers or clinicians have not gone through their own experimental design and experienced the process they are investigating or using in clinical therapy. I suggest that, before teaching biofeedback training, the researcher and clinician first spend 25 hours learning to control his own EEG, EMG, and/or temperature.* By experiencing biofeedback training, the researcher experiences the subtleties involved in autonomic learning.

These subtleties often involve the degrees of competence, attention, warmth, loving, coldness, anxiety, and other parameters that both the trainee and the trainer (experimenter) bring to the learning situation. A major dimension that affects autonomic learning is social pressure, striving, and demand for performance. This anxiety is well illustrated by the urination analogy. During an inter-

---

* The certification procedure for practitioners of autogenic training requires that they experience the entire process as part of their training before they can be accepted.[8] Practitioners in biofeedback would do well to follow the same procedure.

mission at the theater, you are standing at the urinal and a line of people behind you is saying implicitly or explicitly, "hurry up," making it more difficult for you to start urinating. The greater the social pressure, the more difficult it becomes, and so you read the graffiti to try to take your mind off the sense of pressure. Instead of taking 5 seconds to start the urine flow, it takes 30 seconds, and you sweat and feel embarrassed. The urine starts to flow when you finally give up and no longer care. At this point, you are successful.

This paradox often is experienced by subjects during biofeedback training. Usually, when subjects attempt to increase their alpha EEG activity, it initially decreases. When they finally stop trying, alpha EEG may increase. Similarly, one of my migraine patients always "tried" to warm her hand, and each time she tried the temperature dropped. Finally, she literally said, "Damn this study, I'm leaving," and her temperature rose 14°F.

The implicit demand to perform under pressure often permeates university laboratory settings, especially when the researcher must "publish or perish."

An analogy from "forced" urination to voluntary control biofeedback training studies is shown in the research paradigm where the trainee is asked to increase or decrease a certain biological function, such as EMG activity or EEG activity, every 1 or 2 minutes (keep alpha on for 1 minute, off for 1 minute, etc.). Why people learn and do not learn in these situations usually is not understood or explored; but consider what happens if a doctor askes you to urinate into a test tube, and just as you are ready to urinate he says "stop." You wait for 30 seconds, then he says, "Do it now for 5 seconds, and then wait for 30 seconds." Obviously, this would be difficult. Moreover, the more you tried, the more difficult it would be. Our rates of response or adaptation to experimental demands are different. For some of us, 5 seconds would be enough to do the task. For others, this would not be enough time, so that the trainee would still be trying to urinate when the doctor said "stop!" Here, the experimental conditions would not allow the trainee to learn or demonstrate learning; consequently, only a percentage of trainees would learn.

If one wishes to enhance the learning process and mobilize the trainee's own competency, one might try letting the person take responsibility for switching the conditions *when he is ready to switch conditions*. For some people, switching may take 5 seconds, for others, 20 minutes. This was the range found during a program for teaching trainees to tense and relax alternatively with EMG feedback, as is shown in Figure 1.

In this study, 10 subjects sat in a lightproof, sound-attenuated room, in which they received feedback from their integrated frontalis electromyographic activity. Instead of having fixed trial lengths using an A-B design (alternate conditions of voluntary tensing and relaxing of the frontalis muscle), the subjects controlled the 10 sequential trial lengths themselves. They signaled the experimenter when they achieved their optimum performance, which they could gauge from the auditory feedback signal. The distribution of trial lengths is shown in Figure 1. However, had we used 1-minuted fixed trials, 70% of the relaxation trials would have taken less than that time and the subjects would have felt bored,

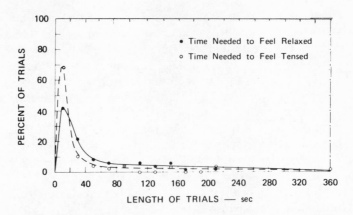

Figure 1. Distribution of trial lengths that were determined by 10 subjects while they received EMG. They signaled to the experimenter when they felt ready to change conditions to feel either relaxed or tense (10 trials for each subject).

while 30% of the trials would have taken longer and the subjects would have felt frustrated. Similarly, during the tense condition, 82% of the trials took less than 1 minute, while 18% were longer than that.[9] Fixed trials would not have allowed the subjects to optimize their performance and probably would have occluded the results with frustration and boredom on the part of subjects.

With these conditions in mind, one can again ask: What is the process for allowing visceral control? Some of the initial assumptions are:

1. You can learn. This is the implicit message the parent gives to a child by "knowing" the child can gain voluntary bladder control. In many research settings, the subject receives a mixed message: Try to do it, but you may not succeed.

2. Patience with the learning process. Again, parents assume children will require many trials before they gain control. But in many research settings, only 2, 3, or 10 training sessions may be used. Negative results indicate only that the person did not learn the task within the experimental constraints and do not prove that learning is not possible.

3. Learning is individualistic and is developed for and by the individual. In urination control, each child is handled differently. The learning is optimized when it corresponds to the mood of the person or to biological readiness. The usual biofeedback training paradigm fits the clinical hour of 50 minutes that includes a certain number of trials. The emotional, physical, and spiritual state of the person usually is not considered. The training is conducted regardless of whether the person is tired, sleepy, anxious, or happy. (Obviously, some experimenters do realize these conditions, since they do not select uncooperative subjects.)

4. Rewards (or reinforcements) in the research setting are too weak and ineffective. They often consist of credits, money, time off, or brownie points. Incentives such as growth, self-respect, love, and self-mastery (which are

often the rewards for a child learning control over urination) might lead to a different outcome.

Luckily, human beings can rapidly learn to habituate to strange conditions or to the factors that inhibit learning. For example, many people find it difficult to urinate in public, but they finally do adjust to the presence of other people—or often can be taught to do this with a technique such as systematic desensitization.[10] However, the researcher usually does not take into account the slowness of habituation. Review the process of urination and the steps will become clearer. What feelings are associated with it? Almost everyone would report that relaxation of the sphincter with a passive gentle attentive focus allows urination to occur. Self-consciousness and thinking about the process or the smells, whether the stream is within the urinal, slows or stops the flow of urine. The process takes longer once inhibition is established, and a vicious circle can be established. The subtleties of social stress in this example are not so different from those that trainees experience in biofeedback training.

Many of the problems of teaching biofeedback are the result of those subtle qualities that similarly affect our control over urination. It is hoped that an introspective analysis of urination may make research experimenters more responsive to the subtleties of autonomic control.

REFERENCES

1. Luce, G., & Peper, E. Biofeedback: Mind over body, mind over mind. *New York Times Magazine*, September 12, 1971.
2. Love, W. A., Montgomery, D. D., & Moeller, T. A. Proceedings of the Biofeedback Research Society, Colorado Springs, February 1974, p. 35.
3. Sterman, M. B. *Seminars in Psychiatry*, 1973, *5*(4), 507.
4. Miller, N. E. In: N. E. Miller, T. X. Barber, L. V. DiCara, et al. (Eds.)., *Biofeedback and self-control, 1973.* Chicago: Aldine, 1974.
5. Miller, N. E. *Science*, 1969, *163*, 434–445.
6. Black, A. H. In: P. A. Obrist, A. H. Black, J. Brener, & L. V. DiCara (Eds.), *Cardiovascular psychophysiology*. Chicago. Chicago: Aldine, 1974.
7. Lapides, J., Sweet, R. B., & Lewis, L. W. Journal of Urology, 1957, *77*, 247.
8. International Committee on Autogenic Therapy. Certification, regulations. Montreal: Central ICAT Registration Office, 1973.
9. Peper, E. Paper presented at the 82nd Annual Convention of the American Psychological Association, New Orleans, 1974.
10. Budzynski, T., & Stoyva, J. In: N. Biraumer (Ed.), *The mastery of anxiety: Contribution of neurophysiology to anxiety research*. Reihe Fortschr. Klini. Psychol., Bd. *3*. Munich; Wein: Verlag, Urban & Schwarzenberg, 1973. p. 248.

5

Clinical Applications of Biofeedback Training: A Review of Evidence

Edward B. Blanchard and Larry D. Young

The published reports on clinical applications of biofeedback training are summarized and critically reviewed. Only in the area of electromyogram feedback for muscle retraining, elimination of subvocal speech while reading, and elimination of tension headaches does the evidence support strong conclusions on the efficacy of biofeedback training.

In the areas of elimination of cardiac arrhythmias, lowering blood pressure, and reducing seizure frequency, the results are encouraging but are subject to a variety of methodological flaws. In other areas no firm conclusions can be drawn from the available evidence.

Within the past few years several reports,[1-3] and even books,[4,5] have appeared in the lay press about the wonders of a new kind of treatment for a variety of ills—biofeedback. Biofeedback training, by which is meant providing the patient with relatively immediate information, or feedback, of some bioelectric response, has been hailed as a panacea for most psychosomatic disorders with diseases as diverse as hypertension, migraine headaches, cardiac arrhythmias, and epilepsy yielding to this mighty new tool. Several companies have begun to manufacture and market biofeedback training devices. This enthusiasm has even penetrated the medical world with the publication of several survey articles in the nonarchival professional journals.[6,7]

This review has been organized around bioelectric response systems and is limited to studies that involved the monitoring and attempted change, through feedback or operant conditioning, of a bioelectric response to achieve some clinical effect in an identified patient. This review is also limited to published reports or to reports presented at national meetings for which abstracts have appeared. For each response system all of the studies will be briefly described, chiefly in tabular form. Then the experimental procedures used and the subsequent conclusions drawn from the data collected will be critically evaluated to determine the "state of the art." In this area, as in any therapeutic endeavor, several rules of evidence should apply: We believe that the clinical applications of biofeedback techniques should be evaluated as to their efficacy by the same standards as one would apply to new drugs or a new form of psychotherapy.

Edward B. Blanchard • Department of Psychology, State University of New York at Albany, Albany, New York 12222.   Larry D. Young • Department of Psychology, University of Mississippi, University, Mississippi 38677.

EXPERIMENTAL PROCEDURES

The studies reviewed differ radically in the experimental procedures used and fall into several general categories. Since the reliability and validity of conclusions about treatment effects are directly related to the experimental procedures, the latter are briefly summarized below.

Anecdotal Case Report. This term refers to a case report without systematic data but which probably includes a description of the patient's symptoms before and after treatment, as well as some description of the treatment. Although it produces few data of use in evaluating treatment effectiveness,[8,9] it can be highly suggestive as to research directions and cannot be discounted. The latter is particularly true if adequate documentation of the baseline, or pretreatment, condition of the patient is included. However, it is not true scientific evidence and hence, valid conclusions cannot be drawn, because the results could possibly be accounted for by other, uncontrolled events in the patient's life.

Systematic Case Study. This term refers to a case report in which data are reported from the systematic measurement of some response over several trials, in a pretreatment or baseline condition and then also during the treatment condition(s). This represents a quasi-experimental design (Campbell & Stanley[9]), or, as described in a recent paper by Barlow and Hersen,[10] an A-B design. It can yield interpretable results, especially if there is a rather long baseline and the change in the target symptoms is coincident with the introduction of treatment.

A variant of the above is the report of *multiple systematic case studies.* This term refers to the situation in which several patients are treated in a similar A-B design. Finding similar changes in the target symptom in several patients at the same point during treatment is fairly strong evidence[10] of the efficacy of a treatment.

Controlled Single-Subject Experiment A stronger design uses the experimental analysis of behavior, or what Barlow and Hersen[10] refer to as the A-B-A design. In this type of report systematic data are collected across at least three conditions: baseline or pretreatment, treatment intervention, and then, and most critically, a return to baseline measurement conditions. If changes in the target symptom occur when going from A to B *and* then revert in going from B to A (the so-called reversal), this constitutes very strong evidence that B is a causal variable for changes in the symptom. A variation on this design is the A-B-A-B design that, as Barlow and Hersen pointed out, is more powerful than the A-B-A since it contains a second test of the efficacy of B as the agent responsible for change in the target behavior.

Single-Group Outcome Study. This is a fairly common design and represents the application of some treatment or treatments to a similar group of patients with pre- and posttreatment measurement of target symptoms. Since this type of study lacks any control procedures, such as a second comparable group of patients who are assessed but not treated, it is difficult, on logical grounds, to conclude that the treatment alone is responsible for any changes found. Conclusions drawn from a study of this design can be strengthened if a prolonged series of baseline measurements are taken, making it similar to a series of multiple systematic case studies. It is possible to have a controlled single-group outcome study, if, after baseline assessment, some other form of treatment is applied before applying the treatment of interest. This enables one to make within-group comparisons, but conclusions are still not as reliable as those made using a controlled group outcome study.

Controlled Group Outcome Study. This last category represents the strongest design.[8,9] The minimum conditions for a controlled group outcome study are an experimental or treatment group and an untreated group of comparable patients who are assessed at the same time as the experimental group. This control for random life events associated with the passage of time and for "spontaneous remission."

A second, even more powerful design (Paul[8]) includes at least three groups: treatment, attention-placebo control, and no-treatment control. The addition of an attention-placebo group controls for changes in target symptoms due to the attention paid patients in treatment and to various placebo or expectancy effects.

ELECTROMYOGRAM (EMG)

Although clinical application of EMG feedback has been reported for several years, the recent interest in biofeedback training has led to its resurgence. One might exclude studies in which EMG feedback was used clinically from this review on the grounds that the bioelectric response being monitored comes from striate muscle; however, since the work on EMG feedback has generally been subsumed under the rubric of biofeedback it is included. Furthermore, in many ways it is the soundest work to be done in the field.

Direct Muscle Retraining

The work on retraining of muscles in paralyzed patients using EMG feedback is the oldest in the biofeedback literature and is summarized in Table 1.

Marinacci & Horande[11] presented a detailed account of the use of EMG feedback in patients with many different kinds of neuromuscular disorders: hemiplegia due to stroke; reversible physiologic blocks such as due to edema; causalgia true motor nerve injury in which some fibers survive; and Bell palsy. In each example a loss of function of long standing was reversed through EMG feedback. All of these can be considered anecdotal case reports with long baselines.

Andrews[12] reports on a series of 20 patients suffering from hemiplegia who had shown no return of function in 1 year since the onset of hemiplegia and who had shown no progress in traditional neuromuscular rehabilitation procedures. Following the training procedure described in Table 1, 17 of the patients were successful in developing strong, voluntary, well-modulated action in the muscle within one trial.

These data represent a single-group outcome study with some degree of control because of the long baseline period and the unanimous failure to respond to previous therapy. What is truly remarkable about the results is the large degree of improvement within such short training periods.

Table 1

Summary of Studies Using EMG Feedback for Muscle Retraining

Authors	Clinical response	Number of Subjects	Frequency and duration of treatment	Training procedure	Concurrent other treatment	Results		Experimental design	
						Bioelectric response	Clinical response	Type of design	Quality of control procedures
Marinacci & Horande[11]	Various neuro-muscular disorders		Variable	Insertion of needle electrodes into muscle and feedback of EMG sound; patient trained to increase sound to generate movement	Variable		Return of some function	Anecdotal case reports	Typically long baseline by history—little data given
Andrews[12]	Hemiplegic patients; response was smooth voluntary movement in arm	20	1- to 5-min sessions	Patients taught normal EMG sound, electrodes inserted in paralyzed arm and auditory feedback given as patient tried to generate sound and movement	None	All patients could produce EMG	17/20 successful in 5 min; one more learned movement with additional 15 min	Uncontrolled single-group study	Long baseline by history; no long-term clinical effects were sought

Reference	N	Sessions	Procedure	Adjunct	EMG	Outcome	Study type	Comments
Johnson & Garton[13]	10	3- to 30-min sessions in hospital; 2 30-min sessions daily at home 2 to 16 wk	Patients taught to produce EMG sounds from foot using direct auditory feedback; training continued at home on portable units with surface electrodes	Some physical therapy after movement returned	All patients could produce EMG	5/10 enough improvement to eliminate brace; improved muscle function in other 5	Uncontrolled single-group study	Long baseline (at least 1 yr of no function and failure to respond to trad. PT) by history; pre- and postfunction
			Hemiplegic patients with leg brace; response was dorsiflexion and walking without brace					
Peper[14]	1	Not given	EMG feedback training for both relaxing spastic muscles and movement in paralyzed arm	Psychotherapy	Not given	Patient recovered function	Anecdotal case report	No data given
			Spasticity and hemiplegia; paralyzed arm					
Booker et al.[15]	1	26, 1-hr sessions over 5 mo	Patient trained to use shoulder muscle nerve for face movement using EMG feedback; (1) independent movement of face muscles; (2) tracking of good side EMG with paralyzed side EMG for facial symmetry; training discontinued for 4 mo, then reinstituted	Home practice before mirror	Patient learned to produce EMG with no noticeable shoulder movement	Patient could close eye; good symmetry at rest; fair symmetry in smiling; deterioration when training stopped —recovered with training	Systematic case study	Baseline by history—3 previous failures of trad. PT; informal A-B-A design on value of training
			Paralysis of left side of face					

Johnson and Garton[13] report on a series of 10 patients with hemiplegia of at least 1 year's duration who each wore a leg brace. In these cases complete rehabilitation was the goal rather than demonstration of return of voluntary movement as in the Andrews study. As outlined in Table 1, treatment proceeded in two phases: first EMG feedback training, similar to that of Andrews,[12] in the hospital. Next the patient was switched to a portable EMG feedback device utilizing surface electrodes, designed for use at home. Patients were continued on home training until use of the short leg brace could be discontinued or there was no further improvement over 1 month.

Of the five "failures," one showed good improvement in muscle function but other problems prevented improvement in walking; one did not use the home-training device properly and three participated only briefly. The latter three did show some improvement in muscle function, however.

This represents a good single-group outcome study. Although there is no formal control group, the prolonged baseline period of 1 year without function lessens this problem, as does the minimal therapeutic contact. The study certainly presents very promising results since most of the feedback training is done at home and functionally significant responses were assessed.

In an anecdotal case report Peper[14] reports in detail on one successfully treated case of hemiplegia, with both spasticity and paralysis in the arm, in which EMG feedback training was given in a graded series of steps.

Booker, Rubow, and Coleman[15] describe a novel use of EMG feedback in the treatment of a patient with no voluntary function in the muscles on the left side of the face, including inability to close the eye or blink. A partial reinervation of the facial muscles was accomplished, surgically, by connecting nerves from the shoulder muscles to the facial musculature. Three separate attempts over 2 years at traditional physical therapy, aimed at teaching control of facial movement by shoulder movement, failed.

Following the EMG feedback training described in Table 1, the patient first learned to control the muscles. Then, since a decided facial asymmetry remained whenever she spoke or smiled, a novel tracing training using EMG feedback was instituted: She was presented, simultaneously, feedback of the EMG from the same muscles on both sides of the face and taught the self-generated target signal (from the uninjured right-side muscle) with the newly inervated muscles on the injured side. At the completion of training the patient was seen in the laboratory once every 2 weeks for 4 months. A second 4-month period during which she was not seen resulted in some deterioration but three training sessions restored the results.

This represents a single-subject experiment without systematic data. However, discontinuation of training did lead to a reversal and reintroduction of it to a return of improvement.

Comment. The work on EMG feedback for muscle retraining has established the therapeutic effect of biofeedback training. Although there are no controlled group outcome studies in the literature, the prolonged baseline periods, during which no function is apparent, and the failure of previous attempts at traditional rehabilitation procedures probably make the data from the single-group studies almost as strong in terms of its reliability and validity as would come from controlled group outcome study.

Elimination of Subvocalization in Reading

Although subvocal speech during reading is well known and constitutes a serious deterent to increasing reading speed, it has proved refractory to many methods of intervention. Hardyck, Petrinovich, and Ellsworth[16] reported on a rapid treatment technique utilizing auditory EMG feedback of the activity of laryngeal muscles as subjects read silently. In one 30-minute feedback session the entire sample of 17 subjects reduced EMG activity to baseline (at rest and not reading) levels. Most subjects showed complete reduction within the first 5 minutes. Follow-up tests at 1 and 3 months with no feedback showed no return of subvocalization.

Although it is an uncontrolled single-group outcome study, the overwhelming results support the conclusion that the biofeedback training was effective. The follow-up data are particularly encouraging and are somewhat rare in the biofeedback area.

McGuigan[17] criticized the Hardyck et al. report on the grounds of a lack of control groups. He presented data on three subjects who were successfully run in a similar EMG feedback paradigm with the exception that the recording site was the chin. His results are examples of systematic case studies.

In a reply to McGuigan, Hardyck, Petrinovich, and Ellsworth[18] presented additional data on comprehension and unsuccessful attempts at voluntary suppression of subvocalization without feedback in support of their techniques.

In a later report Hardyck and Petrinovich[19] report on two controlled outcome studies of their EMG feedback technique. In experiment 1, 43 college students who subvocalized were randomly assigned to two groups. After a baseline recording session, the feedback group received 1 hour's training and showed cessation of laryngeal EMG activity during silent reading. The control group was run for 2 more hours of silent reading during EMG recording and showed no change. Introduction of the EMG feedback training for 1 hour led to complete cessation of subvocalization in this group.

In a second outcome study with 13 high school students, from one to three feedback sessions were necessary to eliminate subvocalization EMG activity. At a 1-month follow-up, it was found that students of average IQ or above did not return to subvocalization (and had learned to stop within one session) while those with a below-average IQ had all returned to the habit and had also required two to three training sessions.

Aarons[20] found similar rapid reduction in subvocalization using the EMG feedback technique of Hardyck et al. and also gains in comprehension in a controlled study comparing subjects high or low in level of subvocal speech.

Comment. The results of the controlled outcome study by Hardyck and Petrinovich coupled with their previous work and the independent replication by Aarons seem to point conclusively to the beneficial effects of this biofeedback technique for reducing target behavior, subvocal speech. It has not been documented whether its elimination leads to an increase in reading speed, however. One reported clinical benefit, in addition to eliminating the habit, has been that students who have undergone the training are less fatigued after several hours of reading than they were previously.

EMG Feedback-Assisted Relaxation

It is fairly well established that people can learn to profoundly relax muscles when given feedback of the level of EMG activity.[21] As summarized in Table 2, this fact has been applied clinically both in studies in which muscle relaxation per se was seen as the major therapeutic intervention and in studies in which training in relaxation was an adjunct to some other form of clinical intervention.

The best study in this area is by Raskin, Johnson, and Rondestvedt,[22] in which 10 patients with chronic anxiety were given EMG feedback-assisted relaxation training as outlined in Table 2. All patients were young adults who had been symptomatic for at least 3 years, the last 2 of which had been receiving individual psychotherapy and possibly minor tranquilizers. As soon as the patient could sustain a deep level of relaxation without feedback, an 8-week assessment period during which he was to continue home practice in relaxation was begun; data from this period were compared to pretreatment data on a number of measures.

This is a single-group outcome study with the prolonged baseline and the 2 prior years of individual psychotherapy serving as a control condition. As shown in Table 2, the results of this study fail to support the efficacy of the biofeedback technique for the chief symptom but do provide good support for efficacy with other problems.

Peper,[14] in an anecdotal case report, described one case of a patient with insomnia who was taught relaxation with the assistance of EMG feedback. Although the case was reportedly a success, its value as scientific evidence of efficacy is nil since it is an anecdotal case report.

Garrett and Silver[23] tested the benefits of biofeedback training of both EMG and EEG alpha in relieving college students of test anxiety. As described in Table 2, two matched groups of college students were assigned to either a no-treatment control condition or to one in which they received biofeedback training both to reduce EMG level and to increase alpha level. The experimental group showed significant physiological effects of biofeedback training. On the posttreatment assessment, the experimental group showed less test anxiety as measured by the questionnaire ($p < .01$) but *did not* differ on the performance measures or on end-of-term grades.

This study, while adequate in terms of design, shows that biofeedback training leads only to a trivial clinical change (response to a questionnaire) but not to changes in any important behaviors.

One other related study was conducted by Jacobs and Felton,[24] who compared patients with neck injuries and normal subjects on ability to relax the trapezius muscle using EMG feedback in a paradigm outlined in Table 2. Results showed significantly higher levels of EMG activity during self-relaxation trials for the patients with neck injuries than for the normals. However, after the feedback training the EMG levels between the two groups were indistinguishable, showing a dramatic reduction in muscle tension with very little training. This well-controlled group outcome study, while highlighting the effects of EMG feedback training on muscle spasm, was not conducted as treatment and no long-term clinical effects were noted.

Wickramasekera[25] has reported an example of EMG feedback-assisted relaxation training used as an adjunct to the treatment of test anxiety with systematic desensitization. Initial relaxation training was conducted using EMG feedback of frontalis muscle activity. During the hierarchial scene presentation, the patient was taught to present herself the scenes and instructed to switch off a scene whenever the EMG feedback signal reached a certain point rather than rely on the typical self-report. The case was successful as the patient passed an examination that she had avoided even taking several times because of high anxiety levels. This anecdotal case report, while interesting, is not evidence for the clinical efficacy of biofeedback training since the basic treatment procedure is well established.

In two other studies Wickramasekera[26,27] has presented evidence that EMG feedback training increases hypnotic susceptibility.

Comment. The best data on EMG feedback to teach relaxation is provided by Raskin et al.,[22] in which the best clinical results, interestingly, came not from direct reduction of reports of anxiety but rather from relief of anxiety-mediated symptoms such as tension headaches and insomnia. Despite its being a single-group study, the Raskin study is, by virtue of using subjects with a very well-documented history of anxiety who were refractory to a previous therapeutic intervention, somewhat controlled and thus fairly valuable as evidence. Procedures used in the other reported studies do not permit evaluation of biofeedback effects.

Tension Headaches

Budzynski and Stoyva, and their associates, have presented a series of three studies[28-30] in which they have systematically applied EMG feedback training to tension headaches. In the first study the equipment and procedure were described as well as data on 15 nonpatients. It was shown that true feedback of frontalis muscle EMG led to greater decreases in muscle activity than pseudofeedback or a relaxation control.

In the second report[29] five patients with tension headaches were treated as outlined in Table 3 with a combination EMG feedback training and home relaxation practice. There was a steady decrease in headache activity (a function of headache intensity and duration) and EMG level over the training period. Tension headaches were eliminated in two patients and reduced markedly in another. For two patients, headaches returned shortly after the end of training. Reinstitution of home relaxation practice for both patients plus feedback sessions for one led to cessation of headaches.

This study represents a series of five systematic case studies and provides evi-

Table 2

Summary of Studies Using EMG Feedback for Relaxation Training

	Clinical response	No. of subjects	Frequency and duration of treatment	Training procedures	Concurrent other treatment	Results Bioelectric response	Clinical response	Experimental design Type of design	Quality of control procedures
Raskin et al.[22]	Chronic anxiety	10	2- to 30-min sessions/wk for 10 to 25 wk	After 8 wk of baseline symptom recording, patients taught to relax using EMB feedback of frontalis muscle, when EMB was low with feedback, patients taught to remain relaxed without feedback by fading out feedback	5/10 minor tranquilizers + daily home practice in relaxation	All patients learned to reduce EMG in session	4/10 moderate or better improvement in anxiety symptoms; 5/6 improvement of insomnia, 4/4 improvement of tension headaches	Uncontrolled single-group study	Long baseline by history; patients refractory to psychotherapy for 2 prior yr
Peper[14]	Insomnia	1	Not specified	EMG feedback relaxation	Home practice in relaxation	Not specified	Patient was cured of insomnia	Anecdotal case report	No hard data given on symptoms or treatment

Garrett & Silver[23]	"Test anxiety"	36	6 to 8 sessions of 40 min: 3 to 4 on EMB reduction	Experimental and control groups pretested on test anxiety and performance items; experimental subjects trained to produce high alpha states and lower EMG levels; controls untreated; both groups posttested and grades compared	3 to 4 sessions on increasing % time alpha in EEG	Experimentals decreased EMG by 40% and increased % time alpha by 21%	Experimentals showed less "test anxiety" than controls on questionnaire at posttest; no difference on performance on test or grade-point average	Controlled group outcome study	Controls were not treated; no attention-placebo control
Jacobs & Felton[24]	Neck muscle spasm	14	1 session with 10, 15-second trials	Experiment 1—relaxation without feedback then with EMG feedback; C-1 same; experiment 2—relaxation with EMG feedback; C-2 same	None	Experimentals and controls show significant reduction in EMG with feedback	Patients able to relax muscle with feedback to level of relaxed controls—no long-term data	Controlled group outcome study	Good design, but no long-term effects noted; C-1 and C-2 were normal subjects
Wickrama-sek era[25]	Test anxiety	1	2 feedback sessions	Patient taught to relax using EMG feedback prior to systematic desensitization; patient monitored self in systematic desensitization by EMG feedback	Systematic desensitization	Patient learned to lower EMG	Patient passed exam that had long been avoided	Anecdotal case report	No systematic data; biofeedback was adjunct

Table 3

Summary of Studies Using EMG Feedback for Tension Headaches

Authors	Clinical Response	Number of subjects	Frequency and duration of treatment	Training procedure	Concurrent other treatment	Results		Experimental design	
						Bioelectric response	Clinical response	Type of design	Quality of control procedures
Budzynski et al.[29]	Tension headaches	5	2 to 3 30-min sessions/wk for 4 to 13 wk	2 wk of baseline recording of EMG, then training to reduce EMG of frontalis muscle using auditory feedback	Home practice in relaxation	No individual data; group data shows steady decrease in EMG	Headaches eliminated or markedly reduced in 3/5; follow-up treatment + home practice eliminated headaches in other 2	Systematic case study with 4 replications	For 2 patients there was an A-B-A-B experiment on use of feedback + home practice; no control group
Budzynski et al.[30]	Tension headaches	18	2 30-min sessions/wk for 8 wk	All groups, 2 wk baseline EMG and headaches; experimental training to reduce EMG of frontalis muscle using auditory feedback C-1—False EMG feedback sessions C-2—No treatment but weekly contact Follow-up for 12 wk on experimental and C-1	Home practice in relaxation for experimental and C-1	EMG lower for experimental thru C-1	Experimental C-1 = C-2 on headache activity; experimental C-1 during follow-up. 4/6 experimental subjects headache-free 1/6 C-1 headache-free	Controlled group outcome study	Attention-placebo + waiting list controls follow-up data; confound of EMG feedback training and home practice in relaxation

Wickrama-sekera[31]	Tension headaches	5	2 30-min sessions/wk for 18 wk	3 wk baseline, 3 wk EMG feedback, 12 wk real EMG feedback on frontalis muscle	None specified	No individual data; group data show decrease in EMG	Apparent decrease in headache intensity and frequency	Controlled single-group study	No statistical analysis of data; no return to baseline
Epstein et al.[32]	Tension headaches	1	24 20-min sessions over several wk and 4 25-min sessions over 4 wk	Baseline and EMG feedback sessions were alternated in A-B-A-B design; patient taught to lower EMG level; ongoing music interrupted by high EMG	Minor tranquilizers and home practice in relaxation during follow-up	EMG reduced during feedback phases	Headache activity decreased during feedback phases returned without feedback. Headaches eliminated when home practice in relaxation instituted with feedback	Controlled single-subject experiment	Good A-B-A-B design; isolates home practice as crucial to permanent reduction in headaches

dence for the efficacy of the combination of EMG feedback training *and* home practice in relaxation. For the two initial failures, the use of home practice was subjected to an unsystematic A-B-A-B design with successful reduction of headaches accompanying each introduction of home relaxation practice and return of symptoms accompanying removal of this intervention.

A control for attention-placebo effects was added in the third study,[30] a controlled group outcome study involving six patients with tension headaches in each of three conditions, as outlined in Table 3. The results, which strongly support the efficacy of the combination of EMG feedback training and home practice in relaxation, showed a significantly lower level of headache activity for the experimental group than either control both at the end of treatment and at end of follow-up. More importantly in terms of individual patients, four of six experimental patients were essentially headache-free as compared with one of six in the group C-1 and none of six for the no-treatment control. In the experimental group there was a significant decrease in amount of analgesics or tranquilizers used by all six patients, with virtual elimination in four of six. For the attention-placebo control patients there was a marked decline in headache medication for two patients.

Interestingly, the two experimental patients who continued to have headaches also reported little or no home practice in relaxation *and* the one successful patient in group C-1 reported very regular home practice in relaxation. Although this study confirms the efficacy of the combination of EMG feedback training and home practice in relaxation, its design does not make it possible to isolate the effects of biofeedback training alone.

And additional study that evaluates the Budzynski technique was a report by Wickramasekera[31] on five patients with tension headaches. After the training procedures outlined in Table 3 the results revealed no drop in headache intensity or duration or in EMG level from baseline to pseudofeedback and a noticeable reduction in the final phase. No statistical comparisons were made between conditions so we are left with only the assumption that the changes reported are significant.

Epstein, Hersen, and Hemphill[32] reported on a single case with long-standing history of tension headaches who was treated with EMG feedback in a controlled single-subject experiment. In the first phases of this experiment (conducted while patient was hospitalized) only EMG feedback was used as treatment with no practice in relaxation. Using an A-B-A-B design, both headache activity and in-session EMG activity were reduced during experimental (B) phases and returned during the second baseline (A) phase.

Further EMG feedback training during outpatient follow-up also showed decreases in headache level with a return of headaches in the return to baseline of the A-B-A design. Institution of home practice in relaxation without further feedback training led to a marked reduction of headache frequency, regardless of medication used, pointing out the apparent value of home practice in relaxation.

Comment. Budzynski and his associates have demonstrated a potent treatment package for intervention in tension headaches: EMG feedback training and home practice in relaxation. This has been confirmed in systematic case studies and controlled group outcome studies. However, it is not clear what the relative contributions of either EMG feedback or relaxation are. We can conclude that EMG feedback training without home relaxation practice is not sufficient for long-lasting reduction of tension headaches as shown by the data from Budzynski et al.[30] and Epstein et al.[32] Whether EMG feedback training is even necessary has not yet been determined.

Summary Comment on EMG Feedback

The work on the application of EMG feedback training to clinical problems is the oldest and the soundest work in the biofeedback area. In such areas as the elimination of subvocal speech during reading and the retraining of paralyzed muscles in hemiplegics, the evidence is quite sound that EMG feedback training has marked therapeutic effects.

It is also fairly well established that a combination of EMG feedback training and home practice in relaxation is very effective in the treatment of tension headaches. This has been demonstrated consistently by several investigators in both uncontrolled and controlled studies. However, the question remains as to the therapeutic contribution of EMG feedback. Finally, there is no clear-cut evidence to support the efficacy of EMG feedback training to teach relaxation either as an intermediary to some other therapeutic endeavor or as the basic training itself.

A final note in this area is that the EMG feedback work is the one area where the response, tensing or relaxing of striate muscle, has traditionally been viewed as being under "voluntary" control. Perhaps this is the reason for the better results than found for any other response.

CARDIOVASCULAR RESPONSES

Within the field of biofeedback research the cardiovascular system has probably been studied more than any other. Numerous studies, summarized in a recent review,[33] have been conducted in which subjects were asked to control their heart rate or blood pressure. However, for the most part these studies were conducted with normal volunteers, were of short duration, and achieved relatively small-scale changes in the response under study.[33] The actual application of this reasearch to clinical problems has been relatively unimpressive.

HEART RATE

Table 4 presents several studies in which patients have been taught to modify heart rate (HR) through feedback training in an effort to obtain a therapeutic effect on some clinical problem.

Table 4

Summary of Studies Using Biofeedback of Heart Rate

Authors	Clinical response	Number of subjects	Frequency and duration of treatment	Training procedure	Concurrent other treatment	Results Bioelectric response	Results Clinical response	Experimental design Type of design	Experimental design Quality of control procedures
Weiss & Engel[34]	Premature ventricular contractions (PVCs)	8	22 to 53 sessions of 17 min 1 to 3 per day	Training in HR control using binary feedback: speeding, slowing, alternate speeding and slowing, maintain HR within range (direct feedback of PVC occurrence), fadeout of feedback	None		Decreases in PVC rate in 5/8 within treatment; decreases in PVC rate in 4/8 at independent check from 10 to 20/min to 1/min	Systematic case study with 7 replications	Long baseline by history; no baseline sessions; follow-up in all cases
Engel & Bleecker[35]	PVC	1	16 daily sessions of 17 min	HR control using binary feedback taught for 4 session each; slowing, speeding, alternation, maintain HR in range	None		Decrease in treatment of PVC rate: 15/min to 1/min	Systematic case study	Long baseline by history plus 2 baseline sessions; follow-up
Engel & Bleecker[35]	Supraventricular tachycardia and PAT	1	26 daily sessions of 17 min	Training in HR slowing	None	In-session decrease of 2/6 BPM	Baseline HR-116 BPM; final session HR-105 BPM; follow-up HR-60-75 BPM; no PATs reported	Systematic case study	Baseline by history; 1 baseline session, 5 follow-up sessions
Engel & Bleecker[35]	Sinus tachycardia	1	21 daily sessions of 17 min	Training in HR slowing (12) and fadeout of feedback (9)	None	In-session decreases of 3 to 4 BPM	Decrease in treatment of HR from 86 to 68 BPM	Systematic case study	Baseline by history; no baseline sessions; no tachycardia in sessions

Study	Condition	N	Sessions	Training procedure	Medication	Learning	Clinical response	Type of study	Comments
Engel & Bleecker[35]	Paroxysmal atrial tachycardia (PAT) and episodic sinus tachycardia	1	40 daily sessions of 17 min	Training in HR control; HR slowing (20 sessions); HR speeding (10); alternation (10)	Diazepam 5 mg, tid	Little learning of slowing, speeding by 15–20 BPM	No data on clinical response during treatment; no report of PAT for 9 mo after treatment	Anecdotal case report	Baseline by history; no in-session baseline; no in-session data on clinical response
Scott et al.[36]	Sinus tachycardia	2	(1) 53 20-min sessions, 1 to 2/day; (2) 30 20-min sessions, 1–2/day	(1) Training in HR slowing using two shaping procedures; (2) training in HR slowing using one shaping procedure	None		(1) Baseline HR-89, no decrease in 26 sessions, then decrease to 72 BPM in 18 sessions; (2) Baseline HR-96, decrease to 78 BPM	Controlled single-subject experiment, A-B-A	Stable baseline established in session; return to baseline in treatment
Bleecker & Engel[37]	Wolff-Parkinson-White syndrome (conduction disorders)	1	Unspecified number daily sessions of 17 min	Patient trained to slow HR, alternate speed and slow, then direct feedback of W-P-W beats	None	Learned alternation	Patient learned to produce WPM or normal beats at will and to increase normal conduction; no overall lasting clinical effects noted	Anecdotal case report	Baseline by history; no systematic data on clinical response; no baseline sessions
Prigatano & Johnson[38]	Approach to feared object (spider)	26	2 60-min sessions	Experimental and control subjects pretested; experimental subjects trained to hold HR constant while viewing picture of spiders	None	Experimental subjects did not learn HR control	No difference between experimental and control subjects at posttreatment test of fear	Controlled group outcome study	Controls matched on pretest, received 2 sessions of tracking task

Cardiac Arrhythmias

The first published reports of clinical application of biofeedback techniques to cardiovascular problems were those of Engel and his associates working with various cardiac arrhythmias.[34,35,39-41] In several brief communications[30-41] the successful treatment of arryhthmias such as atrial fibrillations, atrial and ventricular tachycardia, and premature ventricular contractions (PVCs) "by means of operant conditioning paradigms"[39] was noted. These brief reports can best be considered as anecdotal case reports, and hence of little value in evaluating the efficacy of a treatment. The work reported in the brief communications on patients with PVCs became part of a series of eight cases presented in a major article by Weiss and Engel.[34]

Since they collected systematic data on the principal dependent variable, rate of emission of PVCs, the authors were able to determine in which training phase the major reduction of PVCs occurred. For two patients the major reduction occurred during training in alternating HR. For two others the major reduction was during *range* training; however, one patient did more poorly during range training. Finally, for one patient there was a significant reduction during training in HR slowing and a further reduction during training in alternating HR. Thus there does not seem to be a systematic functional relationship between training phase and decrease in PVC rate. There is, however, a strong relationship between total number of training sessions and improvement: the five patients receiving 47 or more sessions all showed improvement while the three who received fewer sessions did not improve.

While this laudable piece of research is highly suggestive of directions for future investigations, it contains several methodological flaws that seriously detract from its value. First, no baseline data were measured. However, reasonably well-documented histories of PVCs were available in all patients and could be considered as baseline data. Furthermore, since there was no return to baseline conditions, the cases do not represent single-subject experiments but instead should be considered as a series of systematic case studies. Since the major improvement in the dependent variable occurred in different training phases for differnt patients, no functional conclusions can be drawn from the series.

An alternative way of conceptualizing the study is as an uncontrolled single-group study in which there was marked improvement in four of eight cases and some improvement in another case. The lack of a control group seriously detracts from the study, when viewed this way, because of the significant relation between total number of sessions and clinical improvement. The latter relation suggests an alternative explanation of the results in terms of expectancy or placebo effects.

In a recent paper Engel and Bleecker[35] report on the treatment of several more cases of cardiac arrhythmias. One additional patient with PVCs was treated. For the first time laboratory recordings of baseline PVC rate were made and found to be approximately 15 PVC/min. The patient was put through the training outlined in Table 1 that resulted in a decrease in PVC rate to almost zero. Another arrhythmia case treated by Engel and Bleecker[35] involved a man with supraventricular tachycardia and PAT whose HR reportedly was in the range of 130 to 140 beats per minute (BPM) for several years. He was treated as outlined in Table 1.

These two cases represent poor systematic case studies in that only two and one baseline trials were run, respectively. A preferable procedure would be to run baseline trials until the target reponse was stable. the lack of any reversal or control phase seriously hampers the interpretation of the results. This is especially true with the second case since there was a large-scale drop in HR *after discharge* that leads one to suspect that some process other than biofeedback training may have been responsible for the changes noted.

Engel and Bleecker[35] also reported a patient with sinus tachycardia. During the training described in Table 1 his HR as measured in the laboratory decreased from 86 to 68 BPM. The lack of baseline assessment is particularly acute in this case since the baseline value by history was 106 BPM, yet the first session HR was 86 BPM during a trial on which HR did not decrease. This 20-BPM drop without treatment limits the interpretation of the results. Moreover, the steady decline over trials could be due to habituation rather than the feedback training.

A final case reported by Engle and Bleecker involved PATs and episodic sinus tachycardia. After the training outlined in Table 4 there were no recurrences of PAT, and only one episode of tachycardia for which the patient claimed she voluntarily slowed her HR. Since no systematic data were collected on episodes of PAT or sinus tachycardia during treatment, this case is an anecdotal case report.

Scott et al.[36] reported on two cases of chronic sinus tachycardia treated with a biofeedback procedure as outlined in Table 4. In addition to the lowered HR other clinical improvement was noted in both cases: In patient 1, concomitant with the decrease in HR, the patient actively sought and obtained full-time employment after being on disability compensation for his tachycardia for 18 months. The other patient reported feeling less anxious and was able to do more chores at home.

These two cases represent true experiments since (1) a stable baseline was established and (2) a return to baseline conditions was included as a control phase to complete the A-B-A design. However, the failure to find a complete reversal during the return to baseline precludes drawing any definite conclusions from the data of Scott et al. and suggested that some process other than their experimental procedure might account for the results.

This last point highlights a problem in the clinical biofeedback area, particularly in the use of single-subject experimental designs. Because of the difficulty of obtaining a reversal, the A-B-A design may not be appropriate. In fact, the changes may not be reversible except by direct training to reinstate the disorder (see Scott et al.[42] for an example of this) that is difficult to justify on clinical or ethical grounds. Thus either group outcome designs that are difficult to complete in terms of matching patients or multiple subject/multiple base line designs[10] may be more appropriate.

Conduction Disorders

Bleecker and Engel[37] reported on one case of Wolff-Parkinson-White syndrome (WPW) treated by conditioning techniques. This patient showed two types of cardiac impulse conduction: both normal and WPW. Following the training outlined in Table 4 the patient could reliably increase or decrease WPW or normal conduction and maintain normal conduction without feedback.

This report is an anecdotal case report. Although the training stages are clearly spelled out, no systematic data are reported on the principal dependent variable or on overall clinical effects. Its chief value, and that of several other reports[35,42,44] omitted from detailed consideration in this communication, is in contributing to the overall understanding of the functioning of the cardiovascular system.

Other Clinical Applications

One tangential study of biofeedback training of HR was reported by Prigatano and Johnson.[38] In experiment 1, they demonstrated that fearful subjects exposed to the feared object increase their HR variability. In experiment 2, outlined in Table 4, matched groups of spider-fearful subjects were trained to keep HR relatively constant or given a control procedure. Results of a posttreatment assessment involving approach to a spider showed no differences in degree of fear reduction between the two groups; moreover, the biofeedback-trained subjects did not show any better control of HR than did the controls. Thus, while this study was adequate in terms of experimental design, and while it is an interesting application of biofeedback procedures, it tells us little of clinical importance.

Comment. The rationale in the work on cardiac arrhythmias and cardiac conduction disorders seems to have been that teaching patients to control their HR will have a therapeutic effect on the particular disorder. In spite of the methodological problems already noted there are several conclusions we may tentatively draw: (1) In the work on PVCs, the nine cases indicate that a therapeutic effect can be achieved through biofeedback; (2) in the work on sinus tachycardia, the work of Scott et al. in combination with the case reported by Engel and Bleecker indicates that a therapeutic effect can also be achieved with this disorder; and (3) most of the work in this area is inadequate in experimental controls. The two controlled single-subject experiments by Scott et al. present problems of interpretation because of the failure to find a large scale change in HR during the return to baseline conditions.

One final conclusion that may be drawn from this work is that these results are very interesting, and highly suggestive, but that they do not represent strong *scientific* evidence for the efficacy of biofeedback procedures because of the lack of adequate controls. Thus they do not seem to warrant the wholesale enthusiasm they have generated.

BLOOD PRESSURE

The second cardiovascular response that has received major attention is blood pressure (BP), due undoubtedly to the large-scale health problem represented by hypertension.[45] As with HR, several studies[33] report training normotensive subjects to increase or decrease BP through a biofeedback training procedure. There have, however, been several reports of applications of biofeedback procedures to patients with hypertension, and these are summarized in Table 5.

The best known study in this area is one by Benson et al.[46] in which the Harvard group's feedback procedure[47,48] for BP was used to lower the systolic BP of seven hypertensive patients. They were initially run in baseline sessions, during which they sat comfortably relaxed, until their BP showed no further decrease over five consecutive sessions. Next, biofeedback training to lower systolic BP was introduced and continued until systolic BP again showed no further decrease over five consecutive sessions. One patient was not hypertensive at the end of the baseline assessment. Results showed marked (16 mm Hg or greater) decreases in systolic BP in five of seven patients with a range of change for the group of +1 to −34 mm Hg. However, only two of the six hypertensive patients were able to lower BP to within the normal range.

In terms of design this study can be considered either as a series of systematic A-B case studies or as an uncontrolled single-group outcome study. As a group study, the results indicate a significant ($p < .01$) drop in systolic BP. However, the lack of control groups hinders interpretation of these results. As a series of single cases the chief fault is, of course, no return to baseline conditions to complete the experimental analysis.

Schwartz and Shapiro[49] conducted a similar study on a second group of hypertensive patients witht the chief difference being that diastolic BP was the response being monitored. The average diastolic BP for the patients during the baseline condition was 102 mmHg, and it showed no overall decrease in any subsequent condition, despite the fact that there were decreases in BP of approximately 5 mm Hg within individual sessions during the two feedback conditions.

This study is a single-group outcome study. No individual data were presented. Although in terms of design the lack of a control group is a fault, the major problem with the study is that no significant overall changes in diastolic BP were found. Hence, the study is of little clinical importance.

Miller[50] has reported treatment of one case of hypertension that is outlined in Table 5. During baseline her diastolic BP varied from 75 to 115 mm Hg with a mean of 97 mm Hg. With training, both in the hospital and after discharge, her BP decreased to an average of 76 mm Hg and was relatively stable. During training she was withdrawn from antihypertensive medication and diuretics and still maintained the decreases.

This work represents a very good systematic case study, but it cannot be considered as experimental evidence to support the efficacy of biofeedback

Table 5

Summary of Studies Using Biofeedback of Blood Pressure

Authors	Clinical response	Number of subjects	Frequency and duration of treatment	Training procedure	Concurrent other treatment	Results			Experimental design	
						Bioelectric response	Clinical response	Type of design	Quality of control procedures	
Benson et al.[46]	Systolic BP in hypertensive patients	7	13 to 50 daily sessions of 45 min	Lowering of systolic BP taught with binary auditory and visual feedback delivered on beat-to-beat basis	6/7 on constant dosage of antihypertension medication	6/7 show decrease in systolic BP	5/7 show decreases in systolic BP of 16–34 mmHg: 3/7 decreased to normal range	Systematic case study with 6 replications or uncontrolled single-group study	Baseline sessions run until no decrease for 5 sessions—very stable; experimental sessions run until no further decrease for 5 sessions; no follow-up	
Schwartz & Shapiro[69]	Diastolic BP in hypertensive patients	7	20 daily sessions of 45 min	Patients run for 5 sessions in (1) resting baseline; (2) relax and think pleasant thoughts; (3) and 10 sessions in proportional visual feedback delivered approximately once per min and reinforcement for decreases in BP	None specified	Some subjects showed 5-mmHg decrease during feedback sessions	No overall decrease in diastolic BP; 1/7 showed decrease from 99 to 85 mmHg	Controlled single-group study	Subjects used as own controls—included control phase for relaxation; no follow-up	

Reference	Problem	N	Procedure	Detail	Medication	Control	Results	Study type	Comments
Miller[50]	Diastolic BP in hypertensive patient	18	84 daily sessions of 45 min both in and out of hospital	Patient run for 26 baseline trials; in 58 training trials patient taught both to raise and lower BP using binary auditory feedback on beat-to-beat basis	Initially on antihypertensive medication; discontinued during training	Patient could reliably increase or decrease BP by 10 mmHg	Decrease in diastolic BP from 97 mmHg to 76 mmHg; medication withdrawn	Systematic case study	Extended baseline; medication withdrawn during training; loss of control at follow-up due to "emotional stress"
Elder et al.[51]	Systolic and diastolic BP in "hypertensive" patients	1	8 sessions of 40 min, 2/day; 1 baseline, 7 training, also 1 follow-up	Three different conditions ($N = 6$) used; experimental—binary visual feedback on diastolic BP + social reinforcement given once per 2 min; C-1—binary visual feedback on diastolic BP given every 2 min; C-2—BP monitored	Some subjects on minor tranquilizers	BP data given for baseline session only	Experimentals showed decreases of 20% diastolic BP, significantly greater decrease than other 2 groups; C-1 lower than C-2 last trial; no differences on systolic BP	Controlled group outcome study	1. Differential dropout for follow-up; 2. One-session baseline; 3. Several confounds (see text)

procedures since no control conditions were run. Miller[50] himself notes that other factors may have been responsible for the changes.

One controlled group outcome study of the use of biofeedback techniques with BP has been reported by Elder et al.[51] Three groups of six "hypertensive patients" were run in the study outlined in Table 5. Part of the subjects were run in a second baseline session 1 week after the last experimental trial.

Actual BP values are reported only for the baseline trial. The remainder of the data were reported and analyzed as a ratio of experimental trial mean BP to baseline trial mean BP. Using this transformation, there were no significant decreases in systolic BP. For diastolic BP, however, the group receiving feedback and social reinforcement showed greater decreases than the other two. Also the feedback-only control group was significantly lower than the monitoring group by trials 7 and 8.

Despite these seemingly good results, there is some confounding of variables that seriously limit interpretation of these results. (1) The follow-up data are practically worthless since there were large differences in dropout rates among the three groups. (2) There were apparently instructional differences between C-1 and the experimentals that might account for the differences in results that were found: Experimental patients received not only social reinforcement for changes but also instructions to change and a rationale for how to change—"relax." This is important because basic research on HR has shown that instructions alone are effective in generating change,[52] and it has also been shown that relaxation training can lead to substantial decreases in BP.[53-55] One final fault was the use of a single baseline trial: Benson et al.,[46] in the study summarized above, found that four of their seven patients continued to show decreases in BP over 10 or more baseline trials. Despite these faults, an interesting aspect of this study is that feedback given on an intermittent basis was effective. Moreover, the demonstration of a decrease in diastolic BP to 80% of the baseline level, even through a combination of treatment factors, is very encouraging.

Comment. The procedures used to evaluate the clinical application of biofeedback training to BP are better than similar work on HR and the cardiac arrhythmias. Good systematic case studies showing large-scale effects on BP have been reported from two different laboratories. A controlled group outcome study has been reported, which, despite its faults, seems to indicate that large-scale changes in diastolic BP can be obtained. The lack of systematic BP data and of a stable baseline in the Elder et al.[51] study is very critical and precludes drawing definite conclusions, however. In summary, it does appear that biofeedback procedures can have beneficial effects on elevated BP. However, definite conclusions must await a controlled outcome study or a series of single-subject experiments. Also it seems possible that the biofeedback procedures may be only elaborate methods for teaching relaxation.[55]

PERIPHERAL VASODILATION

Although degree of vasoconstriction or dilation of peripheral blood vessels might not ordinarily be considered a cardiovascular response, we have chosen to consider studies of this response here rather than in a separate section. It has been shown that vasodilation can be operantly conditioned, or brought under biofeedback control.[56,57]

Schwartz[58] reports on two cases of Raynaud disease, a problem of peripheral constriction and reduced blood flow that under extreme conditions can lead to gangrene in the hands and feet. The first case was a man in his 60s who had very cold feet. Blood volume was recorded from his big toes and feedback of blood volume in one toe was given. Over 10 sessions the patient began to show "large increases in blood volume," particularly in the foot for which feedback was given. A later switch to the other foot showed similar results. The patient remained symptom-free after an unspecified number of sessions for a year and a half and then requested further training. The second case was a woman who was seen for fewer than 10 sessions. There was no indication of clinically significant changes in blood volume in her hands.

These two cases are anecdotal case reports. Biofeedback training was probably responsible in part for the changes in the first case since a control procedure yielded meaningful data. Thus the results are suggestive but certainly not conclusive; in fact, even the author speculates that the successful case may have been due to a placebo effect.

ELECTROENCEPHALOGRAM (EEG)

Work on the operant conditioning or feedback control of the alpha rhythm (8 to 12 Hz) of the human EEG is some of the oldest work in the biofeedback area, and for a time was some of the best established. There were several reports[59-61] relating increased alpha to various mental states. Recently, however, some authorities have called into question whether there is any true conditioning of alpha activity. For example, Paskewitz and Orne[62] have demonstrated that feedback training can increase alpha density (the percent of the time during which the subject's EEG shows alpha activity) only under conditions in which ambient stimuli are suppressing alpha activity. The increase reported seems due to the subjects learning to disregard environmental stimuli that suppress alpha rather than learning to produce greater alpha densities.

Regardless of the status of alpha biofeedback training, as shown in Table 6, there have been surprising few clinical applications of biofeedback training for control of certain aspects of the EEG.

Alpha Conditioning

Gannon and Sternbach[63] reported on a case in which the patient had frequent vascular headaches as a result of head trauma. Reasoning from reports that Yogis in high alpha states seem relatively insensitive to pain, they tried to teach this patient to produce a high percentage of alpha activity to reduce his headaches. As noted in Table 6, although the patient learned to increase alpha production, there was only minimal improvement in his headaches. As the authors state, "So it seemed that all we were able to do was to make him feel bet-

Table 6

Summary of Studies Using Biofeedback of EEG

Authors	Clinical response	Number of subjects	Frequency and duration of treatment	Training procedure	Concurrent other treatment	Results — Bioelectric response	Results — Clinical response	Experimental design — Type of design	Experimental design — Quality of control procedures
Gannon & Sternbach[63]	Vascular headaches	1	70 sessions of 29 min over several months	Patient trained to produce high % alpha in EEG, first with feedback and then without	None	Increased % time alpha 20% to 70% (with feedback) and to 40% without feedback	No systematic data on headaches; no overall effect on headache; patient felt better in nonheadache state	Anecdotal case report	No systematic data on clinical response
Sterman;[66] Sterman & Friar[64]	Frequency of various kinds of seizures	5	Numerous sessions, 3 to 5/wk, of 20 to 40 min, 4 home feedback training for some 6 to 18 mo	Patients trained to produce bursts of sensorimotor rhythm (SMR) both progressively more frequently and of higher voltage; for 3 patients training was discontinued for 9 wk, then reinstated	None	Increased production of SMR in 4/5 patients	Marked decrease in seizure activity in 4/5 patients (those showing acquisition of SMR) All 3 patients showed return of abnormal EEG and seizure activity in 4 to 6 wk after training stopped; return to low seizure rate with return to training	2 anecdotal case reports and 3 controlled single-subject experiments	Baseline on seizure activity by history; good follow-up; systematic data on only 1 case; use of A-B-A-B design
Miller[67]	Frequency of spikes in EEG and seizures	Not specified	Not specified	Patients trained with audio feedback for spikes to suppress paroxysmal spike activity in EEG	Not specified	Some decrease in spike activity	Not specified	Anecdotal case report	No data presented
Sittenfeld[68]	Sleep-onset insomnia	7	Unspecified number of 20-min sessions	Patients trained to increase theta activity with auditory feedback	EMG training for relaxation (?)	Increased theta production	Useful for 4/7; 4/7 fell asleep in lab with theta training	Anecdotal case report	No systematic data on bioelectric response or clinical response

ter when he felt normal, but that we had no effect when he was already experiencing pain." Since no systematic data were presented on the chief dependent variable of headaches, this must be considered an anecdotal case report that is negative as far as the clinical efficacy of biofeedback application is concerned.

Garrett and Silver,[23] in a study reviewed under EMG, used both EMG feedback and alpha feedback training as treatment for test anxiety in a controlled group outcome study. Despite adequate EEG feedback training to reach a criterion alpha density, the only change was in a self-report measure of test anxiety. There was no difference between treated subjects and untreated controls in performance tests or grade point average.

Sensorimotor Rhythm

Sterman and his associates[64-66] have reported a novel biofeedback procedure that seems to have promise as treatment for various kinds of seizure disorders. In these cases feedback is given of a 12- to 14-Hz rhythm recorded over the sensorimotor cortex in efforts to increase its occurrence through both laboratory and home training.

Data are presented on five cases: (1) a 7-year-old boy with mixed seizure disorder—major motor seizures plus petit mal variant; (2) a 23-year-old woman with focal major motor disorder; (3) an 18-year-old man with mixed seizure disorder—petit mal variant; (4) a 46-year-old adult with petit mal seizures; and (5) an 18-year-old with partial focal seizure disorder. In four of the five cases (1 to 4) decided clinical improvement in terms of reduced seizure frequency was noted as well as marked EEG changes, notably, substantial evidence of learning to emit the SMR at a higher density. In the fifth case there was only a minimal decrease in seizure rate and only minimal evidence of learning to increase SMR.

Although detailed seizure frequency data are presented for only one case,[64] and systematic data on SMR incidence are not provided, nevertheless, three of the cases presented can be considered controlled single-subject experiments. In these three cases training was discontinued after 6 months for approximately 9 weeks. During that interval, which constitutes a true reversal, seizure manifestations were clearly exacerbated after 4 to 6 weeks in each patient. Reintroduction of biofeedback training (to complete the A-B-A-B design) rapidly returned the patients to their improved clinical state.

These results are highly encouraging since beneficial effects have been found in several types of seizure disorders. Moreover, the experimental procedures used provide reliable data on the clinical efficacy of SMR training.

Other EEG Biofeedback Work

Miller,[67] reporting on an unspecified number of patients with abnormal EEG, has noted that giving these patients feedback of the occurrence of paroxysmal spikes has led to a reduction in abnormal EEG activity in the laboratory. No evaluation of transfer of therapeutic effects has been obtained. This work must be considered as anecdotal data of considerable clinical interest.

Sittenfeld[68] has reported beneficial effects for four of seven patients suffering from insomnia who were given biofeedback training to increase theta (4- to 7-Hz) activity. This brief report must also be considered anecdotal data at this point.

Comment. While the work on the biofeedback training in producing high incidence of alpha activity in the EEG is relatively old and has received much publicity,[61] the evidence for clinical efficacy of training to produce alpha or theta is very poor. On the other hand, Sterman's work on biofeedback training to produce a high incidence of sensorimotor rhythm seems quite promising. The data reported to date provide evidence that this training does lead to a suppression of a variety of types of seizure disorders. This avenue certainly seems promising, and worthy of further investigation.

SKIN TEMPERATURE

Migraine Headaches

Although the work of the Menninger group on the use of "hand warming" as a treatment for migraine headaches has been noted in several places,[2,6,69] there is only one published report of their work.[70] Their procedure combines "autogenic training" (Schultz & Luthe[71]) with biofeedback training in raising the temperature of the hands relative to the temperature of the forehead. From their description autogenic training seems to be a combination of self-instruction and relaxation training. The typical patient learns the autogenic phrases and then practices these and relaxation while receiving temperature feedback. After some practice sessions in the laboratory, the patient is switched to home practice with a portable device.

The presentation of the results of this study[70] is poor. Of 75 patients in their total sample, adequate data for clinical ratings were available on 62, of which an unspecified number were migraine sufferers. Of the latter group (number unspecified) 74% were rated as improved. Of the total sample, pretraining data were available on only 32 migraine patients. For these 32 patients, 29 were rated improved based on a global clinical assessment by one member of the team. Two other members judged improvement on the basis of graphs of temperature control data and frequency reports of headache and medications taken: One rater judged 26 patients as improved, the other only 22. There was reportedly "poor agreement" between evaluators. Variability of the data prevented it from showing any degree of statistical significance.

Thus, after running some 75 patients, the authors can only confirm some degree of clincal improvement in 29% to 39% of the total sample. This report is an anecdotal case report although by design it seems to be an uncontrolled single-group outcome study. The procedures for evaluating hand warming are unsatisfactory for three reasons: (1) Little or no data on results are given and it is reported that the posttreatment results do not reach statistical significance; (2) the treatment package itself is a mixture of several factors, suggestion, relaxation training, and biofeedback training, any or all of which may have accounted for the results; and (3) no-treatment or attention-placebo treatment control groups are not provided.

The latter is a particularly critical issue because Mitchell and Mitchell[72] have shown, in a controlled outcome study, an improvement rate of 71% in a group given training in relaxation and instructions as how to use it to counteract their migraine headaches. Moreover, Maslach, Marshall, and Zimbardo[73] have shown that hypnotized subjects can demonstrate 4°C increases in hand temperature in 2 to 4 minutes with no feedback, only instructions and suggestions. Another recent study by McDonagh and McGinnis[74] found autogenic suggestion unrelated to ability to increase hand temperature with biofeedback.

Peper[14] reports on three migraine patients who were initially treated with the Menninger combination of autogenic training and hand temperature feedback. Two of these were successfully treated by this combination; the third was initially unsuccessful and required much more intensive psychotherapy and environmental manipulation to show improvement. These three cases, although only anecdotal data, to provide a degree of confirmation for the work of Sargent et al.[70]

Weinstock,[75] in another anecdotal case report, has reported on seven patients suffering from either tension or migraine headaches, or both, who were treated with the underlying cause (vasoconstriction) as was done by Schwartz.[58] temperature feedback, and psychotherapy. All were reportedly headache-free for several months after treatment.

Raynaud Syndrome

Peper[14] reported on a case of Raynaud disease treated unsuccessfully by hand temperature feedback. While this is a likely approach, it may be that dealing with the surface manifestation (skin temperature) is less effective than dealing with the underlying cause (vasoconstriction) as was done by Schwartz.[58]

Comment. The Menninger group may have discovered an important treatment for migraine headaches. However, based on their published report, it is difficult to assess the role biofeedback of skin temperature plays. The suggestive results warrant further investigation but not the wholesale adoption of this technique.

ELECTROOCULARGRAM (EOG)

One case has been reported by Ballard, Doerr, and Varni[76] of the treatment of a case of essential blepharospasm, a disorder consisting of involuntary clonic and tonic spasms of the eyelids and associated musculature, by a biofeedback training procedure. Several procedures were tried and blink rate recorded: baseline, massed practice during which the patient was instructed to blink as rapidly as possible for 15 minutes; a biofeedback procedure in which a tone was generated by a blink and the patient was taught to delay the tones, first for 1 second, then 2 seconds; and an avoidance procedure in which the patient received a mild shock if she blinked during the delay intervals. The failure to include adequate control conditions (reversal phases) results in this case being a good systematic case study rather than a single-subject experiment. There was marked reduction in blink rate as measured in independent sessions. Moreover, continued practice by the patient at home led to essentially full recovery, i.e., absence of spasms, at a 9-month follow-up.

STOMACH ACID pH

There have been two brief reports of attempts to change the acid concentration in the stomach through biofeedback procedures; however, neither was designed to be a treatment. Gorman and Kamiya[77] presented feedback of stomach pH for three half-hour sessions to nine normal subjects. The results showed some slight degree of control over stomach pH; however, changes were fairly transitory.

In a second study, Welgan,[78] working with patients with duodenal ulcers, was able to demonstrate changes in pH of aspirated stomach secretions. Subjects were given feedback with mixed results: for some trials there was a significant biofeedback training effect; for others there was no training effect. This study was not designed as treatment. Instead it used patients to demonstrate a biofeedback effect and was only moderately successful in doing so.

CONCLUSIONS

By way of summary, what may be concluded about the current status of the efficacy of the application of biofeedback training to clinical problems? The soundest evidence, from point of view of adequacy of the experimental procedures to yield meaningful clinical conclusions, lies in the area of EMG feedback training. In the areas of elimination of subvocal speech during reading and in muscle retraining in paralytic patients, the data support the value of EMG feedback training; in the elimination or reduction of tension headaches, the efficacy of the combination of EMG feedback training plus home practice in relaxation is soundly confirmed; in other applications the evidence for efficacy is marginal at best, resting on anecdotal data, and in some cases the evidence is clearly contradictory.

The next best results are those from the sensorimotor rhythm feedback training. The single-subject experiments and systematic case studies show a definite therapeutic effect, at least while training continues, on various kinds of seizures. The therapeutic value of feedback training producing high proportions of alpha in the EEG has not been demonstrated.

In the cardiovascular area, the evidence of the value of teaching patients with cardiac arrhythmia to control HR is highly suggestive. Taken report by report, the studies yield questionable evidence. However, as a series of replications, there are strong indications of therapeutic value of such training, particularly in patients with PVCs or sinus tachycardia. In the area of hypertension, the evidence is stronger but the demonstration of clinical effects more questionable. Certainly substantial decreases in BP have been obtained using biofeedback training to assist patients with Raynaud disease is interesting but far from conclusive.

Other areas are much less sound with regard to evidence. The single case using EOG feedback provided controlled provocative evidence. Modification of stomach acid pH has not been clearly demonstrated nor have any therapeutic effects. Feedback training for skin temperature in treating migraine headaches has, because of a lack of control procedures, produced questionable evidence from which no substantive conclusions on therapeutic efficacy can be drawn.

Based on this summary, it would seem premature to hail biofeedback training as a panacea for psychosomatic and other disorders. The evidence is often interesting and highly provocative, but with the exception of a few areas mentioned above, no definite conclusions can be made. Wholesale therapeutic application of biofeedback techniques cannot be supported by the available data. This is especially true because of a lack of adequate controls to rule out placebo effects. An exception to the above is the area of EMG feedback for muscle retraining. It may be that clinicians and practitioners are seeking the "ultimate weapon" in the form of biofeedback training before there has been an adequate demonstration that the phenomena are reliable, and certainly before an adequate investigation of the important measures[5] has been made. Without doubt these techniques must be regarded as experimental.

One other conclusion to be drawn from research on biofeedback is the potential of the single-subject design experiment[10] to improve the experimental controls. By way of emphasis, contrast the five cases reported by Sterman[66] using EEG feedback with proper experimental controls and support for feedback effectiveness with the 75 cases of temperature feedback training reported by the Menninger group[70] with few experimental controls and only marginal support for feedback effectiveness. Widespread use of the single-subject experiment approach would provide validity for biofeedback training and would seem a logical intermediate step to doing the necessary controlled group outcome studies.

ACKNOWLEDGMENT. This work was supported in part by grant No. 5-RO1-14906 from the National Heart and Lung Institute.

REFERENCES

1. Pines, M. Train yourself to stay well. *McCall's*, 1970, *48*, 137–138.
2. Morris, S. A heart-stopping, eye-bulging, wave-making idea. *Playboy*, 1972, *19*, 229–230; 244–249.
3. Malloy, M. T. Mind over body. *National Observer*, 1973, *12*, 10.
4. Karlins, M., & Andrews, L. M. *Biofeedback*. New York: Warner Paperback Library, 1972.
5. Lawrence, J. *Alpha brain waves*. New York: Avon Press, 1972.
6. Biofeedback training. *MD*, 1972, *16*, 65–67.

7. Biofeedback in action, *Medical World News*, March 9, 1973, pp. 47–60.

8. Paul, G. L. Behavior modification research: Design and tactics. In C. M. Franks (Ed.), *Behavior therapy: Appraisal and status*. New York: McGraw-Hill, 1969.

9. Campbell, D. T., & Stanley, J. C. *Experimental and quasi-experimental designs for research.* Chicago: Rand McNally, 1966.

10. Barlow, D. H., & Hersen, M. Single case experimental designs: Uses in applied clinical research. *Archives of General Psychiatry*, 1973, *29*, 319–325.

11. Marinacci, A. A., & Horande, M. Electromyogram in neuromuscular re-education. *Bulletin of the Los Angeles Neurological Societies*, 1960, *25*, 57–71.

12. Andrews, J. M. Neuromuscular re-education of the hemiplegic with the aid of the electromyograph. *Archives of Physical Rehabilitation*, 1964, *45*, 530–532.

13. Johnson, H. E., & Garton, W. H. Muscle re-education in hemiplegia by use of electromyographic device. *Archives of Physical Medicine Rehabilitation*, 1973, *54*, 320–325.

14. Peper, E. Frontiers of clinical biofeedback. In L. Birk (Ed.), *Seminars in psychiatry (Vol 5)*. New York: Grune and Stratton, 1973.

15. Booker, H. E., Rubow, R. T., & Coleman, P. J. Simplified feedback in neuromuscualr retraining: An automated approach using electromyographic signals. *Archives of Physcial Medicine and Rehabilitation*, 1969, *50*, 621–625.

16. Hardyck, C. D., Petrinovich, L. F., & Ellsworth, D. W. Feedback of speech muscle activity during silent reading: Rapid extinction. *Science*, 1966, *154*, 1467–1468.

17. McGuigan, F. J. Feedback of speech muscle activity during silent reading: Two comments. *Science*, 1967, *157*, 579–580.

18. Hardyck, D. C., Petrinovich L. F., & Ellwsorth, D. W. Feedback of speech muscle activity during silent reading. Two comments. *Science*, 1967, *157*, 581.

19. Hardyck, C. D., & Petrinovich, L. F. Treatment of subvocal speech during reading. *Journal of Reading*, 1969, *1*, 1–11.

20. Aarons, L. Subvocalization: Aural and EMG feedback in reading. *Perceptual and Motor Skills*, 1971, *33*, 271–306.

21. Green, E. E., et al. Feedback techniques for deep relaxation. *Psychophysiology*, 1969, *6*, 371–377.

22. Raskin, M., Johnson, G., & Rondestvedt, J. W. Chronic anxiety treated by feedback-induced muscle relaxation. *Archives of General Psychiatry*, 1973, *28*, 263–267.

23. Garrett, B. L. & Silver, M. P. *The use of EMG and alpha biofeedback to relieve test anxiety in college students.* Paper presented at the American Psychological Association meeting, Washington, D.C., 1972.

24. Jacobs, A., & Felton, G. S. Visual feedback of myoelectric output to facilitate muscle relaxation in normal persons and patients with neck injuries. *Archives of Physical Medicine and Rehabilitation*, 1969, *50*, 34–39.

25. Wickramasekera, I. Instructions and EMG feedback in systematic desensitization: A case report. *Behavior Therapy*, 1972, *3*, 460–465.

26. Wickramasekera, I. Effects of EMG feedback training on susceptibility to hypnosis: Preliminary observations. In *Proceedings of the 79th Annual Convention, APA*. Washington, D.C.: American Psychological Association, 1971. Pp 783–784.

27. Wickramasekera, I. Effects of electromyographic feedback on hypnotic susceptibility: More preliminary data. *Journal of Abnormal Psychology*, 1973, *82*, 74–77.

28. Budzynski, T. H., & Stoyva, J. M. An instrument for producing deep relaxation by means of analog information feedback. *Journal of Applied Behavior Analysis*, 1969, *2*, 231–237.

29. Budzynski, T. H., Stoyva, J. M., & Adler, C. S. Feedback-induced muscle relaxation: Application to tension headache. *Journal of Behavior Therapy and Experimental Psychiatry*, 1970, *1*, 205–211.

30. Budzynski, T. H., et al. EMG biofeedback and tension headache: A controlled-outcome study. *Psychosomatic Medicine*, 1973, *35*, 484–496.

31. Wickramasekera, I. Electromyographic feedback training and tension headace: Preliminary observations. *American Journal of Clinical Hypnosis*, 1972, *15*, 83–85.

32. Epstein, L. H., Hersen, M., & Hemphill, D. P. Contingent music and antitension exercises in the

treatment of a chronic tension headache patient. *Journal of Behavior Therapy and Experimental Psychiatry*, 1974, *5*, 59–63.

33. Blanchard, E. G., & Young, L. D. Self-control of cardiac functioning: A promise as yet unfulfilled. *Psychological Bulletin*, 1973, *79*, 145–163.

34. Weiss, T., & Engel, B. T. Operant conditioning of heart rate in patients with premature ventricular contractions. *Psychosomatic Medicine*, 1971, *33*, 301–321.

35. Engel, B. T., & Bleecker, E. R. Application of operant conditioning techniques to the control of the cardiac arrhythmias. In P. Obrist et al. (Eds.), *Contemporary trends in cardiovascular psychophysiology*. Chicago: Aldine-Atherton, 1974.

36. Scott, R. W., et al. A shapting procedure for heart-rate control in chronic tachycardia. *Perceptual and Motor Skills*, 1973, *37*, 327–338.

37. Bleecker, E. R., & Engel, B. T. Learned control of cardiac rate and cardiac conduction in the Wolff-Parkinson-White syndrome. *New England Journal of Medicine*, 1973, *288*, 560–562.

38. Prigatano, G. P., & Johnson, H. J. Biofeedback control of heart rate variability to phobic stimuli: A new approach to treating spider phobia. In *Proceedings of Annual Convention, APA*. Washington, D.C.: American Psychological Association, 1972. Pp. 403–404.

39. Engel, B. T., & Melmon, L. Operant conditioning of heart rate in patients with cardiac arrhythmias. *Conditional Reflex*, 1968, *3*, 130.

40. Weiss, T., & Engel, B. T. Voluntary control of premature ventricular contractions in patients. *American Journal of Cardiology*, 1970, *26*, 666.

41. Weiss, T., & Engel, B. T. Operant conditioning of heart rate in patients with premature ventricular contractions. *Psychophysiology*, 1971, *8*, 263–264.

42. Scott, R. W., et al. The use of shaping and reinforcement in the operant acceleration and deceleration of heart rate. *Behaviour Research and Therapy*, 1973, *11*, 179–185.

43. Bleecker, E. R., & Engel, B. T. Learned control of ventricular rate in patients with atrial fibrillation. *Psychosomatic Medicine*, 1973, *35*, 161–175.

44. Troyer, W. G., et al. Learned heart rate control in patients with ischemic heart disease. *Psychophysiology*, 1973, *10*, 213.

45. Pickering, G. R. *High blood pressure*. New York: Grune and Stratton, 1968.

46. Benson, H., et al. Decreased systolic blood pressure through operant conditioning techniques in patients with essential hypertension. *Science*, 1971, *173*, 740–742.

47. Shapiro, D., et al. Effects of feedback and reinforcement on the control of human systolic blood pressure. *Science*, 1969, *163*, 588–590.

48. Tursky, B., Shapiro, D., & Schwartz, G. E. Automated constant cuff-pressure system to measure average systolic and diastolic blood pressure in man. *IEEE Transactions on Biomedical Engineering*, 1972, *19*, 271–276.

49. Schwartz, G. E., & Shapiro, D. Biofeedback and essential hypertension: Current findings and theoretical concerns. In L. Birk (Ed), *Biofeedback: Behavioral medicine*. New York: Grune and Stratton, 1973.

50. Miller, N. E. Postscript. In D. Singh & C. T. Morgan (Eds.). *Current status of physiological psychology: Readings*. Monterey, California: Brooks/Cole, 1972.

51. Elder, S. T. et al. Instrumental conditioning of diastolic blood pressure in essential hypertensive patients. *Journal of Applied Behavior Analysis*, 1973, *6*, 377–382.

52. Bergman, J. S., & Johnson, H. S. Sources of information which affect training and raising of heart rate. *Psychophysiology*, 1972, *9*, 30–39.

53. Jacobson, E. Variation of blood pressure with skeletal muscle tension and relaxation. *Annals of Internal Medicine*, 1939, *12*, 1194–1212.

54. Paul, G. L. Physiological effects of relaxation training and hypnotic suggestion. *Journal of Abnormal Psychology*, 1969, *74*, 425–437.

55. Tasto, D., & Shoemaker, J. E. *The effects of muscle relaxation on blood pressure for essential hypertensives and normotensives*. Paper presented at the Association for Advancement of Behavior Therapy Seventh annual meeting, Miami Beach, Florida, 1973.

56. Snyder, C., & Nobel, M. Operant conditioning of vasocontriction. *Journal of Experimental Psychology*, 1968, *77*, 263–268.

57. Simpson, D. D. *Relaxation training and biofeedback using finger pulse volume.* Ft. Worth: Institute of Behavioral Research, Texas Christian University, 1972.
58. Schwartz, G. E. Clinical applications of biofeedback: Some theoretical issues. In D. Upper, D. S. Goodenough (Eds.). *Behavior modification with the individual patient: Proceedings of third annual Brockton symposium on behavior therapy.* Nutley, New Jersey: Roche, 1972.
59. Brown, B. B. Recognition of aspects of consciousness through association with EEG alpha activity represented by a light signal. *Psychophysiology,* 1970, *6,* 442–452.
60. Nowlis, D. P., & Kamiya, J. The control of electroencephalographic alpha rhythms through auditory feedback and the associated mental activity. *Psychophysiology,* 1970, *6,* 476–484.
61. Kamiya, J. Conscious control of brain waves. *Psychology Today,* 1968, *1,* 57–60.
62. Paskewitz, D. A., & Orne, M. T. Visual effects on alpha feedback training. *Science,* 1973, *181,* 360–363.
63. Gannon, L., & Sternbach, R. A. Alpha enhancement as a treatment for pain: A case study. *Journal of Behavior Therapy and Experimental Psychiatry,* 1971, *2,* 209–213.
64. Sterman, M. B., & Friar, L. Suppression of seizures in an epileptic following sensorimotor EEG feedback training. *Electroencephalography and Clinical Neuropsychology,* 1972, *33,* 89–95.
65. Sterman, M. B. Untitled. In *Highlights of the 17th Annual Conference, VA Cooperative Studies in Mental Health and Behavioral Sciences.* St. Louis: St. Louis VA Center, 1972.
66. Sterman, M. B. Neurophysiological and clinical studies of sensorimotor EEG biofeedback training: Some effects on epilepsy. In L. Birk (Ed.). *Biofeedback: Behavioral medicine.* New York: Grune and Stratton, 1973.
67. Miller, N. E. Visceral learning and other additional facts potentially applicable to psychotherapy. *International Psychiatry Clinics,* 1969, 294–309.
68. Sittenfeld, P. The control of the EEG theta rhythm. In D. Shapiro et al. (Eds.). *Biofeedback and self-control, 1972.* Chicago: Aldine, 1972.
69. Sargent, J. D., Green, E. E., & Walters, E. D. *Preliminary report on the use of autogenic feedback techniques in the treatment of migraine and tension headaches.* Paper presented at the American Association for the Study of Headache, June, 1972.
70. Sargent, J. D., Green, E. E., & Walters, E. D. The use of autogenic feedback training in a pilot study of migraine and tension headaches. *Headache,* 1972, *12,* 120–125.
71. Schultz, J. H., & Luthe, W. *Autogenic therapy* (Vol. 1). New York: Grune and Stratton, 1969.
72. Mitchell, K. R., & Mitchell, D. M. Migraine: An exploratory treatment application of programmed behavior therapy techniques. *Journal of Psychosomatic Research,* 1971, *15,* 137–157.
73. Maslach, C., Marshall, C., & Zimbardo, P. G. Hypnotic control of peripheral skin temperature: A case report. *Psychophysiology,* 1972, *9,* 600–605.
74. McDonagh, J. M., & McGinnis, M. M. *Skin temperature increases as a function of baseline temperature, autogenic suggestion, and biofeedback.* Paper presented at the 81st Annual Meeting, American Psychological Association, Montreal, 1973.
75. Weinstock, S. A. A tentative procedure for the control of pain: Migraine and tension headaches. In D. Shapiro et al. (Eds.). *Biofeedback and self-control 1972.* Chicago: Aldine, 1972.
76. Ballard, P., Doerr, H., & Varni, J. Arrest of a disabling eye disorder using biofeedback. *Psychophysiology,* 1972, *9,* 271.
77. Gorman, P. J., & Kamiya, J. Operant conditioning of stomach acid pH. Paper presented at the Biofeedback Research Society Meeting, Boston, 1972.
78. Welgan, P. *Instrumental control of gastric acid secretions in ulcer patients.* Unpublished doctoral dissertation. Ann Arbor, Michigan, 1972. (University Microfilms, document No. 72-18, 755)

The Possible Uses of Biofeedback in Education

Erik Peper

The concepts underlying biofeedback learning and research are reviewed in relation to their application in education. The basic steps in biofeedback learning are pointed out and consist of: monitoring, self-awareness, control with the feedback equipment, and control without the feedback equipment. In addition, the implications of biofeedback control are reviewed. These include: self-control over the learning process; the concepts of passive attention, nonverbal learning, mind/body synchrony; transfer of learning; and the effect of belief structures. Drawn from these concepts, the paper suggests biofeedback applications for use in educational settings such as the use for teaching science lessons, voluntary control over low arousal and creativity, enhancement of artistic expression, learning of self-awareness and control over internal states, awareness of misplaced efforts, enhancement of visual attention, decreasing subjective striving components, and the use for teaching relaxation and unstressing.

Biofeedback is a tool for self-regulation, so it is ironic that its use in education has not been actively explored. It has great potential as an area for research and application, considering how quickly children learn autonomic control (Russell, 1975; Peper & Grossman, 1974).

The application of biofeedback in education or in any other area depends upon the researcher's results, the practitioner's interest, and the social milieu. The social climate for biofeedback has changed. In the late 1960s and early 1970s, biofeedback was hailed as a means for self-exploration and achieving altered states of consciousness. Biofeedback was considered a tool to develop a psychophysiological language of consciousness (Kamiya, 1974; Peper, 1971), and it was hoped that feedback could be used to achieve an altered state of consciousness, a possible shortcut for meditation.

At present the use of biofeedback for investigating altered states of consciousness has shifted out of the limelight and instead, clinical applications are the main concern of most biofeedback practitioners and researchers. Clinical research was started in the late 1960s and has expanded rapidly. Some of this expansion was encouraged by an increase in monies available for applied research. Clinical applications, although often embedded in or enhanced by other therapeutic techniques, have ranged from the treatment of headaches, Raynaud's disease, cardiac arrhythmia, and epilepsy to the treatment of backaches. (A series

Erik Peper • Center for Interdisciplinary Science, San Francisco State University, San Francisco, California 94134.

of annual collections of papers covering all aspects of research in this area has been published: *Biofeedback and self-control*. See the references.) These applications have recently come so much to the foreground that they may restrict nonclinical potentials of biofeedback.

For example, biofeedback can be used to test research hypotheses from a cybernetic point of view (Mulholland, 1968). One feeds back the physiological signal in such a way that it affects the physiological system from which the feedback signal was generated, with the hope of establishing a positive or negative feedback loop. A typical example of this research tool is testing the relationship between EEG alpha and the visual system. A visual target, contingent upon the presence of the subject's alpha or no-alpha EEG activity, is presented. The effect upon the EEG can be evaluated, to see if the display is tightly linked with the fedback physiological process (Peper, 1970)—i.e., does alpha attenuate each time the subject focuses and accommodates?

Other than using biofeedback to test research hypotheses, to achieve altered states of consciousness, or as a clinical tool, it may be used as a self-educational tool without any pathological (clinical) treatment orientation. One area for which biofeedback use has not been explored is education. After describing some of the underlying concepts in biofeedback, this chapter will suggest a few possible areas for biofeedback application in education.

Biofeedback consists of displaying normally unnoticed physiologial information about an organism back to itself. With such a psychophysiological mirror, a person may become more self-aware and/or be able to change his own psychophysiology. The subtle changes occurring in the organism are amplified and fed back to the person. The information displayed plays the role of an unbiased observer—the information is neutral. How a person uses this information depends on the set and the setting. (However, "control" implies directionality. In many cases, pathology has been well defined but "health" has not. To what level of control does one want to train a subject, and to control what? What is health? For example, is keeping alpha EEG on healthy? Is low EMG healthy?)

The basic steps in feedback learning are:

1. Monitoring the physiological system to feedback changes in that system, since information only exists if there is change,
2. Becoming aware of the feedback and objectively or subjectively linking it to some internal or external sensation. In some cases a person needs to become aware that, for instance, each time the telephone rings, he frowns,
3. Controlling the physiological system with the help of the feedback signal.
4. Maintaining the psychophysiological control without feedback which means that the person has to internalize the learning process.

Learning control over biological functions includes a number of implicit assumptions and concepts that are applicable to the educational process. Some of these implications are as follows.

1. Biofeedback learning implies self-control so that the person is responsible for his own growth. No one can make you control yourself. Hence there is a

change in the source of responsibility—the responsibility rests with the subject. The acceptance of responsibility is an active process rather than a passive one as when a person takes drugs.

2. Feedback control is achieved through passive attention and *not* through active striving or anticipation. One learns control by attending to the process, not the outcome or end goal (Peper, 1976a).

Experientially, the processes affecting and interfering with passive attention are those of anticipation and striving. These effects may be experienced when we try to defecate or urinate. Before you continue to read this essay, you might go to the bathroom and urinate. Become aware of the many physical, emotional, and social constraints, as well as the tension and holding patterns in your body: What are they? Doesn't your body resist complying with the arbitrary demand to urinate? (Note that in order to urinate you merely attend passively and allow the urine to flow.) When you *try* to urinate, such as at a doctor's office when he has asked for a urine specimen, the harder you try the less successful you usually are. The process of passive attention consists of letting go and allowing a process to occur, which is inimical to the "normal" active striving mode which has been programmed into us (Peper, 1976a).

Feedback learning focuses the person on the "here and now". The feedback continuously brings the person back into the present, attending to what is happening now. So often one is thinking about the past (feeling guilty or gloating about achievements) or future (What am I going to do when I see whomever.) Seldom is one *present* and totally in the "here and now."

In the present, *doing* can be an enjoyable process. Often in education the emphasis is on goal rather than process or doing, and therefore learning is boring and forced; the mind drifts away. The student is rewarded for getting a grade or pleasing the teacher, instead of pleasing himself. Even in sports, one learns to run not becuase he likes the feeling of the air flowing past him but because he is forced by the gym teacher to run two laps around the track. Enjoying sports is not the end goal; the "goal" is enjoying the movement and flow of air around the face, the fluid feeling of the body in which arms and shoulders are totally relaxed.

3. Learning is nonverbal. Although most activities one does are nonverbal, one uses language to "tell" someone how to do something. It is not surprising that telling someone "you ought to read" or "you ought to relax" does not work. One needs to define and teach the experience—a behavioral approach. One has to analyze the phenomena involved and develop a learning structure. For example, how do you teach a person to balance and shift his weight? Words merely describe the action and usually do not help. The person trying to learn to balance does not know how to translate verbal instructions into a physiological movement or feeling. However, when the person has the experience of shifting weight (such as by distributing the weight on two scales and feeding back the weight distribution as the person moves from one foot to the other), he can know what you mean (Peper & Robertson, 1976).

Feedback translates and authenticates verbal commands into actual physiological experiences. Hence, *relax* becomes not merely a word, but an actual physiological experience consisting of defined microvolt levels in certain muscles, peripheral warmth, as well as a decrease in electrodermal activity.

With this concept, one looks at the educational process differently: i.e., how can I give an experience—e.g., of reading, to a student—rather than merely repeating verbal instructions.

4. Mind and body are one. There is no mind/body separation. The body somatizes the workings of the mind, so that for every thought there is a corresponding body change. With electromyographic (EMG) feedback from each forearm, one can illustrate that when the person's arm is totally relaxed the EMG is about .5 μV; then, if the person is asked to *imagine* making a fist, the EMG usually shows an increase to 1.5–3. μV.

Experientially, the following exercise may also illustrate this point:

Sit quietly and comfortably; be sure your belt is loose; close your eyes. Spend a minute or so to allow yourself to become relaxed. Now imagine a lemon; visualize it; notice the Sunkist lettering on the side; notice water droplets glistening on the outside of the yellow skin. Notice its two chubby ends. Now imagine your favorite kitchen knife, and cutting the lemon in two. Notice the inside, the white rind, the membranes containing the pulp and the juice; notice the droplets of juice. Imagine squeezing it, tasting and swallowing the lemon juice. Keep tasting for a moment or two.

How did this visualization affect you? Did you smell the lemon? Did you taste it? Did you swallow it? Did you notice an increase in saliva? If you had an increase in saliva, your thoughts directly affected your body. Through simple visualization exercises, the sympathetic and parasympathetic nervous systems have been affected. Similarly, thoughts and emotions affect us and most likely interfere with our study habits.

5. Autonomic awareness implies that if we feel a sensation, we may need to take action in order to stay healthy. If biofeedback mirrors the self, it means that eventually a person will become aware of physiological actions and that the person must (a) look for and attend to the psychophysiological sensations and cues, and (b) act upon those cues. The result of not acting upon those cues allows pathology to occur—such as mild bracing of muscles around the neck and shoulders, which leads to chronic tension headaches. To act is often difficult. For example, while you have been reading this article, have you become aware of the constriction of your belt (panty hose) around your waist? The tightness usually interferes with the abdominal respiratory movement. With such an awareness, one needs to act, i.e., one loosens one's belt. How would that feel if the awareness came while you were teaching a class? Would you still loosen the belt? If not, there is little use for biofeedback training, which increases one's awareness of body cues. Such increased personal awareness may conflict in a mass educational system. Yet the implications are enormous: what about the child whose personal timing makes him an "owl," and who is *never* particularly alert in the mornings? For him, school should start at noon and go till 7:00 p.m.

6. Belief structures limit our experiences. The limits of our beliefs are the limits of our experience. Biofeedback training indicates that people can have fine control over their bodies and minds. However, we often limit the possibilities by limiting what we perceive as "possible." Before the mid-1960s, autonomic control was believed to be impossible; however, feedback training indicated that autonomic self-regulation was possible (Miller, 1969). Similarly, in education our

beliefs are our prophecies: If one believes he is smart, he acts smarter and does better on tests.

The concepts underlying feedback learning are in part the same concepts underlying the educational process. In fact, biofeedback learning is an intensely personal educational process. Some of the potential applications of biofeedback in education are:

1. To teach a science lesson (King, 1975, personal communication). The students can monitor their own behavior and the data from the equipment. This exercise teaches good observation applied to oneself. For example, does anger give the same EEG signal for the same person at different times? Is it different for one person than for another? The purpose here is to use feedback to teach scientific observational techniques and to increase interest in learning by using the students' own behavior as a data base.

2. To teach awareness of one's own anatomy and body functions. A biology class would be more interesting if one could learn, feel, and control some of the processes studied in books.

3. To teach self-awareness and control over internal states. Through feedback of EEG, GSR, temperature, EMG, and self-charting of biological rhythms, students may become aware and "flash" that they can change their own moods. "I wonder how the feeling of love shows electrophysiologically?"

4. To enhance artistic expression. The feedback signals drive a musical instrument, which the person can use to accompany himself. Or in the theater arts, feedback can be used to teach actors the physical expression of internal emotions.

5. To teach voluntary control over low-arousal states and creativity by the use of theta electroencephalography feedback. The student can learn to enter voluntarily a hypnogogic state in which unedited new solutions to a problem may appear. This state may also be used to generate new artistic forms. A slightly different approach has been the use of dream recognition, which alerts a person as he falls asleep. The person stays in the transitional sleep stage, filled with the burst of imagery (C. T. Tart, personal communication).

6. To teach visual attention, through the use of EEG beta feedback. Each time occipital alpha occurs while reading, it means the person is *not* paying visual attention. Possibly one can train students to become more easily aware of momentary drifts in attention. Possibly new educational material would only be presented *contingent* upon their psychophysiological attentive mode such as beta EEG (Mulholland, 1973).

7. To increase the awareness of misplaced efforts and striving components through the use of EMG feedback. For example, the feedback would help a student to stay relaxed and not frown while studying. Totally unexplored is the application to athletics. Feedback could be used to teach an athlete to inhibit any extraneous muscle activity except for those muscle patterns needed for that particular physical activity; for

example, while jogging, the jogger learns to keep his head, shoulders, and neck relaxed; while playing tennis the person does not hold his breath while serving.

8. To indicate striving, through the use of respiratory feedback, because when one is striving he is misplacing physical, emotional, and intellectual efforts. Often when we strive we hold our breath. A small portable breath feedback indicator would make the person aware that he is holding his breath, such as when getting up from a chair or preparing himself to raise his hand in class.

9. To teach a prophylactic course in relaxation, to reduce stress levels, in conjunction with Jacobson progressive relaxation, sensory awareness techniques, and autogenic training. Every student should learn profound voluntary relaxation, so that he can learn and initiate global desensitization to any activity. Relaxation can be easily taught in conjunction with biofeedback, and this is a *basic* skill that all students must master.

10. To train two students to experience similar psychophysiological states and thereby experientially appreciate the other person.

In addition, there are many potential clinical biofeedback applications for education from the training of children with cerebral palsy to reduce their spasticity with EMG feedback (Finley et al., 1976) to the use of temperature training to eliminate migraine in children (Peper & Grossman, 1974). The clinical applications obviously are independent of age. There are a few areas where education and clinical treatment overlap, such as the possible use of EEG alpha feedback and EMG feedback to train hyperactive children to be less hyperactive or to teach destructive children more self-control—since self-control is the basis of biofeedback training.

Biofeedback applications to education are only beginning. This essay outlines only a few of the potential uses. Many of these processes can be used in groups, with the feedback itself providing the individual instruction needed. Once one takes the cybernetic viewpoint that feedback can help the learning process, anything can be used for feedback: audio- and videotape recordings, immediate verbal feedback from the teacher, etc. The major process that biofeedback learning implies and encourages is learning through passive attention, to grasp without grasping—through which we can allow ourselves to open an infinite world in which to expand our own potentials.

ACKNOWLEDGMENTS. This paper was presented in part at the Symposium on Self-Regulation in Education at the American Educational Research Association meeting, San Francisco, 1976. I thank Tim Scully and Susan Chandler for their helpful discussions.

REFERENCES

Biofeedback and self-control, 1971–1975/76 (various editors). Chicago: Aldine, 1971–1976.
Finley, W. W., Niman, C., Standley, J., & Ender, P. Frontal EMG biofeedback training of athetoid

cerebral palsy patients: A report of six cases. *Biofeedback and Self-Regulation*, 1976, *1*, (2), 169–182.

Gibb, J. D., Stephan, E., & Rohm, C. E. T. Belief in biofeedback: A tentative method for the control of short term stress. In *Proceedings of the Biofeedback Research Society*. Denver: Biofeedback Research Society, 1975.

Kamiya, J. Autoregulation of the EEG alpha rhythm: A program for the study of consciousness. In M. H. Chase (Ed.), *Operant control of brain activity (Perspectives in brain sciences*, Vol. 2). Los Angeles: Brain Research Institute (UCLA), 1974.

Miller, N. Learning of visceral and glandular responses. *Science*, 1969, *163*, 434–445.

Mulholland, T. Feedback electroencephalography. *Activitas Nervosa Superior* (Prague), 1968, *10*, 410–438.

Mulholland, T. Biofeedback: It's time to try hardware in the classroom. *Psychology Today*, 1973, December, 103–104.

Peper, E. Feedback regulation of the alpha electroencephalogram activity through the control of the internal and external parameters. *Kybernetik*, 1970, *7*, 107–112.

Peper, E. Reduction of efferent motor commands during alpha feedback as a facilitator of EEG alpha and a precondition for changes in consciousness. *Kybernetik*, 1971, *9* (6), 226–231.

Peper, E. Passive attention: The gateway to consciousness and autonomic control. In P. G. Zimbardo & F. L. Ruch (Eds.), *Psychology and life*. Chicago: Scott Foresman, 1976. (a)

Peper, E. Problems in biofeedback training: An experiential analogy—urination. *Perspectives in Biology and Medicine*, 1976, *19* (3), 404–412. (b)

Peper, E., & Grossman, E. R. *Preliminary observation of thermal biofeedback training in children with migraine*. Paper presented at the Biofeedback Research Society meeting, Colorado Springs, 1974.

Peper, E., & Robertson, J. A. Biofeedback use of common objects: The bathroom scale in physical therapy. *Biofeedback and Self-Regulation*, 1976, *1* (2).

Russell, H. L. Some methodological issues in the training of self-regulation of skin temperature. In *Proceedings of the Biofeedback Research Society*. Denver: Biofeedback Research Soceity, 1975.

7

Passive Attention: The Gateway to Consciousness and Autonomic Control

Erik Peper

Passive control over autonomic functions or altered states of consciousness is the critical process by which both physical and psychological health are modulated. By investigating such processes we may learn new dimensions of our growth and perhaps change traditional views about the nature of health and sickness.

Ideas for this essay have come from two sources: first, my study of "adepts," those remarkable people who demonstrate unusual control over mind and body, and second, the systematic investigation and observation of the mechanisms of voluntary autonomic control. In 1971, I studied my first adept, Ramon Torres, a young man who was able to insert bicycle spokes through his cheeks without reporting any pain. In fact, he was able to sustain a state of relaxation while undergoing this experience, as shown by his increased alpha EEG activity. These findings are similar to those produced by adept Jack Schwarz.

In studying adepts I try to discover: What is going on? By what means or strategies have these adepts attained autonomic control or achieved "cosmic consciousness? How can their internal functioning be translated (that is, made explicit and external), and then learned by ordinary or nonadept people so that they too may be able to use these skills? Adepts illustrate the potentialities of human capabilities and sometimes contradict accepted psychological observations. For example, the observation that we do not learn during deep sleep has been placed in doubt by the study of Swami Rama, an associate Shankaracharya of southern India. While studying this yogi, Dr. Elmer Green of the Menninger Foundation clinic found that the yogi would remember everything that had happened to him while in a state of Yogic sleep (one in which the electroencephalograph showed 40% delta wave activity). Swami Rama was able to recite verbatim 9 of the 10 sentences given to him while in this state and paraphrased the 10th sentence spoken to him.

This single-subject observation casts some doubt upon the accepted theory that learning during deep sleep does not occur. What it indicates is that most likely we simply do not recall the information. The information is encoded in the brain, and we may act upon it, but we do *not* have conscious access to it. Further study

Erik Peper • Center for Interdisciplinary Science, San Francisco State University, San Francisco, California 94134.

of such a subject as Swami Rama supports the observation that information can affect us even when we are in a nonconscious state. For example, there are reported cases of a patient's heart stopping during surgery right after the surgeon said aloud, "I wish the S.O.B. would drop dead"—not meaning the patient, but someone else. The above observation offers us a chance to reevaluate what we accept as the limits of human functioning. The limits are often defined through our cultural bias. The study of adepts allows us to see through those cultural blindfolds and to perceive a different picture of reality—one in which belief in one's own powers sets the limits on what is possible.

What we discovered in studying the adepts and their ability to control unconscious and autonomic functions was that (a) body control is achieved through *passive attention* and not active trying, and (b) the important part of the control is the *process* and the *attention* to it—*not* the outcome or the goal. These dimensions operate in all physical, emotional, and mental activity and are certainly opposed to the teaching of the Protestant ethic, which reinforces us for striving and for achieving goals. Such an orientation gives meaning only to consequences and not to the process—to the ends and not to the means. We can see that in cases of sexual dysfunction a major component of male impotence or female frigidity occurs when the person is actively "trying" to achieve an orgasm instead of letting it happen and knowing it is okay if it does not happen this time. One of the first steps in sexual therapy is to teach the person not to try. The initial homework in such therapy consists of teaching people to perceive through the senses and not the intellect. Actual intercourse is postponed until much later, after each person develops adequate communication skills with the partner. Such exercises aim at removing fear of failure. Success is not the *achievement* of a future goal, but the awareness of the *process* in the present, here and now. This awareness consists of subtle ways of learning passive attention. For example, sexual stimuli may initiate a "turn-on"; this triggers passive attention to the sexual feelings that allow the turn-on to continue. But if one tries actively to be turned on, one is likely to succeed only in turning oneself off. The way to succeed in this business is definitely without really trying!

The dynamics of sexual arousal are similar to the mechanisms that underlie other forms of autonomic control. The process is mediated by *passive attention*. But what is passive attention? It is doing without trying! It is allowing and directing without dictating. To investigate it involves us at once in a contradiction of the usual research approaches; the problem of investigating passive attention lies in the very nature of the process. The moment we try to perform, we inhibit passive attention: In colloquial language, we "break the flow." But research designs are usually demand- and performance-oriented. The phenomenon of passive attention is such that research attempts that focus on performance actually eliminate the thing they are trying to investigate.

Experientially, the processes affecting and interfering with passive attention are those of anticipation and striving. These effects may be experienced when we *try* to defecate or urinate. Before you continue reading this essay, you might go to the bathroom and urinate. Become aware of the many physical, emotional, and social contraints as well as the tensions and holding patterns in your body: What are they? Don't you resent the demand I've placed on you to take this action at this time? Doesn't your body resist complying with that arbitrary demand? (Note that in order to urinate you merely attend passively and *allow* the urine to flow). When you *try* to urinate, such as at the doctor's office when you are asked for a urine sample, or when you sit on the toilet during a theater intermission with people standing in line waiting for you to finish, the harder you try, the less successful you are likely to be. So either you read the graffiti, to distract your mind, or you flush the toilet so that other people will not know that you are so uptight. The process of passive attention consists of *letting go* and allowing a process to occur, which is inimical to the "normal" active striving mode that has been programmed into us.

On the other hand, passive attention is optimized during the practice of meditation. In meditation one learns a focused, passive attention without effort, without anticipation. Instead of focusing on the products of the mind (thoughts and images), which is so often the case in clinical psychology, meditation focuses only on the *process;* whatever happens, we let happen. The being in the present time is maximized. The moment one anticipates, worries, fears, etc., one is out of the present mode, either ruminating about the past or worrying about the future. One should be in a place where one is neither ruminating, worrying, nor falling asleep, but experiencing the internal and the external worlds as they are.

Meditative practices do not focus upon an outcome. It is the inspection of the process that is most important. It is how the person is doing it and never why or what for. Without "grooving" on sensations, or on images or fantasies, one is learning the process of passive attention. It is the feeling of going with the flow, instead of fighting the river. One experiences this process only sporadically in the usual mode of being and one knows this sensation best from joyful sexual experience. Similarly, this occurs in altered states of consciousness: "I want to reach the high point of cosmic consciousness"—yet in most cases, this level of consciousness comes to a person unsuspected, when one is not trying, only attending to the process.

This process of doing without effort modulates all activities. The process is so similar to, yet so different from habitual action patterns. One usually forces while participating in a sport—the braced neck and shoulders—or one tries while studying—the clenched jaw. When one does an exercise without effort, the results are totally different than if the exercise is forced. For example, you may want to do the following toe-touching exercise and note how different it feels from the habitual pattern in which we *force* ourselves to touch our hands to our toes, as we were trained to do in gym classes. Now touch your toes without effort. To do this, let your body, spine, and head lean forward *very slowly*. Pay attention to the minute changes in your body as it slowly changes position. Let your arms hang loose, and let the legs be flexed rather than locked back. Be sure that your head and neck are loose and that you are not holding your head up. Be aware of the stretch, but do not try to stretch or reach down. Breathe slowly and deeply. As you bend more and more, continue to breathe slowly and see if you can bend farther without tensing your neck and lifting your head. Don't push or force, just *allow* your spine to bend and the muscles of the back and legs to stretch. When you have bent over as far as is comfortable, continue to breathe, and with each exhalation feel yourself going down further. Then come up again very *slowly*, vertebra by vertebra, without raising your head, letting your head hang loose. Be aware of the changes in your position, the changes of your spine from a curved to a straighter shape, the changes in your balance. Your head will be the last part of your body to become vertical. At the end, breathe calmly and be aware of how your body feels in its standing position. Do this again; let it take 5 minutes.

If this exercise were done without "trying" but with passive attention to the stretch, two things would probably happen: Muscle activity would decrease and blood vessels would dilate at the areas where passive attention was focused. Recording these physiological changes can indicate to researchers what type of attention the person is using.

The different effects of attentional processes are illustrated by the following clinical example in which a young woman with Raynaud's disease (which leaves the limbs cold) learned to warm her hands with the use of thermal biofeedback. Changes in her skin temperature triggered a signal that indicated when she was getting warmer. Biofeedback creates an external signal the person may use to become aware of subtle variations in internal functioning (such as heart rate or, in this case, skin temperature). You can see the gradual progress the trainee is making during the first 6 minutes of the biofeedback training. At minute 7, she stopped striving actively to control her temperature, she began to attend passively to what she was experiencing. Obviously, she wanted to feel warmer but didn't know consciously how to achieve that goal. But at a physiological level, her body "knew" how to do it—she had merely to tune into that process. At the point that she gave up actively striving, her hand temperature increased dramatically, as illustrated in Figure 1. Even more interesting, once she stopped trying and

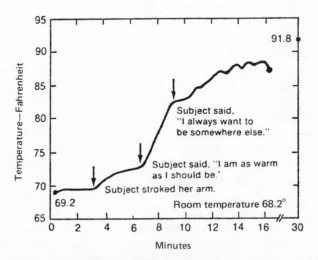

Figure 1. Results of a woman being trained with biofeedback to raise her skin temperature. Gradual improvement over first 6 minutes shifted to marked increase in warmth when she stopped actively trying and passively attended to the process. In 30 minutes she raised her skin temperature 22°F.

allowed the warmth to flow into her hands, she also experienced an insight into how she herself had created her own distressing physical symptoms. By withdrawing her psychological concern and emotional affect from the people around her, she had created the physical symptoms of chronic, peripheral coldness. I find that as the physiological system is alleviated, the underlying psychological difficulty often emerges—a striking demonstration of the interaction between mind and body. In the process of attempting to control her autonomic system through biofeedback learning, this woman came into closer contact with her conscious and unconscious processes and thereby was able to reestablish a harmonious state between mind and body. That is the basis of transforming sickness states into healthy ones.

To help teach autonomic control via passive attention, biofeedback and autogenic training are often used. In autogenic training, a person attends passively to his or her arm and talks to it ("My right arm is heavy" or "My right arm is warm") and something happens: The electromyographic (muscle) activity decreases and the blood flow changes in those areas where the passive attention is focused.

It is important to realize that the prerequisite of passive attention is profound relaxation. Deep relaxation enhances and may even be considered a precondition for this process because the moment we try the body reacts. Most likely for every thought there is a corresponding muscle activity. Hence rumination on emotional events can lead to an increase in anxiety. For instance, I often demonstrate this with my trainees (experimental subjects or patients) using biofeedback. We record the electromyographic activity of the forearm extensors while they allow the muscle to relax. I purposely used the word *allow* instead of *relax*, because "allow" implies not striving while "to relax" may mean you "do something" forcibly. When electrical activity in the muscles is down to 1.0 microvolts (a totally relaxed muscle), I ask the trainees to *imagine* lifting their fingers but not to move them. The EMG often increases up to 2.5 microvolts, illustrating that the muscles contracted even though there were no perceptible movements in the hand or fingers or conscious attempts to move the body.

Dimensions of passive attention can also account for the healthful effect of Hatha Yoga *asanas*—a specific yogic stretch. While doing an asana, the "complete stretch" is not the goal; instead, one gently attends to the area of the stretch, letting the rest of the body relax. One no longer attends to the end goal, or to achievement ("How far can I stretch?"), but instead one gently attends to the process. Hence we would predict that the striate muscle activity would decrease and that change in blood circulation would occur. In the asana, the stretch *captures* our passive attention. The result is the same—a change in physiology. Asanas are body attention-getters to bring passive attention to a specific area. If this is true, some health claims of yoga could be validated. In the Hatha Yoga, the shoulder stand (feet pointed to the ceiling) is said to be done to promote thyroid functioning. But why should that occur? The upside-down posture would cause the throat to compress. What happens is that the person experiences the pressure inside the neck and throat, which captures passive attention. Attending to it could bring about an increased blood flow and affect the thyroid. (This hypothesis is testable through the use of a thermograph and biological monitoring.) Too many of us try to do the asanas without attending passively. Usually one assumes that a person would learn passive attention through doing; however, the person may just continue to strive since we must unlearn the habit of working toward ends and learn to be part of the means. I am currently attempting to explore the occurrences of passive attention during different states of consciousness and during meditative practices.

Passive attention is the wedge through which we join our conscious and unconscious processes. The adepts illustrate some of the possible effects of using it. Autogenic training, biofeedback, and meditative and yogic practices are techniques to develop these same capacities. By this paradoxical process—grasped without grasping—we allow ourselves to open an infinite world in which we can expand our own potentials and participate in the restoration and maintenance of our psychic, spiritual, and physical well-being.

ACKNOWLEDGMENT. The author wishes to thank Susan Chandler and Joanna Taylor for their help in preparing this essay.

8

Biofeedback for Mind/Body Self-Regulation: Healing and Creativity

Elmer E. Green, Alyce M. Green, and E. Dale Walters

As people in this audience know,* the revolution in consciousness we are now talking about was foretold a long time ago. It was thought of as the time when the sleeping giant, humanity, would awaken, come to consciousness, and begin to exert its power. British medical people began to get an inkling of the power of consciousness as long as 250 years ago when they began to study certain Indians who could do some very unusual and interesting things. These people, called yogis, apparently had phenomenal powers of self-regulation, of both mind and body. Of course, medical doctors as a whole did not believe it, but as the decades passed and reports became more numerous, some British and European physicians began the study of mind/body relationships. By the end of the 19th century the physiological phenomena of hypnotism, spiritualism, and various yogic disciplines had attracted some serious medical and philosophical attention, and by 1910 of this century, a mind/body training system, eventually called autogenic training (self-generated or self-motivated training), had begun to be developed by Dr. Johannes Schultz in Germany. This was at approximately the time that Freud gave up the use of hypnosis as a medical tool because it was unpredictable. It occurred to Schultz that perhaps hypnosis was an erratic tool because the patient often unconsciously resisted the doctor. If the patient were able to direct for himself the procedure being used, with the doctor acting as his teacher, then the control technique would come into the realm of *self*-regulation and perhaps be more effective.

It is an interesting fact that the first English translation of Schultz and Luthe's handbook, *Autogenic Training* (1959), contains in its 604 references only 10 that are in English. In addition to telling us that there was much interest on the continent in healing by self-regulation, it also tells us something about the British and the Americans. Freud's ideas became very important in the United

* This chapter was originally a talk given at the symposium called "The Varieties of Healing Experience" at De Anza College, Cupertino, California. The symposium was sponsored jointly by the Academy of Parapsychology and Medicine and by the Lockheed MSC Management Association.

Elmer E. Green, Alyce M. Green, and E. Dale Walters • Biofeedback Center, Research Department, The Menninger Foundation, Topeka, Kansas 66601.

States, whereas the self-regulation techniques of autogenic training were largely confined to Europe. It is also interesting to note that because of his interest in self-awareness, Schultz included in his training system some psychological disciplines that he called "meditative" exercises. These exercises gradually lead into a kind of self-awareness in which the person develops both physiological and psychological self-knowledge.

It was because of our interest in both consciousness and volition that my wife, Alyce, and I decided in 1965 to test autogenic training and find out whether or not people who used the exercises actually could develop some of the physiological controls Schultz talked about. Our research program began with 33 housewives. They practiced autogenic exercises for only 2 weeks and at the beginning and end of their training experience we measured most of the physiological variables that were easy to get, such as brain waves, heart rate, breathing rate, skin potential, skin resistance, blood flow in the fingers, and the temperatures of both hands, front and back. Some of the ladies failed to achieve much temperature control but a couple of them succeeded so well that we decided to continue studying autogenic training. It was clearly a training technique in which volition "entered" into the psychosomatic domain. It was also clear that if psychosomatic disease really existed, then it was logically necessary to hypothesize the existence of psychosomatic health. Both the literature of autogenic training and our research indicate that psychophysiological processes definitely could be self-regulated, and to allow for the existence of psychosomatic disease without postulating its opposite, psychosomatic health, would be an absurdity. If we can make ourselves sick, then we must also be able to make ourselves well.

Since physicians are saying these days that about 80% of human ailments are psychosomatic in origin, or at least have a psychosomatic component, it seems reasonable to assume that about 80% of our disabilities can be cured, or at least ameliorated, by the use of special training programs for psychosomatic health.

Gardner Murphy was very much interested in these research implications and one day suggested that we include biofeedback in our research methodology. He had been interested since 1952 in the possibility of using electrophysiological instrumentation for measuring and presenting to a person some of his own normally unconscious physiological processes, that is, processes of which a person is normally unaware. He knew, for instance, that muscle tension problems were often extremely difficult to handle, and when the doctor says, "Your problem is that you are too tense," he does not give much new information, nor does it help much. Generally, the medical pronouncement is followed by a prescription, but what Gardner was suggesting was that if a person could "see" his tension, could look at a meter and observe its fluctuations, then perhaps he could learn to manipulate the underlying psychophysiological problem. He could practice "making the meter go down" and its behavior would tell him immediately if he was succeeding. In essence, this is an application of the engineering principle of feedback, the servomechanistic principle by means of which automatic machines are controlled. A furnace and its thermostat, for instance, form a closed (self-contained) feedback system. In the analogy, the human who adjusts the thermostat represents volition entering into the system from an energy source outside the closed loop.

Murphy's idea seemed useful, so we combined it with autogenic training and developed in 1967 a system of psychosomatic self-regulation that we called autogenic feedback training. By coupling biofeedback with autogenic training, progress in controlling physiological variables is often highly accelerated. The self-suggestion formula of autogenic training (such as "I feel quite quiet") tells the unconscious section of mind, or brain, the goal toward which the person wishes to move, and the physiological feedback device immediately tells him the extent to which he is succeeding. The objective fact of a feedback meter, as a "truth" detector, has a powerful though not entirely understood effect on a person's ability to control normally involuntary physiological processes. For example, if a person's heart is malfunctioning from psychosomatic causes it is certainly not "all in his head," but knowing that the cause is psychosomatic does not tell him what to do about it. When his heart rate is displayed on a meter, however, he can easily and objectively experiment with the psychological states that influence the rate. While using any kind of biofeedback device as a tool for learning something about yourself, it is interesting and instructive to experimentally induce in yourself a feeling of anxiety and nervousness, then calmness and tranquillity. You can play with anger and with peacefulness. Then you can experiment with muscle tension, relaxation, slow deep breathing, etc. Learning to manipulate physiological processes while seeing the meter (or listening to it if it has an auditory output) is quite similar to learning to play a pinball machine with your eyes open. If you had to learn blindfolded it would be difficult, but if you use your eyes (employing visual feedback), it is easy.

I will summarize the work we have been doing in the Voluntary Controls Project at The Menninger Foundation and later mention our research with Swami Rama, an Indian yogi who demonstrated in the laboratory some of the results of his own psychosomatic training program. If you wish to receive more information on any of this work, a note or postcard to us will be sufficient.

As already mentioned, our first project was to train a group of housewives to increase the temperature of their hands, using only autogenic training methods. After that we began an ambitious program in which an attempt was made to train 18 college men to control *three* physiological variables simultaneously, using autogenic feedback training. Feedback meters showed muscle tension in the right forearm, temperature of a finger on the right hand, and percentage of alpha rhythm in the brain-wave pattern (over the preceding 10-second interval of time).

Muscle tension was picked up from an electrode attached with salt paste to the skin. Temperature was obtained from a thermister taped lightly to the middle finger of the right hand, and brain-wave (EEG) signals were obtained from an electrode pasted to the left occiput (the back of the head). The instruments were adjusted so that if the subject could relax his forearm completely the meter would "rise to the top." Complete relaxation means that there is a complete absence of muscle fiber "firing" and the electrical signal resulting from muscle tension "goes to zero." In this situation, the meter is wired to go to the top, showing complete success in *relaxation*. If the subject's finger showed an increase in *temperature* of 10°F, the temperature meter would rise to the top. It is interesting that if a subject tried to force the temperature to rise, by active volition, it invariably went down. But if he relaxed, "told the body" what to do, and then detached himself from the response, the temperature would rise. This is passive volition. A 10° decrease would cause the meter to go to the bottom. In other words, we set the meter in the center of its scale regardless of the absolute temperature of the hand, and studied only the temperature variations associated with the training program. The third meter showed percentage of alpha rhythm in the visual (occipital) area of the brain. After a period of training in relaxation and temperature control we would say to the subject, "Now while you keep the relaxation and warmth meters up try to make the third meter, the alpha meter, go up without closing your eyes." It is common knowledge that about 90% of the population produce alpha waves when the eyes are closed, so if subjects closed their eyes they could be expected to produce alpha waves, but we wanted them to generate, or bring about, an increase in the percentage of alpha while their eyes were open. One of our research objectives was to test the hypothesis that a person's success in remembering would be a function of, or correlated with, the percentage of alpha waves present while he was trying to remember. The eyes-open condition was useful because it served the purposes of keeping the subject from getting drowsy, permitted the use of a simple visual feedback device (though we could have used auditory feedback if desired), and also enhanced the subject's "coupling" to the outside world. We wanted the subject to be able to look at the outside world and to answer questions without destroying his alpha rhythm, so it seemed useful to train him in awareness of both internal and external "worlds" at the same time by using a visual feedback system for brain waves. Results showed that in the students with whom we worked, the ability to remember was indeed positively correlated with the percentage of alpha ($r = .54$, $p = .1$), and it indicated that an alpha training program might be of great value in assisting students to overcome "mental blocks" during examinations.

Before continuing, however, it is useful to examine Figure 1. It shows the major brain-wave frequency bands and their relation to conscious and unconscious processes, in the general population. When people focus attention on the outside world they usually produce only beta frequencies. If they close their eyes and think of nothing in particular, they generally produce a mixture of alpha and beta. If they slip toward sleep, become drowsy, theta frequencies often appear and there is less of alpha and beta. Delta waves are not normally present except in deep sleep. For example, at this moment I am predominantly in the beta state, and so are you—at least I think so.

Now, alpha waves can be made to appear when the eyes are open if attention is turned inward, away from the outside world, but the way to make the alpha meter go up while looking at it is to learn to "observe without looking." Perhaps

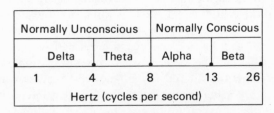

Figure 1. Major frequency bands in the electroencephalographic (EEG) record.

this sounds paradoxical, but it is not as difficult as answering the Zen koan, "What is the sound of one hand clapping?" In any event, we wanted students to be able to produce alpha waves with their eyes open and also to be able to answer questions while in this state.

The attempt to develop simultaneous self-regulation of three physiological variables in 5 weeks proved to be overly ambitious but students usually learned to control one or another of the original three variables quite well, and sometimes could control two at once, but is was not easy for anyone to control all three at the same time.

As we worked with the college group, we also ran pilot subjects in a theta training program and soon we noticed that the psychological state associated with theta contained, in a number of subjects, very clear hypnagogic-like imagery. Pictures or ideas would spring full-blown into consciousness without the person being aware of their creation. The theta "reverie," as we began to call it, was definitely different from a daydreaming state and much to our surprise we found that it seemed to correspond with descriptions given by geniuses of the past of the state of consciousness they experienced while being their most creative. From these observations and from our experiences in training college students we developed our present project called "alpha-theta brain-wave feedback, reverie, and imagery."

Without going into details about the machinery and procedures of theta training, in our present research, in order to signal the presence of both alpha and theta frequencies in the occipital (visual) brain rhythm, we used auditory feedback (musical tones) rather than visual feedback. As already mentioned, alpha production can easily be learned with the eyes open, but theta production is generally possible only with the eyes closed. The imagery associated with theta is often so tenuous that open eyes drive it away. In our currently used EEG feedback devices (these machines are manufactured under licensing agreement from The Menninger Foundation, by a small electronics firm in Lawrence, Kansas), a low frequency feedback tone signifies theta and a higher frequency signifies alpha. For training away from the lab we have developed portable alpha-theta "home trainers," but in the lab we use an auditory feedback system that detects the presence of various brain waves and multiplies their frequencies by 200 (up to the audible range). By this procedure, beta waves are made to produce a "piccolo" type of music. Alpha sounds like a flute, theta like an oboe, and delta like a bassoon. This combination results in an interesting and not unpleasing quartet. We have constructed two identical sets of amplifiers, filters, multipliers, and associated hardware, so that two brain-wave channels can be studied simultaneously, and when we attach electrodes to the two sides of the head, it is possible to feed back to the subject musical information concerning the simultaneous electrical activity of the two cerebral hemispheres.

The right ear "listens" to the right side of the brain and the left ear listens to the left side. We have not used this elaborate laboratory feedback system except in pilot research, but we sometimes claim that we are going to use the machine to train a subject to play "The Star Spangled Banner," with the hope that it will encourage the federal government to release additional funds! That, at least, would demonstrate a high level of control.

In working with research subjects we obviously do not say that the physiological functions they are going to control are involuntary—because if they really believed that, the training would not work. In actuality, it is the "belief" of the subconscious (or unconscious) that is the controlling factor in learning to manipulate a so-called involuntary process. Feedback meters are remarkably powerful in training the autonomic nervous system because seeing is believing, even for the unconscious. There is little room for skepticism or disbelief concerning the practicality of temperature control when the temperature (blood flow) meter is used. Unconscious skepticism, as a factor in the psychophysiological matrix, seems to cause the hand temperature to drop, but this response indicates to the subject that the meter really does tell something, even if at first he does not know what it is. After a bit of practice with a feedback device, the situation is rather like learning to drive a car. The student driver does not question whether the car will move if he steps on the accelerator. And if he thinks that turning the steering wheel to the left will make the car turn to the right, he soon discovers his error.

Without getting involved in details, it seems that a hierarchy of attitudes (or sets) is involved in learning to control normally involuntary processes—first, hypothesis; then, belief, and finally, knowing. A person may start with the *hypothesis* that the temperature of his hand will rise, but because of his previously conditioned response to introspection, his temperature may rapidly drop when he attempts to raise it. This response tells him, however, that something significant is going on in his nervous system in response to his efforts. Then, when he relaxes and begins to think of something else, becomes detached, the temperature begins to rise. So he begins to *believe* that the training system will work. Eventually he *knows* he can control the process and he knows what is happening in himself (in regard to raising or lowering hand temperature) whenever he turns his attention to the matter.

Quite often with beginners the hand temperature will rise at first, but then an insidious thought will creep in, such as, "it may work with other people, but it probably won't work for me." This precipitates vasoconstriction in the hands due to the activation of the sympathetic nervous system and blood flow in the hands is appropriately reduced. Within a few seconds temperature of the hands begins to drop.

From our various research experiences with autogenic training and biofeedback, and with highly trained persons such as Swami Rama and lately with Jack Schwarz, we are beginning to believe, or at least hypothesize, that "*any* physiological process that can be detected and displayed in an objective fashion to the subject can be self-regulated in some degree." Blood pressure, blood flow, heart rate, lymph flow, muscle tension, brain waves, all these have already been self-regulated through training in one laboratory or another. Where is the limit to this capacity for psychosomatic self-regulation? Nobody knows, but research indicates that the limits lie much farther out than was at first suspected by most of those interested in biofeedback.

It is useful here to draw attention to the major areas of the brain and discuss their relation to the process we are calling voluntary control of internal states. The item of particular significance in Figure 2 is that it is divided vertically into

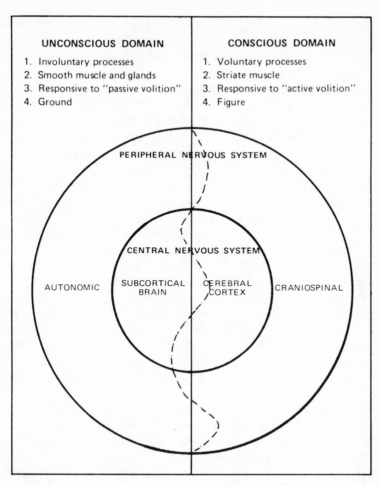

Figure 2. Psychophysiological diagram relating the conscious-unconscious psychological domain to the various sections of the voluntary-involuntary physiological domain. The solid vertical line separates the central and peripheral nervous systems into functional subregions. The dashed line (conceptually visualized to be in continuous undulatory movement) separates the conscious and unconscious areas.

conscious and unconscious domains, on the right and left, respectively. The conscious side contains both the cerebral cortex, which someone in the American Medical Association called the "screen of consciousness," and the craniospinal nervous system, roughly, the voluntary muscular system. The unconscious side includes both the subcortical brain, the "old" lower brain structures that man shares with most of the animals, and the autonomic nervous system, the involuntary nervous system, which lies outside of the brain and brainstem, and which controls, among other things, the skin, the internal organs and glands, and the vascular system of the body. The paleocortex, the old brain, includes a section called the limbic system, which has been given a name of particularly great significance for understanding psychosomatic self-regulation, namely, "visceral brain." It is quite clear from recent research that electrical stimulation of the visceral brain and related neural structures through implanted electrodes causes emotional changes in humans. Conversely, it is well known that perceptual and emotional changes are followed by neural changes, or responses, in the limbic system of the brain, though most of this work was performed with animals. Putting together some of the pieces of the mind/body system as observed both physiologically in the nervous system and behaviorally (through autogenic feedback training), we have found it convenient to postulate a *psychophysiological principle* that goes as follows, "Every change in the physiological state is accompanied by an appropriate change in the mental-emotional state, conscious or unconscious, and conversely, every change in the mental-emotional state, conscious or unconscious, is accompanied by an appropriate change in the physiological state." This closed-loop statement obviously does not allow for volition or free will in humans any more than the furnace-and-thermostat system of your house is "allowed" to have a will of its own, but even as the thermostat is manipulated by a force from the outside, namely, your hand (which would have to be categorized as a metaforce in the furnace-and-thermostat system), so also the psychophysiological principle, or its expression in the psychosomatic unity of mind and body, is manipulated by volition, which at present is of indeterminate origin, but which at least exhibits some of the characteristics of a metaforce. These ideas, incidentally, are quite clearly put forth in the Vedas, sacred scriptures of India, and lie behind the system of Raja Yoga. These basic concepts are well considered in Aurobindo's Integral Yoga, especially in his book called *The Synthesis of Yoga*.

But to return to the diagram, the dashed line represents at a specific moment the actual, rather than the theoretical, division between conscious and unconscious functions in the nervous system. We must visualize the dashed line as continually shifting and undulating between various brain structures as attention shifts from one thing to another. It is clear that when we learn to drive a car, every movement must at first be worked over in the conscious domain. But after we have learned to drive well enough it is possible, when we are thinking of something else, to drive all the way through town without being aware of stopping at stop signs. In other words, what was once conscious becomes unconscious for a time. In other words, the dashed line moves from left to right and extends for a period of time over neurological structures in the neocortex and the craniospinal system. On the other hand, when one learns through biofeedback training to control the flow of blood in his hands, he is obviously extending conscious control for a period of time over an area that lies to the left of center in the diagram. That is, some of the subcortical brain structures and some of the neural circuits in the autonomic nervous system have come under conscious control. It is interesting that when patients using autogenic training reported to Dr. Schultz that they could not achieve control over some physiological process, he would say that they had not made "mental contact" with that part of the body. In other words, again, they had not extended the dashed line of the diagram far enough to the left in a specific neural pathway.

Now we will discuss our research with Swami Rama. Dr. Daniel Ferguson, at the Veterans Administration Hospital in St. Paul, Minnesota, became aware of the "voluntary controls" work at the foundation and one day near the end of 1969 he wrote to me saying that if we were interested in making some tests of an Indian yogi who could control a number of normally uncontrollable physiological processes, he would arrange a meeting in Topeka. The upshot of this was that Swami Rama (of Rishikesh and the Himalayas) and Dr. Ferguson visited us for 3 days in March 1970. The Foundation for the Study of Consciousness, Philadelphia, Pennsylvania, provided research funds for this visit. Later we obtained funding both from the Millicent Foundation, Vancouver, Washington, and from the Joseph and Sadie Danciger Fund, Kansas City, Missouri, to work with the swami over an extended period of time.

During the first visit, Swami Rama demonstrated that he had exquisite differential control over arteries in his right hand. We had "wired" him for brain waves, respiration, skin potential, skin resistance, heart behavior (EKG), blood flow in his hands, and temperature. While thus encumbered he caused two areas a couple of inches apart on the palm of his right hand to gradually change temperature in opposite directions (at a maximum rate of about 4°F per minute) until they showed a temperature difference of about 10°F. The left side of his palm, after this performance (which was totally motionless), looked as if it had been slapped with a ruler a few times—it was rosy red. The right side of his hand had turned ashen gray. During the last session of this visit, he made the comment that according to theory a swami could not be upset or distracted, but that it was a good thing that none of his students were here to demonstrate their powers of physiological control, because he doubted if they would be able to succeed in such a strange scientific setting. Other demonstrations included the speeding and slowing of his heart rate, and finally we concluded the tests, we thought. But during dinner, on the evening before he and Dr. Ferguson were to return to Minneapolis, he suddenly said he was sorry he had not demonstrated "stopping" his heart and that he would do it in the morning.

Both Alyce and I objected to this because he had just finished telling us that in order to demonstrate some of the more physiologically serious controls, such as stopping the heart, it was necessary to fast for a couple of days, taking nothing but fluids. I could well believe this because according to the swami he would stop his heart in this particular demonstration by control of the vagus nerve. Since the vagus nerve also has an important control function over the stomach and other visceral organs, it could logically cause a serious case of indigestion, to say the least.

The swami's answer to our objection, however, was that anything he could do in 3 minutes his guru could do in 3 seconds and that he wanted to perform this experiment in order to test himself. Finally, having satisfied himself that he had answered, or demolished, our arguments, and having said that if necessary he would sign papers to the effect that The Menninger Foundation was not in any way responsible for anything that might happen to him, he said that he could stop his heart in this way for 3 or 4 minutes, and how long would we need for an adequate test. I said that 10 seconds would be quite impressive and he agreed to this limitation.

The next day we hurried to the lab at 9:00 o'clock (we had previously scheduled a lecture for him at 10:00 o'clock) and wired him for the demonstration. Before starting his "inner focusing" procedure, however, he said that when his heart stopped he wanted Alyce to call over the intercom from the control room and say "that's all." This would be the signal for timing the duration of his demonstration and would also remind him not to "go too far." He said that he did not want to interfere with the functioning of his "subtle heart," the one that lay behind the workings of his "physical heart." Having explained this, he made a few trial runs at speeding and slowing his heart, then said, "I am going to give a shock, do not be alarmed." To me this meant that he was going to give himself some kind of neural shock, but later I learned that he was going to shock the research personnel and doctors who were watching the paper records and polygraph pens in the control room, and they were being told not to be alarmed. After about 20 seconds of motionless silence I heard Alyce say, "that's all." At this, the swami pulled in his stomach muscles for a few seconds, then he relaxed. From his look I could see that he felt the test had been a success, so I began asking questions about the "internal" process he used to accomplish such a thing. While he was answering, Alyce called over the intercom and said that the heart record was not what we had expected and suggested that I look at it before going any further.

To my surprise, the heart rate instead of dropping to zero had jumped in one beat from about 70 per minute to about 300 per minute. I returned to the experimental room and described the record to swami. He seemed somewhat surprised and bothered and said, "You know that when you stop the heart in this way, it still trembles in there," and he illustrated with fluttering hands. I speculated then that what we had recorded might be some kind of fibrillation, but later I was told by Dr. Marvin Dunne, cardiologist and professor at the Kansas University Medical Center (Kansas City, Kansas), after he had examined the records, that it was a case of "atrial flutter," a state in which the heart fires at its maximum rate without the blood filling the chambers properly or the valves working properly. He showed me similar records obtained from patients and asked what happened to the swami, he should have passed out, but I had to answer that we quickly "unwired" him so he could get to his lecture on time.

The atrial flutter actually lasted for an interval between 17 and 25 seconds. The exact duration could not be determined from the record because when the Swami drew in his stomach the resulting electrical signal from muscle firing caused the EKG pen to go off the edge of the paper, and after it returned the heart rate was normal again. I asked him why he had moved his stomach and he said that he had established a "solar plexus lock," by means of which the heart condition could be maintained for quite a long time if desired. It is interesting to note that when the heart began to flutter the people in the control room had a hurried consultation among themselves to decide if this was what the swami meant by "stopping" his heart. After about 8 seconds they decided that whatever it was it looked dangerous and decided to give the "that's all" signal.

In summary, we may say that the swami stopped his heart from pumping blood for at least 17 seconds. This was his technique, we discovered, for obliterating his pulse during examination by medical doctors. The "other" kind of heart stopping, he said, involved a hibernationlike state that he might be prepared to demonstrate on some other occasion.

The importance of Swami Rama's demonstrations did not lie in the performances themselves but in their implications. I do not intend to practice stopping my heart or to try to teach anyone else according to the swami's instructions, but the fact that *it can be done* is of major scientific importance. Aside from supporting the psychophysiological theory previously discussed, it more importantly gives us additional reason to believe that training programs are feasible for the establishment and maintenance of psychosomatic health. If every young student *knew* by the time he finished his first biology class, in grade school, that the body responds to self-generated psychological inputs, that blood flow and heart behavior, as well as a host of other body processes, can be influenced at will, it would change prevailing ideas about both physical and mental health. It would then be quite clear and understandable that we are individually responsible to a large extent for our state of health or disease.

Perhaps then people would begin to realize that it is not life that kills us, but rather it is our reaction to it, and this reaction can be to a significant extent self-chosen.

Later in the year Swami Rama returned to the foundation for another series of experiments, especially for correlating internal psychological states (phenomenological or existential states) with brain-wave patterns. At first the experiments appeared disastrous for our general theory of "focus of attention and brain-wave correlates." No matter what psychological state we asked the swami to demonstrate, from a list he had supplied, the only definite brain rhythm was in the beta frequency band, which was presumably associated with (at least in our understanding of the matter) attention on outside-world sensory processes or attention on intense internal activation of a stressful nature. But one day, after about 2 weeks of sessions, the swami said he had some news for us. All the records would have to be thrown away because he had not successfully entered any of the subjective states we had been attempting to study. Since I had not shown him the records and had not discussed my misgivings with him, this unsolicited announcement came like a ray of light through dark clouds. I asked what the problem seemed to be and he answered that it would have been much better if I had not told him that the polygraph paper cost $16 per box. All he could think of, he said, was the terrible expense involved and all the people watching paper shoot out of the machines.

After that came out, we assured him that if necessary we could run paper for 24-hour periods without bankrupting the project, and it was agreed that henceforth he would take as long as necessary to move into a particular state of consciousness and that at the appropriate time he would come out of the state and tell us, essentially, that the last 5 minutes of the record contained what we were looking for. The result of this conversation was a considerable lessening of tension and the swami was subsequently able to enter various states (evidenced by remarkable changes in brain-wave patterns) in no more than 15 minutes, and usually in 5 minutes.

In five 15-minute brain-wave feedback sessions he was able to tie together in his mind the relationship between the tones produced by activation in the various brain-wave bands and the states of consciousness he had learned in a Himalayan cave. Then he produced 70% alpha waves over a 5-minute period of time by thinking of an empty blue sky "with a small white cloud" sometimes coming by. After a number of alpha-producing sessions the swami said, "I have news for you, alpha isn't anything. It is literally nothing." This did not surprise us, because we had already observed that the best way to produce alpha was to close the eyes and think of nothing in particular, but it would have provided a shock, I suppose, to the many mind-training researchers who are telling people all over the country that when in the alpha brain-wave state you can get rid of your diseases, get the most wonderful ideas, and best of all be telepathic. This kind of talk is nonsense to those clinicians and technicians who work in EEG labs. Whether they accept the possibility of telepathy or not, they know that about 90% of the population of the United State produce alpha waves when the eyes are closed, and the majority of our people are certainly not telepathic nor can they rid themselves of disease merely by being in an alpha brain-wave state.

In any event, the swami next produced theta waves by "stilling the conscious mind and bringing forward the unconscious." In one 5-minute period of the test he produced theta waves 75% of the time. I asked him what his experience was and he answered that it was an unpleasant state, "very noisy " The things he had wanted to do but did not do, the things he should have done but did not do, and associated images and memories of people who wanted him to do things came up in a rush and began shouting at him. It was a state that he generally kept turned off, he said, but it was also instructive and important to look in once in a while to see what was there. From what he said I could well understand that his life in India, of rigorous discipline and strenuous practice, had involved a good deal of suppression and that his reverential attitude toward his guru, as a being in whom conflicts were resolved, was partly based on his understanding of the difficulty of creating a true synthesis of forces in oneself. The perfected guru, according to Indian tradition, is a liberated being who, among other things, has consciously examined all parts of his nature, conscious and unconscious, and has established tranquility and harmony there.

After producing theta waves, the swami said he knew exactly how the inner states of awareness were arranged in respect to the brain-wave frequency bands. Then he said, "Tomorrow I will consciously make delta waves for you." I replied that I doubted that he would succeed in that because he would have to be sound asleep in order to produce delta. He laughed at this and said that I would think that he was asleep but that he would be conscious of everything that occurred in the experimental room.

Before this test he asked how long I would like to have him remain in the delta state. I said that 25 minutes would be all right and he said he would bring himself out at that time. After about 5 minutes of meditation, lying down with his eyes shut, the swami began producing delta waves, which we had never before seen in his record. In addition, he snored gently. Alyce, without having told the swami that she was going to say anything (she was in the experimental room observing him during this test) then made a statement in a low voice, "Today the sun is shining, but tomorrow it may rain." Every 5 minutes she made another statement, and after 25 minutes had passed the swami roused himself and said that someone with sharp heels had walked on the floor above and made a click, click, click noise during the test, and a door had been slammed twice somewhere in the building, and that Mrs. Green had said—and here he gave her statements verbatim, except for the last half of the fourth sentence, of which he had the gist correct though not the words. I was very much impressed because in listening from the control room, I had heard her sentences but could not remember them all, and I was supposed to have been awake. Dale Walters, our colleague in this research for the last 5 years, didn't remember much more than I, but we reminded each other that our attention was supposed to be on the physiological records, not on what Alyce was saying.

The swami said that this "yogic sleep," as he called it, was extremely beneficial. He said 15 minutes of it was as good as an hour's normal sleep. Most people, he continued, let their brains go to sleep while their minds were still busy worrying over various matters, with the result that they woke up tired. It is necessary for the mind and brain to sleep at the same time, he explained. In the delta state he had just produced, he said, he told his mind to be quiet, to not respond to anything but to record everything, to remain in a deep state of tranquility until he activated it. He also said that this kind of sleep was called "dog sleep," because a good dog can leap up from a sound sleep and chase after something without any apparent signs of having to reactivate, a very Zen-like condition it seemed to me.

We did not complete all the experiments planned with Swami Rama. He became involved in giving lectures and seminars around the country and eventually went to India to attend the "yoga and science" conference at New Delhi (December 1970). It was interesting that he carried with him two of our biofeedback machines and gave a lecture called "Yoga and Biofeedback Training." His attitude about biofeedback was that it would accelerate the training of young yogis, up to the point where machines could no longer follow. The machines would also eliminate fakers (not fakirs, please note) by the dozens. We hope we will again, one day, have a chance to do more psychophysiological work with Swami Rama.

In our research with the swami we naturally focused a good deal of attention on physiological data because they are easy to put into graphical form, and it is easier to get research money for projects that come out with red ink on green paper. Some of Swami Rama's other accomplishments were of utmost interest, however. For instance, we observed that he could diagnose physical ailments very much in the manner of Edgar Cayce, except that he appeared to be totally conscious, though with indrawn attention for a few seconds while he was "picking up" information. His training program will be made available to medical doctors, he says.

Before concluding, it should be mentioned that when the swami produced alpha, he did not cease the production of beta. And when he produced theta, both alpha and beta were retained, each about 50% of the time. Likewise, when he produced delta he was also producing theta, alpha, and beta during a relatively high percentage of the time. Perhaps this tells us something important. Since alpha is a conscious state, it may be necessary to retain it when theta is produced if one wishes to be aware of the hypnagogic imagery that is often associated with theta. This idea was supported by some of our pilot research with a group of adults who were interested in being experimental subjects for theta research using brain-wave feedback and also some of Swami Rama's breathing exercises for tranquilizing the autonomic nervous system. The main exercise consisted of deep and slow rhythmic breathing, at a constant rate both in and out, with no pauses at the bottom or top of the respiration cycle. After 4 or 5 months had passed, with at least 10 days a month including a "breathing and meditation" period (at home), the breathing rate could be comfortably slowed to once or twice per minute, for a period of 10 minutes. These findings are probably consistent with Wallace's observation, reported in *Science*, that a significant drop in basal metabolism rate (BMR) accompanied the practice of "transcendental meditation" by a group of college students. We did not have metabolism-measuring equipment in our lab, but we might suspect that if the BMR did not drop significantly in our subjects it would be very difficult for them to breath at such an "inadequate" rate without experiencing involuntary diaphragmatic gasping. The swami's instruction, to allow "no jerks," was eventually complied with, much to our surpise.

As a final word, it seems increasingly certain that healing and creativity are different pieces of a single picture. Both Swami Rama and Jack Schwarz, a Western sufi whom we recently had a chance to work with, maintain that self-healing can be performed in a state of deep *reverie*. Images for giving the body instructions are manipulated in a manner very similar to that used by Assagioli for personality and transpersonal integration, as in his *Psychosynthesis*. But this "manner" of manipulation of images is also the same as that in which we find ideas being handled creatively (by two pilot subjects) for the solution of intellectual problems. What an interesting finding! Creativity in terms of physiological processes means then *physical healing*, physical regeneration. Creativity in emotional terms consists then of establishing, or creating, *attitude changes* through the practice of healthful emotions, that is, emotions whose neural correlates are those that establish harmony in the visceral brain, or to put it another way, emotions that establish in the visceral brain those neurological patterns whose reflection in the viscera is one that physicians approve of as stress-resistent. Creativity in the mental domain involves the emergence of a new and valid *synthesis of ideas*, not by deduction, but springing by "intuition" from unconscious sources.

The entrance, or key, to all these inner processes we are beginning to believe, is a particular state of consciousness to which we have given the undifferentiated name "reverie." This reverie can be approached by means of theta brain-wave training in which the gap between conscious and unconscious processes is voluntarily narrowed, and temporarily eliminated when useful. When that self-regulated reverie is established, the body can apparently be programmed at will and the instructions given will be carried out, emotional states can be dispassionately examined, accepted, or rejected, or totally supplanted by others deemed more useful, and problems insoluble in the normal state of consciousness can be elegantly resolved.

Perhaps now, because of the resurgence of interest in self-exploration and in self-realization, it will be possible to develop a synthesis of old and new, East and West, prescience and science, using both yoga and biofeedback training as tools for the study of consciousness. It is also interesting to hypothesize that useful parapsychological talents can perhaps be developed by use of these reverie-generating processes of yoga and biofeedback. Much remains to be researched, and tried in application, but there is little doubt that in the lives of many people a penetration of consciousness into previously unconscious realms (of mind and brain) is making understandable and functional much that was previously obscure and inoperable.

9

The Two Endpoints of an EEG Continuum of Meditation—Alpha/Theta and Fast Beta

Erik Peper and Sonia Ancoli

In this case study, the psychophysiological changes associated with a type of meditation called therapeutic touch were examined. One therapeutic touch healer was studied for 2 days, alone and with three patients. EEG, GSR, EKG, and temperature were recorded. The main finding was a preponderance of fast beta EEG activity present in the healer. The physiological results are interpreted as representative of this type of meditative process. Problems involved in this type of research and suggestions for future research are discussed.

The physiological parameters recorded during meditative practices usually follow the direction of low arousal patterns. For example, the EEG during meditation often shows an increase in alpha and an enhancement of theta electroencephalographic (EEG) activity (Kasamatsu & Hirai, 1969). Yet alpha and theta EEG activity are only part of the many different physiological responses observed during meditation. Das and Gastaut (1955), Peper and Pollini (1976), and Banquet (1973) have observed an enhancement of synchronous beta EEG patterns in advanced meditators. We hypothesize that the different physiological observations are probably related to the *style* of the specific meditative process, with alpha/theta EEG low arousal as one endpoint of a continuum and fast-frequency beta EEG at the other.

The purposes of this chapter are to:

1. Present a hypothesis that EEG findings of meditation are on a continuum. One locus is alpha/theta activity as reported in a number of meditation studies (Bagchi and Wenger, 1957; Anand, Chhina, & Singh, 1961; Banquet, 1973; Kasamatsu & Hirai, 1969; Wallace, 1970); the other is a fast frequency beta, previously cited by Das and Gastaut, reobserved by Peper and Pollini (1976), and reobserved in this case study.
2. Report the observation that fast EEG activity is associated with therapeutic touch (fast EEG activity can also be defined as beta or synchronous beta EEG activity with a frequency range of 18–20 Hz).

Erik Peper • Center for Interdisciplinary Science, San Francisco State University, San Francisco, California 94132. Sonia Ancoli • Langley Porter Neuropsychiatric Institute, University of California, San Francisco, California 94122.

3. Speculate on the meaning of beta EEG frequency as compared to the usual findings of alpha and theta EEG activity in meditation, and how this may relate to the meditative process.
4. Suggest ways by which the psychophysiological outcome can be used to authenticate the meditative process and to assist learning of the meditative process.
5. Examine the psychophysiological changes that occurred during the healing meditation (therapeutic touch).
6. Suggest new strategies by which meditators can be studied.

This research note reports data from a single advanced meditator, Dr. Dolores Krieger (D.K.), who practices a meditation known as "therapeutic touch" (Krieger, 1976). Therapeutic touch has within it components of "the laying on of hands" and "bedside manner." D.K. teaches this meditation at the New York University Division of Nursing and she has practiced it for many years.

D.K. described that in the process of therapeutic touch, the healer becomes quiet, passively listens with her hands, and gently attunes herself to the patient. The healer places her hands upon the areas of "accumulated tension" in the patient and redirects these energies. In the process of touching, the healer reports that she uses herself as a model to "input energy" to help the healee rise to a level of comparative energy.

This is a complex form of meditative practice that involves the control of body energy centers known as chakras (Govinda, 1969, 1976; Evans-Wentz, 1967).

With therapeutic touch, as with other meditative practices, one focuses without effort—the mind is totally focused upon the healing touch and no thoughts enter awareness. Meditation is mindfulness ("attentiveness training"), a process not usually taught in our educational system. As the following exercise illustrates, when we do a task, extraneous thoughts usually enter unaware and we are not mindful: "Sit quietly and for the next two minutes look at your thumbnail. Observe it lovingly, do not judge it. Behold the thumbnail in active contemplation. At the end of 2 minutes, recount how many critical or unaware extraneous thoughts occurred."

With sustained practice, mindfulness can be achieved and the number of distracting thoughts will be reduced while the meditator's mind stays alert and passively focused.

PROBLEMS IN THIS TYPE OF RESEARCH

There are major problems in studying adept meditators, especially single subjects. [Some comparable problems in biofeedback have been described elsewhere (Peper, 1976a,b)].

1. The process is idiosyncratic, and it may not be possible to generalize it or replicate it with other individuals.

2. The conditions of baseline, experimental sessions, and postbaseline are artificial boundaries that the experimenter sets up. For the adept subject, these dichotomies and distinctions may not exist. For example, D.K. uses the therapeutic touch process as soon as she is seated quietly with the patient; therapeutic touch *implies* becoming aware of the patient. This process is automatic for her. She starts attuning to the patient the moment he/she enters. Hence, a "baseline condition" is actually a combined process of that baseline *plus* the healing meditation.

3. There may be no change in physiological functioning in a subject who for years has attuned herself to be in a different state of awareness. For her, there is no longer a difference between meditative and nonmeditative states.

Only a longitudinal study would indicate the physiological transformations of a meditator, a study that to date has not been done. However, a comparative study demonstrating EEG differences of alpha EEG amplitude and theta EEG trains has been reported with beginning, adept Zen meditators and nonmeditators (Kasamatsu & Hirai, 1969).

PATIENTS

Three patients were monitored while D.K. practiced therapeutic touch. They were: H.P., a 60-year-old male with a 5-year history of severe neck, back, and head pain; J.B., a 30-year-old female with a history of fibroid cysts in her breasts; and R.G., a 23-year-old female with a 3-year history of severe chronic migraine as well as one grand mal seizure. A fourth subject, A.B., with a history of severe backache, was eliminated because she was afraid that participation would jeopardize her workmen's compensation claim.

METHODS

D.K. was studied for 2 consecutive days. On Day 1, baseline levels were recorded from D.K. alone. Since most of the healing was done while D.K. was standing, data were collected for eyes open and closed, while sitting and standing.

Different electrode configurations were used to explore the therapeutic touch process. Grass cup electrodes and Grass electrode paste were used for bipolar EEG configurations located at O_2, O_1, F_{p_1}, and F_{p_1}, and the midpoints between (P_4-C_4), (C_4-F_4), (P_3-C_3), and (C_3-F_3) with earlobe as ground (Jasper, 1958). The electrooculograms (EOG) were recorded with slow or nonpolarizing biopotential skin electrodes (Beckman) attached to the outer and inner canthi of each eye. In addition, frontalis electromyographic (EMG) and left palmar galvanic skin response (GSR) leads were recorded. The EEG (O_1-P_3 and O_2-P_4) wrist-to-wrist heart rate (EKG), palmar GSR, and temperature from the hands were were also monitored for each patient.

APPARATUS

All recordings were done with the subjects in a softly lit, electrically shielded, sound-deadened acoustical chamber. The patients were either sitting or in the prone position with D.K. alternating between sitting and standing. All recordings were done on a Grass model 78D polygraph with four model 7P511G amplifiers, two wide-band AC preamplifier integrators (model 7P3B), and two low-level DC preamplifiers (model 7P1E). Sixty-Hz filters were used for each channel. (However, this did not filter out fast EEG frequencies.) In addition, the data from Day 1 were recorded on a Vetter Model A tape recorder.

RESULTS

The major observation was D.K.'s EEG record. Regardless of the experimental condition, it showed a preponderance of fast synchronous EEG activity, often embedded in a mixed EEG record, as is illustrated in Figure 1. (Even though fast beta EEG activity is often associated with certain medications, such as barbiturates [Kooi, 1971], D.K. was not taking any medication.) Since fast

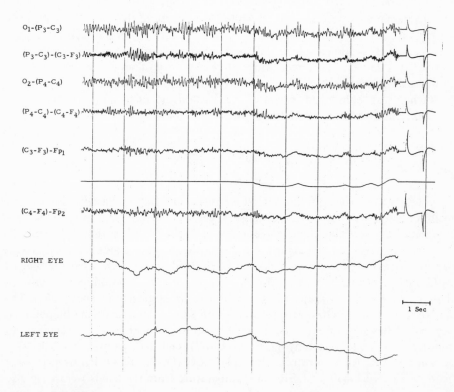

Figure 1. EEG and EOG recording of DK during eyes-open baseline. Note the preponderance of fast EEG (50 μV calibration).

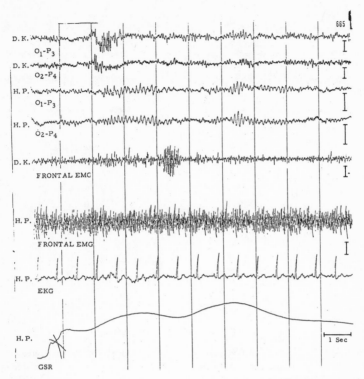

Figure 2. EEG and EMG recording during the therapeutic touch. Simultaneous recording of the patient (H.P.) and healer (D.K.). Observe that the increase in D.K.'s beta EEG is *not* associated with an increase in EMG. Also note the preponderance of alpha in the EEG of H.P. (50 μV calibration).

rhythmic EEG activity would be confused with EMG activity, D.K.'s frontalis EMG was compared with her EEG. As seen in Figure 2, fast EEG activity was also present during low frontalis EMG.

The EEG recording indicated that D.K. was not actively attending to outside cues. The EOG recording showed that her eyes were slightly diverged and showed *no* movement (i.e., no slow rolling or saccadic movements) during therapeutic touch, unless she shifted positions (see Figure 3).

No major changes were seen in the patients' EEG, EKG, EMG, temperature or GSR. All three patients basically showed a relaxed state with an abundance of large-amplitude alpha activity (both with eyes open and eyes closed) (see Figure 2). This was present in the baseline and did not change during the assessment or healing. All three patients reported that the therapeutic touch was relaxing and that they would again volunteer.

We do not know to what extent the improvement of the patients was related to the therapeutic touch experience, because the study was *not* intended to test whether therapeutic touch had healing effect. To study the healing properties of therapeutic touch, controlled studies need to be done. The patients who participated in this study were nominally screened for existing pathology.

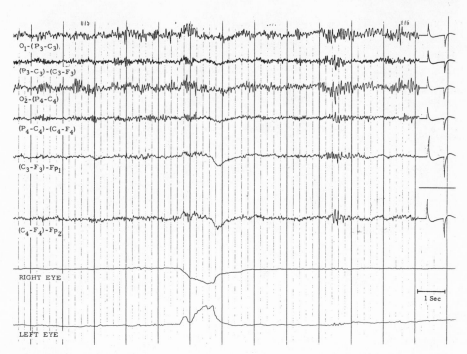

Figure 3. EEG and EOG recording of D.K. during therapeutic touch. Note the preponderance of beta EEG and the extremely stable eye position. Eye movement occurred only when D.K. moved or shifted position (50 μV calibration).

The improvement may not be related to the therapeutic touch experience and no claims can be made. However, the experience was important to the patients. As R.G. pointed out, "This was the first time that I felt that somebody (D.K.) really cared. It is so rare that somebody cares in a medical setting. In addition, I had tried to do something for myself. This made me feel better." Possibly therapeutic touch could be a technique to investigate placebo dynamics.

DISCUSSION

The fast synchronous EEG activity recorded from D.K. is *striking* and *contrary* to the commonly accepted finding that the EEG of meditators is associated with an increase of alpha and theta activity. There are a number of possibilities as to why fast EEG is not usually associated with meditation: (1) It is present in other meditators but not usually observed; (2) it is a parameter of an unstudied meditation process; (3) it is idiosyncratic to D.K.

The fast beta EEG activity may be more common than previously reported. Past researchers often could not observe this phenomenon because EEG was not analyzed for fast frequencies. In most studies of meditation, low pass filters were used, which filtered out frequencies greater than 15 Hz, therefore masking the observation of fast beta frequencies (Peper & Pollini, 1976). In addition, the data from EEG feedback studies are also meaningless, since in most studies alpha was defined but beta and theta were seen as "not alpha" (Peper, 1974; Ancoli & Kamiya, 1978).

The fast beta activity is probably not idiosyncratic to D.K., since fast beta activity and a decrease in alpha EEG activity have been reported in other meditators and most likely are associated with their particular meditative style (Das & Gastaut, 1955; Banquet, 1973; Peper & Pollini, 1976).

The predominant presence of beta in D.K.'s EEG during her meditation may represent the physiological style of her meditation. For example, in a meditation such as raja yoga, one can meditate upon a word or *mantra*. However, as one meditates upon the mantra, the "mind" may get distracted. One can be distracted by an itch, or hypnogogic imagery. This drifting may account for the high percentage of alpha and theta as well as for the Stage 1 sleep spindles observed in transcendental meditation (TM) meditators (Pagano, Rose, Stivers, & Warrenburg, 1975). However, meditation can also be focused passive attention, in which the mind is so well trained that the moment one sits quietly and meditates, *no* extraneous images or thoughts come in; one is totally attentive without effort.

For D.K., extraneous thoughts are no problem. She focuses without effort. As she reports, there are no longer ever any extraneous thoughts when she meditates—she passed through that process many years ago. Her eyes would focus at nothing in the distance so that she could passively attend to the sensation of the therapeutic touch experience (Figure 3). This carried over into her baseline periods. We interpret the presence of fast EEG activity in the subject as a learned passive control over her meditation to such an extent that she is totally focused and alert without ever drifting into hypnogogic imagery. We suspect that it is not the type of meditation that a person does that is important but rather *how* the person does it. For example, the person's mind (internal dialogue) is totally quiet. There are no extraneous thoughts while the person is focusing *passively with intention* upon a task.

When past psychophysiological data were recorded during meditation, the concurrent subjective reports or experiences were often lacking. This made any subjective interpretation of the data impossible. We suggest that fast EEG activity be used in combination with subjective reports to identify the style of an advanced meditator. The study of meditation must account for these psychophysiological (EEG) differences. This can be done by grouping meditators into those who show a preponderance of fast beta EEG activity during meditation and those who show an increase in slow alpha/theta EEG activity. This type of research would help to clarify the hypothesis that fast beta EEG indicates a passive-focused attention without interruptive thoughts, a meditative state separate from the usual alpha/theta EEG state in which some subjects allow themselves to drift into quiet pleasantness.

We hope that this report will suggest and encourage a more precise investigation of meditation both by studying the quality of the meditative experience and concurrently initiating an open-ended psychophysiological recording to avoid some of the pitfalls we have encountered.

We suggest that future research in therapeutic touch and meditation:

1. Look for other healers and meditators for similar psychophysiological patterns.

2. Explore new baseline paradigms so that the meditation is not confounded with the baseline condition, such as by having the patient and the healer in separate rooms, or by giving the meditator an active task to keep him from meditating.

3. Look at additional physiological measures for the relaxation response in the patient.

4. Feedback those components of the physiological response that were most meaningful to the meditative experience of the subjects. Both patients and healers could describe which feedback signal was associated with the healing qualities of the meditation.

5. Initiate EEG feedback training with subjects to explore the subjective and objective experience of EEG beta activity.

6. Include spectral analysis of the EEG data to more fully explore and understand the exact frequency distribution.

SUMMARY

A pilot investigation of therapeutic touch indicated that the healer showed a preponderance of fast EEG activity. These data suggest that EEG changes may be linked to attentive meditation styles.

ACKNOWLEDGMENTS. We appreciate the cooperation and discussion with Dr. Joe Kamiya, Dr. Dolores Krieger, Joanne Kamiya, and Jim Johnston, and the helpful assistance of Christopher Brown, Noel Mapstead, Tamar Morgan, Dr. Karen Naifeh, and Laura Stratachik. The material in this chapter was originally presented at the Biofeedback Society of America meeting at Orlando, Florida, March 1977.

REFERENCES

Anand, B. K., Chhina, G. S., & Singh, B. Some aspects of electroencephalographic studies in yogis. *Electroencephalography and Clinical Neurophysiology*, 1961, *13*, 452–456.

Ancoli, S., & Kamiya, J. Methodological issues in alpha biofeedback training. *Biofeedback and Self-Regulation*, 1978, *3*(2), 159–183.

Bagchi, B. K., & Wenger, M. A. Electrophysiological correlates of some yogi exercises. *Electroencephalography and Clinical Neurophysiology*, 1957, supplement no. 7, 132–149.

Banquet, J. P. Spectral analysis of the EEG in meditation. *Electroencephalography and Clinical Neurophysiology*, 1973, *35*, 143–151.

Das, N. N., & Gastaut, H. Variations de l'activité électrique du cerveau, du couer et des muscles sequielettiques au cours de la meditation et de "l'extase" yoguique. *Electroencephalography Clinical and Neurophysiology*, 1955, *6* (Suppl.), 211–219.

Evans-Wentz, W. Y. (Ed.). *Tibetan yoga and secret doctrines* (2nd ed.). London: Oxford University Press, 1967.

Govinda, Lama Anagarika. *Foundations of Tibetan mysticism*. London: Rider, 1969.

Govinda, Lama Anagarika. *Creative meditation and multidimensional consciousness*. Wheaton: Theosophical Publishing House, 1976.

Jasper, H. H. Report of the committee on methods of clinical examination in electroencephalography. *Electroencephalography Clinical and Neurophysiology*, 1958, *10*, 371-375.

Kasamatsu, A., & Hirai, T. An electroencephalographic study of the Zen meditation (Zazen). In C. Tart (Ed.), *Altered states of consciousness*. New York: Wiley, 1969, 489-501.

Kooi, K. A. *Fundamentals of electroencephalography*. New York: Harper, 1971.

Krieger, D. Healing by the laying-on of hands as a facilitator of bioenergetic exchange: The response of in-vivo human hemoglobin. *International Journal for Psychoenergetic Systems*, 1976, *2*.

Pagano, R. R., Rose, R. M., Stivers, R. M., & Warrenburg, W. S. Sleep during transcendental meditation. *Science*, 1975, *191*, 308.

Peper, E. Problems in heart rate and alpha electroencephalographic feedback: Is the control over the feedback stimulus meaningful? *Kybernetik*, 1974, *14*, 217-221.

Peper, E. Problems in biofeedback training: An experiential analogy—urination. *Perspectives in Biology and Medicine*, 1976, *19*(3), 4012-412. (a)

Peper, E. Passive attention: The gateway to consciousness and autonomic control. In P. G. Zimbardo & F. L. Ruch (Eds.), *Psychology and life*. Chicago: Scott Foresman, 1976. (b)

Peper, E., & Pollini, S. J. Fast beta activity: Recording limitations, problems and subjective reports. In *Proceedings of the Biofeedback Research Society*, Colorado Springs, 1976.

Wallace, R. K. Physiological effects of transcendental meditation. *Science*, 1970, *167*, 1751-1754.

10

Biofeedback Training: Holistic and Transpersonal Frontiers

Erik Peper, Kenneth R. Pelletier, and Barbara Tandy

Biofeedback is one of many tools in the current revolution in psychotherapy and medicine which places the responsibility for illness, health, and personal growth upon the individual. In this model, the therapist acts as a guide or a teacher in order to maximize the conditions for the trainee's growth and self-healing.

CONCEPTS OF DISEASE IN BIOFEEDBACK TRAINING

In order to benefit from biofeedback training, trainees usually have to change lifelong patterns. This challenging process is similar to stopping smoking, losing weight, or starting regular exercise programs. In the process of learning, the person realizes that the "dis-ease" has probably been related to an established stress and response pattern. As with any other tool in education, psychotherapy, or self-exploration, biofeedback training without a motivated subject and without the therapist's consideration of the multiplicity of physical and psychological aspects of a disorder may be useless or even harmful. The approach in clinical biofeedback is holistic and considers the individual's physical, psychological, and spiritual needs.

Trainees are not only ill with their symptoms but are also trapped with their self-images ("I cannot lose weight"; "I cannot control my migraine"). The limits of their personal beliefs limit their health. Over the course of many years they have developed rationalizations such as "I cannot take time from my family to practice relaxation." For trainees to attain wellness they need to change these beliefs and learn to reduce their illness-producing patterns. Trainees are encouraged to develop a new feeling about themselves and their bodies by learning skills that can be used to regulate themselves. Personal responsibility is an important aspect of the learning process. The knowledge "I have control" is the experiential counterpart of the undefined healing quality, often transmitted in the phenomenon of "bedside man-

Erik Peper • Center for Interdisciplinary Science, San Francisco State University, San Francisco, California 93134.   Kenneth R. Pelletier • Department of Psychiatry, University of California School of Medicine, San Francisco, California 94143.   Barbara Tandy • Institute for Research in Social Behavior, Oakland, California 94612.

ner," which a physician can generate in a patient—the inner confidence of getting well. The trainee is programming himself for success instead of failure. The therapist plays an important role by developing and supporting feedback signals that are meaningful to the trainee so that he does not experience failure. Thus biofeedback, rather than being crisis-oriented and placing responsibility for disease on others, aims for self-control, self-help, and self-responsibility. Many of the components of biofeedback also fulfill the major tenets of holistic health. These components include (1) positive wellness, not just absence of disease, as the goal; (2) the idea that the causes of most illness are found in the environment, life-style, and emotional–sensory balance; (3) prevention of illness is encouraged by the transformation of one's life; (4) healing of many chronic diseases may be possible; (5) illness is a process from which we can learn; (6) we are responsible for our own health.

THE PROCESS OF BIOFEEDBACK TRAINING

Feedback of various kinds shapes our responses and behavior in all aspects of life. Learning how to change or control the feedback signal may also mean changing and gaining control over other aspects of everyday life. In this way, the therapist helps the trainee understand how the biofeedback signal reflects the trainee's own body, and, in a larger sense, his life attitudes.

A common way to begin biofeedback training is to guide a trainee with relaxation exercises, in conjunction with electromyographic (EMG) feedback, so that he can allow himself to relax deeply. Usually as trainees learn to recognize and control relaxation, they feel less helpless. As the trainee learns to control the feedback signal, he also integrates relaxation exercises into his life at home and at work.

One major behavioral way to help this integration and transfer of learning is through the use of home practice, as well as keeping a daily log to enhance self-assessment (see Figure 1). Doing homework practices means the trainee has to interrupt a stress-producing routine, thus putting distance between himself and the stressor and becoming more detached—an unprogrammed global desensitization process. This process is usually supplemented by discussion or verbal education therapy.

Relaxation feedback training goes beyond learning to lower EMG levels. The trainee learns to sense the tension levels in everyday life. In the clinic, the person learns to tense, to feel the tensing, and to let go, and to correlate the physical experience with the feedback signal. At home, the trainee practices this control without equipment. The focus in relaxation training is both to *recognize* and to *control* the response, since autonomic control implies both the ability to increase and decrease a particular biological function.

Effective biofeedback training often takes many hours of practice. Trainees usually come for 2 to 4 months once or twice a week for feedback and/or discussion. During this time, the trainee also practices daily exercises at home.

Date _____ Name _____

1. What time did you go to bed?_____ How long did it take you to fall asleep? _____

   What time did you wake up? _____ Was your sleep restful or not? _____

   Did you dream?_____ Were the subjects pleasant or unpleasant? _____

2. Chemical intake during the day, including all medication:

   Coffee _____ cups   Cola drinks_____   Liquor _____   _____

   Tea_____cups   Beer _____   Others: _____

   Cigarettes _____   Wine _____   _____

3. List and identify the practice sessions you performed, the time of day you did them, and what you experienced while doing them.

   1. _____

   2. _____

   3. _____

   4. _____

   5. _____

   6. _____

Physical exercise (when, what) _____
_____

When did you feel most tense today?_____

Why? _____

Were you tired during the day? _____

Intensity of symptoms (please label medication on chart):

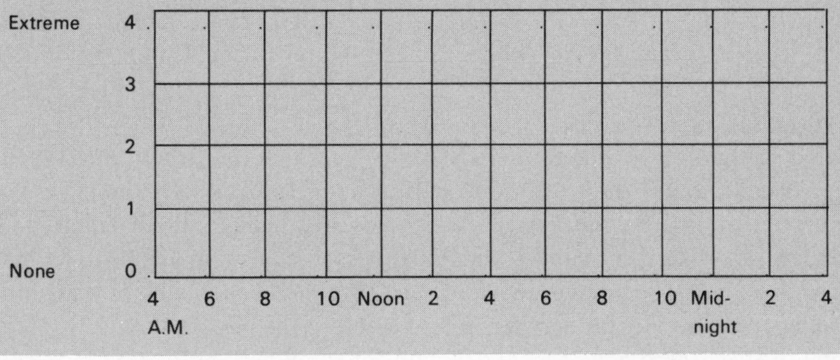

Figure 1. Daily log that trainees fill out. It is helpful in monitoring long-term changes (clinical efficacy) in identifying daily stressors that may be related to symptoms, and as a reminder for the trainee to practice the newly learned skill to encourage transfer of learning.

TYPICAL CLINICAL APPLICATIONS OF BIOFEEDBACK

Biofeedback in Physical Rehabilitation

Biofeedback for muscle reeducation, as in physical rehabilitation, has not been emphasized enough. It is an instrumental method by which a person may recontrol his own body. Training should be started rapidly after any neuromuscular accident and should be incorporated into the rehabilitation program before compensating habits develop. Many successes of this type have been reported by Marinacci (1968), who has applied EMG feedback for muscle reeducation since the 1950s. Here feedback is used to let the trainee hear the muscle spasm and teach him to decrease it. In addition, the trainee may learn to tense muscles and discriminate among movements if the feedback is given from several muscles and shaping procedures are used. With portable equipment, trainees can have intensive daily training sessions at home.

In the case of one of our trainees, who had mild left hemiplegia with spasticity and paralysis in the left arm due to stroke, feedback was given from the extensor and then the flexor muscles and finally from both. The purpose was to allow the muscles in her hand, which was in a claw position, to relax so that the spasticity might stop. Then she began to learn to tense other muscles independently and differentially. After 20 weeks of diligent practice, she could do such tasks as opening a door and using an electric toothbrush. Even for such seemingly "pure" physical disorders, biofeedback training tends to point out psychological problems or connections. In the course of training, this woman's sense of her arm as a dead and useless appendage changed, and she began a psychological reconnection with it as she began to use it more.

We worked with another trainee who for 5 years had suffered from a spastic torticollis. Previous biofeedback therapy had aggravated her symptoms by having her tense the trapezius muscles opposing the contraction. We instructed her to passively attend to relaxing the stressed muscle, "allowing" her head to turn. This modification from active to passive volition proved successful.

Encouraging results have been reported in many other rehabilitation cases. Marinacci has trained patients with Bell's palsy, causalgia, nerve injury, residual anterior poliomyelitis, and CVAs, while Booker, Rubow, and Coleman (1969) have successfully facilitated retraining of the facial muscles in a patient with severance of the facial nerve.

A related category of trainees includes cases in which the person developed incorrect physical habits, such as subvocalization (Hardyck, Petrinovich, & Ellsworth 1966). In this category such symptoms did not fulfill an emotional need. Feedback is an external path by which the person can sense and redirect his internal programming. The process is similar to that of a coach who is teaching someone the correct motion for serving in tennis. Here the person should be able to learn rapidly since there is no secondary gain for the illness-producing pattern. In cases where the trainee needs only to correct misapplied physiological tension, such as in subvocalization, feedback training alone may suffice. The more the symptom is entwined with the trainee's personality, the more the trainee needs other nonbiofeedback skills.

Biofeedback in Psychotherapy

At the opposite end of the continuum lie the uses of biofeedback in formal psychotherapy. Changes in physiology reflect psychological processes that point out to the trainee and therapist that the body/mind has acted. Physiological changes can be used to help focus the trainee on recognizing their inner experience. In a therapeutic setting, feedback signals can help the therapist direct the therapy. For instance, in the case of feedback of hand temperature, the trainee's temperature occasionally goes *down* after the instruction for warmth. To the therapist, such a reversal may indicate some type of psychological resistance.

An overlooked method of potential value in psychotherapy is galvanic skin response feedback and monitoring. Toomim and Toomim (1975) have used the method in their clinical practice. They differentiate among overreactors, whose GSR responds excessively; underreactors, whose GSR does not respond to emotional stimuli; and medial reactors, whose GSR clearly reflects emotional changes; and they train each type differently. Using GSR, both the therapist and the trainee are aware of the trainee's body–mind processes. The GSR is a useful device for showing graphically the subject's different physiological arousal levels.

Biofeedback Training for Unstressing and Health Maintenance

Broadly stated, the major application of clinical biofeedback is to teach deep relaxation and self-control for health restoration and health maintenance. It is ironic that biofeedback, like many innovative techniques, has often been applied to the most seriously ill trainees for whom standard medical treatment is of no avail; only recently has it been applied to the currently healthy potential patient.

The greatest efficacy can be expected when relaxation skills are learned in cases where only minor symptoms have occurred. The most promising application is educational—overcoming habitual chronic stress responses in reasonably healthy people. For example, muscle feedback relaxation can be used to wean subjects from their tranquilizers or soporifics (Love, personal communication, 1973). A person in preventive training learns to achieve deep relaxation so that he can avoid developing somatic symptoms of stress after experiencing external and internal stresses (Stoyva & Budzynski, 1973). This approach may avoid the development of illness as predicted by Holmes and Rahe (1967), who have indicated that illnesses of all kinds are often precipitated by prolonged or transient life stresses—such as marriage, divorce, vacation, death in the family, or even job promotion—in the preceding 2 years. Biofeedback training assumes the hypothesis that if a person learns to unstress himself consciously from chronic pressure or trauma, he may be able to avoid chronic stress-induced illness.

In our own experience, subtle positive side effects often occur as a result of preventive biofeedback training for unstressing. For example, one migraine trainee slowly learned control and her headaches became shorter in duration. An unexpected side effect of the training was that she no longer had palpitations of the heart, a symptom she used to have before training. Another trainee with migraine reported that she no longer needed her before-dinner cocktail—she could now let go of the tensions of the day without it.

Unstressing is a major factor for amelioration of hypertension. Moeller and Love (1972) used EMG feedback from the frontalis in conjunction with multiple homework exercises to train hypertensive patients in deep relaxation, and achieved an 11% decrease in both systolic and diastolic pressure after 16 weeks of training.

These relaxation concepts can be applied to everyday stresses long before disease begins to appear. For example, one of our trainees, an opera singer who keyed himself up before the performance to project his voice, needed several hours to dissipate built-up internal tension after a performance. With EMG training, he rapidly learned to quiet down and could go to sleep within a half hour after a performance. In addition, in Europe and Japan autogenic training has been used to prevent tensing before athletic contests. One of our trainees used relaxation before gymnastics and found that she performed better. Deep relaxation feedback training can also be used before surgery or as an adjunct technique for natural childbirth. Relaxing before the event can also be applied to stressful business and social situations.

Many common behavior problems and neuroses and many somatic symptoms, such as migraine and tension headaches, ulcerated colitis, and spastic colon, are habitual responses to stress. For instance, one of our trainees, who had achieved some control over migraines, lapsed into a headache under the stress of learning that her son was involved in illegal activity.

When everyday stresses include the roles at home or at work, the trainee not only has to learn a new skill but also has to readjust his life-style to accept new and different responsibilities. Often communication skills and family counseling are necessary in order to create enough flexibility in the environment to support trainees' new life patterns. Such trainees need to learn biofeedback skills in a holistic setting.

The following case example illustrates the holistic approach in which multiple factors interact to help a trainee regain control.

The subject was a 39-year-old professional woman, married, with children. She had had a spastic colon for 5 years, with heavy drug intake and restricted diet. She had frequent lower abdominal pain, constipation, and diarrhea. Our training program consisted of teaching her relaxation and hand warming with feedback, and finally having her subjectively "move a warm blanket" over her colon to relax it (an internal transfer-of-learning situation). Feedback helped develop a reacquaintance with her body and a sense of control; however, biofeedback was only a segment of the reeducational process. Early in the training, a hypnotic induction was used to ask her to find a mental sanctuary where she could be and do what she wanted. This led to an important therapeutic situation because since childhood she had never been asked what *she* would like to do. She was also taught other relaxation exercises and encouraged to go to a yoga class for breathing techniques. After attaining some voluntary control and practicing the exercises at home and at work, she recognized the massive tensions she was enduring on her job. The experience of looking for and being offered another job greatly enhanced her self-image. Although she kept her old job, she handled its tensions differently. She independently took herself off all her medication,* and after suffering the classic delayed barbiturate withdrawal symptoms, was drug-free and increasingly symptom-free. She continued seeing a psychiatrist. After a year, she said of herself, "Cheerfulness no longer seems a mask but a part of my fundamental outlook. The physical symptoms are well under control but I realize now that they always were secondary. I think the greatest validity of biofeedback was in getting me to think about my own needs instead of seeing myself only in the role of servicing others." For her, biofeedback was the door opener that allowed the process of growth. The success was due also to numerous other techniques, including family and job couseling, rational therapy, hypnotic guidance, assertiveness training, and psychotherapy.

Deep Relaxation States for Advanced Self-Teaching

Biofeedback training is a potent tool for teaching deep relaxation. When deeply relaxed, one can listen to oneself more clearly without preconceptions. In many ways, deep relaxation means letting the mind go and loosening the bonds of the ego. A person who is quiet enough to stop verbalizing may be able to enter a hypnogogic state and gain access to his unconscious.

Hypo-aroused states, such as electroencephalographic (EEG) theta, or very low electromyographic levels, can be used for self-programming and sleep learning (Budzynski & Peffer, 1974). Green (1974) used theta EEG feedback training to develop imagery, creativity, and integrative experiences. Or one can use these states of consciousness for enhanced self-awareness. For example, Peper has had trainees use this deeply relaxed state to "ask" their unconscious some question important for their personal growth. One of those trainees asked herself, when deeply quiet, how she should grow, and waited for hypnogogic images. The message, "love yourself," inscribed cartoon-style on a balloon, was deeply meaningful for her. Deeply relaxed states, used attentively by a receptive trainee, offer unlimited potential for personal growth.

Biofeedback training and the closely allied autogenic training and meditation skills require a person to face himself: He has the ultimate responsibility for the training. The person may develop a positive attitude by focusing on positive, objectively measured feedback skills. Biofeedback training emphasizes the trainee's active participation by promoting independence from the therapist and by encouraging intensive therapeutic work at home. Success lies in stopping the critically analytical intellect and in physical relaxation. With considerable

---

* It is strongly recommended that individuals do not independently withdraw medications but rather do it under the supervision and consultation of a health professional.

practice, a person learns enough subtle nonverbal cues to enter this quasi-meditative state on command.

FRONTIERS IN CLINICAL BIOFEEDBACK

Emphasis in this discussion has been on a few pragmatic applications of biofeedback. As with any dynamic discipline, the directions and capabilities of biofeedback are constantly expanding while incorporating new technologies and new perceptions about body, mind, and spirit interactions. When put in the context of autogenic training (Luthe, 1969) and progressive relaxation (Jacobson, 1938, 1970), the frontiers of biofeedback are multifold. Sensitively applied, biofeedback can be helpful in many clinical and psychiatric disorders such as gastrointestinal, cardiovascular, and neuromuscular disorders. The potentials of biofeedback in therapy are vast and are limited only by the practitioner's ingenuity. For example, French, Fahrion, and Leeb (1973) have successfully trained five human subjects to induce hand warming, and subsequently to attain scrotal heating with thermal feedback. This paradigm arose from data indicating that external applications of heat to the scrotum would cause the sperm count to decrease. After 5 consecutive days of scrotal heating the sperm count was reduced below fertility levels in all five subjects. Such warming may thus prove feasible as a potential means for nonpharmaceutical male birth control.

On the other hand, negative research results should not necessarily deter further experimentation. Simonton (personal communication, 1973) was unsuccessful in attempting to control his own white blood cells. When he attempted to increase his white cell count, his conceptual medical training interfered, for each attempt was thwarted by the knowledge that an increase in white blood cells might indicate leukemia and his thoughts, "I do not want leukemia," countermanded thoughts of increasing his white blood cell count. Similarly, his fear of leaving himself open to infection confounded his attempt to lower his white cell count. This "negative" result does not illustrate the impossibility of the proposed task but rather shows how the subjective ambivalence of the researcher-subject affected the learning process.

Several highly specialized and so far little-used forms of biofeedback seek to achieve localized control of different biological functions with specific sensors. Here, the emphasis is on developing the proper sensors for a specific function to be controlled. For example, a small strain gauge around the penile shaft has been developed to give penile erection feedback so that the subject and therapist may become aware of penile changes in overcoming impotence. Gorman and Kamiya (1972) have trained subjects to change their stomach pH, a procedure that could be a treatment for ulcers. Temperature feedback has become an efficient way to train patients with Raynaud's disease. Air-resistance feedback to teach changes in bronchial diameter may have applications to asthma and other respiratory diseases (Vachon & Rich, 1976) while Peper (1977) has explored vaginal photoplethysmographic feedback and pubococcygeal muscle feedback for awareness of sexual arousal. However, many of these sensors are at present elaborate and experimental, and therefore not used widely. Future developments could range from a vaginal pH feedback system to control fertility and yeast infections to intraocular pressure feedback for the treatment of glaucoma.

Even when a trainee is learning localized control, he has to be quiet to allow internal changes to take place. It is not necessary for him to understand how the control takes place in order to succeed. the stage of quieting is fundamental to more generalized uses of biofeedback and autogenic training. An important point to note in the clinical applications we have discussed is that physical changes are accompanied by profound alterations in the individual's perceptions of himself and others. Frequently, trainees report vivid altered states of consciousness that are strikingly analogous to experiences of persons during meditation.

Clinical biofeedback and meditative practices share a common ground in transpersonal psychology since they emphasize the attainment of a state of relaxed internal awareness as a prerequisite to achieving insight and growth. In both systems, the person is asked to attend passively in a quiet environment. During this time, the individual attempts to identify and develop a synchrony between body/mind/spirit consciousness. This practice is rare in the Western world, where a person usually does not sit, listen, or reflect upon himself, but continuously acts externally. A more internally oriented posture needs to be adopted in order to achieve autonomic control whether through biofeedback or meditation.

In biofeedback, the control of subtle psychophysiological functions such as change in blood flow is dependent upon the individual's ability to turn his attention away from active mental concentration toward a state of passive attention so that autonomic control can be achieved (Pelletier and Peper, 1977). Similarly, in the Tibetan Buddhist tradition, the initial step is Kum Nye, a technique for physical relaxation accompanied by a state of passive attention. Other meditative systems, such as transcendental meditation or Zazen, require a similar passive, waiting attitude. A meditation master, or guru, in effect provides feedback to the meditator, gauging his progress and instructing his further development.

One of the differences between biofeedback training and meditation is that biofeedback amplifies biological signals. This information is neutral, and biofeedback training is only a technique with no accompanying dogma. An advantage of biofeedback over nonfeedback techniques is that the physiological information tells an individual precisely how he is functioning. With feedback, the person knows exactly how tense certain muscles are, and whether certain techniques relax those muscles. Another similar role in giving feedback occurs in the therapist–trainee exchange in body therapies. In fact, a body therapist can use feedback monitoring and training as an additional tool to make manifest various subtle changes occurring in the trainee's body, and to enhance the trainee's sensitivity to such changes. In order to assess the trainee's progress in clinical biofeedback, meditation, and body therapies, both therapist and trainee need accurate, objective, ongoing information, which biofeedback can provide.

Biofeedback is a technique that mirrors a person's psychophysiology. In order to use the information from the mirror, the person needs to be aware that the image reflected is his; be aware that he might desire to change the image; believe that he is capable of changing the image; and experience change, growth, and control so that he knows he is actually changing.

How the individual changes depends upon how he uses the information presented in the mirror. The emphasis in clinical biofeedback (as in meditative practice) is placed upon maximizing a person's self-awareness so that he can sense an alternative manner of acting and being in his environment. How this process takes place is difficult to verbalize. The establishment of autonomic control is equally difficult to explain or describe. One link between voluntary and autonomic learning is that both are dependent upon an unobservable internal process involving the person's attention and attitudes.

Investigating passive attention to simple biological and psychological functions such as breathing, heart rate, defecation, thought processes, and muscle contractions is a basic tenet of all meditative systems. Autonomic control in biofeedback is based upon the same principle of passive attention. All autonomic learning depends on focusing passive attention on a simple function and creating a harmonious interaction of mind and body. The necessity of achieving this synchrony is clearly recognized in meditative systems but is often ignored in the purely technological, conditioning approaches to biofeedback. When the interaction between mind and body is ignored or eliminated in biofeedback, training in autonomic control is, not surprisingly, often unsuccessful.

Although biofeedback is perceived as a Western scientific approach to enhance control, in practice the trainee learns to allow unusual internal phenomena to occur. He slowly allows the muscle tension to decrease and/or the alpha/theta EEG to stay on. During the feedback learning the trainee for the first time actively participates in "doing nothing"—sitting quietly and relaxing. He sits down and listens to himself, neither grasping nor suppressing any thoughts or emotions. After reaching a certain criterion of relaxation, the trainee has entered, without knowing and without instruction, a spontaneous Vipasana meditation. Through biofeedback learning and its related techniques, the trainee experiences the concept of passive volition. Through the many phases of this process (especially if autogenic training is used) the trainee experiences spontaneous shifts of consciousness and corresponding body sensations in a nonthreatening unfolding. Deep relaxation and passive attention are the window to the unconscious.

With this experience, trainees become aware of the richness of quietness and often seek additional guidance for internal development. By this time the trainee is not hostile to transpersonal concepts. This self-development is encouraged and we suggest to the trainee either additional reading material or classes in meditation.

Sometimes, however, trainees experience anxiety in deeper relaxed states. The sensations of relaxation feel threatening. Such trainees avoid these sensations by tensing. Possibly these sensations trigger a reexperience of past physically traumatic events (Luthe, 1969). In such situations, we teach the trainee merely to allow the sensations to pass through him. This process of release appears to be similar to the Kryas in meditation, which occur when consciousness shifts and relaxes. In this way, a trainee may allow himself to change subjective avoidance behavior that has shaped his inner life. The person in effect desensitizes himself to the sensations of the altered state of awareness, as well as to the discharges of body/mind-held tensions. As in autogenic training, before growth can continue, the body/mind has to discharge these painful experiences so that they are no longer avoided and blocked. The importance of previous traumas has been underscored by Luthe (1969). After the person is familiar with moving through different levels of consciousness, the process of transpersonal growth can continue. Consequently, during the deep relaxation that follows, the trainees often experience sensations of unity—they merge with the room, the chair, the light, the therapist. . . .

Such marked altered states constitute a vast area of inquiry, which cannot be adequately covered here. Our observation has been that the process of self-healing by means of biofeedback and guided visualizations inevitably involves the individual in a process of growth and profound transpersonal experiences. These experiences are extremely important in the alleviation of many disorders.

Too often, such profound altered state experiences are dismissed or ignored as simply interesting anecdotes with few objective implications. Actually, we have found that these experiences create a marked transformation of the personality and have pragmatic applications in holistic therapy. Evoked through clinical biofeedback training, these experiences are vital in maintaining, correcting, and enhancing psychological and physical health.

For example, Peper, Robinson, Craig, and Jampolsky at the Center for Attitudinal Healing, using such a self-healing approach with open-angle glaucoma patients, found that in 10 of the 19 patients (average age 53.6 years; "mean" years of disease, 12.1) that eye pressures dropped significantly, as shown in Figure 2 (Peper, 1978). A number of the trainees reported that this program has changed their lives.

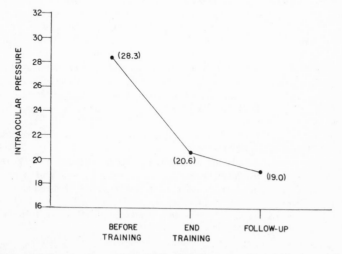

Figure 2. The average intraocular pressure (IOP) of the 10 successful trainees (out of the 19 who participated). Success was defined as a significant decrease in IOP or medication during and following the 10-week holistic training program. Average follow-up was 1.6 years.

Finally, the true frontiers of biofeedback lie not in the indiscriminate application of machines to bodies but in the sensitive adaptation of multiple therapies to each individual. Thus the frontiers are limited only by current technology and by the creativity of therapists in constructing a system in which the trainee's dignity, self-regulation, and growth are enhanced and developed.

ACKNOWLEDGMENTS. We wish to thank Gay Luce for her help in formulating research and drafting this paper, and Sonia Ancoli for her helpful comments.

REFERENCES

Booker, H. E., Rubow, R. T., & Coleman, P. J. Simplified feedback in neuromuscular retraining: An automated approach using electromyographic signals. *Archives of Physical Medicine and Rehabilitation*, 1969, *50*, 621–625.

Budzynski, T., & Peffer, K. Twilight state learning: The presentation of learning material during a biofeedback produced altered state. *Proceedings of the Biofeedback Research Society*. Denver: Biofeedback Research Society, 1974.

French, D., Fahrion, S., & Leeb, C. Self-induced scrotal hyperthermis in man followed by a drecrease in sperm output: A preliminary report. *Andrologie*, 1973, *5*(4), 311–316.

Forman, P., & Kamiya, J. *Voluntary control of stomach pH*. Research note presented at the Biofeedback Research Society, Boston, November 1972.

Green, A. Brainwave training, imagery, creativity and integrative experiences. *Proceedings of the Biofeedback Research Society*. Denver: Biofeedback Research Society, 1974.

Hardyck, C. D., Petrinovich, L. F., & Ellsworth, D. W. Feedback of speech muscle activity during silent reading: Rapid extinction. *Science*, 1966, *154*, 1467–1468.

Holmes, T. H., & Rahe, R. H. The social readjustment rating scale. *Journal of Psychosomatic Research*, 1967, *1*, 213–218.

Jacobson, E. *Progressive relaxation* (2d ed.). Chicago: University of Chicago Press, 1938.

Jacobson, E. *Modern treatment of tense patients*. Springfield, Illinois: Charles C Thomas, 1970.

Luthe, W. (Ed.). *Autogenic therapy*. New York: Grune and Stratton, 1969.

Marinacci, A. A. *Applied electromyography*. Philadelphia: Lea & Febinger, 1968.

Moeller, T. A., & Love, W. A. *A method to reduce arterial hypertension through muscular relaxation*. Paper presented at the Biofeedback Research Society, Boston, November 1972.

Pelletier, K. R., & Peper, E. The chutzpah factor in altered states of consciousness. *Journal of Humanistic Psychology*, 1977, *17*, 63–73.

Peper, E. Presidential address to the Biofeedback Society of America, Orlando, Florida, March 1977.

Peper, E. Problems in biofeedback training: An experiential analogy—urination. *Perspectives in Biology and Medicine*, 1976, *19*, 404–412.

Peper, E. Putting caring back into health care. Presidential Address of the Biofeedback Society of California, Millbrae, California, 1978.

Stoyva, J., & Budzynski, T. Cultivated low arousal—an anti-stress response? In L. V. DiCara (Ed.), *Recent advances in limbic and autonomic nervous system response*. New York: Plenum, 1973.

Toomim, M. K., & Toomim, H. GSR biofeedback in psychotherapy: Some clinical observations. *Psychotherapy: Theory, Research and Practice*, 1975, *1*, 33–38.

Vachon, L., & Rich, E. S. Visceral learning in asthma. *Psychosomatic Medicine*, 1976, *38*, 122–130.

COMPLEMENTARY TECHNIQUES

This section focuses on the complementary techniques that enhance the effectiveness of biofeedback. To fully understand biofeedback, clinicians, students, and researchers need to be familiar with autogenic therapy techniques (AT), progressive relaxation techniques (PR), as well as many other approaches ranging from meditation, hypnosis, and behavior therapy to assertiveness training (see Appendix A).

Learning autonomic control has no innate philosophy of its own but incorporates those of other disciplines. One major technique, which for the last 50 years has systematically explored homeostatic self-regulation, is autogenic training.

Autogenic therapy has been used for numerous clinical problems ranging from diabetes, angina, hypertension, and stuttering to childbirth and sports. Guidelines and precautions have been developed for its use and are applicable to biofeedback and any other stress management program that incorporates relaxation techniques. By using the AT model, the biofeedback professional can avoid autonomic training strategies that can be deleterious to the trainee, e.g., teaching subjects to warm their foreheads, a procedure that causes headaches.

Finally, by incorporating AT into biofeedback procedures, new clinical as well as personal growth strategies can be developed, e.g., teaching hay fever subjects to cool their nose and throat to allow the nasal passage to decongest.

Luthe (Chapter 11) describes the encompassing field of AT. We want to reinforce the idea that persons planning to do clinical or educational biofeedback would be well advised to familiarize themselves with autogenic therapy.

In addition, anyone seriously investigating biofeedback should also be familiar with the technique of progressive relaxation. Developed by Edmund Jacobson in the first part of the century, PR was one of the first relaxation techniques systematically studied. Its components have been incorporated into almost all relaxation procedures, stress management feedback training programs, and home practice techniques to encourage transfer of learning of the feedback skill. Patterson (Chapter 12) gives a short overview of this important technique.

Issues to consider in many of the following clinical articles are how much of the success or failure is due to the incorporation of these relaxation techniques in the treatment methods, and what other variables might be influencing the clinical outcome in these studies.

One major unexplored area, which underlies all learning strategies, is experimental bias, set, and placebo. We included these topics in this section because of the powerful effects they have on outcome. It is hoped that we can learn to *use* these phenomena to enhance biofeedback learning.

Placebo is important in the care of patients. The dimensions underlying it (experimental belief, trainees' expectations) are often difficult to assess. It is critical that research procedures are developed to optimize the placebo effect. Components of the placebo effect include the trainee's beliefs and attitudes. Quinn (Chapter 13) focuses upon the significant role belief and attitude play in the therapeutic process by presenting several belief categories. The constant interaction between belief and experience is one process that occurs during the biofeedback training. Belief affects experience (performance) and performance affects belief. In the end, the trainee no longer believes but "knows" that visceral control is possible. This delicate difference between belief and knowing is illustrated in the following anecdote:

A married couple are sitting on a bench with their five kids—the husband believes the kids are his, while his wife knows . . .

Although belief is important, it needs to be matched with performance at the feedback task. This is the issue that Stroebel and Glueck eloquently address in Chapter 14. Finally, Gibb, Stephan, and Rohm (Chapter 15) describe an experiment exploring the effects of mental expectation involved in the relief of stress in various groups, thus suggesting that belief structure should be enhanced to maximize biofeedback learning in clinical and educational settings.

The major questions and issues to remember from this chapter when reading the other sections are:

1. What additional relaxation techniques are used?
2. How did the relaxation techniques affect the biofeedback training results?
3. What was the investigators' belief bias?
4. What was the trainee's belief bias?

For overviews on PR, the reader is referred to Bernstein and Borkovec (1973) and Jacobson (1970, 1974, 1976), as well as to Waterman, Tandy, and Peper (1978) for an extensive relaxation bibliography. For an overview of AT, an exhaustive collection of materials and case reports may be found in Luthe's series of books on autogenic therapy (Luthe & Schultz, 1969a,b,c; Luthe, 1970a,b, 1973). The reader is also advised to read Rosa (1976) and the manual of the training workshop sponsored by the Biofeedback Society of America which was written by Luthe (1977). Further information on AT can be obtained from the International Committee on Autogenic Training (see Appendix B). Relaxation tapes are also available (see Appendix B).

Two other important readings in the area of placebo are by Beecher (1959) and Shapiro (1960).

REFERENCES

Beecher, H. K. *Measurement of subjective responses: Quantitative effects of drugs.* New York: Oxford University Press, 1959.

Bernstein, D. A., & Borkovec, T. D. *Progressive relaxation training: A manual for the helping professions.* Champaign, Illinois: Research Press, 1973.

Jacobson, E. *Modern treatment of tense patients.* Springfield, Illinois: Charles C Thomas, 1970.

Jacobson, E. *Progressive relaxation* (3rd rev. ed.). Chicago: University of Chicago Press, 1974. (Originally published, 1938.)

Jacobson, E. *You must relax* (5th ed.). New York: McGraw-Hill, 1976. (Originally published, 1934.)

Luthe, W. *Autogenic therapy* (Vol. 4). *Research and theory.* New York: Grune and Stratton, 1970. (a)

Luthe, W. *Autogenic therapy* (Vol. 5). *Dynamics of autogenic neutralization.* New York: Grune and Stratton, 1970. (b)

Luthe, W. *Autogenic therapy* (Vol. 6). *Treatment with autogenic neutralization.* New York: Grune and Stratton, 1973.

Luthe, W. *Introduction to the Methods of Autogenic Therapy.* Manual for a workshop sponsored by the Biofeedback Society of America. Denver: Biofeedback Society of America, 1977.

Luthe, W., & Schultz, J. H. *Autogenic therapy* (Vol. 1). *Autogenic methods.* New York: Grune and Stratton, 1969. (a)

Luthe, W., & Schultz, J. H. *Autogenic therapy* (Vol. 2). *Medical applications.* New York: Grune and Stratton, 1969. (b)

Luthe, W., & Schultz, J. H. *Autogenic therapy* (Vol. 3). *Applications in psychotherapy.* New York: Grune and Stratton, 1969. (c)

Rosa, K. *You and AT.* New York: E. P. Dutton & Co., Inc. 1976.

Shapiro, A. Contribution to a history of the placebo effect. *Behavior Science*, 1960, *5*(2), 109–135.

Waterman, D., Tandy, B., & Peper, E. *Relaxation bibliography*, Denver: Biofeedback Society of America, 1978.

11

About the Methods of Autogenic Therapy

Wolfgang Luthe

One of the most important assumptions of autogenic therapy is that nature has provided man with homeostatic mechanisms not only to regulate fluid and electrolyte balance, blood pressure, heart rate, wound healing and so on, but also to readjust more complicated functional disorders that are of a mental nature. In autogenic therapy the term *homeostatic self-regulatory brain mechanisms* is often used.[38,39,51] This concept assumes that when a person is exposed to excessive disturbing stimulation (either emotional or physical trauma), the brain has the potential to utilize natural biological processes to reduce the disturbing consequences of the stimulation (i.e., neutralization). At the mental level some of this self-regulatory neutralization or recuperation occurs naturally during sleep and dreams.[40,48]

The techniques developed and used in autogenic therapy have been designed to support and facilitate the natural self-healing mechanisms that already exist. Thus the emphasis is not in trying to control the natural system but rather on helping natural systems use their inherent potentials of self-regulatory adjustment more fully.

There has been a tendency in American medicine to overemphasize symptomatic treatment and to overlook the unity of the individual. This "left-hemispheric" approach[9,21,43,56] has resulted in a preference for easy clearcut mechanical solutions (e.g., inject, operate, prescribe more medication).

These pragmatic solutions all attempt to control or modify certain functional or structural variables through manipulative procedures imposed onto the biological system from outside. The approach often adopted is analogous to the way one would go about repairing a defective television set. In many situations (e.g., pneumonia, acute appendicitis) this outside manipulation of the defective biological system is clearly the best solution to the problem. However, there exists a great variety of functional and psychosomatic disorders where such a mechanical, "nonhomeostatic" approach is not the best answer and may even be deleterious.[17,18]

Autogenic therapy has always seen the mind and body as a unit and approaches mental and bodily functions simultaneously. Autogenic methods permit adaptation of the treatment program to the individual. Of practical

Wolfgang Luthe • Medical Centre, Montreal, Canada.

importance is the fact that patients learn to do most of the therapeutic work by themselves at home, and that the most frequently used clinical method, autogenic standard training, can be applied in groups ranging from elementary school children to the elderly. In certain disturbances such as sleep disorders[48] or examination anxiety[52] significant improvements within 2 weeks or less are not exceptional. Often patients are freed of their reliance on tranquilizers and hypnotics. The practical implications are obvious. The degree of dependence on the physician is kept at a low level. In addition, the therapist using autogenic approaches is able to make more efficient use of his time than with most other psychotherapeutic methods. An increased number of patients can be treated in the same amount of time. (See Figure 1.)

The combination of methods available provides effective and flexible treatment techniques for many organic, psychosomatic, and psychiatric disorders.

In the area of nonclinical application, autogenic methods have been used in everyday life both to improve the efficiency of various bodily or mental activities and as a psychophysiologic self-protection against the damaging effects of stress. The encouraging results of regular practice of AT and specifically adapted approaches have stimulated increasing application and research in the areas of education, industry, sports, and creativity.

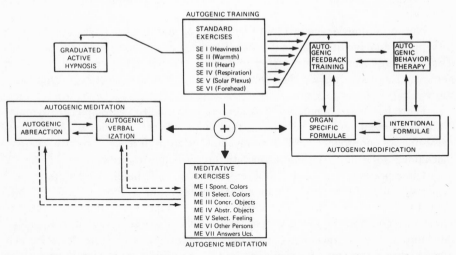

Figure 1. Autogenic methods: combinations and procedural interaction. This illustrates the various methods that can be applied in autogenic therapy. *Autogenic Training* (AT) is the foundation for all other approaches and is therefore the most important and widely used technique. Of the many methods, autogenic training alone is sufficient for the majority of treatment situations. However, in 10–20% of patients, because of the history or the nature of the disorder, a more intensive method called *Autogenic Neutralization* (AN) may be necessary. *Meditative Exercises* (ME), *Autogenic Modification* (AM), and *Graduated Active Hypnosis* (GAH) are less frequently employed and are reserved for special situations. *Autogenic Feedback Training* (AFT) and *Autogenic Behavior Therapy* (ABT) are relatively new techniques that are the result of interdisciplinary interaction.

Over the past 10 years an increasing number of studies of the effects of autogenic training (AT) have provided information pointing toward the practical usefulness of psychophysiologic relaxation in the area of education. University professors, schoolteachers, adolescent high school students, and younger elementary school children who learn AT for noneducational reasons consistently report favorable effects that directly or indirectly influence their behavior and performance in the educational sector.[52] Such individual observations have been confirmed by controlled studies focusing on specific areas in the field of education.[2,3,7,49,50,53]

The results of AT-related investigations with different educational levels (i.e., elementary grades to postgraduate studies) have been consistently favorable irrespective of sociocultural differences between countries (e.g., Canada, France, Germany, Japan, Romania, USA, USSR) in which observations were obtained.[52] Such studies have focused, for example, on observation of classroom behavior of young Japanese children after their overconcerned mother began to practice AT[71]; on improvement of athletic performance and psychodynamic changes in high school students; on reduction of examination anxiety in Canadian, American, French, and German university students; on improvement of academic performance in American high school students as well as in disadvantaged 7-year-old black students in Philadelphia[24]; on the use of AT by students of pedagogical institutes and on its application to neurotic school children in the Soviet Union.

In the area of sports, a variety of reports indicate that the regular practice of autogenic methods leads to better performance with improved reactivity and coordination, better endurance, faster recuperation, and reduction or elimination of psychoreactive disturbances that tend to occur before important tournaments.

AUTOGENIC TRAINING

Standard Exercises

Autogenic training (AT) is the basic and most frequently applied treatment technique that a patient can carry out himself by using passive concentration upon certain combinations of psychophysiologically adapted stimuli. Passive concentration on autogenic standard formulas can be so tailored that a measurable normalizing influence upon various bodily and mental functions will result.[38,39,40,67]

Psychophysiologically, autogenic training is based on three main principles: mental repetition of topographically oriented verbal formulae for brief periods (e.g., 30 seconds); mental activity known as "passive concentration"; and reduction of exteroceptive and proprioceptive afferent stimulation (specific training postures). The mental practice periods are always terminated in three consecutive steps by briskly flexing the arms, taking a deep breath, and opening the eyes.[67]

The verbal formulas are organized into six standard exercises (SEs) that are physiologically oriented. The content of these formulas is focused on the general topics of heaviness and warmth in the extremities, and on calm and regular function of the heart, self-regulation of respiration, soothing warmth in the upper abdomen (solar plexus) area, and agreeable cooling of the forehead. Occasionally, a complementary exercise called the First Space Exercise (SP-1)[44,45,46] is taught prior to beginning work with the orthodox series of standard exercises. (The first space exercise has only recently been adapted from Fehmi's biofeedback procedure and used with patients in AT. It involves the sequential imagination of spaces between symmetrical parts of the body. The pattern of formulae is as follows: "I imagine the space between my eyes . . . [about a 5-second interval] I imagine the space between my ears . . . [5-second interval] I imagine the space between my shoulders . . . [5-second interval]" and so on for elbows, wrists, hands, fingers, knees, heels, feet, toes, and legs. The aim is to more specifically mobilize nondominant right hemispheric functions.)

Passive Concentration. The patient's attitude while repeating a formula in his mind is conceived of as "passive concentration." Passive concentration (and passive volition) may best be understood by comparing it to what is usually called "active concentration" and active volition.

Concentration in the usual sense has been defined as "the fixation of attention" or "high degrees of attention" or "the centering of attention on certain parts of experience." This type of concentration involves the person's interest, goal-directed investment of mental energy and effort, and concern about the result during the performance of the task.

In contrast, passive concentration implies a casual attitude during the performance of a task and complete indifference about the result. Any goal-directed effort, active interest of apprehensiveness must be avoided. The patient's casual and passive attitude toward the effects of a given formula is regarded as one of the most important factors of the autogenic approach.

The effectiveness of passive concentration on a given formula depends on two other factors, namely, the mental contact with the part of the body indicated by the formula, and keeping up a steady flow of filmlike (verbal, acoustic, visual) representation of the autogenic formula in one's mind.

The duration of passive concentration (PC) on a formula should be adapted to the functional situation of the trainee (e.g., 5, 10, 30, or 60 seconds in the beginning). Later, when the trainee has no difficulty in maintaining an adequate level of passive concentration and there are no undesirable reactions (e.g., circulatory), the exercises may be extended to 3, 5, or 10 minutes and longer.

Holistic Concept of Therapy

To the autogenic therapist the level of functional harmony is of central importance; it is determined both by a person's adaptation to environmental demands and by adaptation to inner realities that evolve from (a) his genetic constellation (i.e., "authentic self") and (b) the developmental consequences of his life experience (i.e., the "natural self"). In other words, the assumption is that reaching and maintaining a desirable level of inner harmony and living in favorable agreement with the "authentic self" means (a) the recognition of (genetically and otherwise) given limits of functional possibilities and (b) the use of the circumstances of life to promote development in agreement with the biologically determined potential (i.e., self-realization); (c) the avoidance, reduction, or elimination of those stimuli and circumstances that are known to produce antihomeostatic and harmony disturbing effects.

Practically, the development of inner harmony with the "authentic self" is accomplished in several ways. Autogenic training plays the key role by mobilizing self-regulatory homeostatic forces (shift to a trophotropic state that is diametrically opposed to stresslike states). The patient, through the combination of autogenic techniques, not only experiences functional adjustments (e.g., reduced anxiety level) but also develops increased sensitivity as to "what is good" and "what is not good" for his system.

Patients often need explanations why, from a homeostatic point of view, it is advisable to avoid situations that would further accumulate anxiety stimuli. For instance, the avoidance of violent movies, attendance at funerals, or visits to dying persons might be suggested to a person who has an overload of anxiety or aggression. Likewise, it may be recommended to a person to give up risky motorcycle driving or skydiving; or a change in a conflict-loaded work situation may be advised. The techniques used to communicate these suggestions include confrontation, "paradoxical intention,"[20] and support.

The Role of Medication

Since autogenic therapy aims at restoring and supporting natural homeostatic functions as quickly and effectively as possible, the reduction or elimination of psychopharmacological agents (particularly diazepam, trifluoperazine, barbiturates, amphetamines, and monoamine oxidase inhibitors) that tend to interfere with this process is important. Among the various families of psychopharmacological agents, certain drugs have been found to interact better with AT than others. The following agents have been observed to interfere the least with the homeostatic action of AT: anxiolytic—chlordiazepoxide, meprobamate; antidepressant—imipramine; neuroleptic—chlorpromazine, promazine.

Reduction in medication is the rule in a variety of disorders, e.g., chronic bronchial asthma, constipation, epilepsy, hayfever, essential hypertension, primary glaucoma, migraine, sleep disorders, and certain disorders of cardiac rhythm. Particularly important in the management of diabetic trainees is that a progressive lowering of insulin requirements occurs as experience in the practice of AT increases.

AT and Other "Relaxation Response"-Promoting Approaches

There is general agreement that different methods such as transcendental meditation (TM), various forms of yoga (Y), Zen meditation (Z), progressive relaxation (PR),[5,28] certain approaches of heterohypnosis (HH),[61] and autohypnosis (AH),[34,37] certain biofeedback techniques (BF),[22,23] and certain approaches in behavior therapy (BT)[75] can contribute desirable elements for improvement of mental and physical health through the elicitation of a "relaxation response."[4] The trophotropic nature of the "relaxation response" and the underlying "integrated nervous system reaction" is functionally diametrically opposed to stress and provides a favorable but relatively nonspecific situation that permits certain homeostatic mechanisms to work with greater efficiency (e.g., recuperation from stressor effects).

In comparing the technical elements of these approaches, we find that in addition to common basic elements (e.g., nature of mental device, passive attitude, decreased muscle tone, quiet environment, trained instructor)[4] there are psychophysiologically important differences (e.g., heteroinstructed, self-instructed; topographic, nontopographic; directive, nondirective; symptomatic, nonspecific; verbal, nonverbal) in procedural details.[58,61] Each of these procedural details may exert therapeutically desirable, undesirable, or relatively nonspecific effects depending on the patient's history and actual functional situation. This leads to the question: Who should practice what technique, in what manner, for how long and under what kind of treatment control?

In certain specific situations (e.g., intractable pain, hyperemesis gravidarum) "monosymptomatic" approaches may be the method of choice. For example, in hyperemesis gravidarum, symptomatic treatment with heterohypnosis is the best approach. However, symptomatic treatment of headache by heterohypnosis or biofeedback could be a serious technical error when, for example, the headache is a homeostatic signal calling for a release of a suppressed need for crying. When a history of serious accidents is prominent and is likely to constitute a major part in psychophysiological disorders it is therapeutically unrealistic to expect TM, Z, Y, BF, HH, AH, PR, BT, AT, or psychoanalysis to be adequate. Such cases require the combined application of AT and AA. From a pathophysiologic and homeostatic point of view, long-term treatment results tend to be better as the natural forces of homeostasis are given support to achieve and maintain favorable levels of functional adjustment.

AUTOGENIC MODIFICATION

Autogenic modification consists of two complementary approaches: (a) psychologically oriented "Intentional Formulas" (IF) and (b) physiologically oriented "Organ Specific Formulas" (OF). Both approaches are designed to use the peculiar psychophysiological nature of the autogenic state as a functional vehicle for obtaining specific desirable effects that were not obtained through the regular standard exercises. For example, when chronic constipation has not improved sufficiently after 10 weeks of AT, the formula "My lower abdomen is warm" may be added to the end of the series of SEs in order to stimulate organ-specific activation of peristalsis in the colon, and to increase blood flow in the colon wall.[51] Or, when the regular practice of AT does not readjust (anxiety) dream-related awakening within 2 months, desirable readjustments of the patient's dream behavior and sleep pattern may be obtained by adding the IF: "In my dreams I remain passive and go along with the messages of my brain."[40,48]

AUTOGENIC MEDITATION

The practice of the seven meditative exercises is not indicated if a trainee has difficulty in maintaining an adequate level of passive concentration over longer periods (e.g., 30 to 50 minutes) and if there is evidence of disturbing autogenic discharges. However, occasionally the visual imagery components of the meditative exercises have been successfully used in the management of specific psychosomatic problems, in combination with autogenic behavior therapy techniques,[69,70-73] and as a complementary approach in psychoanalytic therapy.

The orthodox procedure as conceived by J. H. Schultz[67] distinguishes the following steps: (a) preparatory training; (b) ME I: spontaneous experience of colors; (c) ME II: experience of selected colors; (d) ME III: visualization of concrete objects; (e) ME IV: visualization of abstract objects; (f) ME V: experience of a selected state of feeling; (g) ME VI: visualization of other persons; (h) ME VII: answers from the unconscious.

AUTOGENIC NEUTRALIZATION

The hypothesis that there exist biological self-regulatory brain activities is not new. One of the elements that distinguishes autogenic therapy from others is the assumption that the patient's own system knows best how certain functional disturbances come about and how to reduce their disturbing effects (neutralization). This assumption is based on the puzzling observation that the regular practice of passive concentration on the autogenic formulas helps to improve many medical and psychological disorders. Since it was difficult to understand how the repetition of the formulas together with passive concentration was solely responsible for the significant improvements in patients' symptoms, it was hypothesized that unknown brain functions participated and that the altered state of consciousness produced by the technique (the autogenic state) facilitates the activity of (otherwise inhibited) self-regulatory mechanisms that promote the normalization of bodily and mental disorders.[39,67]

Observations of spontaneous training symptoms or autogenic discharges that occur during the autogenic state indicate that they have no apparent relationship to the content of the formulas. Detailed studies of these discharges showed that they occurred in great variety and had a unique profile for each patient. Often there was a close relationship to the patient's complaints, his clinical condition, and certain events of his past. In some ways, they resembled phenomena described during "sensory isolation," during certain stages of sleep (e.g., motor discharges, dreams), and responses obtained by direct electrical stimulation of cortical and subcortical structures.[60] It was therefore hypothesized that the autogenic state facilitates spontaneous discharges from certain parts of the brain that have a need for "unloading," and that this discharge activity is one of the therapeutic factors at work during AT. On the basis of this hypothesis, two different techniques of autogenic neutralization—autogenic abreaction (AA)[39,40] and *autogenic verbalization* (AV)[67]—were developed to enhance the therapeutic effect of AT by giving the brain a better opportunity to neutralize and release whatever it needs to discharge.

Autogenic Abreaction

This method is not required if the training symptoms are not particularly disturbing and satisfactory progress is being made with AT alone. However, if an increasing number of disturbing phenomena are noted, the introduction of AA may be necessary. Restlessness, vestibular discharges such as unpleasant dizziness and marked body image distortions, pain, headaches, bursts of anxiety, repeated episodes of disagreeable somesthetic sensations, inability to continue the exercises, massive interference from intruding thoughts, and the frequent appearance of differentiated visual phenomena are some of the autogenic discharges that indicate that there is a need in the patient to unload disturbing material.

Clinical observations have shown that certain events in patient's history have particularly damaging effects and therefore increase the likelihood that AA will be necessary. These factors include life-threatening accidents (especially when followed by unconsciousness); inhalation anesthesia; near drowning; severe drug intoxications (e.g., unconsciousness following an overdose); sexual deviations (e.g., homosexuality)[8]; and anxiety-provoking forms of religious education.

The technique of AA includes the following elements: (a) The patient is asked to mentally shift from the initial use of passive concentration on autogenic formulas to a spectatorlike attitude called *passive acceptance*. The mental shift comes during or after a 2- to 3-minute period of repetition of the heaviness formulas. (b) In the autogenic state and with this "carte blanche" attitude, the patient verbally describes, without restriction, everything that he experiences. The description may include sensory, motor, visual, intellectual, auditory, olfactory, affective, or vestibular phenomena. (c) Both the patient and the therapist must observe and respect the therapeutic *principle of noninterference*. Interventions are limited to the management of resistance and should be made only after it repeatedly becomes obvious that the neutralization is blocked from proceeding in a direction already indicated by the patient's self-regulatory elaborations. (d) The period of description should be prolonged until a sufficient level of neutralization is reached. (e) The AA is terminated in the usual three-step sequence by flexing the arms, taking a deep breath, and opening the eyes. (f) The entire AA is tape-recorded by the patient, and as soon as possible after the session, he types a verbatim transcript and, after reading it aloud (verbal reexpression during an unaltered state of consciousness) includes a commentary (feedback, integration). (g) The patient carries out unsupervised AAs at home as soon as he has acquired a satisfactory level of competence with the technique.[39,40]

When autogenic abreaction is applied, it is important that the patient practices the standard exercises regularly and demonstrates that his therapeutic cooperation is reliable. The notes on his training symptoms during AT are usually a good indication of motivation. Unless it is practical to carry out a large portion of the therapy in the office, AA should not be started with patients who do not seem to have the motivation to work intensively on their own.

During a typical AA session, the therapist may initially assist and hetero-verbalize the heaviness formula. The patient begins to describe his experience as soon as he notices the onset of training symptoms. If the patient does not begin to talk by the end of the heaviness sequence, the following supportive formula may be added: "And now you imagine yourself in a meadow, and tell me how the meadow looks today or whatever else you see, or feel or think." The supportive "meadow image" was chosen since it is a relatively neutral situation that can be taken as a convenient beginning point. However, when this technical support is used it must be clear to the patient that the "meadow" is merely another stimulus (like heaviness) and that no mental effort should be made to obtain or maintain the image.

Generally, one can distinguish four large groups of initial patterns of dynamics of autogenic neutralization:

a. Patterns of predominantly intellectual elaborations, which may or may not be associated with sporadically occurring visual phenomena or other bodily oriented modalities of discharges.
b. Patterns dominated by a variety of sensory (viscerosensory) and motor (visceromotor) phenomena with or without sporadically interjected intellectual or visual elaborations.
c. Patterns in which visual elaborations assume central importance and bodily oriented phenomena or intellectual elaborations are of secondary nature, which may or may not participate occasionally.
d. Mixed patterns in which all known modalities of brain-directed elaborations may participate with variable intensities.

An AA may last 15 to 150 minutes, and it is important that the patient keeps describing until the pattern of homeostatic elaborations indicates that nothing further is happening and he feels quite comfortable. However, if such a self-regulatory ending is not reached and premature termination cannot be avoided, it is possible to minimize disagreeable aftereffects (e.g., headaches, depressive feelings, anxiety attacks, nightmares) by ending the AA during a positive or relatively neutral phase.

Although limitations of space do not permit a comprehensive presentation of the mechanisms of autogenic neutralization, a few observations and theoretical issues do deserve special mention.

On the surface, it may seem that the technique simply involves the pairing of a relaxed "trophotropic" state with a continuous uncensored description of spontaneous elaborations (e.g., sensory, motor, vestibular, visual, ideational, affective), thereby producing neutralization. However, this explanation is an oversimplification of the complex and unique dynamics observed. The elaborations are often symbolic, primary process, or dreamlike, and seem to be closely related to (nondominant) right-hemispheric functions.[43]

The emphasis on right-hemisphere activity observed during AA is in keeping with the hypothesis that part of the transmission from one hemisphere to the other can be selectively and reversibly blocked. Bogen and Bogen proposed that "certain kinds of left-hemisphere activity may directly suppress certain kinds of right-hemisphere action. Or, they may prevent access to the left hemisphere of the products of right-hemisphere activity."[9] Similarly, Galin[21] considered the hypothesis that "in normal intact people, mental events in the right hemisphere can become disconnected functionally from the left hemisphere (by inhibition or neuronal transmission across the cerebral commissures), and continue a life of their own. This hypothesis suggests a neurophysiological mechanism for at least some instances of repression and an anatomical locus for unconscious mental contents."[21] The corollary of this theory is that a functional imbalance or inhibition between the two hemispheres participates in the development of psychodynamic and psychosomatic disorders. One can further hypothesize that AA facilitates communication between the two cerebral hemispheres and allows repressed, primary-process-like, disturbing material (presumably right hemispheric) to become integrated into logical, analytical, verbal awareness (largely left hemispheric).[43] The result is a reduction in the disturbing potency of traumas (neutralization, resolution of intrapsychic conflict).

During AA the patient's homeostatic brain mechanisms automatically select and control the release of disturbing material, adapt the process of neutralization to the patient's level of tolerance, modify and repeat certain themes until sufficient neuralization is achieved, shift to other "pressure areas" once neutralization of a given theme is sufficiently advanced, neutralize negative transference, and signal that the neutralization of certain themes is terminated. Although the reason for some of these or other dynamics may be unclear to both the patient and the therapist, it invariably turns out that the patient's homeostatically directed brain mechanisms knew the reasons for proceeding in a particular manner.[39]

Accidents and Traumatizing Events. Extensive clinical experience with AT and particularly AA indicates that the damaging effects of accidents and traumatizing medical procedures (e.g., inhalation anesthesia, bone marrow puncture, ECT), particularly in conjunction with artificially induced alteration or loss of consciousness, have been underestimated. The neglect of this area may stem from the fact that no detectable neurological lesions are involved and no approach, other than autogenic therapy, has the tools to cope with the disruptive psychophysiologial effects. Thus these patients are often dismissed as malingerers with a "compensation neurosis."

The effects of such physical traumas tend to become functionally linked to other unrelated events and thereby aggravate existing problems (e.g., homosexuality,[8] psychosomatic disorders). Since the experience and its consequences are nonverbal, exploration of this field is difficult or impossible by verbal approaches alone. During AT and AA, some patients may transitorily have feelings of being about to lose consciousness, unpleasant vestibular phenomena (e.g., spinning, dizziness, falling), and unpleasant physical sensations in a previously injured area of the body accompanied by anxiety. Such phenomena are usually seen in patients who have a history of disturbing physical traumas.[39,40]

Autogenic Verbalization

Autogenic verbalization is a more limited method of neutralization.[67] This approach is different from autogenic abreaction in that it does not involve a carte blanche attitude, but rather focuses on a predetermined specific topic such as aggression, anxiety, or obsessive material. For instance, in the autogenic state, after the heaviness formulas, the patient is instructed to verbalize about all the things that make him angry and is encouraged to keep expressing his aggression. A typical verbalization consists of many repetitions of the same theme and usually lasts 10 to 40 minutes. The patient practices the method at home. For correct use of this technique, it should be emphasized that he must verbalize continuously until he is certain that his mind is "empty" and there is nothing more to say. If a verbalization is cut short, disturbing effects may remain mobilized the disagreeable aftereffects may ensue (e.g., headache, anxiety, irritability, chest pain). The approach is particularly useful when there has been a recent acute disturbance. Close supervision of patients using autogenic verbalization is important because incorrect use of the techniques may spontaneously convert into unwanted complicated processes of autogenic abreaction.

The following case illustrates the usefulness of autogenic verbalization in a patient with severe migraine headaches:

Case 4 is a 33-year-old single, female secretary. For 14 years, she had been treated medically and with psychotherapy (nonautogenic) for migraine headache of variable severity. Despite high doses of anxiolytics, antidepressants, and analgesics, for the 6 months prior to her referral for autogenic therapy, her symptoms continued to increase, to the point where she was no longer able to work. She was anxious, "all tied up in knots," depressed, and crying. Her main complaints were unceasing migraine headaches, insomnia, vomiting, anorexia, and very low self-confidence. After 3 months of AT, she was no longer dependent on diazepam, was less anxious, and generally felt better, but she still had several headaches per week and was somewhat depressed. Therefore, imipramine therapy was started, but no further improvement occurred in the next 3 months. Autogenic verbalization on aggression was then taught. In addition to AT, she did a daily verbalization of about 30 minutes with great subjective relief. Almost immediately her symptoms began to dissolve. She returned to work, signed up for an evening course, and began to socialize more. After 1 year of follow-up she was still free of headaches, sleeping well, and free of anxiety and depression.

GRADUATED ACTIVE HYPNOSIS

In contrast to all other autogenic methods, the combination of AT with elements of orthodox techniques of hypnosis aims at obtaining a shift to hypnotic states.[34] The method emphasizes the exclusive use of self-instruction (i.e., self-hypnosis).[37] After about 2 weeks of preparatory practice of the first and second standard exercise, the hypnotic element of eye fixation (sometimes in combination with monotonous auditory stimuli, e.g., metronome) is added in order to promote the shift to a hypnotic state. Then, after preparatory technical discussion, the patient continues to regularly use the self-induced hypnotic state exercises for implanting (mental repetition) sloganlike phrases that are designed to support therapeutically desirable developments. Kretschmer[20,37] recommended this approach for neurotic patients and personality disorders with strong obsessive-compulsive components and as a complementary method to "problem-focused" analytic psychotherapy (i.e., "Zweigleisige Standardmethode," "double-track standard method").[34,37]

AUTOGENIC BEHAVIOR THERAPY

Behavior therapists who were interested in finding a more satisfactory alternative to Jacobson's Progressive Relaxation (PR)[5,28] initiated the use of behavior therapy (BT) techniques (e.g., systematic desensitization) together with autogenic methods (i.e., autogenic behavior therapy).[1,4,27,41] To effectively support the application of behavioral techniques (e.g., systematic desensitization, assertive training, behavioral rehearsal, modeling, flooding) preparatory periods of intensive home practice of standard exercises (e.g., five to eight sets of SE I, SE II per day for 2 weeks) are frequently used. Other ABT procedures may include frequent practice of the partial exercise, "my neck and shoulders are heavy;" case-adapted use of meditative exercises when therapeutic procedures wish to emphasize work with visual imagination (e.g., preparatory visual rehearsal); occasional use of intentional formulas when additional support in a specific functional area is needed; or the use of autogenic verbalization when massive overload of aggression or anxiety require "deflation" before and during assertive training or systematic desensitization.[22,25,26,69-72]

The complementary use of AT and autogenic abreaction may be valuable when the conventional strategies of BT encounter special problems when attempting to desensitize patients—for example, in cases "in whom it is not possible to reduce anxiety by any of the standard methods"[76] or "in situations where the patient does not experience increased tension upon presentation of stimulus scenes, situations where tension does not decrease, or where it actually increases upon repetition and situations where the procedure itself disturbs the patient."[19]

The substitution of AT for PR led independent investigators to conclude that ABT (a) augments the effects of traditional BT with PR; (b) effects in unit time a more substantial improvement in stress defenses; (c) augments of degree of defense against extrapsychic pressures; (d) facilitates the conditioning routine; (e) provides improvement in personality dynamics that are different from the removal of a symptom or a symptom complex and, in addition that (f) fewer cases fail to respond adequately; (g) there is no abrupt termination of therapy by patients who continue AT; and finally (h) AT "supplies essential therapeutic ingredients at present missing from traditional behavior therapy methods."[25,30]

In behavioral medicine the combination of autogenic therapy with BT techniques can provide satisfactory treatment resulting in specific areas (e.g., food allergy, phobic reactions, writer's cramp, contact dermatitis, cold-induced dermatitis, muscular dystrophy, collagen disease, recent cerebellar ataxia); of 208 ABT patients, 84% were significantly improved or cured after follow-up periods of 6 to 30 months. [1,26,41,69-73]

AUTOGENIC FEEDBACK TRAINING

The combination of biofeedback techniques (BT) with autogenic approaches began around 1965 under the influence of Gardner Murphy at the Menninger Foundation with the work of Green, Green, and Walters. [23] As in autogenic behavior therapy, independent investigators hypothesized that biofeedback combined with AT yields better results than biofeedback without AT. [22,23,42,62-64,68]

A variety of clinical studies supported or confirmed this assumption. For example, in 468 migraine and tension-headache patients, the use of EMG (or hand) temperature feedback in combination with AT resulted in improvement in 56% and better results were noted in straight vascular headaches (76% improved; $N = 105$) than in psychogenic or mixed forms of headaches. [14] In a 1-year follow-up, study of 25 migraine and/or tension-headache patients found that a 5-day intensive autogenic feedback training program (hand temperature) was successful in 82.4%. [59] Cowings, Billingham, and Toscano, in search for a means to control the debilitating effects of motion sickness, found that groups of subjects who used biofeedback together with AT to simultaneously control multiple autonomic responses (i.e., heart rate, respiration rate, blood volume, pulse of face and hands) withstood the stress of Coriolis acceleration significantly better than did the control group. [10-13]

Available findings in the area of AFT show that the combination of BF and AT is a powerful tool in learning to voluntarily control a variety of bodily functions. Although this appears to be very encouraging from a mechanistic point of view of symptomatic treatment, further research is needed to clarify certain questions. Some of those questions are related to occasional observances that specific functional disturbances may occur after successful BF learning of the voluntary control of autonomic functions (e.g., local blood flow regulation, paresthesia, spermatogenesis). [42] Such functional disturbances may mean that forceful nonhomeostatic interferences in homeostatically controlled functions can lead to undesirable disturbances of specific sectors of the human system.

ABOUT NONINDICATIONS AND CONTRAINDICATIONS OF AUTOGENIC TRAINING

This section attempts to provide a general orientation on practical circumstances, functional disorders, and pathological conditions that affect or preclude the beneficial application of autogenic training (for details see Vols. I–III of *Autogenic Therapy*). [51,52,67]

Generally, a distinction between "nonindications," "relative nonindications," "contraindications," and "relative contraindications" is made.[57]

The listings here included are subject to change as more information from clinical and experimental research becomes available.

The term *nonindication* signifies that it is not advisable to use autogenic training. The subcategory of *relative nonindications* is reserved for all those diseases and conditions that require other forms of treatment, but where the simultaneous practice of autogenic training (AT) is not known to cause undesirable effects. For example, in hyperemesis gravidarum (severe vomiting of pregnancy) heterohypnosis is considered the most effective approach; however, there is no reason why the patient should not practice AT as well. Similarly, a patient with acute appendicitis requiring surgery may derive certain benefits from practicing AT before and after the operation.

Nonindications

- Persons with severe mental deficiencies.
- Children below the age of 5 (age-adapted management for children age 5 and onwards required).
- When careful and critical control of the patient's training symptoms is not possible.
- Persons with lack of motivation to apply AT in an adequate manner (e.g., recalcitrant psychopaths).
- When a differential diagnostic evaluation of training symptoms (e.g., autogenic discharges versus nature of unrecognized pathological processes) is not possible (e.g., pain, disturbances of blood flow, hypoglycemia).
- During acute episodes of schizophrenic reaction.

Contraindications

Contraindication has been defined as "any condition, especially any condition of disease, which renders some particular line of treatment improper or undesirable."[57] Generally it is implied that the treatment in question may or is known to produce unfavorable reactions, functional changes, and sequels that are detrimental to the patient's health. Consequently, the therapeutic modality should not be used. Contraindications include:

- Persons with doubtful or impending myocardial infarction unless monitored (e.g., in intensive care units), and supervised by a physician with AT experience.
- During and directly after myocardial infarction, and in the presence of complicating disorders (e.g., arrhythmias, pulmonary embolism, extension of the infarct to the endocardial surface with systemic embolism) unless monitored and supervised by a physician with AT experience.[32]
- Trainees repeatedly showing significant (paradoxical) increases in blood pressure during AT.

- Diabetic patients (a) lacking reliable collaboration, or (b) in circumstances that do not permit careful clinical control over longer periods of time (18–24 months).
- Patients with hypoglycemic conditions: (a) when the differential diagnostic evaluation has not been completed, (b) when there is a lack of reliable collaboration, (c) when clinical or other circumstances are therapeutically unfavorable.
- Patients with glaucoma (i.e., primary chronic open angle or acute or chronic angle closure) when weekly tonometric control of intraocular tension is not guaranteed. At must be discontinued when increases of intraocular tension are noted on two consecutive control measurements within 7 days.
- Involutional psychotic reaction (subacute psychotic outpatients require careful individual evaluation before AT may be used).
- Trainees with paranoid reaction showing increase of persecutory or grandiose delusions during or after AT.
- Dissociative (nonpsychotic) reactions (e.g., depersonalization, dissociated personality, stupor, fugue, amnesia, dreamy state, somnanbulism) unless under clinically well-supervised conditions.

Relative Contraindications

Relative contraindications are conditions that require particular caution in the application of a therapeutic approach. Such precautions may include modifications in procedure (e.g., not using certain standard formulas) or abandoning the line of treatment (e.g., AT) when undesirable reactions are noticed. Relative contraindications include:

I. Supportive background formula "I am at peace"
   - Persons who are prone to experience unfavorable antithematic reactions (e.g., anxiety, restlessness, massive motor discharges).
II. Supportive association of peaceful images
   - Persons who have difficulties on finding or holding a "peaceful image"; who report that selected peaceful images assume dynamic (filmlike) qualities; who notice that the selected peaceful image changes spontaneously to include disturbing features.
III. Trainees who frequently report the onset of anxiety or restlessness during and after the exercises should not practice AT without close supervision. They should be instructed to practice long series of exercises (e.g., 20 to 40), each of very short duration (e.g., 5–10 seconds). If improvement is not observed within about 2 weeks, AT should be discontinued.
IV. First standard exercise (heaviness formulas)
   - When trainees report strong and largely disagreeable cardiac and vasomotor reactions (e.g., congestion of the cranial region, flushing of face, chest pain, tachycardia, sensations of palpitations), one should proceed slowly with carefully adapted reduced formulas.

  V. Second standard exercise (warmth formulas)
   • When the environmental temperature is unusually high; or when SE II
     formulas elicit strong vasomotor reactions (e.g., swelling of training
     limb, disagreeable pulsating or "pressure," dizziness, feeling of empti-
     ness in head, initial symptoms of fainting). Such reactions require a step-
     by-step approach with "reduced formulas" and brief exercise.
 VI. Third standard exercise (heart)
   • Frequent occurrence of disagreeable and disturbing modalities of heart-
     related autogenic discharges (e.g., anxiety, uneasiness, tenseness, cramp-
     like pain, precordial pressure, tachycardia).
   • Patients with cardiac disorders or others who are unduly heart-conscious
     (e.g., "infarctophobia," "cardiac neurosis") and show marked apprehen-
     siveness toward their heart, unless very careful and consistent supervision
     is possible.
   • Trainees with a pattern of undesirable reactions during SE I and SE II
     (e.g., sharp drop in blood pressure, marked decrease of heart rate,
     disagreeable chest sensations, dizziness, headache anxiety) may try SE
     III after all other standard exercises have been practiced and the disturb-
     ing reactivity has subsided.
   • Hypertensive patients reacting with sudden and marked decrease in
     blood pressure and feelings of uneasiness and anxiety.
   • Patients on regular hemodialysis treatment when disagreeable cardiac
     sensation or complaints are reported.
   • Hyperthyroid conditions.
   • In children under the age of 10.
 VII. Fourth standard exercise (respiration)
   • Trainees suffering from functional disorders or acute pathological
     processes of the respiratory system (e.g., bronchial asthma, pulmonary
     tuberculosis). In many of these cases the fourth standard formula should
     be postponed till the end of the autogenic standard exercises.
   • Trainees who previously practiced methods that included voluntary con-
     trol of respiratory functions and who find it unusually difficult to relearn
     a passive oriented attitude while practicing "Breathing calm and
     regular," "It breathes me." In these cases, SE IV should be postponed
     until all standard exercises have been practiced satisfactorily.
VIII. Fifth standard exercise (solar plexus)
   • When the nature and location of the solar plexus cannot be adequately
     explained, or cannot be adequately understood (e.g., children).
   • Onset of pain in the abdominal area during SE V.
   • Trainees with disorders of the digestive tract.
   • Diabetic patients showing a marked decrease in insulin tolerance with
     frequent episodes of rapid onset of hypoglycemia.
   • Patients with hyperinsulinism of other forms of hypoglycemia.
   • Trainees with angina pectoris and frequent disagreeable reactions during
     SE V.

- During pregnancy.
- In children.

IX. Sixth standard exercise (forehead)
- Trainees who repeatedly report onset or worsening of headache or migraine during or after SE VI.
- Trainees with brain injuries: 50% require a case-adapted modification of SE VI or have to stop the formula
- Epileptic patients with marked vasomotor instability affecting the cranial region and other undesirable reactivity.

X. Partial exercise ("My neck and shoulders are heavy")
- Not during stages of sleep deficiency or exhaustion while engaged in potentially hazardous activities because of the risk of sudden onset of sleep.
- Not to be used in a standing or simple sitting posture by patients suffering from narcolepsy, epilepsy, hypotension, and marked degrees of vasomotor instability.

XI. Space exercises
- The first space exercise ("I imagine the space between my eyes," etc.) when unduly disturbing reactions (e.g., anxiety, dizziness, vomiting) occur more than twice during or after the exercise and/or when paradoxical increases in heart rate or blood pressure are recorded.
- The second space exercise ("My right arm is filled with space," etc.) should not be practiced when frequent control of blood pressure (i.e., before, after exercises) is not possible and when increases in blood pressure are noted on two subsequent occasions (i.e., within 7 days).

ACKNOWLEDGMENT. The material in this chapter was taken in part from W. Luthe and S. Blumberger, Autogenic therapy. In E. D. Wittkower and H. Warnes (Eds.), *Psychosomatic medicine. Its clinical applications.* New York/ London: Harper & Row, 1977.

REFERENCES

1. Abe, T. Behavior therapy and blepharospasm, hyperhydrosis, Raynaud's syndrome or collagen disease, myasthenia gravis, ataxia, dystrophia muscularis, and Schilder's disease. *Japanese Journal of Psychosomatic Medicines*, 1971, *11*(2), 33–33.
2. Angers, P., Bilodeau, F., Bouchard C., Luthe, W., et al. Application of autogenic training in an elementary school. In W. Luthe & F. Antonelli (Eds.), *Autogenic methods: Application and perspectives* (Proceedings of the 3rd Congress of the International College of Psychosomatic Medicine and the 2nd International Symposium on Autogenic Therapy, Vol. IV). Rome: Edizioni Luigi Pozzi, 1977.
3. Angers, P., Bilodeau, F., Bouchard, C., Luthe, W., et al. Application of autogenic training in an elementary school. Part III: Conclusions and recommendations. In W. Luthe & F. Antonelli (Eds.), *Autogenic methods.* Rome: Edizioni Luigi Pozzi, 1977.

4. Benson, H. *The relaxation response.* New York: Morrow, 1975.

5. Bernstein, D. A., & Borkovec, T. D. *Progressive relaxation training: A manual for the helping professions.* Champaign, Illinois: Research Press, 1973.

6. Blizard, D. A., Cowings, P., & Miller, N. E. Visceral responses to opposite types of autogenic training imagery. *Biological Psychology*, 1975, *3*, 49–55.

7. Blumberger, S. R. Similarities between autogenic approaches and W. Luthe's "Creativity mobilization technique." In W. Luthe & F. Antonelli (Eds.), *Autogenic methods.* Rome: Edizioni Luigi Pozzi, 1977.

8. Blumberger, S. R., & DeRivera, J. L. G. Homosexual dynamics studied with autogenic abreaction and psychotherapy of analytic orientation. In W. Luthe & F. Antonelli (Eds.), *Autogenic methods.* Rome: Edizioni Luigi Pozzi, 1977.

9. Bogen, J. E., & Bogen, G. M. The other side of the brain III: The corpus callosum and creativity. *Bulletin of the Los Angeles Neurological Society*, 1969, *34*,(4), 191–220.

10. Cowings, P. S. Combined use of autogenic therapy and biofeedback in training effective control of heart rate by humans. In W. Luthe & F. Antonelli (Eds.), *Autogenic methods.* Rome: Edizioni Luigi Pozzi, 1977.

11. Cowings, P. S. Observed differences in learning ability of heart rate self-regulation as a function of hypnotic susceptibility. In W. Luthe & F. Antonelli (Eds.), *Autogenic methods.* Rome: Edizioni: Luigi; Pozzi, 1977.

12. Cowings, P. S., Billingham, J., & Toscano, B. W. Learned control of multiple autonomic responses to compensate for the debilitating effects of motion sickness. In W. Luthe & F. Antonelli (Eds.), *Autogenic methods.* Rome: Edizioni Luigi Pozzi, 1977.

13. Cowings, P. S., & Toscano, B. W. Psychosomatic health: Simultaneous control of multiple autonomic responses by humans—a training method. In W. Luthe & F. Antonelli (Eds.) *Autogenic methods*, Rome: Edizioni Luigi Pozzi, 1977.

14. Diamond, S., & Franklin, M. Autogenic training and biofeedback in treatment of chronic headache problems in adults. In W. Luthe & F. Antonelli (Eds.), *Autogenic methods.* Rome: Edizioni Luigi Pozzi, 1977.

15. Degossely, M., & Bostem, F. AT and states of consciousness: A few methodological problems. In W. Luthe & F. Antonelli (Eds.), *Autogenic methods.* Rome: Edizioni Luigi Pozzi, 1977.

16. DeRivera, J. L. G. Autogenic abreaction and psychoanalysis. In W. Luthe & F. Antonelli (Eds.), *Autogenic methods.* Rome: Edizioni Luigi Pozzi, 1977.

17. Dongier, M. Foreword. In E. D. Wittkower & H. Warnes (Eds.), *Psychosomatic medicine: Its clinical applications.* New York: Harper, 1977.

18. Engel, G. L. The need for a new medical model: A challenge for biomedicine. *Science*, 1975, *196*, 129–136.

19. Fensterheim, H. Technical problems in the clinical use of systematic desensitization. *Tenth Annual Convention of the Association on Advancement of Behavior Therapy*, New York, December 1976. Workshop 17, p. 30.

20. Frankl, V. Paradoxical intention: A logotherapeutic technique. *American Journal of Psychotherapy*, 1960, *14*, 520.

21. Galin, D. Implications for psychiatry of left and right cerebral specialization. *Archives of General Psychiatry*, 1974, *31*,(4), 572–583.

22. Green, E. Biofeedback for mind–body regulation: Healing and creativity. In D. Shapiro, T. X. Barber, L. V. DiCara, J. Kamiya, N. E. Miller, and J. Stoyva (Eds.), *Biofeedback and self-control, 1972.* Chicago: Aldine, 1973.

23. Green, E. D., Green, A. M., & Walters, A. D. Voluntary control of internal states: Psychological and physiological. *Journal of Transpersonal Psychology*, 1970, *2*(1), 1–26.

24. Harlem, S. H. *The effects of psychophysiological relaxation upon selected learning tasks in urban elementary school children.* Doctoral dissertation, University of Pennsylvania, 1975.

25. Haward, L. R. C. Reduction in stress reactivity by autogenic training. In W. Luthe (Ed.), *Autogenic training: Correlationes psychosomaticae.* New York: Grune and Stratton, 1965.

26. Ikemi, Y., Nakagawa, S., Kusano, T., & Sugita, M. The application of autogenic training to psychological desensitization of allergic disorders. In W. Luthe (Ed.), *Autogenic training: Correlationes psychosomaticae.* New York: Grune and Stratton, 1965.

27. Ikemi, Y., Nakagawa, T., Suematsu, H., & Luthe, W. The biologic wisdom of self-regulatory mechanisms of normalization in autogenic and oriental approaches in psychotherapy. *Psychotherapy and Psychosomatics*, 1975, *25*, 99–108.

28. Jacobson, E. *Progressive relaxation* (2nd ed.). Chicago: University of Chicago Press, 1944.

29. Julien, R. A., Almaric, R., & Plantey, F. Le training autogène et son exploration telethermographique par l'appareil AGA 680 Medical (Thermovision). In W. Luthe & F. Antonelli (Eds.), *Autogenic methods*. Rome: Edizion: Luigi Pozzi, 1977.

30. Kazdin, A. E. The sparse evidence for active ingredients in systematic desensitization. *Tenth Annual Convention of the Association on Advancement of Behavior Therapy*, New York, December 1976, Symposium 4.

31. Klumbies, G., & Eberhardt, G. Results of autogenic training in the treatment of hypertension. In J. J. Lopez-Ibor (Ed.), *IV World Congress of Psychiatry, Madrid, 5–11, IX, 1966* (Int. Congr. Series 117). Amsterdam: Excerpta Medica, 1966.

32. Koleshaeo, A. A., Savitsky, V. V., & Sapchenko, G. V. The use of autogenic training in the complex treatment of patients with myocardial infarction in the ward of intensive therapy. In A. S. Romen (Ed.), *Psichicheskaya Samoregulyatsiya*. Alma Alta (USSR), 1974.

33. Körmendy, E. Psychische Störungen und Autogenes Training: Erfahrungen mit dem Autogenen Training in einer Volkshochschule. *Rheinisches Arzteblatt*, 1975, *18*, 541–546.

34. Kretschmer, E. *Medizinische Psychologie* (8th ed.). Leipzig: G. Theime Verlag, 1945.

35. Laberke, J. A. Über eine psychosomatische Kombinationsbehandlung (mehrdimensionale Therapie) bei sogenannten inneren Krankheiten. *Münchener Medizinische Wochenschrift*, 1952, *94*, 1718–1724, 1809–1816.

36. Laberke, J. A. Klinische Erfahrungen mit dem Autogenen Training bei Herz- und Kreislauferkrankungen. In W. Luthe (Ed.), *Autogenic training: Correlationes psychosomaticae*. New York: Grune and Stratton, 1965.

37. Langen, D. *Die gestufte Aktivhypnose* (2nd ed.). Stuttgart: G. Thieme Verlag, 1967.

38. Luthe, W. *Autogenic therapy: Research and theory*. New York: Grune and Stratton, 1970.

39. Luthe, W. *Autogenic therapy: Dynamics of autogenic neutralization*. New York: Grune and Stratton, 1970.

40. Luthe, W. *Autogenic therapy: Treatment with autogenic neutralization*. New York: Grune and Stratton, 1973.

41. Luthe, W. Autogenic behavior therapy (1965–1972). *Japanese Journal of Hypnosis*, 1974, *19*(2), 23–29.

42. Luthe, W. Autogenic feedback training. *Japanese Journal of Hypnosis*, 1973, *18*(2), 3–15.

43. Luthe, W. Hemispheric specialization and autogenic therapy. In W. Luthe & F. Antonelli (Eds.), *Autogenic methods*. Rome: Edizioni Luigi Pozzi, 1977.

44. Luthe, W. On the development of space exercises in autogenic training. In W. Luthe & F. Antonelli (Eds.), *Autogenic methods*. Rome: Edizioni Luigi Pozzi, 1977.

45. Luthe, W. The first space exercise: Observations in long-term trainees. In W. Luthe & F. Antonelli (Eds.), *Autogenic methods*. Rome: Edizioni Luigi Pozzi, 1977.

46. Luthe, W. The second space exercise: Observations in short- and long-term trainees. In W. Luthe & F. Antonelli (Eds.), *Autogenic methods*. Rome: Edizioni Luigi Pozzi, 1977.

47. Luthe, W. The first space exercise: Blood pressure and heart rate changes in long-term trainees. In W. Luthe & F. Antonelli (Eds.), *Autogenic methods*. Rome: Edizioni Luigi Pozzi, 1977.

48. Luthe, W. The dream formula. In W. Luthe & F. Antonelli (Eds.), *Autogenic methods*. Rome: Edizioni Luigi Pozzi, 1977.

49. Luthe, W. *Creativity mobilization technique*. New York: Grune and Stratton, 1976.

50. Luthe, W., Mailhot, D., & Vallieres, G. L'utilisation du training autogene comme technique de médecine preventive chez les enfants de cinq ans. In W. Luthe & F. Antonelli (Eds.), *Autogenic methods*. Rome: Edizioni Luigi Pozzi, 1977.

51. Luthe, W., & Schultz, J. H. *Autogenic therapy: Medical applications*. New York: Grune and Stratton, 1970.

52. Luthe, W., & Schultz, J. H. *Autogenic therapy: Applications in psychotherapy*. New York: Grune and Stratton, 1970.

53. Luthe, W., Trudeau, M., Mailhot, D., & Vallieres, G. Blood pressure and heart rate variations in

elementary school children with and without autogenic training. In W. Luthe & F. Antonelli (Eds.), *Autogenic methods*. Rome: Edizioni Luigi Pozzi, 1977.

54. Marks, I. M. Sexual and phobic-obsessive disorders: Clinical studies. In *Tenth Annual Convention of the Association on Advancement of Behavior Therapy*, New York, December 1976.

55. McKusick, V. A., & Ruddle, F. H. The status of the gene map of the human chromosomes. *Science*, 1977, *196*, 390–405.

56. Mirabile, C. S., Glueck, B. C., & Stroebel, C. F. Spatial orientation, cognitive processes and cerebral specialization. *Psychiatric Journal of the University of Ottawa*, 1976, *1*(3), 99–104.

57. Newman, N. A., Adriani, J., et al. *Dorland's illustrated medical dictionary*. Philadelphia: Saunders, 1974.

58. Ogawa, K. Differences of the subjective nature between hypnosis and autogenic training (AT). *Educational Sciences Journal of Yokohama National University*, 1975, *15*, 50–62.

59. Pearse, B. A., Walters, E. D., Sargent, J. D., & Meers, M. *Exploratory observations of the use of an intensive autogenic feedback training procedure in a follow-up study of out-of-town patients having migraine and/or tension headaches*. Accreditation (B.A.) study, Washburn University, Topeka, Kansas, 1974.

60. Penfield, W., & Jasper, H. *The functional anatomy of the brain*. Boston: Little, Brown, 1954.

61. Rush, J. C. *A study of self-hypnosis under alternative procedures*. Doctoral dissertation, Stanford University, 1972.

62. Sargent, J. D. Biofeedback and biocybernetics. In E. D. Wittkower & H. Warnes (Eds.), *Psychosomatic medicine: Its clinical applications*. New York: Harper, 1977.

63. Sargent, J. D., Green, E. E., & Walters, E. D. Preliminary report on the use of autogenic feedback training in the treatment of migraine and tension headaches. *Psychosomatic Medicine*, 1973, *35*, 129–135.

64. Sargent, J. D., Walters, E. D., & Green, E. E. Psychosomatic self-regulation and tension headaches. *Seminars in Psychiatry*, 1973, *5*(4), 411–428.

65. Schaeffer, G. Das autogene Training in einer medizinischen Poliklinik. In W. Luthe (Ed.), *Autogenic training: Correlationes psychosomaticae*. New York: Grune and Stratton, 1965.

66. Schenk, T. Das autogene Training in der Behandlung von Asthmakranken. *Psychotherapie*, 1958, *3*, 148–150.

67. Schultz, J. H., & Luthe, W. *Autogenic therapy: Methods*. New York: Grune and Stratton, 1969.

68. Sheridan, C. L., Boehm, M. B., Ward, L. B., & Justesen, D. R. *Autogenic-biofeedback, autogenic phrases and biofeedback compared*. Paper presented at the 7th annual meeting of the Biofeedback Research Society, Colorado Springs, 1976.

69. Takaishi, N., Hosaka, M., Minami, R., & Kaneko, Z. Systematic desensitization therapy by the use of autogenic training. *Japanese Journal of Hypnosis*, 1968, *12*(1), 24–28.

70. Uchiyama, K. Effects of autogenic training relaxation in the systematic desensitization treatment. *Japanese Journal of Counseling Science*, 1970, *3*(2), 65–75.

71. Uchiyama, K. The efficacy of behavior therapy for anthropophobia: Systematic desensitization with autogenic training. *Clinical Psychiatry (Japan)*, 1972, *48*(7), 57–61.

72. Uchiyama, K. A study on writer's cramp treatment by systematic desensitization with autogenic training. *Bulletin of Clinical Consulting Psychology*, 1973, *13*, 1–2.

73. Ujimori, H., & Uchiyama, K. The amplitude's fluctuation of the plethysmogram under images of anxiety situation: Study on AT relaxation 5. *Bulletin of Clinical Consulting Psychology*, 1970, *10*, 85–94.

74. Wittkower, E. D., & Warnes, H. Preface. In E. D. Wittkower & H. Warnes (Eds.), *Psychosomatic medicine: Its clinical applications*. New York: Harper, 1977.

75. Wolpe, J. *Psychotherapy by reciprocal inhibition*. Stanford: Stanford University Press, 1958.

76. Wolpe, J. Special problems in behavior therapy cases. *Tenth Annual Convention of the American Association on Advancement of Behavior Therapy*, New York, December 1976. Symposium 4.

12

Progressive Relaxation Training: Overview, Procedure and Implications for Self-Regulation

Dale M. Patterson

Relaxation is something that most persons in our complex, rapidly moving society could use as an effective means for dealing with everyday stress as well as stress induced by situational or medical conditions. Drs. Thomas Budzynski and Johann Stoyva, former presidents of the Biofeedback Research Society, feel that deep muscular relaxation is far more valuable to individuals than Westerners currently consider it to be. One effective means by which an individual might attain deep states of relaxation is *progressive relaxation training,* a method of learning generalized and specific reductions in muscular tension through the systematic tensing and relaxing of a number of appropriate muscle groups in the body.

The pioneer of progressive relaxation training was Edmond Jacobson, who in 1908 at Harvard began formalizing a theory that, stated simply, postulated that low levels of muscle tension and anxiety are incompatible responses. That is, he believed that anxiety and tension are diametrically opposed to deep states of muscular relaxation. He published his first comprehensive book on progressive relaxation in 1938, which outlined the 15 major muscle groups involved in bodily tension and relaxation. However, a major problem with his methods was that each muscle group was to require 1 to 9 one-hour-per-day sessions, with 56 sessions of systematic training in all!

In response to this problem, Joseph Wolpe elaborated on Jacobson's physiological theory in 1948 (which ultimately led to *systematic desensitization*, a behavior therapy technique that uses relaxation as an aid in eliminating fear responses) and abbreviated Jacobson's relaxation methods effectively. Wolpe's major contributions have thus been to develop a program wherein relaxation became integrated with behavior therapy, and the effective abbreviation of Jacobson's original techniques. Specifically, he developed an effective method of learning relaxation which required only six 20-minute clinical training sessions, with two 15-minute daily home practice sessions between training sessions. He employed basically the same muscle groups as Jacobson.

Dale M. Patterson • Center for Self-Regulation and Biofeedback, Carrier Clinic Foundation, Belle Mead, New Jersey 08502.

CURRENT STATUS

One of the more valuable areas of evidence supporting the efficacy of progressive relaxation training is the demonstration of psychophysiologic changes that occur during or following use of the technique. Such research has been conducted in the past, with favorable results, and will certainly continue to be conducted in the future (see following section).

In general, however, progressive relaxation is in a phase where it is being evaluated for its appropriateness and the behavioral problems for which it is most suited. Thus far, it is being used effectively within behavior therapy (mostly desensitization and covert sensitization), differential relaxation training, and various anxiety relief techniques (Bernstein & Borkovec, 1973; Lamont & Edwards, 1967). More recently, progressive relaxation (often combined with autogenic phrases; see Schultz & Luthe, 1969) has been used as a preliminary step toward acquiring psychophysiologic self-regulation skills via biofeedback training (Budzynski, 1973; Budzynski, Stoyva, & Adler, 1970).

PSYCHOPHYSIOLOGIC RESEARCH WITH RELAXATION

Progressive relaxation as a low arousal technique was one of the earliest to be systematically investigated. Decreased pulse rate, blood pressure, skin conductance, respiration rate, muscle tension, heart rate, and subjective tension have been reported to occur following progressive relaxation by Jacobson, Wolpe, and others (e.g., Paul, 1969).

Self-regulated low arousal states attained with similar techniques have resulted in physiologic effects consistent with those above. For example, dominant EEG frequency has been shown to decrease during low arousal biofeedback training (DeGood, 1977; Patterson, 1977), transcendental meditation (TM) (Levine, 1976; Levine, Herbert, Haynes, & Strobel, 1975), and self-hypnosis (Lecron, 1964). In addition to brain-wave slowing (thus giving rise to greater incidence of alpha/theta rhythms), increases in generalized phase synchrony of the EEG have been reported to occur during TM (Levine, 1976; Levine et al., 1975). Moreover, somatocognitive movement toward low arousal via intensive biofeedback training was found to effect relative increases in right (nondominant) hemisphere electrical activity along with concomitant decreases in left (dominant) hemisphere activity (Patterson, 1977). Finally, in the same experiment, successful hemisphere-specific EEG biofeedback training was found to elicit activation of the spatial-intuitive (vs. verbal-analytic) cognitive mode.

Together, these studies indicate that progressive relaxation, as well as other low arousal techniques, can produce salient, patterned psychophysiologic changes within an individual. Such changes have proven to be extremely important toward an individual's success at gaining voluntary control over stressful stimuli elsewhere in his life.

COMPARATIVE AND BEHAVIORAL STUDIES

In 1969, Gordon Paul at the University of Illinois conducted an experiment to compare the effectiveness of progressive relaxation and hypnotic induction to effect patterned psychophysiologic changes within college students. One-third of his subjects were trained in progressive relaxation, one-third in direct hypnotic suggestion toward relaxation, and one-third were told to simply sit quietly and relax as they would normally. The results showed that progressive relaxation elicited greater reductions in psychological tension, as well as in muscle tension, heart rate, skin conductance, and respiration rate, than did the other groups. Paul thus concluded that progressive relaxation was superior to hypnotically induced or self-induced relaxation.

Other studies have shown that progressive relaxation training facilitates increased verbal recall, but only in highly anxious persons. Moreover, in persons with low anxiety levels, progressive relaxation training produced a *decrease* in verbal recall ability (Straughan & Dufort, 1969). Psychotic children became quiet and relaxed during and after relaxation training (Graziano & Kean, 1968), while severe insomnia was improved significantly following progressive relaxation sessions (Borkovec & Fowles, 1973; Geer & Katkin, 1966).

CAUTION: RELAXATION IS NOT A PANACEA

Despite Budzynski and Stoyva's claims that relaxation is far more valuable than we realize, it cannot alone be considered a cure-all for biomedical or psychosocial problems. In fact, other than its obvious benefits for dealing with the effects of daily stress, it is actually considered appropriate for a limited range of difficulties within a limited range of individuals (Bernstein & Borkovec, 1973).

If any general statement is to be made regarding its primary target behavior, progressive relaxation is ideal for individuals with *high* tension levels, regardless of the context in which the training is undertaken (e.g., clinical vs. nonclinical). However, for individuals with relatively low tension levels, undertaking progressive relaxation training within a clinical setting might result in disappointment, since expectations of benefit could remain unmet (Bernstein & Borkovec, 1973). Of course, outside such a setting (e.g., in one's home), progressive relaxation training may provide valuable psychophysiologic benefit to individuals, regardless of their daily tension level.

BIOMEDICAL APPLICATIONS

Since stress-related, functional, or psychosomatic problems often include psychogenic features or secondary gain, relaxation training alone cannot be expected to deal effectively with the latter components of such disorders. Consequently, the use of progressive relaxation training in the treatment of these disorders is usually included among a more comprehensive cognitive-behavioral (or other) treatment program. Examples of symptoms treated in such a manner with progressive relaxation, where medication may or may not currently be effective, include muscle-contraction headache, migraine headache (prior to cardiovascular reeducation), low back pain, paroxysmal atrial tachycardia (cardiac arhythmias), insomnia, hypertension, chronic rumination, excessive muscular or psychological tension ("tight nerves," free-floating anxiety), relaxation within various behavior therapies, and preliminary elicitation of parasympathetic dominance prior to (or during) biofeedback training.

ASSESSING THE APPROPRIATENESS OF RELAXATION TRAINING

Medical Clearance. A thorough physical examination should be given, as well as relevant laboratory tests completed, before any rigorous progressive relaxation training is initiated. This is to ensure that no strictly organic or physical bases exist for problems that might be more effectively and more easily treated with drugs. In the case of headache, for example, skull X ray, brain scan, and clinical EEG data are customarily reviewed before stress management training is prescribed.

Contraindications. Progressive relaxation should not be undertaken by individuals who should not tense certain muscle groups or those who are advised not to terminate the use of strong relaxant drugs. The latter contraindication is particularly important, since progressive relaxation is learned more easily and effectively without the concurrent use of such medications (Bernstein & Borkovec, 1973).

Clinical Appropriateness. Progressive relaxation may not be appropriate for all muscle groups in some conditions. An example of this is in specified varieties of lower back pain, where certain muscles should be strengthened rather than relaxed.

Assessment of Reported Tension. The first question to be asked regarding tension is whether it is appropriate or not. For instance, is the reported tension response clearly unnecessary, or is it a rational one to realistic circumstances? An example of the former might be debilitating test-taking anxiety, the latter where a person is regularly confronted with a life-threatening stimulus.

More specifically, the tension response must be evaluated as to its primary versus secondary role. Tension itself would be considered secondary where external circumstances exist that are as salient as the tension response itself (e.g., major financial problems, interpersonal problems, threats on one's life). These represent serious and definable problems in living that require attention before long-term relief would be acquired. Relaxation training would, at most, provide transient aid in such situations and should thus comprise only a portion of the total therapeutic effort. On the other hand, tension would be considered primary if an individual is found to consistently overrespond to both major *and* minor problems in his life. Progressive relaxation in such a case is likely to be very effective.

Stimuli Underlying the Tension Response. If a person is clearly responding with tension and/or anxiety to a specific object or situation in his environment, such as spiders, heights, or testing situations, then progressive relaxation training alone, as indicated, is likely to be less effective than progressive relaxation used in conjunction with behavior therapy (e.g., systematic desensitization). Such a convergent approach would not only help the individual learn to relax but would extinguish a conditioned response of anxiety to the phobic object or situation, replacing it with one of relaxation to the same stimulus conditions. However, it should be noted that in moving toward the use of systematic desensitization, individuals often note dramatic improvements in dealing with the stimuli eliciting their tension or anxiety response from the initial use of progressive relaxation alone.

ROLE OF THE CLIENT

In order for progressive relaxation to be undertaken successfully, the trainee must be able to maintain passively focused attention on the muscles of his body and to the voice of the trainer/therapist. In addition, he must be able to systematically tense and relax specified muscle groups. Finally, and most important, he must be motivated to regularly practice the techniques presented in clinical training sessions, so that effective learning of the patterned low arousal response can take place.

PHYSICAL SETTING

Room. The room chosen for progressive relaxation training should be very quiet and free from as many sources of extraneous stimulation as possible. The idea here is to maximize one's ability to maintain passively focused attention on the sensations of both tension and relaxation during the exercise. Specifically, windows and doors should be closed and the drapes drawn. Ringing telephones and loud conversations should be avoided. Air-conditioning, heating, or ventilation systems are generally no problem, since habituation by most trainees to such continuous sounds is rapid. Lighting should be dark or as dim as possible.

Chair. The chair used for progressive relaxation training should be completely supportive (Bernstein & Borkovec, 1973). The individual learning to relax should not need to tense any muscles in order to stay supported comfortably, as he will need to relax these muscles during training. Thus the ideal chair would appear to be a well-padded recliner. Pillows may be used to prevent head turning, enabling the neck muscles to relax (see Jacobson, 1964; Bernstein & Borkovec, 1973).

Although recliners are commonly found in relaxation laboratories, it should be noted that such completely supportive chairs may actually inhibit, rather than facilitate, deep states of relaxation (i.e., beyond the reduction of initially high tension levels). A review of the current literature in biofeedback training, as well as consideration of Eastern meditative practices, suggests that a low-back, over-stuffed chair, or even a cross-legged posture with minimal back support, facilitates deeper states of relaxation than those attained through the use of a conventional recliner. This is due to the tendency of trainees to relax "too far" and consequently fall into Stage 2 sleep using completely supportive chairs, instead of relaxing to a hypometabolic, *conscious* state.

The rationale for this, depending on the specific application, is that conscious awareness must be maintained in order to attain maximum benefit from relaxation. More specifically, the trainee must be *aware* of his relaxed state and, through this awareness, learn that he can recreate it as desired without fear of falling asleep. Consequently, biofeedback training is usually undertaken in a low-back chair or while sitting on the floor, thus allowing the disruption of head or body balance to signal overshooting of the desired psychophysiologic state.

Clothing. Attire worn during progressive relaxation training should be comfortable and loose-fitting (with loose-fitting undergarments) to allow unrestricted blood circulation. Contact lenses should not be worn. Shoes, watches, and regular glasses may be removed to maximize comfort during training.

RATIONALE AND PROCEDURE

Progressive relaxation training basically involves tensing and relaxing various groups of muscles throughout the body, while simultaneously paying very close attention to the *feelings* associated with *both* tension and relaxation. The goal of the training is to learn to recognize, pinpoint, and reduce tension not only during relaxation sessions but as it arises during daily activity as well.

Learning relaxation is not unlike learning any other skill such as tennis, swimming, golf, or bicycle riding. Consequently, in order to improve one's ability to relax deeply, one must practice it in a manner similar to other skills requiring practice for improvement. The trainer/therapist administering progressive relaxation training is not really doing anything *to* the trainee. He is simply directing the trainee's attention to various aspects of procedure and to the feelings associated with his fluctuating muscle tension levels. Thus, without cooperation and regular practice, the procedures are of little use.

The rationale for tensing before relaxing in training is so that, upon relaxing, the level of muscular activity will drop far below the *adaptation level*, or the amount of tension each person operates under each day (Bernstein & Borkovec, 1973). By tensing first, the electrical activity in the muscles is raised considerably above adaptation level. But by subsequently releasing the increased tension all at once, momentum is created, and the electrical activity will drop far below adaptation level, much as the swing of a pendulum takes itself beyond center when released from one side. This gives the trainee a "running start" toward deep relaxation via the momentum created by the release of tension. Moreover, the tensing procedure makes a vivid contrast between tension and relaxation and thus allows the trainee to directly perceive and compare the two, appreciating the difference in feeling associated with each of these states (Bernstein & Borkovec, 1973).

Throughout the procedure, the trainee uses the relaxation level of earlier muscle groups as a reference for the relaxation of subsequent ones. He is constantly making comparisons to those already relaxed, so that all groups become equally relaxed. When tensing each muscle group, the trainee holds the tension for 5–7 seconds (somewhat shorter for the feet). As indicated, the tension should be released quickly, not gradually.

BASIC MUSCLE GROUPS

Muscle groups used in the standard abbreviated progressive relaxation procedure and techniques for relaxing them are listed below. A standard session involves tensing and relaxing these muscle groups in the order listed, twice through (e.g., hand and forearm to feet, hand and forearm to feet again). The trainee should be instructed to keep his eyes closed throughout. (For more detailed information, see Jacobson, 1934, 1938, 1964; Bernstein & Borkovec, 1973.)

1. *Dominant* hand and forearm* (make tight fist, inhale; feel tension in hand, over the knuckles, and up into lower arm; exhale when releasing)
2. *Dominant biceps* (push elbow down against arm of chair and simultaneously pull elbow inward toward body, inhale; keep muscles in lower arm and hand relaxed; exhale when releasing)
3. *Nondominant hand and forearm*
4. *Nondominant biceps*
5. *Forehead* (lift eyebrows as high as possible and make exaggerated frown, inhale; feel tension in forehead and up into scalp region; exhale when releasing)
6. *Upper cheeks and nose* (squint eyes very tightly and simultaneously wrinkle nose, inhale; feel tension in central part of face; exhale when releasing)
7. *Lower cheeks and jaws* (bite teeth together, not too hard, and pull corners of mouth back, inhale; feel tension all through lower part of face and jaw; exhale when releasing)
8. *Neck and throat* (pull chin downward toward chest and simultaneously prevent it from actually touching chest, or, press head back against the chair, inhale; feel a bit of shaking or trembling in these muscles; exhale when releasing)
9. *Chest, shoulders, and upper back* (take a deep breath and hold it while simultaneously pulling shoulder blades together, trying to touch them, or, hold an exaggerated "shoulder shrug"; feel tension in chest,

* Right hand is dominant, left hand nondominant in right-handed persons, vice versa for most left-handed persons.

shoulders, and upper back; exhale when releasing; notice slow and regular breathing after releasing tension)

10. *Abdominal or stomach region* (take a deep breath and hold it, make stomach hard, feel tightness in stomach area; exhale when releasing)

11. *Dominant thigh* (take a deep breath and hold it, make thigh hard; feel tightness there; exhale when releasing)

12. *Dominant calf or lower leg* (take a deep breath and hold it, pull toes upward toward head; feel tension in lower leg; exhale when releasing)

13. *Dominant foot* (Take a deep breath and hold it, point the toe, turn foot inward, and simultaneously curl toes, not too hard; feel tension under the arch and in ball of foot; exhale when releasing)

14. *Nondominant thigh*

15. *Nondominant calf or lower leg*

16. *Nondominant foot*

The trainee should repeat the entire procedure, then focus on and enjoy the whole-body relaxation for as long as he likes.

Helpful Hint: Conditioned Relaxation. Each time the trainee exhales when releasing tension, he should be instructed to softly vocalize or subvocalize the word *calm* or *relax*. This word might then become a low arousal cue for him and could subsequently be used to elicit relaxation in the future (e.g., once he has learned to relax well using standard progressive relaxation techniques). However, the trainee should also be instructed not to use his low arousal cue indiscriminantly. That is, to maximize its personal effectiveness, he should use it only when actually attempting to lower his arousal level, such as when practicing relaxation. This is to prevent the cue from acquiring surplus meaning, so that intrusive thought elicited via semantic (or other) association is minimized.

Finally, it should be noted that the tensing–relaxing procedures delineated above may be altered if necessary. However, alteration is not recommended *unless* it is necessary, since these techniques have been shown to involve the maximum number of muscles available in each group (Jacobson, 1964).

SUMMARY OF PROCEDURE: THE FIVE BASICS

The following sequence of events is summarized by Jacobson with respect to effectively relaxing each muscle group.

1. Attention is passively focused on the muscle group.

2. At signal from trainer/therapist or tape, the muscle group is tensed.

3. The tension is maintained for 5–7 seconds (shorter with feet).

4. At signal from trainer/therapist, the muscle group is released *quickly* (i.e., all at once).

5. Passively focused attention on the muscle group is maintained as it relaxes. The difference between relaxation and the tension that preceded it is felt and noted.

GENERAL PROCEDURAL CONSIDERATIONS

In an attempt to train an individual at his own rate, successive muscle groups should not be focused on until the groups previous are deeply relaxed. Procedurally repeating the tense–release cycle should facilitate this. Moreover, hand signals used between the trainer/therapist and the trainee can eliminate the need for distracting verbal communication during the session (e.g., the trainee might raise his finger to signal the successful relaxation of each muscle group). The trainee should also be instructed to be honest with himself with respect to perceived tension and relaxation, rather than to simply go through the motions.

A good sign that deep relaxation has been achieved is a report from the trainee that warmth or heaviness is felt in any or all muscle groups following the session. Muscles that have a tendency to cramp should not be overly tensed. That is, the tension time for these muscles should be shortened, or they should not be tensed as hard, or both. In terminating the session, the legs and feet should be moved first, followed by the arms and hands, head and neck, and finally, the eyes should be opened.

The trainee should be instructed never to rise quickly from the chair following a relaxation session. Rather, generalization of his relaxed psychophysiologic posture can begin immediately by having the trainee sit in the chair for 3–5 minutes following the session, with his eyes open, attempting to maintain an uncritical acceptance of the relaxed state attained. Over the course of several weeks, his memory and awareness of the feelings associated with low arousal states can be generalized, bits at a time, to his daily activity. Behavioral techniques for the generalization of acquired psychophysiologic skills have been used to facilitate this process (see Bram Amar, 1977; Budzynski, 1977a; Graham, 1977; Steiner, 1977).

COGNITIVE STRATEGIES

Any cognitively useful information that facilitates the learning process should be supplied to the trainee when appropriate. Although the trainer/ therapist's voice, as well as the tense–release exercise itself, can often act to inhibit evaluative rumination during the session, this is rarely the case with trainees who display strong obsessive/compulsive or overcontrolled features, or with those who prefer verbal-analytic cognitive strategies or vocations. In such instances, it should gently be pointed out to the trainee that, in order to let go of unnecessary cognitions and the related tension they induce, one must passively attempt termination of effortful, directive thinking.

More specifically, thoughts must be allowed to "flow in one side of the head and out the other," so to speak, while the trainee witnesses or observes their "flow" in an unobstructed, nonjudgmental, nondirective manner. As such, characteristic attachment to thoughts must be abandoned in order to make room for emergent sensations of relaxation.

Analogies drawn from the descriptive and functional differences existing between the two cerebral hemispheres during both active and passive states are often helpful toward explaining the rationale for this strategy. Above all, the trainee should be instructed to remain *nonreactive*, in thoughts, feelings, and behavior, to his attempts to implement such a strategy, regardless of the quality of his actual performance. That is, his performance in the relaxation session, as well as his perceived success at inhibiting "mental chatter" and other such cognitive intrusion, should be ignored at all times, being effectively replaced with passive, uncritical attention on the sensations coming from the appropriate muscle group. Moreover, his failure, if any, to remain nonreactive to his own successes and failure at the task should also be gently handled via a nonreactive response set. The trainee's diligence or "gentle persistence" at maintaining a nonreactive set to all perceived consequences of his behavior may very well shape the likelihood of his attaining the somatocognitive, low arousal state during his training, and acquiring useful relaxation or psychophysiologic self-regulation skills during his life.

HOME PRACTICE

The importance of practicing progressive relaxation cannot be overemphasized if relaxation skills are to be learned and eventually generalized. For this reason, cassette tapes designed for home practice of progressive relaxation are recommended. Such tapes may be purchased commercially or they may originate from tape recordings of actual trainer–trainee relaxation sessions. Care should be taken, however, to secure tapes that approximate as closely as possible the techniques and procedures described here (e.g., choice of muscle groups, tense–release instructions), if utilization of Jacobson and Wolpe's methods is desired. (For more detailed information, see Jacobson, 1964; Bernstein & Borkovec, 1973.)

To maximize efficiency during the learning process, it is suggested that trainees practice twice every day (with the tape), for periods of approximately 15–30 minutes. These practice sessions are in addition to clinical sessions with the trainer/therapist, which may vary from once to three times per week. At least 3 hours should separate the two daily home practice sessions. A rule of thumb might be one in which practice sessions are not too far removed from daily activity (e.g., before breakfast and before dinner versus early evening and at bedtime).

It should be emphasized to the trainee that the use of a tape-recorded relaxation procedure is temporary and that it is not to be used on a long-term basis. Specifically, the tape should be used no longer than it requires for the trainee to achieve deeply relaxed states at home and/or to memorize the procedure. If dependency on the tape becomes apparent, systematic weaning should be initiated immediately. One such method is to have the trainee begin to use the tape at one of his daily practice sessions only, and eventually at neither of them. He might be instructed instead to recreate the step-by-step, tension–relaxation exercise on his own.

If the latter procedure proves unsuccessful, the following alternative method may be attempted. The trainee should be instructed to listen only to as much of the tape at each session as he requires in order to attain deep relaxation, himself turning off the recorder when such states are achieved. This may initially amount to his playing two-thirds of the tape, followed by one-half, one-third, and finally none of it, at each practice session. Above all, it should be emphasized that maximum benefit from relaxation training will be accrued only upon the emergence of the trainee's ability to reliably self-induce low arousal states on his own (i.e., without the aid of the tape or the trainer/therapist).

Practice should be undertaken where interruption is unlikely, external stimulation is minimal, and no time pressure exists (e.g., one should not practice 15–30 minutes prior to a scheduled appointment). The ideal practice session is one in which the trainee has nothing to do for a reasonably long period of time, perhaps 45–50 minutes, and can passively focus his attention on relaxation practice. These considerations (e.g., time, lack of interruption and distraction, quietness) should take precedence over reserving any particular time of day. Of course, as with any low arousal technique, one should avoid practicing progressive relaxation following meals, since the desired physiologic effects at such times are counterposed to those occurring as a result of the digestive process.

Finally, the cognitive strategies described earlier should be reiterated by the trainer/therapist for the trainee's benefit prior to prescribing home practice sessions. Casual reference to such strategies may also be included on the cassette tape used for home practice, in the form of relaxation "patter" (see Bernstein & Borkovec, 1973). As indicated, the nonreactive response set should be emphasized, so to minimize the emergence of frustration, anger, or boredom during practice in the absence of the trainer/therapist.

FURTHER APPLICATIONS

Tension during Daily Activity. Individuals often waste considerable amounts of energy through the maintenance of unnecessarily exaggerated muscle tension during daily activity, such as in automobile driving, walking, and running. Using a related procedure in combination with progressive relaxation training (called *differential relaxation*), an individual can learn to sustain low levels of tension in muscles unnecessary for a given activity, while maintaining sufficient levels of tension in those required for the activity (see Bernstein & Borkovec, 1973).

Tension-Exacerbated Illness. As indicated, chronic tension can aggravate or even cause physical symptoms, which can subsequently result in additional tension. Progressive relaxation training can directly reinforce the body's elicitation of recuperative parasympathetic and hypometabolic activity, out of which the healing and discontinuance of aggravated physical conditions is facilitated.

Communication and Psychological Integration. Cultivated low arousal states can often increase one's ability and willingness to communicate with himself and others. If one's tension or bracing response is so frequent and intense that communication with himself and others about possible causes for his tension is difficult or impossible, progressive relaxation training can effectively alter physiologic and metabolic activity to allow constricted perspectives to "open up."

This phenomenon appears directly related to the earlier reported electrophysiologic changes that occur within the cerebral hemispheres during deep, self-regulated relaxation: In a descriptive sense, the nonverbal, holistic, cognitive properties of the right (nondominant) hemisphere are relatively increased in their expressiveness, whereas the often restrictive and judgmental, logicorational properties of the left (dominant) hemisphere are concomitantly flattened.

The potential for enhanced communication skills, creativity, and/or personality integration resulting from cultivated low arousal training are even greater when the suggestibility of the nondominant hemisphere is constructively used in such a setting. More specifically, when carefully prepared verbal information or instructive material is presented to the nondominant hemisphere under predetermined psychophysiologic conditions (e.g., during sustained theta EEG and/or extremely low upper body EMG states), while the dominant hemisphere is "kept busy" and cannot interfere, significant changes in personality and behavior can apparently be produced. This procedure is called *twilight state learning* and is currently being researched by Drs. Thomas Budzynski and his colleagues in Denver, Ian Wickram in Peoria, Elmer and Alyce Green and their colleagues at The Menninger Foundation, and our group at the Carrier Foundation near Princeton (see Budzynski, 1976, 1977b; Green, 1977; Wickramasekera, 1976).

IMPLICATIONS AND FUTURE DIRECTIONS

Progressive relaxation training is thus firmly established as an effective low arousal technique. In psychophysiologic effects, it is not unlike techniques such as meditation, autogenic training, self-hypnosis, and low arousal biofeedback training. In the larger sense, however, its ideal conception and application fits into the much broader model of *psychophysiologic self-regulation.*

For example, when an individual controls or modifies his responses to his environment, whether it is to avoid the biological consequences of an adverse personal or social situation, or to simply come in out of the rain, he is self-regulating his behavior. Although we have known how to do the latter for quite some time, the former has been a problem for us. During the past century this has been particularly true, since we have chosen to direct our technological skills in such a way that the effects of stress on us are both chronic and devastating. However, over the past 15 years, through the "inward" direction of our technological efforts, we have discovered that our self-regulatory abilities might extend to the very core of our physiology or at least to biological areas once thought to be uncontrollable, viz., autonomic nervous processes.

Theories of psychophysiologic self-regulation are relatively nonexistent at this time. However, when developed they will undoubtedly draw on data from research with progressive relaxation training, biofeedback training, and related techniques in support of statements made about the human potential for "complete" self-regulation. Current models of holistic health care, for example, already hold self-regulatory concepts and techniques as fundamental to their premises, goals, and procedures.

Consequently, in view of our past successes and increasing wisdom to date, we need to gather still more data in support of a better understanding of the relationship between consciousness, human biology and physiology, and our self-regulatory abilities. Specifically, as Schwartz (1975) has pointed out, the self-regulation of multiple physiologic processes elicits cognitive/emotional experience that is quite distinct from the self-regulation of single physiologic processes. Therefore, we need to design experiments along this line whose data will (1) clarify the long-term psychophysiologic differences among the low arousal techniques currently available, (2) guide us in developing our ability to effectively control multiple physiologic systems, and (3) facilitate our use of that ability to voluntarily alter undesirable, unhealthy, or inappropriate behaviors.

In this connection, such data can only help us to refine and improve our efforts with such tools, especially, for example, in as potentially fruitful an area as twilight state learning. More specifically, pilot data from current twilight learning studies, as impressive as they are, invariable rely on the presence of a single EEG rhythm (e.g., theta), and occasionally on low frontal or upper body EMG activity, for the presentation of target material. This would appear to be an extremely crude though bona fide attempt to isolate an as yet unknown but desirable psychophysiologic state, seemingly tantamount to an attempt to locate a large needle within a haystack aided only by a small but reliable magnet! Unfortunately, we can at this time only guess how modifiable an individual's personality or behavior might be if material presented in such a setting were contingent upon multiple, whole-body physiologic systems (or even biochemical processes), as determined and controlled by a psychobiologic computer. Ironically, the implementation of such an idea, although distant from simple progressive relaxation training, may not be as far away as we think.

NOTE. The material in this chapter was originally prepared for a class taught by the author entitled Stress Management Procedures, sponsored by the University for Man, Manhattan, Kansas. University for Man (UFM) is a free university network under the auspices and funding of Kansas State University, Manhattan, Kansas.

REFERENCES

Bernstein, D., & Borkovec, T. *Progressive relaxation training: A manual for the helping professions.* Champaign, Illinois: Research Press, 1973.

Borkovec, T., & Fowles, D. A controlled investigation of the effects of progressive and hypnotic relaxation on insomnia. *Journal of Abnormal Psychology*, 1973, *82*, 153–158.

Bram Amar, P. Transfer of learning: Can new biofeedback learned behaviors be maintained in the real world? In W. A. Love, Jr. (Chair), *Generalizing self-regulatory ability from the clinic to life.* Symposium presented at the meeting of the Biofeedback Society of America, Orlando, 1977.

Budzynski, T. H. Biofeedback procedures in the clinic. *Seminars in Psychiatry*, 1973, *5*, 537–547.

Budzynski, T. H. Biofeedback and the twilight states of consciousness. In G. E. Schwartz & D. Shapiro (Eds.), *Consciousness and self-regulation* (Vol. 1). New York: Plenum, 1976.

Budzynski, T. H. Facilitating transfer of biofeedback skills to real life. In W. A. Love, Jr. (Chair), *Generalizing self-regulatory ability from the clinic to life*. Symposium presented at the meeting of the Biofeedback Society of America, Orlando, 1977. (a)

Budzynski, T. H. Tuning in on the twilight zone. *Psychology Today*, 1977, *11*, 38–44. (b)

Budzynski, T. H., Stoyva, J. M., & Adler, C. Feedback-induced muscle relaxation: Application to tension headaches. *Journal of Behavior Therapy and Experimental Psychiatry*, 1970, *1*, 205–211.

DeGood D. E. *A multiple response comparison of parietal EEG and frontalis EMG biofeedback*. Paper presented at the meeting of the Biofeedback Society of America, Orlando, 1977.

Geer, J., & Katkin, E. Treatment of insomnia using a variant of systematic desensitization: A case report. *Journal of Abnormal Psychology*, 1966, *71*, 161–164.

Graham, C. Techniques to maximize transfer of biofeedback training to the life situation. In W. A. Love , Jr. (Chair), *Generalizing self-regulatory ability from the clinic to life*. Symposium presented at the meeting of the Biofeedback Society of America, Orlando, 1977.

Graziano, A., & Kean, J. Programmed relaxation and reciprocal inhibition with psychotic children. *Behaviour Research and Therapy*, 1968, *6*, 433–437.

Green, E. E. Theta feedback and hypnogogic imagery. In I. Wickramasekera (Chair), *Biofeedback and the twilight state*. Symposium presented at the meeting of the Biofeedback Society of America, Orlando, 1977.

Jacobson, E. *You must relax*. New York: McGraw-Hill, 1934.

Jacobson, E. *Progressive relaxation*. Chicago: University of Chicago Press, 1938.

Jacobson, E. *Anxiety and tension control*. Philadelphia: Lippincott, 1964.

Lamont, J., & Edwards, T. The role of relaxation in systematic desensitization. *Behaviour Research and Therapy*, 1967, *3*, 11–25.

Lecron, L. M. *Self hypnotism: The technique and its use in daily living*. Englewood Cliffs, New Jersey Prentice-Hall, 1964.

Levine, P. H. The coherence spectral array (COSPAR) and its application to the study of spatial ordering in the EEG. *Proceedings of the San Diego Biomedical Symposium*, 1976, *15*.

Levine, P. H., Herbert, J. R., Haynes, C. T., & Strobel, U. EEG coherence during the transcendental meditation technique. MERU report 7501, Neurophysiology Laboratory, Center for the Study of Higher States of Consciousness, Maharishi European Research University, Weggis, Switzerland, 1975.

Patterson, D. M. *Differential biofeedback training, pre–post cognitive style changes, and the role of the "preferred" hemisphere in spatial-intuitive vs. verbal-analytic subjects*. Paper presented at the meeting of the Biofeedback Society of America, Orlando, 1977.

Paul, G. Physiological effects of relaxation training and hypnotic suggestion. *Journal of Abnormal Psychology*, 1969, *74*, 425–437.

Schultz, J. H., & Luthe, W. Autogenic methods. In W. Luthe (Ed.), *Autogenic therapy* (Vol. 1). New York: Grune and Stratton, 1969.

Schwartz, G. E. Biofeedback, self-regulation, and the patterning of physiological processes. *American Scientist*, 1975, *63*, 314–324.

Steiner, S. S. Use of EMG biofeedback to control compulsive symptoms in the natural environment. In W. A. Love, Jr. (Chair), *Generalizing self-regulatory ability from the clinic to life*. Symposium presented at the meeting of the Biofeedback Society of America, Orlando, 1977.

Straughan, J., & Dufort, W. Task difficulty, relaxation, and anxiety level during verbal learning and recall. *Journal of Abnormal Psychology*, 1969, *74*, 621–624.

Wickramasekera, I. (Ed.). *Biofeedback, behavior therapy, and hypnosis*. Chicago: Nelson-Hall, 1976.

13

Beliefs and Attitudes: Their Significance in Therapeutics

Michele Quinn

A number of subtle, often unsuspected, and neglected variables affect biofeedback learning and its clinical efficacy. These include the beliefs and attitudes of the patient. In this chapter, several categories of beliefs that are significant in therapeutics are classified and specified. These are based upon (1) verbal communications during training sessions, (2) observations of trainee's learning processes, (3) summary charts of learning curves, (4) patient reports of changes in symptom patterns, and (5) trainee's overall success or lack of success in accomplishing necessary life-style changes. These appear to be relevant in training, in trainee motivation, and in progress of therapy. Though biofeedback training is used in the examples, the categories are stated in terms that retain their applicability to many therapeutic processes.

This discussion covers the following four areas: (1) the paradigm that distinguishes and defines the concepts of belief, attitude, and intention; (2) a personal example that illustrates the effects of preconscious beliefs on the performance of a self-regulation task; (3) a classification of belief types; and (4) comments on the relationship between placebo, faith healing, experimental bias, experimenter effects, and beliefs about the therapeutic (or experimental) mode.

THE PARADIGM

Beliefs, attitudes, intentions, and behaviors are four major classes of variables that can affect therapeutic outcome. While behaviors are observable, beliefs, attitudes, and intentions are hypothetical constructs that must be inferred from the behaviors. They operate or exert their influence on behavior from unconscious, preconscious, or conscious levels. Each concept is independent though systematically related and often proceeds in a sequential fashion.

A belief is thought of as the link between some object and an associated attribute. An attitude reflects a person's feelings about an object. Beliefs, as the precursors of evaluative affective response, generate an attitude. This attitude, in turn, is the antecedent of a set of intentions that affect a number of related

Michele Quinn • Psychophysiological Treatment Center, Oxnard, California 93030.

behaviors (Fishbein & Ajzen, 1975). [For a more comprehensive discussion on beliefs, attitudes, and intentions, the reader is referred to Fishbein & Ajzen (1975); McGuire (1969).]

For example, a person has several beliefs about biofeedback training (BFT), such as, "BFT is used for the relief of stress and tension" or "BFT is difficult for the average person to learn." These beliefs may form a weak positive attitude toward BFT. As a result, the person intends to talk to a neighbor about biofeedback, or read a biofeedback article in a weekly magazine, but does not intend to talk to a physician about it. This set of intentions reflects the weak positive attitude the person holds toward BFT.

Each intention corresponds to a behavior while an attitude corresponds to a total behavioral pattern. Information obtained by performing these actions may then result in a change in belief (i.e., "BFT is learned without difficulty by the average person"), and this then may produce a change of attitude (moderately positive) and have concomitant effects on further intentions and behaviors. Beliefs are the cornerstone of this structure and in order for an affective evaluative (i.e, attitude) change to occur, they must be changed by direct observation (experience), knowledge from external sources, or inference processes.

PERSONAL EXAMPLE

My first effort to warm my right hand, using a temperature feedback device, involved an explicitly stated intention in my mind. I intended to warm my hand by imagining the vessels dilating and more blood flowing into it. As I imagined these events, the instrument informed me that my finger was cooling quickly! In surprise and fright, I tried harder; the finger cooled even further. I stopped, touched both hands to my face, and discovered that the finger connected to the thermistor was the coolest, the rest of my right hand warmer, and my left hand warmer still. I could hardly believe it; I had failed! This was a terrible event. I could not possibly teach temperature regulation if I couldn't do it. The finger cooled further still.

In behalf of my own salvation, I asked myself, "Do you believe you can warm your hand?" A little unsure "yes" bubbled from the depths of fear that I couldn't really warm it. I realized that I was afraid and that my fear had to be disarmed. I continued asking myself the same question, each time concentrating more fully and intensely on the depth of the question and the strength of the "yes" rising within me. My fear subsided quickly as my affirmed belief grew stronger and pronounced itself in a peaceful calm. I then asked myself, "Do I want to? Yes, I want to, and I believe I can. I believe I can and I want to. I know I can . . ." and the feedback tone began to rise, indicating a corresponding rise in the temperature of my finger.

Using the conceptual framework to analyze my experience retrospectively, it could be explained as beliefs that (a) I (object) can warm my hands (attribute); (b) I can use imagery to increase my finger temperature; (c) I want to be able to regulate my peripheral blood flow; (d) I cannot warm my hands; (e) I cannot self-regulate using imagery. Based on my evaluation of each of those attributes, my attitude might have been that I would like to warm my hand, it is important to me, but I am afraid that I can't. [Value, attraction, sentiment, valence, and utility "can be assumed under the category of 'attitudes' due to their similar bipolar nature," according to Fishbein and Ajzen (1967), whereas habits, traits, drives, and motives can be distinguished from attitudes by requiring the affective/evaluative dimension that is distinctively characteristic of attitudes.] The overall valence of my attitude was likely to be negative due to a strong fear of failure. Having received the information that I had indeed failed, I recognized my fear, chose to examine my salient beliefs, and began to nurture the belief that I could perform the task successfully. This process of consciously strengthening selected beliefs eventually created a more positive attitude, which was assured rather than afraid. Without any awareness of intentions or behaviors on my part, the outcome I valued came about.

An alternative way to explain this is in volitional terms. The concepts of active and passive volition are often used to explain the dynamics of a vasomotor response similar to that given in this example. However, looking deeper than these broad terms, volition (willing, choosing, or deciding) is very similar conceptually to intending (planning, destining). Perhaps these volitional concepts could be better understood by exploring the nature and strength of beliefs and attitudes that underlie them.

BELIEF CATEGORIES

The sets of beliefs that make up the content of the following categories comprise important factors that significantly influence a patient's actions. The patients' behaviors, in turn, are crucial to their progress in therapy and success in biofeedback or related training procedures. (Surely they are not the only influences; motives, persistent ideals, habitual modes of conduct, and components of the behavioral setting are also of great importance.)

This allocation of belief types to a system of classes does not mean to imply discrete, absolute, or unrelated groupings; to a certain extent, they overlap due to the variety of elements and relationships involved. This arrangement serves only to categorize beliefs according to broad and related objects to which many different attributes can be associated. The few examples are to demonstrate the nature of implicit beliefs that are commonly encountered.

Beliefs about Psychological Relations to Physiological Processes. (I believe my thoughts _____.) Commonly heard are such implicit statements as "My pain is real, " "My mind has nothing to do with my physical problems" "It is not in my head, it is in my body." (It can be helpful here, with the EMG and GSR attached, to ask the trainee if his car keys are locked in the car. The cacophony of the auditory feedback usually helps to demonstrate the fact that the mind and body are not two separate functions.)

Beliefs about the Factors that Determine Health. (I believe my health is determined by _____.) This category primarily includes a person's opinions about what factors are relevant to health. Heredity and genetics are commonly believed to be important factors, as are familial traits and weaknesses, bacterial invasions, toxins, eating, sleeping and/or exercise practices, and detrimental habits such as smoking and alcohol consumption. Luck, chance, and/or fate are also often viewed as contributors. Many people do not, however, recognize the role of emotional stress, their beliefs about themselves (self-concepts), about the world (i.e., hostile or benign), about other people (as threats or resources), and associated attitudes that determine their readiness to respond in a consistently favorable or unfavorable manner to experience.

Beliefs about the Causes of One's Particular Expressions of Illness or Disease. (I believe my illness is caused by _____.) Most often this category will include personal stories that describe mishaps, accidents, inflicted injuries, neoplastic diseases, infections, drug side effects, old age degeneration, and factors such as those listed in the previous category along with fatigue, boredom, and affective states. [Anger, fear, guilt, shame, grief, jealousy, and frustration are considered stressful emotional states (Lazarus, 1976).]

Beliefs about the Possibility of Cure or Relief. (I believe a cure; I believe relief of my problem is _____.) Here, common statements include, "No cure exists," "Nobody knows what is wrong," "No one can help me," "Nothing will work," "Somebody has got the answer," "I am just going to have to live with it."

Beliefs about the Competence and Credibility of the Therapeutic Model and Practitioner. (I believe this treatment/practitioner is _____.) Little is usually said to the practitioner concerning the patient's disbelief in the therapeutic approach, but beliefs such as "chemotherapy (my doctor, medication, biofeedback, physical therapy, etc.) can/will cure me" are frequently expressed. Beliefs about the therapist can strongly influence beliefs about the method of treatment and its efficacy for the patient. But here again, little is usually said directly.

Beliefs about Personal Self-Regulation. (I believe self-control is _____.) In this category, one might hear, "Self-regulation is important to learn; facilitates stress management; requires daily practice; is easy to learn; is easier said than done; is great if you can do it." The beliefs of this category may be intimately associated with the beliefs of the previous categories in the formation of belief systems, attitudes, and intentions. Beliefs about self-regulation may be shaped by previously formed beliefs about psychologic effects on physiological processes, factors relevant to health and disease, the possibility of cure or relief, and/or beliefs about the therapeutic model. Conversely, beliefs about self-regulation may strongly influence the beliefs held in other categories.

COMMENTS

The influence of belief systems held by both trainee and practitioner permeate the healing arts. In research they are often labeled as placebo effects (nonspecific effects), faith healing, experimental bias, and experimenter effects. Placebo effects can be seen as related to beliefs about the therapeutic method, that is, the belief, and even expectation, that the methods of treatment will be effective in the relief or cure of illness or disease. William James, in *The Varieties of Religious Experience*, suggested that faith can operate as a healing agent (Miller & Buckhout, 1973). This idea that faith can affect health and disease has been a part of eastern philosophical systems for centuries. Central to the notion of faith healing is a strong expectant belief, conviction, or certainty that the treatment will bring about relief. Experimental bias also involves belief—the preconceived notion and possibly expectation that the design of the variables operating in an experimental situation and the methods of measurement will elucidate and possibly prove the verity of a predicted outcome. Experimenter effects are always present. They involve subtle behaviors by the experimenters that tend to influence the subjects to respond in a manner favorable to the experimenter's bias or belief in predicted outcomes.

In summary, the matrix of beliefs and the constellation of attitudes that are held within and throughout the classifications presented are of major consequence to the range of patient behaviors. They therefore effect the patient's present health status, his or her learning progress, symptom changes, and motivation dynamics. Because belief systems are enduring organizations of cognitive assumptions, and any goal-oriented action is based on these cognitions about the form, meaning, and efficacy of that action, it is important to assess and make salient the content and strength of relevant beliefs and attitudes.

REFERENCES

Fishbein, M. (Ed.) *Readings in attitude theory and measurement.* New York: John Wiley & Sons, 1967.

Fishbein, M., & Ajzen I. *Belief, attitude, intention and behavior: An introduction to theory and research.* Menlo Park, Calif.: Addison-Wesley, 1975.

Lazarus, R. S. *Patterns of adjustment.* New York: McGraw-Hill, 1976.

McGuire, W. J. The nature of attitudes and attitude change. In G. Lindzey & E. Aronsen (Eds.), *The handbook of social psychology* (2d ed.). Reading, Massachusetts Addison-Wesley, 1969.

Miller, C. A., & Buckhout, R. *Psychology: The science of mental life.* New York: Harper & Row, 1973.

14

Biofeedback Treatment in Medicine and Psychiatry: An Ultimate Placebo?

Charles F. Stroebel and Bernard C. Glueck

Speculation about the potentials of biofeedback in the treatment of psychiatric, psychosomatic, and somatopsychic disorders is widespread. Enthusiasts view biofeedback as an objective scientific means for achieving control of neural and visceral processes that are normally outside the range of conscious awareness, even though they are also associated with attention, perception, emotions, and feelings. A subjective parallel is an apparently comparable degree of control reportedly achieved through inner suggestion by practitioners of various yogic techniques.

Biofeedback actually has both objective and subjective components. The participant is placed in a closed feedback loop where information about one or more of his normally unconscious physiologic processes is made available to him as a visual, auditory, or tactile signal. The subject's progress in controlling the process (e.g., density of EEG alpha, muscle tension, or blood pressure) can be monitored objectively with a polygraph. His subjective mental state in achieving such control and his interpretation of it cannot be monitored, except by introspective report.

At present, adequate psychophysiologic data to substantiate clinical expectations for biofeedback are scarce. Because of increasing concern with issues of deception and informed consent, most present and future clinical studies will be of the demonstration type, where controls necessarily will be inadequate. The critical question of a subjective placebo effect will be raised for most of these studies, as will a variety of corollary issues, such as cotreatment contaminants, suggestion, autohypnosis, etc. Debate among experimentalists will center on this issue: Is the subject really learning biofeedback control, is he merely altering his cognitive set, or is he responding to a suggestion-placebo effect by whatever means?[6,12,14]

As clinicians, we have wondered if it ever will be possible to separate out the "real" versus the placebo effects of biofeedback in human subjects. Probably not, much to the anguish of our scientific side, which demands objectivity, experimental precision, and epistemologic surety in our quest for a scientific understanding of man and his problems.

Charles F. Stroebel • Psychophysiology Clinic and Laboratories, Institute of Living, Hartford, Connecticut 06106, and Department of Psychiatry, University of Connecticut Health Center and Medical School, Storrs, Connecticut 06268. Bernard C. Glueck • Institute of Living, Hartford, Connecticut 06106.

On the other hand, the perplexing objective–subjective mix that characterizes biofeedback may force us to recognize the existence of a "soft" clinical issue that has eluded attempts at clarification by many psychologists and physicians in the post-Watsonian era of scientific medicine. Recognition that the placebo effect, per se, is inextricably interwoven with the illness onset and illness recovery process is long overdue. The "contaminating" placebo effect may be a crucial clinical variable of utmost importance that we have minimized in our zeal for a scientific medicine.

Of course, placebo effects have not escaped scientific scrutiny. Observe the classic studies of its profound effects on pathologic pain by Beecher[2] and numerous controlled drug and psychophysiologic studies.[13,21-23,26] However, routine clinical application of our knowledge about placebos varies from disdainful neglect by "scientific" doctors, who ignore the effect, to "shamed" discomfort on the part of "unscientific" general practitioners, who recognize its influence.

This chapter will explore the possibility that biofeedback procedures may prove to be an "ultimate placebo" by squarely placing both the placebo effect and the patient himself in a position of importance in the prevention and treatment of illness. Seen in this light, the placebo component of a biofeedback procedure may assume an importance greater than its potentially active component, particularly in transfer of the active psychophysiologic principle of biofeedback out of the laboratory into daily life, and in eventual persistence of its effects.

A placebo has been defined as "any medication [treatment] used to alleviate symptoms, not by reasons of specific pharmacologic action, but solely by reinforcing the patient's favorable expectancies from treatment."[10]

Placebo procedures have been used by psychophysiologists to resolve those effects of treatment that are primary, i.e., produced by the active treatment principle, from effects that may result from implicit or explicit response predispositions on the part of the subject–patient and/or experimenter–clinician. Increasing concern with the issues of deception and informed consent in research with human subjects will significantly restrict use of such placebo procedures in future clinical research. Experimental studies with normal volunteer or paid subjects and contrived instruction procedures will likely not solve the problem, since the implicit expectations of such subjects, now almost universally high with regard to biofeedback, are hardly neutral or random.

An "ultimate placebo" might be defined as a procedure that provides the patient with an effective means of preventing illness and/or potentially curing himself by helping him regulate the pace of his daily life-style, of his thought patterns, of his body processes, his habits, and his perceptual style, reducing, it is hoped, susceptibility to pathologic levels of hyperactivation when faced with stressful life events. Suggesting that biofeedback may serve as "an ultimate placebo" does not imply that it will be universally effective, just as drug placebos vary in effectiveness with a variety of individual perceptual–coping styles (field dependence–independence, kinesthetic enhancing or reducing intolerance of sonality styles and defense mechanisms of patients to be able to optimally interact continuum of placebo reactors-nonreactors.[22] Just as physicians identify the personality sytles and defense mechanisms of patients to be able to optimally interact with them clinically,[11,19] biofeedback procedures should permit patients to use trial-and-error experience to personally optimize their own perceptual and coping styles in dealing with daily stress. Hence, usage here of the word *ultimate* implies a self-individualized path with many different options, where the person himself senses responsibility for achieving the goal of therapy.

Suggesting that biofeedback may serve as an ultimate placebo does not minimize its potential as an active therapeutic principle. Rather, it shifts the focus in a positive direction toward clinical pragmatism away from an experimental impasse with human subjects, which may never be solved with satisfaction by the rigorous standards of modern science.

BIOFEEDBACK AS REAL EFFECT

Impressive evidence for the active therapeutic principle of biofeedback does exist in animals, where the question of a subjective placebo response is minimized. Of special interest is the fact that most of these data were acquired while the animals were curarized, minimizing the possibility of feedback control via effects from setting, tensing, or manipulating of skeletal musculature. The variety of autonomic responses controlled (both decreased and increased) through instrumental feedback during the 1960s is impressive, including heart rate, intestinal contractions, kidney function, hyperemia of stomach mucosa, blood flow in specific regions of the skin, blood pressure independent of heart rate, as well as control of brain-wave activity.[16] Professor Neal Miller, a leader in this effort, has speculated (1969) that "biofeedback should be well worth trying on any symptom, functional or organic, that is under neural control, that can be continuously monitored by modern instrumentation, and for which a given direction of change is clearly indicated medically . . . for example, cardiac arrhythmias, spastic colitis, and asthma, and those cases of high blood pressure that are not essential compensation of kidney damage."[16]

Miller's stature as a leading psychobiologist gave credibility to biofeedback and its medical potential. The mass media, and not a few scientists, began to serve biofeedback up as the "new magic bullet-cure for all ills." Dozens of firms began to capitalize on this publicity by producing inexpensive over-the-counter feedback boxes. However, unpredictably, reports began emanating from Miller's laboratory that the exciting early work with operant autonomic control under curare could not be replicated. Whereas the earlier studies actually demonstrated faster acquisition of control under the curare state (explantation: muscle movement apparently interfered with visceral learning) and transfer of control to the noncurare state, studies since 1970 have demonstrated very little acquired control of variables, such as heart rate, under the curare condition. A number of explanations for the replication failure have been advanced, e.g., the usual pharmaceutical supplier of curare changed sources in 1969. It is conceivable that the curare agent available since then is less pure with some antihomeostatic effect that alters learning.

Despite the replication failure under curare, evidence for the active principle of biofeedback (i.e., acquiring voluntary control of autonomic and neural responses) remains convincing in animal studies without curare, and is affirmative, although not conclusive, in human studies.[5,9,20]

RESULTS WITH BIOFEEDBACK AS A PLACEBO EFFECT

The previous section concluded that a substantive data base now exists to assume that the active principle of biofeedback can work. However, if the active principle really were not effective, could placebo effects conceivably account for the physiologic changes that actually have been observed in human subjects? Data from a number of nonbiofeedback studies confirm this possibility. For example, Franks explored the potential role of suggestion in psychotherapy and concluded that even death was not immune from psychologic influence (voodoo death).[7] Shapiro has widely reviewed the placebo literature and cites data to support the potential of this effect in virtually every therapeutic area, including "incurable malignancies."[18]

Uncertainty about the degree of physiologic specificity obtained with placebo phenomena has been clarified in an experiment by Sternbach.[21] He gave three sets of instructions in a "drug" experiment stating that one kind of pill would relax the stomach, that a second was a placebo pill having no effect, and that the third was a stimulant to the stomach. In actuality, all three pills were identical plastic-coated magnets used to monitor gastrointestinal activity. In most subjects, the stomach motility responded in accordance with the anticipated effect of the drug.

Graham and colleagues have studied the attitudes of patients suffering from 13 different psychosomatic conditions; subsequently they suggested three specific attitudes to healthy subjects under hypnosis and observed physiologic changes partially mimicking the associated psychosomatic disorders.[8] Barber has argued that hypnosis, per se, is not needed to obtain such results, and documents numerous case studies where suggestion alone could be used to elicit and dissipate various psychosomatic disorders.[1]

If animal studies documenting the active principle of biofeedback were not available, the foregoing evidence would probably be sufficient to conclude that all of the human results with biofeedback could be explained by invoking a subjective-placebo, cognitive, expectancy, suggestion-type rationale.

SUBJECTIVE INTERPRETATION OF ALTERED STATES

A distinction should be made between the foregoing physiologic changes as opposed to psychologic concomitants of the placebo effect. Once an altered physiologic state has been achieved (via active principle or placebo effect), psychologic factors again come into operation to determine how the altered physiologic state is subjectively interpreted. Orne has described these psychologic factors as the "demand characteristics" of the situation[17]; e.g., the subject-patient's expectations of a possible alteration in mood or "high" from the experience, or implicit/explicit suggestions or cues provided by the experimenter-physician. This rationale may explain the variety and range of subjective reports obtained by Brown and others when feedback is provided within specific EEG frequency bands.[4] Figure 1 summarizes these data from several sources, including our own experience using the Clyde Mood Scale as a rating device.

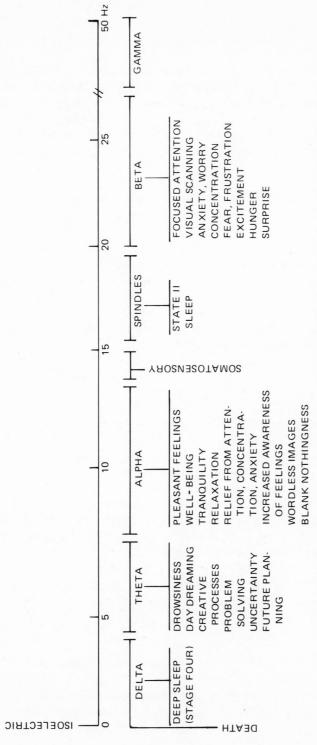

Figure 1. Moods and psychophysiologic states associated with various bands within the spectrum of EEG activity.

It is a distinct possibility that certain of the EEG states (theta and alpha) may make subjects especially prone to suggestion and/or uncritical or primary process thoughts, conceivably enhancing hypnotic phenomena and/or free association in psychoanalytic psychotherapy.

An alternative explanation for variations in subjects' mood reports correlated with a specific band of EEG activity would be the dissociation of EEG and behavioral arousal that has been demonstrated pharmacologically and in sensory deprivation experiments.[3,15,27] For example, Lynch and Paskewitz have suggested that alpha biofeedback has certain similarities to sensory deprivation, including elimination of patterned external stimulation and unfocusing of attention.[14]

EFFECTIVENESS OF BIOFEEDBACK AS BALANCE OF ACTIVE AND INACTIVE PRINCIPLES

For didactic purposes, the preceeding sections examined biofeedback separately as primarily an active or a placebo process. In reality, the two principles operate simultaneously in varying proportions. The problem is, what proportions? Obviously, some index of the interaction and balance between inactive (placebo) and active (voluntary control) components is needed for meaningful evaluation of (1) current effectiveness at any point during training and (2) prediction of long-range effectiveness.

Evaluation of the active component is straightforward, essentially being derived from a subject's "learning curve." An example would be measuring the percent of time that alpha density is above criterion during an alpha enhancement session.

Unfortunately, there has not been any description of the means for evaluating the placebo component and its interaction with the active principle in determining effectiveness of treatment. Understandably, most of us find even semiquantitative assessment of placebo effects notoriously difficult, a fact that may account for their neglect by scientific medicine.

Impressed as we are by the significant role of placebo effects in evaluating biofeedback, we have placed high priority on developing tentative models that could aid in better understanding the successes and failures with biofeedback that we have observed in our patients and subjects. It is our hope that these efforts will help overcome the previously noted experimental impasse regarding placebo effects and permit clinically effective application of biofeedback techniques; conceivably these models may advance our treatment rationale with other placebo-sensitive medical therapies.

PLACEBO–ACTIVE THERAPY INDEX MODEL

The model that we propose, called the Placebo–Active Therapeutic Index (PATI), requires the input of two easily obtained pieces of information, and calculation of two indices (Current PATI and a Prognostic PATI index) that are used to enter a table to obtain an objective estimate of (1) current effectiveness and (2) prediction of long-term effectiveness of treatment. A step-by-step procedure for using the PATI model is presented in Tables 1 and 2.

Figure 2 schematically illustrates the rationale behind the PATI model. Balanced against one another are two opposing but independent sigmoid curves representing cumulative distributions of active (on the left) and placebo (on the right) components of treatment. Once the active control and expectancy scores have been obtained (steps 1 through 3 in Table 1), each can be marked at the appropriate point on its respective sigmoid curve. Their combined (interaction) effect can be visualized as a single line connecting the two points for each trial. This line represents "current effectiveness" and indicates the degree of balance

Table 1

Placebo–Active Therapeutic Index (PATI) Procedures

Step 1: Obtain two pieces of information from each training trial as follows:
(1) *Active control score:* Estimate the degree of voluntary control achieved by the subject-patient. This estimate, easily obtained from a cumulative learning curve, is made to the nearest quartile and is assigned a score value from the following chart:

Quartile	Percent control	Score
Q_4	75%–100%	+2
Q_3	50%–74%	+1
Q_2	25%–49%	−1
Q_1	0%–24%	−2

(2) *Expectancy score:* The subject-patient is asked to rate the degree of expectancy, enthusiasm, and confidence that he has in the treatment procedure on a 3×5 card after each trial. The rating scale and its assigned score values are as follows:

Expectancy rating	Score
Very high	+2
High	+2
Moderate	−1
Low	−2

Step 2: Calculate two indices as follows:
(1) Current PATI = Active control score + Expectancy score

(2) Prognostic PATI = $\sum_{A=0}^{A=75} \dfrac{\text{Active Score}}{\text{Expectancy Score}}$

= Cumulative algebraic sign (plus, zero, minus)

of the ratio $\dfrac{\text{Active control score}}{\text{Expectancy score}}$

summed over trials until active score exceeds 75% (where the curve becomes asymptotic and nonlinear).

Step 3: (A) Obtain an adjective estimate of *Current Effectiveness of Treatment* by entering Table 2 with the current PATI (range of +4−−4).
(B) Obtain an adjective estimate predicting *Long-Term Effectiveness of Treatment* by entering Table 2 with the cumulative algebraic sign of the prognostic PATI (plus or zero vs. negative).

Table 2

Current and Long-Range Effectiveness of Therapy

Current effectiveness		Long-term effectiveness	
		Sign of Prognostic PATI	
Current PATI		Plus or zero	Negative
+4	Very high	Excellent	Questionable
+3			
+2	High	Good	Poor
+1			
0	Moderate	Questionable	Poor
−1			
−2	Low	Poor	Very poor
−3			
−4	Very low	Very poor	Very poor

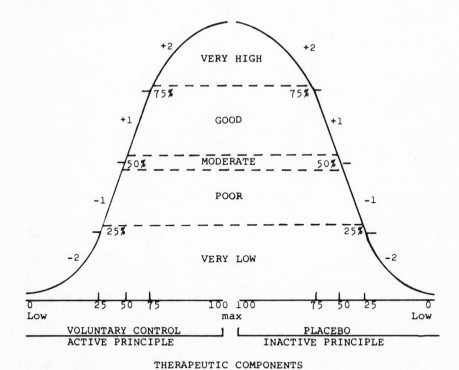

Figure 2. Schematic representation of the Placebo–Active Therapeutic Index model (PATI). Dotted lines indicating balance of a variety of active and expectancy scores are included to demonstrate the basis for the "current effectiveness" scoring scale.

and relative elevation of placebo and active components on their respective cumulative curves.

Unbalanced conditions (high active, low placebo, or low active, high placebo) counterbalance one another to contribute to current effectiveness, but tend to be unstable, carrying an unfavorable prognosis. These occur when a subject's expectations (overly enthusiastic) consistently exceed his actual success at active control, or when his expectations (overly pessimistic) are consistently less than his degress of voluntary control. In other words, a cumulative active/expectancy ratio that is negative implies that the subject is is generally unrealistic in coupling his expectancies with his degree of active control. If his expectancies have been too high, he will very likely discontinue practice of his biofeedback technique when he is not immersed in the demand characteristics surrounding his training sessions. If his expectancies are consistently too low, his motivation for continuation away from the demand characteristics of the laboratory will be even lower.

The PATI model implies that biofeedback training can be optimized by maintaining a relative balance between active control and placebo expectancies. If expectations by the subject are too high or too low over the course of training sessions, the eventual long-term effectiveness (transfer out of the laboratory and persistence) is likely to be low, even though the subject apparently performs well in the laboratory setting.

DATA TO SUPPORT THE PATI MODEL

General support for the PATI model is provided by data obtained in our laboratory in studying 50 normal and 25 psychiatric inpatient subjects in 2,150 sessions of alpha training with auditory feedback when alpha density exceeded 25% of that in an eyes-closed, control session. The data for all subjects who eventually achieved a high degree of discriminative control of alpha density can be partitioned into three groups: Group A, low expectancy; Group B, moderate expectancy; and Group C, high expectancy.

Group A subjects with consistently low expectancies generally reported that the alpha "on" condition was a "nothing" state, their minds being blank of images and words. These subjects were ambivalent, frequently missed scheduled sessions, felt that they had received very little benefit from their training experience, and stated that they did not plan to continue practicing the alpha technique when they finished training. Retests 1 month later demonstrated a significant loss of ability to achieve previous alpha densities under feedback and no-feedback conditions. This outcome was predicted by mean PATI scores for the final training session as follows: active score = +2; expectancy score = −2; current PATI = 0; prognostic PATI = (−); current effectiveness = moderate; long-term effectiveness = poor. Lines A and B in Figure 3 represent this group on the final training session (A) and 1 month later (B).

Group B subjects tended to consistently balance moderate expectancies with success at active control. They generally interpreted the alpha "on" condition as a kind of "inner calmness" that helped them regulate the style and pace of their

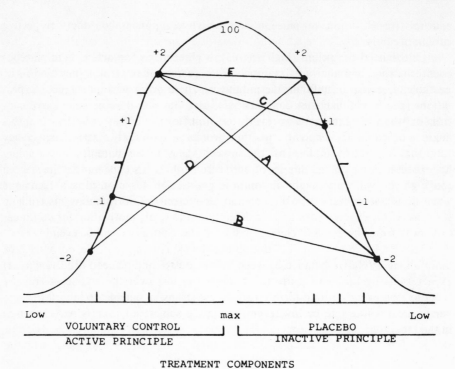

Figure 3. Illustration of five possible outcomes (A through E) for the PATI model for specific cases discussed in the text.

daily lives. At 1 and 3 months after training, they maintained their ability to control alpha and reported that they practiced alpha control daily to give perspective to their previously "rushed" daily schedule. Mean PATI scores for the last training session predicted this apparently successful outcome as follows: active = +2; expectancy = +1; current PATI = +3; prognostic PATI = 0; current effectiveness = high; long-term effectiveness = excellent; line C in Figure 3 represents this group on the final training session and at 3 months.

Group C subjects, those consistently expressing very high expectancies, tended to be evangelistic, seeking extra sessions for themselves, and recruited friends for training; they reported pleasant, tranquil, relaxed, and frequent "high" feelings during the alpha "on" condition. Retest at 1 months showed no loss of their ability to control alpha and a continuing degree of enthusiasm. While at 3 months these same subjects retained their ability to control alpha (active principle), all but two had lost their enthusiasm, reporting that they seldom had time to practice except as a means for inducing sleep. The placebo component of their training had apparently dissipated. Mean PATI scores at the last training session were consistent with this outcome: active = +2; expectancy = +2; current PATI = +4; prognostic PATI = (−); current effectiveness = very high; long-term effectiveness = questionable. In Figure 3, line D represents this group during early training; line E represents the end of training and at 1 month; line A demonstrates the loss of expectancy at 3 months.

The PATI model and data supporting it suggest that biofeedback results can be optimized if active control and expectancies of outcome are maintained in relative balance during the course of training sessions. In subsequent applications of EEG alpha and EMG as relaxation techniques, and with patients receiving differential temperature and EMG training for migraine and tension headaches, we seek to adjust a subject's expectancies to keep pace with his degree of active control. Subjects are told that their biofeedback training will be effective only to the extent that they use it to gain perspective in regulating the pace of their lives on a daily basis. They acquire their training with the expectation that the experience should be used as something more than a novel, quick "high" or as an occasional "stop-gap" self-therapy.

Regular practice and body awareness are also encouraged by daily completion of the *Psychophysiological Diary*,[24] a computer-scored record of moods, body changes, and life events. While the *Diary* does provide a continuing link with the demand characteristics of the laboratory, it also encourages the subject to view himself as the responsible agent in regulating his life-style and health. He becomes the crucial link in maintaining his own placebo-expectancy response.

This transformation in the old adage of "Physician, heal [by] thyself" to "Patient, heal thyself" has promising potential for reasonably intelligent, middle-class patients.

FURTHER IMPLICATIONS OF THE PATI MODEL

Examination of the time-course of active/expectancy ratios during training for a variety of biofeedback procedures reveals a differentiating principle that is a useful guideline for the experimenter-clinician in regulating his own role as a placebo agent in optimizing long-term effectiveness. This principle, which emerges from analysis of Figure 4, suggests that biofeedback procedures can be categorized into one of two types, general or specific, as listed in Table 3.

"General-type" biofeedback procedures, including EEG alpha and theta enhancement and frontalis muscle EMG reduction, require what has been described as "passive volition" or defocusing of attention for achieving relaxation and lower levels of general arousal, external attention, and tension, states thought to be incompatible with a flight-or-fight response to stress. For these procedures, the expectancy score tends to be significantly greater than the active score, particularly during early training, as shown in Figure 4.

"Specific-type" biofeedback techniques include a variety of procedures used to regulate or lower the activation of a target organ system that presents clinically as a psychosomatic symptom. Like the general type, voluntary control in the specific situation also involves a kind of passive volition, but also permits a much greater degree of mental activity and attention to external cues. Hence, these procedures can more easily be incorporated into a behavioral therapy desensitiza-

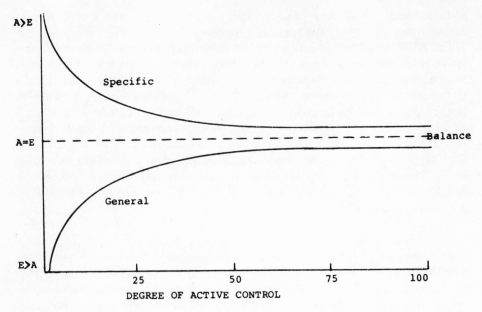

Figure 4. Biofeedback procedures can be differentiated into general and specific types based on study of relative predominance of active (A) or expectancy (E) scores over the course of training (see Table 3).

Table 3

Types of Biofeedback

General[a]	Specific[b]
EEG alpha	Thermal
	Migrane headache
	Raynaud's disease
EEG theta	Neck EMG
	Tension headache
Frontalis EMG	Back EMG
	Muscular back pain
	pH
	Gastric ulcer
	Pressure
	Irritable colon
	Blood pressure
	Ulcerative colitis
	EKG
	Cardiac dysrhythmias

[a] Objective: relaxation and lowering of tension.
[b] Objective: to regulate or lower the activation of a target organ system.

tion framework. For specific-type procedures, the active control score usually exceeds the expectancy score until the subject begins to experience symptom relief from his training (see Figure 4).

These derivations of the PATI model predict that long-term effectiveness of training can be optimized through regular use of PATI ratings, permitting the experimenter-clinician as a placebo agent to verbally suppress a subject's tendencies toward high expectancies during early trials in general-type training; in contrast, low expectancies should be actively boosted during early phases of specific types of training.

The PATI model may prove useful in predicting current and long-term effectiveness of any procedure or treatment that is placebo-sensitive. Two examples will be cited.

An incredible range of benefits (improved memory and concentration, controlled headaches, solved problems, sleep without drugs, complete relaxation, improved schoolwork, controlled bad habits, development of your intuition and ESP) is being advertised nationally for several varieties of nonbiofeedback "alpha–theta mind control," which are taught as intensive courses lasting 30–40 hours. Testimonials and high-pressured confrontation apparently are used to create exceedingly high expectancies and a heightened state of autosuggestibility in participants. The actual degree of alpha or theta control achieved is not routinely measured, and has been quite low in several ex-participants who requested postcourse testing in a biofeedback laboratory. Given the conditions of very high expectancy and very low active control (see line D, Figure 3), the PATI model would predict that these techniques for achieving advertised benefits will be moderately effective during the course, but will possess very poor long-term effectiveness when participants are no longer immersed in the demand characteristics of the course itself, including social interaction with other participants and the instructor.

A second extension of the PATI model can be made into a nonbiofeedback technique for achieving deep relaxation: transcendental meditation (TM). Traditionally, TM training involves 4 hours of lectures, during which the instructor seeks to create very high expectancies about potential benefits from learning the technique ("creative intelligence," "unstressing the nervous system") followed by 1 hour of actual meditation instruction and 3 hours of group discussion and meditation. While Wallace[25] has demonstrated that experienced meditators do achieve a state of deep relaxation by psychophysiologic criteria, the percentage of new meditators rapidly achieving a significant degree of relaxation ("active control") is not routinely measured and is uncertain. For subjects who are slow in achieving active control, the PATI model would predict a moderate degree of current effectiveness during training succeeded by very poor long-term effectiveness. In fact, a significant attrition rate has been observed 2–3 months after training. The PATI model suggests several ways TM training could be optimized. First, instructors should be moderate in creating high expectancies during initial lectures before the actual technique for achieving active control is provided; second, active contact should be continued with the initiate to maintain his expectancies until it is reasonably certain that he can consistently achieve a degree of active control-relaxation equivalent to his expectations. A number of TM instructors have reportedly begun incorporating a program of continuing contact into their training procedure with significant reduction of the attrition rate.

DISCUSSION

Experience with a variety of biofeedback techniques with normal subjects and patients led us to the conclusion that exclusive consideration of the active component of biofeedback, without consideration of the placebo-expectancy component, was an inadequate basis for meaningful clinical application of the procedures. Persistence and transfer of training to real-life situations outside the laboratory on a continuing basis apparently require consideration of additional factors in the form of a self-reinforcing placebo effect or other type of reward.

A simple model called the Placebo–Active Therapeutic Index (PATI) was developed to incorporate and legitimate placebo-expectancy effects as an important component of biofeedback training to be evaluated and manipulated, rather than ignored or neglected.

The model, which has proved useful with a variety of general and specific biofeedback procedures, emphasizes the need for achieving a relative balance of active and expectancy factors to optimize long-term effectiveness of training. Improvements and potential correlates (e.g., personality style) of the model and its relatively crude scoring scheme (to the nearest quartile) are under continuing investigation.

Analysis of the model lends support to the concept of biofeedback procedures as an "ultimate placebo." For example, the successes of modern scientific medicine have been widely impressed upon the populace by the mass media in various forms: medical soap operas, documentaries, and commercials for patent medicines. The public has come to expect a "magic-bullet" pill or a "60-minute TV-doctor cure" by an omnipotent physician who allegedly possesses a vast armamentarium of infallible cures. So well has this message been received that physicians are no longer expected or permitted to make occasional mistakes. According to this modern prescription, the doctor has become solely responsible for the cure, not the patient.

It is true that once tissue pathology has occurred, whether through infection, trauma, poison, congenital defect, or tumor, external intervention by modern medicine to patch the defect is often impressive and largely beyond the subjective control of the patient. However, the vast majority of ills and the illness-onset situation itself[18] are clearly not beyond subjective control. These cannot be the private domain of the doctor-scientist but are a matter of responsibility for each individual.

Modern medicine probably does not sufficiently emphasize this need for individual responsibility. Acclimated as he is to be a recipient rather than a participant in treatment, modern man may require personal demonstration through a structured period of self-learning to incorporate the concept of individual responsibility into his daily life-style in times of both health and illness. Biofeedback may serve as an optimal procedure for a structured self-learning experience, since individuals can learn firsthand about regulating the effects of daily stress on body functioning.

Many scientist-physicians wonder "what is missing" and become defeatists when they observe widespread lack of compliance by patients in taking prescribed medications, in following dietary restrictions, and in regulating their pace of life. The "something" that is missing may be the more active involvement of the patient himself in the prevention–treatment process. Balanced recognition and application of both active and expectancy factors in biofeedback may provide a meaningful basis for helping man acquire this involvement, becoming, in essence, his own ultimate placebo.

ACKNOWLEDGMENTS. The authors are indebted to the following for assistance: Jane Archer, Laverne Barbagallo, R. N., Brooke Craven, Charles Glueck, and Michael Scammon. We are also grateful to Erik Peper and Gay Luce for their advice at the early stages of our work with biofeedback.

REFERENCES

1. Barber, T. X. *LSD, marihuana, yoga and hypnosis*. Chicago, Aldine, 1970.
2. Beecher, H. A. Pain: One mystery solved. *Science*, 1966, *151*, 840.
3. Bradley, P. B. Central action of certain drugs in relation to the reticular formation of the brain. In H. H. Japser (Eds.), *The reticular formation of the brain*. Boston: Little, Brown, 1958.
4. Brown, B. Recognition of aspects of consciousness through association with EEG alpha activity represented by a light signal. *Psychophysiology*, 1970, *6*, 442.
5. Budzynski, T., Stoyva, J., & Adler, C. Feedback-induced muscle relaxation: Application to tension headache. *Journal of Behavior Therapy and Experimental Psychiatry*, 1970, *1*, 205.
6. Crider, A., Schwartz, G. E., & Shnidman, S. R. On the criteria for instrumental autonomic conditioning: A reply to Katkin and Murray. *Psychological Bulletin*, 1969, *71*, 455.
7. Franks, J. D. *Persuasion and healing*. Baltimore: Johns Hopkins Press, 1961.
8. Graham, D. T., Kabler, J. D., & Graham, F. K. Physiological response to the suggestion of attitudes specific for hives and hypertension. *Phychosomatic Medicine*, 1962, *24*, 159.
9. Green, E. E., Green, A. M., & Walters, E. D. Voluntary control of inner states: Psychological and physiological. *Journal of Transpersonal Psychology*, 1970, *2*, 1.
10. Hirsie, L. E., & Campbell, R. J. *Psychiatric Dictionary* (3rd ed.). New York: Oxford University Press, 1960.
11. Kahana, R. J., & Bibring G. L. Personality types in medical management, In N. Zinberg (Ed.), *Psychiatry and medical practice*. New York: International University press, 1964. Pp. 108–123.
12. Katkin, K. E., & Murray, E. N. Instrumental conditioning of autonomically mediated behavior: Theoretical and methodological issues. *Psychological Bulletin*, 1968, *70*, 52.
13. Lasagna, L., Mosteller, F., von Felsinger, J., et al. A study of the placebo response. *American Journal of Medicine*, 1954, *16*, 770.
14. Lynch, J. J., & Paskewitz, D. A. *On the mechanisms of the feedback control of human brain wave activity. Biofeedback and self control*. Chicago: Aldine, 1971.
15. Mathews, A. M. Psychophysiological approaches to the investigation of desensitization and related procedures. *Psychological Bulletin*, 1971, *76*, 73.
16. Miller, N. E. Learning of visceral and glandular responses. *Science*, 1969, *163*, 434.
17. Orne, M. T. On the social psychology of the psychological experiment: With particular reference to demand characteristics and their implications. *American Psychologist*, 1962, *17*, 776.

18. Shapiro, A. K. Factors contributing to the placebo effect: Their implications for psychotherapy. *American Journal of Psychotherapy*, 1964, *Suppl.*, 73.
19. Shapiro, D. *Neurotic styles*. New York: Basic Books, 1965.
20. Shapiro, D., & Schwartz, G. E. Biofeedback and visceral learning clinical applications. *Seminars in Psychiatry*,. 1972, *4*, 171–184.
21. Sternback, R. A. The effects of instructional sets on autonomic responsivity. *Psychophysiology*, 1964, 1, 67.
22. Sternbach, R. A. *Pain: A psychophysiological analysis*. New York: Academic Press, 1968.
23. Stroebel, C. F. Psychophysiological pharmacology. In N. S. Greenfield & R. A. Sternbach (Eds.), *Handbook of psychophysiology*, New York: Holt, Rinehart & Winston, 1972.
24. Stroebel, C. F., Luce, C. G., & Glueck, B. C. *Psychophysiological diary: A computer scored daily record of moods, body changes and life events*.Hartford: Institute of Living, 1971.
25. Wallace, R. K. Physiological effects of transcendental meditation. *Science*, 1970, *167*, 1751.
26. Wolf, S., Doering, C., Clark, M., & Hagans, J. Chance distribution and the placebo "reactor." *Journal of Laboratory and Clinical Medicine*, 1957, *49*, 837.
27. Zubek, J. P. Physiological and biochemical effects. In *Sensory deprivation: Fifteen years of research*. New York: Appleton-Century, 1969.

15

Belief in Biofeedback for the Control of Short-Term Stress

J. Douglas Gibb, Eric Stephan, and C. E. Tapie Rohm, Jr.

This research explores the effect of biofeedback training and mental expectation or "belief" on the relief of short-term stress. Three experiments using a total of 165 subjects demonstrated that similar low levels of tension could be achieved with physical training using biofeedback instruments or with "belief" training using a biofeedback machine for a demonstration only. Two physiological indicants of short-term stress were the subjects' muscle tension and finger temperatures. The results seem to indicate the possibility of a method of instruction for educators and therapists that, when coupled with traditional biofeedback training, may produce superior results at a reduced monetary investment.

One problem of concern to persons undertaking to master the performing disciplines is that of remaining calm while anticipating a pressure situation. Development of a reliable method for doing this would have value to such persons. Biofeedback has been touted as such a method. Despite the concern and recent research in biofeedback, where subjects are able to reach low levels of relaxation within a few sessions (Budzynski & Stoyva, 1969; Green, Walters, Green, & Murphy, 1969), compared to the lengthy training required with other techniques (McCroskey, Ralph, & Barrick, 1970; Schultz & Luthe, 1958), there has been little time devoted to the study of the potential importance of mental expectation or the belief aspects of the process (see Pelletier & Peper, 1974).

Our work in the past three years, relating to the reduction of anxiety prior to performance in speech, drama, music, and athletics using biofeedback techniques, has developed an awareness of a certain pattern of behavior with respect to naive subject's physical responses. Sally was typical; when requested to give an impromptu speech she would tense herself in preparation for the task. Two physiological indicants of her tension were muscle contraction and peripheral vascular system constriction, which resulted in lowering the temperature of her fingers. Though this kind of reaction is self-defeating, she was able to give an adequate speech. With the aid of feedback instrumentation, which provided a monitor of her inner physical activity, she soon realized that she had been associating

J. Douglas Gibb • Department of Speech and Dramatic Arts, Brigham Young University, Provo, Utah 84602.   Eric Stephan • Communications Department, Interpersonal and Organizational Division, Brigham Young University, Provo, Utah 84602.   C. E. Tapie Rohm, Jr. • College of Osteopathic Medicine, Ohio State University, Athens, Ohio 45701.

good speaking with high levels of muscular tension and cold hands, and repeated this error at every speaking performance. Now, however, she wanted help. She felt that her performances were not improving as they should be with practice, and further, she felt unhappy and uncomfortable with the whole speaking experience.

At this point Sally was taught how to relax when anticipating a speech by using electromyograph feedback training. Surface electrodes were attached to her frontalis muscles and a small meter with a needle reading from 0 to 50 microamperes was placed before her (Model PE-2, Biofeedback Systems Inc.,2736 47th St., Boulder, Colorado 80301). She was encouraged to relax her frontalis muscles, thus lowering the meter reading, while thinking about giving the speech in a manner used by Budzynski, Stoyva, and Adler 1971. After a short period of training, Sally was able to reach a low level of muscle tension. She could hold the meter needle steady at this low limit even while she was thinking about the speech. The electromyograph reading suggested desensitization had occurred.

Since the mind's expectation seems to play such an important role in biofeedback achievement, we decided to alter the desensitization method in order to determine whether or not Sally had reached her lowest physical relaxation limit. We asked her to tense her body muscles and then quickly release them and try to lower the meter reading to the lowest level. This she did repeatedly for four trials. Each time she reached a low-level reading of 18. She could not get lower but she could reach 18 on that trial.

The instrument used on Sally provided three sensitivity settings so that a meter reading of 18 on the low-sensitivity setting would read 26 on the medium setting although the subject would still be at the same tension level. On a subsequent trial with Sally, we asked her to tense her muscles by gritting her teeth and squinting her eyes. While she was doing this we changed the machine sensitivity level from low to medium without her awareness of the change. Our thinking was that if she had truly reached her lowest physical relaxation level then we would get a reading of 26 when she relaxed. This would be the same microvolt output as the earlier readings of 18. To our surprise, Sally returned the needle to 18. She could achieve a much lower relaxation level by believing she could.

This same procedure was then used with other subjects and essentially the same results were achieved. All the subjects tended to move in the direction of

Table 1

Analysis of Covariance—Deviations from Regression

Source	df	MS	F
Between groups	1	5.48	30.44[a]
Within groups	29	.18	
Total	30		

[a] $p = .05$.

Table 2

Mean Scores in Microvolts between Groups for the Data in
Table 1

	3rd trial	4th trial
Control group (no change in electrical sensitivity setting)	5.74	5.78
Experimental group (change from low to medium sensitivity)	6.04	5.23

their "belief level" rather than stopping at the original "physical level." Results from eight male and eight female experimental subjects and eight male and eight female control subjects were analyzed with a covariance design. Tables 1 and 2 show the results.

We now became quite interested in the "belief" factor and its influence on relaxation during short-term stress. One hundred and eight students participated in the next experiment. At the first instruction session they were told that their task was to learn to relax during the anticipation stage of receiving a topic for an impromptu speech. We explained that after selecting their topic they would have 15 seconds to prepare the speech. The quality of their presentation would be judged and their muscle tension and hand temperature would be measured and recorded just seconds before they received the impromptu topic. At the second instruction session the students were divided into three groups. One group was trained with the use of biofeedback machines to achieve a low of tension while thinking about the impromptu speaking assignment. Another group was given a demonstration, which helped them believe that biofeedback training really worked, by observing one of their peers producing a low meter reading during an EMG relaxation measured exercise. They were then asked to form a clear image

Table 3

Analysis of Variance of the Data in Experiment
II—Muscle Tension

Groups (A)	2	269.80	5.13[a]
Between groups 3 & 1, 2	1	401.17	7.63[a]
Between groups 1 & 2	1	138.42	
Sex (B)	1	223.32	4.25[a]
Behavioral intention (C)	2	30.62	
A × B	2	167.80	
A × C	4	10.01	
B × C	2	19.92	
A × B × C	4	39.83	
Within cells	90	52.56	
Total	107		

[a] $p = .05$.

Table 4

Analysis of Variance of the Data in Experiment II—Finger Temperature

Source	df	MS	F
Groups (A)	2	122.06	—
Sex (B)	1	.67	—
Behavioral Intention (C)	2	49.80	—
A × B	2	2.45	—
A × C	4	13.13	—
B × C	2	41.62	—
A × B × C	4	94.54	—
Within cells	90	50.82	
Total	107		

in their minds of a low EMG needle reading a successful lowering of muscle tension to deep levels of relaxation even while thinking about the impromptu speech. The third group was a control group and received no physical or mental training in biofeedback. An intention factor and a sex factor were included in the experiment as further investigative variables. As Tables 3 and 4 indicate, both methods, belief and physical, showed highly significant muscle tension reduction.

As we had not predicted, there were no significant differences in hand temperatures among the three groups. We hypothesized that the subjects never set or were trained to set a belief level or physical level expectation of the blood flow in their fingers. Consequently, nothing happened, except that we tried one last experiment. Twenty-four subjects with no feedback training experience were informed that their task was to keep their hands warm during the anticipation stage of receiving a topic for an impromptu speech. We followed the previous pattern of instruction for training, gave them a demonstration and an explanation that it could be done successfully, and then asked them to visualize themselves warming their hands, and set a successful temperature reading in their minds. Again controlled comparisons demonstrated that the subjects trained in "belief" could raise the temperature of their hands successfully.

We conclude these exploratory studies by suggesting that a "belief method" is equal to, or in some cases superior to, methods generally used today in the process of controlling short-term stress. Undoubtedly, the use of "belief" together with a sound understanding of biofeedback training offers new frontiers of development for all who are engaged in the performing and therapeutic arts.

REFERENCES

Budzynski, T. H., & Stoyva, J. M. An instrument for producing deep muscle relaxation by means of analog information feedback. *Journal of Applied Behavioral Analysis*, 1969, *2*, 231–237.

Budzynski, T. H., Stoyva, J. M., & Adler, C. Feedback-induced muscle relaxation: Application to tension headache. In T. X. Barber et al. (Eds.), *Biofeedback & Self-Control: 1970*. Chicago: Aldine, 1971.

Green, E. E., Walters, E. D., Green, A. M., & Murphy, G. Feedback techniques for deep relaxation. *Psychophysiology*, 1969, *6*, 371–377.

McCroskey, J. C., Ralph, D. C., & Barrick, J. E. The effects of systematic desensitization on speech anxiety. *Speech Teacher*, 1970, *19*, 32–36.

Pelletier, K. R., & Peper, E. The chutzpah factor in psychophysiological parameters of altered states of consciousness. In *Proceedings of the Biofeedback Research Society 1974*. Denver: USMC, 1974, No. 202.

Schultz, J. H., & Luthe, W. *Autogenic training: A psychophysiologic approach in psychotherapy.* New York: Grune and Stratton, 1958.

TECHNICAL CONSIDERATIONS IN BIOFEEDBACK

The use of biofeedback requires a working knowledge of instrumentation since successful outcome of biofeedback training is totally dependent on the appropriate technology and accurate use and interpretation of the equipment. Hence a basic understanding of how, why, and what the machines do is essential. The electrodes (sensors) must be placed correctly on skin that has been prepared properly. Batteries may need to be checked. The user must be sure that when the equipment indicates an increase or decrease in psychophysiological functioning, it represents an actual physiological change and is not an artifact such as the movement of an electrode wire, or electromagnetic interference produced by a building elevator moving between floors.

The articles in this section cover some of the basic and fundamental ideas that we consider minimum requirements. Peper (Chapter 16) reviews behavioral methods that can be used to test the relative accuracy of the equipment when calibration equipment is not available. Beck and Peper (Chapter 17) humorously encapsulate some of the problems encountered in biofeedback research. This is included to assure those new in the field (and those of us not so new) that we are not alone in our mistakes. In fact, anyone who has ever used biofeedback equipment (or for that matter has ever done research) will attest that, when new techniques, machines, procedures, or pilot studies are being explored, errors are always made. Most of these errors are never discussed in scientific publications and are newly reexperienced by students and practitioners. Yet Murphy's Law applies in the scientific laboratory: "If anything can go wrong, it will." Let us hope that, by being aware and properly educated, the reader can avoid the most common errors.

As previously mentioned, knowledge of instrumentation is critical. Gaarder and Montgomery (Chapter 18) review and explain the function and mechanics behind the equipment used for the different feedback training modalities. This will be especially helpful for the biofeedback trainer just getting involved in this field. The last three articles cover the more technical aspects of equipment. Strong (Chapter 19) defines and explains how electrodes work. Toomim, Schandler, Spiegel, Freeman, and Elder give the standard specifications of different equipment, explaining what it all means (Chapter 20), and provide a glossary of terms (Chapter 21) with which every person using biofeedback should become familiar.

Finally, knowing what the equipment *cannot* do is also critical. One needs to know the technical limitations of the equipment. The user must be aware that the signal recorded and fed back is only *that* signal which the equipment selectively records. This does *not* mean that it represents the total psychophysiological signal. This point was made earlier in regard to fast EEG activity (Peper & Ancoli, Chapter 9). They pointed out that traditional EEG recordings usually filter out fast beta EEG activity. Often this filtering is done to eliminate 60-Hz artifact, induced by the ever-present alternating current. However, when 60-Hz artifact is eliminated, the possibility of observing a real 60-Hz biological signal is also eliminated. By understanding the limitations of the equipment and the band width of recording, one realizes that other parameters not recorded also exist and these too may reflect actual psychophysiological changes. By knowing the boundaries, we can avoid wearing equipment-limited blinders.

While this section is far from complete and quite short of providing a full technical background, the reader who carefully completes this section should have a basic understanding of the technical considerations of the equipment.

The following sources are suggested for additional technical considerations encountered with psychophysiological recording: Brown (1967), Cromwell, Weibell, Pfeiffer, & Usselman (1973), Geddes and Baker (1975), Greenfield & Sternbach (1972), Hassett (1978), Strong (1967), and Venables & Martin (1967).

REFERENCES

Brown, C. *Methods in psychophysiology*. Baltimore: Williams & Wilkins, 1967.

Cromwell, L., Weibell, G. J., Pfeiffer, E. A., & Usselman, L. B. *Biomedical instrumentation and measurements*. Englewood Cliffs, New Jersey: Prentice-Hall, 1973.

Geddes, L. A., & Baker, L. E. *Principles of applied biomedical instrumentation*. New York: Wiley, 1975.

Greenfield, N. S., & Sternbach, R. *Handbook of psychophysiology*. New York: Holt, Rinehart & Winston, 1972.

Hassett, J. *A primer of psychophysiology*. San Francisco: W. H. Freeman, 1978.

Strong, P. *Biophysical measurements*. Beaverton, Oregon: Tektronix, 1967.

Venables, P. H., & Martin, I. *Manual of psychophysiological methods*. Amsterdam: North Holland Publications, 1967.

16

A Beginner's Behavioral Test Guide to Biofeedback Instrumentation

Erik Peper

This chapter focuses on a few techniques that a practitioner should know when he uses biofeedback equipment. Since biofeedback is a psychophysiological mirror, it is useful only if the equipment records and amplifies the biological signal accurately. The techniques discussed will apply to electromyographic (EMG), thermal, electrodermal (EDR or GSR), or skin potential response (SPR), and electroencephalic (EEG) biofeedback equipment. Obviously these concepts can be extended to other feedback devices not discussed here. The recorded measures must be accurate so that the practitioner can interpret changes in the feedback signal as indications of changes in the psychophysiology or autonomic self-regulation of the trainee (Peper, 1974). (The term *trainee* is used instead of *patient* or *client* as I perceive biofeedback training as a learning tool.) For example, the EMG of the forearm extensor could be as high as 18 μV even though there is no voluntary muscle tension. The reading may imply that the person had tensed his forearm extensors through lifting the fingers or bending the hand back at the wrist, and that the reading is *not* due to artifacts such as 60-Hz or sensor (electrode) lead movements. To avoid misinterpretation of the recorded physiological data, the practitioner should be familiar with the human interface of the equipment: (1) knowledge of the equipment, i.e., the flow diagram, which is a schematic representation of how the signal is processed; (2) external, internal, and physiological factors affecting the biological functions recorded; and (3) suggested behavioral testing procedures to assess whether the biofeedback equipment is working. This knowledge is crucial for a practitioner who works independently and has no quick and easy access to precision laboratory test procedures. The practitioner must be confident that the feedback equipment is operating appropriately.

KNOWLEDGE OF THE EQUIPMENT

The practitioner should have a basic understanding of the equipment's function and operation through the flow diagram and a thorough knowledge of the

Erik Peper • Center for Interdisciplinary Science, San Francisco State University, San Francisco, California 94134.

owner's manual. He should understand the transformation from input of the signal to output of the physiological data inside the "black box." (This information is often found in the manufacturer's equipment manual or can be obtained from the sales personnel.) The practitioner should know which segments of the biological signal *are* or *are not* recorded, amplified, filtered, or integrated. For example, in electromyographic feedback equipment, the frequency band pass is typically set between 100 and 200 or 1000 Hz. This means that muscle signals of less than 100 Hz or greater than 200 or 1000 Hz are not recorded; there are muscle frequency spectra outside this bandpass which could contain valuable information, especially in the lower frequency range, which increases in power as the muscles relax more.

Once the flow diagram is understood, the practitioner may test the equipment and sensor. To test the accuracy of a thermal feedback device, the practitioner compares it with standardized thermometers and thereby recalibrates his equipment. To measure the basal level of the EDR (GSR), the practitioner inserts a resistor of known value such as 50 kΩ between the electrodes and compares it to the observed recording and recalibrates the equipment. To observe the combined noise level of the equipment and especially of the ambient 60-Hz effects on the sensor cable for EEG and EMG, the practitioner uses a "dummy subject." Usually the dummy subject consists of using two 10 kΩ resistors. Each resistor is placed between the active and ground sensor. The observed active noise level, which could be as high as 2 μV, would then be subtracted from the subject's reading to ascertain a true EMG or EEG level. When doubtful readings occur, the practitioner must initiate problem solving, through checking in sequence each part of the feedback circuit.

Other problems can also be expected. The probability of inaccurate, artifact-filled recording is enhanced by poor sensor contact (resulting in excessive or unbalanced sensor impedence); therefore, the practitioner must check the impedance of sensors. Often poor sensor contact, broken sensor leads, or poor electrical contacts of switches in the equipment cause transient or intermittent problems. In many cases, the life-span of the EEG and EMG sensors is less than one year. In addition, offset problems are often caused by miscalibrated equipment, different sensors, or low battery voltage. Every time the equipment is used, the batteries must be tested. When the battery voltage is low, unreliable readings usually occur. Thus basic knowledge of the equipment can reduce or eliminate most transient and constant offset errors.

KNOWLEDGE OF THE EXTERNAL AND INTERNAL FACTORS WHICH AFFECT THE PSYCHOPHYSIOLOGICAL SIGNAL

The practitioner must know the following.
1. The External Factors Affecting the Recording at the Sensor (Electrode) Site. The most common external factors affecting the physiological recording are

environmental artifacts. Examples of transient external factors include CB radio interference with EEG and EMG, or an increase in apparent EEG and EMG activity due to the additional 60-cycle input each time the practitioner touches the trainee. Constant offset might include such factors as increased EMG readings (15 μV instead of 4 μV) due to constant 60-cycle artifact.

Whenever doubtful readings occur, possibly due to external artifacts, one or more of the four following steps should be taken to see if the recording levels are affected:

A. Change the relative physical position of the trainee and the biofeedback unit.
B. Turn on and off lights and other operating machines such as air-conditioners, typewriters, neighbor's TV, etc.
C. Disconnect sensors from unit and then ground the trainee to earth (e.g., a water pipe), then reattach sensors. Be sure there is no AC or DC voltage on the sensor leads before re-attaching to a grounded trainee.
D. Re-prepare sensor site and reapply sensors.

There are a number of other external factors that may affect the readings. For example, thermal feedback is affected by room temperature. If the room is warm, the trainee's hand is likely to be warmer than if the room is cold. In addition, where and how the thermistor is attached affects the reading. If the person covers the thermistor with another finger or rests it on another part of the body, the temperature will usually increase due to additional warmth from that body part. In this case the apparent increase in peripheral temperature obviously does *not* signify that the subject has learned to control temperature, only that the thermistor has touched a warmer object. Finally, with EDR, artifactual recordings can be obtained if the trainee gently squeezes the electrode pads and thereby increases the conductance. Movement of electrodes or sensors is another common cause of signal artifact.

2. The Internal Factors Affecting the Various Physiological Systems. One common internal factor affecting the recorded date is incorrect knowledge of body functioning. The function and limits of the physiological system should be understood, e.g., what is the range of peripheral temperatures which can be expected or which is the antagonistic muscle. Often it is impossible to teach a certain type of physiological control since two parts of the task are incompatible. For example, when one records the EMG activity of a muscle being used for lifting an object, that muscle cannot relax unless the person stops lifting the object.

Body position can also be critical since in certain positions the body, or parts of it, cannot relax.

Finally, the internal physiological system may be difficult to bring under voluntary control because it is being regulated by medication. In the case of EEG, fast beta is often associated with barbiturate intake. Peripheral temperature is affected by nicotine intake, since the nicotine causes vasoconstriction and thereby a decrease in peripheral temperature.

KNOWLEDGE OF BEHAVIORAL TECHNIQUES WHICH CAN ASSESS THE FUNCTIONING OF THE BIOFEEDBACK EQUIPMENT

Behavioral techniques to test the relative accuracy of the equipment consist of a series of exercises that the trainee performs while the practitioner monitors the effect upon the feedback recording. They are used "on line" to test the function of the equipment. These tests are done routinely after the trainee has been attached to the sensors. With this approach, the practitioner observes the behavior of the trainee to see if it is synchronous with the feedback signal. *He observes both the trainee's behavior and the feedback signal.* Only if the two are congruent (the apparent behavior of the trainee and the appropriate direction of the feedback signal) does the practitioner accept the relative accuracy of the biofeedback equipment.

The behavioral testing for the biofeedback devices can be done as follows.

EMG. The surface sensors are attached over the appropriate muscle bundle and the trainee is asked to tense and relax that muscle. For example, if the sensors are placed over the frontal area (Basmajian, 1976), the EMG should increase when the trainee wrinkles his forehead and decrease as the trainee smooths his forehead. This test gives a relative indication of whether the EMG is working.

Temperature. Before the thermistor is attached to the trainee, the practitioner gently exhales his warm breath over the thermistor. The recorded temperature should increase. Then the practitioner inhales cool air over the thermistor and the recorded temperature should decrease. If the thermistor is already attached to the trainee, then the practitioner could touch his own finger to the thermistor. If his fingers are warmer than the trainee's fingers, the temperature feedback device will indicate an increase in temperature, while if his fingers are colder than the trainee's, the feedback will indicate a decrease in temperature. This test will give a relative indication of whether the thermal feedback device is working.

A fairly accurate measure can be obtained by placing the thermistor underneath the arm and the axillary temperature can be used as a relatively accurate standard measure; the meter should read $96° \pm 2°$.

EDR (GSR and SPR). Have the trainee take a deep breath, hold for a count of 30, and then exhale rapidly; this will usually elicit a rapid increase in skin conductance. Another technique is to have the practitioner touch or scratch the trainee, make a loud unexpected noise, or ask the trainee to think of an unpleasant situation. Any one of these orienting techniques should show a temporary increase in sympathetic activity. The response indicates that the EDR feedback unit is in relative working order.

EEG. The practitioner places the sensors over the trainee's occipital area. The trainee is instructed to close his eyes. In the condition of eyes closed and relaxed, 80% of the trainees will exhibit some alpha EEG activity. If the feedback indicated that the alpha EEG occurs in the trainee, ask him to open his eyes and focus on a near object; the alpha EEG should totally disappear. The EEG feedback should be used only if the alpha activity disappears when the trainee opens his eyes and focuses. If alpha EEG unit indicates alpha with the eyes focusing, the feedback signal is in most cases incorrect (Mulholland & Peper, 1971).

These tests increase confidence in the recorded data. Note, however, that this approach demonstrates the relative function of the equipment but does not usually test absolute levels.

A subjective "sense of accuracy" is slowly learned through familiarity with the equipment. With time, the practitioner learns the idiosyncratic behavior of his equipment and thereby may be able to estimate its performance. Generally, any unusual monitoring and/or feedback patterns are suspect until proven correct.

Every trainee routinely should be taken through these behavioral tests to check the relative functioning of the equipment. A successful behavioral test is one in which the feedback signal varies in the appropriate direction with the biological activity. When the feedback confirms the behavioral tests, the practitioner can trust the feedback as a relatively accurate psychophysiological mirror, reflecting the internal physiological changes, and can have confidence in the relative accuracy of the data.

Obviously, the problems described and their solution are *not* exhaustive but constitute a brief description of some of those most commonly encountered. There are many more sources of artifact and error, which can range from polarization of electrodes through impedance testing to the poor condition of electrode cream. For a more comprehensive treatment, the reader is referred to Brown, 1967; Cromwell, Weibell, Pfeiffer, and Usselman, 1973; Geddes and Baker, 1975; Greenfield and Sternbach, 1972.

ACKNOWLEDGMENTS. The author thanks Michael James, Francine Butler, and Thomas Budzynski for their helpful suggestions.

REFERENCES

Basmajian, J. V. Facts vs. myths in EMG biofeedback. *Biofeedback and Self-Regulation*, 1976, *1*(4), 369–371.

Brown, C. *Methods in psychophysiology*. Baltimore: Williams & Wilkins, 1967.

Cromwell, L., Weibell, G. J., Pfeiffer, E. A., & Usselman, L. B. *Biomedical instrumentation and measurements*. Englewood Cliffs, New Jersey: Prentice-Hall, 1973.

Geddes, L. A., & Baker, L. E. *Principles of applied biomedical instrumentation*. New York: Wiley, 1975.

Greenfield, N. S., & Sternbach, R. *Handbook of psychophysiology*. New York: Holt, Rinehart & Winston, 1972.

Mulholland, T. B., & Peper, E. Occipital alpha and accommodative vergence, pursuit tracking and fast eye movements. *Psychophysiology*, 1971, *8*(5), 556–575.

Peper, E. Problems in heart rate and alpha electroencephalographic feedback. *Kybernetik*, 1974, *14*, 217–221.

17

Common Errors Made during Biofeedback Training and Research Studies

René Beck and Erik Peper

Errors made by clinicians and experimentalists in biofeedback studies are often forgotten and not taught or passed on. Hence, each beginning student, researcher, or practitioner has to reexperience the morass of possible mistakes—who, as a professional, wants to look like a fool? The following essay illustrates some mistakes that commonly occur, based on our own hard-won and sometimes painfully embarrassing experience. Murphy's Law states that if anything can go wrong, it will; it is our hope that if we illustrate some of the obvious and not so obvious mistakes, they will not be repeated. Making mistakes is *not* stupidity; repeating a mistake, however, is; and correcting a mistake is the learning process by which we grow and expand our knowledge and competence.

Some of our mistakes are illustrated in the transgressing of a number of obvious but often neglected rules.

Rule 1. Be sure you have access to the room where the client, subject, or trainee is sitting. "Don't panic," we told ourselves, as we yelled to a trainee through a locked laboratory door. As we waited for her reply, it seemed to us that unplugging oneself from the biofeedback equipment was a simple task, but as the silence endured we began to picture the trainee strangled in electrode wires. However, having locked ourselves out of the experimental room, leaving the trainee attached to an electromyograph (EMG), galvanic skin response (GSR) unit, and two temperature feedback units, we were hardly in a position to make judgments. When the trainee finally opened the door, carrying two $400 units still attached to her arms, we tried to maintain a cool researcher's air as we disentangled her and the equipment.

Rule 2. Be a subject in your own experiment. After an hour and a half of answering a battery of psychological tests and questionnaires, our subjects began to complain of writer's cramp. We agreed to allow them to take the forms home. Although the forms were to be returned immediately (within the next few days), they trickled in for weeks. Subjects complained of questions being repetitive. It wasn't until the study was nearly over that we decided to read the material straight through ourselves—and we found that the subjects' complaints had been justified.

René Beck • Department of Psychology, San Francisco State University, San Francisco, California 94134. Erik Peper • Center for Interdisciplinary Science, San Francisco State University, San Francisco, California 94134.

Rule 3. Check and recheck the collected data. After we collected the returned inventory tests (CPI, etc.), we found a number to be incomplete—some had no name or date, some had other vital information missing, so that, for instance, we could not always distinguish the beginning from the final baseline. We should have read the tests thoroughly before and after handing them out to the trainees, to make sure the forms were without error, and that they asked pertinent questions. Afterwards, we should have checked immediately to be sure the trainee had answered them completely. As it stood, we seemed to be merely collecting information for its own sake.

Rule 4. Reward for appropriate performance. Our trainees were instructed to fill out daily diary forms in which they recorded their home practices, moods, and symptoms. We faithfully collected these forms each session. As they came in, it would have been appropriate for us to sit down and look over the week, acknowledging and discussing the home practice, rather than merely stuffing these diaries into a drawer. We were preoccupied with collecting data for our statistical use, instead of actively searching for clues with which to help subjects with their life-style patterns. After the first couple of weeks, subjects failed to submit their homework forms and the data began to shrink in quantity and usefulness. When the subjects asked what patterns we had observed in their practices, we had nothing to say. The best way to keep trainees from following instructions is not to notice and reinforce their behavior when they give the desired response.

Rule 5. Always label all data, completely. After having studied subjects for alpha training for six weeks, we wanted to analyze the data six months later. However, who was the person with the 30-μV alpha? Was condition A baseline with eyes closed or with eyes open? The circular file (wastebasket) became the journal for publication of these data.

Rule 6. Pretest all handout material. To enhance learning the biofeedback relaxation skill, all trainees received relaxation tapes to practice with at home. When the prerecorded exercises were transferred onto blank tapes, using two tape recorders, we had assumed that both tape recorders were working. After unintentionally distributing a couple of blank tapes, we learned to listen to each tape before handing it out. For those subjects who seemed determined to erase tapes, we discovered the punch-out tabs on the back side of the cassettes which prevent accidental erasing. A similar problem was reported in a large biofeedback clinic. During the first session for a severely disturbed patient, a new assistant put on a cassette tape and left the room for almost half an hour. When the assistant returned to the room, the patient wondered what was going on, what games the clinicians were playing, expressing definite feelings of confusion and anger. It was no wonder—the assistant had played a blank tape.

Rule 7. Be sure the instructions are very clear. We wanted to assess biochemical changes in urine before and after the biofeedback relaxation training—the collection of urine to be done by the trainees at home. The written instructions called for the trainee to record diet, date, and time of collection and to store the filled urine bottle temporarily in a home freezer. A special note did caution trainees to warn other household members of the contents of the bottle, lest it be mistaken for something else. There was, however, no lecture on basic physics—specifically the expansion of liquids under freezing temperatures. One woman learned the hard way not to fill the bottle to the top; as she later expressed, "I went to my freezer to get ice cream and got 'pee-cicles' instead."

Rule 8. Be assertive and precise. Not realizing that dropouts were a fact of research and not necessarily a reflection of our own competence, we spent hours waiting for trainees who missed or were late for their appointments, only to reschedule them so we could wait some more. We supposedly were helping people assume responsibility for themselves (their health and otherwise), but we projected that they were doing us a favor by coming. We soon found that being precise about our expectations for reasonable promptness and cooperation improved our communication in other areas with trainees, and enabled us to separate out willing from reluctant trainees.

Rule 9. Be sure the trainees are comfortable for relaxation training. In our research lab, the trainees began to complain of the harsh fluorescent lights and the seemingly comfortable chair that in fact put pressure on one's legs when the feet were elevated. One claustrophobic subject who showed no alpha EEG, a high amount of EMG activity, and cool hands, found the entire atmosphere intolerable, and suggested we opt for a more natural setting, namely, "real" light and "real" air.

Rule 10. Know and pay attention to your equipment and clinical methods. During his second session, one trainee showed remarkable GSR readings—"zero conductance." We had never seen such low conductance recordings, so for the first ten minutes we kept our astonishment to ourselves. Finally, we decided to do a behavioral test with the subject (these tests should always be done, for obvious reasons; see Chapter 16). When the dial didn't move, we concluded that either this person was quite remarkable or really sick, or the unit was broken. As we silently pondered what to do next, the trainee asked if we were going to attach the GSR electrodes to his hand, as we had done the previous week.

Problems with equipment, or in using equipment, were everlasting. During the fifth session, after completing all the baseline recordings on one trainee, we noticed that some of the dials on the units had been changed and a plug had been pulled from the back of the unit. With the trainee still attached, we ran for assistance. The dials could be reset, but where should the plug go?

The next day the batteries were low in the EMG. Pleased that we were prepared for this disaster, we removed the batteries we had been saving in their sealed packages and tested the equipment once again. Once again we found ourselves unprepared. The "new" batteries were no good. Leaving another trainee attached to the equipment, we left to search for more batteries. A gracious colleague with less trust in modern technology gave us new batteries that had been stored in a refrigerator.

Rule 11. Be willing to doubt the feedback signal. The "auditory hallucinations" of one subject during twilight alpha/theta EEG training were not prophetic visions, but Big Mama of the CB radio, which was interfering. As we painfully found out, artifacts can infiltrate any recording and may be fully amplified by the equipment.

Rule 12. Be aware of linguistic implications. Trainees were often unclear when they tried to describe their experiences. We found that we were not phrasing the questions in such a way that we could elicit useful answers. When we asked,

"Did you experience anything?" the answer was inevitably a yes or a no. When we asked, "How did you feel?" or "What did you experience?" the trainees expanded with more detailed descriptions. When responses were limited to "It felt OK" or "Good," we needed to delve into what those words meant to the trainee. After such probing, we realized that the subject may not necessarily say exactly what he means or easily verbalize new feelings and sensations.

Rule 13. Enhance a positive, nonstriving attitude. Our first mistake in this category was sitting high above the subject on a chair to record the success of biofeedback training. Since the trainee was positioned like a lowly pauper, his temperature decreased and the muscle tension increased as we taught him how to "relax." Somehow we were projecting a striving attitude: "Try to relax." As a remedy, we left the room to relieve any performance pressure the trainee might be feeling. Learning improved, but with our presence in the room again, the subject was back where he started. Obviously, our expectations were being communicated to the trainee: Warm your hands so we can see what great trainers we are. After several frustrating sessions, we learned to share with trainees that it was OK if they didn't raise their temperature or reduce their tension. Keeping a detached attitude and changing our own belief system as therapists to one of positive support in a nonpathological framework proved the key (Peper, 1976). Almost miraculously, our trainees began to learn.

The mistakes go on, and little things add up. The researcher and practitioner emerge slowly from many mistakes and begin to realize that, after all, growth is not necessarily in avoiding all errors but in learning from the ones that occur.

REFERENCES

Peper, E. Problems in biofeedback training: An experiential analogy—urination. *Perspectives in Biology and Medicine*, 1976, *19*(3), 404–412.

18

Biofeedback Equipment

Kenneth Gaarder, Charles Burgar, and Penny Montgomery

Caveat Emptor

INTRODUCTION

This section will concern itself with helping the practitioner with relatively little electronics background in the selection of equipment for clinical use. We will attempt to explain the elementary functions of a particular kind of equipment, the nature of the component parts, some of the specifications of the components, and useful features to be sought. We will not recommend specific manufacturers, since the available instruments are rapidly changing and recommendations would soon be obsolete, but will attempt to provide guidelines that will allow the reader to make his own discriminations.

Before discussing specific equipment, we will take up general considerations about biofeedback equipment. Then we will discuss research grade equipment. This will be followed by discussion of electromyographic (EMG) feedback equipment. After this there are sections on skin temperature feedback equipment, electroencephalographic (EEG) feedback equipment, galvanic skin response (GSR) feedback equipment, and finally other feedback equipment.

GENERAL CONSIDERATIONS

There are a number of general considerations to be weighed concerning biofeedback equipment which we will take up in order. These include the basic types of equipment available, the manufacturers of the equipment, the specifications of the equipment, whether to use battery-operated equipment, what basic instruments a clinic should purchase, whether to buy equipment with complex special features, and what cost will be. We will briefly describe our experiences with each of these questions.

Basic Types of Equipment. Biofeedback equipment is currently available in three major forms—portable units, modular components, and polygraphic.

Kenneth Gaarder • Gerontology Research Center, National Institute of Aging, Baltimore City Hospitals, Baltimore, Maryland 21224.   Charles Burgar • Department of Psychiatry, University of Texas Health Science Center, San Antonio, Texas 78284.   Penny Montgomery • Department of Psychiatry/Division of Psychology, University of Texas Health Science Center. San Antonio, Texas 78284.

Portable units are the type for most clinical practices. These are the self-contained complete portable units that carry out a particular kind of measurement and then have a feedback display of that particular measurement available for the patient. They include the typical EMG unit, the typical finger temperature unit, and the typical alpha and theta unit. When well designed, they offer the clinician the ideal instrument for his practice. In terms of cost, ease of operation, simplicity, and fulfillment of function, the portable unit is far ahead of the alternatives.

Modular component biofeedback equipment has not yet been reduced to a form where it will appeal to many clinicians, although it is very useful for research. Those unfamiliar with electronics can best understand this equipment as analogous to component high fidelity equipment, in which a user selects a number of optional building blocks out of which to build a particular high fidelity set. A number of single-function modular components are held in an equipment rack and interconnected in the desired way by wires. The user must purchase a number of modules, but once they are purchased, he can use them to "build" particular biofeedback instruments by interconnecting the modules. Besides amplifying and displaying signals in auditory and visual modes, the modules can perform such logical functions as analog-to-digital or digital-to-analog conversion, filtering, and/nand gating, or/nor gating, timing, integrating, etc. The equipment is particularly useful for the programming of complex experiments.

Polygraphic equipment represents the standard used by researchers trained in the era when the quality of amplified signals was of great concern because of the uncertainty of electrode technique, the unreliability of amplifiers, and the need for complete electronic shielding. Advances in modern equipment technology lessen the need of these concerns. However, the polygraph may still be justifiably viewed as the workhorse instrument of the psychophysiologist and is the basic starting point of many biofeedback laboratories. Both research grade types of equipment are generally offered by older, larger and more established manufacturing companies, many of whom have long-standing reputations of deep concern for the quality of their products. Most of these companies have not yet entered the portable unitary equipment market, whose manufacturers will be considered next.

Manufacturers. Currently, there are fewer than a dozen manufacturers making clinical portable biofeedback equipment of quality worth considering. We and our engineering staffs have examined equipment and specifications from all of these and have not found a single manufacturer whose entire line of equipment is so complete and outstanding that it can be recommended without reservation. It appears justified to conclude that the portable biofeedback instrument manufacturing industry has not yet stabilized and may not do so for a number of years. It began and has continued with a number of small firms recognizing a demand and meeting it by providing the needed instruments. It has passed beyond the hand-to-mouth stage for the larger firms but has not yet reached the stage where the manufacturing is profitable enough to stabilize the companies, nor are there any companies known by us to have been bought out by larger firms to provide stability in this way. Some of the current firms operate marginally; others have well-financed backers and advertise extensively. Some firms provide good value for the dollar; others are overpriced. Some firms have imaginative engineering; others follow the pack. Some firms provide basic fundamentals; others feature gimmicks, appendages, and attachments. Some of the best do not advertise well, while some of the more dubious merit their main praise for promotion. Some have good repair policies; others not. Some have instruments that can be repaired by competent electronic workshops; others have epoxy-potted components that must be replaced by the manufacturer. Some provide complete schematic diagrams of their instruments; others maintain a veil of secrecy because the components are epoxy-potted and diagrams are not available.

Recent government regulations of biofeedback devices will provide some help by eliminating firms that make extravagant claims. It will also improve the quality control of instruments but will not address many of the problems considered above. The only reliable guideline in instrument selection is *caveat emptor*.

Three methods of choosing a manufacturer can be recommended. The first is for the clinician to obtain complete specifications for instruments under consideration from as many manufacturers as possible, examine the specifications, talk to manufacturer representatives when they are available, and then make his own choices. The main disadvantage of this method is that it does not provide unbiased authoritative guidance. The next method is to talk with other clinicians who have used equipment and get their opinions. The disadvantages of this method are that the clinician's opinion may not be informed and that the clinician may have no experience with a particular good line of equipment. The third method is to consult with an electronics engineer regarding equipment purchases. The disadvantage of this method is that it may be difficult and costly to find the right engineer, who must fully understand the clinician's needs, should have knowledge of the product's internal circuits, and ideally should know most of the companies by reputation. All of these methods can also be combined. When possible, the clinician purchasing equipment should seek to buy it on approval and, once it has been obtained, to have it inspected by an electronics engineer or qualified electronics technician, to use it as much as possible during the trial period, and to compare it with units owned by colleagues.

Specifications. In describing biofeedback instrument specifications, we will use the technical terminology of electronics without explaining the meanings of all of the terms. Table 1 reviews a few of the basic units. Further information on electronics in psychophysiology can be found in standard texts on psychophysiological methods, such as Brown (1967), Venables and Martin (1967), Sternbach (1972), Cromwell, Weibell, Pfeiffer, & Usselman (1973), or Geddes and Baker (1975). Some of the specifications we recommend are routinely supplied by manufacturers in their advertising material. Other specifications can only be determined by electonic tests—this applies particularly to EEG feedback equipment. Manufacturers often give noise levels and input voltage ranges in different forms. Therefore we have provided Table 2 to allow conversion of AC voltages to the root-mean-square value, which is the most accurate form for complex physiological signals.

Battery Operation. For the sake of safety and simplicity, we make the general recommendation that all portable clinical biofeedback equipment be battery-powered unless it is to be used by someone quite familar with electronics or is in a research setting where electronic consultation is available. The reason is that it is inevitable with line-powered equipment that eventually there will be accidental shocks received, while with battery-operated equipment mishaps will not occur unless other electrical equipment that is line-powered is connected to the biofeedback equipment. Rechargeable batteries are a convenient, but not essential, feature of a portable unit and should be weighed against other features in making a decision about equipment.

Basic Instruments to Purchase. We recommend that the clinician contemplating the general use of biofeedback in the treatment of stress-related conditions have available portable EMG and skin temperature feedback equipment. After experience with these instruments, the clinician should be able to see from his own situation what further instruments to purchase. Having both instruments available is particularly desirable because of the flexibility it offers in having alternate routes of treatment when a particular method does not work well.

Complexity of Instruments. As a general rule we have not found that the addition of special processing options to clinical feedback equipment is necessarily an advantage. Some companies have a series of models for a particular biofeedback function; often their least expensive model is as good as the higher priced line. In some instances, high-priced options do not do what is advertised. One particularly useful optional item is the time-period integrator, which gives the average score over a preset time interval. For trial periods of 10 seconds up to several minutes this can be quite useful, especially in comparing performance from session to session and trial to trial, since the alternative is to try to guess at an average reading from a constantly moving needle on a meter.

Cost. The clinical portable units most clinicians should be considering vary in cost from several hundred dollars to about $2000 per unit. Generally, the very cheapest equipment may not be satisfactory but one cannot assure quality by purchasing the most expensive. A rule of thumb is to try to shop in the lower-middle price range. Skin temperature instruments are among the least expensive and EMG units are in the middle price range, so that a basic starting package can be purchased for around $1000. Psychotherapists are generally unfamiliar with

Table 1

Simple Definitions

Unit	Measures	Use
Ampere = A	Current flow	Milliampere = 1/1000 A (mA)
Volt = V	Electrical energy	Millivolt = 1/1000 V (mV)
		Microvolt = 1/1,000,000 V (μV)
Ohm = Ω	Electrical resistance	Kilohm = 1000 Ω
Hertz = Hz	Cycles per second	Alpha rhythm = 8–12 Hz
Decibel = dB	Logarithmic ratios	Filter design
		Frequency response
Root-mean-square = rms	Wave quantity	Best single measure of complex signals

Table 2

Wave Measure Conversions for a Sine-Wave Signal[a]

E (peak) = 1.414 × E (rms)
E (peak to peak) = 2.828 × E (rms)
E (average) = 0.9 × E (rms)

[a] To be used in comparing instrument specifications of different manufacturers. Usually given in microvolts for EMG and EEG.

instrument costs, but physicians from fields where a great deal of equipment is needed to practice, such as radiology, pathology, ophthalmology, or urology, will recognize that the cost of this equipment is very modest indeed if actually used much in patient care.

Special Equipment. Every clinician using EEG or EMG equipment needs an ohmmeter in order to measure electrode impedances. In many instances the inexpensive volt-ohmmeter available for about $20 in electronics shops will prove satisfactory. However, these ohmmeters have the disadvantage of polarizing skin electrodes, which can potentially cause signal-processing difficulty if the first stage amplifier is DC-coupled with a high gain. Since the meter is inexpensive, it is worthwhile to find out from the manufacturer if there would be difficulties with its use. The alternative instrument is a battery-operated AC impedance meter, which prevents polarization of electrodes. This costs more than $100 and is unnecessary if the problem mentioned above is not present.

RESEARCH GRADE EQUIPMENT

We are not addressing ourselves in this book to the problems of the psychophysiological researcher attempting to purchase biofeedback equipment, because he is almost sure to have other adequate sources of information available to him through colleagues, through engineering consultants, and through his own past experiences in the field. One of the typical paths chosen by researchers is to purchase a standard 8- or 12-channel polygraph with plug-in modular amplifiers for some of the major parameters of interest, such as EMG, EEG, GSR, heart rate, skin temperature, or blood pressure. The output of the modular amplifiers is then readily subjected to signal reduction and display by fairly inexpensive circuits, which the researcher or his engineering support personnel can fabricate.

Some investigators will wish to depart from the tradition of the polygraph to record and collect data in other forms. Other types of equipment often help in this process, especially the now widely available modular switching equipment and medium-sized laboratory computers, which can simultaneously collect and analyze data as well as control the experimental setting. We have not attempted to provide guidance on these matters.

One particular instrument of great value to any biofeedback research is the four-channel variable persistence storage oscilloscope with widely variable sweep speeds. It is an effective display for many forms of feedback and can be made integral to numerous experiments. When seeking understanding, the way often becomes clear after staring at data at varying sweep speeds for several hours. The four-channel storage scope is also the simplest flexible display for rehabilitation muscle retraining work.

EMG FEEDBACK EQUIPMENT

Function. The portable modular EMG biofeedback unit is designed to detect muscle activity and feed back suitable information to the subject about the activity level of the muscles measured. It almost always uses skin surface electrodes as transducer and has the typical component configuration of transducer, signal amplifier, signal processor, and signal display.

Safety. The battery-powered unit does not have the shock hazard of the line-powered units and is therefore recommended. Equipment design must ensure that no more than 5 mA of direct or 500 μA of 60-Hz alternating current would enter the subject in the event of a component failure.

Equipment Specifications. Differential (bipolar) signal input is to be greatly preferred over single-ended (unipolar) input. This permits the use of the EMG in electrically noisy environments such as most offices and homes provide. Impedance of the input circuitry should be at least 1 megohm. The common mode rejection ration (CMRR) at 60 Hz should be at least 80 dB (80,000:1) measured at the output of the signal amplifier. Notch filters are a valuble asset for additional attenuation of 60-Hz interference.

A high-quality device should respond to signals in the 20- to 1000-Hz frequency range having amplitudes of 1 to 100 μV rms. For clinical use, however, it does not appear crucial to cover the entire frequency spectrum. For monitoring muscle activity in the neck or back region, a lower frequency cutoff of 100 Hz can help eliminate EKG artifact. Input equivalent noise (the noise generated by the signal amplifier) should be less than 1.0 μV rms. The time constant of the output circuits should fall between 0.25 and 1.0 seconds. A built-in circuit for measurement of electrode-to-electrode resistance is a worthwhile feature, but should give a range on a meter and not just consist of an *on* or *off* light.

Feedback Modalities. Having both auditory and visual modes of feedback is to be greatly preferred in an EMG. The most common auditory feedback used is a clicking sound or tone that increases in frequency as the input signal increases in amplitude. Visual feedback is normally given by an analog meter that provides amplitude information as well as a means for comparing performance during and between sessions. Either those instruments equipped with meters provide a gain control, giving several full-scale sensitivity ranges, or they incorporate a nonlinear (usually log or semilog) display that covers the entire range of input amplitude. The latter method has the advantage of providing a larger meter deflection for a given change in amplitude at the low end of the scale where further reduction becomes more difficult. This method also eliminates the need to change ranges, and therefore to establish new goals, as relaxation progresses. Digital numerical displays as a continuous visual feedback are not very practical, since most subjects find it hard to follow the registered changes in numbers. On the other hand, a digital readout of average amplitude during a trial period can be quite useful.

TEMPERATURE FEEDBACK EQUIPMENT

Function. The portable skin temperature feedback instrument is designed to measure and display changes in skin temperature from a selected body site. Skin temperature is mainly controlled by the thermal transfer from blood flow to the part and blood flow is controlled largely by autonomically mediated arteriolar changes. This is one of the simplest of the biofeedback instruments electronically. The temperature is picked up by a thermistor, which is usually taped to the skin with a small piece of adhesive tape. The temperature measurement is usually read from a simple bridge circuit by a meter calibrated to read in degrees.

Safety. Most available portable units are battery-powered, but since there is no electrical connection directly to the patient there is minimal danger.

Equipment Specifications. Most available instruments monitor one location for absolute temperature changes. Some include provisions for measuring the difference in temperature between two parts of the body, but this particular method has been abandoned by most clinicians so the feature is not needed. One reason the feature is not useful is because in following the progress of the subject, it is better to have means of making absolute temperature measurements. The units should have a meter output and sensitivity should be changeable to permit full-scale deflections ranging from several degrees Fahrenheit to 10 or 20°. Without the high-sensitivity setting the subject may not be able to work as well with the instrument.

The analog meter output is preferable to digital LED readout as trends and small changes are more easily followed. Instruments are also available with auditory feedback in the form of a tone, the frequency of which is usually proportional to absolute temperature.

EEG (BRAIN WAVE) FEEDBACK EQUIPMENT

Function. Portable EEG feedback equipment is designed to detect and amplify electrical signals generated by the brain, discriminate among the various frequency components, and give information to the subject concerning the amplitude or frequency of these components. Skin surface electrodes are usually used as transducer and the other components are signal amplifier, signal processor, and signal display. There are technical problems in making good brain wave feedback equipment which are far greater than for any other feedback instrument that we consider. These are reflected in the details mentioned below. We have only provided details for alpha, theta, and beta feedback equipment, which are the commonly used types. Other brain wave feedback instruments are mentioned later.

Safety. Battery operation is recommended. Input circuitry should be designed to allow no more than 5 mA of direct current or 500 μA at 60 Hz of alternating current to flow through the subject in the event of a component failure. Any accessories used with EEG feedback equipment should also be battery-operated or be insolated electrically through the use of optical or magnetic (transformer) techniques.

Equipment Specifications. Input to the device should be differential (bipolar) with an impedance exceeding 2 megohms. Common mode rejection should be at least 80 dB (80,000:1) at 60 Hz. The frequency response of the amplifier alone should be at least 40 dB down at 60 Hz. Input DC current should be less than 50 nA. An equivalent input noise level of .5 μV rms or less is recommended. (This measurement should be made at the output of the signal amplifier section, before the filter section, and should be made over the entire frequency range covered by the instrument.)

A calibrated control must be provided to set the threshold amplitude above which feedback is given and it should at least cover the range of 1.5 to 35 μV rms. Some units perform this task by providing an amplifier gain control and comparing the filtered signal to a fixed voltage reference. Another approach is to fix the gain of the amplifier (usually between 2000 and 100,000) and compare the filtered signal to an adjustable reference. A desirable feature is the incorporation of artifact inhibit circuits to squelch feedback resulting from movement artifact. One of the early stages of amplification should incorporate AC coupling to prevent saturation of the amplifier due to electrode offset potential.

It is recommended that equipment utilize analog filter design with at least −18 dB per octave attenuation of signals outside the passband (e.g., three-pole Butterworth filters). Digital filters have a more ideal frequency response but give poor results if the signal of interest is accompanied by slower waves having amplitudes approaching that of the desired signal. Analog filters, on the other hand, are subject to "ringing"—an output near the center frequency when the filter is excited by spiking activity in the EEG or by movement artifact. This tendency to ring increases as the filter skirts are made steeper. Some manufacturers utilize both types of filters in series, giving improved performance over either type alone.

For alpha and theta feedback, the instrument must respond to signals with frequencies between 4 and 13 Hz. Beta feedback requires an upper frequency limit of 28 Hz. Adjustable upper and lower filter controls allow one device to be used for any of the above ranges. Most devices on the market employing only one frequency range control have filters with undesirable response characteristics. The filter section should have a flat (±1 dB) response across the band selected, dropping to −3 dB at the upper and lower cutoff frequencies. Use of silver/silver-chloride electrodes is recommended. An internal means of checking electrode-to-electrode resistance is a desirable feature available in some units.

Feedback Modalities. Whereas the means by which information is presented to the subject remains somewhat a matter of personal preference, we have found auditory methods preferable over visual since the subject can work with eyes open or closed, as desired. A steady tone that is made to warble when the feedback criteria are met has been found less alerting by some users when compared to techniques in which the tone is either on or off to signal success. Whichever method is utilized, feedback should appear to be instantaneous, lagging the onset of the triggering signal by not more than .5 seconds. Devices use different criteria for signaling the signaling the presence of the desired brain wave. We feel that it is important for information to come as soon as possible and we prefer that the continuous discrimination of amplitude be given in some way.

GSR FEEDBACK EQUIPMENT

Function. The purpose of portable modular GSR feedback equipment is to detect and display changes in the skin resistance (or conductance) caused by changes in the subject's emotional state. GSR is a reflection of autonomic nervous system activity. Although this is also a very simple instrument electronically, methodological problems complicate the widespread acceptance of its use.

Safety. Instruments should be battery-operated and design must preclude the passage of more than 5 mA through the subject in the event of a component failure.

Equipment Specifications. Equipment using the constant current method of skin resistance measurement is suggested. These units pass a small controlled current through the skin and measure the resulting voltage drop. Current density should be maintained below 10 μA per cm^2 (calculated by dividing the current output of the device by the area of one of the electrodes). In no case should the current normally passed through the subject exceed 50 μA. The instrument should be capable of accepting skin impedance from 2 to 2000 kilohms (basal level) and should reflect resistance changes as small as 200 ohms. To display phasic changes adequately, the indicating device should be AC-coupled to the input signal through a circuit having a time constant of 3 to 5 seconds.

Feedback Modalities. While accurate measurement of the basal resistance level is sometimes done in research work and may someday be important clinically, at present only a relative indication of the amplitude and direction of transient resistance changes is usually provided. This is normally performed by an analog meter and/or changing tone.

OTHER BIOFEEDBACK EQUIPMENT

Biofeedback has been used for treatment of a number of specific disease conditions in which special instrumentation is necessary. Here we will briefly mention these uses and the equipment and where to find further information on the subject. It is fairly obvious what the general principles of such instruments are—a bodily function must be measured in real time, the function must have some moment-to-moment variation, and the subject must be shown some indication of this variation. Sometimes this merely means taking an already used instrument and turning it around so that the patient as well as the operator can see the readout.

Epilepsy. A number of laboratories are studying the treatment of epilepsy with biofeedback. The methods depend upon special brain wave filtering and differ from most biofeedback in that the length of treatment is very long, with an upper limit not yet having been established. Investigators using the methods do not recommend them for widespread clinical use yet. An introduction to the area is provided by Sterman (1973).

40-Hz Brain Waves. Besides the usual brain wave frequencies, investigators have recently become interested in studying the properties of a frequency of about 40 Hz. Equipment to analyze the brain waves has been designed and is available. Sheer (1975) is the major investigator responsible for this work, and has described the rhythm in his papers.

Thermography. Modern technology has produced an instrument that operates on the same principles as television, except that it measures infrared radiation instead of visible light. This device can very precisely map the temperature of the surface of any part of the body and presents an alternative to the single-probe skin temperature feedback instrument. Currently, the instrument is mainly used diagnostically by radiologists to diagnose blood vessel conditions and screen for breast cancer and is extremely expensive. However, it meets the requirements of a biofeedback instrument mentioned at the beginning of this section and is sometimes available in institutional settings for collaborative work. Its main drawback is lack of sensitivity.

Anal Sphincter Feedback. The method of this treatment has been well worked out and described. The needed equipment is a special catheter, three pressure transducers, a write-out or display instrument, and necessary tubing and balloons. Engel, Nikoomanesh, and Schuster (1974) have described the equipment and procedure in detail.

Esophageal Sphincter Feedback. Nikoomanesh, Wells & Schuster (1973) have controlled the sphincter between the esophagus and the stomach with biofeedback. The basic equipment is already available in many gastroenterologists' offices in the instrument measuring intraluminal pressure at several sites on the catheter. Several methods of measurement are used, but as long as continuous measures from several close-by sites on a stationary catheter are obtainable, the procedure is straightforward.

Hypertension. A few words are in order concerning instrumentation in the treatment of hypertension with biofeedback. We have worked with or examined most of the methods of blood pressure biofeedback and feel it is uncertain at present what sort of procedure may eventually be found most useful. The current elaborate methods may not necessarily give better results than very simple ones using standard relaxation parameters such as EMG and skin temperatures. However, this remains to be demonstrated.

Cardiac Arrhythmia Feedback. The methods of treating cardiac arrhythmias by directly related feedbacks have not yet been reduced to clinical practice and require special equipment as described by Engel and co-workers (see Birk, 1973, for references).

SUMMARY

Biofeedback equipment is most readily available for clinical use in low-cost portable units that are often of good quality. Many factors need to be considered in making a decision about a particular instrument. A beginning clinical facility should have EMG and skin temperature feedback available and later add other parameters as experience is acquired. Specifications of these and other instruments are described.

REFERENCES

Birk, L. *Biofeedback: Behavioral medicine*. New York: Grune & Stratton, 1973.

Brown, C. *Methods in psychophysiology*. Baltimore: Williams & Wilkins, 1967.

Cromwell, L., Weibell, G. J., Pfeiffer, E. A., & Usselman, L. B. *Biomedical instrumentation and measurements*. Englewood Cliffs, N.J.: Prentice-Hall, 1973.

Engel, B., Nikoomanesh, P., & Schuster, M. M. Operant conditioning of rectosphincteric responses in the treatment of fecal incontinence. *New England Journal of Medicine*, 1974, *290*, 646–649.

Geddes, L. A., & Baker, L. E. *Principles of applied biomedical instrumentation* (2d ed.). New York: Wiley, 1975.

Nikoomanesh, P., Wells, D., & Schuster, M. M. Biofeedback control of lower esophageal sphincter contraction. *Clinical Research*, 1973, *21*, 521.

Sheer, D. E. Biofeedback training of 40-Hz EEG and behavior. In N. Burch & H. L. Altshuler (Eds.), *Behavior and brain electrical activity*. New York: Plenum, 1975.

Sterman, M. B. Neurophysiologic and clinical studies of sensorimotor EEG biofeedback training: Some effects on epilepsy. In L. Birk (Ed.), *Biofeedback: Behavioral medicine*. New York: Grune & Stratton, 1973.

Sternbach, R. A. *Principles of psychophysiology*. New York: Holt, Rinehart & Winston, 1972.

Venables, P., & Martin, I. *A manual of psychophysiological methods*. New York: Wiley, 1967.

19

Electrodes

P. Strong

The electronics engineer, accustomed to measuring potentials between various points on an electronic circuit, may tend to regard two physiological electrodes simply as two probes applied to a subject in order to measure a potential difference. Such an oversimplification cannot be made as the conduction of current in tissue, as in any other liquid system, is ionic, that is, by the migration of positive and negative ions from point to point. To measure electrical effects in tissue it is necessary to make a transfer from this ionic conduction to the electronic conduction that occurs in the measuring circuit. This transfer is accomplished at the tissue–electrode interface.

ELECTRODE OFFSET POTENTIAL

If two dissimilar metals are inserted into a container of electrolyte, a potential difference can be measured between these metals. If one of these metals were silver and the other copper, this potential would be referred to as the silver/copper cell potential and would be on the order of .4 volts. This potential is composed of two separate components added algebraically together: a "half-cell" potential due to the silver electrode and a "half-cell" potential due to the copper electrode. These half-cell potentials, although difficult to measure, are the potentials produced across the metal–electrolyte interfaces. To a first order approximation, neglecting many chemical factors that would be important if the electrodes were used in a chemical measuring application rather than a biophysical measuring application, the half-cell potential is approximately equal to the electrode potential of the metal concerned. Thus the potential produced between the silver electrode and the copper electrode will be approximately equal to the difference in the electrode potentials of silver and copper, that is, approximately equal to .80 V minus .34 V, or .46 V. The exact value of this potential will depend on many chemical factors, the important of which are the electrolyte used and the concentration of this electrolyte; however, the value given is probably within about 100 mV of the actual value that may be measured in a physiological environment. A list of the electrode potentials for the more common metals is shown in Figure 1. This listing is referred to as the electrochemical

P. Strong • Tektronix, Inc., Beaverton, Oregon 97077.

	METAL	IONIC SYMBOL	ELECTRODE POTENTIAL (EP)*
CORRODED END (ANODIC OR LEAST NOBLE)	ALUMINIUM	Al^{+++}	-1.66VOLTS
	ZINC	Zn^{++}	- .76
	IRON	Fe^{++}	- .44
	LEAD	Pb^{++}	- .12
	HYDROGEN	H^+	0
	COPPER	Cu^{++}	+ .34
	SILVER	Ag^+	+ .80
PROTECTED END (CATHODIC OR MOST NOBLE)	PLATINUM	Pt^+	+ .86
	GOLD	Au^+	+1.50

*APPROXIMATELY EQUAL TO HALF-CELL POTENTIAL
IN PHYSIOLOGICAL ENVIRONMENTS.

Figure 1. Electrode potentials of metals, the electrochemical series.

series. The example given of a silver and copper electrode is illustrated in Figure 2, which shows the similarity between electrodes in a container of electrolyte and electrodes on a subject. In electrophysiology the difference in half-cell potentials that can be detected between two electrodes is referred to as "offset potential."

It is important not to confuse the electrode offset potential produced between two electrodes connected to a subject and the DC-differential offset potential available in many differential amplifiers. The DC-differential-offset-potential capability in differential amplifiers is intended to be used to cancel the electrode offset potential produced between electrodes.

In the biomedical situation, the electrode offset potential produced between electrodes may be unstable and unpredictable. Thus it is desirable that this potential be as low as possible. In order to reduce electrode offset potential it is first necessary to understand its origin. At any electrode–electrolyte interface

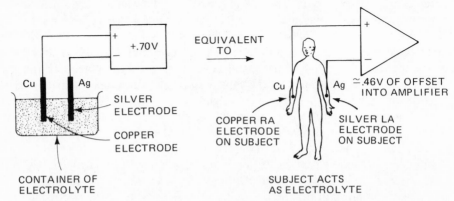

Figure 2. Electrode offset potential. Offset potential produced by dissimilar metals approximately equals difference in electrode potentials. Offset $\simeq$ EP Ag – EP Cu, $\simeq$ .80 V – .34 V, $\simeq$ .46 V.

there is a tendency for the electrode to discharge ions into solution and for ions in the electrolyte to combine with the electrode. These chemical reactions may be represented as follows:

$$\text{Metal} \rightarrow \text{electrons} + \text{metal ions}$$
(Oxidization reaction)

$$\text{Electrons} + \text{metal ions} \rightarrow \text{metal}$$
(Reduction reaction)

The net result of these reactions is the creation of a charge gradient, the spatial arrangement of which is called the electrode double layer. This double layer may be represented, as shown in Figure 3A, in its simplest form as two parallel areas of charge of opposite signs. Electrodes in which no net transfer of

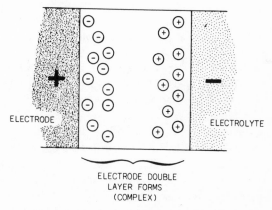

ELECTRODE DOUBLE
LAYER FORMS
(COMPLEX)

POTENTIAL EXISTS BETWEEN THE ELECTRODE AND
ELECTROLYTE DUE TO THE FORMATION OF THE
ELECTRODE DOUBLE LAYER.

(A) METALLIC ELECTRODE

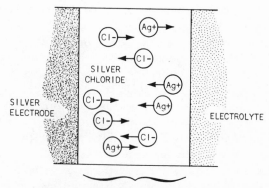

SILVER CHLORIDE FORMS FREE SILVER IONS (Ag+)
AND CHLORIDE IONS (Cl-) WHICH PREVENT THE
FORMATION OF THE ELECTRODE DOUBLE LAYER.

Figure 3. Electrode–electrolyte interface.   (B) SILVER/SILVER CHLORIDE ELECTRODE

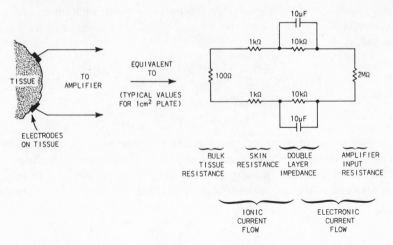

Figure 4. Electrode equivalent circuit for partially reversible electrodes.

charge occurs across the metal–electrolyte interface are referred to as perfectly polarized or perfectly nonreversible electrodes, that is, only one of the two chemical reactions shown above can occur. Electrodes in which unhindered transfer of charge is possible are referred to as perfectly nonpolarizable or perfectly reversible electrodes, that is, both of the equations referred to above occur with equal ease. Practical electrode systems have properties that lie between these ideal limits. The electrode double layer existing between a practical electrode and electrolyte may be regarded as a battery in parallel with a reasonably high impedance as shown in Figure 4. This impedance may typically be 10,000 ohms and the battery may be equivalent to a 10-μF capacitor. The potential of the battery, or the charge on the capacitor, will be the half-cell potential of the electrode.

The silver/silver-chloride electrode shown in Figure 3B consists of either a solid silver surface coated with a thin layer of solid silver chloride or, as is the case with Tektronix silver/silver-chloride electrodes, consists of silver powder and silver chloride powder compressed into a solid pellet. The presence of the silver chloride allows the electrode to behave as a near-perfect nonpolarizable or reversible electrode as it prohibits the formation of the electrode double layer, the silver chloride dissociating to silver ions and chloride ions that are free to migrate between the electrode and the electrolyte, thus opposing the formation of the double layer. The net result is a low-impedance, low-offset-potential interface between the silver and the electrolyte. Both silver/silver-chloride and zinc/zinc-sulfate electrodes exhibited this characteristic.

Most electrodes form soluble metallic salts and thus are highly toxic and can be used only as surface electrodes on intact skin. Silver electrodes are, however, nontoxic, as silver chloride is almost insoluble in a chloride-containing solution; therefore very few free silver ions exist and tissue damage from them is negligible. Thus silver or silver/silver-chloride electrodes are definitely preferred for use on exposed tissue. Although, as stated previously, zinc/zinc-sulfate electrodes produce low-offset-potential characteristics similar to silver/silver-chloride electrodes, they are highly toxic to exposed tissue due to the passage into the tissue of free zinc and/or sulfide ions.

A layer of silver chloride may be deposited on silver electrodes, converting them to silver/silver-chloride electrodes, by a process known as chloriding. This is achieved by making the silver electrodes positive to a solution containing sodium chloride or saline (.9% concentration) and passing a current through the electrode at the rate of 1 mA/cm² of surface for several minutes. The silver electrode should be cleaned to remove surface contaminants before chloriding.

Mechanical disturbance of the electrode double layer causes electrode noise because the double layer acts as a region of charge gradient, disturbance of which gives rise to a change in capacitance and thus a change in voltage. The electrical stability of an electrode is considerably enhanced by mechanical stabilization of the electrode–electrolyte interface. This is achieved by the use of indirect-contact floating electrodes, which interpose an electrolyte "jelly" or "paste" between the electrode and the tissue.

The preceding discussion of electrode offset potential has been highly simplified, as in electrophysiology it is unnecessary to know the exact value of the electrode offset potential produced, and it is therefore unneccessary for users of electrodes to understand all of the chemistry involved. Interested readers wishing to more fully understand the chemical process involved should refer to Geddes and Baker (1968, Sections 9.2, 9.3, 11.1, 11.2, and 11.3) and also Dewhurst (1966, Section 21.2, specifically Chapters 21, 22, 26, and 28).

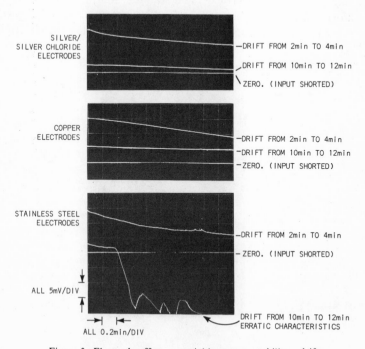

Figure 5. Electrode offset potential long-term stability—drift.

ELECTRODE OFFSET POTENTIAL CHARACTERISTICS

The previous section dicusses the electrode offset potential produced at an electrode–electrolyte interface and states that this potential is unstable and unpredictable. When electrodes are connected to a subject in order to record a bioelectric event on a DC-coupled oscilloscope, long-term changes in electrode offset potential appear as baseline drift and short-term changes appear as noise on the trace. If a pair of new electrodes are applied to a subject, an electrode offset potential will exist, as the electrodes can essentially be regarded as two batteries. When these electrodes are then connected to a DC-coupled oscilloscope amplifier, the input impedance of this amplifier will act as a load on the batteries and tend to discharge them. Since these electrodes form a very poor battery, a typical Tektronix oscilloscope differential-input impedance of two megohms will discharge the batteries over a period of several hours. It is recommended that new electrode pairs be shorted together in .9% saline for a few hours before use in an effort to accelerate this process. As these batteries are discharged, their effective potential is reduced, this decreasing potential appearing as electrode offset potential drift, as shown in Figure 5. Although the source is represented as a battery in preceding discussions, it may equally well be represented as a capacitor with the amplifier differential-input impedance tending to discharge the capacitor, as depicted in the equivalent circuit shown in Figure 4. Either analogy is only a first order of approximation to the true situation.

Referring to Figure 5, the electrode offset potential drift for silver/silver-chloride electrodes, copper electrodes, and stainless stell hypodermic needle electrodes is shown. In each case the electrode offset potential drift is shown over a 2-minute segment after the amplifier load had been applied to the electrodes for 2

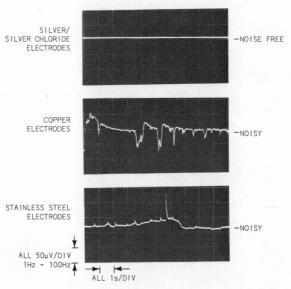

Figure 6. Electrode offset potential short-term stability—noise.

minutes and for 10 minutes. A "zero" trace is also included on each photograph. The electrode offset potential produced by the silver/silver-chloride electrodes and the copper electrodes appears to decrease exponentially; however, the stainless steel electrodes are clearly erratic and, for the particular pair of electrodes used for this investigation, show an abrupt change in potential after about 10 minutes. The electrode offset potential drift for the silver/silver-chloride electrodes and the copper electrodes would be considered acceptable; however, the erratic performance of the stainless steel electrodes may make them undesirable for physiological recording.

Short-term changes in electrode offset potential are referred to as electrode noise. If electrodes are used in conjunction with an AC-coupled high-sensitivity amplifier as shown in Figure 6, the long-term drift characteristics will be rejected by the low-frequency characteristic of the amplifier.

REFERENCES

Dewhurst, D. J., *Physical instrumentation in medicine and biology*. New York: Pergamon, 1966.

Geddes, L. A., & Baker, L. E., *Principles of applied biomedical instrumentation*. New York: Wiley, 1968.

20

Standard Specifications for the Description of Biofeedback Instruments

Hershel Toomim, S. L. Schandler, T. H. Spiegel, J. A. Freeman, and W. Elder

Currently there exists a variety of biofeedback instruments available for clinical application and research purposes. The existence and extent of this variety is evidenced by the increasing number of instruments available not only for the presentation of different types of physiological information but also for the presentation of information from a particular physiological system. As instruments increase in diversity and number, confusion may arise in the attempt to understand specific capabilities and functions within and across instrument types.

It has been the intent of the Instrumentation Committee of the Biofeedback Society of California to examine, develop, and recommend standard specifications for describing various forms of biofeedback instruments. Emphasis has been placed on providing specifications that are directly related to practical instrument applications and can be readily understood and tested by both the manufacturer and the user of the devices. The primary types of instruments examined by the committee included EMG, EEG, GSR, and temperature feedback devices. In addition, supplementary equipment including digital integrators and isolation units were considered.

The present report is intended to provide a summary of the committee's recommendations.

GENERAL EQUIPMENT SPECIFICATIONS

Though there exists a wide variety of biofeedback instrument types, there are certain specifications that may be commonly applicable to most instruments. The committee has therefore developed a series of general recommended specificatons for all feedback devices. It is stressed that these specifications are designed to be supplemented with specifications developed for individual instruments.

Feedback Modality Specifications. The sensitivity and range of all available feedback modalities should be specified. This specification could be stated in the

Hershel Toomim, T. H. Spiegel, and W. Elder • Biofeedback Research Institute, Los Angeles, California 90048.   S. L. Schandler • Department of Psychology, Chapman College, Orange, California 92666, and Human Physiology Research, Veterans Administration Medical Center, Sepulveda, California 91343.   J. A. Freeman • Autogenic Systems, Inc., Berkeley, California 94710.

form of a transfer function giving the relationship between input signal to the feedback instrument and output signal displayed by the feedback modalities. Transfer function should be given as a graph, or, at a minimum, the end points of the function. If the latter method is used, the linearity of the transfer function should be specified. The accuracy of the transfer function should be given in relation to the specified ambient temperature range and battery life.

Feedback meter response can be an important feedback parameter. In some applications, it should respond quickly, whereas in other applications an averaged response is optimum. The committee therefore recommends that the speed with which a feedback meter registers from 0 to 63% of full-scale reading should be specified.

Auditory forms of feedback are recognized as being difficult to examine in terms of speed of response. However, the committee feels that information should be given as to whether a specific auditory frequency can be accurately reproduced across sessions.

Output Jacks. The maximum external output load values that will allow the instrument to be operated to guaranteed specifications should be provided. In addition, it is recommended that the loading effects (if any) on the instrument's feedback systems should be specified as a guaranteed minimum change in percent of full scale measured at full-scale output. The transfer function from input to the output jacks should also be given at recommended load. Effects of multiple external loads (if allowed) should also be specified, as should the effects of connecting external AC-operated loads.

Electrodes. For specifications where electrodes are required at one input of the instruments, electrode type, size (area), and electrode cream should be specified. If different electrode types are provided as standard equipment with an instrument, the effects of each electrode type should be specified. If different electrodes are available as options, the effects of these electrodes should be examined by the manufacturer and provided on request. Recommended electrode-application procedures should also be provided.

Battery Life. For battery-operated equipment, the committee recommends at least three battery specifications: maximum life of the battery, maximum life of the battery that will allow the instrument to operate at guaranteed operational specifications, and the expected battery life encountered over typical continuous operational periods of eight hours each.

Temperature. The committee recommends that the ambient temperature specifications be given representing the range in which the instrument will operate at guaranteed specifications. It is further suggested that a storage temperature range be provided.

General. In all instances where specifications such as accuracy, resolution, and band pass are given, it is assumed that these specifications are guaranteed within the given temperature and battery range specifications.

The committee further recommends that the manufacturer consider within-session and between-sessions operational stability of the feedback instruments. For example, how effectively can the user reproduce a given instrument–subject interaction across several sessions with the same subject or different subjects?

Also how closely will instruments of the same model match each other in these aspects?

TEMPERATURE FEEDBACK INSTRUMENT SPECIFICATIONS

Among the numerous forms of physiological information currently being used in feedback applications, temperature is possibly the least difficult to measure and feed back. Placing and securing the thermistor electrode requires little preparation, while the instrumentation for monitoring and feeding back temperature information is relatively straightforward.

Temperature is, however, one of the more ambiguous forms of physiological information, being dependent on a variety of conditions within and outside the subject. As a possible step toward minimizing ambiguity, the committee has suggested a series of recommendations concerning the description of temperature feedback instruments.

Accuracy of Temperature Response. Most feedback manufacturers specify the accuracy of their instruments in terms of accuracy of tolerance of the thermistor probe. The committee recommends that it is more useful to specify accuracy of the probe *and* temperature measurement of a portion of the unit together. It is recommended that this specification be stated in degrees Fahrenheit or Celsius rather than in a percentage, since the former may be more readily understood by the user. Accuracy should be measured using fixed input to simulate end points of a normally encountered temperature range, such as 70° and 90°F. Accuracy would then be expressed as a difference between simulated input temperature and temperature recorded by the instrument.

Rapidity of Temperature Response. It is acknowledged that the thermistor probe possesses a specified speed of response given by the probe manufacturer. Of greater importance to the user is the inclusion of a specification concerning the time required for a given change at the thermistor probe to be displayed on the temperature measurement portion of the feedback instrument. This specification would be derived by producing a known change in the temperature of the probe and noting the time required for 98% of this change to be displayed on the instrument.

Drift. Drift is intended as an indication of within-session measurement stability of the temperature feedback instrument. As such, drift is defined as the indicated change in a constant input temperature as measured over a typical operational period, such as eight hours' continuous use. Whether drift is at a constant rate across the operational period (linear) or occurs at particular points during the period should be noted.

GSR FEEDBACK INSTRUMENT SPECIFICATIONS

While GSR feedback may prove to be one of the most useful forms of feedback, the physiological properties underlying this activity and the instrumentation required for its measurement are not generally understood.

A major source of ambiguity exists in the terminology applied to describing the activity and the instrument. *GSR* has been generally taken to mean either galvanic skin resistance or the more general galvanic skin response. While the latter meaning is most often implied, the confusion that has arisen in the meaning of the term and the general opinion that the term is archaic has resulted in the adoption of the term *EDR* or electrodermal response to describe this activity. Depending on the type of instrumentation being used, EDR activity may be measured as skin conductance (SC), skin resistance (SR), or skin potential (SP). Within each of these measures long-term changes are termed *levels* (L) and short-term changes, to a stimulus for example, are termed *responses* (R). Thus there exist SCR and SCL measures.

Measurement ambiguity may be further compounded by the fact that certain instruments may measure one form of activity and record that activity in a different form. For example, skin resistance may be measured, but the instrument may transform this measure and display it as skin conductance.

The committee feels that the use of proper terminology is exceedingly important to use of these devices. Regardless of what the manufacturer calls his instruments, the actual measurements that the equipment is capable of recording should be specified in a standard manner.

Given SC, SR, and SP instruments, the committee proposed certain specifications related to each.

Conductance Devices. If the unit measures and records SC data, the polarizing voltage and maximum expected deliverable current during operation should be specified. Application of current values greater than 100 μA/cm^2 (microamperes per square centimeter) may result in skin irritation, while currents in excess of 20 μA/cm^2 may produce nonlinearity. Whether the voltage supplied is AC or DC should be specified: If AC, it is recommended that a conversion factor to DC values be supplied. Scale ranges should be specified using the standard micromho conductance units.

Resistance Devices. If the unit measures and records SR data, the polarizing current and maximum expected deliverable voltage should be stated. Excessive voltage can also result in skin irritation. If AC, then the AC to DC conversion should be provided. Scale ranges should be specified in standard units of resistance (ohms).

Potential Devices. If the unit measures and records SP data, the input impedance with input current and offset voltages should be stated. Scale ranges should be specified in units of voltage, such as the millivolt.

General. In addition to the specific instrument specifications, there are certain general specifications that the committee recommends. If the unit contains a zero suppression system, the zero suppression values should be provided along with the accuracy of these values over the stated operational temperature and battery life ranges. These instruments may also provide a polarizing voltage that can be affected by or can affect other instruments. Any such effects should be stated. Further, the possible effects of electrode polarization and means for its measurement should be provided.

EMG FEEDBACK INSTRUMENT SPECIFICATIONS

Muscle or EMG biofeedback has been shown to be useful in a variety of clinical and experimental applications. However, the actual components of the EMG signal and the meaning and importance of EMG instrument specifications are not often understood.

In actual use, EMG generally consists of a low-level (weak) signal often found in the presence of artifact signals. These artifacts are primarily composed of amplifier noise, environmental noise, and activity from other physiological systems. The committee therefore decided to derive specifications that would be most applicable to the actual usage of EMG feedback instruments rather than a theoretical application on the test bench.

Amplifer Input Noise. Noise present at the input of the EMG amplifier during actual use may consist of both amplifier voltage noise, which is usually considered, and amplifier current noise. Noise may be further influenced by the band pass of the amplifier and electrode impedances. To arrive at specifications that consider all these factors, the committee proposes that amplifier input noise be specified as a noise factor. Noise factor represents the ratio of input noise present at given practical input resistances to the theoretical noise level of the resistance. Noise factor accounts for both current noise and instrument band pass, and is recommended as a plotted curvilinear function over varying electrode impedances. The committee recommends that a curve of guaranteed maximum noise factor values be supplied for differential source resistances of 1000 to 100,000 ohms. The committee further recommends that a single point, consisting of the noise factor at a differential input resistance of 20,000 ohms, be stated.

Common Mode Rejection. The committee recommends that guaranteed minimum common mode rejection ratios be specified with a 20,000-ohm source imbalance at both the center of the band pass and at 60 Hz. The voltage level for this measurement shall be stated.

Rejection of AC Power Line Interference. The largest environmental artifact is electrical interference generated by AC power line and power line-operated equipment. Although the power lines radiate frequency components that are higher than the fundamental 60 Hz, it is this fundamental frequency that is the strongest and provides the greatest interference to EMG amplifiers. The committee therefore recommends that the minimum guaranteed differential rejection at 60 Hz be specified in decibels.

Differential Input Impedance. The committee recommends that the guaranteed minimum differential input impedance be stated at the center of the band pass with the electrodes connected to the instrument. That the electrodes be connected to the instrument is quite important, since the type of electrode system can have a significant influence on common mode rejection and differential input impedance. Consequently, the committee recommends that impedance and common mode specifications be given with the electrode system supplied with the instrument.

Band Pass. The band pass should be specified at the high and low 3-dB points and in minimum guaranteed attenuation in dB 2 octaves below the low 3-dB point and 2 octaves above the high 3-dB point.

Detection. It is very convenient for an amplifier to be calibrated with a known peak, average, or RMS value sine wave, since the relationship involving all these values is well defined. Although approximations can be made, there is no exact correlation between peak, average, and RMS for an actual EMG signal. Therefore, it is recommended that the readout of the amplifier or instrument be calibrated in the same units as the detector design.

Absolute Accuracy. The absolute accuracy of the instrument readout should be stated as a guaranteed maximum error expressed in percent of full scale of the scale being used.

Amplitude Range. The amplitude range of each scale should be stated in the appropriate calibrated units. It is further recommended that the range of the most sensitive scale also be stated in average units, although this unit may not have been used to calibrate the scale. This will provide a uniform indication across designs of the sensitivity of the most sensitive scale regardless of units used in its calibration.

EEG FEEDBACK INSTRUMENTATION SPECIFICATIONS

Both EMG and EEG are relatively low-level signals, sharing a number of common problems associated with the general amplification of these signal types. Consequently, the specifications previously discussed for EMG feedback devices generally pertain to EEG feedback devices as well. However, unlike EMG, EEG activity may contain a number of specific frequency and amplitude characteristics that are crucial to its recognition and classification. For this reason, the committee recognizes that the type and function of frequency and amplitude detection systems contained within EEG devices must be carefully described and specified. Where such systems involve filters, the role of each filter and the description of the filter type are critical specifications. Where frequency and phase detection systems are in operation, these system characteristics require specification and description.

The committee believes that the problem of supplying concise and understandable EEG feedback specifications is critical, and we are currently devoting a great deal of time and effort toward this goal.

TIME PERIOD DIGITAL INTEGRATOR SPECIFICATIONS

Though time period digital integrators are not generally considered as biofeedback instruments themselves, they greatly extend the measurement precision of physiological activity recorded by certain feedback devices. Integrators are, however, relatively complex and sensitive, requiring certain fundamental performance specifications.

Method of Detection. The method of detection should be specified for the integrator unit. For example, if the detection method involves peak to peak or averaging of wave forms, the detection time constant should be stated. Method of threshold detection should also be stated as instantaneous or average.

Frequency Response. If the integrator measures an AC signal, the frequency response of the integrator should be assessed and specified with the unit interfaced to a common feedback instrument. Further, a statement should be provided indicating the effects of various feedback interfaces on integrator functioning. Frequency response should be specified in terms of 3-dB points of the band pass of the integrator.

Zero Offset. Specified as either the accumulated count with zero input or the required input to bring the zero count to one least significant digit.

Linearity. Specified as the greatest error as a percentage of full scale that can be measured anywhere on the scale with varying inputs.

Resolution. Worst case stability of least significant digit on scale that can be measured anywhere on the scale with varying inputs.

Calibration. The method in which the integrator is calibrated is crucial. Any calibration specifications should include the wave form type and frequency of the calibration signal at selected input sensitivities.

General. The committee stresses the importance of the manufacturer's indicating at least which of his instruments may be used with the integrator and any changes in specifications that may occur when the integrator is so used. Whether the integrator is single-ended or differential should also be specified.

EQUIPMENT ISOLATION UNIT SPECIFICATIONS

Isolation units are generally employed when the output of a particular feedback instrument is intended to be displayed on a peripheral instrument such as a polygraph or an oscilloscope. The function of an isolator is to ensure safety of the subject when using the peripheral line-operated equipment and to minimize electrical interference from the peripheral devices. The types of isolation units available include transformer, acoustic, and optical isolators. The committee recommends that the manufacturer consider both the effects of recommended isolators on the safety of the subject and the effects of coupling the feedback signal to a peripheral instrument. Concerning the latter, a transfer function should be stated in terms of percent attenuation between isolator input and isolator output.

21

A Bioelectric Glossary

H. Toomim, S. Schandler, T. H. Spiegel, J. A. Freeman, W. Elder, and
Barbara Silverberg

AC—See *alternating current*.

alternating current (*AC*)—A signal whose direction of flow (polarity) varies with time in a periodic manner (though not necessarily at a fixed or predictable rate). If this variation with time occurs at a fixed rate, this periodicity will determine the *frequency* of the signal.

ampere—The unit in which electrical current flow is measured (see *volt*).

amplifier—A device (usually an electronic circuit) that converts a small signal into a larger signal, the amount of amplification determined by the *gain* of the amplifier.

amplitude—A measure of the size of the signal. For an electrical signal, the amplitude is measured in *volts*, but this unit is not sufficient to unequivocally define the size of a wave. The amplitude of a signal may be measured in *peak* volts (a), or *peak-to-peak* volts (b), or volts *rms* (c), or *average* volts (d). These are all mathematically defined, and for a known wave form their ratio to one another is fixed. However, for a wave form that cannot be described completely (e.g., EMG), amplitude must be measured in the unit most meaningful for the modality being monitored.

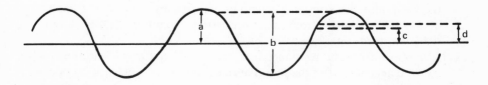

analog signal—A signal that varies directly with the physiological signal being monitored; e.g., a voltage that rises as skin temperature increases, or a tone whose pitch increases with an increase in skin temperature.

artifact—Any electrical signal detected by a biomedical instrument which does not originate in or directly reflect the activity of the physiologic function

H. Toomim, T. H. Spiegel, and W. Elder • Biofeedback Research Institute, Los Angeles, California 90048. S. Schandler • Department of Psychology, Chapman College, Orange, California 92666, and Human Physiology Research, Veterans Administration Medical Center, Sepulveda, California 91343. J. A. Freeman and Barbara Silverberg • Autogenic Systems, Inc., Berkeley, California 94710.

being monitored; e.g., EKG picked up by an EEG or EMG amplifier is an artifact to the EEG or EMG measurement.

average—See *amplitude.*

band pass—See *filter.*

binary signal (*logic signal, digital signal*)—A signal that can hold either of two permissible values or states, indicating that some parameter or requirement is (*true* state) or is not (*false* state) being fulfilled; e.g., a voltage that is either positive (logic true) or zero (logic false).

bipolar recording—Measurement of one active electrode with respect to another active electrode, through the use of a differential amplifier. A third electrode, referred to as the "ground" electrode, is usually placed midway between the two active electrodes, or on an electrically inactive location, and connected to the "common" terminal of the amplifier input.

common-mode rejection—See *differential amplifier.*

DC—See *direct current.*

differential amplifier—An amplifier that amplifies the difference between two signals. Such an amplifier is particularly useful in examining bioelectric signals, which occur as a potential difference between two active electrodes (see *bipolar recording*). Any signal that is common to the two electrodes would be completely ignored by an ideal differential amplifier; in practice, some of this *common-mode* signal comes through. The *common-mode rejection* of a differential amplifier is the ratio of its differential gain to its common-mode gain, and should be extremely high for successful differential amplification of bioelectric signals.

digital signal—See *binary signal.*

direct current (*DC*)—A signal that is nonvarying. It may have either a positive or a negative polarity.

dominant frequency—The frequency component having the highest amplitude present in the entire spectrum being monitored at any given time (usually used with reference to EEG frequency).

electrode—A device for converting the ionic bioelectric potentials generated by the body into the electrical potentials required by conventional measuring devices. (The transfer from ionic to electronic conduction takes place at the tissue–electrode interface.)

electrode resistance—The resistance measured between a pair of electrodes when they are in contact with the skin. This measure, since it includes the skin–electrode interface, is an indication of how well the electrodes have been applied. The lower the electrode resistance achieved, the lower will be the effects of noise and signal attenuation on the overall signal conditioning. (See *input impedance; ohm.*)

filter—An electronic device (either active or passive) that determines the frequency response characteristics of a circuit, attenuating certain frequency components while passing others unmodified. A *filter* is described by its band width, its mid-band gain, its corner or cutoff frequencies (the frequencies at which it starts to attenuate the signal—actually the frequency at which the voltage of the signal is down to .707 of its mid-band value), and its slope or rate of attenuation (expressed in dB/octave).

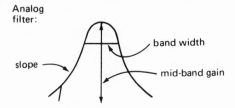

Analog filter:

band width

slope

mid-band gain

Fourier analysis—See *spectral analysis.*

frequency—The number of times each second that a period wave repeats itself, usually expressed in cycles per second (cps) or hertz (Hz).

gain—The ratio of the output to the input in an electronic amplifying system (measured in dB, or in volts/microvolt).

ground—An electrical connection to the earth or to the metal framework of the electrical circuit. If this framework is not connected to earth through a power cord connection or a ground wire (as in a battery-power instrument), it is referred to as *common.*

impedance—A measure of the barriers to current flow in an AC circuit (composed of resistance, capacitive reactance, and inductive reactance). See *ohm, input impedance, electrode resistance.*

imput impedance—The impedance (or resistance) measured across the input terminals of an amplifier or preamplifier. In biomedical instrumentation, it is particularly important that the input impedance be extremely high, at least 100 to 1000 times the source impedance (the resistance across the skin–electrode interface) to prevent attenuation or distortion of the very small biopotentials being measured. Input impedance is measured in megohms (see *ohm*).

integral average—See *amplitude* and *time integral.*

integration—See *time integral.*

logic signal—See *binary signal.*

megohm—See *ohm.*

microvolt—See *volt.*

millivolt—See *volt.*

monopolar recording—Measurement of a single active electrode with respect to a "ground" electrode placed in an electrically inactive location. This can be done using a single-ended amplifier, or a differential amplifier with one of its inputs grounded.

ohm (Ω)—The unit in which electrical resistance or impedance is measured (see *volt*). A megohm (MΩ) is one million ohms, a kilohm (kΩ) is one thousand ohms.

peak-to-peak—See *amplitude.*

preamplifier—The first stage of amplification in a system that requires several stages of amplification to convert a very small electrical signal into a signal that is large enough to be viewed or measured by conventional instruments. Because the input signal to the preamplifier is by definition extremely small, high-input impedance and low amplifier noise are of particular concern in the design of biomedical preamplifiers.

rectification—The conversion of alternating current into direct current (performed electronically by a rectifier or a diode); following rectification, the signal is usually filtered to produce a smooth DC signal, which is directly proportional to the energy contained in the AC signal prior to rectification. Thus *rectified EMG* is a DC measure of the energy contained in the complex AC EMG signal at any given time.

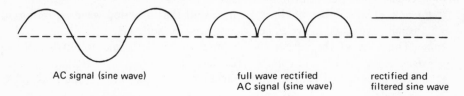

AC signal (sine wave)   full wave rectified   rectified and
                                     AC signal (sine wave)   filtered sine wave

resolution—A measure of the ability of an instrument to respond to small changes in signal level; the smallest *change* in signal that an instrument is capable of measuring. Note the distinction between *resolution* and *sensitivity*.

RMS—See *amplitude*.

sensitivity—A measure of the ability of an instrument to respond to extremely small signals; the smallest signal that an instrument is capable of measuring. This is usually limited by the noise level of the instrument, since signals so small as to be buried in the noise cannot be measured by conventional techniques. Note the distinction between *sensitivity* and *resolution*.

spectral analysis (*Fourier analysis*)—According to *Fourier's theorem*, any smooth periodic function may be represented as the sum of a number of sinusoidal waves with frequencies that are multiples of one basic frequency. A complete spectral analysis divides a signal into its sinusoidal components and measures the amplitude and phase of each of these components to completely define the wave form. Mathematically, it is extremely difficult to perform an accurate spectrum analysis of an EEG signal, since it is not time-invariant for a period long compared with the lowest frequencies present.

subdominant frequency—Any frequency component having an amplitude less than that of the dominant frequency.

time integral—Mathematically, this is the area under the curve over a specified time interval; thus it is a measure of the average energy contained in a signal over a defined period of time.

transducer—A device capable of converting energy from one form to another; e.g., a thermistor, which converts thermal energy into electrical energy.

volt—The unit of electrical potential required to move a unit charge or electron through a resistive field—or, in other words, the force required to cause a current to flow through a resistance. The current is measured in *amperes* (or amps), the resistance in *ohms*. A *microvolt* (one-millionth of a volt) is more common in biomedical measurement.

voltage-controlled oscillator (*VCO*)—A signal generator whose output frequency is a function of the voltage applied at its input. This is a particularly common device in biofeedback instruments; it might be used, for example, to generate an audio tone whose pitch is proportional to the frequency of an EEG signal, or to generate a click whose rate is proportional to EMG activity.

ELECTROENCEPHALOGRAPHY
BIOFEEDBACK

The field of biofeedback had its beginning in the area of electroencephalography (EEG), and with this came the excitement that biofeedback might become a research strategy for exploring consciousness. Since the mid-1960s, many studies have been published, exploring the association between a broad EEG spectrum and consciousness and neurological mechanisms. Some of this excitement is conveyed by one of the early investigators, Dr. Barbara Brown, in her book *New Mind, New Body* (1974).

We begin this section with a brief neurophysiological review by Green (Chapter 22), which helps clarify the basis of EEG. In Chapter 23, Strong gives a short description of EEG electrode placements and recording problems.

Chapter 24 by Kamiya, one of the earliest investigators, covers some history, data, and philosophy of the EEG alpha rhythm. Kamiya brings to light the importance of subjective awareness and examines the use of alpha biofeedback to study consciousness. The study of consciousness and introspection for many years was lost in the mazes of behaviorism. Only in recent years has the *Zeitgeist* changed to reallow the investigation of man's uniqueness: consciousness.

Mulholland and Benson (Chapter 25) illustrate a totally different approach. By studying the effects of feedback on visual attention, Mulholland and associates devised a model for the fluctuation of alpha and nonalpha and this was used in an attempt to understand more about the relationship between EEG and visual attention. Mulholland (1977) has gone on from there to employ a cybernetic model and uses feedback systems to test research hypotheses. Cybernetics involves the theoretical study of controller processes in mechanical and biological systems, especially the analysis of information within the system. A perfect example is the thermostat.

> There is a setting for the desired room temperature; and if the actual temperature of the house is below this, an apparatus is actuated which opens the damper, or increases the flow of fuel oil, and brings the temperature of the house up to the desired level. If, on the other hand, the temperature of the house exceeds the desired level, the dampers are turned off or the flow of fuel oil is slackened or interrupted. In this way the temperature of the house is kept approximately at a steady level. Note that the constancy of this level depends on the design of the thermostat, and that a badly designed thermostat may send the temperature of the house into violent oscillations not unlike the motions of a man suffering from cerebellar tremor. (Wiener, 1961, pp. 96–97)

Though some readers may find Mulholland and Benson's chapter slightly more difficult, it does provide a novel approach to biofeedback theory and helps illuminate the psychobiological mechanisms.

Two research studies are then presented to acquaint the reader with different types of research in alpha biofeedback. As a student of Mulholland, Peper (Chapter 26) presents a series of experimental studies within a cybernetic framework, showing how one can stabilize the EEG. Feedback stabilizes the natural variations of the EEG alpha pattern. Once the system is stabilized, one can see the effect of different internal and external stimuli.

In Chapter 27 Lynch and Paskewitz present their data in light of the possible mechanisms involved in alpha biofeedback. After reading these two articles, the reader should begin to realize the problems involved in alpha biofeedback training. Ancoli and Kamiya (Chapter 28) outline some of the methodological issues and problems, and suggest strategies for improving the state of the art. For a fuller review of the methodological issues in all the alpha biofeedback literature published from 1968 to 1976, the reader should see Ancoli and Kamiya (1978), and for an older annoted bibliography, Brown and Klug (1974).

While the use of EEG (alpha) biofeedback studies has been an elegant research tool, sensorimotor rhythm (SMR) for the treatment of epilepsy is one of the few applications of EEG biofeedback training with large clinical potential. In the last article in this section, Chapter 29, Sterman and Macdonald describe the details of this approach.

EEG feedback is in its infancy. It has been constricted by difficulties in investigating subjective experience as well as by technological problems. There have been many other suggested research and applied explorations of EEG feedback, which the reader may wish to explore. These range from pain control (Gannon & Sternbach, 1971; Pelletier & Peper, 1977), creativity (Green, Green, & Walters, 1971), and twilight learning (Budzynski, 1977) to teaching in the classroom (Mulholland, 1973). At present, new and exciting areas are opening up, as feedback training explores other frequencies and amplitudes besides alpha, beta, and theta, i.e., the work of Sheer and collaborators (1975) on 40-Hz EEG and the exploration by Peper and Ancoli on 18–20 Hz (see Chapter 9). In addition, there exists the exciting work on brain lateralization and possible localized feedback training of different scalp locations suggested by Davidson and Schwartz (1977); Galin (1974); and Peper (1971).

Finally, with the rapid technological changes and complexities of feedback left to explore, EEG at this stage is still an area with many more questions than answers.

Further suggested readings on the basis of EEG are Hill and Parr (1963), Kooi (1971), Craib and Perry (1975), and Walter (1953).

REFERENCES

Ancoli, S., & Kamiya, J. Methodological issues in alpha biofeedback training. *Biofeedback and Self-Regulation*, 1978, *3*(2), 159–183.
Brown, B. *New mind, new body*. New York: Harper & Row, 1974.
Brown, B., & Klug, J. W. *The alpha syllabus: A handbook of human EEG activity*. Springfield, Illinois: Charles C Thomas, 1974.

Budzynski, T. Tuning in on the twilight zone. *Psychology Today*, August 1977, pp. 39–44.

Craib, A. R., & Perry, M. *EEG handbook*. Beckman Instruments, 1975.

Davidson, R., & Schwartz, G. The influence of musical and non-musical self-generation tasks. *Psychophysiology*, 1977, *14*(1), 58–63.

Galin, D. Implications for psychiatry of left and right cerebral specialization. *Archives of General Psychiatry*, 1974, *31*, 572–583.

Gannon, L., & Sternbach, R. Alpha enhancement as a treatment for pain: A case study. *Behavior Therapy and Experimental Psychiatry*, 1971, *2*, 209–213.

Green, E. Biofeedback for mind–body self-regulation: Healing and creativity. In *Varieties of healing experience: Exploring psychic phenomena in healing, a transcript from the Interdisciplinary Symposium*. Cupertino, Calif., October 1971.

Hill, D., & Parr, G. *Electroencephalography*. London: Macdonald., 1963.

Kooi, K. *Fundamentals of electroencephalography*. New York: Harper & Row, 1971.

Mulholland, T. Biofeedback: It's time to try hardware in the classroom. *Psychology Today*, 1973, *6*, 103–104.

Mulholland, T. Biofeedback as scientific method. In G. Schwartz & J. Beatty (Eds.), *Biofeedback theory and research*. New York: Academic Press, 1977. Pp. 9–28.

Pelletier, K., & Peper, E. Developing a biofeedback model: Alpha EEG feedback as a means for pain control. *International Journal of Clinical and Experimental Hypnosis*, 1977, *25*(4), 361–371.

Peper, E. Comment on feedback training of parietal-occipital alpha asymmetry in normal human subjects. *Kybernetik*, 1971, *9*(4), 156–158.

Sheer, D. Biofeedback training of 40 Hz EEG and behavior. In N. Burch & H. Altschuler (Eds.), *Behavior and brain electrical activity*. New York: Plenum Press, 1975.

Walter, W. G. *The living brain*. New York: Norton, 1953.

Wiener, N. *Cybernetics* (2nd ed.). Cambridge: M.I.T. Press, 1961.

22

Brain Rhythms and the EEG

Judith Green

Exploration of the organization and function of the brain has been paced by gradual developments in understanding of the electrical nature of the nervous system. Walter (1953) tells the story of two Prussian army physicians dashing about the battlefield with their primitive Galvanic current stimulator, applying electric currents to the exposed brains of recently deceased soldiers. Like Galvani's dramatic demonstration with frog legs, they demonstrated limb movement in response to stimulation of contralateral brain areas. That was 1870. Today extensive technical advances have been made in methods of stimulation and recording from the brain, and stimulation continues to be a principal technique for investigation of neuronal pathways and behavior. The use of microelectrodes and stereotaxic techniques enables accurate placement of depth electrodes in subcortical and cortical targets. Neuronal responses to stimulation can be recorded by electrodes placed in strategic locations and can be analyzed for time delays between various electrode placements, wave formation changes, and other parameters with the hope of elucidating the mechanisms of neuronal transmission and responsivity. Obviously, this technique cannot be used extensively with human subjects, and it presents a methodological problem in being a nonphysiological technique; the stimulation is an artificial input not generated by the brain's own mechanisms. Human studies using depth electrodes must be justified by disease and are limited to electrode placements that are needed for analysis of the disease process. Given these limitations and the complexity of neuronal organization, it is not surprising that so little is known of the cellular and intercellular mechanisms underlying the electroencephalographic (EEG) recording made from large electrodes placed on the human scalp.

It has long been assumed that the cortical surface or scalp EEG recording reflects the activity of underlying neurons, and it was originally thought that the gross EEG was the summation of cortical action potentials. With the development of microelectrode techniques, however, it became difficult to explain the relatively slow EEG wave on a basis of the extremely high frequency action potentials that are measured from single neurons. Consequently, it has been

Judith Green • Biofeedback Consultant, Aims Biofeedback Institute, Aims Community College, Greeley, Colorado 80631. This chapter is taken from the author's doctoral thesis, "Brain Wave Feedback Training for Seizure Reduction in Epilepsy," The Union Graduate School, Yellow Springs, Ohio, 1976.

hypothesized that the EEG reflects the summation of waxing and waning inhibitory and excitatory postsynaptic potentials, that is, the dendritic, nonpropagating response, which varies with intensity of presynaptic electrical stimulation (Vorontsov, 1960; Grossman, 1969; Pollen, 1969; Morrel, 1967). However, several researchers have noted dissimilarities between cortical surface electrodes and cortical and subcortical depth electrodes during simultaneous recordings (Vorontsov, 1960; Elul, 1972; Peronnet, Sindou, Lavirou, Quoex, & Gerin, 1972; Creutzfeldt, 1973) and there seems to be no simple explanation for the genesis of the EEG during normal and abnormal states.

One of the great challenges to neurophysiologists has been to find an explanation for the appearance and disappearance in the EEG of high-amplitude, rhythmical alpha waves, a phenomenon so striking that Berger with his crude instruments immediately noticed the shifts between alpha and nonalpha (Gloor, 1969). Alpha activity represents two puzzling aspects of EEG that also occur in epileptiform activity, *synchronization* and the possible existence of a *pacemaker* in subcortical regions. *Synchrony* has two meanings: first, that the wave pattern appears at two or more recording sites nearly simultaneously and in phase, and second, that the pattern results from the simultaneous activation of masses of neurons. One theory to account for amplitude changes that occur with different wave patterns is that the potentials generated by single neurons are additive (Gastaut, 1954). Hence, when all the neurons in a pool are simultaneously stimulated, high-amplitude synchronized waves are generated. This theory is supported by the observation that alpha is present most abundantly in a quiet, awake, eyes-closed state, whereas alerting and activation correlate with a sudden decrease in the EEG amplitude and replacement of the smooth rhythmical alpha waves by choppy, high-frequency beta. It is assumed that under the impact of alerting and attending to incoming stimuli, cortical neurons fire in a more random, nonsynchronized manner. To some extent this model may need to be amended by the finding that different cortical neurons, at different depths, in themselves produce responses of different amplitude (Verzeano, 1972).

Verzeano (1972) also amends the second meaning of synchronization, showing that groups of neurons recorded from closely spaced electrodes in the cortex and thalamus respond sequentially, and only partially in synchrony, when a rhythmical "synchronous" wave is being generated. Verzeano adds this interesting report to the picture of neuron firing:

> Further studies of the pathway of circulation of neuronal activity by means of arrays of micor-electrodes whose tips are arranged in such a way that they form a triangle and, thus, provide a tri-dimensional view of the process . . . have shown that the circulation is not limited to one plane but shifts continually from one plane to another. If the series of loops followed by the pathway of circulating activity in one plane . . . are extended to three-dimensional space, the three-dimensional pathway might conform to a helix. (Verzeano, 1972)

We might speculate that helical or not, when waves of activity are transmitted through the scalp and displayed on a two-dimensional EEG chart, the positive and negative wave activity that we see is the transposition of a three-dimensional signal to two dimensions (if we call "time" a dimension). This lack of synchronized neuronal activity during synchronous waves is also noted by Elul (1972). These are very circumscribed studies, however, and the results may not be relevant to the generation of the extremely high-amplitude "hypersynchronous" waves of epilepsy.

The fact that synchronized waves may appear over large areas of the cortex simultaneously (or nearly so) led to the hypothesis that alpha must be paced by centers in the brain that have connections with both hemispheres. A natural candidate for such a pacemaker role is the thalamus, which projects off all areas of the cortex and is a midline structure. This hypothesis, with extensive supporting data, has been thoroughly discussed by Andersen and Andersson (1968) in their review of research on the physiological basis of the alpha rhythm. The evidence supports the theory that the rhythmic spindles seen in certain thalamic nuclei and corresponding cortical recordings is generated by "powerful recurrent inhibition." In this type of inhibition, an excitatory neuron gives off an axon collateral, which synapses on an inhibitory neuron, and the inhibitory neuron in turn synapses back on the excitatory cell. Thus, through recurrent inhibition, excitatory cells "self-regulate" via connections with inhibitory cells. Andersen and Andersson wrote: "The timing of the rhythmic periods is given by the duration of the inhibitory potentials. Furthermore, the wide distribution of the recurrent inhibition causes the synchronous behavior of many thalamic neighboring neurons in the rhythm." In a summary paragraph, these researchers add: "Admittedly, it is not possible to know whether the spindle behavior has any particular meaning at all. It could be a physiological artifact, an unavoidable process that goes with the powerful thalamic recurrent inhibition that is needed for some other purpose, perhaps a lateral inhibition of sensory information. However, because the organism has many other mechanisms at its disposal for the control of sensory information . . . it is not unlikely that the thalamic inhibition serves a particular purpose."

The ambiguity of the "meaning" of brain rhythms and of the electrophysiological genesis of the electroencephalogram raises an essential question: To what degree does the EEG reflect the complex hierarchy of events in the communication between neuron and neuron, nucleus and nucleus, subcortex and cortex, cortex and subcortex, hemisphere and hemisphere? And more importantly for human study, to what degree does the EEG reflect the inherent plasticity and capacity of brain functioning to mediate physiological and psychological processes? From the perspective of both neuronal and psychophysiological complexity of the organism, the human EEG seems to reveal very little, and a cautious approach to interpretation is warranted.

It is not ambiguous, however, that the smooth operation of the nervous system necessitates intact and unimpeded excitatory and inhibitory neuronal pathways, a supportive, nutritive environment of glial cells, sufficient production, release and uptake of neurotransmitter substances at the synaptic junction, and chemical balance within and without the neuron. And it is clear that in spite of backup systems and plasticity, the central nervous system is vulnerable to irregularities that, for reasons as yet uncertain, may result in the phenomenon known as epilepsy.

REFERENCES

Andersen, P., & Andersson, S. A. *Physiological basis of the alpha rhythm*. New York: Appleton-Century-Crofts, 1968.

Creutzfeldt, O. D. Synaptic organization of the cerebral cortex and its role in epilepsy. In M. A. B. Brazier (Ed.), *Epilepsy and its phenomena in man, UCLA Forum #17*. New York: Academic Press, 1973.

Elul, R. Randomness and synchrony in the generation of the EEG. In H. Petsche & M. A. G. Brazier (Eds.), *Synchronization of EEG activity in epilepsies*. New York: Springer-Verlag, 1972.

Gastaut, H. *The epilepsies: Electro-clinical correlations*. Springfield, Illinois: Charles C Thomas, 1954.

Gloor, P. Hans Berger on the electroencephalogram of man. *EEG Clinical Neurophysiology*, 1969, Suppl. 28.

Grossman, S. P. *A textbook of physiological psychology*. New York: Wiley, 1969.

Morrell, F. Electrical signs of sensory coding. In G. C. Quarton, T. Melechuk, & F. O. Schmitt (Eds.), *The neurosciences: A study program*. New York: Rockefeller University Press, 1967.

Peronnet, F., Sindou, M., Laviron, A., Quoex, F., & Gerin, P. Human cortical electrogenesis: Stratigraphy and spectral analysis. In H. Petsche & M. Brazier (Eds.), *Synchronization of EEG activity in epilepsies*. New York: Springer-Verlag, 1972.

Pollen, D. A. Microelectrode studies of penicillin foci. In H. Japser, A. Ward, & A. Pope (Eds.), *Basic mechanisms of the epilepsies*. Boston: Little, Brown, 1969.

Verzeano, M. Pacemakers, synchronization and epilepsy. In H. Petsche & M. Brazier (Eds.), *Synchronization of EEG activity in epilepsies*. New York: Springer-Verlag, 1972.

Voronstov, D. S. What does the electroencephalogram express? *Pav. J. Higher Nerv. Acta.*, 1960, *10*, 42–54.

Walter, W. G. *The living brain*. New York: Norton, 1953.

23

Electroencephalography

P. Strong

The following is necessarily a short and therefore somewhat incomplete survey of the EEG and EEG measuring techniques. Interested readers will find W. Grey Walter's text (1953) invaluable for further study.

Electroencephalography, conveniently abbreviated EEGy, is the study of the electrical activity of the brain. Usually this activity is recorded from electrodes placed on the scalp, although some relatively rare diagnostic procedures require electrodes on or beneath the cerebral cortex. The EEG has been known for some 40 years and has made many contributions to man's knowledge of brain function. For reasons that are examined later, it has been of greater help to neurology (the study of brain function) than to psychiatry (the study of mental processes).

THE CHARACTERISTICS OF THE NORMAL EEG

The EEG of a normal adult human, *normal* being used in the everyday sense of the word, is relatively easily described. When the subject is relaxed, but not drowsy, a relatively smooth oscillation, whose frequency is seldom less than 8 Hz or more than 13 Hz, can be recorded from the area of scalp immediately over the occipital lobes. Typically this oscillation, the α rhythm, has an amplitude of 50 μV peak to peak, although in rare subjects it may be twice this amplitude and in about 10% of the population it is absent or very small. This rhythm is responsive to mental activity; in most subjects, attempting a task such as mental arithmetic will attenuate or abolish it.

Most EEGs are recorded using multichannel ink-writing oscillographs, as shown in Figure 1, historically because they were widely available to physiologists. If some more sophisticated method of display is used it is found that more than one generator is involved, that there are generally several different frequencies, that there are differences in responsiveness between the cerebral hemispheres, and that often the frequency of the signal measured in a transverse plane is consistently different from that observed with laterally placed electrodes. Frequency information is particularly significant since the basic frequency of the EEG varies greatly with different behavioral states. To assist in the EEG analysis,

---

P. Strong • Tektronix, Inc., Beaverton, Oregon 97077.

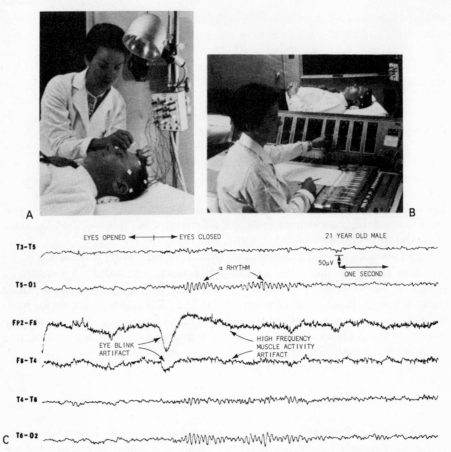

Figure 1. A typical adult EEG from a normal subject. (A) Electrodes are applied to the scalp and plugged into the junction box. (B) A switch selector allows the desired electrode configuration to be chosen. (C) A segment of the record obtained showing six of the sixteen channels recorded.

the normal frequency range of the EEG (0.5 Hz to 30 Hz) has been subdivided into five bands:

delta	(δ).	0.5 Hz– 4 Hz
theta	(θ).	4 Hz– 8 Hz
alpha	(α).	8 Hz–13 Hz
beta	(β).	13 Hz–22 Hz
gamma	(γ).	22 Hz–30 Hz

Various techniques for signal display are discussed later in this chapter. Although the α rhythm is the most prominent activity in the EEG of healthy adults, it is not seen in very young children and its absence does not indicate a lack of mental health or any deficiency in intelligence.

A segment of an EEG record from a normal adult male is shown in Figure 1. Six of the 16 channels commonly recorded by an EEG instrument are shown. The tracing is read from left to right. Initially, the subject's eyes were open but after about 2.5 seconds he was asked to close them. The large downward deflection in leads FP2-F8 and the smaller one in F8-T4 are the "eye-blink artifact". The α rhythm can be seen in the occipital channels T5-O1 and T6-O2 after the eyes were closed. Although the subject was completely normal, the α rhythm is somewhat smaller and less persistent than usual. The high-frequency component in the two middle tracings is an artifact due to muscle activity and is not from the brain. The EEG shown in Figure 1 represents only about 8 seconds of recording; however, in practice, a recording may be maintained for an hour or more, producing a vast quantity of information for analysis.

From an engineering standpoint the design of an EEG instrument and its accessories (electrodes, etc.) is nowadays a routine matter requiring little more than ordinary care and attention to detail. As is so often the case in electronic design, the overall system limitations are almost all in the input devices (the electrodes), which interface the equipment to the subject, and in the methods of storing the output data.

The input electrodes are the most critical components of the recording chain. To be of use for routine EEG recording they must be small, be easily affixed to the scalp with minimal disturbance of coiffure, cause no discomfort, and remain in place for extended periods of time. They must also have some fairly rigid electrical specifications if the signals are to be recorded with acceptably low levels of distortion.

We have noted that many EEG signals are of microvolt levels and it should be remembered that the signal is arising not at the scalp but in the cerebral cortex, which is separated from the scalp by the cerebral spinal fluid (in which the brain is suspended) and by the skull. Parenthetically, we should note that engineers often suppose the skull to be an insulator because they usually see it dried and mounted. The living brain, however, is encased in living bone, which is well permeated with conducting fluid. The amplifying system thus sees signals that arise in generators, which have large, complex, and variable source impedances. There may be large electrode offset potentials of the order of many millivolts developed between the electrode and the scalp unless a suitable electrode material is used. The high common-mode rejection ratio of the modern EEG amplifier will cancel the common-mode part of this signal, but in practice small movements of the subject's head can cause substantial variations in the standing potential and if these are different in each lead they will of course appear as differential signals.

A further cause of problems in EEG recording is the presence in the modern clinic of many pieces of line-operated equipment so that there are substantial magnetic and electric fields at the line frequency. The CMMR of the amplifier can, in principle, reduce these signals to insignificance but only if the entire system, including the electrode impedances, is balanced with respect to the common (ground) point on the amplifier. Thus electrode resistance must be reduced as far as possible; with good technique interelectrode resistances of 1–2 kΩ can be obtained. The alternative technique of reducing the line interference by the use of a shielded cage is not generally satisfactory since the degree of physical isolation it entails can be an emotionally upsetting experience, especially for a child. A relaxed subject is a necessity if good recordings are to be obtained.

The most widely used electrodes are small silver pads electrolytically coated with silver chloride and attached to the scalp with a quick-drying adhesive, usually collodion. A harness of rubber straps is also often used to hold the electrodes in place. Before the electrodes are applied, the scalp area is degreased and cleaned with alcohol and the surface resistance reduced by the use of a conducting paste. These electrodes are satisfactory for most recordings in the range 1–60 Hz. If, however, the low-frequency limit is to be extended, which is the case in some research applications of the EEG, then electrodes that more closely approximate truly nonpolarizable electrodes, such as Tektronix Ag/AgCl electrodes, must be used. Electrodes are generally placed at standard locations on the scalp to facilitate communication between electroencephalographers. These positions, with their usual designations, are shown in Figure 2. The usual abbreviations are: F = frontal, T = temporal, C = central, P = parietal, O = occipital.

Turning now to the output end of an EEG recording system, multichannel ink-writing oscillographs are used for many reasons. The recording material is relatively cheap, the record is available for inspection as it is being written, the electroencephalographer can quickly flip through a long recording and obtain an "eyeball" impression of its contents, and he may study interesting or complex parts of the record for as long as is necessary. Other media such as magnetic tape do not possess these properties and have not become popular in the routine clinical laboratory. If visual analysis is to be supplanted by computer or other automated data-processing techniques, then the written record must be supple-

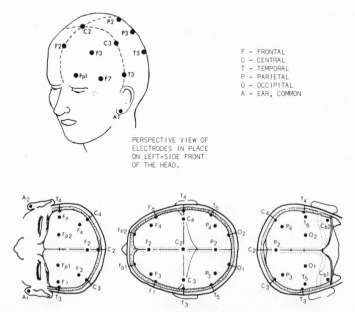

F – FRONTAL
C – CENTRAL
T – TEMPORAL
P – PARIETAL
O – OCCIPITAL
A – EAR, COMMON

PERSPECTIVE VIEW OF
ELECTRODES IN PLACE
ON LEFT-SIDE FRONT
OF THE HEAD.

Figure 2. EEG electrode positions.

mented by a magnetic recording or a curve reader (e.g., the multichannel high-speed curve reader described by Barlow in 1968) must be used. The frequency response of most EEG systems is limited by the characteristics of the recorder to something of the order of 60 Hz, but this is adequate for most clinical purposes.

EEG recording systems are usually self-contained units consisting of electrode switching networks, high-gain differential amplifiers, and graphic recorders. Multichannel recording is almost invariably used, the number of channels ranging between 6 and 32 with 8 or 16 channels being the numbers preferred for routine work.

A multiplicity of electrodes is affixed to the scalp as shown in Figure 2 and the recording channels are connected to them via a switching network. The amplifiers are invariably designed to accept differential inputs and their design is usually optimized for low noise and good common-mode rejection. The low-frequency response usually extends to about .1 Hz; however, the high-frequency response need not be in excess of about 100 Hz due to the limited high-frequency response of the graphic recorder following the amplifier. Since most EEG activity occurs below 50 Hz, a notch filter tuned to line frequency is often included in EEG instruments to minimize line frequency interference, but its use is strongly discouraged except as a last resort.

Although the gain of most modern EEG instruments is stable to within a few percent, a 50-μV square-wave calibrator may be included in the instrument. Although the sensitivity of the amplifier may be adjusted to suit particular subjects, the electroencephalographer rarely changes the sensitivity during the recording of an EEG. He usually selects a gain that makes the initial record "look right" and uses the same gain throughout all phases of recording the EEG. Since the electroencephalographer is concerned with relative amplitudes between the channels, it is necessary that each channel has the same sensitivity. It is desirable to standardize on both sensitivity and paper speed to achieve aspect ratio consistency, which allows comparison with other EEGs recorded from other subjects. No firm standard exists here; however, many workers prefer a sensitivity of about 7 mm per 50 μV for adult subjects, a somewhat lower sensitivity for children, and a somewhat higher sensitivity for the aged. The range of sensitivities used is usually within the range of 4 mm per 50 μV to 15 mm per 50 μV.

REFERENCES

Walter, W. G. *The living brain*. New York: Norton, 1953.

24

Autoregulation of the EEG Alpha Rhythm:
A Program for the Study of Consciousness

Joe Kamiya

In keeping with the functionalist outlook of contemporary Western psychological research, most studies of the behavior of organisms employ procedures that require the behavior to be externally directed so as to involve the organism in gross interaction with the environment. In contrast, the new studies in trained autoregulation or "biofeedback training" require the organism to produce an internal effect. The methods of experimental control are external, as before, but the goal-directed behavior specified by the experimenter is an internal physiological effect.

The point of departure we have taken in our studies with the new methods is that these trained physiological effects seem to have behavioral properties. At the human level one of these behavioral properties is experiential or subjective concomitants. The fact that humans can compare the effects of the physiological training with other behavioral states, by verbal reports and by other discriminative behaviors, poses interesting questions.

We will describe the various studies we have done to establish that humans can be trained to discriminate and to control the average amplitude of their occipital electroencephalographic alpha rhythms. We will then describe a general methodology that we hope will be fruitful in specifying the dimensions of experiential qualities associated with such trained control.

But first a word of commentary on the concepts that seem to be reflected by the recent surge of interest in this field. What we seem to be witnessing is an increasing convergence of several diverse methodologies, concepts, and interests. These include the application of behavioral technology and electronic instrumentation to the historically controversial area of such private internal events as feelings, conscious control, attention, etc. This surge of interest appears to be spurred by studies that show physiological concomitants of Eastern-style meditation practices, by a growing interest in expanded awareness of body and mind through sensitivity training, and by an increasing number of studies relating physiological and pharmacological variables to states of consciousness. The studies of dreaming and of the effects of the hallucinogenic drugs are good examples of these convergent trends.

Joe Kamiya • Langley Porter Neuropsychiatric Institute, University of California, San Francisco, California 94143.

These trends seem to be signs of progress. First, psychology appears to be getting less stiff about accepting "mentalistic" concepts such as dreaming as reasonable, hypothetical processes to account for the facts of dream-reporting behavior. Second, there appears to be growing recognition of the notion that the body is not only a part of the O side of the Organism–Environment dichotomy, but that it is also a proximal environment in which behaviors can take place (for example, trained control of peripheral blood flow) and have their effects more centrally (as in headache control) as well as have effects in the more distal environment (as in controlled blushing by actors). The recognition of the body as a discriminable and controllable entity points to its status both as an environment itself and as an interface with the more distal ecology. Biofeedback training seems to me to be especially helpful in emphasizing this unitive concept in which behavior and experience are no longer incompatible but are instead intrinsic to biological organization.

Clearly, however, the theoretical tools for sharpening our comprehension of the entire range of phenomena are still quite primitive. As a way of helping progress toward the development of a more adequate theory, or at least in pointing out issues that seem to be relevant, the following points may be worthwhile. Initially, we might ask why trained physiological control sometimes, if not always, appears to have behavioral concomitants at all. Whether these concomitants are in the form of observable responses or are restricted to internal experience, why should they ever occur in association with operantly trained physiological activity? Three possible reasons occur to me: First, the same reinforcers that control externally directed behaviors appear to work for training physiological control. Food, water, termination or avoidance of aversive stimuli, and electrical stimulation of brain centers have all been used successfully in training physiological control in animals. For humans, monetary rewards, course credits, and praise or status seem to work for many physiologically defined behaviors as well as for externally oriented behaviors. A consequence of this similarity may be that, at least for the period of the experiment, the functional significance of the arbitrarily chosen physiological change (for example, a decrease in heart rate) is similar to that of an already established external operant (for example, a bar press), since both obtain the same reinforcer (for example, food). Also, whatever physiological events constitute the process of reinforcement should be similar, whether the specific response is behaviorally or physiologically defined; and they might be expressed as secondary effects in behavior or experience.

Second, whatever the physiological processes underlying responses to discriminative stimuli may be, such processes should have similar effects on behavior if they can be initiated by the organism itself as a result of trained physiological control.

Third, the very physiological processes that are being brought under operant control have evolved phylogenetically, at least in part as mechanisms subserving externally directed behavior. For example, cardiac acceleration assists the organism in stressful emergencies. Animals trained by operant methods under nonstressful conditions to increase heart rate, therefore, might well be expected later to show altered signs of emotional responsiveness in stressful conditions, as in DiCara and Weiss's study (1969).

Although these considerations are couched in the language of external behavior, they can be stated in terms of internal behavior as well. That is, operantly controlled physiological activity can be thought of as behavior itself, albeit purely internal. The subjective concomitants, then, may well be a reflection of internal discriminative activity associated with the behavior, either as mediators or as resultants of the behaivor. That is, the internal behavior has stimulus properties that are discriminable.

At any rate, an empirical search for physiological and psychological concomitants seems worthwhile. We turn now to a brief description of work done in our lab along these lines, with feedback training of the EEG.

The first of our studies on the EEG alpha rhythm and consciousness was done in 1958 at the University of Chicago. William Dement had just introduced me to the techniques of EEG recording and dream detection in the sleep laboratory of Professor Nathaniel Kleitman, and there was much talk about dreaming, consciousness, and Stage I sleep. Because the waxing and waning alpha rhythm of the subject who had yet to fall asleep fascinated me (and perhaps partly because studying awake subjects was less demanding than studying all-night sleep subjects), I found myself gradually defecting from sleep and dream research.

What I wanted to know about the waxings and wanings of the alpha rhythm was whether they were accompanied by changes in consciousness. A conditioned discrimination was tried in which a bell was rung from time to time, and the subject's task was to guess each time whether or not he had been generating alpha at the moment just before the bell was rung (Kamiya, 1971). The fact that subjects could learn this task was gratifying, not only because of the specific evidence relating alpha to an apparently discriminable state of awareness, but also because the method seemed to provide a promising paradigm for the behavioral study of many other physiological measures.

Retrospective reports by the subjects implicated close-up visual imagery as being associated with the absence of alpha. Since the experiments were conducted with the eyes closed and in total darkness, their imagery was not from actual seeing. The presence of alpha was reported as being associated with less visual imagery, and as being more relaxed, less attentive to anything in particular, and less intense. Quite by accident of experimental whim we found that subjects trained in making these discriminations were, by virtue of the training, able to produce the fluctuations in alpha at our command. Thus it appeared that discrimination of the internal state of alpha–nonalpha was intimately related to control of the state.

Subsequently, in 1961 in our laboratory at the Langley Porter Neuropsychiatric Institute, we decided to train for alpha control directly, and devised the first of our audio feedback systems for this purpose (Kamiya, 1969). A tone in the subject's room was made to go on (or off) when the amplitude of the filtered, full-wave rectified and smoothed alpha rhythm reached a criterion threshold. When the amplitude fell below this level, the tone went off (or on). Additional feedback was provided in the form of a numerical score shown every 30 seconds, indicating the percent of time the tone had been on (or off). The subject's task was to increase the percent of time the tone was on. He sat with his eyes closed in a dark room. The equipment was in an adjacent room.

Most subjects learned quite quickly, within one or two sessions of about 45 minutes each, to suppress alpha significantly. Specific coaching by suggesting close-up visual imagery, and especially instructions to attent to phosphenes, helped subjects to suppress alpha even further. Learning to increase alpha in relation to baseline percentages was more difficult, often requiring four or more sessions to demonstrate such increases. Some subjects failed to reach scores that were consistently higher than baseline scores. All subjects showed a decrease in alpha, relative to pretraining baselines, in the first one or two trials of feedback training to increase their alpha. This decrease was sometimes not fully recovered even after an entire hour of training. The early parts of alpha-increase trials were, therefore, very much as described by Lynch and Paskewitz (1971)—a matter of overcoming the factors that inhibit alpha.

It was found that the training produced a change in alpha during the baseline trials that followed immediately, where no feedback was given and where the subject was instructed to wait quietly with his eyes closed and not try to control his EEG. These were given after every five training trials. If the training trials were *increase* trials, the baseline scores went up by approximately the same amount as did the training scores. If the training trials were *decrease* trials, the baseline scores went down, also to the same degree as the training scores. There thus appeared to be an inertial effect of training trials on the resting baseline scores.

The subject's feelings during alpha-increase trials were described in general as being relaxed though alert, calm, and sometimes pleasant. The alpha-decrease trials were described as more involved with close-up visual imagery and with more tension, anxiety, and fatigue than the increase trials.

Experiments using an alternating sequence of increase and decrease trial blocks, sandwiched by baseline trials, were more useful in determining the degree of control achieved by subjects. Alternation also permitted a test of the behavior of the baseline scores. The sequence of trial blocks in one study was five 30-second increase trials, two 30 second baseline trials, and five 30-second decrease trials. This sequence was repeated over the entire session of about 45 minutes.

The results were as follows: (1) Both increase and decrease trial scores departed significantly from initial baseline values in the expected direction. (2) Alpha-decrease scores became significant in relation to initial baseline scores more quickly than did increase scores. (3) The basal scores followed the same course as the increase trial scores and were not distinguishable from them.

Thus, when subjects were allowed to rest between alternations of increase and decrease trial blocks, they clearly behaved like alpha-increase subjects. This result was replicated in additional studies using the same design and the same equipment. Again, Lynch and Paskewitz's interpretation seems, in general, to apply (Lynch & Paskewitz, 1971). However, in subsequent experiments some modifications designed to improve the efficiency of learning resulted in data that throw serious doubt on the interpretation that learning to increase alpha is merely a matter of learning to overcome its inhibitors.

The first modification was a change in the method of feedback. Rather than continue the use of a dichotomous on–off feedback signal triggered by an arbitrary criterion amplitude, we changed to a continuous tone whose loudness varied monotonically with the amplitude of the alpha envelope. This gave a more faithful reproduction of the manner in which trains of alpha activity actually varied in amplitude. Second, we turned to scoring for the time integral of the area under the alpha envelope, thus giving a measure that was proportional to the average amplitude. This measure is especially important for giving appropriate feedback to subjects who appear to level off in alpha production in terms of percentage of alpha time, but who might continue to increase the amplitude of their alpha rhythms. Third, we changed to a 2-minute trial period instead of a 30-second period, thus giving the subjects a greater opportunity to move into a sustained high-amplitude state.

With these modifications in use over the last 4 years of work, we have consistently found that after about four sessions of training of about 45 minutes each, subjects being trained to increase alpha tend to go above their pretraining baseline levels, as well as above their baseline scores taken during rest periods in the training sessions. This is true whether the training consists of increase trials only or of alternating blocks of five trials of increase or decrease training. For training subjects to decrease alpha, the earlier method is not appreciably different from the modified methods.

One interpretation of the results is that alpha amplitude increases are learned, much like other skills are learned, and that, if it is a matter of learning to overcome inhibitors, such learning is aided by feedback training. A current study utilizing noncontingent feedback supports this view. However, the results presented so far tend to give an overly simple account of the factors affecting alpha. A persistent and serious problem in the interpretation of alpha amplitude feedback learning presents itself in the following observations.

Alpha-increase trials were interrupted in the middle of the session, and the experimenter entered the subject's room for 3 or 4 minutes to ask the subject to relate the states of mind he felt were most conducive to the control of the rhythm. When the training was resumed immediately thereafter, the average amplitude of the subject's alpha was found to be increased in the next one or two trials by considerably more than would occur if the subject were left alone to continue his trials. The gain lasted for only 2 or 3 minutes, with the scores then returning to their previous trend of a more gradual increase characteristic of feedback alpha training. More than half of all subjects have shown this effect.

This increase is puzzling. It does not appear to be the result of merely taking a break, for equal periods of time-out without the reporting do not result in an increased alpha level. Neither does such an increase result when the subject is not in the feedback training situation at all, but is merely waiting during a period corresponding to the length of the training period, and is then engaged in conversation for a period equal to the time of interruption of the experimental subjects. This increase is seen even in highly trained subjects.

We seem to be seeing a kind of potentiation of the effect of alpha-increase trials by the self-reporting period. Further studies are needed to determine the component of these periods which is responsible for the increase. Several possibilities need checking, including the possibility that personal contact between experimenter and subject is responsible. Meanwhile, the results serve to remind us that a factor not encompassed by the feedback training method can affect alpha amplitude very substantially. If the increases are being *elicited* by a factor not yet understood, a modification of methodology to include classical conditioning procedures might be useful in augmenting experimental control.

The work described thus far has to do with the control of the average amplitude of the alpha rhythm. We have also observed that subjects can be trained to control alpha frequency (Kamiya, 1969). In this study, an electronic device sent either a high-pitched or a low-pitched click into the subject's room, depending on whether the duration of each alpha cycle detected by the circuit was longer or shorter than the median duration of his pretraining alpha cycles. With the aid of these signals, subjects learned to control the predominance of slow waves relative to fast waves.

Theta waves are likewise subject to trained control through the use of feedback devices (Green, Green, & Walters, 1970; Brown, 1971). In our own laboratory a system for feeding back an auditory signal that was a function of the difference between theta and alpha envelope amplitudes was successfully used in an effort to sharpen the subject's differentiation between theta and alpha. We also found that subjects could control the cross-correlation between simultaneous values of left- and right-side alpha recorded between central and occipital electrodes if they were presented a tone controlled by the fluctuations in the correlation (computed from a moving 1-second window).

Finally, following the lead of Galin and Ornstein (1972), we have found that a tone feedback system can be used by subjects to control the asymmetry between the amplitude of the left bipolar occipital-to-central alpha envelope and the amplitude of the right bipolar occipital-to-central alpha envelope. In this system, the asymmetry between the two alpha envelopes is computed by on-line computer for a half-second moving window by the function (L. ampl − R. ampl)/(L. ampl + R. ampl). Changes in the index are translated into variations in pitch.

The assessment of the subjective experiences associated with control of these EEG parameters of frequency, differences in envelope amplitude, cross-correlation, etc., is, of course, one of our primary aims. It is too early to describe with adequate reliability what the subjective concomitants are. The individual differences in retrospective verbal reports for any one parameter are very large, and within a single subject the reports change over time, in part because precision of control increase with training. What was felt subjectively to be important at one stage is often later considered unimportant, new concepts emerge to abstract the various experiences of the subject in a more general way, and so forth.

The aim of mapping the subjective qualities of controlled physiological activity is difficult to achieve for at least two reasons. First, the physiological response discriminations necessary for the achievement of control are often quite difficult for subjects to acquire. Second, it commonly occurs that simple verbal labels available to the subject are not satisfactory for describing the experiences associated with physiological control. This is not surprising in light of the fact that he has never heard others describe their experiences with feedback. Nor has he ever had others label his specific experience with the feedback task, as he often had other experiences labeled in his childhood (for example, when his mother used the word *hurt* to describe his sensations from a bruise).

It is important to recognize that the natural language of the subject for referring to internal events is perhaps the best medium currently available for assessing his descriminative repertoire for the physiological processes under discussion, and that rating scales, adjective check lists, etc., should be developed to optimize the validity of the verbal data. However, it also seems that the verbal reports in even the most articulate subjects simply do not match the discriminative precision implied by the high degree of control over physiological processes that is frequently seen, or by his capacity to differentiate one feedback task from another.

The aim of determining subjective experiences, fortunately, need not be limited to verbal report methods. In principle, a program of research combining features of both multidimensional psychophysics and operant training of physiological parameters could yield a more rigorous mapping of the subjective qualities of physiological self-control than any method now available. The general approach described below would seem to be required.

First, subjects should be trained to a high degree of control of the physiological measure to strengthen their discriminative grasp of the ability involved.

Second, each subject should be trained over a wide variety of measures. For example, in the EEG field, this would include alpha amplitude, alpha frequency, theta and beta patterns, and left–right and posterior–anterior dominance of each of these. Control of local circulation, EMG at different body sites, respiratory patterns, gastric motility and acidity, and many more measurable processes, singly and in various combinations, would be other examples.

Third, assessment of the behavioral or subjective equivalence of control among all the measures should be undertaken, and matrices of indices comparing each physiological measure with each of others should be attempted. I can think of three types of these indices:

a. Ask the subject to provide simple ratings of the degree of similarity of one controlled meaure to the others. For example, how similar is alpha to theta, to low EMG at frontalis muscle, to warm hand? Ratings along other dimensions such as *calmness* might also be tried.

b. In a detection type of task, ask the subject, upon a signal, to guess which one of each of two parameters is showing the more extreme state at that moment. For instance, ring a bell for either left-side alpha or right-side alpha, and ask the subject to guess which is present. Determination of the frequency with which one parameter is mistaken for another would provide a measure of their stimulus equivalence.

c. Ask the subject to produce changes in one state. Observe the covariation with the other states as a measure of response equivalence.

Fourth, from such matrices for each subject, the best reference axes (factors) for descriptive purposes should be extracted mathematically, so that any one parameter can be characterized as a combination of "loadings" along such axes.

Fifth, adjectives commonly used to describe experiential states should be matched to these axes.

Such a program would obviously require an effort not realizable within any single laboratory in the foreseeable future, and doubtless would need considerable modification before it could be implemented. But several gains could result.

1. Currently the choice of physiological parameters as candidates for operant training is highly arbitrary. This is especially true in the field of electroencephalography, where so little is known of the functional significance of the parameters extracted. It is reasonable to expect that the approach outlined would reduce the frequency of blind selection and would provide some guideposts based on knowledge of functionally equivalent parameters.

2. If individual differences in the axes were low enough, the language of subjective states for specifiable physiological states would be much more precise, and serious comparisons of the distances between points in the subjective space could be attempted.

3. Exploration of new areas in the subjective space could be tried, partly as a validation of the descriptive system. For example, if particular combinations of values of several physiological measures have never occurred before in the person, training in the production of such combinations should lead to experiences the subject had not had before, but whose qualities might be predicted in advance.

4. Characterization of the degree to which different subjects yielded different axes would change many of the all too speculative and philosophical disputes concerning the similarity of private experiences among different persons into empirically resolvable disputes.

5. A most important gain that we can hope for is that the mapping operation described above, or some replacement of it, will help to bridge both the conceptual and the empirical gaps among physiology, behavior, and subjective experience.

NOTE. This investigation was supported in part by a Research Scientists Development Award #MH 38897 from the National Institute of Mental Health, and in part by the Advanced Research Projects Agency of the Department of Defense under contract N-0014-70-C-350 to the San Diego State College Foundation, monitored by the Office of Naval Research.

REFERENCES

Brown, B. B. Awareness of EEG—subject activity relationships detected within a closed feedback system. *Psychophysiology*, 1971, *7*, 451–464.

DiCara, L. V., & Weiss, J. M. Effect of heart-rate learning under curare on subsequent noncurarized avoidance learning. *Journal of Comparative and Physiological Psychology*, 1969, *69*, 368–374.

Galin, D., & Ornstein, R. Lateral specialization of cognitive mode: An EEG study. *Psychophysiology*, 1972, *9*, 412–418.

Green, E. E., Green, A. M., & Walters, E. D. Voluntary control of internal states: Psychological and physiological. *Journal of Transpersonal Psychology*, 1970, *2*, 1–26.

Kamiya, J. Operant control of the EEG alpha rhythm and some of its reported effects on consciousness. In C. T. Tart (Ed.), *Altered states of consciousness*. New York: Wiley, 1969. Pp. 507–517.

Kamiya, J. Conditioned discrimination of the EEG alpha rhythm in humans. Abstract of a paper presented at the Western Psychological Association meeting, 1962. Reprinted in T. Barber et al. (Eds.), *Biofeedback and self-control: A reader*. Chicago: Aldine-Atherton, 1971. P. 279.

Lynch, J. J., & Paskewitz, D. A. On the mechanisms of feedback control of human brain wave activity. *Journal of Nervous and Mental Disease*, 1971, *153*, 205–217.

Detection of EEG Abnormalities with Feedback Stimulation

Thomas Mulholland and Frank Benson

A feedback method for testing the reactivity of the occipital-parietal EEG in selected brain-lesioned patients revealed abnormalities of (a) insufficient reactivity, (b) bilateral differences in reactivity, and (3) asynchrony. These abnormalities were more evident during feedback stimulation than in the baseline conditions. The utility of feedback method for detecting EEG abnormalities rests on the increased stability or decreased "noisy" variation in the EEG during feedback. The EEG becomes more predictable even to the "on-line" human observer. This makes it easier to detect aberrations or deviations from normal effects. Some effects can only be seen with feedback such as the bilateral differences that occur when the left side controls the feedback compared to when the right side controls it. The results show that feedback EEG is a useful tool in clinical research and indicate that a clinical diagnostic test could be developed with more research. However, the feedback EEG method is not yet a proven diagnostic technique.

Clinical and experimental studies of the typical human bilateral parietal–occipital EEG have shown that the recordings from the left and right sides are similar, although some mismatching of details always occurs. Both visual observation and measurement schemes, which classify the EEG recording into intervals of synchronous and desynchronous activity, emphasize gross similarities, while more refined and precise measurements, e.g., phase differences, emphasize the dissimilarity of details. On all levels of observation, a large and recurring bilateral mismatch compared to norms is a pathological sign.

Recordings of occipital alpha rhythms are bilaterally similar during continuous darkness or steady light and also following visual stimulation. The decline (habituation) of EEG response to repeated visual stimulation is also bilaterally represented.

The evaluation of the magnitude, bilateral symmetry, and synchrony of the response of the posterior alpha rhythms to stimulation has been an important part of "functional EEG" and has been studied in a wide range of brain disorders (Gastaut, 1949; Bancaud, Hecaen, & Lairy, 1955; Fischgold & Mathis, 1959; Cobb, 1963; Hill, 1963). The bilateral absence or marked reduction of alpha blocking by stimuli is an abnormal sign (Liberson, 1944; Blum, 1957;

Thomas Mulholland • Veterans Administration Hospital, Bedford, Massachusetts. Frank Benson • Neurobehavior Center, Veterans Administration Medical Center, Boston, Massachusetts.

Kooi & Thomas, 1958; Wells, 1962; Holloway & Parsons, 1971). Unilateral hyporeactivity or unilateral changes of alpha frequency are less commonly reported (Cobb, 1963). Disturbances of normal habituation and a reduction or absence of dishabituation of the alpha suppression response have also been documented for the brain-damaged (Wells, 1962; Holloway & Parsons, 1971).

METHOD

In this study, changes in the occurrence of the occipital alpha rhythms were used as an index of the orienting response in normal subjects and selected brain-lesioned patients. The description of the EEG index of the orienting response presented here is different from the familiar description of the singular alpha "block" or suppression following visual stimulation (Jus & Jus, 1960). The response of the occipital EEG is described here as a *disturbance* followed by a *recovery* of the ongoing alternation between alpha and intervals of little or no alpha. These latter intervals are collectively called no-alpha. The time series is called the "alpha-attenuation" cycle (Milstein, Stevens, & Sachdev, 1969). There is no mechanism or physiological process implied by the term; it is simply a name for a familiar EEG phenomenon (Bagchi, 1937).

Alpha and no-alpha durations are extremely variable between and within individual records. To reduce variation, we have utilized a *biofeedback method*. A visual stimulus causes a blocking of the EEG alpha, which is connected to the stimulus through an external path of electronic instruments, controlling both its presentation and removal. In this study, alpha caused a visual stimulus to go on; no-alpha caused it to go off. The feedback EEG method markedly reduces unsystematic variation of alpha duration and no-alpha durations after recovery from the initial disturbance, both within and between subjects, and produces a more stable alternation between intervals of alpha and intervals of little or no-alpha (Mulholland, 1968/1970, 1973).

Through feedback EEG *is* a quantitative method, the EEG record can be read by an experienced electroencephalographer to detect abnormal "feedback" effects. In the first part of this chapter examples were selected that are best seen with feedback stimulation compared to a baseline "resting" EEG. This extension of the EEG as a diagnostic test reflects the increased control over the EEG that feedback offers. The examples are not exhaustive and only salient effects that can be observed on-line in the recording are presented in the first part of this chapter. They permit the experienced electroencephalographer to judge the utility of the feedback method for revealing abnormal effects.

The second part of this chapter presents a computer-generated graphical display for the quantitative analysis of individual responses features, e.g., reactivity, which is the initial disturbance and subsequent recovery from the effect of the stimulus and the bilateral similarity of the response. They are intended to be "read" in the same way an EEG record is read, that is, by the experienced electroencephalographer who knows the advantages and limitations of the method. These graphs provide a standardized characterization of the responsivity of the EEG on a trial-by-trial basis.

The feedback method is also useful for testing higher mental functions when the proper complex feedback stimuli are used. Since different kinds of feedback stimuli produce different effects on the occipital EEG (Mulholland, 1973), the ability of the person to react differently to different stimuli can be evaluated. An indirect test of stimulus discrimination can be provided at the same time that other features of the EEG are being tested.

The feedback methods used here have been described elsewhere (Mulholland & Gascon, 1972; Mulholland, 1973). In all cases, occiptal alpha was detected and, by means of external electronic instruments, was associated with a visual stimulus flashed on a screen in front of the subject. The stimulus was either a word, a picture, or an unpatterned spot of light. The visual stimulus was on with alpha and off with no-alpha (Loop 1) or reversed so that the stimulus was off with alpha and on with no-alpha (Loop 2). At the level of on-line monitoring of an EEG during feedback, the experienced examiner can identify the *reactivity* to feedback stimulation, the *recovery* (habituation), the *stability* of the EEG features during feedback after habituation has progressed, the *bilateral symmetry* during feedback, and the *system response* when the left hemisphere EEG is controlling the stimulus compared to when the right side is controlling. The latter conditions are called "left-contingent" and "right-contingent," respectively.

Clinical Material

The examples were selected from an ongoing study aimed at developing instrumentation, test protocols, and data analysis for a clinical feedback EEG method. All cases were from an aphasia therapy unit; all were ambulatory and able to follow simple instructions. For comparison, two EEG typical records and one atypical record from three nonpatient volunteers are presented. All of the patients with brain lesions did not show the effects described here. Also, since recordings were made of the occipital–parietal EEG, abnormal responses in other EEG locations, if they occurred, were missed.

Selected Examples

In the illustrations herein, recordings from left (O_1-P_3) and right (O_2-P_4) are compared. The response of the alpha detector that controls the feedback stimulus is also marked on the record. In some records only the side that controls the feedback is marked; in other records, alpha is marked for both sides. This mark is called "alpha relay." Unless indicated otherwise, the start and stop of feedback is marked by two arrows. In some illustrations, a continuous epoch is shown; in others, samples that are discontinuous are selected.

The first example (Figure 1) is from a normal subject. The stimulus was a picture of a nude woman. The upper two sets of tracings are continuous and show the response to the first 4 stimuli; the lower two sets are continuous and show the response to the last 9 of 30 stimuli, after habituation had occurred.

When feedback begins, controlled by alpha from the left side, a prominent bilateral disturbance of the alternation between alpha and no-alpha (the alpha-attenuation cycle) occurs. After recovery from the disturbance (habituation) a regular alternation between alpha and attenuation with feedback stimulation can be seen. Bilateral symmetry is easy to evaluate because of the enhanced stability of the alpha-attenuation cycle during feedback. A similar pattern is seen in more than 50% of normals.

The second example (Figure 2) is also from a normal subject. It was selected because, though within normal limits, there is a mixture of alpha and other frequencies and a diminished bilateral symmetry that could be appraised visually. Despite this visual impression, the alpha marker shows a normal response. First, a prominent and prolonged attenuation response to the first 2 stimuli (nude woman) is shown in the upper two sets of tracings. The response to the last 12 out of 30 stimuli in the lower two sets of tracings shows the characteristic stability of the alteration between alpha and attenuation after habituation. Bilateral symmetry of the alpha marker is obvious, though asymmetry does occur occasionally as in all normal subjects.

Figure 3 is from the record of a patient with a bilateral carotid occlusion. The only atypical feature is *reduced reactivity* to the stimuli. Because reactivity is reduced, the period of alternation between alpha and no-alpha is brief. This permits the whole series of 27 stimuli to be shown in Figure 3. Low reactivity at

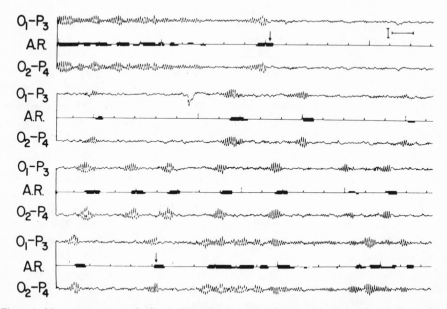

Figure 1. Normal response to feedback. Note the alternation between bilateral alpha spindles and no-alpha intervals at the beginning (top two tracings). The alternation between alpha and no-alpha is more stable after habituation (bottom two tracings). Feedback begins with the first arrow and ends with the second. Calibration is 50 μV and 1 second. A. R. indicates "alpha relay."

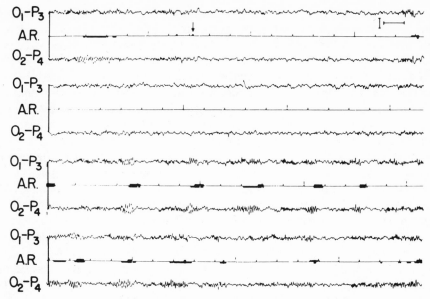

Figure 2. Normal response to feedback. Same format as Figure 1.

onset of feedback is unusual but can be seen in a normal subject who is habituated or who is stimulated with simple or excessively redundant stimuli. This patient showed a diminished reactivity to stimuli that are usually quite evocative for normals such as pictures of nudes, emotional words such as *bitch* or *raped*, and a "real person" stimulus. The generalized low reactivity is definitely atypical, yet stability and bilateral symmetry are normal, i.e., it is a "borderline" record.

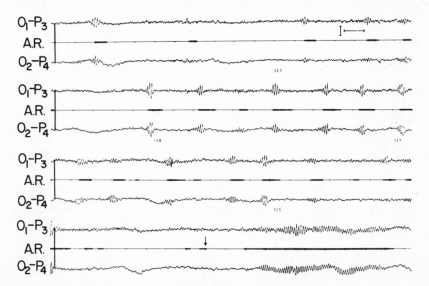

Figure 3. Atypical hyporeactivity to feedback in a patient with bilateral carotid occlusion. Same format as Figure 2.

The next patient, with an old aphasic disturbance, and gait difficulties including right foot drop, was frankly *hyporeactive* to a variety of pictorial, verbal, and "real person" stimuli (Figure 4). The feedback stimulus in this example was a picture of a nude woman. Bilateral symmetry of the alpha attenuation and stability are good, but the low reactivity is abnormal for this stimulus.

The next case had surgical occlusion of the left carotid artery for ruptured left posterior communicating artery aneurysm. He had right hemiparesis, alexia, and anomia. Reactivity is prominent but abnormally *asymmetrical* at the start of feedback (middle set of tracings of Figure 5). The attenuation response, though prolonged on the right side, has much shorter duration on the left. This asymmetry is not seen in the resting "eyes-open" EEG (top set of tracings) and in the EEG after habituation to the feedback stimulus (bottom set of tracings). No abnormal wave forms are evident. This patient's abnormally asymmetrical response to verbal and pictorial stimuli will be illustrated later, using a computer-generated graphical display.

The next individual had a diagnosis of posttraumatic temporal lobe seizures and illustrates a different kind of asymmetry, which was seen primarily at the beginning of feedback (see Figure 6). The asymmetry due to slow waves (7–8-Hz) in the left recording could be seen in the resting record but becomes more evident during feedback. The right side shows a normal attenuation of synchronous rhythms in response too the stimulus. This accentuates the *asynchrony*, due to the slow waves appearing on the left side. After the third presentation of the stimulus (a picture of a nude woman), slow activity (7–8-Hz) appears on the left side, while alpha attenuation continues on the right. This is seen clearly in the second set of tracings. The two sets of tracings show 7–8-Hz continuing on the left along with increasing alpha in the left and right EEGs. The difference between left and right is not obvious after habituation because of increased bilateral alpha.

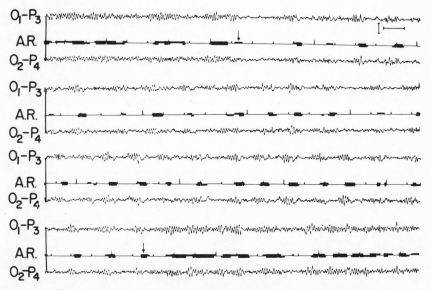

Figure 4. Abnormal hyporeactivity to feedback in a left-lesioned patient.

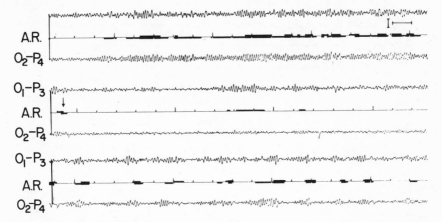

A.R.

O_2-P_4

O_1-P_3

A.R.

O_2-P_4

O_1-P_3

A.R.

O_2-P_4

Figure 5. Abnormal asymmetry of the EEG response to feedback stimulation (middle tracings). Desynchronization persists on the right side while alpha returns sooner on the left. In the resting record (top tracings) or after habituation (bottom tracings) asymmetry is much less and within normal limits. Patient has temporal lobe seizures, posttraumatic.

The next two cases illustrate the utility of feedback for on-line testing of a hypothesis about asymmetry. In both cases the alpha-attenuation cycle was normal on the right. When the feedback was controlled by the right side, the alpha bursts on the left were either poorly developed or did not occur (see Figure 7). The first case had occlusion of the left posterior cerebral artery from its source in the posterior fossa to the occipital area. The top set of tracings was made during an eyes-open condition in the dark before feedback. The relatively lower-amplitude alpha on the left is evident.

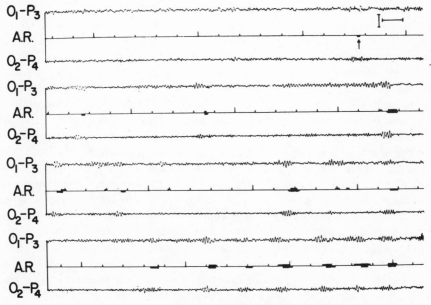

O_1-P_3

A.R.

O_2-P_4

O_1-P_3

A.R.

O_2-P_4

O_1-P_3

A.R.

O_2-P_4

O_1-P_3

A.R.

O_2-P_4

Figure 6. Abnormal asynchrony at the beginning of feedback stimulation.

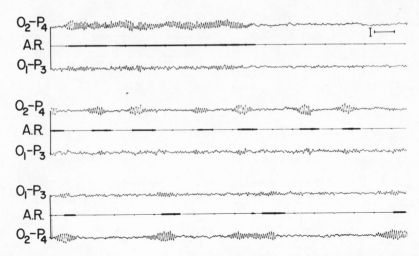

Figure 7. Abnormal asymmetry and asynchrony greatly exaggerated during two kinds of feedback: right side controlling the stimulus (middle tracings) and left side controlling the stimulus (bottom tracings) and left side controlling the stimulus (bottom tracings). Alpha relay (A.R.) marks only the *one* side controlling the stimulus. Patient has occlusion of the left posterior cerebral artery.

During feedback (a spot of white light) controlled by the *right* side (A.R. marks alpha in the contingent channel) the stable alpha-attenuation cycle is seen on the right; on the left, minimal alpha occurs.

One could hypothesize that even though a bilateral attenuation of alpha frequencies occurred in response to stimulation, when the stimulus was off it took much longer for alpha to recover on the left. The right-sided alpha always would occur sooner and cause a stimulus that again blocked alpha bilaterally. Thus alpha on the left could not develop. This hypothesis can be tested by connecting the left side into the feedback loop. The bottom set of tracings shows what happens. (Note that O_1-P_3 is now the top tracing in the bottom set.) Since the simulus does not occur until sufficient alpha on the *left* occurs, alpha bursts can develop on the left. However, since alpha on the right occurs sooner once the stimulus is off, long, prominent asymmetrical alpha spindles develop on the right. By applying the feedback to one side and then to the other, the degree and kind of asymmetry can be manipulated to emphasize the pathological asymmetry. A similar effect has not been observed in normals.

The next case had suffered a left frontal infarct. In Figure 8, an effect similar to that in Figure 7 is shown (A.R. is marking alpha in the contigent channel only). The left recording was abnormal during the eyes-open in the darkness prior to feedback, as shown in the top set of tracings. The shift from shorter to longer alpha spindles with a shift from right-contingent (middle set of tracings) to left-contingent (bottom set of tracings) is evident, though not as clearly as in the previous example. Note that the position of O_1-P_3 and O_2-P_4 are reversed in the bottom set of tracings.

Figure 9 presents a rare asymmetry recorded from a nonpatient several years ago in an unrelated study. During the condition of resting with eyes open in the

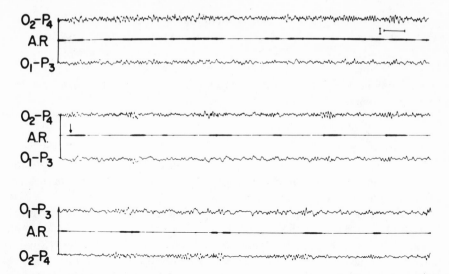

Figure 8. Abnormal asymmetry and asynchrony exaggerated with left feedback and right feedback as in Figure 6. Alpha relay (A.R.) marks only the *one* side controlling the stimulus. Patient diagnosed as left frontal infarct.

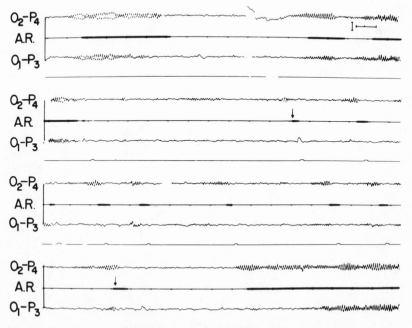

Figure 9. Abnormal asynchrony and asymmetry of EEG activity. Subject is a nonpatient.

dark (top set of tracings), the record is bilaterally symmetrical. With the onset of feedback stimulation (spot of white light), the record is markedly asymmetrical. With the cessation of feedback (bottom set of tracings), the delayed return of alpha on the left side is evident. This degree of asymmetry has not been seen in any other nonpatient so far, i.e., it has occurred in less than 1 in 1000 nonpatient volunteers who have been tested in various experiments since 1960.

Graphical Display

The evaluation of reactivity, habituation, and the bilateral similarity during feedback is facilitated by computer-generated graphical displays of the response of the occipital EEG to feedback stimulation.

The response of the EEG to a series of feedback stimuli is a *disturbance* followed by a *recovery* of the attenuation between intervals of alpha (Δta) and intervals of no-alpha (Δtna), as defined by the feedback control system (Boudrot, 1972). This series is extremely variable with eyes open in the dark, i.e., the "before-feedback" condition. With the initiation of Loop-1 feedback (alpha turns the stimulus on; no-alpha turns it off), the intervals of alpha become brief, much less variable, and quite stable over repeated stimuli; the intervals of no-alpha increase and then decrease irregularly to a level near initial values. Though the variance of no-alpha is also reduced by feedback, this reduction is not as marked as for the alpha durations.

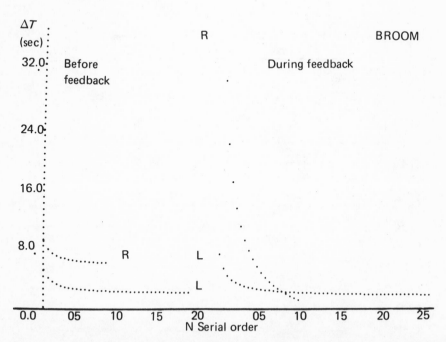

Figure 10. Alertograph for patient shown in Figure 5. Reactivity is definite for the right side but is much less on the left. The stimulus was the word *broom*.

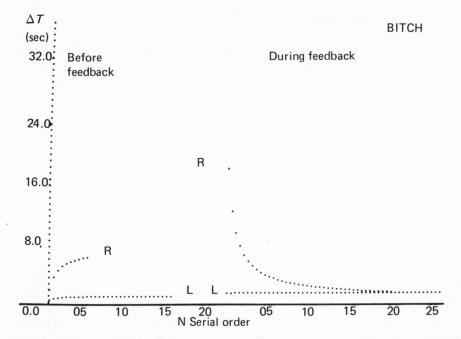

Figure 11. Same as Figure 9 except that the reactivity on the left is nil while on the right it is attenuated. Stimulus is the word *bitch*.

In previous studies (Mulholland & Runnals, 1962; Mulholland, 1973) it was shown that the disturbance and recovery of the occipital alpha-attenuation cycle could be described by fitting curves to the series of alpha durations and to the series of no-alpha durations using the method of Least Squares. A straight line can be fitted to the alpha (Δta) and a hyperbola to the no-alphas (Δtna) to describe the response during feedback. Each best-fit function has statistical measures which determine it: N is the serial number of alpha and no-alpha events. The scatter of actual data around the best-fit lines is shown by the standard error of estimate SE. As shown below, A, B, C, and D are parameters of the functions.

$$1. \quad \Delta \text{ta} \ = (A \cdot N + B) \pm SE$$
$$2. \quad \Delta \text{tna} - (C/N + D) \pm SE$$

From these best-fit functions, graphs are computed which we call "alertographs." They show the disturbance and recovery of alpha and no-alpha durations before feedback, during feedback, and for left and right EEGs. For more details concerning the computerized curve-fitting procedures, see Goodman (1973).

The following examples in Figure 10 and 11 were taken from single trials from the patient whose EEG is presented in Figure 5. They are intended to illustrate the graphical description of an abnormal EEG response to two visual stimuli, the word *broom* and the word *bitch*. Normal subjects usually show a definite bilateral reactivity, initially with a reduction in reactivity with repetition over trials, but not the unilateral reduction shown here in the left EEG. Normal subjects usually show a greater response to the word *bitch* than to the word *broom* if they can read. In Figures 10 and 11 the curves are the estimated durations of intervals of no-alpha (Δtna). Alpha best-fit functions are not shown. Before feedback, the estimated no-alphas on the right are greater than on the left, and stable. In Figure 10, the response to the word *broom* is shown. At the start of feedback the estimated value of no-alpha definitely increases on the *right* but only slightly on the left. In Figure 11, the second visual stimulus, the word *bitch*, produced some response on the right but none on the left. In Figure 10, an *abnormal asymmetry* of response is seen; in Figure 11, an *abnormal hyporeactivity* is illustrated.

DISCUSSION

The use of a closed-loop feedback method has advantages for estimating EEG reactivity. First, the alpha-blocking response is made to recur again and again in a relatively stable way. In our terms, visual feedback stabilizes the alpha-attenuation cycle bilaterally. Against the background of a regular recurring response, aberrations from the expected pattern are more observable. For instance, asymmetries of reactivity if they occur can be visually identified because of the regular alternation of alpha and no-alpha intervals on the unaffected side. Feedback *emphasizes* and may *exaggerate* asymmetries of EEG reactivity and EEG asynchrony.

The evaluation of EEG reactivity is more accurate since the response pattern is more predictable because of feedback, and many responses are sampled. evaluated with computer methods, but the experienced electroencephalographer familiar with this method can appraise reactivity from the ink record.

The cases illustrated here were all diagnosed as having focal, localized brain lesions. Such a sample would be expected to show a higher proportion of bilateral asymmetries. On the other hand, the feedback evaluation involved only the parietal–occipital EEG. We did not use feedback from other EEG locations, which could have increased the number and kind of abnormalities that would be observed. We examined only alpha-rhythms. Much more research on feedback from differnt EEG locations and with EEG rhythms at other frequencies needs to be done.

The present report is only a beginning. The full potential for feedback method in clinical EEG is not yet known. The results are encouraging and indicate that further research on this topic is reasonable and likely to yield useful results.

The use of this feedback method to test stimulus discrimination was not shown, though such tests could be useful. Also tests of voluntary control of the response to feedback like those shown with normals (Mulholland, 1973) were not tested. Both *stimulus discrimination* and *voluntary modulation* of the response could be included in a clinical evaluation. More research is required here.

For a better estimation of the *abnormality* of feedback effects, normative data are most desirable. However, standardization and reliability of the method had to be established before meaningful norms could be established. The present method is sufficiently standardized and reliable so that the collection of normative data could begin, especially if a number of researchers were to try the method.

The effects shown here are not claimed to be diagnostic signs of known reliability. To appraise the frequency of occurence of that type of feedback phenomena that would assist the diagnostician, more extensive data would be required. However, from the standpoint of clinical EEG, asymmetry of EEG reactivity, asynchrony, and hyporeactivity that are effectively revealed by the feedback method are diagnostically relevant.

ACKNOWLEDGMENTS. The assistance of Erik Peper, Sylvia Runnals, Rosemary Billingslea, and Thomas McLaughlin in the EEG recording and data analysis was indispensable to this study.

REFERENCES

Bagchi, B. K. The adaption and variability of response of the human brain rhythm. *Journal of Psychology*, 1937, *3*, 463–465.

Bancaud, J., Hecaen, H., & Lairy, G. C. Modifications de la réactivité E.E.G., troubles des fonctions symboliques et troubles confusionnels dans les lesions hemispheriques localisees. *Electroencephalography and Clinical Neurophysiology*, 1955, *7*, 179.

Blum, R. H. Alpha-rhythm responsiveness in normal, schizophrenic and brain-damaged persons. *Science*, 1957, *126*, 749–750.

Boudrot, R. An alpha detection and feedback control system. *Psychophysiology*, 1972, *9*, 461–466.

Cobb, W. A. The EEG of lesions in general. In D. Hill & G. Parr (Eds.), *Electroencephalography. A symposium on its various aspects*. New York: Macmillan, 1963.

Fischgold, H., & Mathis, P. *Obnubilations, comas et stupeurs*. Paris: Masson et cie, 1959.

Gastaut, H. L. L'activité électrique cérébral en relation avec les grande problemes psychologiques. *L'Année Psychologique*, 1949, *51*, 61–88.

Goodman, D. ALFIE: Collection of EEG alpha under feedback control using time series analysis. *Psychophysiology*, 1973, *10*, 437–440.

Hill, D. The EEG in psychiatry. In D. Hill & G. Parr (Eds.), *Electroencephalography. A symposium on its various aspects*. New York: Macmillan, 1963.

Holloway, F., & Parsons, O. Habituation of the orienting reflex in brain-damaged patients. *Psychophysiology*, 1971, *8*, 623–634.

Jus, A., and Jus, C. Etude de l'extinction par répétition de l'expression EEG du réflexe d'orientation et de l'action du frein externe dur les réactions EEG aux différents stimuli chez l'homme. *Electroencephalography and Clinical Neurophysiology*, 1960, *Suppl. 13*, 321–333.

Kooi, K. A., & Thomas, M. H. Electonic analysis of cerebral responses to photic stimulation in patients with brain damange, *Electroencephalography and Clinical Neurophysiology*, 1958, *10*, 417–424.

Liberson, W. T. Functional electroencephalography in mental disorders. *Diseases of the Nervous System*, 1944, *5*, 357–364.

Milstein, V., Stevens, J., & Sachdev, K. Habituation of the alpha attenuation response in children and adults with psychiatric disorders. *Electroencephalography and Clinical Neurophysiology*, 1969, *26*, 12–18.

Mulholland, T. Feedback electroencephalography. *Activitas Nervosa Superior (Prague)*, 1968, *10*, 410–438. Reprinted in T. Barber et al. (Eds.), *Biofeedback and self control: A reader*. Chicago: Aldine, 1970.

Mulholland, T. Objective EEG methods for studying covert shifts of visual attention. In F. J. McGuigan & R. A. Schoonover (Eds.), *The psychophysiology of thinking*. New York: Academic Press, 1973.

Mulholland, T., & Gascon, G. A. Quantitative index of the orienting response in children. *Electroencephalography and Clinical Neurophysiology*, 1972, *33*, 295–301.

Mulholland, T., & Runnals, S. Evaluation of attention and alertness with a stimulus-brain feedback loop. *Electroencephalography and Clinical Neurophysiology*, 1962, *14*, 847–852.

Wells, C. E. Response of alpha waves to light in neurologic disease. *Archives of Neurology*, 1962, *6*, 478–491.

26

Feedback Regulation of the Alpha Electroencephalogram Activity through Control of the Internal and External Parameters

Erik Peper

Experiments with feedback stimulation triggered from the subject's electroencephalogram result in changing the sequential time series of intervals of occipital alpha and
intervals of little or no alpha EEG activity. The rate of recurrence of alpha and no-alpha
EEG can be changed by regulating the external feedback stimuli or by asking the subject to change his internal state. Four different paradigms were investigated and the
results interpreted in terms of the hypothesis that oculomotor functions regulate the
occurrence and nonoccurrence of alpha.

INTRODUCTION

Biological feedback, specifically electroencephalographic (EEG) alpha feedback
(Mulholland & Runnals[1], Mulholland[2], Kamiya[3]) can be used to elucidate the
relationship between a subject's behavior and his EEG. In feedback EEG, a
stimulus is presented to the subject which is contingent upon the presence of a
certain EEG pattern. The parameters of this pattern are determined by the
experimenter. The feedback method reduces the variability of the EEG and
demonstrates the functional relationships between behavior and the EEG.

The occurrence of occipital alpha rhythms can be increased or decreased by
changing the parameters of the feedback in certain subjective states such as attention, visual imagery, and looking behavior.

Study 1. Oculomotor functions. The subject is asked to perform certain
visual tracking tasks.

Study 2. Internal feedback loop changes. The subject is instructed to change
his internal state.

Study 3. External feedback loop changes. The experimeter changes the feedback stimulus.

Study 4. Autoregulation of the EEG. The subject voluntarily attempts to
regulate his own EEG.

Erik Peper • Center for Interdisciplinary Science, San Francisco State University, San Francisco,
California 94134.

METHODS

The four approaches have a common feedback methodology similar to that described previously by Mulholland,[2] as shown in Figure 1.

The EEG was recorded from bipolar electrodes (Grass) usually O_2–P_4, O_1–P_3 (Jasper.[4]) Ground was connected to the right or left mastoid.

Alpha was defined as an 8- to 13-Hz signal with greater than 25% of the maximum amplitude at the frequency recorded with eyes closed, with duration greater than 0.3 seconds. The low-pass filter was set at ± 1 Hz of the subject's resting alpha frequency. Alpha turned the "state" relay on. With alpha frequencies less than 20% of "resting" amplitude, the relay was off. Between 20 and 25% of "resting" amplitude, it was unpredictably on. For each subject the input attenuators were adjusted so that maximum alpha with eyes closed was approximately 1 cm peak to peak.

The state relay controlled the stimulus function. Two feedback modes were used. In Loop 1, the time-delay relay, having negligible time delay when the control turned to zero, was on when the state relay was on (alpha). In Loop 2, the delay relay was on when the state relay was off (no-alpha).

The electrooculograms (EOG) were recorded with slow or nonpolarizing biopotential skin electrodes (Beckman) attached to the outer canthi of the eyes.

The unpaid subjects were college students and Veterans' Administration Hospital employees. Each subject was evaluated under standard conditions for a specific experiment. All recordings were obtained with the subject inside a lightproof, sound-attenuated, electrically shielded room. An intercom linked the experimental chamber with the experimenter.

Approach 1. Oculomotor Functions

Oculomotor relationships to the EEG activity have often been suggested (Mulholland[2], Dewan[5]). Specifically, Mulholland has shown the oculomotor involvement in the blockage of occipital alpha activity by having subjects look at a stationary or moving target under conditions of tracking a near target with focused accommodation, with relaxed accommodation that is blur tracking, and no-tracking with relaxed accommodation. Alpha was most prevalent during blur no-tracking and least prevalent during focus tracking. A series of experiments designed to study this oculomotor involvement in the EEG is described below (Peper[6]).

The stimulus and subject were in the sound-attenuated, lightproof room. The subject was instructed to track a small target, a small incandescent light. The bulb was taped so that a ¼-inch opening with a thinly lined cross was visible. When visible, the target, which was approximately 5 inches in front of the subject, was always moving in a quasi-sinusoidal path. The visibility of the target was controlled through the external EEG feedback path so that in Loop 1 the target was visible when the alpha was on, and in Loop 2 when the alpha was off. After baseline recordings, the experimenter alternated between Loop 1 and Loop 2 every minute.

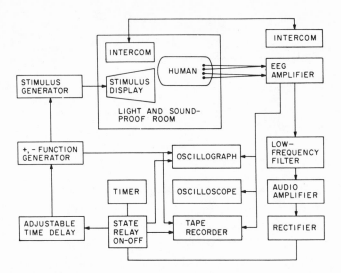

Figure 1. Flow diagram of electroencephalographic alpha feedback loop.

The subjects were selected according to one criterion: Their alpha EEG activity had to have enough amplitude to be recorded at 1 cm p–p on the oscillograph. Subjects were seated and told to track the moving target whenever it was visible. The subject's EEG and EOG alpha indicator, target-visibility marker, and target position were recorded.

Results. All 13 subjects behaved identically and showed two extremes. During Loop 1, regenerative feedback developed in which there was a constant oscillation between alpha and no-alpha. The frequency of oscillation is dependent upon the fixed delays (~0.3 s) and two variable delays: the time between stimulus on and alpha off and the time between stimulus off and the alpha recurrence in the dark. In *no* case could a subject initiate or continue to track without blocking his alpha EEG.

During Loop 2 a runaway positive feedback system developed in which the EEG erratically went from alpha, during which there was no tracking, to no-alpha, during which there was continuous tracking. Sample recordings of Loop 1, Loop 2, and the experimenter's switching between Loops 1 and 2 are shown in Figures 2, 3, and 4.

The means between the feedback modes of Loops 1 and 2 of alpha and no-alpha are shown in Table 1.

Discussion. The task of tracking a near target comprises orientation, acquisition of the target, convergence, accommodation, and smooth-pursuit tracking. The data indicate that whenever the subject initiates tracking, his occipital alpha desynchronizes. In other words, whenever the subject gives efferent oculomotor commands, desynchrony occurs. Previous experiments by Mulholland[2] and new experiments by Pollen,[7] who inactivated the accommodation system by means of drugs and replaced it by an external lens system to accommodate for the subject, have shown that the efferent oculomotor functions—specifically, accommodation—block the alpha rhythm. In Pollen's experiment, the subjects produced

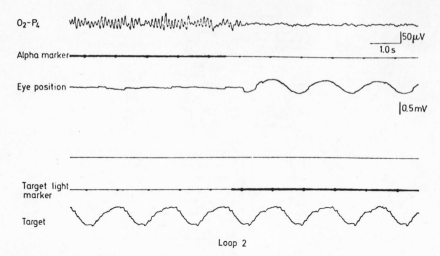

Loop 2

Figure 2. Tracking of target in which target luminance is contingent upon the subject's no-alpha EEG.

occipital alpha activity while reading text, after they got used to the artificial accommodation system; the subject did not have to look, the image was always in focus. Similarly, the tracking experiments with the use of Loop 1 demonstrate this by the occurrence of regenerative feedback.

The previous attention hypothesis (Lindsley[8]), which states that alpha blockage is due to attention to stimuli, is incorrect; instead, oculomotor efferent commands block alpha. The attention state is usually associated, however, with oculomotor commands so that it initially appears to be attention that blocks alpha.

The oculomotor efferent command theory resolves the paradox of the previous attention hypothesis, in which persistent occipital alpha occurred when a

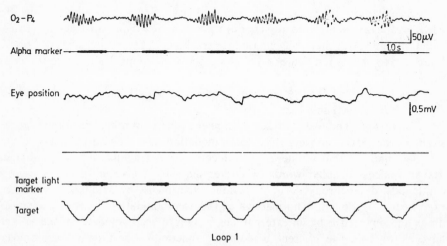

Loop 1

Figure 3. Tracking of target in which target luminance is contingent upon the subject's alpha EEG.

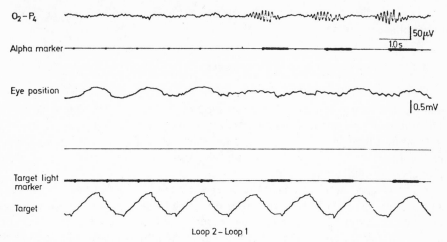

Loop 2 – Loop 1

Figure 4. Tracking of target in which experimenter changes contingency of target luminance from no-alpha to alpha occurrence.

subject was attending to an auditory stimulus. The initial alpha blockage to a loud auditory stimulus is caused by the orientation response; the eyes are directed to the focus of the sound, and this response habituates rapidly.

The performance of the subject while using the Loop 2 feedback mode measures his tracking ability. As long as alpha EEG activity is present, the target is invisible. When the EEG "spontaneously" desynchronizes, the target reappears and the subject starts to track. In this case momentary lapses in tracking, reflected in the EEG by alpha recurrence, is reinforced by the target disappearance and causes the subject to sit in the dark, which enhances spontaneous alpha activity. Consequently, the subject has to motivate himself continuously to track or not track at all. The use of Loop 2 optimizes either oculomotor commands (no-alpha tracking) or no oculomotor commands (alpha darkness). The frequency of these erratic jumps from alpha to no-alpha (no track) in this positive runaway feedback system appears to be related to the control of "internal looking commands." There is a trend indicating that the college group had fewer erratic jumps between alpha and no-alpha per minute intervals than the matched kitchen helpers.

The possibility of applying this method to explore the complete relationship between the occipital alpha and the oculomotor system, and its possible use as an

Table 1

Difference in Alpha and No-Alpha Lengths during Feedback Modes 1 and 2

	Feedback mode							
	Loop 1	Loop 2	Loop 1	Loop 2	Loop 1	Loop 2	Loop 1	Loop 2
Mean alpha length (sec)	0.7	4.6	.7	.9	.8	1.3	.7	1.4
Mean no-alpha length (sec)	3.9	19.5	2.8	22.3	2.5	25.8	2.0	24.8

indicator to identify the biological basis of "visual attention," should be explored (Mulholland[2]).

Approach 2. Internal Feedback Loop Changes

The previously described oculomotor efferent commands, the "attentive looking–tracking commands," are assumed to be operating in this experiment. The effect of different instruction sets was investigated. The subjects were seated in front of a light that had slow rise and decay times. The stimulus was arranged in the Loop 1 feedback mode so that the stimulus went on when the subject produced occipital alpha EEG.

The subjects were instructed to keep their eyes open and look at the light. Two conditions, each lasting 35 consecutive alpha–no-alpha intervals were investigated. Condition A: The subject was instructed to "pay attention" to the light as it went on. Condition B: The subject was instructed "not to pay attention" to the light as it went on.

Results. All subjects behaved similarly. In Condition A the sequential ΔT alpha/ΔT no-alpha is stable, while in Condition B it became unstable, as is shown in Figure 5a.

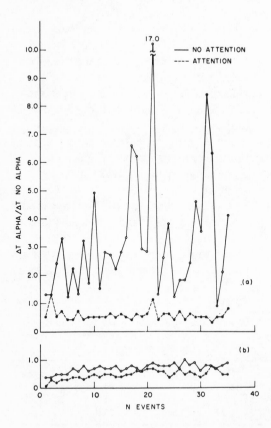

Figure 5. (a) Time series of attention, no-attention subjective state for $35\Delta T$ alpha/ΔT no-alpha periods using a slow on/off-set light. (b) Time series of attention, no-attention subjective state for 35 ΔT alpha/ΔT no-alpha periods using a fast on/off-set light.

Discussion. The difference between the two conditions (attention–no attention) may be the absence or presence of oculomotor commands, such as accommodation and convergence. During the "attention" mode the subject gives these "looking commands"; during the "no-attention" mode the subject does not give these looking commands. Even with his eyes open, the subject can rapidly habituate his visual orientation to the light, which has a slow on and off transition. By not giving efferent commands to his eyes whenever the stimulus goes on in the no-attention conditions, the regenerative feedback does not occur. The regenerative feedback does develop during the attention condition because the subject tells his eyes "to look" when the light goes on.

By optimizing the feedback stimulus, the experimenter can force the subject to give oculomotor commands, as has been shown in the tracking behavior or by the use of orienting evoking stimuli. If the stimulus is of high orientation value such as a light that has a fast on and off transition, the subject is forced by the experimental condition to orient, that is, to give oculomotor commands in his nonattention state. Under this condition, it is extremely difficult to separate attention from no attention, as shown by Fig. 5b in which a bright light having fast rise and decay times was used.

The data from the attention–no attention experiment indicate a need to optimize the feedback stimulus in order to measure the internal state or the response activation by the stimulus. To measure the internal state, the subject must be able to rapidly disengage himself from the stimulus, that is, habituation of the orienting response to the stimulus. This was possible in the first case, with the relatively slow light; this was not possible in the second case, with the relatively fast-onset light.

The feedback method shows a potential for estimating the internal state of the subject when involved in a visual task. The possibility of applying this method to line monitoring of "visual attention" linked to TV screen teaching machines should be explored, as suggested by Mulholland.[9] The methodology can also be used to examine which stimulus causes visual orientation and which depends upon internal visual orienting.

Approach 3. External Feedback Loop Changes

The previous experiment demonstrated that the ΔT alpha/ΔT no-alpha curve in the no-attention state changed when the external stimulus was changed. In this experiment the effect of different external stimuli is investigated. Male subjects were instructed to look at the screen in front of them on which different pictures or white light were projected. The pictures or white light were presented by using feedback Loop 1, in which the visibility is contingent upon the subject's alpha occurrence. Each picture or its white-light condition was presented for 25 consecutive alpha, no-alpha intervals.

Two pictures were investigated. Picture 1: A nude girl (P_1). Picture 2: A small flower (P_2).

Two conditions were investigated. Condition 1: Look at the picture, either P_1 or P_2. Condition 2: Imagine picture P_1 or P_2 when the white light is shown (conditions I_1 and I_2).

Results. Figures 6 and 7 illustrate the results. The no-alpha lengths that occurred during the presentation of P_1 showed continued orienting (long no-alpha burst) whenever the picture was shown; at the same time, the alpha durations were very constrained. In conditions P_2, I_1, I_2 the alpha lengths are much less constrained; and at the same time the no-alpha lengths are much shorter.

Discussion. Alpha blockage is due to the oculomotor "looking" command to the eyes; consequently, the mean alpha lengths increase when the picture is not worth looking at or the subject has to imagine the picture. On the other hand, the no-alpha intervals result from the orienting (activation) of the subject by the stimulus. Is it possible that the subject continues to look *for* the slide of the nude and not look *for* the slide of the flower? It is this looking command, the oculomotor efferent command, that blocks alpha activity; consequently, the no-alpha intervals are extremely long, as shown by comparing pictures P_1 and P_2 in Figures 6 and 7.

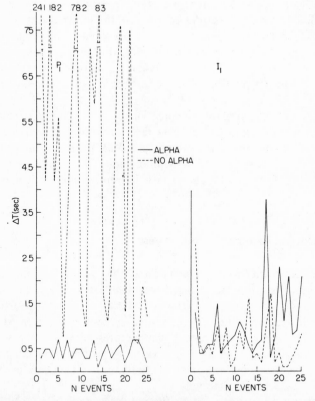

Figure 6. Time series of picture and imagination conditions. P_1 is a slide of a nude. I_1 asks the subject to imagine a nude picture when a white light occurs. Both picture and light visibility are contingent upon the subject's alpha occurrence.

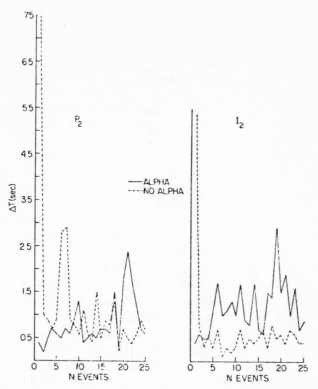

Figure 7. Time series of picture and imagination conditions. P_2 is a picture of a flower. I_2 asks the subject to imagine the picture of the flower when a white light occurs. Both picture and light visibility are contingent upon the subject's alpha occurrence.

It is hypothesized that this method will allow one to select two different types of visual orientation (internal activation to the stimulus).

Type A: The initial attractiveness of the stimulus to the subject. This is reflected in the length of the first no-alpha burst (initial orienting response).

Type B: The continued attractiveness of the stimulus to the subject. This is reflected in the slope and asymmetry of the habituation curve of the no-alpha intervals (Mulholland[9]).

The possibility of applying this method to visual teaching machine situations in which the stimulus changes as the no-alpha length decreases, as a means of developing new subjective attentive audiovisual displays and of measuring the subjects' responses to visual stimuli such as advertising should be explored (Mulholland[2,9]).

Approach 4. Autoregulation of the EEG

In these experiments, which have been described previously by Peper and Mulholland,[10] the subject's ability to control his alpha EEG in the dark was investigated. The subject was instructed to relax, keep his eyes closed, listen to a tone, and "somehow" keep this tone either on or off during alternating 2-minute trials, contingent upon the experimenter's instructions. The tone occurred concurrently with the subject's alpha EEG. Specifically investigated was the subject's ability to alternate between keeping alpha on and off for 2-minute trials. At the end of each session, a final trial was given without feedback to test "learning" to control alpha either on or off from "inner cues."

Results. The summed results of those who learned during the first session are shown in Figure 8. The first session was the discriminative session for learning to control occipital alpha. The five subjects who showed control during the first session showed control during subsequent sessions, while those who did not show control during the first session did not show control during subsequent sessions. Approximately 20% of the subjects learned control. Of the subjects who learned, most learned to block alpha but not to increase alpha activity.

Discussion. The method of control depends upon the initial baseline, and appeared to be a continuous shifting between active vigilance: low voltage, high frequency (>13 Hz); passive relaxing, high voltage, alpha frequency (8–13 Hz); and drowsiness, low voltage, slow frequency (<8 Hz).

Subjects were instructed to control the tone on/off (alpha on/off) in the dark by means of mental states. Subjects had been instructed not to move or control the tone by body movements, and so forth. The subjects who learned were highly discriminative of their own internal cues; moreover, they had to change rapidly from one state to another every 2 minutes. The task is difficult, and we found no reason why some subjects could discriminate and learn and others could not.

On the other hand, when a dim light is kept on in the room so that subjects can look around, 80 to 90% of the subjects learn to control the tone (Waitzkin, personal communication). It is hypothesized that in this case the subjects learn to "look–not look" in order to control the tone. This task is much more difficult in the dark, as there are no cues from the environment, whether you are looking or not, especially when the eyes are closed. Again, we assume that alpha on is the absence of oculomotor commands, while alpha off is the giving of oculomotor

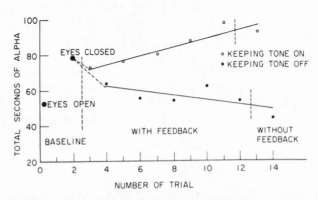

Figure 8. Mean alpha production in seconds for 2-minute trials (for first session of subjects with their eyes closed who participated more than once and showed control).

efferent commands, since in informal experiments most subjects can learn to control their alpha EEG if they are instructed to use oculomotor commands, such as focus, blur, do not look, and so forth.

Nevertheless, the high alpha state appears to be associated with passive relaxation and a pleasant, quiet, subjective state without drowsiness.

The possibility of applying this method to attain different levels of consciousness, to train the attentional process (visual looking), or to aid epileptics to block seizure through control of their own EEG should be explored.

CONCLUSION

The experiments show a methodology that uses variations of a feedback technique to explore biological potentials. With this method the EEG patterns can be manipulated, highly ordered, and regulated. Specifically investigated, was the occipital alpha activity, but the same technique can be applied to any biological pattern. In these experiments two factors affect the EEG:

1. The external feedback path, external feedback stimuli.
2. The internal feedback path, internal mediation of the stimuli.

In all cases we can show, or not be able to exclude, the possibility that oculomotor functions, probably accommodation, cause the alpha blockage. The experiments reported here show that feedback EEG can be used as an index of behavior, and suggest that this methodology is a new approach to reanalyzing the electrophysiological correlates of behavior. By optimizing the feedback path, the system can be a highly sensitive measure of a subject's "internal state."

ACKNOWLEDGMENTS. This work was supported by NIGMS Grants 5 PO1 GM 14940-04 and GM 15006-03. Most of this research was conducted at the Perception Laboratory, Veterans' Administration Hospital, Bedford, Massachusetts, with the cooperation of Dr. Thomas B. Mulholland.

REFERENCES

1. Mulholland, T., & Runnals, S. A brain response-sensory stimulus feedback system. *Digest of Papers*, 1961 International Conference on Medical Electronics. Princeton, 1961, p. 166.
2. Mulholland, T. Feedback electroencephalography. *Activas Nervosa Superior*, 1968, *10*, 410–438.
3. Kamiya, J. *Conditional discrimination of the EEG alpha rhythm in humans*. Paper presented at the meeting of the Western Psychol. Assoc., San Francisco, 1962.
4. Jasper, H. H. Report of the committee on methods of clinical examination in electroencephalography. *Electroencephalography and Clinical Neurophysiology*, 1958, *10*, 370.
5. Dewan, E. M. Occipital alpha rhythm, eye position and lens accommodation. *Nature (London)* 1967, *214*, 975–977.
6. Peper, E. *Alpha feedback EEG and the oculomotor system*. Paper present at the American Society for Cybernetics, Gaithersburg, Maryland, October 14–16, 1969.
7. Pollen, D. Lecture. Harvard University, January 8, 1970.

8. Lindsley, D. B.: Attention, consciousness, sleep and wakefulness. In J. Field, H. W. Magoun, & V. E. Hall (Eds.), *Handbook of physiology, Sect. I: Neurophysiology III*. Washington, D.C.: American Physiological Society 1960. Pp. 1553–1593.
9. Mulholland, T. The automatic control of visual displays by the attention of the human viewers. In C. M. Williams & J. L. Debes (Eds.), *Proceedings of the First National Conference on Visual Literacy*. New York: Pittman, 1970. Pp. 70–80.
10. Peper, E., & Mulholland, T. Methodological and theoretical problems in the voluntary control of electroencephalographic occipital alpha by the subject. *Kybernetik* 1970, 7(3) 10–13.

27

On the Mechanisms of the Feedback Control of Human Brain-Wave Activity

James J. Lynch and David A. Paskewitz

The recent attention given to the feedback control of human brain-wave activity and the implications of such control prompts a careful analysis of this phenomenon. Particular emphasis is placed on the learned control of the alpha rhythm. A review of possible factors that might influence the density of alpha rhythms led to the differentiation of three general sources of influence: constitutional, physiological, and cognitive–attentional factors. Each of these factors is discussed as a possible mediator of the learned control of the alpha rhythm. The view is advanced that increases in alpha density during feedback training arise from a diminution of those factors that block this rhythm, and some implications of such a view are discussed. Several of the issues raised appear generalizable to the whole question of the operant control of autonomic activity.

In recent years an ever-growing number of studies have reported the possibility of using operant conditioning techniques to control a wide variety of physiological and neurophysiological processes.[15,48,49,67,68,112] Of special interest are reports that the human S can learn to control various electroencephalographic (EEG) wave forms by these operant techniques. Clinical applications of these techniques have been suggested by several authors. Miller[67] has, for instance, suggested the possibility of using operant techniques to train epileptic patients to suppress the abnormal paroxysmal spiking in their EEG. In addition to the potential therapeutic application of operant techniques to the human EEG, an ever-increasing number of studies have presented evidence to suggest that the amount of alpha activity that occurs in the human can, through appropriate feedback conditions, be either increased or decreased.[14,31,38–41,76–78,80,84,85,96,97] These reports have stimulated a great deal of excitement, not only because of the potential of controlling specific neurophysiological processes but also in regard to the potential of this approach in gaining an understanding of the relationship between alpha activity and subjective mood states.[40] Further, it has been suggested that these techniques may lead to a more precise definition of the various states of consciousness.[13,105]

James J. Lynch and David A. Paskewitz • Department of Psychiatry, University of Maryland School of Medicine, Baltimore, Maryland 21201.

Kamiya[40] has, for instance, reported the possibility of changing the mood state of a S by having the S "turn on his alpha." The possibility of not only controlling brain-wave activity itself but also influencing subjective feelings associated with brain-wave activity has naturally elicited a wave of enthusiasm among behavioral scientists. In commenting on this research, Maslow[65] recently stated:

> What is seminal and exciting about this research is that Kamiya discovered quite for-tuitously that bringing the alpha waves to a particular level could produce in the subject a state of serenity, meditativeness, even happiness. Some follow-up studies with people who have learned the Eastern techniques of contemplation and meditation show that they spontaneously emit EEGs that are like the "serene" ones to which Kamiya was able to educate his subjects. That is to say, that it is already possible to teach people how to feel happy and serene. The revolutionary consequences not only for human bet-terment, but also for biological and psychological theory, are multitudinous and obvious. There are enough research projects here to keep squadrons of scientists busy for the next century. The mind–body problem, until now considered insoluble, does appear to be workable after all. (p. 728)

Gardner Murphy[83] suggests that by using Kamiya's techniques, "before the year 2000, there will be both identification of many kinds of phenomenological states that are anchored upon particular types of EEGs and the invention of appropriate names, appropriate language, to describe the newly identified and newly integrated components" (p. 526).

Because of the broad implications of controlling the human alpha rhythm, both as a process in and of itself and because of the stated implications that such control may lead to the altering and control of subjective mood states, it is imperative that a very close analysis be made of the phenomenon. Specifically, at least four questions are elicited by the previous research: (1) What is alpha activity? (2) What factors influence the production of alpha activity and how might control be gained over it? (3) How does one evaluate the acquisition of con-trol? (4) How and to what extent does the control of alpha activity influence the subjective mood state of the individual?

THE NATURE OF ALPHA ACTIVITY

Among the intrinsic rhythms of the human brain, perhaps the most widely investigated has been the alpha rhythm, a rhythm of 8 to 13 Hz, usually averag-ing around 30 μV and occurring most frequently in the human during the state of relaxed wakefulness.[57] One of the first reported characteristics of the alpha rhythm was the fact that it would block when the human was presented with any of a variety of sensory or attentional stimuli, but that after a few repetitions of these stimuli, this rhythm would no longer block.[10] Berger[10] believed that alpha blocking resulted from the focus of attention upon the specific sensory system being stimulated, with inhibition then spreading to other systems. This view was subsequently supported in studies by Adrian and Matthews[2] and has ultimately led to the inclusion of attention as part of the official definition of alpha activity by the terminology committee of the International Federation for Electroencephalography and Clinical Neurophysiology; "alpha rhythm: rhythm, usually with a frequency 8–13 c/sec in adults, most prominent in the posterior areas, present most markedly when eyes are closed, and attenuated during attention, especially visual."[104]

The relationship of alpha activity to the visual system has even led recently to the suggestion that the alpha rhythm is an artifact produced by a tremor of the extraocular muscles,[58] but alpha activity has also been recorded in humans even when these muscles have been eliminated.[102] The possibility that the alpha rhythm is an artifact is by no means a recent suggestion.[66] The proposal was made some years ago that alpha rhythm recordings were an artifact produced by mechanical pulsation (choroid plexus pump) of a gel, in this case the human brain, causing differential electrical pulsations.[46] Lindsley[56] and Mudy-Castle[82] have suggested that alpha rhythms reflect a fluctuation in the excitability of individual neurons, with fluctuations then synchronized for many neurons. Bard[9] suggests that alpha rhythms represent basic cellular metabolic processes. Eccles[20] has suggested that the alpha rhythms are due to reverberating chains in the cortex. Recently the possibility that alpha rhythms are generated by thalamic activity has gained widespread neurophysiological support. In a comprehensive textbook review of the physiological basis of alpha rhythms, Andersen and Andersson[5] have concluded: "The available evidence strongly indicates that the thalamus is the prime mover of the thalamocortical rhythmic activity. . . . The large degree of thalamic control over the cortical alpha rhythm advocates that studies on this rhythm and the control of its should be directed toward the thalamic mechanisms involved" (p. 209).

One of the most perplexing aspects of the alpha rhythm is the high degree of variability found both within and between Ss. Although it is generally agreed that an individuals's EEG is characteristic,[33] Davis and Davis,[17] summing up the then available evidence, stated: "All of the features of the EEG show variations from person to person, even when the records are taken under strictly standard conditions. Most of the features, however, are quite stable and characteristic for each individual person on successive tests. The least stable feature is the amount of alpha rhythm" (p. 53).

In spite of the many factors contributing to alpha rhythm variability, however, the within-S stability of alpha activity has been sufficiently high to suggest a constitutional basis for difference among Ss[16] Grey Walter[114] has stated:

> These observations have shown clearly that, unlike most physiological phenomena, the alpha rhythms must be considered in relation to each individual of a given species, and not merely as a specific or genetic character. In other words the alpha rhythm patterns, in terms both of spatial distribution, frequency and relation to function, are highly characteristic of every individual. The variation is so wide that classification of alpha type must include a class of normal persons in whom no alpha activity whatever is visible even in those conditions which are most favorable to the appearance of these rhythms in other people. At the other extreme there are people in whom alpha rhythms persists even in circumstances which are most inclined in other subjects to interrupt or suppress this activity. (p. 287)

The hypothesized constitutional basis for differences in alpha density has led to a variety of schemata for classifying individuals on this dimension.[16,29,95] For example, Golla, Hutton, and Walter[29] have divided Ss as follows: (1) those with no alpha, even with eyes closed and their mind at rest; (2) those with alpha only with their eyes closed and their mind at rest; (3) those with alpha present even with their eyes open and their mind active.

Numerous reports have attempted to link alpha activity to various personality traits, but in this complex area no clear definitive results have yet emerged.[22,24,30,55,99]

FACTORS IN THE PRODUCTION AND CONTROL OF ALPHA ACTIVITY

There are several aspects to the feedback control of alpha activity that require further elucidation, but none seems more central to understanding the phenomenon of alpha control than the suggestion that this control occurs as the result of operant conditioning.[39]

In a recent review of the operant control of autonomic responding, Katkin and Murray[43] have proposed a set of criteria for evaluating whether the autonomic response observed is truly an example of operant conditioning. Briefly, they pointed out that if a response is mediated, either cognitively or physiologically by some other system, then it is that system that is being conditioned and not the autonomic response system one happens to be measuring. While this proposal seems simple enough, the thrust of their argument is perhaps deceptively so.

A pair of analogies may serve to illustrate both the proposal and the dilemma it creates. No one would be surprised if an individual claimed he could control his heart rate by jumping up or down, or by running, or holding his breath; in such cases the mediation of heart rate activity via other physiological mechanisms would be clear to us all. In such a case it is also clear that the individual has not "learned" to control his heart rate directly, rather he has altered other mechanisms, which in turn reflexively affect heart rate. What is "learned" in such a case is an operationally bewitching problem, but clearly one did not learn to control his heart rate directly. But the alternative question, albeit pushed to its logical extreme is equally bewitching. Is it ever possible for a physiological system to be conditioned without some sort of mediation? Can we, for instance, increase heart rate without affecting changes in blood flow, blood pressure, or peripheral vasomotor tone? This would seem to be a hydraulic impossibility and, therefore, following the strictest interpretation of Katkin and Murray's[43] proposals, heart rate cannot be operantly conditioned in any direct sense. Furthermore, in light of the many variables affecting alpha activity, it is equally unlikely that alpha activity may be operantly conditioned according to such a proposed criterion.

Even the Pavlovian conditioning of alpha activity has been questioned. It was the observation of the sensory blocking of alpha activity that led to the investigation of whether this blocking response could be classically conditioned. Indications that conditional alpha blocking was possible first came with reports by Durup and Fessard[19] and Loomis, Harvey, and Hobart.[59] Following these initial reports, a more detailed analysis of a variety of conditioning parameters of alpha blocking was made by Jasper and Shagass.[36] Since these reports, a large number of studies have indicated that alpha-blocking responses could be obtained with Pavlovian conditioning techniques, and that various types of alpha-blocking and alpha-enchanced responses could be elicited with various conditioning contingencies.[115] The Pavlovian methodology for eliciting these changes has been, however, usually restricted to very short time periods (1 to 10 seconds) during the conditional stimulus, and, in addition, the changes are subject to a great deal of variability caused both by environmental and organismic influences.[50,51,71,72] Much of this classical conditioning literature, however, has evoked questions as to whether or not the alpha blocking observed is really a "conditional response."[4,50,109]

Although a number of authors[45,47,53,74,75,103] have held that autonomic functions could be conditioned only through the use of Pavlovian techniques, this assumption has been challenged by evidence indicating that autonomic and neurophysiological responses can be conditioned by operant or instrumental techniques.[15,48,49,67,68,112] It appears, however, that the recent avalanche of reports on the successful operant conditioing of autonomic systems, rather than convincing large numbers of people that such a phenomenon can occur, has instead elicited an operational crisis in psychology as to just what is meant by conditioning. An in-depth discussion of this problem would take us far from the central theme of this article, but the general question cannot be avoided. It is becoming abundantly clear that the very nature of the meaning of conditioning is being cast in doubt, and this doubt extends to both classical and operant conditioning.[21,26,62,63,94,100,101] One aspect of this operational crisis is exemplified in the recent discussions of the proper controls necessary in conditioning[43,44,94] and the suggestion that there are limits to the usefulness of such controls.[101] One conclusion does seem apparent, however; alpha activity is mediated by a whole host of factors, and the likelihood of ever controlling or eliminating all these factors to observe only simple alpha conditioning is extremely small. Thus, in the more restricted sense, any discussion of the "operant control of alpha activity" seems to us, operationally indefensible.

Having then for the moment assumed that any demonstration of the operant control of "nonmediated alpha activity" is highly unlikely, it becomes necessary to understand those factors, both physiological and cognitive, that mediate alpha activity and that are possible mechanisms by which a S could control such activity.

GENERAL FACTORS THAT INFLUENCE ALPHA ACTIVITY

A large number of environmental and organismic variables have previously been documented as altering the density of alpha activity observed in the human EEG. These may be roughly broken down into two major categories, physical or somatic influences, and attentional–arousal factors.

Physical or Somatic Influences on Alpha Activity

Perhaps the most dominant influence on alpha activity and its variability is the visual system, through direct visual stimulation, attention to visual stimuli, or

oculomotor activity. it has long been recognized that visual stimulation and oculomotor activity can markedly affect alpha levels.[1,2,19] Recently this oculomotor
activity has been implicated as a major mediating mechanism for how some Ss
"learn" to control their own alpha activity during feedback training.[18,79,92] On the
other hand, it has also been reported that in some Ss alpha activity is not significantly related to eye position[25] and that Ss can control their alpha activity with
their eyes in either an up or a down position.[39]

In addition to this type of movement, the ambient illumination of the room
and the concomitant possibility of visual scanning and fixation clearly influence
the amount of alpha activity observed, with significantly greater densities being
seen when a S is in a dark room or has his eyes closed.[57] In fact, the entire visual
system, whether muscular activity, visual stimulation, or visual attention, appears
to have such massive effects on alpha activity that a close analysis must be made
to assess the degree to which the visual system can be controlled adequately in
order to assess the learned control of alpha activity. Whether other systems are
involved in the mediation of alpha activity in the feedback situation, systems such
as respiration, muscle tension, cardiovascular activity, and so forth, is, as yet,
unclear. Changes in respiration rate, tidal volume, and O_2 consumption during
Zen meditation have been linked to the occurrence of more alpha activity during
meditative states,[8,34,107] but whether these changes occur during alpha feedback is
again not certain. In all, few attempts have been made thus far to critically
evaluate the possibilities in the somatic mediation of alpha activity.

Attentional–Arousal Factors in Alpha Activity

From the extant research data on human alpha activity, it appears that some
type of "optimal level of arousal" exists for the occurrence of alpha activity. If
the S is too aroused, alpha activity will be diminished, and conversely, if the S
becomes too drowsy, alpha will be diminished. When a S passes into this optimal
level, from either a state of alertness or a drowsy state, alpha activity tends to be
activated almost in proportion to the amount that the individual S is constitu-
tionally able to produce it. A large and varied assortment of research data seems
to reinforce this statement.[56]

Alpha activity tends to occur most frequently when an individual is in a state
of relaxed awakening, either with eyes closed or when the individual is in a dark
room. It is usually diminished either in states of extreme arousal or in sleep.[37,52,90]

Related to the state of arousal of an individual is the fact that ongoing alpha
activity will usually block when an awake individual is presented with a variety of
environmental stimuli with visual stimulation usually eliciting the most marked
blocking.[2,10] However, the rate of extinction of this alpha-blocking orienting
response depends on a number of organismic and environmental variables: for
example, the type of sensory stimulus used, the definition of an alpha-blocking
response, the number of times the sensory stimulus is presented, the length and
intensity of the stimulus, and the emotional state of the organism.[7,23,51,70,111,113]
Furthermore, it appears that this alpha-blocking response can also be elicited by
conditional signals paired with these unconditional alpha-blocking stimuli.[115]

While factors that block alpha activity have received the greatest amount of research interest, numerous reports since the first observations on the existence of alpha activity have also noted the frequent occurrence of the reverse of alpha blocking for example, stimulus-induced alpha activity.[2,7,117] In reviewing this phenomenon Lenore Morrell[69] has identified at least four situations in which stimulus-induced alpha enhancement has been observed: during sleep, during aspects of Pavlovian conditional inhibition, during studies on attention, and during periods in which no alpha activity is occurring just prior to stimulation. She notes that this phenomenon has been frequently observed and given a variety of labels, including paradoxical activity, inverted reaction, alpha activation, alpha enhancement, alpha facilitation, alpha augmentation, or stimulus-provoked alpha activity.[69] Alpha activity labeled as paradoxical or inverted reaction is that which occurs against a background that contains no alpha activity.[11,28] A series of studies have also noted that if stimuli are presented to Ss who are going to sleep,[12,60,89] or if stimuli are presented to Ss who have been sleep-deprived,[6] alpha activity can be elicited. Alpha enhancement has been frequently noted in studies involving Pavlovian conditional inhibition, including inhibition of delay, differential conditioning, and extinction.[27,35,72,73,98,115] Research on aspects of sustained attention, such as prolonged visual attention or prolonged mental arithmetic, have also noted the phenomenon of alpha enhancement.[61,108,116] A similar phenomenon has been reported in studies of directed or focused attention.[54,81] Noting that all of these various situations involve some type of inhibition, Morrell[69] hypothesizes that "stimulation-provoked alpha activity may be an electrical sign of central inhibitory processes" (p. 560). Perhaps stimulus-evoked alpha is an indication that the S has been aroused to a level where alpha activity would normally occur.

Because of the paucity of evidence concerning the role of cognitive factors in the alpha feedback situation, we can only suggest some of the factors that may influence the production of alpha activity. Among them is the feedback situation itself, the attention that it demands of the S, the eventual boredom of the task, and the feeling he has about being evaluated by the experimenter. The amount of success that a S experiences in the form of trial-to-trial increases also determines, in part, his congitive–emotional state during the feedback situation, not only relative to the point at which he starts but also in relation to his expectations concerning his performance. Previous research with other physiological systems, such as the galvanic skin response, has clearly indicated that the S's experiences, feelings of success, and motivations can interact with each other to influence the physiological responses observed.[32,88] The whole fact of being in a particular place for the purpose of participating in an experiment can have subtle and far-reaching effects on physiology.[3] The method of feedback, whether visual, auditory, tactual, or otherwise, will lead to certain variable difficulties in habituating to its presence. It has long been known, for instance, that when a stimulus is first presented to a S, any alpha activity that is occurring will usually be blocked.[10] Adrian and Mathews[2] as early as 1934 noted that focusing of attention, or any "disturbance of the mind" such as mental arithmetic, will usually block the alpha rhythm. As noted earlier, the rate at which this alpha-blocking orienting response will extinguish is contingent upon a number of variables: the type of sensory stimulus used, the definition of a blocking response, the length and intensity of the stimulus, and the emotional state of the organism.[23,51,70,111,113] The number of factors that enter into the rate of extinction of the alpha-blocking orienting response have to be considered in the feedback situation, if for no other reason that the fact that the changing feedback stimuli can themselves be partly considered as orienting stimuli to which the S must habituate.

EVALUATING RESPONSE ACQUISITION AND CONTROLS IN THE FEEDBACK CONTROL OF ALPHA ACTIVITY

In addition to their comments on mediation in operant conditioning, Katkin and Murray[43] discuss two additional factors to be considered in evaluating evidence that conditioning has occurred. First of all, they point out that an increase in the response should be demonstrated above the level observed during a baseline period, that is, an increase should really be an increase. Secondly, appropriate controls should be present such that the procedure can be related to observed increases directly, and that increases are not merely a chance or natural occurrence.

The problem of defining response acquisition is perhaps one of the most difficult methodological problems to appear in evaluating the feedback control of alpha activity. There are two basic strategies that have been employed. The first of these is to define the desired result of the experimental procedure in terms of demonstrating that a S can gain control over the production of alpha activity, and to seek significant differences between periods when Ss are told to keep their alpha activity on and periods when they are instructed to keep the activity off. Such differential control in the density of alpha activity as the result of instructions has been demonstrated by a number of studies.[18,39,40,85,93] Some authors have noted, however, that although Ss can very quickly learn to suppress their alpha activity, often within the first trial, increases during instructions to augment alpha densities are far more difficult to achieve, and rarely rise above alpha levels that naturally occur under optimal conditions.[91,93] In light of the many known factors that may block alpha activity, such differential control, while of interest, indicates only that Ss can bring these factors into use with little difficulty. The other side of the coin, that is, the degree to which such factors may be voluntarily excluded, has perhaps more important consequences.

In such a case, it is imperative to know whether or not a S has, by means of the feedback procedure, increased alpha density above that observed during optimal baseline periods. In light of many factors influencing alpha density, however, the establishment of appropriate or optimal baseline conditions from which to measure increases becomes difficult. Almost any initial baseline will be contaminated by apprehensions about the forthcoming experiment, the novelty of the situation, or other such influences. As a result, unless measurements of baseline density are obtained during the course of the feedback training, it is impossible to establish whether or not any increase is due to training or only to factors involved in the situation which relate to the rapport or ease of the S. Indeed, Ss who receive false feedback, or those who are simply told at the end of each session how well they did, have been shown to increase their alpha densities.[31,64,91] Even the procedure of including frequent baseline determination, however, has been questioned as a method for establishing differences between baseline and feedback conditions. Noting that his Ss do not exceed baseline levels during periods when they were getting the feedback stimulus, Kamiya[41] suggests that the procedure itself alters the baseline:

> The increase in the curve for the Enhance Alpha condition is much more striking (than the Suppress Alpha condition), and it is clear that there is a very significant difference in percent alpha time between the enhance and suppress conditions for these Ss. Thus it's not merely a function of alpha decreasing with the passage of time; there does seem to be some measure of volitional control. Now, consider the third curve (labeled basal level) which represents the percent alpha score Ss got in the rest periods when they weren't getting the tone; as a matter of fact they were specifically told not to try producing tones, they were told that the tones would be switched off and just merely to wait until we got our machine aligned. This curve shows a generally upward trend, yet if this were really a baseline sort of thing one would have expected it to have stayed level. My interpretation of this upward trend is that the experimental tasks apparently set them into certain preferred modes of waiting, and the preferred mode is the higher alpha state. (p. 513)

Such an explanation appears to be based on the assumption that all increases in alpha density arise from training, rather than from the sorts of rapport factors considered earlier. Irrespective of the various interpretations of the source of baseline shifts in alpha density, it is clear that no proper controls have been established. Unless the task of the S can be specified during baseline periods in a way that allows a standard assessment of resting alpha level which will be stable from time to time, there appears little possibility of conclusively demonstrating that Ss can be trained to increase their alpha densities above those observed during optimal resting conditions. To our knowledge no such demonstration has yet appeared.

SUBJECTIVE MOODS AND ALPHA FEEDBACK

Much of the interest in the relationship between alpha activity and subjective mood has come from reports that Zen and Yoga practitioners show high and almost continuous levels of alpha activity during meditation, usually slowing in frequency during the course of a session.[8,42,86] Additional interest has been generated by reports that Ss in the feedback situation generally find the experience pleasant, and relaxing and wish to return, often reporting dissociative phenomena such as feelings of floating, being unaware of the immediate environment, and distorted time perception.[13,31,39–41,85]

The source of these feedback statements and the process through which they come about are both somewhat obscure. Although the study of the relationship between brain-wave activity and mental processes began quite early in the EEG literature, and subjective reports of mental blankness and abstract thinking were associated with alpha activity,[110] to say, as does Maslow,[65] that we can now "teach people how to feel happy and serene" appears premature. Certainly no simple and direct relationship exists between alpha density and subjective feelings. Individuals with high chronic alpha density have not been shown to be markedly different from others with lower levels. Simple physical maneuvers like closing or opening the eyes have not been related to mood changes of the sort reported in feedback situations and yet such eye maneuvers markedly affect alpha density. It would appear fruitful to examine some aspects of the feedback situation itself in some detail.

Subjective reports are frequently influenced by the experimental setting and the course of the experiment itself. It is certainly possible that some of the reports of Ss in the feedback situation are influenced by what Orne[87] has called the "demand characteristics" of the situation; that is, Ss enter the experiment expecting to experience alterations in mood, expecting the session to be pleasant, perhaps a "high," or if they don't feel this way initially, the experimenter may reinforce such feelings, both in the preexperimental interview and in the actual instructions given during the experiment. It would be interesting to speculate on the effects of an alternative orientation, that alpha feedback would permanently warp one's personality, for instance. It is, indeed, somewhat surprising to find such general agreement on the pleasantness of the situation, since some Ss with naturally low alpha densities can be expected to fail at the task of increasing alpha density; conversely, some of the positive affect in the situation may arise from the S's feelings of success at the task. Some of the dissociative phenomena, however, are less easily explained by S expectations.

One aspect of the situation that bears consideration is its similarity to perceptual and sensory deprivation environments where Ss are cut off from patterned external stimulation. Many of the effects that have been reported by Ss in the feedback situation have also been noted as concomitants of sensory deprivation experiments, even with durations as short as 1 hour.[106,118] Although noted after several days, rather than the shorter time span common in feedback experiments, a slowed alpha frequency with sensory deprivation may suggest common aspects between this and the meditative situation.

One aspect of the feedback task that must be considered as a possible source of subjective reports is that a great deal of literature, as noted earlier, stresses the importance of attention in blocking alpha activity. It is likely that those who exhibit alpha activity during feedback sessions do so, in part, through a process of "unfocusing" attention, that is, trying not to attend to any one aspect of the surroundings, thus creating a sort of perceptual deprivation. Whether this may have psychological or physiological effects that contribute to subjective mood states is certainly unclear at present.

A VIEWPOINT TOWARD ALPHA DENSITY INCREASES DURING FEEDBACK

A consideration of the phenomena of the feedback control of alpha activity, based on previous data and consideration of the many factors that can influence alpha density, has led us to formulate a hypothesis to account for the trial-to-trial increases in alpha activity noted in previous research, as well as other related effects. We suggest that *alpha activity occurs in the feedback situation when an individual ceases to pay attention to any of a number of stimuli which normally block this activity*. These stimuli may be cognitive, somatic, emotional, or anything, in fact, that will lead to alpha blocking. The alpha densities that can occur in the feedback situation may approach those seen in that same individual under optimal baseline conditions, but will not significantly exceed them. While the feedback process may yield trial-to-trial increases that resemble learning curves, these curves are the result of inhibition, as the S gradually removes from his attention most or all of the influences that block the production of alpha activity. The resulting density is limited only by the Ss own natural ability to generate this activity. In addition to the feedback process, any other process by which these influences may be removed will result in increased alpha activity, and the process need not be an active one. It may be a process similar to falling asleep, or something analogous to "highway hypnosis," that is, something that occurs naturally unless blocked. Working at the task may, indeed, lead to a result quite the opposite of that intended by focusing attention on those aspects of the situation that lead to alpha blocking.

The implications of this approach to the study of alpha activity are several. One implication is that the feedback situation may be not necessarily the best method for producing a high index of alpha activity in a S, but only one way of producing it in a situation that would not normally be expected to yield a great deal of alpha activity. If the feedback situation could be shown to produce amounts significantly greater than those achieved in other conditions, it would deserve special attention, but such demonstrations have not been reported.

A second implication is that not every S can be expected to successfully inhibit blocking influences, particularly in the feedback situation, and thus feedback may not assure high alpha densities. A corollary to this implication is that those Ss having a high degree of naturally occurring alpha activity would probably be less able to block such activity for sustained periods of time, compared to those with low alpha densities; that is, some Ss would be able to generate alpha activity better than they could block it. Yet another implication of this approach is that much of the literature on attentional processes, orienting, habituation, and the factors that influence these processes becomes relevant to the question of alpha control. A fourth implication concerns the etiology of the subjective mood states that are reputed to accompany the control of alpha activity. If, as hypothesized, the lack of attention to blocking stimuli results in alpha increases, and other methods may produce similar increases in alpha levels, then these other methods should lead to changes in mood states similar to those reported during feedback control.

REFERENCES

1. Adrian, E. D. The dominance of vision. *Transactions of the Ophthalmological Societies of the United Kingdom*, 1943, *63*, 194–207.
2. Adrian, E. D., & Matthews, B. H. C. The Berger rhythm: Potential changes from the occipital lobes in man. *Brain*, 1934, *57*, 355–385.

3. Agnew, H. W., Webb, W., & Williams, R. L. The first night effect: An EEG study of sleep. *Psychophysiology*, 1966, *2*, 263–266.
4. Albino, R., & Burnand, G. Conditioning of the alpha rhythm in man. *Journal of Experimental Psychology*, 1964, *67*, 539–544.
5. Andersen, P., & Andersson, S. A. *Physiological basis of the alpha rhythm*. New York: Appleton-Century, 1968.
6. Armington, J. C., & Mitnick, L. L. EEG and sleep deprivation. *Journal of Appled Physiology*, 1959, *14*, 247–250.
7. Bagchi, B. K. The adaptation and variability of response of the human brain rhythm. *Journal of Psychology*, 1937, *3*, 463–485.
8. Bagchi, B. K., & Wenger, M. A. Electrophysiological correlates of some Yogi exercises. In *EEG, clinical neurophysiology and epilepsy*. London: Pergamon Press, 1959. Pp. 132–149.
9. Bard, P. B. Some further analyses of the functions of the cerebrum. In P. B. Bard (Ed.), *Medical physiology* 11th ed., St. Louis: Mosby, 1961.
10. Berger, H. Über das Elektrenkephalogramm des Menschen. *Archiv fuer Psychiatric und Nervenkrankheiten*, 1929, *87*, 527–570.
11. Bjerner, B. Alpha depression and lowered pulse rate during delayed reactions in serial reaction test. *Acta Physiologica Scandinavica*, 1949, (Suppl. 65), 1–93.
12. Blake, H., Gerard, R. W. Brain potentials during sleep. *American Journal of Physiology* 1937, *119*, 692–703.
13. Brown, B. Recognition of aspects of consciousness through association with EEG alpha activity represented by a light signal. *Psychophysiology* 1970, *6*, 442–452.
14. Bundzen, P. V. Autoregulation of functional state of the brain: An investigation using photostimulation with feedback. *Fiziologicheskii Shurnal SSSR imeni I. M. Sechenova*, 1965, *51*, 936. (Republished: *Federal Proceedings [Trans. Suppl.]*, 1966, *25*, T551–T554.
15. Crider, A., Shapiro, D., & Tursky, B. Reinforcement of spontaneous electrodermal activity. *Journal of Comparative Physiology and Psychology*, 1966, *61*, 20–27.
16. Davis, H., & Davis, P. A. Action potentials of the brain in normal persons and in normal states of cerebral activity. *Archives of Neurology (Chicago)*, 1936, *36*, 1214–1224.
17. Davis, P. A., & Davis, H. Electrical activity of the brain, its relation to physiological states and to states of impaired consciousness. *Research Publications, Association for Research in Nervous and Mental Disease*, 1939, *19*, 50–80.
18. Dewan, E. M. Occipital alpha rhythm, eye position and lens accommodation. *Nature (London)*, 1967, *214*, 975–977.
19. Durup, G., & Fessard, A. L'électroencéphalogramme de l'homme. *Année Psychologique*, 1935, *36*, 1–32.
20. Eccles, J. C. *The neurophysiological basis of mind*. London: Clarendon Press, 1953.
21. Efron, R. The conditioned reflex: A meaningless concept. *Perspectives in Biology and Medicine*, 1966, *9*, 488–514.
22. Ellingson, R. J. Brain waves and problems of psychology. *Psychological Bulletin*, 1956, *53*, 1–34.
23. Esecover, H. B., Torres, A. A., Taylor, R. M., Wilkens, B., & Malitz, S. Contingent alpha blocking and sensitization. *Nature (London)*, 1964, *201*, 1247–1248.
24. Fenton, G. W., & Scotton, L. Personality and the alpha rhythm. *British Journal of Psychiatry*, 1967, *113*, 1283–1289.
25. Fenwick, P. B. The effects of eye movement on alpha rhythm. *Electroencephalography and Clinical Neurophysiology*, 1966, *21*, 618. (Abstract)
26. Gantt, W. H., B. F. Skinner and his contingencies. *Conditional Reflex*, 1970, *5*, 63–74.
27. Gastaut, H., Jus, A., Jus, C., Morrell, F., Storm van Leeuwen, W., Dongier, S., Naquet, R., Regis, H., Roger, A., Bekkering, D., Kamp, A., & Weere, J. Etude topographique des réactions d'electroencéphalographiques conditionées chez l'homme. *Electroencephalography and Clinical Neurophysiology*, 1957, *9*, 1–34.
28. Goldie, L., & Green, J. M. Paradoxical blocking and arousal in the drowsy state. *Nature (London)*, 1960, *187*, 952–953.
29. Golla, F. L., Hutton, E. L., & Walter, W. G. The objective study of mental imagery: I. Physiological concomitants. *Journal of Mental Science*, 1943 *89*, 216–223.

30. Gottlober, A. B. Relationship between brain potentials and personality. *Journal of Experimental Psychology*, 1938, *22*, 67–74.

31. Hart, J. T. *Autocontrol of EEG alpha*. Presented at the Seventh Annual Meeting of the Society for Psychophysiological Research, San Diego, October 20–22, 1967.

32. Hicks, R. G. Experimenter effects on the physiological experiment. *Psychophysiology*, 1970, *7*, 10–17.

33. Hill, D. The EEG in psychiatry. In D. Hill & G. Parr (Eds.) *Electroencephalography: A symposium on its various aspects*. New York: Macmillan, 1963.

34. Hirai, T. Electroencephalographic study on the Zen meditation (Japan). *Folia Psychiatrica et Neurologica Japanica*, 1960 *62*, 76–105.

35. Iwama, K. Delayed conditioned reflex in man and brain waves. *Tohoku Journal of Experimental Medicine*, 1950, 53–62.

36. Jasper, H., & Shagass, C. Conditioning occipital alpha rhythm in man. *Journal of Experimental Psychology*, 1941, *28*, 373–388.

37. Johnson, L., Lubin, A., Naitoh, P., Nute, C., & Austin, M. Spectral analysis of the EEG of dominant and non-dominant alpha subjects during waking and sleeping. *Electroencephalography and Clinical Neurophysiology*, 1969, *26*, 361–370.

38. Kamiya, J. *Conditional discrimination of the EEG alpha rhythm in humans*. Presented at the Meeting of the Western Psychological Association, San Francisco, April 1962.

39. Kamiya, J. EEG operant conditioning and the study of states of consciousness. In D. X. Freedman (Chairman), Laboratory Studies of Altered Psychological States. Symposium at American Psychological Association, Washington, D.C., September 4, 1967.

40. Kamiya, J. Conscious control and brain waves. *Psychology Today*, 1968, *1*, 57–60.

41. Kamiya, J. Operant control of the EEG alpha rhythm and some of its reported effects on consciousness. In C. Tart (Ed.), *Altered states of consciousness: A book of readings*. New York: Wiley, 1969.

42. Kasamatsu, A., & Hirai, T. An electroencephalographic study on the Zen meditation (Zazen). *Folia Psychiatrica et Neurologica Japanica;* 1966, *20*, 315–336.

43. Katkin, E. S., & Murray, E. N. Instrumental conditioning of autonomically mediated behavior: Theoretical and methodological issues. *Psychological Bulletin*, 1968 *70*, 52–68.

44. Katkin, E. S., Murray, E. M., & Lachman, R. Concerning instrumental autonomic conditioning: A rejoinder. *Psychological Bulletin*, 1969, *71*, 462–466.

45. Keller, F. L., Schoenfeld, W. N. *Principles of Psychology*. New York: Appleton-Century, 1950.

46. Kennedy, J. L. A possible artifact in electroencephalography. *Psychological Review*, 1959, *66*, 347–352.

47. Kimble, G. A. *Hilgard and Marquis, conditioning and learning*. New York: Appleton-Century, 1961.

48. Kimmel, H. D., & Hill, F. A. Operant conditioning of the GSR. *Psychological Reports*, 1960, *7*, 555–562.

49. Kimmel, E., & Kimmel, H. D. A replication of operant conditioning of the GSR. *Journal of Experimental Psychology*, 1963, *65*, 212–213.

50. Knott, J. R. Electroencephalography and physiological psychology: Evaluation and statement of problem. *Psychological Bulletin*, 1941, *38*, 944–974.

51. Knott, J. R., & Henry, C. E. The conditioning of the blocking of the alpha rhythm of the human EEG. *Journal of Experimental Psychology*, 1941, *28*, 134–143.

52. Knott, J. R., Gibbs, F. A., & Henry, C. E. Fourier transformations of the EEG during sleep. *Journal of Experimental Psychology*, 1942, *31*, 465–477.

53. Konorski, J., & Miller, S. Further remarks on two types of conditioned reflex. *Journal of General Psychology*, 1937, *17*, 405–407.

54. Kreitman, N., & Shaw, J. C. Experimental enhancement of alpha activity. *Electroencephalography and Clinical Neurophysiology*, 1965, *18*, 147–155.

55. Lemere, F. The significance of individual differences in the Berger rhythm. *Brain*, 1936, *59*, 366.

56. Lindsley, D. B. Basic perceptual processes and the EEG. *Psychiatric Research Reports*, 1956, *6*, 161–170.

57. Lindsley, D. B. Attention, consciousness, sleep and wakefulness. In J. Field (Ed.) *Handbook of*

physiology, section 1: Neurophysiology (Vol. 1). Washington, D.C.: American Physiological Society, 1960.

58. Lippold, O., & Novotny, G. E. K. Is alpha rhythm an artefact? *Lancet*, 1970, 976–979.

59. Loomis, A. L., Harvey, E. N., & Hobart, G. A. Electrical potentials of the human brain. *Journal of Experimental Psychology*, 1936, *19*, 249–279.

60. Loomis, A. L., Harvey, E. N., & Hobart, G. A. Distribution of disturbance patterns in the human electroencephalogram with special reference to sleep. *Journal of Neurophysiology*, 1938, *1*, 413–430.

61. Lorens, S. A., & Darrow, C. W. Eye movements, EEG, GSR, and EKG during mental multiplication. *Electroencephalography and Clinical Neurophysiology*, 1962, *14*, 739–746.

62. Lynch, J. J. The stimulus-the ghost-the response: The carousel of conditioning. *Conditional Reflex*, 1970, *5*, 133–139.

63. Lynch, J. J., & Kakigi, S. *Some theoretical implications of CS-UCS intervals in classical conditioning*. Presented at the Annual Meeting of the Society for Psychophysiological Research, Washington, D.C., October 1968.

64. Lynch, J. J., Paskewitz, D. A., Orne, M. T., & Costello, J. An analysis of the feedback control of alpha activity. *Conditional Reflex*, 1970, *5*, 185–186. (Abstract)

65. Maslow, A. Toward a humanistic biology. *American Psychologist*, 1969, *24*, 724–735.

66. Miller, H. L. Alpha waves: Artifacts. *Psychological Bulletin*, 1968, *69*, 279–280.

67. Miller, N. E. Learning of visceral and glandular responses. *Science (Washington)*, 1969, *163*, 434–445.

68. Miller, N. E., & Carmona, A. Modification of a visceral response, salivation in thirsty dogs, by instrumental training with water reward. *Journal of Comparative Physiology and Psychology*, 1967, *63*, 1–6.

69. Morrell, L. K. Some characteristics of stimulus-provoked alpha activity. *Electroencephalography and Clinical Neurophysiology*, 1966, *21*, 552–561.

70. Morrell, F., & Jasper, H. H. Electrographic studies of the formation of temporary connections in the brain. *Electroencephalography and Clinical Neurophysiology*, 1956, *8*, 201–215.

71. Morrell, F., Roberts, L., & Jasper, H. H. Effect of focal epileptogenic lesions and their ablation upon conditioned electricl responses of the brain in the monkey. *Electroencephalography and Clinical Neurophysiology*, 1962, *14*, 724–730.

72. Morrell, F., & Ross, M. Central inhibition in cortical conditioned reflexes. *Archives of Neurology (Chicago)*, 1953, *70*, 611–616.

73. Motokawa, K., & Huzimori, B. EEG and conditioned reflexes. *Tohoku Journal of Experimental Medicine*, 1949, *50*, 214–234.

74. Mowrer, O. H. On the dual nature of learning: A reinterpretation of "conditioning" and "problem-solving." *Harvard Educational Review*, 1947, *17*, 102–148.

75. Mowrer. O. H. *Learning theory and personality dynamics. Selected papers.* New York: Ronald Press, 1950.

76. Mulholland, T. Variations in the response duration curve of successive cortical activation by a feedback stimulus. *Electroencephalography and Clinical Neurophysiology*, 1964, *16*, 394–395.

77. Mulholland, T. The concept of attention and the electroencephalographic alpha rhythm. In C. R. Evans & T. Mulholland (Eds.). *Attention in neurophysiology.* London: Butterworths, 1969. Pp. 100–127.

78. Mulholland, T. Feedback electroencephalography. *Activitas Nervosa Superior*, 1968, *10*, 410–438.

79. Mulholland, T., & Evans, C. R. An unexpected artefact in the human electroencephalogram concerning the alpha rhythm and the position of the eyes. *Nature (London)*, 1965, *207*, 36–37.

80. Mulholland, T., & Evans, C. R. Oculomotor function and the alpha activation cycle. *Nature (London)*, 1966, *211*, 1278–1279.

81. Mulholland, T., & Runnals, S. Increased occurrence of EEG alpha during increased attention. *Journal of Psychology*, 1962, *54*, 317–330.

82. Mundy-Castle, A. C. An appraisal of electroencephalography in relation to psychology. *J. Nat. Inst. Personnel Res.*, 1958. (Monograph suppl.).

83. Murphy, G. Psychology in the year 2000. *American Psychologist*, 1969, *24*, 523–530.

84. Nowlis, D. P. Early observations on a system providing EEG alpha feedback. Hawthorne House Research Memorandum 78, 1968.
85. Nowlis, D. P., & Kamiya, J. The control of electroencephalographic alpha rhythms through auditory feedback and the associated mental activity. *Psychophysiology*, 1970, *6*, 476–484.
86. Okeima, T., Kogu, E., Ikeda, K., & Sugiyama, H. The EEG of Yoga and Zen practitioners. *Electroencephalography and Clinical Neurophysiology*, 1957, *51* (*Suppl. 9*).
87. Orne, M. T. On the social psychology of the psychological experiment: With particular reference to demand characteristics and their implications. *American Psychologist*, 1962, *17*, 776–783.
88. Orne, M. T., Thackray, R. I., & Paskewitz, D. A. On the detection of deception: A model for the study of the physiological effects of psychological stimuli. In N. Greenfield, & R. Sternbach (Eds.). *Handbook of psychophysiology*. New York: Holt, Rinehart & Winston, 1968.
89. Oswald, I. *Sleeping and waking* Amsterdam: Elsevier, 1962.
90. Paskewitz, D. A. *The quantification of nocturnal electroencephalographic patterns in Man.* (Doctoral dissertation, University of Oklahoma, 1967). Ann Arbor, Michigan. (University Microfilms, No: 67-14140.)
91. Paskewitz, D. A., Lynch, J. J., Orne, M. T., & Costello, J. The feedback control of alpha activity: Conditioning or disinhibition. *Psychophysiology*, 1970, *6*, 637–638.
92. Peper, E. Feedback regulation of the alpha electroencephalogram activity through control of the internal and external parameters. *Kybernetik*, 1970, *7*, 107–112.
93. Peper, E., & Mulholland, T. Methodological and theoretical problems in the voluntary control of electroencephalographic occipital alpha by the subject. *Kybernetik*, 1970, *7*, 10–13.
94. Rescorla, R. A. Pavlovian conditioning and its proper control procedures. *Psychological Review*, 1967, *74*, 71–80.
95. Rubin, M. A. The distribution of the alpha rhythm over the cerebral cortex of normal man. *Journal of Neurophysiology*, 1938, *1*, 313–323.
96. Runnals, S., & Mulholland, T. A method for the study of bilateral asymmetry of cortical activation. *American Journal of EEG Technology*, 1964, *4*, 15–18.
97. Runnals, S., & Mulholland, T. Selected demonstrations of voluntary regulation of cortical activation. *Bedford Research*, 1965, *11*, 26.
98. Rusinov, V. S. General and localized alterations in the electroencephalogram during the formation of conditioned reflexes in man. *Electroencephalography and Clinical Neurophysiology*, 1960, *Suppl. 13*, 309–320.
99. Saul, L. J., Davis, H., & Davis, P. A. Correlations between electroencephalograms and psychological organization of the individual. *Transactions of the American Neurological Association*, 1937, *63*, 167.
100. Schoenfeld, W. N. Some old work for modern conditioning theory. *Conditional Reflex*, 1966, *1*, 219–223.
101. Seligmann, M. E. Control group and conditioning: A comment on operationism. *Psychological Review*, 1969, *76*, 484–491.
102. Shaw, J. C., Foley, S., & Blowers, G. H. Alpha rhythm: An artefact? *Lancet*, 1970, 1173.
103. Skinner, B. F. *The behavior of organisms: An experimental analysis*. New York: Appleton-Century, 1938.
104. Storm van Leeuwen, W. (Chairman), Bickford, R., Brazier, M. A. B., Cobb, W. A., Dondey, M., Gastaut, H., Bloor, P., Henry, C. E., Hess, R., Knott, J. R., Kugler, J., Lairy, G. C., Loeb, C., Magnus, O., Oller Daurella, L., Petsche, H., Schwab, R., Walter, W. G., & Widen, L. Proposal for an EEG terminology by the terminology committee of the International Federation for Electroencephalography and Clinical Neurophysiology. *Electroencephalography and Clinical Neurophysiology*, 1966, *20*, 293–320.
105. Stoyva, J., & Kamiya, J. Electrophysiological studies of dreaming as the prototype of a new strategy in the study of consciousness. *Psychological Review*, 1968, *75*, 192–205.
106. Suedfeld, P. Changes in intellectual performance and in susceptibility to influence. In J. P. Zubek (ed.). *Sensory deprivation: Fifteen years of research*. New York: Appleton-Century, 1969.
107. Sugi, Y., & Akutsu, K. *Science of Zagen—energy metabolism*. Tokyo: 1964.
108. Toman, J. E. P. The electroencephalogram during mental effort. *Federal Proceedings*, 1943, *2*, 49.

109. Torres, A. A. Sensitization and association in alpha blocking "conditioning." *Electroencephalography and Clinical Neurophysiology*, 1968, *24*, 297–360.
110. Travis, L. E. Brain potentials and the temporal course of consciousness. *Journal of Experimental Psychology*, 1937, *21*, 302–309.
111. Travis, L. E., & Egan, J. B. Conditioning of the electrical response of the cortex. *Journal of Experimental Psychology*, 1938, *22*, 524–531.
112. Trowill, J. A. Instrumental conditioning of the heart rate in the curarized rat. *Journal of Comparative Physiology and Psychology*, 1967, *63*, 7–11.
113. Visser, S. L. Correlations between the contingent alpha blocking EEG characteristics and clinical diagnosis. *Electroencephalography and Clinical Neurophysiology*, 1961, *13*, 538–548.
114. Walter, W. G. Intrinsic rhythms of the brain. In J. Field (Ed.). *Handbook of physiology: Section I, Neurophysiology* (Vol. 1). Washington, D.C.: American Physiological Society, 1959. Chap. 11, pp. 279–313.
115. Wells, C. E. Electroencephalographic correlates of conditioned response. In G. H. Glasser (Ed). *EEG and behavior*. New York: Basic Books, 1963.
116. Williams, A. C. Some psychological correlates of the electroencephalogram. *Archives of Psychology*, 1939, *240*, 1–48.
117. Williams, A. C. Facilitation of the alpha rhythm in the electroencephalogram. *Journal of Experimental Psychology*, 1940, *26*, 413–422.
118. Zubek, J. P. Physiological and biochemical effects. In J. P. Zubek (Ed). *Sensory deprivation: Fifteen years of research*. New York: Appleton-Century, 1969.

28

Alpha Biofeedback Training: Some Methodological Issues and Future Considerations

Sonia Ancoli and Joe Kamiya

This chapter attempts to help resolve some of the controversies in the field of alpha biofeedback training. Long before feedback training was developed, it was known that alpha activity was suppressed by visual and oculomotor processes. Many of the details of this relationship have been investigated in a wide variety of studies (Fenwick & Walker, 1969; Jasper & Shagass, 1941; Mulholland, 1969).

One question that has never been adequately resolved, however, is whether all increases in alpha activity are only the result of reduced visual and oculomotor activity. This question arose from those studies that suggested that alpha activity can be enhanced with biofeedback above resting, eyes-closed, pretraining baselines. Complicating this issue is the fact that other studies suggested that alpha activity does not exceed pretraining levels. In order to be able to answer this question, the more central issue of whether alpha can be enhanced over eyes-closed baseline must be resolved. These controversies concerning outcomes of EEG alpha feedback training are at least in part due to methodological differences between studies. The aim of this discussion is to provide future and present researchers in this field with an analysis of methods used in most of the studies published since 1968, and to comment on those methodological issues we think most important. Our comments on these issues are not meant to be exhaustive. Some points are offered not so much as conclusions derived from our review of the work of others but rather as comments based on our own work.

The following methodological points were considered: (1) how EEG alpha is assessed, (2) subject selection, (3) feedback parameters, (4) baseline assessment, (5) training schedules, and (6) uni- versus bidirectional training. In addition, a commentary follows suggesting the parameters one might use for improved alpha enhancement training.

ALPHA ASSESSMENT

Frequency. The range defining alpha activity often varies among studies. This is true even if the specified cutoff frequencies are the same, since these

---

Sonia Ancoli and Joe Kamiya • Langley Porter Neuropsychiatric Institute, University of California, San Francisco, California 94143.

merely indicate where the half-amplitude points are. The slope of the filter beyond these points (the extent to which signal frequencies adjacent to alpha are rejected by the filter) is important but not always reported. This is especially relevant in considering the extent to which theta activity (usually thought to involve psychological states different from alpha) entered into the alpha score. Eight studies do include this information; the rest do not. Many studies, in fact, do not even include the frequencies used.

Amplitude. There is ample evidence by now that the method of assessing the degree of alpha activity can affect the outcomes of studies. Dichotomous scoring (which involves the use of an arbitrary amplitude criterion and the assessment of the total duration of time that the amplitude exceeded the criterion) sometimes provides a poor approximation of the average alpha amplitude (Hardt & Kamiya, 1976). The two are not equivalent. Dichotomous scoring also poses the difficulty of comparing studies that have used different amplitude criteria. In the analysis of the 45 studies, 4 used 10-uV p-p, 9 used 15-uV p-p, and 5 used 20-uV p-p.

Electrode Location. It is known that the relative amplitudes of alpha at different scalp sites are not constant over time. This implies that alpha training at site A may not be the same physiologically or psychologically as training at site B. The reference electrode location is also important, with the ipsilateral ear as reference being easier to interpret than active scalp reference sites. While most studies use the occipital (either O1, O2, or Oz) as the active site referenced to either A1, A2, or linked ears, some record from OzC4, O2Cz, O2F4, O2P4, and O102. Thus, though the results of these studies all state some conclusion about alpha, they may not in fact refer to the same phenomenon.

Eyes Open versus Eyes Closed. Since this variable strongly affects the amount of alpha activity present, the 32 studies using eyes-open (EO) training are not comparable with the 15 using eyes-closed (EC) training. (Note that 5 studies used both.) In addition, results from one condition, assessed against baseline recordings in the other condition, are not comparable with studies using the same condition for both training and baselines. For example, some studies have found that feedback training for alpha enhancement (AE) with eyes open yielded gains in alpha abundance. However, the gains during such eyes-open training did not result in alpha levels higher than eyes-closed baselines, taken before training. To conclude from such results that training for alpha enhancement is ineffectual, before examining data from eyes-closed training under comparable conditions, is unjustified.

Room Illumination. Room illumination interacts with the variable of EO-EC. While most EO studies have been conducted in ambient light and EC studies in darkness, there are eight studies that ran subjects with EO in darkness. In addition, not all studies reported the lighting conditions. Interpretation of those studies, and comparison with studies that do, is therefore made difficult.

Artifacts. Because drowsiness, electrode artifacts, eye movement, and EMG activity can all affect the alpha score, it is important that graphic records with adequate band width be taken at all times. When this is not possible, the contribution of these should be experimentally determined. Graphic records also enable determination of whether "nonalpha" is theta or beta activity. We recognize that in this age of portable EEG feedback units graphic records are often difficult to obtain, but we see no alternative.

FEEDBACK PARAMETERS

Evidence is growing that continuous feedback, where the signal is not merely on or off but rather varies in proportion to the amplitude of alpha, is superior in training alpha control. Eleven studies used continuous feedback while the rest used binary signals. Different results among studies are probably traceable in part to this variable. The giving of scores at regular intervals during each session also adds to the total sense of progress for the subject, especially in long-term training. Subjective appreciation of overall performance is difficult with just the momentary feedback signal, yet that is the most common feedback parameter used.

BASELINE ASSESSMENT

To evaluate performance as a result of training, the measurement of pretraining baseline (BL) is essential. Thirteen studies either did not include baselines as part of the basic methodology or did not report them. Of those studies that do include baselines, most use an inadquate time sample for assessment of both average and variability. Also important, but rarely reported, is the specification of the instructions given to the subjects during the baseline period.

Finally, it is becoming increasingly clear that the assessment of feedback training against the average value of a few minutes under a single condition is not adequate. More care needs to be taken to sample the entire range of spontaneous alpha activity that can occur, using experimental conditions designed to maximize the range. For example, some subjects show an initial decline of eyes-closed alpha due to drowsiness. It is important not to take these values as typical of the subjects' baseline levels, but to take them in combination with values of alpha obtained immediately following full arousal, such as are seen following breaks in conversations with the experimenter, walking about, etc. In short, a family of pretraining baselines makes possible a much stronger and more accurate assessment of alpha feedback training.

TRAINING SCHEDULES

The duration, number, and spacing of feedback trials and sessions is highly varied among different studies. Trials are defined by that period of time during which the subject is asked to control the signal in a particular direction, and which is followed by either a rest period or a trial during which the subject controls the signal in the opposite direction. Trial lengths have varied from 2-minute trials (in 12 studies) to 10-minute trials (4 studies). In our opinion, trial periods as short as 2 minutes, especially for alpha enhancement, are too short for effective training, particularly if alpha enhancement is alternated with alpha suppression. From our experience, we would judge that 10 minutes in early training sessions and 15 to 20 in later training sessions are more reasonable. Scores, if given, should be presented more often, e.g., every 1 or 2 minutes.

Typically, a single session is all that is given, leaving no indication of effects of more sustained training. There is some evidence indicating temporary performance decrements following initial success for many subjects (Hardt, 1975), and training to asymptote may often be prematurely terminated. Four studies have given up to six sessions; however, total training time (TTT) has been as short as a few minutes and as long as 4½ hours.

In addition, intermittent rest periods are sometimes used. The information or instructions subjects are given, the explanation given about this time, and whether or not the subjects are allowed to move about may also contribute to the outcome of some studies. Yet few studies report this information.

UNI- VERSUS BIDIRECTIONAL TRAINING

The relative merits of including both enhancement and suppression training trials versus just enhancement trials in a single study are still somewhat uncertain. Despite the power of data evaluation provided by bidirectional training, in some studies this is lost since the two kinds of trials are alternated so rapidly that learning is made difficult. Assessment of control in terms of difference between enhancement (or suppression) and baseline scores is a different matter from simply assessing the difference between enhancement and suppression, or the amount of alpha increase over trials; yet they are treated as if they are the same. Of the studies that gave enhancement and suppression training, six analyzed their enhancement and suppression data with respect to baselines while eight looked at the "on minus off" scores. Some studies used both methods. Among those studies with only an alpha enhancement task, six looked at increases above baselines while eight looked at increases over trials. It is therefore almost impossible to compare the results of these three different types of studies, although at first glance they all seem to be concerned with the same question.

Exploratory periods (play periods), where the subject is allowed to experiment freely with the signal rather than being required to control the signal in a particular direction, have been employed in seven studies. Although this method does not permit moment-by-moment assessment of performance scores, it may be important and deserves more systematic investigation as a potential facilitator of performance.

SUBJECT SELECTION

Subject sampling is another important factor affecting the outcome of studies, but it is often ignored. Especially important is the motivation for participation in the study. Twenty-seven studies used volunteer subjects, 10 paid their subjects, while 14 used psychology students.

In subjects, the following information, though important, is often not reported: (a) the exact manner of recruitment, including subject's motivation for participation and criteria for rejection of subjects; (b) subjects previous experience and knowledge of biofeedback; and (c) the kind of experiences the subject has had in meditation, athletics, psychotherapy, arts, and other activities involving exploration or differentiation of one's self and body.

We think the time is rapidly arriving for a more systematic basis for comparing subject samples in different studies, particularly along dimensions that are related to "aptitude" for learning the specific biofeedback tasks (or for learning all biofeedback tasks). Perhaps helpful would be a life history questionnaire, as well as some widely used personality inventory. With both of these, item analysis with biofeedback performance as a criterion could be conducted to develop a biofeedback personality profile of scale scores that provide optimal prediction of individual differences in this area. If used by all researchers, these would be valuable for providing a basis for comparing subject populations in different studies.

COMMENTARY

In our view, many of the studies reviewed suffer from important methological weaknesses. The quality of training, including training times that have been too short and conditions that have not been optimum, has precluded success in many studies. We think the probabilities of successful feedback enhancement of alpha above eyes-open and eyes-closed baselines can be substantially improved by incorporating the following suggestions: (a) the use of at least four training sessions; (b) the use of continuous rather than dichotomous feedback, supplemented by periodic quantitative scores of progress; and (c) using training trials of at least 10 minutes' duration.

One important factor not previously reviewed here is the social interaction conditions surrounding the experiment. In some of our own work, we have observed strong facilitative effects that seem to emerge as a combined product of feedback training and certain personal interaction (Kamiya, 1974). The influences are subtle and require careful experimental analysis to determine exactly what is involved. We believe that this area of social facilitation of feedback learning deserves much more exploration. It is highly possible that many of the conflicting results in alpha training could be partly due to differences in experimenter–subject interactions. Since such interactions are rarely described in research reports, it is difficult to evaluate them. It is possible that experimenters that have tried to minimize these social interactions (in the interests of scientific rigor) may have had the effect of handicapping the subjects' biofeedback learning.

Another important factor not always mentioned is the instructional set given to the subject, as well as the amount of additional information given about the alpha state. To aid in the more complete evaluation of results, it is important to know if the subjects were told just to increase the tone or to explore the relationship between the tone and their feelings, told how difficult or easy the task would be or given hints such as "relax, don't worry, you're doing fine, don't try too hard," etc. Some of these are examples of kinds of casual comments by experimenters that are seldom reported, but contribute an important part of the total instruction set of all studies, and their general nature should be specified as accurately as possible.

Although in the early stages in this field, diversity of method was to be expected and even encouraged, the time has arrived for optimization of training conditions as well as improved coverage of the methodological details reported. We believe that the methodological points covered in this chapter will be helpful and hope that they will lead to improvement over methods used in the past.

NOTE. For a fuller version of this chapter, including tables and references, see the article "Methodological issues in alpha feedback training" in *Biofeedback and Self-Regulation*, 1978, *3*(2), 159–183.

REFERENCES

Fenwick, P. B. C., & Walker, S. The effect of eye position of the alpha rhythm. In C. R. Evans & T. B. Mulholland (Eds.), *Attention in neurophysiology*. New York: Appleton-Century-Crofts, 1969.

Hardt, J. V. The ups and downs of learning alpha feedback. *Proceedings of the biofeedback research society*. Monterey, California: Biofeedback Society of America, 1975. p. 118.

Hardt, J. V., & Kamiya, J. Conflicting results in EEG alpha feedback studies: Why amplitude integration should replace percent time. *Biofeedback and Self-Regulation*, 1976, *1*(1), 63–75.

Jasper, H., & Shagass, C. Conditioning the occipital alpha rhythm in man. *Journal of Experimental Psychology*, 1941, *28*, 373–387.

Kamiya, J. Autoregulation of the EEG alpha rhythm: A program for the study of consciousness. In M. H. Chase (Ed.), *Operant control of brain sciences* (Vol. 2). Los Angeles: BIS/Brain Research Institute, University of California, 1974.

Mulholland, T. B. The concept of attention and the EEG alpha rhythm. In C. R. Evans & T. B. Mulholland (Eds.), *Attention in neurophysiology*. New York: Appleton-Century-Crofts, 1969.

29

Effects of Central Cortical EEG Feedback Training on Incidence of Poorly Controlled Seizures

M. B. Sterman and L. R. Macdonald

INTRODUCTION

A growing literature in recent years suggests that operant conditioning of certain central cortical EEG patterns may provide a behavioral approach for the control of seizure disorders. Research in this area developed from studies in the cat which indicated that animals could learn to voluntarily increase the incidence of rhythmic 12- to 16-Hz sensorimotor cortex EEG activity (Sterman & Wyrwicka, 1967; Wyrwicka & Sterman, 1968). When challenged with a convulsant dose of the toxic hydrazine derivative, monomethylhydrazine, animals overtrained in this task demonstrated increased threshold for seizures, as compared with untrained or oppositely trained animals (Sterman, LoPresti, & Fairchild, 1969; Sterman, 1976). Other studies in cats confirmed the previously noted association between this activity and behavioral immobility (Chase & Harper, 1971; Howe & Sterman, 1972; Rougeul, Letalle, & Corvisier, 1972) and demonstrated a corre-lated reflex suppression (Babb & Chase, 1974) and attenuation of unit discharge in sensorimotor pathways (Harper & Sterman, 1972). Recent studies in primates have documented similar behavioral correlates in this species (Bouyer, Dedet, Konya, & Rougeul, 1974; Holcombe, Sterman, Goodman, & Fairchild, 1979).

The application of central cortical EEG feedback training in poorly con-trolled epileptics has produced numerous reports of significant seizure reduction (Sterman & Friar, 1972; Sterman, Macdonald, & Stone, 1974; Finley, Smith, & Etherton, 1975; Ellertsen & Kløve, 1976; Lubar & Bahler, 1976; Wyler, Lock-hard, Ward, & Finch, 1976; Kuhlman & Allison, 1977; Sterman, 1977a; Quy, Hutt, & Forrest, 1979). Research in this new area must address a number of unique problems in evaluating both independent and dependent variables. Unlike drug studies in which dose or blood levels of anticonvulsants can be specified with some accuracy in large numbers of patients, the idiosyncratic EEG parameter in epileptics, altered by both pathology and drugs, poses numerous problems for a

M. B. Sterman and L. R. Macdonald • Veterans Administration Hospital, Sepulveda, California 91343 and Departments of Anatomy and Psychiatry, University of California, Los Angeles, California 90024.

comparable assessment of training "dose." Quantitative evaluation of clinical seizure manifestations also presents serious difficulties. Drug studies using large numbers of patients with appropriate control conditions can achieve sufficient consensus to inspire some confidence, despite the variability among epileptics and the considerable problem of seizure quantification. Because of the technical nature of the EEG feedback training approach, and the frequent patient contacts required, studies have been limited to relatively small numbers of subjects. This fact, together with lack of control groups in early experiments, has led some to remain skeptical, particularly when "equivocal" results were reported by Kaplan (1975), and enthusiastically endorsed by Gastaut (1975). Finally, the marked variability in seizure characteristics among the population of poorly controlled patients to whom this approach was directed has made group design studies difficult.

In the present investigation these realities led, once again, to a focus upon a relatively small group of patients. A multiple, single case study design and corresponding statistical analytic procedures were employed to provide answers to at least some of the basic issues in this area. This approach produced a substantial amount of data from each patient, all of which were eventually examined. This chapter will be restricted to a consideration of only one dependent variable from this study, i.e., clinical response patterns.

METHODS

Patient Selection

Eight epileptic subjects were recruited for this study through a referral program with the UCLA Neurology Clinic and other local neurologists. Criteria for selection were (1) confirmed diagnoses of seizure disorder with primary motor or motor and complex partial seizures, or generalized atonic or tonic–clonic seizures; (2) history of poor seizure control with anticonvulsant medications for a period of at least 3 years, with systematic logging of seizure incidence for at least 3 months; (3) age between 10 and 40 years; and (4) no additional neurologic or significant psychiatric symptomatology. Informed consent was obtained from all patients who participated in the study.

Experimental Design

The objective of this study was to determine the specific relationship between EEG feedback training, using various central cortical EEG frequencies, and clinical seizure rate. The experimental design established to accomplish these goals was necessarily complex, as outlined in Table 1. A double crossover, single-blind ABA design was employed, with the patient as his or her own control (Blanchard & Young, 1974). This was accomplished by making reward contingent on the occurrence of activity within one EEG frequency band in the absence of activity in a second frequency band, and then reversing these contingencies at

Table 1

Outline of Counterbalanced, Double-Crossover ABA Design Used in the Study of EEG Operant Conditioning with Seizure Disorder Patients Reported Here[a]

	Condition							
Group	Baseline		A_1		B		A_2	
1	Lab EEG Sleep EEG Clin. EEG Anticonv. Lev.	B training repeated where appropriate	12–15 Hz (+) 6–9 Hz (−)	Repeat of sleep and clinical measurements	12–15 Hz (−) 6–9 Hz (+)	Repeat of sleep and clinical measurements	12–15 Hz (+) 6–9 Hz (−)	Laboratory training period
2	Lab EEG Sleep EEG Clin. EEG Anticonv. Lev.		12–15 Hz (−) 6–9 Hz (+)		12–15 Hz (+) 6–9 Hz (−)		12–15 Hz (−) 6–9 Hz (+)	
3	Lab EEG Sleep EEG Clin. EEG Anticonv. Lev.		18–23 Hz (+) 6–9 Hz (−)		18–23 Hz (−) 6–9 Hz (+)		18–23 Hz (+) 6–9 Hz (−)	
4	Lab EEG Sleep EEG Clin. EEG Anticonv. Lev.		18–23 Hz (−) 6–9 Hz (+)		18–23 Hz (+) 6–9 Hz (−)		18–23 Hz (−) 6–9 Hz (+)	

[a] Training contingencies for each 3-month phase of the design are indicated. Reward was obtained when one central cortical EEG frequency band was present for 0.5 seconds (+) in the absence of a paired frequency band (−). Two patients were studied in each of the four groups detailed here.

systematic intervals without the patient's knowledge. To evaluate an extended range of appropriate central cortical EEG frequencies, the combinations derived were focused on three specific frequency bands—6- to 9-Hz, 12- to 15-Hz, and 18- to 23-Hz. The 6- to 9-Hz band was selected in order to evaluate central cortical low frequencies while still avoiding the even lower frequencies associated with abnormal acitivity. Moreover, this frequency band corresponded to the "slowed" alpha activity seen in many of our patients and therefore addressed the potential therapeutic role of learned relaxation suggested by Kaplan (1975). The 12- to 15-Hz band was selcted because of previous animal and human studies in our laboratory. Additionally, this frequency corresponds to normal sleep spindle or sigma activity which we have found to be attenuated or disrupted in many of our patients (Sterman, 1977a). Finally, the 18- to 23-Hz band was selected as a representative frequency for beta activity, which is associated with EEG activation and behavioral arousal. This band was of interest because of the suggestion by Wyler et al. (1976) that therapeutic results with EEG feedback training could result from increased attention associated with reward for activating frequencies.

In all instances, the 6- to 9-Hz band was paired with either the 12- to 15-Hz or the 18- to 23-Hz band. Pairing of 12- to 15-Hz and 18- to 23-Hz bands was avoided after preliminary studies suggested that these two frequencies may covary functionally (Sterman, 1977b). The order of training with each of these frequency pairs was counterbalanced, establishing the four separate training schedules shown in Table 1.

Two patients were assigned to each of these four schedules in random order. After obtaining baseline data, as indicated in Table 1, patients were given preliminary laboratory training to assure competence and to familiarize them with the use of portable training equipment. This equipment would eventually be assigned to the patient for continuation of training at home. The laboratory training period (2 to 3 weeks) also provided for determination of individual EEG voltage characteristics and appropriate adjustment of signal detection channels on the feedback unit. The experimental design was initiated with the beginning of home training, and training contingencies were reversed at 3-month intervals. Patients whose initial training (condition A_1) provided positive reward for one of the two higher frequencies [12–15 Hz (+) or 18–23 Hz (+)] were followed for an additional 3 months at the end of training. This follow-up period provided for one recorded laboratory training session every 2 weeks for a total of six sessions over the 3-month period. Patients who began with reward for 6–9 Hz (+) were not allowed to end with this schedule. In this case, training required 12 months, since a second 3-month period was provided with positive reward for the appropriate higher frequency (i.e., a B_2 condition). A 3-month follow-up period then terminated these schedules as well.

Equipment and Training Procedures

EEG feedback training was accomplished with a portable feedback unit (NFI Neuroanalyzer, model 4000), which utilized tuned active filters, analog analysis circuits, timing circuits, and logic circuits for training of a *pattern* of events (Figure 1). This unit provided simultaneous positive feedback for a given

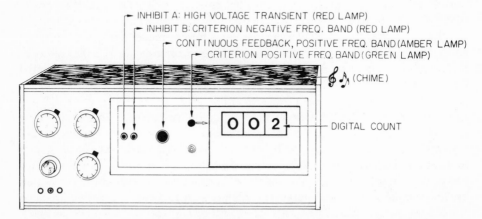

Figure 1. Diagram of portable feedback equipment (Neurofeedback Instruments, model 4000) used for laboratory and home EEG feedback training described in text. Instrument is 15 inches wide, 6 inches high, and 12 inches deep. Target area for patient attention is set off by bold white outline and contains feedback signals as indicated here and described in text. Other features shown include channel sensitivity and EEG gain control dials, as well as reset button and input receptacles.

EEG frequency band and negative feedback for an alternate band. Additionally, the reward system was aborted whenever a high-voltage transient ($50\,\mu V$ or more) occurred in the signal. The latter feature prevented abnormal EEG activity or movement artifact from activating the reward channel. Positive reward consisted of a green light, a digital count display, and a tone (Figure 1), and was activated only in the absence of the negative frequency band or any high-voltage transient. The occurrence of either of these events was signaled by one of two red lamps. A modulated amber lamp provided continuous information concerning the positive frequency band, changing intensity in direct relation to the incidence of this activity in the EEG. The subject was thus provided both with continuous feedback and with discrete reward when criterion conditions were met. The portable unit also connected to a portable 4-channel strip chart recorder which registered for later tabulation the time of each home training session, its duration, and the number of rewards obtained.

During laboratory training sessions, gold-plated cup electrodes were placed over left central cortex at positions 10% and 30% lateral to vertex (slightly medial to the standard T_3 and C_3 placements of the International 10–20 System). The resulting bipolar signal was fed into the portable feedback unit and to a Grass model 8 electroencephalograph. The output of the feedback unit amplifier was recorded also on the polygraph. Thus, signal detection criteria were established with reference to individual EEG characteristics, and laboratory training was carried out with comparison of EEG recordings directly from the patient and indirectly through the portable feedback instrument. Reward (positive and negative) was provided for *trains* of the appropriate frequency band lasting more than 0.5 seconds at $5–20\,\mu V$, depending on the frequency and on the patient.

After a minimum of ten laboratory training sessions, the patient was initiated into the ABA design, with training continued at home. A technician accompanied the patient to set up the home training situation and establish a fixed location and time of day for practice. Patients were instructed to work with the instrument for a minimum of 30 minutes per day, 6 days per week. A custom-made elastic headband, with special low-impedance electrodes attached, was used to obtain recordings in the home. Patients and their families were instructed in the application of these electrodes during the final phase of laboratory training. The home training unit was preset in the laboratory for appropriate function with each patient. Setup or maintenance problems were handled by return visits with portable test equipment.

The patient returned to the laboratory at 2-week intervals for a recorded training session. The strip chart record was removed from the unit at this time to document compliance with training instructions. The unit was retained by the laboratory for the succeeding 2-week period (for use by another patient) and then returned to the original patient. In this manner, each patient worked with the unit for 2-week periods (12 training sessions) and was off training for the subsequent 2-week period. This arrangement provided an on–off training schedule and allowed for the sharing of these expensive instruments among patients. At the end of each 3-month interval, reward contingencies were reversed without the patient's knowledge. In one patient (no. 6) it was necessary to extend both the A_1

and B_1 training conditions to 5 months because of unavoidable disruptions in the training schedule for this subject.

Recording of Clinical Seizure Incidence

Subjects who participated in this study were selected, in part, because of a history of careful seizure logging. Primary seizures in all of these patients involved major motor symptoms, which lent themselves to relatively accurate detection. Seizure logs showing all detected motor seizures for a period of at least 3 months were required from all patients prior to the initiation of training. With entrance into the study, each patient was issued a special seizure log form and instructed to record all detected seizures for each 2-week design interval throughout the period of participation. It was usually necessary to have a close family member assist in this logging of seizures.

At the end of participation in the study seizure incidence for each patient was calculated from these logs. The number of seizures reported for each 2-week period were summed to provide sequential monthly rates; mean values for each 3-month period were tabulated and plotted according to the schedule of the experimental design. These calculations were made independently and without knowledge of the reward contingencies for a given patient during a given phase of the study. Data from each patient were treated as an independent experiment. The Analysis of Variance Test was used to evaluate treatment effects (ABA conditions) which, if significant, were further tested with the Multiple Comparison t-Test.

Anticonvulsant blood levels were evaluated before the initiation of training and at each point of reversal in training contingencies. While somewhat variable, the results of these measures suggested that all patients had continued to comply with previously established drug regimens, as instructed. A more detailed description of these findings will be provided in a later report of corresponding EEG responses.

RESULTS

A classification of seizure disorders and seizure types for the 8 patients studied here is presented in Table 2, together with information concerning the duration of the disorder and anticonvulsant medications during the period of study. The latter were kept constant once the patient was accepted. As mentioned above, determination of plasma levels of the various medications used, obtained at 3-month intervals, suggested compliance with this requirement. Six of the patients had generalized tonic–clonic seizures, and 4 of these also had partial motor seizures. One patient had primary focal motor seizures, while another had a mixed pattern of complex-partial and akinetic seizures. The history of poorly controlled seizures in these patients ranged from 8 to 24 years.

Pretraining seizure rate tabulation was available for periods of at least 3 months in all patients and in excess of 9 months in 4 patients (Tables 3 and 4).

Table 2

Summary of Seizure Disorder Classifications, Duration, and Associated Anticonvulsant Medications in 8 Patients Provided Here with EEG Feedback Training

Patient no.	Age	Disorder: seizure type	Duration (years)	Medications
1	23	Generalized: tonic–clonic	12	Dilantin Tegretol
2	26	Mixed: focal motor tonic–clonic	16	Mysoline Diamox Eskabarb Tridione
3	18	Generalized: tonic–clonic	15	Dilantin Phenobarbital
4	35	Mixed: psychomotor tonic–clonic	24	Tridione Mysoline Dilantin
5	22	Partial: focal motor	21	Dilantin Valium Phenobarbital Synthroid
6	28	Mixed: psychomotor tonic–clonic	8	None
7	28	Mixed: psychomotor akinetic	14	Dilantin Tranxine
8	30	Mixed: psychomotor tonic–clonic	18	Dilantin

Data from these 4 patients were utilized to assess the reliability of 3-month, rate-per-month tabulations by calculating multiple Pearson product moment correlations between successive, nonoverlapping 3-month data blocks over a 9-month period (Downie & Heath, 1959). Correlation values ranged from 0.62 to 0.81, with a mean overall $r = 0.74$. These findings suggest that a 3-month tabulation of monthly seizure rates in these patients provided a reasonable, stable estimate of the more general incidence of detected seizures.

Tables 3 and 4 also show reported monthly seizure rates during all phases of training and follow-up. Analysis of Variance and subsequent Multiple Comparison t Tests were carried out with the data from each subject, and resulting F and p values are presented. Statistically significant deviations from baseline seizure rates are indicated also by asterisks next to qualifying mean seizure-rate values. Corresponding data indicating percent of baseline seizure rates are shown in the far-right column of these tables.

In order to visualize these results more easily, plots of percent change from baseline seizure rates are shown in Figures 2 and 3. Figure 2 presents data from 4 subjects in whom seizure-rate changes more or less paralleled training contingencies (i.e., seizure-rate reversals followed training contingency reversals), while

Table 3

Seizure Rate Data Reported Before, During, and After EEG Feedback Training with ABA and ABAB Designs in 4 Poorly Controlled Seizure Patients Rewarded for Alternating Combinations of 12–15 and 6–9 Hz

Subj. no.	Condition	Seizure rate reported per month									Mean rate per period	Percent pretrain rate
		1	2	3	4	5	6	7	8	9		
1	Pretrain	17	29	23							23 ± 6.0	100
	A_1(12–15+)	5	6	7							6 ± 1.0^a	26
	B_1(6–9+)	18	26	22		$F = 8.27, p = <.01$					22 ± 4.5	96
	A_2(12–15+)	12	6	19							12 ± 6.5^a	52
	Posttrain	7	11	12							10 ± 2.14^a	44
2	Pretrain	37	34	39	47	42	38	23	27	34	36 ± 7.3	100
	A_1(12–15+)	34	37	32							34 ± 2.5	94
	B_1(6–9+)	46	28	42		$F = 6.66m, p = <.01$					39 ± 9.4	108
	A_2(12–15+)	17	25	20							21 ± 4.0^a	58
	Posttrain	26	17	22							22 ± 3.7^a	61
3	Pretrain	1	0	2	1	1	1	1	1	2	1.1 ± 0.6	100
	A_1(6–9+)	1	2	1							1.3 ± 0.6	118
	B_1(12–15+)	0	0	2							0.7 ± 1.1	64
	A_2(6–9+)	1	2	0		$F = 2.24, p = <.05$					1.0 ± 1.0	91
	B_2(12–15+)	0	0	0							0.0 ± 0.0^a	0
	Posttrain	0	0	0							0.0 ± 0.0^a	0
4	Pretrain	105	62	73	102	116	100	93	88	94	93 ± 16.5	100
	A_1(6–9+)	74	72	104							83 ± 17.9	89
	B_1(12–15+)	97	94	102							98 ± 4.0	105
	A_2(6–9+)	110	90	77		$F = .497, p = NS$					92 ± 16.6	99
	B_2(12–15+)	100	61	63							75 ± 22.0	81
	Posttrain	81	125	55							87 ± 28.9	94

$^a p < .05.$

Figure 3 shows data from 4 patients showing other response patterns. In 2 of these, seizure rates were consistently reduced, in spite of contingency reversals, and in 2 others seizure rates showed no consistent change.

Significant reductions in seizure rate were recorded by all 4 patients whose data are shown in Figure 2. In 3 of these patients, seizure reductions occurred exclusively during reward for 12–15 Hz in the absence of 6–9 Hz. This was true regardless of the phase of the design in which this contingency was rewarded. The reduction was greatest during the initial 3-month period of 12- to 15-Hz (+) training (A_1) in patient no. 1, but was maximal during the second period of 12- to 15-Hz (+) training in patients 2 (A_2) and 3 (B_2). The fourth patient in this group (no. 7) was provided training with 18–23 and 6–9 Hz and showed a significant reduction in seizures during the initial 6- to 9-Hz, A_1 condition. However, with reversal to the 18- to 23-Hz (+) contingency, this patient's seizure rate dropped even more impressively (B_1). A return to 6–9 Hz (+) was associated with a slight increase in rate, followed again by a decline after contingency reversal (B_2) and into the 3-month follow-up period. In all of these patients, reported seizure incidence remained significantly reduced during the 3-month follow-up period.

Table 4

Seizure Rate Data Reported Before, During, and After EEG Feedback Training with ABA and ABAB Designs in 4 Poorly Controlled Seizure Patients Rewarded for Alternating Combinations of 18–23 and 6–9 Hz

Subj. no.	Condition	Seizure rate reported per month									Mean rate per period	Percent pretrain rate
		1	2	3	4	5	6	7	8	9		
5	Pretrain	52	45	40							46 ± 6.0	100
	$A_1(18\text{--}23+)$	13	32	31							25 ± 10.7^a	54
	$B_1(6\text{--}9+)$	6	18	10			$F = 10.14, p = <.01$				11 ± 6.1^a	24
	$A_2(18\text{--}23+)$	5	18	9							11 ± 7.2^a	24
	Posttrain	22	4	4							10 ± 10.4^a	22
6	Pretrain	7	9	11							9.0 ± 2.0	100
	$A_1(18\text{--}23+)$	5	1	2	0	0					2.0 ± 2.1^a	22
	$B_1(6\text{--}9+)$	0	1	0	0	0	$F = 25.71, p = <.01$				0.2 ± 0.4^a	2
	$A_2(18\text{--}23+)$	0	0	0	0						0.0 ± 0.0^a	0
	Posttrain	0	0	0	0						0.0 ± 0.0^a	0
7	Pretrain	54	42	40							45 ± 7.6	100
	$A_1(6\text{--}9+)$	36	35	36							36 ± 0.6^a	80
	$B_1(18\text{--}23+)$	21	22	22			$F = 16.92, p = .01$				22 ± 0.6^a	49
	$A_2(6\text{--}9+)$	30	25	33							29 ± 4.0^a	64
	$B_2(18\text{--}23+)$	14	25	25							21 ± 6.3^a	47
	Posttrain	18	17	19							18 ± 1.0^a	40
8	Pretrain	10	17	13	14	12	6	12	9	13	12 ± 3.1	100
	$A_1(6\text{--}9+)$	12	4	7							8 ± 4.0^a	64
	$B_1(18\text{--}23+)$	12	13	7			$F = 4.72, p = <.05$				11 ± 3.2	92
	$A_2(6\text{--}9+)$	14	17	12							14 ± 2.5	117
	$B_2(18\text{--}23+)$	14	18	14							15 ± 2.3^a	125
	Posttrain	7	12	8							9 ± 2.2	75

$^a p < .05.$

Among the patients whose data are presented in Figure 3, numbers 5 and 6 showed a similar pattern of seizure reduction, with a significant decrease during an initial (A_1) 3-month period of reward for 18–23 Hz (+), 6–9 Hz (−). However, this effect was not reversed during the subsequent B_1 condition which, in fact, was associated with a further decline. Seizure rates in both of these patients were markedly reduced at this point and remained so throughout subsequent training and follow-up periods. Patient no. 4 showed no significant change in reported seizure rate throughout 15 months of tabulation. Data from patient number 8 were unique in demonstrating an initial reduction during the A_1 period, with reward for 6–9 Hz (+), an increase during B_1 with 18–23 Hz (+), and then a further increase during the next 6- to 9-Hz (+) period (A_2). This trend was continued to the final training period (B_2), with reward once again for 18–23 Hz (−), where it reflected a significant increase in seizure rate. The follow-up period was associated with a sharp drop in rate to pretraining levels.

Significant and consistent seizure reductions were thus reported by 6 of the 8 patients studied. Data from these patients are compiled separately in Table 5, which compares the circumstances of training during phases with maximum and

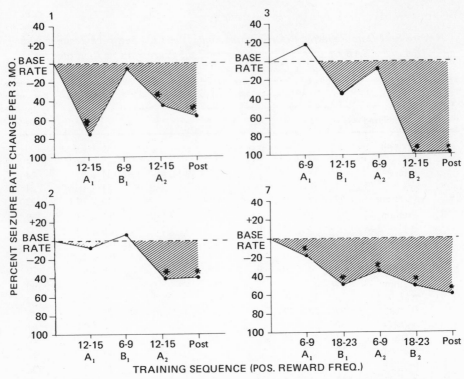

Figure 2. Graphic presentations of percent seizure rate change per 3-month period of the experimental design are shown here for 4 seizure disorder patients who demonstrated a more or less contingency-specific response to EEG feedback training. Base rate values were derived from a minimum of 3 months of seizure tabulation. Asterisks indicate significant rate changes ($p = <0.05$) from base rate as determined by Multiple Comparison t test. Each phase of the ABA or ABAB design is shown together with the frequency band which was positively rewarded during that period (negative band not indicated but was always band shown for subsequent phase). Data from 3-month posttraining follow-up period are shown also.

Table 5

Summary of Design Characteristics Associated with Maximum and Minimum Therapeutic Outcomes in 6 Patients Showing Systematic Seizure Reduction with EEG Feedback Training

Subject no.	Maximum therapeutic effect			Minimum therapeutic effect		
	Condition	Schedule	% Rate change	Condition	Schedule	% Rate change
1	A_1	12–15+	−74	B_1	6–9+	−4
2	A_2	12–15+	−42	B_1	6–9+	+8
3	B_2	12–15+	−100	A_1	6–9+	+18
5	A_2	18–23+	−76	—	NONE	—
6	A_2	18–23+	−100	—	NONE	—
7	B_2	18–23+	−53	A_1	6–9+	−20
Mean percent change			−74.2			+0.5

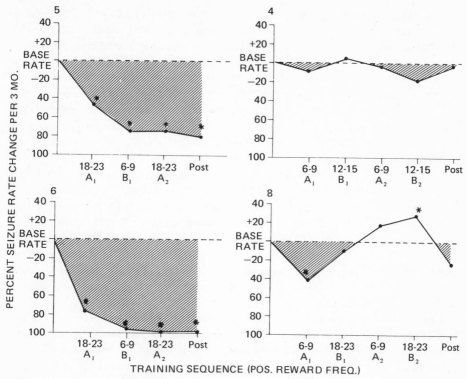

Figure 3. Graphic presentation of percent seizure rate change as in Figure 2. The 4 patients shown here demonstrated seizure rate changes which were not contingency specific. Two of these patients showed significant seizure rate reductions during initial 3 months of reward for 18–23 Hz (+), 6–9 Hz (−) which were not altered by contingency reversals. Two others failed to demonstrate any consistent response to training.

minimum reported therapeutic effects. In the 6 responding patients it can be seen that maximum seizure reductions were noted after at least 6 months of training (A₂) in 5 of these patients and occurred during reward for 12–15 Hz or 18–23 Hz in all 6. For these 6 patients the mean optimal seizure reduction was 74.2%. Conversely, minimal effects were noted during the first 6 months of training (A₁ or B₁), and with reward for 6–9 Hz, in the 4 patients who showed contingency-specific effects. The mean rate change under these conditions was +0.5%.

DISCUSSION

The most important outcome of this study was the report of sustained seizure reductions by 6 of 8 epileptic patients during and after central cortical EEG operant conditioning. Before discussing this finding in detail, we should consider the experimental dependent variable on which it is based, i.e., reported seizure incidence. There is clearly no way to tabulate seizure rate accurately in such patients, short of maintaining constant visual and telemetered EEG surveillance in a restricted hospital ward environment. This approach, however, was neither practical nor economically feasible. Reported seizure incidence, despite its shortcomings, reflects the patient's personal awareness of his or her disorder or the observations of individuals in close contact with the patient. Traditionally, this has been an important index of treatment outcome in medicine. Moreover, the reliability of this measure was increased in the present study by its focus on primary motor seizures in patients with long and relatively stable histories of seizure disorders. The use of a multiple-crossover design in a series of counterbalanced, single-case studies provided the most reliable approach feasible for such an investigation. Finally, EEG data to be described in a forthcoming communication indicated significant changes related both to training and reported seizure incidence.

The temptation to attribute seizure reductions with EEG operant conditioning to nonspecific factors such as attention or the so-called "placebo effect" has been strong. There is no question that nonspecific influences can lead to seizure reductions in epileptics. However, such influences cannot account for the bulk of the present findings. Despite the fact that patients were attended to most directly and frequently during the first month of involvement in the study, seizure reductions were generally greatest *after 6 months* of training. In the 3 patients responding to training with the 12- to 15-Hz and 6- to 9-Hz frequency combination, significant seizure reductions were restricted to periods of positive reward for 12–15 Hz, even when this contingency was presented 3, 6, and 9 months after the initiation of training. In the 3 patients responding to training with the 18- to 23-Hz and 6- to 9-Hz combination, seizure reductions were sustained for periods in excess of 9 months. Finally, it should be recalled that training was carried out primarily in the patient's home with only two visits per month to the laboratory.

A number of other studies have presented data which argue against a nonspecific interpretation of seizure response to central cortical EEG operant conditioning. Kuhlman and Allison (1977) and Wyler et al. (1976) both reported no reduction of seizures in poorly controlled patients during initial periods of noncontingent training. When reward was subsequently made contingent on central cortical 9–14 and 14–26 Hz, respectively, both of these laboratories found significant seizure reductions. Wyler et al. also reported that training to reduce frontalis electromyographic activity had no therapeutic effect when tested in 1 patient.

The patients studied here had not responded well to previous chemotherapeutic efforts. The significant seizure reductions noted thus suggest that some element of the EEG feedback training produced a meaningful therapeutic effect. Since nonspecific influences appear to be ruled out, we are left with a finite number of potential therapeutic factors. These include (a) suppression of movement, (b) suppression of abnormal EEG discharge, (c) reward for the presence of high frequency activity, or (d) all of the above.

As described earlier (Sterman et al., 1974), patients undergoing extended EEG feedback training learn to sit quietly in the training situation and focus attention on the feedback signals provided. Postural adjustments or "time out" periods of movement tend to occur at regular intervals. Several of our animal studies indicated that restraint or paralysis raised seizure thresholds in cats, while at the same time enhancing sensorimotor cortex 12- to 15-Hz activity (Sterman,

Fairchild, Allison, & Goff, 1972; Bowersox, Siegel, & Sterman, 1978). The relative suppression or reorganization of movement during training, however, was a constant element of response throughout the various phases of the design employed here. Since seizure reduction occurred mainly or exclusively during specific reward contingencies, it is unlikely that this element of the training was a primary therapeutic factor. Similarly, negative feedback for high-voltage abnormal discharge was provided during all phases of training. It should be mentioned, however, that Upton and Longmire (1975) have reported impressive therapeutic effects in epileptic patients using feedback training for suppression of EEG focal discharge, and Cott, Avloski, and Black (personal communication) have found that negative reward for high-voltage transients (large slow waves and spikes) alone was as effective as positive reward for 12–15 Hz in the absence of these transients.

It should be noted that 4 patients in the present study reported significant seizure reductions during periods of reward for 6–9 Hz in the absence of 18- to 23-Hz activity. This effect was never observed in data reported by patients who received the 12- to 15-Hz, 6- to 9-Hz training combination. Two patients showing seizure reduction with 6- to 9-Hz (+) reward received 18- to 23-Hz (+) training initially and demonstrated primary seizure reduction during this phase of training. Evaluation of EEG data from these patients indicated a failure to increase previously suppressed low-frequency components of EEG power after reward was reversed (Sterman, 1977a). Thus, in these patients sustained seizure reduction during a secondary 6- to 9-Hz (+) training condition could reflect a failure to reverse therapeutic changes achieved during the initial 18- to 23-Hz (+) training contingency.

Two other patients reported seizure reduction during initial periods of 6- to 9-Hz (+) training. One patient had participated in the study reported by Wyler et al. (1976) and had shown seizure reduction with reward for frequencies between 14–26 Hz. The patient's seizure rate had eventually returned to baseline after acute termination of involvement in the previous study. It is reasonable to assume that this patient initiated training in the present study with a previously developed strategy. This possibility will be evaluated through analysis of corresponding EEG response. The second patient showed a seizure reduction with initial 6- to 9-Hz (+) training followed by a seizure increase during the second phase of reward for this contingency. This unstable response pattern suggests that the initial response in this patient could also have reflected expectation rather than a true therapeutic effect. As a result of these considerations and the data presented in Table 5, we conclude that reward for 6- to 9-Hz central cortical EEG activity cannot be considered an effective training condition for seizure reduction.

A number of investigators have reported seizure reductions with single-contingency training providing reward for frequencies ranging from 9 to 23 Hz (Sterman & Friar, 1972; Ellertsen & Kløve, 1976; Kuhlman & Allison, 1977). Other studies combined low-frequency suppression and reward for these higher frequencies with equally good results (Sterman et al., 1974; Finley et al., 1975; Lubar & Bahler, 1976; Wyler et al., 1976; Quy et al., 1979). In the present study, reward for 12–15 or 18–23 Hz in the absence of 6–9 Hz produced the greatest and most reliable therapeutic effects. Thus, it would appear that reward for central cortical frequencies above 8 Hz, with or without suppression of lower frequencies, can be effective in reducing seizures.

This conclusion led Wyler et al. (1976) to propose a general desynchronization or alerting hypothesis as the most parsimonious explanation for observed seizure reductions. However, reward for frequencies above 25 Hz may be contraindicated since Wyler (personal communication) has recently found that such training increased seizure rates dramatically in monkeys made epileptic with cortical alumina cream implants. Thus, a simple activation hypothesis may not be feasible.

We have previously reported that many of these patients showed a significant disruption of sleep spindle activity in pretraining recordings when compared with normal subjects (Sterman, Macdonald, & Berntsen, 1977). It is possible, therefore, that enhancement of this normal EEG pattern in patients rewarded for 12- to 15-Hz activity provided protection against abnormal discharge utilizing the thalamocortical pathways involved. Similarly, patients rewarded for 18- to 23-Hz activity may have increased normal discharge along reticulocortical activating pathways, the primary effect of which was desynchronization of abnormal cellular recruitment producing large slow waves. Data reported by both Kuhlman and Allison (1977) and Wyler et al. (1976) also suggested that the enhancement of normal activity in potential seizure propagation pathways could be therapeutic. Thus, a concept of EEG "normalization" might provide an explanation for the therapeutic effects reported in this study and other investigations employing different feedback strategies. Evidence in support of this possibility has been suggested by preliminary findings from analysis of concurrent EEG data obtained from the patients described here.

SUMMARY

This study examined the clinical effects of central cortical EEG feedback training in 8 patients with poorly controlled seizures. After baseline recordings, patients were trained in the laboratory and then initiated on a double- or triple-crossover design using portable equipment at home, with bimonthly laboratory test sessions. Performance at home was monitored by a strip chart recorder with the portable unit. Training was based on the simultaneous detection of two central cortical (C_3-T_3) EEG frequency bands (6- to 9-Hz and either 12- to 15-Hz or 18- to 23-Hz), with reward provided for the occurrence of one in the absence of the other. The design consisted of successive 3-month periods of training, with reward contingencies reversed after each period without the subject's knowledge. Seizure incidence records were compared statistically before, during, and after the design. Six of the 8 patients reported significant and sustained seizure reductions, which averaged 74%, following reward for either 12–15 or 18–23 Hz in the absence of 6–9 Hz. Response to positive reward for 12–15 Hz was specific, with seizure rates returning to baseline when reinforcement contingencies were reversed. Reduced seizure rates following positive reward for 18–23 Hz were not altered with contingency reversals. A nonspecific interpretation of these effects is rejected in favor of an EEG normalizing hypothesis.

ACKNOWLEDGMENTS. The authors wish to acknowledge the valuable clinical assistance in these studies of Drs. G. O. Walsh and M. Lucia of the Department of Neurology, UCLA, and the significant contributions of S. Sarnoff and I. Berntsen from our laboratory, V. A. Hospital, Sepulveda. This research was supported by the Verterans Administration and U.S. Public Health Service grant 2 R01 NS10726-04.

REFERENCES

Babb, M. I., & Chase, M. H. Masseteric and digastric reflex activity during conditioned sensorimotor rhythm. *Electroencephalography and Clinical Neurophysiology*, 1974, *36*, 357–365.

Blanchard, E. B., & Young, L. D. Clinical applications of biofeedback training. *Archives of General Psychiatry*, 1974, *30*, 573–589.

Bouyer, J. J., Dedet, L., Konya, A., & Rougeul A. Convergence de trois systémes rythmiques thalmocorticaux sur l'aire somestlfsique du chat et du babouin normaux. *Review of Electroencephalography and Neurophysiology*, 1974, *4*, 197–406.

Bowersox, S., Siegel, J. M., & Sterman, M. B. Effect of restraint on EEG variables and monomethylhydraxine induced seizures in cats. *Experimental Neurology*, 1978, *61*, 154–164.

Chase, M. H., & Harper, R. M. Somatomotor and visceromotor correlates of operantly conditioned 12–14 c/sec sensorimotor cortical activity. *Electroencephalography and Clinical Neurophysiology*, 1971, *31*, 85–92.

Downie, N. M., & Heath, R. W. Other correlational methods. In *Basic statistical methods*. New York: Harper & Brothers, 1959. Pp. 187–188.

Ellertsen, B., & Klove, H. Clinical application of biofeedback training in epilepsy. *Scandinavian Journal of Behavioral Therapy*, 1976, *5*, 133–144.

Finley, W. W. Operant conditioning of the EEG in two patients with epilepsy: Methodologic and clinical considerations. *Pavlovian Journal of Biological Science*, 1977, *12*(2), 93–111.

Finley, W. W., Smith, H. A., & Etherton, M. D. Reduction of seizures and normalization of the EEG in a severe epileptic following sensorimotor biofeedback training: Preliminary study. *Biological Psychology*, 1975, *2*, 189–203.

Gastaut, H. Comments on "Biofeedback in epileptics: Equivocal relationship of reinforced EEG frequency to seizure reduction" by Bonnie J. Kaplan. *Epilepsia*, 1975, *16*, 487–490.

Harper, R. M., & Sterman, M. B. Subcortical unit activity during a conditioned 12–14 Hz sensorimotor EEG rhythm in the cat. *Federation Proceedings* (abstract), 1972, *31*, 404.

Holcombe, V., Sterman, M. B., Goodman, S. J. and Fairchild, M.D. The immobilization response in Rhesus monkeys: A behavioral and electroencephalographic study. *Experimental Neurology*, 1979, in press.

Howe, R. C., & Sterman, M. B. Cortical-subcortical EEG correlates of suppressed motor behavior during sleep and waking in the cat. *Electroencephalography and Clinical Neurophysiology*, 1972, *32*, 681–695.

Kaplan, B. J. Biofeedback in epileptics: Equivocal relationship of reinforced EEG frequency to seizure reduction. *Epilepsia*, 1975, *16*, 477–485.

Kuhlman, W. N., & Allison, T. EEG feedback training in the treatment of epilepsy: Some questions and some answers. *Pavlovian Journal of Biological Science*, 1977, *12*(2), 112–122.

Lubar, J. F., & Bahler, W. W. Behavioral management of epileptic seizures following EEG biofeedback training of the sensorimotor rhythm. *Journal of Biofeedback and Self-Regulation*, 1976, *1*, 77–104.

Quy, R. J., Hutt, S. J., & Forrest, S. Electroencephalographic feedback training for the treatment of epilepsy. *Epilepsia*, 1979, in press.

Rougeul, A. A., Letalle, A., & Corvisier, J. Activité rythmique du cortex somesthésique primaire in relation avec l'immobilité chez le chat libre éveille. *Electroencephalography and Clinical Neurophysiology*, 1972, *33*, 23–39.

Sterman, M. B. Effects of brain surgery and EEG operant conditioning on seizure latency following MMH intoxication in the cat. *Experimental Neurology*, 1976, *50*, 757–765.

Sterman, M. B. Effects of sensorimotor EEG feedback training on sleep and clinical manifestations of epilepsy. In J. Beatty & H. Legewie (Eds.), *Biofeedback and behavior*. New York: Plenum Press, 1977a. Pp. 167–200.

Sterman, M. B. Clinical implications of EEG biofeedback training: A critical appraisal. In G. E. Schwartz & J. Beatty (Eds.), *Biofeedback: Theory and research*. New York: Academic Press, 1977b.

Sterman, M. B., Fairchild, M. D., Allison, T., & Goff, W. R. *Effects of monomethylhydrazine (MMH) on evoked cerebral neuroelectric responses*. Technical Report AMRL-TR-72-52. Aerospace Medical Research Laboratory, Air Force Systems Command, Wright-Patterson Air Force Base, Ohio, 1972.

Sterman, M. B., & Friar, L. Suppression of seizures in an epileptic following sensorimotor EEG feedback training. *Electroencephalography and Clinical Neurophysiology*, 1972, *33*, 89–95.

Sterman, M. B., LoPresti, R. W., & Fairchild, M. D. *Electroencephalographic and behavioral studies of mononiethylhydrazine toxicity in the cat*. Technical Report AMRL-TR-69-3. Air Force Systems Command. Wright-Patterson Air Force Base. Ohio. 1969.

Sterman, M. B., Macdonald, L. R., & Berntsen, I. Quantitative analysis of EEG sleep spindle activity in epileptic and non-epileptic subjects. *Electroencephalography and Clinical Neurophysiology* (abstract), 1977, *42*(5), 724.

Sterman, M. B., Macdonald, L. R., & Stone, R. K. Biofeedback training of the sensorimotor EEG rhythm in man: Effects on epilepsy. *Epilepsia*, 1974, *15*, 395–416.

Sterman, M. B., & Wyrwicka, W. EEG correlates of sleep: Evidence for separate forebrain substrates. *Brain Research*, 1967, *6*, 143–163.

Upton, A. R. M., & Longmire, D. Effects of feedback on focal epileptic discharges in man. *Canadian Journal of Neurological Science*, 1975, *3*, 153–168.

Wyler, A. R., Lockhard, J. S., Ward, A. A., & Finch, C. A. Conditioned EEG dyssynchronization and seizure occurrence in patients. *Electroencephalography and Clinical Neurophysiology*, 1976, *41*, 501–512.

Wyrwicka, W., & Sterman, M. B. Instrumental conditioning of sensorimotor cortex EEG spindles in the waking cat. *Physiological Behavior 3*, 703–707.

ELECTROMYOGRAPHY BIOFEEDBACK

Technology for muscle tension—electromyography (EMG)—recording has been available since the 1930s. While most electromyographers used EMG as a passive diagnostic recording technique, two groups of clinicians were the exception. In the 1950s, Whatmore in Seattle and Marinacci in Los Angeles independently started using EMG feedback.

Whatmore, extending the steps taken by Jacobson, started using EMG biofeedback training in combination with progressive relaxation. By recording from multiple muscle locations in a variety of patients, he noted that EMG recordings from a single site were insufficient since trainees often activated other muscles. He observed that patients involved in different tasks (ranging from cognitive to physical activity) tended to produce inappropriate bracing. Whatmore and Kohli (Chapter 33) labeled this inappropriate bracing process, along with other inappropriate covert efforts, "dysponesis" (misdirected efforts). Their major contributions were the observations that patients needed to become aware of their misdirected efforts, learn how to correct these effort errors, and learn to lower their overall tension levels. In a 6- to 21-year follow-up (mean of 13.4 years) with their patients, Whatmore and Kohli found that long-term clinical success was highly correlated with the patient's final skill in detecting and controlling minimal changes in muscle tension at the end of the treatment, in both the "increase" and "decrease" conditions (Whatmore & Kohli, 1974). This increase and decrease in minimal tension illustrates bidirectional control and is applicable in most biofeedback applications.

Independently, Marinacci (1968), a neurologist, applied EMG feedback in rehabilitation medicine and reported major clinical improvement in stroke, Bell's palsy, and polio patients.

Although Whatmore and Kohli, and Marinacci both used biofeedback techniques, the concepts of biofeedback did not catch on until the 1960s. At this time, Harrison and Mortenson (1960) showed that single motor unit control (SMU) was possible (a motor unit is the subset of striated muscle that is innervated by a single motor neuron. Such muscle activity is described by Strong in Chapter 30. Based on the observation that SMU training was possible, Basmajian (Chapter 31) illustrates and reports upon this novel biofeedback research. Success in learning SMU control was variable, and although some subjects showed exquisite SMU control, they were still unable to explain how they did it. This phenomenon illustrates that voluntary control is not necessarily equivalent to awareness of the mechanisms involved.

Striate muscle activity is perceived as being under voluntary control, while single motor unit control seems difficult to learn. If one is asked to move a single finger, it can easily be done. However, learning voluntary control of fine motor movement takes long hours of practice. For example, move the middle toe of your right foot and observe the difficulty in inhibiting the other toes. Learning control involves not only controlling the muscle to be moved but also inhibiting adjacent muscles. This process of control and inhibition is involved in *all* motor learning, ranging from playing tennis or the violin, or grasping a spoon, to learning to walk and talk. When the inhibition of extraneous muscle groups is not learned, the result is dysponesis.

EMG recordings, as described above, were often done with needle or fine wire electrodes, i.e., needles were inserted into the muscle tissue. More recently, however, this technique has been abandoned in most research and clinical work in favor of noninvasive surface electrodes. With this advancement, EMG became a useful tool in biofeedback.

Unlike the needle electrode technique in which one is sure as to which muscle is being recorded, surface electrodes pick up muscle potentials from a much greater area. The recorded EMG often integrates the activity of adjacent muscles. Basmajian (Chapter 32) describes some of the problems associated with EMG biofeedback as recorded from the most common site, the frontalis muscle, located above the eyebrows on the forehead.

EMG activity from the frontalis area often reflects the habitual and unconscious tensing of the facial muscles (brow, nose, jaw, and mouth) used in expressing emotions. This may support Edmund Jacobsen's statement, made in the 1930s, that for every thought or mental state there is a corresponding muscle activity. Most of this activity is so minute, like microscopic facial expressions, that it remains beneath our level of awareness. EMG feedback, by amplifying these small changes, has become a powerful tool for investigating the mind/body reactivity. When trainees listen to their own EMG activity and observe a change, they can ask, "What am I feeling? Where did I brace or relax? What was I thinking?" and in this way learn to make the association between cognitive and emotional states and corresponding muscle activity.

Although Whatmore and Marinacci were previously mentioned as being pioneers in the field of EMG, it was not until Budzynski and Stoyna's initial work (Chapter 34) that EMG biofeedback became a legitimate tool. They demonstrated the clinical utility of EMG feedback by doing and reporting on the first EMG feedback study with tension headache patients (Budzynski, Stoyva, & Adler, 1970). Much of their work combined EMG biofeedback training with progressive relaxation, behavior therapy, and homework practice. EMG treatment procedures are usually confounded by these additional variables; therefore, it is difficult to assess which component is causally related to success. This question still has not been totally resolved, though the answer seems to lie in the interaction of the feedback, progressive relaxation, and homework. We support the concept that it is the holistic integration of the approach, not the separate parts, that is the major success contributor.

Along these lines, the articles by Otis, Low, and Turner (Chapter 35) and Schneider and Culver (Chapter 36) collate and summarize the practical issues and problems involved in the use of biofeedback training.

Another important application of EMG biofeedback, described by Fernando (Chapter 37), is in the area of physical rehabilitation. For more of an overview of biofeedback work in rehabilitation, the reader is referred to Owen, Toomin, & Taylor (1975).

The articles in this section cover a broad range and are suggestive of many other applications. Within the context of dysponesis, EMG training, embedded in generalized unstressing procedures, is a powerful tool for teaching the reduction of misdirected effort. This concept goes beyond the treatment of clinical pathology and suggests that each of us must learn unstressing procedures for continued health.

For more information, we suggest the following books by Whatmore and Kohli (1974) Marinacci (1968), Basmajian (1975), Malmo (1975), and Owen et al. (1975).

REFERENCES

Basmajian, J. V. *Muscles alive* (3d ed.). Baltimore: Williams & Wilkins, 1975.

Budzynski, T., Stoyva, J., & Adler, C. Feedback induced relaxation: Application to tension headache. *Journal of Behavior Therapy and Experimental Psychiatry*, 1970, *1*, 205.

Harrison, V. F., & Mortenson, O. A. Abstract of work in *Anatomical Record*, 1960, *136*, 207; 1962, *144*, 109.

Malmo, R. B. *On emotions, needs, and our archaic brain*. New York: Holt, Rinehart and Winston, 1975.

Marinacci, A. A. *Applied electromyography*. Philadelphia: Lea & Febiger, 1968.

Owen, S., Toomim, H., & Taylor, L. P. *Biofeedback in neuromuscular reeducation*. Los Angeles: Biofeedback Research Institute, 1975.

Whatmore, G. B., & Kohli, D. R. *The physiopathology and treatment of functional disorders*. New York: Grune & Stratton, 1974.

30

Muscle Action and the Sensory System

P. Strong

Fundamental relationships exist between muscle function, the sense receptors, the brain, the nervous system, and the peripheral nerves. The discussion of muscle function that follows includes a discussion of the physiology of the nervous system and the peripheral nerves. The brain is, at this stage, regarded as a processor.

THE MOTOR UNIT

The motor unit, as the name implies, is the biological unit of muscle function. A motor unit consists of a motor nerve arising from motoneurons in the brain stem or spinal cord and branching into various motor end plates. These motor end plates are each connected to an individual muscle fiber; stimulation of these motor end plates causes contraction of the single muscle fiber attached to it, as shown in Figure 1. The number of motor units varies among the different muscles of the body; generally speaking, the larger the muscle, the more motor units will be found in that muscle. The size of the motor unit, that is, the number of muscle fibers activated by the same nerve fiber, can be quite different for different muscles; in man, one motor unit may contain from 25 to 2000 muscle fibers. The force developed by a motor unit may range from 0.1 to 250 grams weight. *The muscle fibers of a motor unit are not clumped together in one part of the muscle, but rather the muscle fibers of different units are interlaced as shown in Figure 1.*

MUSCLE ACTION

A cell can only exist in its polarized or depolarized state; that is, it is a bistable device and intermediate potential levels are not stable. Motor nerves are also cellular in nature; therefore, any individual motor nerve can only exist in a polarized or depolarized state and will transmit only two potential levels to the motor end plates causing a bistable "on–off" action of the muscle fibers. Thus the individual muscle fibers of one motor unit can exist in only two states, a relaxed state and a tensed state. Normal muscular activity is characterized by smoothness

P. Strong • Tektronix, Inc., Beaverton, Oregon 97077.

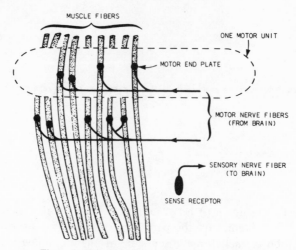

Figure 1. Relationship between nerve and muscle.

of movement, steadiness, and precision. These characteristics are due to the large number of motor units constituting any one muscle. If a small muscular effort is required, only one motor unit will be called into action; as increasing muscular effort is required, many more motor units are called into action until the muscle is providing maximum effort, at which time all motor units connecting to this muscle are being used. In this way, some smoothness of movement is obtained.

Additional smoothness of movement is obtained by modulating the number of muscle fiber contractions per unit time. Although an individual motor unit can result in only one level of muscular contraction, the number of times that this contraction occurs per unit time (the number of depolarizations and repolarizations executed by the motor end plate cells) will effectively increase the power of these muscle fibers. Thus the smoothness of movement of a muscle is controlled both by the number of motor units activated and by the rate at which these motor units are being activated.

THE MUSCULAR SERVOMECHANISM

A highly simplified block diagram of the nervous system controlling muscle action is shown in Figure 2. The system is similar to a servomechanism control system: A sense receptor or transducer produces a position or velocity signal, which is sent to the brain via the sensory nerve. The brain in turn initiates an "error" or control signal by comparing the measured position with the desired one stored in the memory. This signal is sent via the motor nerve to the muscle to control its action.

This servosystem can be demonstrated by the following experiment. When one's finger is placed on a cool object, the sense receptor in the finger senses the temperature and relays this information to the brain. The brain interprets this signal as coming from a cool object and thus does not necessarily initiate any signal to the motor nerves. If the finger is then placed on a warm object, the brain will interpret the information received from the sensory nerves as relating to a warm object and will activate the motor nerves controlling the muscles in the arms and the hand causing the finger to be lifted from the warm object. There is a time delay of several hundred milliseconds between the time that the sense receptor feels the warm object and the time that the finger is lifted from the warm object. This delay is governed largely by the degree of attention that the subject is paying to the warm object. Now, if the finger is placed on a hot object, a reflex is obtained and the finger is removed from the hot object in about 150 milliseconds. This reflex is active at all times although it is most marked for the hot object.

REFLEX RESPONSE

An emergency gate has been shown in Figure 2; this emergency gate is not markedly involved in normal receptor/muscle operation. When a reflex response is called for, however, this emergency gate bypasses the signal path to and from the brain and initiates a reflex response. This emergency gate is usually located within the spinal cord. Thus a reflex response results from a "large" signal, i.e., a high repetition rate signal, being received from a sense receptor. This signal bypasses the brain in the initiation of muscle action. These reflex responses protect the body from serious damage.

THE POTENTIAL GENERATED DURING MUSCLE ACTION

Depolarization initiated within a sense receptor travels to the brain along the sensory nerve fiber as a series of traveling depolarization waves. The brain then initiates another series of traveling waves of depolarization along the motor nerves to cause a series of depolarizations of the motor end plates. Depolarization of the motor end plates depolarizes cells within the muscle fiber causing contraction of these fibers. The actual internal cell potentials involved here are the normal cell polarized potential of -90 mV and the normal cell depolarized potential of $+20$ mV.

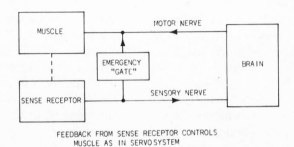

Figure 2. Block diagram of the nervous system.

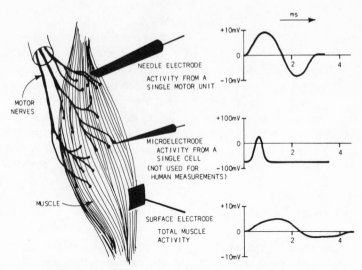

Figure 3. The EMG obtained with various electrode types.

In dealing with muscles and nerves, it is unusual to use microelectrodes to record the action potential within individual cells. More commonly, needle electrodes are used to record the net result of a number of cells such as one motor unit, or surface electrodes are used to record the results of many motor units. If a microelectrode were inserted into a muscle cell to observe the depolarization and repolarization process, the total process would occur in less than one millisecond. If, however, a needle electrode is placed near these muscle cells, it will detect current flow from many fibers of the corresponding motor unit. These fibers are being fired at their motor end plates at practically the same instant by the branching nerve. The different fibers of a motor unit do not, however, develop their action currents simultaneously; small time variations between the different fibers occur. These varying delays are due to the varying lengths of the terminal branches between the motor nerves and the muscle. Thus the excitation as it travels along is slightly ahead in some fibers compared with others. The result is that current flow in any small area from the cells constituting one motor unit lasts from 2 to 5 milliseconds, which is several times the duration of the current from any single muscle fiber. This asynchronous action helps produce smoothness of muscle tension.

With anything other than microelectrodes, the basic electrical activity detected in any muscle is the single motor unit action potential. These potentials from single motor units are best detected by concentric-needle electrodes or by insulated-needle electrodes, as shown in Figure 3. Single motor unit activity may sometimes be detected by placing a small electrode on the skin over the muscle. The volume of muscle influencing such an electrode is, however, considerable, and the actual recording is typically the total activity from many motor units having random relationships to one another. The potential produced by muscle action, whether recorded by needle electrodes or by surface electrodes, is known as the electromyogram or the EMG.

31

Control and Training of Individual Motor Units

John V. Basmajian

Experiments clearly demonstrate that with the help of auditory and visual cues man can single out motor units and control their isolated contractions. Experiments on the training of this control, interpreted as the training of descending pathways to single anterior horn cells, provide a new glimpse of the fineness of conscious motor controls. After training, subjects can recall into activity different single motor units by an effort of will while inhibiting the activity of neighbors. Some learn such exquisite control that they soon can produce rhythms of contraction in one unit, imitating drum rolls, etc. The quality of control over individual anterior horn cells may determine rates of learning.

It is a commonplace observation that very gentle contractions of skeletal muscles recruit only a few motor units and that, on relaxation, human beings can promptly repress all neuromuscular activity in large areas under voluntary control.[1] However, little attention has been paid to the fine voluntary control of individual motor units. In 1960 Harrison and Mortensen[2] reported that subjects were able to maintain isolated activity of several different motor units in the tibialis anterior as recorded from surface electrodes and confirmed by needle electrodes. The implications of this finding led to an intensive systematic investigation with special indwelling electrodes.

By definition, a motor unit includes a spinal anterior horn cell, its axon, and all the muscle fibers on which the terminal branches of the axon end (Figure 1). This motor unit "fires" when an impulse reaches the muscle fibers, the response being a brief twitch. The electrical potential accompanying the twitch is now well documented. The twitch frequency has an upper limit of about 50 per second. With indwelling electrodes, individual motor units are identifiable by their individual shapes; these remain relatively constant unless the electrodes are shifted.

The subjects of these experiments were provided with two modalities of "proprioception" that they normally lack, namely, they heard their motor unit potentials and saw them on monitors. The subjects were 16 normal persons ranging in age from 20 to 55. All but 5 were under 24 and only 1 was female.

The main muscle tested in all subjects was the right abductor pollicis brevis (Figure 2). In two subjects the tibialis anterior was also tested; in another, the biceps brachii and the extensor digitorum longus were tested on other occasions. The recording and monitoring apparatus is illustrated in Figure 2.

John V. Basmajian • Department of Medicine, McMaster University, and Chedoke Hospitals, Hamilton, Ontario, Canada.

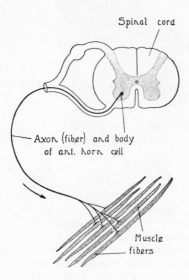

Figure 1. Diagram of a motor unit of skeletal muscle.

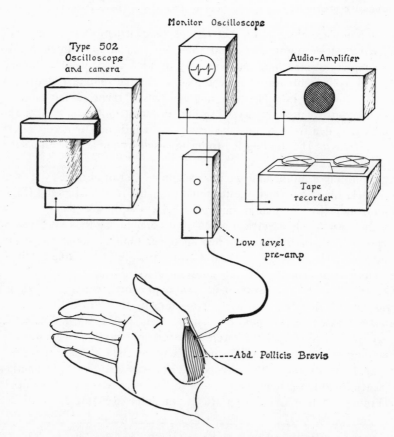

Figure 2. Technique of recording from abductor pollicis brevis.

The indwelling electrodes used have already been described in detail.[3] They are nylon-insulated Karma alloy wires .025 mm in diameter, which are introduced into the muscle as a pair by means of a hypodermic needle that is immediately withdrawn. In the case of a small muscle like the abductor pollicis brevis, the activity of all its motor units are probably detected while the fascial coat of the muscle isolates the pickup to this muscle alone.

After placement and connection of the electrodes, the subjects spent 5 to 10 minutes becoming familiar with the response of the electromyograph to a range of movements and postures. They were invariably amazed at the responsiveness to even the slightest effort. Then they began learning how to maintain very slight contractions, which were apparent to themselves only through the response of the apparatus. This led to increasingly more demanding effort involving many procedures intended to reveal both their natural talent in controlling individual motor units and their skill in learning and retaining tricks with such units. Individual units were identified by the characteristics of their potentials, which show considerable difference on the oscilloscope and, to a lesser extent, on the loudspeaker. Film recordings of potentials were made for confirmation (Figure 3).

Generally, experiments on one muscle were limited to about half a day. Within 15 to 30 minutes all subjects had achieved notably better willful control over gentle contractions. In this time almost all had learned to relax the whole muscle instantaneously on command and to recruit the activity of a single motor unit, keeping it active for as many minutes as desired. A few had difficulty maintaining the activity of such a unit, or in recruiting more units. No relationship was obvious to age, manual dexterity, or anything that might have been invoked as an underlying explanation of the differences in performance. Two of the apparently most dexterous persons performed only moderately well. The youngest persons were among both the worst and the best performers. General personality traits did not seem to matter.

After about 30 minutes the subject was required to learn how to repress the first motor unit he had become familiar with and to recruit another one. Most subjects were able to do this and gain mastery of the new unit in a matter of

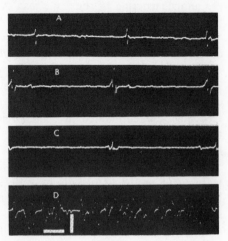

Figure 3. Electromyograms of potentials from motor units, A, B, and C, and a weak-to-moderate contraction (tracing D) in the abductor pollicis brevis of one subject. Calibrations lines: 25 msec and 200 μV.

minutes; only one subject required more than 15 minutes. More than half of the subjects could repeat the performance with a third new unit within a few minutes. A few subjects could recruit a fourth or a fifth isolated unit. The next problem facing a subject was to recruit, unerringly and in isolation, the several units over which he had gained control.

Here there was a considerable variation in skill. About one in four could respond easily to the command for isolated contractions of any of three units. About half the subjects displayed much less skill in this regard, even after several hours and even though they may have learned other bizarre tricks. Several subjects had particular difficulty in recruiting the asked-for units. They groped around in their conscious efforts to find them and sometimes, it seemed, only succeeded by accident.

The subjects with the finest control were then trained to learn various tricks. Several were tested for their powers of recalling specific units into activity in the *absence* of the aural and visual feedbacks that were so important to most of the subjects. Three subjects could recall units voluntarily under these handicaps, but they were unable to explain how they could do it.

Other tests showed that in all subjects the aural feedback is more useful than the visual display on the cathode ray tube monitor. The latter served only a subsidiary purpose.

After 60 to 90 minutes, most of the subjects were tested and trained in the production of specific rhythms. Almost all could reduce and increase the frequency of a well-controlled unit. It soon became apparent that motor units do not have a single characteristic frequency. Rather, they have an individual maximum rate below which their firing can be greatly slowed and single isolated contractions can be produced. Above the maximum rate that is characteristic for a specific unit, overflow takes place and other motor units are recruited.

Subjects learned to control units so that they could produce various rhythms. Almost all the subjects in the later experiments who were asked to try these (10 of 11) succeeded. Various gallop rhythms, drumbeat rhythms, doublets, and roll effects were produced and recorded. Excerpts of tape recordings were played to the annual meeting of the American Association of Anatomists, April 1963, as part of a paper of mine.

The experiments reported above suggest that pathways from the cerebral cortex can be made to stimulate single anterior horn cells while neighboring anterior horn cells remain dormant or are depressed. Although the skills learned in these experiments depended on aural and visual feedbacks from muscles, the controls are learned so quickly, are so exquisite, and are so well retained after the feedbacks are eliminated in some subjects that one must not dismiss them as tricks. The underlying mechanisms seem to involve active suppression of neighboring anterior horn cells.

A number of obvious problems emerge from the differences in the rates of learning of motor unit skills by different subjects. New but limited studies by Harrison[4] suggest that accomplished athletes have no better control than other subjects over their motor units. Future studies to ascertain the relation of rates of motor unit learning to dexterity, special abilities, and techniques of teaching motor skills are called for.

The extremely fine ability to adjust the rate of firing of individual motor units is a novel concept. Above a characteristic frequency, which varies from cell to cell, overflow to neighbors occurs. Detailed studies of these characteristics should expose some of the underlying control mechanism in the spinal cord.

ACKNOWLEDGMENT. This work was supported by grants from the Muscular Dystrophy Association of Canada and the Medical Research Council of Canada. Glenn Shine provided technical assistance.

REFERENCES

1. Basmajian, J. V. *Muscles alive: Their functions revealed by electromyography*. Baltimore: Williams and Wilkins, 1962. P. 7.
2. Harrison, V. F., & Mortensen, O. A. *Anatomical Record*, 1960, *136*, 207; 1962, *144*, 109. (Abstract)
3. Basmajian, J. V., & Stecko, G. *Journal of Applied Physiology*, 1962, *17*, 849.
4. Harrison, V. F. *Anatomical Record*, 1963, *145*, 237. (Abstract)

32

Facts versus Myths in EMG Biofeedback

John V. Basmajian

A rapidly thickening cloud of mythology about the technical aspects of electromyography that seriously affects professional use of biofeedback compels the writing of this essay. The impression grows daily that most users of EMG biofeedback have little or no understanding of the electrical events involved. Further, a substantial number seem not to care; apparently (to paraphrase the poet Thomas Gray), where ignorance is bliss (and money), 'tis folly to be wise!

The facts can be easily separated from the myths by those with long experience in EMG kinesiology. But few practitioners of biofeedback can have now or can acquire soon a clear knowledge of EMG from their present practices. They require clarification of the problems of technical gathering, recording, measuring (and so, the conscious influencing) of myopotentials.

Myopotentials are the electrical discharges from the surface membranes of the striated muscle fibers that make up the skeletal (voluntary) muscles. In normal whole muscles, these myopotentials are produced individually by a group of muscle fibers supplied by a single motor nerve fiber that runs from the body of a single motor nerve-cell in the gray matter of the spinal cord or brain stem. Each such group is a motor unit, and the spike potential produced each and every time a *motor unit* gives a mechanical twitch is a *motor unit potential* or *myopotential*.

At rest, the twitching of normal motor units is completely and easily stilled, but then they are recruited in increasing numbers and frequency as a contraction is increased in strength.

Individual myopotential spikes from intramuscular electrodes (needles or wires) measure about 500 μV in amplitude (with a wide range). With surface electrodes, however, they are often undetected, except when grouped together by a substantial contraction and gathered up from a wide area of the body. With superb surface-electrode techniques, single myopotentials from motor units near the surface can be detected. However, the standard electrode techniques current among most EMG biofeedback practitioners are quite inadequate to reflect single myopotentials, and of course this is not a problem, since surface electrodes are to be preferred except in special research. Fortunately, the better manufacturers provide circuits to integrate the substantial numbers of myopotentials that can come from muscular activity over a wide area. The output provides a useful (but

John V. Basmajian • Department of Medicine, McMaster University, and Chedoke Hospitals, Hamilton, Ontario, Canada.

unspecific) measure of the level of general muscular tension of the whole area of the body in a tense subject. Neither localization nor specification serves a purpose in relaxation training, because general tension is the target condition most biofeedback practitioners are working to reduce. Thus, the current craze over "microvolt levels" is just that—crazy.

To the EMG specialist, such pseudospecificity seems amusing, because it reflects vague and variable activities from a wide area, many muscles, and varying functions. For example, the electrode placements of many biofeedback workers who are supposedly picking up "frontalis muscle activity" actually reflect repeated swallowing, breathing, and movements of the jaws, tongue, lips, eyelids, and eyeballs, rather than real myopotentials originating in the frontalis muscle. At rest, all parts of the frontalis muscle in most people relax completely, but the muscle springs into vigorous EMG acctivity whenever the eyebrows are raised.

The foregoing facts mean that to be useful in biofeedback practice, integrated EMG from the forehead or frontal region need not come from frontalis muscle. Indeed, a wide source of myopotentials is much to be preferred as a reflection of general nervous tension. But we should know that (1) wide-source myopotentials are *not* "frontalis EMG," and (2) the numbers of "microvolts" produced on the meter of a commercial device or any other device simply indicate a microvolt reading at the input of the device. The integrated EMG from forehead surface electrodes generally reflects the total or global EMG of all sorts of repeated dynamic muscular activities down to about the first rib—along with some postural activity and nervous tension overactivity. The exact meter readouts can be taken with a grain of salt by the knowledgeable electromyographer at the same time as he is deliberately and wisely using them as (1) a rough indicator of progress in a clinical relaxation training program and (2) a visual placebo in reinforcing the patients' responses. Any higher level of reliance on such inflated numbers is self-deception.

Finally, a word on muscle reeducation with EMG biofeedback. To consider it as anything other than a modified form of rehabilitation medicine is to invoke mysticism once more. Rehabilitation therapists have been the basic technique without electronics for many years; electromyography simply gives the experienced practitioner instant reinforcement and conditioning of patients' responses, and this reinforcement and conditioning have permitted dramatic acceleration or initiation of recovery in some neuromotor conditions in some patients.

Once more, users of biofeedback techniques should be warned about the localizing and generalizing of EMG pickups that depend heavily on the placement of electrodes. Most novices seem to be completely deceived by generous "cross talk" from muscles other than the target. Even experienced physical therapists and physicians can be confused for a time, but their knowledge of anatomy and muscular function should get them out of trouble. For biofeedback specialists who do not have a thorough training in rehabilitation therapies, it is folly to proceed on specific muscle retraining. Indeed, it may be medical or professional malpractice.

33

Dysponesis: A Neurophysiologic Factor in Functional Disorders

George B. Whatmore and Daniel R. Kohli

This chapter discusses a physiopathologic state that is a hidden etiologic factor in a number of common clinical syndromes, and can give rise to a variety of functional disturbances within the organism. It is basically a reversible physiopathologic state composed of errors in energy expenditure that interfere with nervous system function and thus with control of organ function. Its detrimental influence is exerted by means of excitatory and inhibitory patterns of signal input at widespread points within the complex networks of the nervous system, resulting in reduction in the organism's productivity and disturbance of its emotional reactivity, ideation, and central regulation of various organs of the body. Most of this energy expenditure, covert in nature, goes unnoticed by both the person expending it and those who observe him. Diagnosis is based upon history, physical examination, and laboratory and psychological tests. Electromyometric studies are a necessary part of each patient work-up whenever dysponesis is suspected.

Treatment is a form of neurophysiologic engineering wherein basic principles of neurophysiology are used to carry on a retraining within the nervous system. Specific instances to which the patient overreacts are identified so that he can be "desensitized" to them through application of the principles of effort management. The patient is trained to observe at least some of the covert efforts that he makes unknowingly. Electromyometry, electromyophony, electromyoscopy, and other procedures are used for teaching purposes to delineate and objectify these efforts and bring them into the realm of observable phenomena, and much electronically monitored instruction and practice are necessary. The patient is then trained to take these energy expenditures into account with a minimum of fuss and attention as he goes about his daily activities. The quality of therapeutic result is directly proportional to the proficiency attained by the patient.

The purpose of this chapter is to discuss a fairly common physiopathologic state that is to a large extent overlooked in present-day medical practice. Its importance lies in its being a hidden etiologic factor in several clinical syndromes. The condition has been overlooked, hence ineffectively treated, until recently because ordinary examination procedures do not detect it. Recent advances in neurophysiologic knowledge and instrumentation have made recognition as well as treatment of this condition possible.

Most diseases consist of physiologic reactions that lead to organ dysfunction. These physiologic reactions constitute the response of the organism to some

George B. Whatmore and Daniel R. Kohli • Pacific Northwest Research Foundation; and Private Practice (Internal Medicine and Functional Disorders), Medical-Dental Building, Seattle, Washington 98101.

noxious agent, whether microbial, chemical, or mechanical. For example, pneumonia is the outpouring of leucocytes and exudate into the lung spaces in response to the presence of a microbe. Hay fever consists of vasodilatation, lacrimation, and mucous secretion in response to an allergen. Silicosis is the organism's attempt to isolate a penetrating foreign substance. The physiologic reaction is the disease, and the result is organ dysfunction.

The present discussion will extend this concept of disease to include a physiopathologic state composed of neurophysiologic reactions to various agents. To avoid semantic confusion while discussing this entity, we suggest the descriptive name *dysponesis*—"dys" meaning bad, faulty, or wrong, and "ponos" meaning effort, work, or energy. The term thus identifies the basic nature of the condition, namely, a physiopathologic state made up of errors in energy expenditure within the nervous system.

Dysponesis is capable of producing a variety of functional disturbances within the organism. By affecting nervous system function, it can alter the regulation and thereby organ function of almost any system of the body. Among the numerous clinical manifestations are fatigue and exhaustion, insomnia, headache, backache, hyperventilation, anxiety and depression, "indigestion," impotence, frigidity, and spastic colon.

Dysponesis can occur by itself or can accompany and complicate other illnesses. It can produce symptoms that might be attributed to a neurosis but it is not a neurosis in the sense that symptoms are symbolic of unconscious conflicts. It can also produce symptoms that might be attributed erroneously to anatomical or biochemical pathology. If a patient's symptoms have their origin in dysponesis but he is treated only for structural disease or only to resolve psychological problems, results will be disappointing, for dysponesis is a neurophysiologic response pattern that will survive these forms of treatment. On the other hand, if the patient's symptoms are the result of factors other than dysponesis, or in addition to dysponesis, results will be disappointing if treatment is limited to measures for correcting dysponesis. It therefore becomes important for us to have a clear understanding of the entity dysponesis if we are to recognize it in our patients and if we are to treat it effectively.

PRELIMINARY CONSIDERATIONS

Before we can obtain a clear picture of the basic nature of dysponesis, we must first examine from a neurophysiologic point of view the types of effort of which the human organism is capable.

By effort, or ponesis, we mean the production of nerve impulses (or action potentials) in pathways extending from motor and premotor cortical neurons through pyramidal and extrapyramidal tracts to and including the peripheral musculature. This portion of the nervous system is referred to as the voluntary, volitional, or somatic portion of the motor system, as contrasted to the autonomic, visceral, or involuntary portion. Its pathways participate in all voluntary motor activity. Action potentials constituting effort can be recorded by appropriate electronic instruments at any point along these pathways from the cerebral cortex to the peripheral musculature.

Our daily lives are made up of various sequences and combinations of effort. Although some of these efforts are observable outwardly in the form of overt performances, many are not detectable with the unaided eye. These latter efforts usually go unnoticed by both the person making them and others observing him, but they must be taken into consideration if we are to obtain a clear picture of dysponesis and its effects on the organism. Any classification of effort from a neurophysiologic standpoint must include them.

One such classification that assists us greatly in understanding dysponesis divides the efforts making up daily life into four basic categories as follows.

Performing Efforts. These are the efforts by which we walk, talk, lift objects, drive a car, hammer a nail, and so on. We carry out some "performance" that is observable outwardly. These efforts are readily recognized as effort by everyone and consist mainly of learned motor skills.

Bracing Efforts. These are the efforts by which we hold the body, or a part of the body, rigid or "on guard." A steady effort is maintained that prepares us for quick initiation of performing efforts, for "fight or flight" in many instances. Often one effort is pitted against another, one muscle contracted against its antagonist. These efforts can be made in any or all parts of the body such as the extremities, the breathing musculature, the neck, the back, the jaw, the tongue, and the throat.

Bracing efforts can be violent or extremely small. Although some of them are readily observable, most of them go unnoticed by both the person making them and others observing him.

Representing Efforts. These are the efforts by which we bring forth within ourselves, in substitute form, objects or events or phenomena that are not at the moment impinging upon our sense organs. They constitute a form of self-signaling. We can represent objects we have seen but which are not now before us, sensations we have experienced but which are not present at the moment, past events, possible future events, problems or issues, goals, concepts, and so on. Specific sequences and constellations of effort are a necessary part of this process. Without these efforts, representations do not occur. Thinking, remembering, anticipating, daydreaming, and worrying are partly made up of representing efforts.

The efforts that play a vital role in representation are for the most part not recognized as effort by the person making them unless he has been trained to observe them, and are not detectable by external observers using only the naked eye.

For example, minute eye efforts participate in the production of visual images and the particular eye efforts made vary with the characteristics of the visual image (Deckert, 1964; Dement & Kleitman, 1957; Jacobson, 1930, 1938; Lorens & Darrow, 1962; Totten, 1935). Without the eye effort there is no visual image. Tongue, throat, and other speech region efforts participate in the formation of auditory images of words or other sounds (Gould, 1949, 1950; Jacobson, 1931, 1938; Max, 1937). They are part of the process of carrying on inner speech or subvocal speech. Visual imagery and auditory imagery are two common forms of representation.

Representation of movement of a part of one's body can be accomplished (1) by eye efforts to picture or visualize the part in motion (2) by very slight efforts in motor pathways to the part "as if" to move that part of the body, or (3) by both of these simultaneously (Allers & Scheminzky, 1926; Jacobson, 1930a,b,d, 1931, 1938; Max, 1937; Shaw, 1940). Efforts of inner speech can also participate.

Additional evidence for the participation of efforts in the process of representation is found in studies of dreaming and in studies of deaf-mutes. Dreams of a visual nature are accompanied by eye efforts that correspond in pattern to what is being visualized. These efforts can be so large that gross eye movements are observable through the dreamer's lids or they can be smaller and recorded graphically by measuring corneoretinal potentials (Aserinsky & Kleitman, 1955; Dement & Kleitman, 1957). Dreams of carrying out bodily movements are accompanied by efforts, measurable electromyographically and sometimes overtly observable, in the corresponding parts of the body and in patterns corresponding to the movement dreamed of (Wolpert, 1960). Deaf-mutes who have learned sign language to communicate with others make upper extremity efforts, measurable electromyographically, as part of dreaming and also as a part of abstract thinking (Max, 1935, 1937). In addition, we have all heard persons speaking aloud in their sleep as a part of the dreaming process and talking audibly or making visible lip movements as they think about something while awake.

Thinking or ideation is a complex process involving widespread circuits within the nervous system, and there are many details of this mechanism yet to be worked out. But the combinations of effort and sensory image that we call "representing" make up an important part of it.

Attention Efforts. These are the efforts by which the organism allows impulses arriving from some sense organs to have a greater influence on nervous system function than those arriving from others. They are the efforts by which we direct our attention from one thing to another or hold our attention on something. Attention can be directed to events in our external environment or to events within ourselves, including our representations, and it can shift very quickly from one item to another. What we observe at a given moment is dependent upon the state of our attention at that moment. Eye efforts are an essential part of the act of directing attention. (This holds true only for persons not born blind.) Attention can be directed by means of gross eye efforts to turn the eyes toward a source of stimulation or by means of minute efforts "as if" to turn the eyes toward a source of stimulation. The tiny attention efforts go unnoticed as such by the person making them unless he has been trained to observe them, and they are not detectable by external observers using only their unaided eyes (Amadeo & Shagass, 1963; Jacobson, 1938; Whatmore, unpublished data).

Although many efforts in the bracing, representing, and attention categories are made unknowingly and go unnoticed as such by both the person making them and others observing him, they play an important role in nervous system function and in the production of disturbances in its function.

BASIC NATURE OF DYSPONESIS

Dysponesis is a reversible physiopathologic state composed of neurophysiologic reactions to various agents and the repercussions of these reactions throughout the organism. The agent to which the organism is reacting can be an environmental event, a bodily sensation, an emotion, or a thought. The neurophysiologic reactions consist mainly of covert errors in energy expenditure via motor and premotor cortical neurons, pyramidal and extrapyramidal tracts, and their extensively ramifying side branches and feedback pathways, as the organism attempts to cope with, or adapt to, the agent. Instead of assisting the organism, these energy expenditures act as an interference phenomenon in nervous system functioning.

The term *energy expenditure* is used here in a physiologic sense, referring to the occurrence of action potentials in motor nerve fibers and in muscle fibers, contraction in muscle fibers, and the biochemical changes associated with these processes. We are not referring to the abstract "psychic energy" used in psychodynamic theory since we are discussing a basic physiopathologic state.

Dysponesis is thus made up principally of those covert misdirected efforts we make each day that have a detrimental influence on the organism. Most of them lie in the bracing, representing, and attention categories and, being covert in nature, go unnoticed by both the person making them and others observing him. They occur concomitantly with our productive efforts and interfere with the efficiency, productivity, and health of the organism. The detrimental influence of these misdirected efforts results from the fact that action potentials (or nerve impulses) constituting effort not only follow the well-known pathways from motor and premotor cortex to anterior horn cells, and thus to muscle fibers, but also feed signals (by way of side branches and feedback mechanisms) into the reticular activating system, the hypothalamus, the limbic system, and the neocortex, thus producing widespread additional effects. These signals exert excitatory and inhibitory influences that are inappropriate to the immediate objectives of the organism. The result is an interference with many aspects of nervous system function including the organism's emotional reactivity, its ideation, and the regulation of various organs of the body. The known pathways by which dysponesis can produce such diverse effects in the organism are summarized in Figure 1.

An example may help to clarify the basic nature of dysponesis. If a person is being attacked by a wild animal, or by a bandit in a dark alley, a certain amount of bracing effort is appropriate. In conjunction with an appropriate fear response, it prepares the person for quick initiation of performing efforts (such as fight or flight) and activates autonomic mechanisms that give physiologic and biochemical support to violent exertion. If a person braces similarly in a social gathering or when he has to speak before an audience, the bracing becomes inappropriate and interferes with effective functioning. The autonomic responses it arouses are also inappropriate. Increased heart rate, elevation of blood pressure, secretion of adrenalin and other hormones, mobilization of glucose and fatty acids, and numerous other emergency responses all prepare the organism for vio-

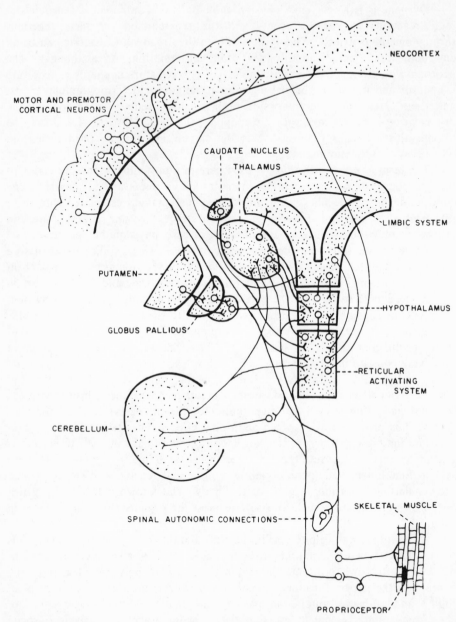

Figure 1. Diagram showing known pathways by which effort (ponesis) can affect structures playing an important role in autonomic activity (hypothalamus), emotional reactivity (limbic system), and ideation (neocortex).

lent muscular exertion, yet no such exertion is called for. Both the bracing and the autonomic responses interfere with a person's productive efforts (carrying on a conversation or speaking before an audience) and give rise to discomfort. In addition, they interfere with normal organ function. If frequent and prolonged, they may give rise to tissue alteration of a pathological nature. Thus the well-intentioned but misdirected bracing efforts operate to the organism's detriment. They constitute one of the numerous forms of energy expenditure that make up dysponesis.

The efforts composing dysponesis constitute one process in a complex system of interacting processes and can disturb the entire system. These interactions are shown in Figure 2. In this diagram, broken lines indicate connections that can be modified by learning or conditioning and continuous lines those that are inborn.

Dysponesis can be intermittent or continuous. In its early stages it is often intermittent, the misdirected efforts being made only in response to particular environmental situations, bodily sensations, emotions, or thoughts. But as time passes—often a matter of years—and the organism unknowingly becomes more proficient in making dysponetic responses, they tend to be made more frequently, until finally the person can be maintaining this type of energy expenditure continuously. Although this energy expenditure makes the organism more vulnerable to various disturbances in bodily function, it is possible for dysponesis to be present for variable periods, perhaps even for a lifetime, without symptoms of any great significance as far as the individual himself perceives them, or with only intermittent symptoms that concern him. Yet he is made vulnerable by the presence of dysponesis, and some chance event in life can trigger incapacitating symptoms.

ETIOLOGY AND PATHOGENESIS

The etiology of dysponesis has not been clearly established because of the myriad of influences to which each individual is subjected during a lifetime. Whether dysponesis is inherited or acquired, or is a combination of these, is not known. If inherited factors are present, their elucidation will come with further advances in our knowledge of genetics. If we assume that dysponesis is acquired, a fairly reasonable etiology and pathogenesis can be postulated.

We suggest that the physiopathologic reactions constituting dysponesis are basically learned responses. Each person, as a result of his own particular life experiences, learns many different motor responses. Some of these are appropriate in one situation but become inappropriate and a detriment to him in other situations. Others are inappropriate at any time. For example, the southern drawl of a person raised in South Carolina or the umlaut vowels of a German are learned speech-muscle sequences that are appropriate in their original setting but become not only inappropriate but actually a handicap when they are carried over into other languages and other locales. The inadvertent motor responses that cause the golfer to slice, hook, or top the ball are inappropriate whenever they

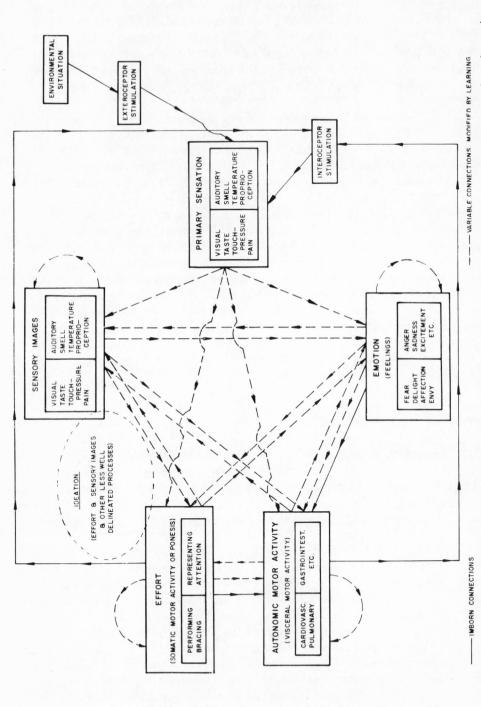

Figure 2. Diagram showing the position of effort in the interaction of several basic nervous system processes. Inborn connections are shown by continuous lines, and connections that can be modified by learning are shown by segmented lines.

occur. These examples illustrate how learned motor responses can be disadvantageous to an individual.

The physiopathologic motor responses constituting dysponesis may originate in a similar manner. For example, a person may learn at one time to brace appropriately to threatening environmental situations that require the quick initiation of performing efforts (such as fight or flight) and then unknowingly utilize these covert bracing efforts in his attempt to meet intellectual threats or challenges not requiring the rapid initiation of performing efforts. The bracing under these circumstances becomes inappropriate and a detriment to him by mechanisms described in other sections of this chapter. Since the bracing efforts are made unknowingly and there is no automatic signaling system to correct these errors, the person tends to persist in making them and through repetition to become more proficient in making them. Misdirected representing and attention efforts may be learned inadvertently during trial-and-error behavior in the attempt to cope with or adapt to life situations. Or they may be learned by imitation through constant association with a person who makes such efforts frequently and often expresses his representations aloud. They may also result partly from the presence of inappropriate bracing efforts and the disorganizing effects of these on the limbic system and neocortex (see Figures 1 and 2).

Although we do not attempt at present to delineate the precise conditioning experiences or the genetic factors, if any, that give rise to dysponesis, further observation and investigation should enable us to be more specific. Basic principles of instrumental and classical conditioning, and of learning theory in general, will undoubtedly assist us in eventually elaborating the etiology and pathogenesis of dysponesis.

PHYSIOLOGIC EFFECTS OF DYSPONESIS, WITH SUPPORTING EVIDENCE

Although the hypotheses concerning dysponesis and its effects on the organism are based upon available evidence that is neither complete nor fully conclusive, it is sufficient to justify the concept, and so far no contrary evidence has been found. It is our hope that further research will be stimulated by this presentation.

The specific effects that dysponesis will have in a given person at a given time are determined by several factors:

1. The inherited constitutional characteristics of the individual. This includes the gene-determined aspects of such characteristics as the number of neurons composing the nervous systems, their location, size, shape, biochemical composition, interconnections, and the composition of the internal environment bathing the neurons. It also includes gene-determined characteristics of other systems of the body.
2. Acquired characteristics of the individual, characteristics resulting from the person's total past experience. This includes the results of previous learning as well as any changes in structure or metabolism resulting from injury, disease, or pharmacologic agents.

3. Activity going on within the neuronal networks of the nervous system at the time they are subjected to dysponetic influences.
4. The duration, magnitude, and distribution of the particular dysponesis present at that time.

Dysponesis affects emotional reactivity. The ability to experience many different emotions is built into the human organism, and emotions are of value to us when they are appropriate in amount and kind. Dysponesis can inhibit some emotional reactions, exaggerate others, or lead to inappropriate emotions depending upon the circumstances of the moment. This makes it difficult for a dysponetic person to know his real feelings (emotions) about persons or events in his life. These effects of dysponesis on emotional reactivity are probably mediated by way of connections between pyramidal–extrapyramidal pathways and the reticular activating system, the hypothalamus, and the thalamus and thereby to the limbic system (see Figure 1). In addition, there are probably direct connections between pyramidal–extrapyramidal pathways and the limbic system. The limbic system occupies an important position in emotional experience (MacLean, 1955; Papez, 1937).

Laboratory evidence for the influence of somatic motor activity on emotional reactivity is found in (1) diminished emotional reactivity in cats following administration of curarelike substances (anectin) in dosages sufficient to produce only an effect on the neuromuscular junction (Gellhorn, 1957; Gellhorn & Loofbourrow, 1963); (2) the decreased hypothalamic excitability resulting from such dosages of curare as measured with implanted electrodes (Gellhorn, 1957, 1958; Gellhorn & Loofbourrow, 1963); (3) the effects of a learned reduction in somatic motor activity on emotion (Jacobson, 1938); and (4) the increased hypothalamic excitability produced by proprioceptive impulses (Bernhaut, Gellhorn, & Rasmussen, 1953). There is clinical evidence that dysponesis may play an etiologic role in the production of depression (Whatmore, 1966; Whatmore & Ellis, 1962).

Dysponesis is also able to affect a person's ideation. For example it can distort his perception of environmental events, what he thinks is happening to him, and what he thinks he would like to do about it. It may also play a role in the production of delusions and hallucinations. This effect of dysponesis on ideation is probably brought about by a direct effect on neocortical function and also by way of an action on the reticular activating system, the hypothalamus, the limbic system, and the effects of these in turn on the neocortex (see Figure 1).

Evidence for an influence of effort on ideation comes from several sources. First, the necessary pathways and connections that would enable effort to affect structures participating in ideation are present within the nervous system (see Figure 1). The neocortex is an important component of these structures in contrast to the limbic system, which plays a more important role in emotion (MacLean, 1955; Papez, 1937). Second, specific effects of effort on the neocortex have been demonstrated. Proprioceptive impulses, which are ordinarily initiated by effort, have been shown by direct recordings to produce a diffuse increase in cerebral cortical excitability (Bernhaut et al., 1953; Gellhorn, 1957, 1958; Hodes, 1962). In addition, descending effort impulses as well as the ascending proprioceptive ones give evidence of playing a role in maintenance of consciousness (Jacobson, 1938; Kleitman, 1963; Magoun, 1963) and through this effect on the waking state can affect ideation. Cortical motor neurons also affect the excitability of other cortical neurons directly by intracortical and association fibers and by short pathways through subcortical nuclei (Bubnoff & Heidenhain, 1949; Dusser de Barenne & McCulloch, 1939; Lorenté de No, 1943). Laboratory studies on human subjects give support to an influence of effort on thought processes (Jacobson, 1938). Clinical studies suggest that dysponesis may play a role in the ideational disturbances of acute schizophrenic episodes (Gould, 1949, 1950; Whatmore, 1966; Whatmore & Ellis, 1964).

Dysponesis can disturb autonomic function. This is accomplished not only by way of its effect on emotion but also by a direct effect on autonomic centers. This fact supplies an additional mechanism to help explain various disturbances in visceral and vascular function not related to emotional states.

It has been demonstrated experimentally that effort can directly influence autonomic activity by means of at least three levels within the nervous system. At the farthest downstream level, it initiates proprioceptive impulses that, in laboratory studies, have been shown to increase hypothalamic excitability (Bernhaut et al., 1953; Gellhorn, 1957, 1958), the hypothalamus being one of the higher centers of autonomic control. Motor and premotor cortical neurons can also affect autonomic activity at the hypothalamic level by way of circuits through the basal ganglia and by direct connections (Kennard, 1947). Pyramidal tract impulses can also effectively augment autonomic functions at the spinal level, separately from the hypothalamus and its descending path (Landau, 1953).

Studies in dogs have shown that effort without emotion is sufficient to produce autonomic changes (Rushmer, 1955). Studies in human beings have shown the effect of effort on blood pressure and heart rate, on sweat secretion, and on smooth muscle tonus of the gastrointestinal tract independent of emotion (Freeman & Simpson, 1938; Jacobson, 1925, 1936, 1939, 1940a,b).

Dysponesis can also alter primary sensation (Buytendijk, 1955; Miller, 1926) and reflexes. It can augment or inhibit reflexes, depending upon the circumstances. Clinical evidence for the effect of somatic motor activity on reflex activity is found in the well-known effect of hand clasping in augmenting the knee-jerk. Laboratory studies have demonstrated the effect of effort on the knee-jerk, the flexion response to a painful stimulus, and the startle response to a loud sound (Jacobson, 1926; Jacobson & Carlson, 1925; Lundervold, 1952; Miller, 1926).

It is likely that dysponesis can overstimulate the pituitary–adrenal axis by way of its effect on the hypothalamus and a humoral connection between the hypothalamus and the anterior pituitary. If prolonged, this overstimulation could lead to cardiovascular and other tissue damage. Dysponesis may also affect thyroid and other endocrine gland function in some persons through the hypothalamus and anterior pituitary.

There is considerable evidence that stress and emotion can affect endocrine function and that hypothalamic neurons can activate a humoral mechanism enabling the nervous system to affect the anterior pituitary and hence its target endocrine organs (Nalbandov, 1963). However, the authors are not aware of any studies demonstrating a direct effect of effort, as here defined, on endocrine function. There is, however, indirect evidence for such a relationship at least with regard to the adrenotropic hormone of the anterior pituitary. It has been shown by implanted-electrode studies that direct stimulation of the posterior hypothalamus evokes secretion of ACTH by way of a portal system connection with the anterior pituitary (Mason, 1958), and that proprioceptive impulses increase the excitability of the posterior hypothalamus (Bernhaut et al., 1953; Gellhorn, 1957, 1958; Gellhorn & Loofbourrow, 1963). Effort could thus affect anterior pituitary and adrenal–cortical function by way of its excitatory effect on the posterior hypothalamus.

There are numerous further indications that motor activity, particularly covert motor activity, occupies a fundamental position in nervous system functioning (Bender, 1956; Bull, 1962; Haugen, Dixon, & Dickel, 1958; King, 1954; Kleitman, 1963; Max, 1934; Sperry, 1952). It is not just an end product of ideation and emotion, but instead is intimately involved in both of these processes.

ROLE OF DYSPONESIS IN VARIOUS CLINICAL SYNDROMES

By way of these effects of effort on nervous system function, dysponesis is capable of giving rise to a variety of clinical entities and provides physiologic methods of treatment to be described in a later section of this chapter. In understanding how these occur, the reader should keep in mind the circuits of Figure 1. The following explanations are based upon available laboratory and clinical evidence and are proposed not as final answers but as tentative hypotheses.

Anxiety

Dysponesis is able to activate the limbic system in such a way as to give rise to acute or chronic anxiety (for data related to this concept, see Barlow, 1955; Bernhaut et al., 1953; Dickel, Dixon, Shanklin & Davidson, 1955; Garmany, 1952; Gellhorn, 1957, 1958; Gellhorn & Loofbourrow, 1963; Haugen et al., 1958; Jacobson, 1926, 1938, 1964; Malmo & Shagass, 1949; Malmo, Shagass, & Davis, 1951; Sainsbury & Gibson, 1954). The mechanism is similar to that by which stimulating electrodes inserted into the limbic system can give rise to anxiety. It is a neuronal stimulation effect brought about by dysponesis feeding signals into this system. Both bracing and representing efforts contribute to the process.

Bracing raises the level of arousal of the organism and increases excitability of the limbic system, and when inappropriate it leads to an exaggeration of appropriate fear responses. Under some circumstances, bracing can elicit inappropriate fear or anxiety directly.

The representing of a dreaded event, one that may or may not actually occur, tends to elicit an appropriate fear or concern that is of value to the organism, but when it is accompanied by inappropriate bracing and when it goes on to a repetitious and inappropriate representing and rerepresenting of the event, the organism experiences exaggerated fear or anxiety, even panic.

Digestive System Disturbances

By affecting autonomic function via the mechanisms described previously, dysponesis often disturbs secretion and smooth muscle activity of the digestive tract (Jacobson, 1925, 1938). Increased peristaltic activity, decreased peristaltic activity, segmental spasm or diffuse spasm, and hypersecretion of gastric juice or of colon mucous are common manifestations. Altered autonomic outflow also produces vascular changes seen as mucosal hyperemia or blanching. Some of the resulting clinical entities are known as globus hystericus, spastic esophagus, duodenal ulcer, spastic colon, irritable colon, and mucous colitis.

Circulatory System Disturbances

Also by way of its influence on autonomic function, dysponesis is able to produce tachycardia and elevate blood pressure, and probably plays a role in conjunction with hereditary factors in the production of essential hypertension (Jacobson, 1936, 1939, 1940a,b,c).

Impotence and Frigidity

Penile erection in the male, vaginal secretion in the female, and orgasm in both are autonomic functions and are inhibited by certain patterns of dysponesis. The result is impotence and frigidity.

Headache and Backache

Sustained bracing in the back and neck musculature and in the frontalis muscle, whether in response to pleasant or unpleasant events, is a common cause of backache and headache. These efforts can lead directly to pain but often fatigue-spasm and myostatic contracture (a reversible physiologic contracture) resulting from the efforts are mediating agents (Davis & Malmo, 1951; Dickel, Dixon, Stoner, & Shanklin, 1958; Dixon & Dickel, 1967; Dixon, O'Hara, & Peterson, 1967; Gasser, 1930; Holmes & Wolff, 1952; Malmo, Shagass, & Davis, 1950; Rinehart & Dixon, 1961; Sainsbury & Gibson, 1954; Shagass & Malmo, 1954; Wolff, 1963). Migraine headaches originate in a disturbance of autonomic function leading first to vasoconstriction in localized portions of the cerebral cortex followed by vasodilatation of the extracranial or dural branches of the external carotid arteries. The head pain is produced by arterial distention and also by edema of the artery wall. This sequence of autonomic changes is readily triggered in predisposed individuals by a variety of dysponetic patterns (Whatmore, unpublished data).

Insomnia

If a person continues to make bracing and representing efforts after retiring for the night, he keeps the reticular activating system active, and sleep is prevented, resulting in insomnia (Jacobson, 1938, 1964; Kleitman, 1939/1963). The mechanism is similar to that by which a person who walks instead of getting into bed will keep himself awake by his own performing efforts. In sleep deprivation experiments, it was found that one of the best ways to keep a sleep-deprived subject awake was to keep him walking (Kleitman, 1939/1963). Sleep deprivation has to be extreme before sleep can occur during the act of walking. Bracing and representing efforts keep a person awake by the same basic mechanism, namely, stimulation of the reticular activating system, but they are not so readily noticed as performing efforts.

Fatigue States

Fatigue and exhaustion are commonly the result of dysponesis. A pleasant fatigue, wherein the person feels tired yet "wonderful" follows moderate or marked performing efforts. This is a normal physiologic process. Dysponesis leads to an unpleasant fatigue, often occurring in the absence of performing efforts. Sustained bracing effort is one form of dysponesis capable of bringing this about. The human organism is constructed to carry out a reciprocal, rhythmical, intermittent type of motor activity and is not constituted to maintain prolonged bracing. Reciprocal activity tends to build up energy reserves in muscle tissue, whereas sustained bracing tends to deplete them, resulting in fatigue (Dixon, Peterson, Dickel, Jones & West, 1952; Rinehart & Dixon, 1961; Watkins, Cobb, Finesinger, Brazier, Shands, & Pincus, 1947).

However, dysponetic mechanisms other than sustained bracing also lead to unpleasant fatigue. Misdirected representing efforts are able to lead to the subjective experience of fatigue, in the presence of adequate energy reserves, simply by their failure to arouse the organism sufficiently. It is a common observation that some types of representing are activity-propelling whereas other types lack this quality. A person who is continually representing and rerepresenting his plight or predicament and doesn't go beyond this to the representing of possible solutions and goals is simply failing to activate the emotional and autonomic responses that give physiologic and biochemical support to overt action; hence performing efforts are experienced as a difficult task.

Attention efforts also play a role in the production of fatigue sensations. Attention to a specific sensory input has been shown to lower the sensory threshold to that input by an action on the primary cortex or some more peripheral structure (Deutsch & Deutsch, 1963). The giving of excessive attention to how we feel lowers our threshold for the perception of bodily discomfort. Mild sensations of fatigue that would ordinarily not be noticed are then "ballooned" out of proportion, giving rise to undue fatigue.

Depression

Dysponesis is at least one factor in the production of depression, and the role it plays is similar to that which it plays in the production of fatigue. Fatigue and depression are probably closely related physiologically. One can shift readily to the other and both are often present simultaneously. Anxious patients who are both fatigued and depressed exhibit a marked reduction of high energy phosphates in muscular tissue (Dixon et al., 1952). High energy reserves of nervous tissue are probably reduced still further. Whether neuronal fatigue leads to subjective sensations of fatigue or of depression may depend upon such variables as the location of the neurons involved.

In many instances of depression, an increased bracing has been present for a long time before the depression begins, and it is also present during the depression (Whatmore & Ellis, 1959, 1962). Sustained bracing, by its action on the limbic system and its tendency to deplete high energy phosphate reserves, makes a person more prone to depression and can change an appropriate feeling of sadness into severe depression.

Misdirected representing efforts also play a role in the production of depression. They often occur immediately prior to an episode of depression and appear to act as triggering agents (Beck, 1963, 1964; Whatmore, unpublished data). If a person begins to represent and rerepresent his plight or predicament (as he perceives it) and doesn't go beyond this to the representing of possible solutions and goals, he is doing a type of representing that brings no solutions but only arouses emotion such as sadness or depression. The presence of concurrent bracing efforts exaggerates the emotion, even to the point of severe depression, and impels the person to continue making the same misdirected representing efforts compulsively, thus keeping himself depressed. Furthermore, the repetitiveness of the representing distorts the person's perception of his predicament, perhaps through a neuronal fatigue mechanism. If, in addition, the person braces to that which he represents, this additional bracing still further distorts his perception of the predicament, increases the emotional response further, and produces more depletion of high energy reserves.

Hyperventilation Syndrome

Increased performing efforts in the breathing musculature, carried out unknowingly as one copes with a threat not requiring violent exertion, can lead to hyperventilation and its consequent syndrome. This is not a reflex increase in rate and/or depth of breathing but a voluntary participation in breathing carried out unintentionally. Increased bracing efforts in the breathing musculature sometimes lead to hypoventilation and this in turn to hyperventilation (Kaufman, 1951; Wolf, 1947).

Eczema and Neurodermatitis

There is reason to believe that increased performing efforts in the form of scratching play a role in the production and maintenance of eczema and neurodermatitis (Bobroff, 1962). However, misdirected bracing, representing, and attention efforts also play a role by lowering sensory thresholds and contributing to compulsive scratching.

Obsessions, Compulsions, Hypochondriasis, and Schizophrenia

Disturbances in limbic and neocortical function resulting from dysponesis contribute to the production of obsessive–compulsive states and hypochondriasis and may even play a role in acute schizophrenic episodes (Haugen et al., 1958; Jacobson, 1938, 1941; Whatmore, 1966; Whatmore & Ellis, 1964).

Myocardial Infarction

A particular type of overt behavior pattern has been reported to be associated with a high incidence of clinical coronary artery disease in young and middle-aged persons, and etiologic significance has been attributed to this way of life (Friedman & Rosenman, 1959; Rosenman & Friedman, 1961, 1963). The behavior pattern consists of such elements as enhanced drive, competitiveness, ambitiousness, and an excessive sense of urgency of time, with habitual involvement in multiple pursuits subject to "deadline" pressures. The covert behavior patterns (dysponetic patterns) of these people have not been determined but may be of even greater significance than the overt behavior in the etiology of coronary artery disease.

DIAGNOSIS OF DYSPONESIS

The diagnosis of dysponesis is made on the basis of the history, physical examination, and indicated laboratory and psychological studies. Multichannel electromyometric studies are a necessary part of each patient work-up whenever dysponesis is suspected. The general procedure and equipment used by the authors for this special type of electromyography, with a sample electromyometrogram (EMMG) and findings in certain patients, can be found in previous publications (Whatmore & Ellis, 1958, 1959). More recent equipment has a still lower noise level and greater amplification than that described in the previous publications.

Presently available office EMMG procedure measures mainly bracing efforts. Briefly, it consists of measuring action-potential output simultaneously from eight different motor regions through four channels, each channel recording from two regions. The patient can be either sitting or lying. The regions selected for recording can be a standard sampling of motor regions or an individualized selection. Both standard and individualized procedures are often used in the same patient. Action potentials are stored in each amplifier for a period of one minute, and the resulting potential is then automatically recorded every minute on a slowly moving paper. In addition, four readout meters and four pairs of earphones, and sometimes oscilloscopes as well, follow second-to-second changes for monitoring purposes. Continuous recordings are made for 15- to 30-minute intervals. Following this, additional 10- or 15-minute recordings are made in which the patient is subjected to various forms of stress or nonstressful stimulation. Subjecting the patient to stress during electromyometric recordings is a useful diagnostic procedure, since one characteristic of dysponesis is its tendency to occur when the person is working at tasks or dealing with problems, emotions, or other experiences of life. The stress can be a simple task, such as an arithmetic assignment, or a stress tailored to the individual patient. The way the patient manages his efforts in meeting stress has diagnostic value.

A comparison can be made here to the situation that exists when a resting electrocardiogram is normal but an exercise EKG brings out the findings of coronary heart disease. In the same way, a resting electromyometrogram (EMMG) can be normal but an EMMG in which the person is subjected to some form of stress may bring out the findings of dysponesis. The presence of positive findings on either a resting EKG or a resting EMMG, however, is diagnostic without further testing.

Positive electromyometric findings are almost pathognomonic of dysponesis. Negative electromyometric findings do not rule out dysponesis because of the intermittency of the condition during early stages of its development and because a dysponesis made up largely of representing efforts and attention efforts would not be expected to show on routine electromyometry, which measures mainly bracing efforts. As mentioned previously, a person in the intermittent phase is in and out of the dysponetic state depending upon the life circumstances in which he finds himself. It is only later that the dysponesis becomes continuous.

In the presence of a negative EMMG, it is then necessary to rely more heavily upon other findings or to run subsequent EMMGs or more elaborate stress EMMGs. The history and physical examination including gross observation of the patient will have to be given more weight. There are no pathognomonic findings from these sources, although clinical experience becomes more and more valuable just as it does in any phase of medical practice. Direct observation of the patient, combined with clinical judgment derived from having seen many patients who gave conclusive EMMG evidence of dysponesis, enables the physician to suspect an intermittent dysponesis. The physician who is interested in dysponesis will soon learn to be an astute observer, recognizing clues in the form of stance, facial expression, automatic movements, gestures and gesticulations, breathing, pupillary responses, skin dampness, speech control, and the general account the patient gives of himself and his illness. If treatment of a suspected dysponesis is undertaken without positive EMMG confirmation, subsequent observation of the patient and numerous electronically monitored teaching sessions will confirm or refute the diagnosis.

TREATMENT OF DYSPONESIS

The treatment of dysponesis is a technical procedure that is difficult to describe in a few words without conveying many misconceptions. The reader of the following brief verbal description should keep in mind that live demonstrations and supervised "doing" are necessary to obtain a thorough grasp of treatment procedure.

The present discussion of treatment will be confined to measures for the correction of dysponesis. When factors other than dysponesis, or in addition to dysponesis, are involved in the production of a given illness, they must be dealt with accordingly, since the correction of dysponesis cannot be expected to alleviate symptoms of a different origin.

Ineffective Forms of Treatment

Psychotherapy (treatment limited to interview techniques) appears to have no correcting effect on dysponesis (Whatmore, unpublished data). Patients we have studied who have undergone prolonged psychoanalysis and other forms of psychotherapy have shown no significant reduction in their dysponetic patterns. In fact, a dysponetic individual treated with psychotherapy alone sometimes becomes more dysponetic. The procedure uncovers material to which the patient is possibly reacting but it does not directly alter his effort response to this material. Some forms of psychotherapy may reduce the stress-value of a troublesome factor in a person's life without altering his effort response to stress itself, hence leaving him equally vulnerable to future stress. Psychotherapy can be used, when there are indications for it, along with definitive treatment of dysponesis, but it is a separate procedure that attacks a different aspect of the individual and does not alter dysponetic response tendencies. However, the presence of dysponesis in a patient can interfere greatly with any attempts to carry out psychotherapy, and many psychotherapeutic failures are due to the presence of an unrecognized, hence untreated, dysponesis (Whatmore, 1962; unpublished data).

Hypnosis cannot correct dysponesis because it cannot teach a person new skills. For example, it cannot teach a person to fly an airplane or to play the piano. Learning a skill similar to that for flying an airplane is necessary for the correction of dysponesis.

Pharmacologic agents likewise fail to correct dysponesis because they cannot teach. There is no drug, for example, that will teach a person to drive a car. Drugs can sometimes diminish symptoms resulting from dysponesis or diminish motor activity by paralyzing certain enzyme systems, but they do not alter the underlying response tendencies of the organism and often lose their effect in time. They have a place as temporary measures to be used in conjunction with definitive treatment but should not be looked upon as corrective measures.

General Principles of Effective Treatment

What is needed in treating dysponesis is a way of retraining specific circuits within the nervous system, a way of systematically altering the patient's covert effort responses to the many experiences of life, to the memory of such experiences, and to the anticipation of future experiences.

Such a procedure is supplied by the techniques of effort training or ponesiatrics. These are an outgrowth of earlier, less sophisticated procedures that do not utilize so extensively the teaching advantages of modern instrumentation and do not direct the training so extensively to a monitoring of effort during daily activities (Barlow, 1955; Dickel et al., 1955; Garmany, 1952; Haugen et al., 1958; Jacobson, 1938, 1964).

A product of the physiology laboratory, effort training is a form of neurophysiologic engineering applied to man wherein basic principles of neurophysiology are used to carry on a retraining within the nervous system. As far as possible the methods are based upon laboratory and clinical evidence and not upon philosophic concepts. The possible origin of the dysponesis in a given patient is not considered important for treatment purposes, since this information has proven to have little practical value in the training process.

The specific portions of the nervous system that need retraining are delineated and subjected whenever possible to instrumented learning, wherein electronic and other instruments are used to engineer into the nervous system the desired response patterns. In addition, the specific items to which the patient is overreactive are identified, whether they be environmental situations, bodily sensations, emotions, or thoughts, so that he can be "desensitized" to them through application of the principles of effort management. Therapeutic suggestion, although it cannot be eliminated entirely from any form of treatment, is intentionally kept as low as possible in the treatment of dysponesis because it produces a premature and temporary symptomatic improvement not based upon adequate physiologic change. Highly suggestible patients are difficult to train.

Much further research is needed to develop new and better training procedures but a fair amount of progress has been made to date. With further improvement in training methods it may be possible to shorten what is now a lengthy procedure.

Training in the Recognition and Regulation of Energy Expenditures

Before a patient can begin to manage any given set of efforts he must first learn to recognize them. This involves a training of neuronal circuits employed in attention and observation. The patient is trained to observe at least some of those covert efforts, mentioned previously, that he makes unknowingly. There is no way of conveying to a patient by words alone what he is to be observing. He has to learn what it is mainly by direct experience. Electromyoscopy, electromyometry, electromyophony, and electromyography are employed here for teaching purposes, along with other devices, to delineate and objectify these unnoticed efforts and bring them into the realm of observable phenomena. Readout devices for these procedures, respectively, consist of oscilloscopes, meters, earphones or loudspeakers, and graphs, used singly or in various combinations. They are so arranged that the physician alone or both physician and patient can observe them. Once a person has learned to observe a given effort, that effort comes directly under his control and he can make the effort or diminish it (go "on with the power" or "off with the power") to whatever degree he chooses. It becomes truly a "voluntary" effort. Numerous studies have demonstrated that the human organism can learn to recognize extremely minute amounts of effort and bring them under voluntary control, even to the extent of activating single motor units (Basmajian, 1963; Jacobson, 1934a,b, 1938, 1942, 1943, 1955; Whatmore, unpublished data). Much electronically monitored instruction and practice are necessary.

Having learned to recognize and control a given set of efforts to some extent, the person is then trained to take these efforts into account as he goes about his daily activities. This is a separate skill in itself. At first, it requires a fair amount of the patient's attention, but with practice he becomes able to reduce the amount of attention until finally he can take these efforts into account with a bare minimum of attention, scarcely any at all. An important aid to the development of this skill is electronic monitoring of bracing efforts while the patient is engaged in conversation on both stressful and nonstressful subjects. The physician is kept informed of the patient's efforts by means of earphones and meter while the patient uses only his learned ability to regulate them. When the physician observes that the patient is failing to monitor his bracing responses adequately, he signals to the patient to do a better job. On some occasions it is desirable to halt the conversation for an interval while the patient gives full attention to correcting the errors he has begun to make. At other times the patient is allowed to observe the monitoring instruments himself while he is engaged in conversation.

At first just a few basic bracing efforts are dealt with, and the patient is given training in recognizing and managing them. Often training starts with a single forearm effort, one of the least difficult to observe. Then step-by-step he is exposed to additional efforts and more difficult ones. The specific bracing efforts studied in great detail can vary with the individual but commonly include arms, legs, jaw, throat, breathing regions, and forehead. After some acquaintance with bracing efforts, the patient progresses to representing efforts and finally to attention efforts, learning to recognize and regulate the specific energy expenditures involved in each. Each new addition to his total of observable effort is immediately included in the efforts to be managed during his daily life. The patient is taught to go "on with the power" in some categories of effort and "off with the power" in other categories in such a way that his efforts serve him instead of hindering him and harming him. Effective use of energy is taught.

The patient gradually comes to observe for himself that in modern civilized life most bracing efforts are misdirected and that his representing and attention efforts can be either a great service to him or a detriment depending upon how he uses them and what specific efforts he makes. He learns to judge for himself when he is making errors in energy expenditure. For example, he finds that he tends to brace whenever he feels insecure or anxious but that learning not to brace at these times enables him to do a better job of detecting and coping with whatever is leading to his insecurity or anxiety. In addition, he finds (1) that a continued representing and rerepresenting of his plight or predicament, as he perceives it, can lead to sadness and even severe depression, (2) that a continued representing and rerepresenting of dreaded future events can lead to fear and even panic, and (3) that excessive attention to a bodily sensation can lead to undue discomfort from that sensation. He also finds that there are times when it is to his advantage for him to go "on with the power" in the representing or attention categories, even though he may not want to. He discovers that through the regulation of efforts (energy expenditure) he has a control of representing and attention not otherwise available to him and that these efforts can be trained just as other efforts can be trained. Some patients need more training in various forms of going on with the power than they do in going off with the power.

During his daily life the patient practices going on with the power and off with the power in the various categories of effort with a minimum of attention and fuss. He learns to expect that he will be continually making errors in the management of his efforts and that his job is to catch just a portion of them. We never eliminate all of our misdirected efforts and it is only when we start making too many of them that treatment becomes necessary. As the patient continually corrects a portion of his errors in energy expenditure, he develops a certain automatic tendency to carry on his daily activities with fewer misdirected efforts. But this automatic tendency cannot be depended upon by itself because it is not that reliable, and furthermore it depends for its maintenance upon a continual correcting of errors.

Observational Skill versus Intellectual Understanding

An intellectual understanding of effort management, by itself, is not sufficient to correct the dysponetic state. Improvement depends mainly upon applications of what the patient can learn to observe for himself, the misdirected efforts he can actually catch himself making. The physician must be constantly on the watch for the ever-present danger that the patient will become top-heavy with intellectual understanding and give only lip service to observation. Such top-heaviness will greatly impede his accomplishments. However, the patient should understand intellectually that every benefit to be obtained is to come from his own applications. He is given competent instruction and the opportunity to learn. The rest is up to him. His doctor will not accomplish any of his objectives for him, not in the slightest measure, but will clearly show him the way.

At the observational level, it is essential that the patient learn to distinguish between effort and other types of experience such as discomfort. These are easily confused. Effort can give rise to discomfort but the discomfort is not the effort, and the effort giving rise to the discomfort need not have the same location as the discomfort. Labeling a given discomfort as effort and proceeding to try to diminish it will lead the person only further into a dysponetic state.

It is also essential that the patient learn to distinguish between effort and emotion. The untrained observer will often believe that anyone experiencing anger, fear, or other emotion is necessarily dysponetic at the moment. This is incorrect. The ability to experience a wide variety of emotions is built into the human organism and is of great value to us, and emotion need not be accompanied by dysponesis. Our effort state of the moment can influence our emotional reactions to situations and we can become dysponetic in response to emotions, but the efforts and the emotions are separate processes. It can be said that emotion is a way of feeling, whereas effort is something we do. One goal of effort training is to develop a certain proficiency in managing efforts in the presence of emotion so that our emotions can be of greater service to us. Cultivation of this proficiency can be assisted by single-channel or multichannel monitoring of efforts, using visual and auditory readouts, while the patient engages in conversation on emotion-arousing subjects. The monitoring instruments can be placed so that the patient uses them for training purposes, or the physician alone can use them to evaluate the patient's proficiency. The more skillfully a person manages his efforts in any situation, the more likely he is to experience the appropriate emotion in the appropriate amount for the given situation.

Duration of Treatment

There are all degrees of skill in effort management and there is no way of telling in advance how much skill a given patient will need to meet his own individual requirements or how long it will take him to acquire that much skill. After the patient has some observational acquaintance with all four categories of effort, he is in a position to start deciding for himself when his technique is meeting his requirements. Prior to this he is not qualified to do so because he does not have the full picture and he may decide during a spontaneous remission of his functional symptoms that his technique is adequate. To cover the four basic categories of effort with present training procedures takes the superior patient who applies himself diligently a little over a year of twice-weekly instruction periods, daily practice periods at home or work, and a sincere interest in applying what he learns. Most patients take longer. Often it is necessary to carry a patient through several relapses before he learns essential lessons about effort management.

Goals of Effort Training and Quality of Results

Correction of dysponesis, as indicated by objective measures, leads to alleviation of the illness that was a consequence of the dysponesis. In addition, the patient acquires something that goes far beyond. He discovers a way of managing his energy expenditures, a way of living, that is extremely valuable to him in everything he does. He discovers a technique that enables him to reach goals and accomplish things that he could never do otherwise. He also discovers a way of dealing with problems and a way of meeting the hardships, disappointments, and misfortunes of life that is more effective than any method he has used. In addition he discovers that the joys, the satisfactions, and the pleasures of life can become richer experiences when he applies these same principles.

A high quality of therapeutic result can be expected and is uniformly obtained in those patients in whom objective evidence indicates that a good technique in effort management has been learned. Lesser qualities of improvement are the result of lesser degrees of skill in the recognition and management of efforts. A statistical analysis of results with long-term follow-ups will be reported at a later date. In the meantime, illustrative case histories at the end of this chapter will demonstrate the nature of results and the problems involved in obtaining them. Treatment evaluation for any functional illness requires long-term follow-ups, since it is the reduction in recurrence rate that is to be sought and not just removal of a given episode of functional illness.

The greatest challenge in treating dysponetic patients is to get across to them what they need most to learn. The task for the future is one of developing still better training methods, still better methods of neurophysiologic engineering wherein instrumentation and instrumented learning will undoubtedly play an increasing role.

The ultimate goal of effort training is to teach the patient to be independent in the recognition and management of his daily energy expenditures so that he can, on his own, increase his efficiency and productivity, his enjoyment of life, and his freedom from functional disturbances.

ILLUSTRATIVE CASE HISTORIES

Case 1

Mr. A, a 30-year-old electrical engineer, had been troubled with headaches since childhood as had numerous other members of his family. These were most often in his right eye, in the right side of his head, and extending into the right side of his neck. They were intense, accompanied by nausea and often vomiting, lasted anywhere from a day to several days, and recurred on an average of two to three times per month. In recent years ergotamine was used to relieve them.

He was first seen in 1957. For the previous four years, since taking a job with a large corporation, he had had increasing difficulty with another type of headache, namely, posterior nuchal and suboccipital pain bilaterally. In the previous year it had been present almost every day and had spread upward so that he had pressure sensations throughout his head, his ears felt plugged and would ring frequently, and his nose was stuffy. He also had sharp shocklike sensations in his neck while lying down at night. He had become depressed, fatigued, and irritable.

Over the years he had always been an energetic person but was also excitable. He almost always developed anxiety before examinations at school, at which time his hands perspired, his heart pounded, and he felt out of breath. He also became shaky when talking to his superiors. Whenever he had to speak before a group or at a meeting, he would have a lump in his throat and felt as if he had to keep swallowing or he would be unable to talk. Also at these times he would get sharp pains in his upper abdomen. This interferred with his job performance since he was required to give presentations to audiences. For many years, his symptoms would subside when the stressful situation had passed, but in recent years he had begun to experience these symptoms increasingly between periods of stress.

Before being referred for neurophysiologic evaluation he had had extensive work-ups by an internist, a neurologist, and an allergist. Treatment included medication, heat, massage, neck traction, and a course of desensitization to allergens.

The history and gross examination of the patient suggested that dysponesis might be a factor in his disability. Electromyometric studies, using standard leads with the patient sitting at rest with eyes closed, showed moderate elevation of readings in one lead and nothing distinct in the patterns exhibited. Opening the eyes led to significant elevations in one additional lead and a further increase in the one already elevated. Giving him a mathematical task to perform led to significant further elevations in these two leads. These findings were sufficient to establish the diagnosis of dysponesis. Further evidence was obtained during training periods, when increased values became still more evident.

Here, evidently, was a capable engineer who met intellectual challenge with certain errors in physiologic energy expenditure. His history indicated that he probably responded to a number of other situations with similar misdirected effort.

Effort training was begun in 1957. Seventy-two training sessions on a twice-weekly basis were required before the patient developed a fair control of bracing efforts in a statistical sampling of possible regions, namely, forearm, leg, masseter-temporalis, tongue-throat, breathing regions, frontalis-corrugator-orbicularis, and the neck-shoulder regions. When the electrodes picking up the action potentials in a given region were connected to an oscilloscope or meter that the patient could see, the readings were at first much higher than those found in the initial diagnostic electromyometric studies. This further confirmed the diagnosis of dysponesis by demonstrating dysponetic responses to challenge, namely, having to perform in the face of a device that would measure accurately how well he was doing. After learning to correct his errors during the training sessions, the patient was trained to monitor his efforts as he went about his daily activities. He found that whenever he was confronted with a challenge or was unsure of himself or whenever he was rushed he tended to brace. He discovered that this was basically an error in energy expenditure, an attempt to help himself that actually worked against him, and that by reducing this form of energy expenditure he increased the quality of his performance and decreased the price he had to pay in the form of symptoms.

By the time he had practiced managing bracing efforts for several months, the persistent daily nuchal and suboccipital pain, with pressure sensations extending throughout the head, had largely subsided, as had the plugged sensation in the ears, but his nose was still stuffy most of the time and this annoyed him greatly. The ringing in the ears and the shocklike sensations in his neck at night had also subsided. The vascular-type headaches had decreased somewhat in frequency but were still severe when they occurred.

Training in the recognition and regulation of representing efforts took this patient 97 instruction periods to develop a fairly adequate technique. The eye efforts involved in visualization and the tongue and throat efforts involved in subvocal speech were studied in detail, first one at a time and then simultaneously.

After further training in both representing and bracing efforts, he discovered that whenever the demands of his job required him to do the impossible, such as being three different places at the same time, he would tend to carry out a type of misdirected representing and in turn brace to the representation in such a way that a vascular headache would be triggered. If he caught these errors in energy expenditure in the first few minutes and "went off with the power," he could abort the headache. However, if these misdirected efforts were allowed to continue too long, the headache mechanism seemed to develop a momentum of its own and no amount of effort control would abolish the headache. It then had to run its course or be alleviated by medication. By learning to catch this type of representing and bracing error at an early stage and dealing directly with the physiologic energy expenditures, he developed a way of preventing the vascular-type headaches. However, if he became negligent of his efforts during these critical minutes when the headache mechanism was in the process of being triggered, a full-blown headache could result.

Training in recognizing attention efforts to some extent, and tying them in with what he had learned previously, took another 30 training sessions. When he had become somewhat adept at this, he observed that he was giving far too much attention to his nasal passages and would repeatedly test them and try to clear them a little by sniffing. Although the air would pass he was greatly annoyed by how the passages felt. He evidently had lowered his discomfort threshold in the nasal passages to such an extent, by giving so much attention to them and testing them so frequently, that sensations ordinarily unnoticed had come to be markedly annoying. When he practiced giving less attention to the sensations in the nasal passages, checking them less by sniffing, and diminishing a tendency to brace whenever he noticed annoying sensations in the nose, this problem progressively subsided.

With regard to the symptoms he would develop in anticipation of having to talk to his superiors or speak before an audience, this patient made several significant observations after he had been trained sufficiently to observe. He found that not only did he brace markedly but he also tended to represent dreaded events, events that he thought would be terrible if they actually occurred. For example, among other errors, he found himself making tongue and throat efforts as if to say "What if I would get up there and be unable to talk," or "What if I fainted," and he found himself making eye efforts to picture himself sprawled on the floor. By dealing directly with the physiologic energy expenditures involved in this bracing and costly representing and diminishing them effortlessly whenever he became engaged in them, he found he could be more at ease anticipating these situations and could direct his energies to a more effective presentation to his audience. With practice he found himself actually beginning to enjoy giving talks.

During the course of approximately two years of effort training, not only did this patient experience a subjective relief from discomfort and improvement in his performance, but relatives, friends, and fellow employees noticed a remarkable change in his personality and responsiveness. This patient continued on his own to apply what he had learned about energy expenditure and eight years later has had no recurrence of his previous difficulties.

Case 2

Mrs. B, a 52-year-old dynamic, vivacious extrovert, was seen in 1958 by referral because of severe back pain, mainly interscapular but sometimes lumbar. It had begun in about 1940, occurring at first in occasional mild episodes but became more frequent and more severe as the years passed. By 1950 pain was present every day and intermittently unbearable. She required hospitalization three to four times per year during the next eight years. During this time numerous forms of treatment were tried under orthopedic supervision. These included local injections of procaine and cortisone, traction, heat and massage, electrical stimulation, and exercise. For the past several years she had worn a brace with steel supports constantly except while in bed at night.

The pain would be less in the morning but would increase in intensity as the day progressed. A sudden effort, such as in catching her balance after slipping, would trigger an episode of severe pain. Being subjected to a lot of excitement and having too many things to do would also aggravate the pain.

Examination for possible neurophysiologic factors, including electromyometric studies, led to a diagnosis of dysponesis.

Effort training was begun in the spring of 1958. It took 46 training sessions to cover 9 sets of bracing efforts that were selected for training. They were forearm, leg, masseter-temporalis, tongue-throat, breathing regions, erector spinae muscles, shoulder retractors and elevators, and the frontalis-corrugator-orbicularis group. In addition, she was instructed to continue the back exercises previously prescribed by her orthopedist, and these were modified somewhat as she learned more about bracing efforts.

It took another 169 training sessions along the lines described in Case 1 to cover representing efforts and attention efforts along with numerous interspersed sessions that were devoted to instructing her further in bracing efforts and their control. As situations came up in her daily life, when she failed to apply her training or applied it incorrectly, these were discussed. She found that she tended to brace inappropriately in just about everything she did and that learning to cut down on this had a favorable influence on her back discomfort. She also discovered that whenever a sudden postural adjustment was required as in a slipping of her foot, she reacted with violent and exaggerated covert bracing and that she could learn to reduce the extent of this overreaction. She further discovered that she gave far too much attention to her back, that the very beginnings of discomfort were spotted immediately and were followed by bracing and by inappropriate and costly forms of representing that served only to aggravate the condition rather than to help it. Earlier, she contested the need to study representing efforts but soon recognized her errors in energy expenditure in this category and the role they played.

The patient's improvement was a gradual process over a period of about five years. This was a long time, but it must be remembered that it had also taken a long time for the disability to develop to such a severe degree. The episodes of severe pain became less frequent and less severe, and between these she had periods of increasing length when she was free of pain. She became able to leave her back brace off for short periods and gradually lengthened the intervals until she went all day without it. Having to make a sudden adjustment of her posture, as in falling, ceased to be an occasion for an episode of severe pain. Often no pain followed but sometimes, especially if she failed to control her inappropriate bracing and representing soon enough, she would have a few hours or days of mild to moderate discomfort.

One objective measure of this patient's success in effort management is the finding that whereas hospitalization for back pain was required three to four times per year for eight years prior to effort training, hospitalization has not been necessary in the nine years since effort training began.

Case 3

Mrs. C, a 52-year-old housewife, complained of recurrent episodes of severe depression accompanied by anxiety. The first episode occurred at age 27, and in the ensuing 25 years she had eight additional episodes occurring in increasing frequency and severity. The last six required hospitalization.

In the present episode, which began in 1958, she had lost 22 pounds in a 2-month period. She cried much of the time and felt there was no hope for her. An "awful feeling" was present in her body and all feelings were "dead." She considered herself a perfectionist and ordinarily had much energy, but now she dreaded each day.

Electromyometric studies gave clear evidence of a marked dysponesis.

Effort training along the lines described in Case 1 was begun in 1958. Thirty-seven periods were devoted initially to training in the recognition and control of bracing efforts. Then 48 sessions were devoted to representing efforts. The next 103 sessions were devoted to a further study of both bracing and representing efforts and their applications, since the depressed and anxious patient often exhibits an intricate interplay of errors in both the bracing and representing categories. Very little training in attention efforts was given to this patient.

After sufficient training, this patient was able to observe for herself that she tended to overreact in effort to predicaments that confronted her and to represent them inaccurately. She discovered that a representing and rerepresenting of her plight, or predicament (as she perceived it), on a background of sustained bracing led invariably to depression. This was especially so if the predicament involved some defect in her own performance. She also found that once depression was present it tended to impel her to continue making the same misdirected bracing and representing efforts. She learned, however, that she could break this cycle by managing her efforts and representing her predicaments more accurately, such as when she failed to achieve one of her perfectionistic goals.

When she had become sufficiently adept that she was functioning effectively and feeling well (a total of 188 sessions), the intervals between her instruction periods were progressively lengthened to help ensure that she would continue effort management as a way of life. One objective measure of her success is that whereas she had been hospitalized six times (and with increasing frequency) prior to effort training, no hospitalizations have been necessary in the nine years since effort training began.

Case 4

Mr. D, a 45-year-old businessman, was referred because of multiple functional symptoms, including extrasystoles that were frightening to him. He had experienced extrasystoles for the previous 25 years but in the past year they had become more frequent. Only the extrasystoles will be used here to illustrate a type of disability. After one occurred he would be weak and have to lie down. Often he would be unable to work for the rest of the day. A run of extrasystoles had a still more profound effect on him. He had consulted several cardiologists over the years and each had reassured him that his extrasystoles were of no consequence. The reassurance had no effect and the patient continued to be incapacitated by these sensations. He knew intellectually that they were harmless yet he wondered why they continued to have such a devastating effect on him. Surely, he reasoned, the doctors must be missing something. Three years of psychodynamic psychotherapy had not altered this problem.

The history and electromyometric studies gave evidence of a marked dysponesis, and a program of effort training was begun. It took 134 training sessions along the lines described in Case 1 before it was felt that his technique was sufficient to meet his requirements. One of the big lessons he had to learn was that his effort reaction to the extrasystoles, and not the extrasystoles themselves, was what led to his weakness and incapacitation. He had to be trained so that whenever an extrasystole occurred he could recognize immediately the errors he started to make in energy expenditure and could "nip them in the bud." They were mainly in the bracing and representing categories. He tended to brace in a generalized fashion, but especially in the breathing regions, and to represent dire consequences such as death itself. By monitoring his efforts effectively he became able to experience extrasystoles without discomfort or alarm. Five years later he is still doing well.

ACKNOWLEDGMENT. Preparation of this chapter was supported by a grant made by Richard E. Lang to the Pacific Northwest Research Foundation, 1102 Columbia Street, Seattle. The authors wish to thank Drs. George A. Davidson, Ralph W. Gerard, Gerhard B. Haugen, Robert E. Rinehart, and Herbert S. Ripley for reading the manuscript and making valuable suggestions.

REFERENCES

Allers, R., & Scheminzky, F. Über Aktionssträme der Muskelin bei motorischen Vorstellungen und verwandten Vorgängen. *Archives of Physiology*, 1926, *212*, 169–182.

Amadeo, M., & Shagass, C. Eye movements, attention, and hypnosis. *Journal of Nervous and Mental Disease*, 1963, *136*, 139–145.

Aserinsky, E., & Kleitman, N. Two types of ocular motility occurring during sleep. *Journal of Applied Physiology*, 1955, *8*, 1–10.

Barlow, W. Anxiety and muscle tension. In D. O'Neill (Ed.), *Modern trends in psychosomatic medicine*. New York: Paul B. Hoeber, 1955. Pp. 285–309.

Basmajian, J. V. Control and training of individual motor units. *Science*, 1963, *141*, 440–441.

Beck, A. T. Thinking and depression. I. Idiosyncratic content and cognitive distortions. *Archives of General Psychiatry*, 1963, *9*, 324–333.

Beck, A. T. Thinking and depression. II. Theory and therapy. *Archives of General Psychiatry*, 1964, *10*, 561–571.

Bender, L. *Psychopathology of children with organic brain disorders*. Springfield, Illinois: Charles C Thomas, 1956.

Bernhaut, M., Gellhorn, E., & Rasmussen, A. T. Experimental contributions to the problem of consciousness. *Journal of Neurophysiology*, 1953, *16*, 21–35.

Bobroff, A. *Eczema: Its nature, cure, and prevention*. Springfield, Illinois: Charles C Thomas, 1962.

Bubnoff, N., & Heidenhain, R. In P. C. Bucy (Ed.) *The precentral motor cortex* (2nd ed.). Urbana: University of Illinois Press, 1949. Pp. 173–210.

Bull, N. *The body and its mind*. New York: Las Americas Publishing Co., 1962.

Buytendijk, F. J. Über den Schmerz. *Psyche*, 1955, *9*, 436–542.

Davis, F. H., & Malmo, R. B. Electromyographic recording during interview. *American Journal of Psychiatry*, 1951, *107*, 908–916.

Deckert, G. H. Pursuit eye movements in the absence of a moving visual stimulus. *Science*, 1964, *143*, 1192–1193.

Dement, W., & Kleitman, N. The relation of eye movements during sleep to dream activity: An objective method for the study of dreaming. *Journal of Experimental Psychology*, 1957, *53*, 339–346.

Deutsch, J. A., & Deutsch, D. Attention: Some theoretical considerations. *Psychological Review*, 1963, *70*, 80–90.

Dickel, H. A., Dixon, H. H., Shanklin, J. G., & Davidson. G. A. Observations on the anxiety tension syndrome. *Canadian Medical Association Journal*, 1955, *72*, 1–6.

Dickel, H. A., Dixon, H. H., Stoner, W., & Shanklin, J. G. Electromyographic studies on patients with chronic headaches. *Northwest Medicine*, 1958, *57*, 1458–1462.

Dixon, H. H., & Dickel, H. A. Tension headache. *Northwest Medicine*, 1967, *66*, 817–820.

Dixon, H. H., O'Hara, M., & Peterson, R. D. Fatigue contracture of skeletal muscle. *Northwest Medicine*, 1967, *66*, 813–816.

Dixon, H. H., Peterson, R. D., Dickel, H. A., Jones, C. H., & West, E. S. High energy phosphates in the muscles of depressed and fatigued patients. *Western Journal of Surgery*, 1952, *60*, 327–330.

Dusser de Barenne, J. G., & McCulloch, W. S. Factors for facilitation and extinction in the central nervous system. *Journal of Neurophysiology*, 1939, *2*, 319–355.

Freeman, G. L., & Simpson, R. M. The effect of the experimentally induced muscular tension upon palmar skin resistance. *Journal of General Psychology*, 1938, *18*, 319–326.

Friedman, M., & Rosenman, R. H. Association of specific overt behavior pattern with blood and cardiovascular findings. *Journal of the American Medical Association*, 1959, *169*, 1286–1296.

Garmany, G. *Muscle relaxation as an aid to psychotherapy*. London: Actinic Press, 1952.

Gasser, H. S. Contractures of skeletal muscle. *Physiological Reviews*, 1930, *10*, 35–109.

Gellhorn, E. *Autonomic imbalance and the hypothalamus*. Minneapolis: University of Minnesota Press, 1957.

Gellhorn, E. The influence of curare on hypothalamic excitability and the electroencephalogram. *Electroencephalography and Clinical Neurophysiology*, 1958, *10*, 697–703.

Gellhorn, E., & Loofbourrow, G. N. *Emotions and emotional disorders: A neurophysiological study*. New York: Hoeber Medical Division of Harper & Row, 1963.

Gould, L. N. Auditory hallucinations and subvocal speech. *Journal of Nervous and Mental Disease*, 1949, *109*, 418–427.

Gould, L. N. Verbal hallucinations as automatic speech. *American Journal of Psychiatry*, 1950, *107*, 110–119.

Haugen, G. B., Dixon, H. H., & Dickel, H. A. *A therapy for anxiety tension reactions*. New York: Macmillan, 1958.

Hodes, R. Electrocortical synchronization resulting from reduced proprioceptive drive caused by neuromuscular blocking agents. *Electroencephalography and Clinical Neurophysiology*, 1962, *14*, 220–232.

Holmes, T. H., & Wolff, H. G. Life situations, emotions, and backache. *Psychosomatic Medicine*, 1952, *14*, 18–33.

Jacobson, E. Voluntary relaxation of the esophagus. *American Journal of Physiology*, 1925, *72*, 387–394.

Jacobson, E. Response to a sudden unexpected stimulus. *Journal of Experimental Psychology*, 1926, *9*, 19–25.

Jacobson, E. Electrical measurements of neuromuscular states during mental activities: I. Imagination of movement involving skeletal muscle. *American Journal of Physiology*, 1930, *91*, 567–608. (a)

Jacobson, E. Electrical measurements of neuromuscular states during mental activities: II. Imagination and recollection of various muscular acts. *American Journal of Physiology*, 1930, *94*, 22-34. (b)

Jacobson, E. Electrical measurements of neuromuscular states during mental activities: III. Visual imagination and recollection. *American Journal of Physiology*, 1930, *95*, 694-702. (c)

Jacobson, E. Electrical measurements of neuromuscular states during mental activities: IV. Evidence of contraction of specific muscles during imagination. *American Journal of Physiology*, 1930, *95*, 703-712. (d)

Jacobson, E. Electrical measurements of neuromuscular states during mental activities: V. Variation of specific muscles contracting during imagination. *American Journal of Physiology*, 1931, *96*, 115-121. (a)

Jacobson, E. Electrical measurements of neuromuscular states during mental activities: VI. A note on mental activities concerning an amputated limb. *American Journal of Physiology*, 1931, *96*, 122-125. (b)

Jacobson, E. Electrical measurements of neuromuscular states during mental activities: VII. Imagination, recollection and abstract thinking involving the speech musculature. *American Journal of Physiology*, 1931, *97*, 200-209. (c)

Jacobson, E. Electrical measurements concerning muscular contractions (tonus) and the cultivation of relaxation in man: Studies on arm flexors. *American Journal of Physiology*, 1934, *107*, 230-248. (a)

Jacobson, E. Electrical measurements concerning muscular contractions (tonus) and the cultivation of relaxation in man: Relaxation times of individuals. *American Journal of Physiology*, 1934, *108*, 573-580. (b)

Jacobson, E. The influence of skeletal muscle tension and relaxation on blood pressure. *American Journal of Physiology*, 1936, *116*,86.

Jacobson, E. *Progressive relaxation* (2nd ed.). Chicago: University of Chicago Press, 1938.

Jacobson, E. Variation of blood pressure with skeletal muscle tension and relaxation. *Annals of Internal Medicine*, 1939, *12*, 1194-1212.

Jacobson, E. Variations of blood pressure with brief voluntary muscular contractions. *Journal of Laboratory and Clinical Medicine*, 1940, *25*, 1029-1037. (a)

Jacobson, E. Variation of blood pressure with skeletal muscle tension and relaxation: II. The heart beat. *Annals of Internal Medicine*, 1940, *13*, 1619-1625. (b)

Jacobson, E. Cultivated relaxation in "essential" hypertension. *Archives of Physical Therapy*, 1940, *21*, 645-654. (c)

Jacobson, E. The physiological conception and treatment of certain common "psychoneuroses." *American Journal of Psychiatry*, 1941, *98*, 219-226.

Jacobson, E. The effect of daily rest without training to relax on muscular tonus. *American Journal of Psychology*, 1942, *55*, 248-254.

Jacobson, E. The cultivation of physiological relaxation. *Annals of Internal Medicine*, 1943, *19*, 965-972.

Jacobson, E. Neuromuscular controls in man: Methods of self-direction in health and in disease. *American Journal of Psychology*, 1955, *68*, 549-561.

Jacobson, E. *Anxiety and tension control: A physiologic approach*. Philadelphia: Lippincott, 1964.

Jacobson, E., & Carlson, A. J. The influence of relaxation upon the knee jerk. *American Journal of Physiology*, 1925, *73*, 324-328.

Kaufman, W. Syndrome of spontaneous hypoventilation. *Mississippi Valley Medical Journal*, 1951, *73*, 133-142.

Kennard, M. A. Autonomic interrelations with the somatic nervous system. *Psychosomatic Medicine*, 1947, *9*, 29-36.

King, H. E. *Psychomotor aspects of mental disease: An experimental study*. Cambridge: Harvard University Press, 1954.

Kleitman, N. *Sleep and wakefulness*. Chicago: University of Chicago Press, 1963. (See also 1st ed., 1939.)

Landau, William. Autonomic responses mediated via the corticospinal tract. *Journal of Neurophysiology*, 1953, *16*, 299-311.

Lorens, S. A., Jr., & Darrow, C. W. Eye movements, EEG, GSR, and EKG during mental multiplication. *Electroencephalography and Clinical Neurophysiology*, 1962, *14*, 739–746.

Lorenté de No, Rafael: Cytoarchitecture of the cerebral cortex. In J. F. Fulton (Ed.), *Physiology of the nervous system*. New York: Oxford University Press, 1943. Pp. 274–301.

Lundervold, A. J. S. Electromyographic investigations of tense and relaxed subjects. *Journal of Nervous and Mental Disease*, 1952, *115*, 512–525.

MacLean, P. D. The limbic system ("visceral brain") in relation to central gray and reticulum of the brain stem. *Psychosomatic Medicine*, 1955, *17*, 355–366.

Magoun, H. W. *The waking brain*. Springfield, Illinois: Charles C Thomas, 1963.

Malmo, R. B., & Shagass, C. Physiologic studies of reaction to stress in anxiety and early schizophrenia. *Psychosomatic Medicine*, 1949, *11*, 9–24.

Malmo, R. B., Shagass, C., & Davis, F. H. Specificity of bodily reactions under stress. *Research Publications, Association for Research in Nervous and Mental Disease*, 1950, *29*, 231–261.

Malmo, R. B., Shagass, C., & Davis, J. F. Electromyographic studies of muscular tension in psychiatric patients under stress. *Journal of Clinical and Experimental Psychopathology*, 1951, *12*, 45–66.

Mason, J. W. The central nervous system regulation of ACTH secretion. In H. H. Jasper, L. D. Proctor, R. S. Knighton, W. C. Noshay, & R. T. Costello (Eds.), *Reticular formation of the brain*. Henry Ford Hospital International Symposium. Boston: Little, Brown, 1958. Pp. 645–670.

Max, L. W. An experimental study of the motor theory of consciousness: I. Critique of earlier studies. *Journal of General Psychology*, 1934, *11*, 112–125.

Max, L. W. Experimental study of the motor theory of consciousness: III. Action-current responses in deaf-mutes during sleep, sensory stimulation, and dreams. *Journal of Comparative Psychology*, 1935, *19*, 469–486.

Max, L. W. Experimental study of the motor theory of consciousness: IV. Action-current responses in the deaf during awakening, kinesthetic imagery, and abstract thinking. *Journal of Comparative Psychology*, 1937, *24*, 301–344.

Miller, M. Changes in the response to electric shock by varying muscular conditions. *Journal of Experimental Psychology*, 1926, *9*, 26–44.

Nalbandov, A. V. (Ed.). *Advances in neuroendocrinology*. Urbana: University of Illinois Press, 1963.

Papez, J. W. A proposed mechanism of emotion. *Archives of Neurology and Psychiatry*, 1937, *38*, 725–743.

Rinehart, R. E., & Dixon, H. H., Sr. Muscular dysfunction. *Northwest Medicine*, 1961, *60*, 707.

Rosenman, R. H., & Friedman, M. Association of specific behavior pattern in women with blood and cardiovascular findings. *Circulation*, 1961, *24*, 1173–1184.

Rosenman, R. H., & Friedman, M. Behavior patterns, blood lipids, and coronary heart disease. *Journal of the American Medical Association*, 1963, *184*, 934–938.

Rushmer, R. F. *Cardiac diagnosis: A physiologic approach*. Philadelphia: W. B. Saunders, 1955.

Sainsbury, P., & Gibson, J. C. Symptoms of anxiety and tension and the accompanying physiological changes in the muscular system. *Journal of Neurology, Neurosurgery, and Psychiatry*, 1954, *17*, 216–228.

Shagass, C., & Malmo, R. B. Psychodynamic themes and localized muscular tension during psychotherapy. *Psychosomatic Medicine*, 1954, *16*, 295–314.

Shaw, W. A. The relation of muscular action-potentials to imaginal weight lifting. *Archives of Psychology*, 1940, *35*, 5–55.

Sperry, R. W. Neurology and the mind-brain problem. *American Scientist*, 1952, *40*, 291–312.

Totten, E. Eye movements during visual imagery. *Comparative psychology monographs, Vol. XI, Serial 53*. Baltimore: Johns Hopkins Press, 1935. Pp. 1–46.

Watkins, A. L., Cobb, S., Finesinger, J. E., Brazier, M. A. B., Shands, H. C., & Pincus, G. Psychiatric and physiologic studies on fatigue. *Archives of Physical Medicine*, 1947, *28*, 199–206.

Whatmore, G. B. A neurophysiologic view of functional disorders. *Psychosomatics*, 1962, *3*, 371–378.

Whatmore, G. B. Some neurophysiologic differences between schizophrenia and depression. *American Journal of Psychiatry*, 1966, *123*, 712–716.

Whatmore, G. B., & Ellis, R. M., Jr. Some motor aspects of schizophrenia: An EMG study. *American Journal of Psychiatry*, 1958, *114*, 882–889.

Whatmore, G. B., & Ellis, R. M., Jr. Some neurophysiologic aspects of depressed states: An electromyographic study. *Archives of General Psychiatry*, 1959, *1*, 70–80.

Whatmore, G. B., & Ellis, R. M., Jr. Further neurophysiologic aspects of depressed states: An electromyographic study. *Archives of General Psychiatry*, 1962, *6*, 243–253.

Whatmore, G. B., & Ellis, R. M., Jr. Some neurophysiologic aspects of schizophrenia: An electromyographic study. *American Journal of Psychiatry*, 1964, *120*, 1166–1169.

Wolf, S. Sustained contraction of the diaphragm, the mechanism of a common type of dyspnea and precordial pain. *Journal of Clinical Investigation*, 1947, *26*, 1201.

Wolff, H. G. *Headache and other head pain* (2nd ed.). New York: Oxford University Press, 1963.

Wolpert, E. A. Studies in psychophysiology of dreams: II. An electromyographic study of dreaming. *Archives of General Psychiatry*, 1960, *2*, 231–241.

34

Cultivated Low Arousal—
An Antistress Response?

Johann Stoyva and Thomas Budzynski

ASSUMPTIONS

Our basic working hypothesis, and the unifying principle behind most of our experiments, has been the idea that frequently stressed individuals will show physiological hyperarousal in one or several bodily systems. A complementary hypothesis has been that frequently stressed (or overreactive individuals) are likely to lose the ability to relax well; i.e., to shift into a low arousal condition.

When faced by recurring stresses, the individual must repeatedly mobilize his physical and mental resources. Such responding characteristically involves sympathetic activation and elevated muscle tension, a readiness to respond to threats and challenges—the *fight-or-flight* response or *defense-alarm* reaction. Individuals forced frequently to mobilize themselves to meet stresses are likely to lose their ability to execute the opposite response, i.e., to shift into the parasympathetic mode in which bodily recuperation normally occurs. Support for this position can be drawn from the work and theories of scientists such as Charvat, Folkow, Malmo, Sternbach, Cannon, Wolff, Lader, and Mathews.

The other major component of our theoretical orientation has been the assumption that the individual's reaction to psychological stress is capable of at least some learned modification. Such learned modification can, we think, be strengthened by means of feedback techniques. Generally, biofeedback techniques employed in our laboratory have been designed to produce low arousal—a condition we assume has physiological effects opposite to those produced by stress.

Although our beginning experimental work focused on alpha feedback, growing evidence for the clinical usefulness of muscle relaxation caused us to shift our efforts to electromyographic (EMG) feedback. Various sources suggested that muscle relaxation would be useful in producing a low arousal condition with certain antistress properties. For example, there was Jocobson's (1938) important pioneering work with progressive relaxation, a technique that he employed for a variety of anxiety and stress-related disorders. Also, the German-developed autogenic training (Luthe, 1963, 1969)—essentially a series of exercises designed to

Johann Stoyva • Department of Psychiatry, University of Colorado Medical Center, Denver, Colorado 80262. Thomas Budzynski • Biofeedback Institute of Denver, Englewood, Colorado 80111.

produce a shift toward a parasympathetic response pattern—similarly pointed to the clinical usefulness of "cultivated low arousal" and allied techniques. Of more recent origin was the behavior therapy technique of systematic desensitization (Wolpe, 1958), a valuable new approach in reducing anxiety to both real and symbolic situations. In the most commonly used variant of the latter technique, muscle relaxation forms an integral part of the procedure.

A further consideration in favor of muscle relaxation was that since the striate musculature makes up at least 50% of body mass, it would seem likely to have powerful effects on the organism as a whole. Also, there was the obvious fact that muscular activity is an inescapable part of adaptive behavior (and of the response to stress). Without it, there is no behavior. We therefore felt that training in muscle relaxation—and its accompanying low arousal condition—would be an important *first step* in the search to find ways of *moderating the reaction to stress*.

TWO CLINICAL EXAMPLES OF MODIFYING THE RESPONSE TO STRESS

Is there any convincing evidence that the individual's response to stress can be modified? Actually, there are at least two useful clinical examples that may be cited. One is the just-mentioned behavior therapy technique of systematic desensitization. In essence, this technique involves substituting a relaxation response for an anxiety response. When desensitization is complete, the patient is able to think calmly about things that formerly made him extremely anxious.

Systematic Desensitization

In his development of systematic desensitization, Wolpe (1958) drew on the important pioneering work of Jacobson (1938). Over the years, Jacobson had noted that anxious patients typically show elevated levels of muscle tension. On the basis of clinical observations, he developed the parallel idea that cultivating a condition of thorough muscular relaxation could be useful in reducing a patient's anxiety.

It was for this reason that Wolpe (1958) incorporated the Jacobson technique into the practice of systematic desensitization. Specifically, he postulated that a condition of muscular relaxation is physiologically incompatible with an anxiety response. On the strength of this postulate, muscle relaxation came to play a central role in systematic desensitization.

In Wolpe's desensitization technique, the patient is first taught muscle relaxation by means of an abbreviated Jacobson progressive relaxation technique (usually two to six training sessions). He is next presented with a graded series of anxiety scenes, known as a *hierarchy*. A given hierarchy is focused around a single theme, such as public-speaking anxiety, and the items are ranked from the one that is the least anxiety-producing to that which is most anxiety-producing. When the actual desensitization is begun, the least anxiety-evoking scene is used first. The task of the patient is to maintain a condition of thorough relaxation while he imagines the anxiety item. After he masters a given scene, the patient progresses to a more difficult one until finally he becomes able to remain calm even while visualizing the scene that formerly made him the most anxious. Wolpe (1958) reports that transfer from the clinic to everyday life occurs readily, and in the case of specific anxieties, such as phobias, Wolpe and Lazarus (1966) report an impressive successful outcome rate of 80 to 90%.

Tension Headache

In this laboratory, we began working with tension headache. This is a stress-related disorder likely to occur when the patient feels under external pressures (e.g., deadlines, plenty of unfinished work, or mutually conflicting tasks) or feels burdened by emotional conflicts. since it had been experimentally demonstrated (Wolff, 1963) that the immediate cause of tension headache is the sustained contraction of the head or neck muscles, we hypothesized that systematic training in muscular relaxation might be useful in treating this disorder.

To assist the process of muscular relaxation, we employed an EMG feedback device originally developed by T. H. Budzynski (see Budzynski & Stoyva, 1969). Its essential operation is as follows: Surface electrodes detect the EMG activity produced by a particular muscle, such as the frontalis. Through his headphones, the patient hears a train of discrete clicks. If EMG activity is high, the click rate is fast. When EMG activity decreases, the click rate also decreases. The task of the patient is to relax as thoroughly as possible—aided by the information feedback provided by the clicks.

Pilot Work. The EMG feedback technique was applied to several tension headache patients—the first five individuals available for the study (see Budzynski, Stoyva, & Adler, 1970). With EMG feedback training in muscle relaxation, these patients not only learned to produce lowered EMG activity (frontalis monitored) but showed associated reductions in headache activity. Follow-up results over a 3-month period indicated that for these five patients, headache activity remained at a low level, especially if they continued to practice relaxation for a short time every day. An interesting collateral observation was that many patients, when they felt tension headache beginning to develop in a stress situation, learned to abort the headache by deliberately relaxing their upper body musculature.

Controlled-Outcome Study. In view of our favorable pilot observations, we initiated a controlled-outcome study (Budzynski et al., unpublished observations). The experimental design involved one treatment group and two control groups. The six patients in the experimental group (group A) received accurate information feedback as to their frontalis EMG levels. Over a 9-week period, they received two EMG feedback sessions per week. The six patients in the *pseudofeedback* group (group B) were given the same number of laboratory sessions of relaxation training, but instead of true feedback they listened to feedback signals that had been tape-recorded from the experimental group. To help in applying the relaxation response to everyday life, all patients in both the experimental and pseudocontrol groups were told to do the relaxation training at home or work twice a day. The six subjects in the second control group (group C) received no treatment at all.

All persons chosen for the study suffered from frequent tension headaches and had been afflicted for an average of 7 years or more. Patients in all three groups kept daily records of headache activity (a rating scale of intensity recorded on an hour-by-hour basis) during the entire experiment, and for a 3-month follow-up period.

Results. In brief, the results showed that, with training, frontalis EMG levels in the experimental group fell to less than 40% of baseline values. In the pseudofeedback group, levels remained at about 80% of baseline values. This difference between the two groups was even greater at the end of the 3-month follow-up period (mean frontalis EMG levels for group A = 3.92 mV, and for group B = 8.43 mV; $p < .01$).

Figure 1 shows the headache activity over a 23-week period for the three groups. Group A levels of headache activity toward the end of training (weeks 8 and 9) were significantly lower than in groups B and C ($p < .001$, Kurskal-Wallis analysis of variance by ranks).

Group A patients also showed a sharply reduced medication usage when assessed at the end of the 3-month follow-up period. Such a reduction was not characteristically shown by the group B patients.

In summary, then, patients in the treatment group showed diminished headache activity, greatly decreased drug usage, and markedly reduced frontalis EMG levels relative to those of the two control groups. Since the controlled study was completed, a number of additional patients have been run on a case-by-case basis, so that by now over 60 persons have undergone the training. Approximately 75% of them have shown substantial reductions in headache activity. Of the control patients run to date (total of 12), fewer than 25% have shown substantial improvement.

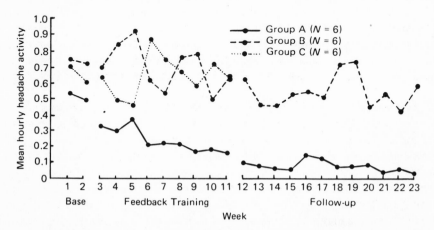

Figure 1. Headache activity during baseline period, during 2-month feedback training period, and during 3-month follow-up period (A and B only). Group A was experimental group receiving EMG feedback training. Groups B and C were controls.

Also, of great interest, from the point of view of modifying the stress response, is that patients typically passed through several stages in terms of their ability to use a *cultivated* relaxation response to reduce headache activity. At first they were able to relax only with deliberate effort. Later, the relaxation response became easier to do, even when the patient felt under some pressure. Finally, with some patients, the relaxation response appeared to have become virtually an automatic reaction, no longer requiring conscious effort.

EXPERIMENTS ON FEEDBACK-INDUCED MUSCLE RELAXATION

The two foregoing clinical examples show that systematic training in muscle relaxation can be useful in treating certain stress-related disorders. It should be noted, however, that in the older techniques of inducing a relaxed, low arousal condition—such as Jacobson's progressive relaxation, systematic desensitization, and autogenic training—the training is generally conducted without continuous physiological monitoring. Such a practice can lead to difficulties. For example, is the subject really relaxed or simply reporting that he is? Or, if he has trouble relaxing—likely to be the case with patients having stress-related disorders—how can he be efficiently and reliably taught to relax?

In view of these problems, and in view of the demonstrated (and potential) clinical value of muscle relaxation, we decided to explore the idea that feedback techniques could be used to improve the learning of muscle relaxation. Therefore, in tandem with our clinical studies (on tension headache and sleep-onset insomnia), we undertook a series of validation and parameter studies addressed to questions such as the following. Is EMG feedback superior to the absence of it in producing muscle relaxation? Does muscle relaxation have effects on other bodily systems, e.g., cortical or autonomic activity? Are some muscles more useful than others for inducing a relaxed, low arousal condition? Can subjects learn to maintain the relaxation response even in the absence of feedback? Described below is a series of interlocking experiments bearing on these questions. Although these studies are chiefly drawn from work in our own laboratory, it should be noted that other investigators have worked with EMG feedback, for example, Green, Green, and Walters (1970). A strong interest of this group has been the experiential correlates of low arousal conditions.

Frontalis Feedback

In our first validation study (Budzynski & Stoyva, 1969), we made use of the frontalis, a muscle frequently involved in anxiety and hyperarousal disorders (see Sainsbury & Gibson, 1954; Shagass & Malmo, 1954). If subjects could learn to achieve a high degree of control over this hard-to-relax muscle (see Balshan, 1962), then the feedback procedure should presumably be readily applicable to other less difficult muscle groups.

Three groups of five subjects each were compared with respect to depth of relaxation achieved. The experimental group received accurate feedback of frontalis EMG levels (a tone varying in frequency combined with a shaping procedure). Of the two control groups, one received irrelevant feedback (a steady low tone); the other received no feedback at all (silent condition). Of the approximately 30 subjects who volunteered, the 15 with the highest baseline EMG levels were selected for the experiment.

As indicated in Figure 2, subjects received one baseline session with no feedback. Next came three training sessions conducted on 3 separate days. Finally, there was a postbaseline day on which there was no feedback of any kind, and subjects were instructed to relax as thoroughly as possible. Additionally, all subjects were given a money reward—the better their performance, the greater the payment for each of the five sessions.

The results clearly showed the superiority of the feedback approach. Following only three training sessions, the feedback subjects had lowered their frontalis EMG levels by 50%, the silent group had decreased by 24%, and the irrelevant feedback group had increased by about 28%.

As Figure 2 shows, although the irrelevant feedback group had the poorest mean performance, the most salient characteristic of this group was its great variability—range of 6.1 to 28.4 mV in Session 5. For the feedback group, the range for Session 5 was 5.3 to 10.8 mV, indicating that correct feedback more reliably produced low levels of EMG activity than did irrelevant feedback.

Further support for the statement that correct feedback more reliably produced thorough relaxation than does irrelevant feedback was demonstrated by comparing one of the subjects from the low tone group under both irrelevant feedback and correct feedback conditions. This subject, who had been one of the two poorest performers in the irrelevant feedback group, was provided with cor-

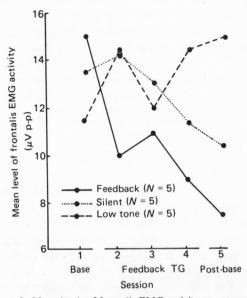

Figure 2. Mean levels of frontalis EMG activity across sessions.

rect feedback training over four additional sessions (sessions 6, 7, 8, and 9 in Figure 3). For this subject, EMG levels had been high throughout the five previous sessions. But, as may be seen in Figure 3, the mean level dropped sharply with accurate feedback training.

Cortical Rhythms. An additional observation of interest, especially to electroencephalographers, was that cortical rhythms could be quite clearly distinguished in the forehead EMG after thorough relaxation had been achieved. This phenomenon, although previously noted by Davis (1959), is difficult to observe under ordinary conditions because the dense, high-frequency muscle action potentials from the frontalis mask the cortical rhythms. After feedback training, however, most of the EMG activity drops out of the tracing. Then bursts of cortical frontalis rhythms, in particular alpha (8 to 12 Hertz) and theta (4 to 7 Hertz), are likely to become quite apparent (provided that filter band-pass characteristics are such as to allow the passage of EEG signals).

Masseter Feedback

The aim of the second validation study (Budzynski & Stoyva, 1973a) was to see whether the merits of the feedback technique would be apparent even in the course of a single training session. Eighty subjects were told to relax the masseter muscle as deeply as possible. Experimental group I consisted of 20 subjects who received accurate auditory feedback (a tone of varying pitch). Experimental group 2 consisted of 20 subjects who received a visual *digital-light* feedback (a small red signal light flashed on or off depending on EMG level). There were two control groups. Twenty control subjects received irrelevant feedback (a steady low tone); and another 20 received no feedback at all. Again the results spoke clearly in favor of the feedback approach.

Mean EMG levels for the *steady low tone* control group ran 70% above those of the two experimental groups. And mean EMG levels for the *silent* control group ran 100% higher than those of the experimental groups (average EMG levels for entire session).

Frontalis versus Forearm Feedback

A recent study (Ball et al., unpublished observations) examined whether some muscles are better than others for promoting general bodily relaxation and low arousal. Since work with both patients and normals had suggested that when subjects reached very low EMG levels on the frontalis, that other muscles, especially of the upper body, were also likely to be relaxed, we decided to compare a frontalis feedback group with a forearm (extensor) feedback group. Worth noting in this context is Jacobson's (1970, p. 41) challenging assertion that when EMG activity in the facial and laryngeal muscles falls to very low (close to zero) levels, then the individual is inevitably asleep.

In this study, we ran college-age male volunteers under one of three following conditions: (1) Group A received variable rate auditory clicks from fontalis ($N = 7$); (2) Group B received variable rate clicks from forearm extensor ($N =$

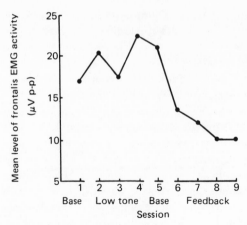

Figure 3. Mean levels of frontalis EMG activity in same subject under irrelevant (low tone) feedback condition, and under subsequent correct feedback condition.

7); (3) Group C, the control group, received tape-recorded clicks produced by the frontalis subjects.

The three groups were comparable in age ranges, and with respect to means and ranges of EMG levels. Each subject was run for a total of 10 laboratory sessions—including 1 throwaway adaptation session, 2 baseline sessions, 5 training sessions, and 2 postbaseline sessions (the last without feedback).

Only group A (frontalis feedback) showed a significant decline in frontalis EMG activity when pretraining EMG levels were compared with posttraining levels ($p < 0.01$, one-tailed). But perhaps more revealing were pre–post decreases for the three groups expressed as *percentages* (baseline EMG levels minus post-baseline levels).

These results confirmed our hypothesis regarding superiority of the frontalis muscle over the forearm muscle for feedback training purposes. The data showed that only the frontalis feedback subjects decreased on *both* frontalis and forearm EMG levels. In other words, when the frontalis is low, the forearm is also likely to be low. But the reverse relationship does not hold. Subjects receiving forearm feedback decreased 41% on forearm EMG levels but remained virtually the same on their frontalis EMG levels. Actually, the control subjects showed as much change as did the forearm feedback subjects.

High versus Low EMG Subjects. Another observation in this experiment—and one likely to be of practical training value—was the differing results for 7 high EMG and 7 low EMG subjects. (Although 14 frontalis subjects were originally available, it proved possible to match only 7 of them with the available forearm and control subjects. However, all 14 received the same frontalis feedback training. For the following comparison, these 14 subjects were divided, on the basis of frontalis EMG, into 7 high EMG subjects and 7 low ones.)

Figure 4 shows that, in the low frontalis EMG group, pre–post decreases were slight (13%). But in the high frontalis EMG group, decreases were substantial (46%).

This result is in close agreement with an experiment conducted independently at the University of Dusseldorf by Engel and Sittenfeld (personal communication). In their experiment, frontalis EMGs were measured on 200 medical students. Three groups were then chosen for further training—a low frontalis EMG group (N = 12), a medium-level frontalis EMG group (N = 12), and a high frontalis EMG group (N = 12). Subjects were given four feedback training sessions on 4 consecutive days. Control subjects received auditory feedback of their own respiration. High EMG subjects receiving frontalis EMG feedback showed sharp reductions in EMG levels, compared to high EMG subjects receiving only respiratory feedback. However, differences between experimentals and controls were nonexistent in the subjects who had *started* with low frontalis EMG levels.

This finding is valuable in that it helps define the population for whom feedback-induced relaxation is likely to be useful, namely, subjects with high EMG levels. Our impression is that the latter are likely to be older subjects, those with anxiety or stress-linked disorders, people in demanding jobs, or some combination of the foregoing. The observed differences between high and low EMG subjects show that individuals with high muscle tension levels improve considerably in their ability to relax after EMG feedback training. But for subjects who are already quite relaxed, the feedback training produces only minimal changes (a result clearly in keeping with the law of initial values).

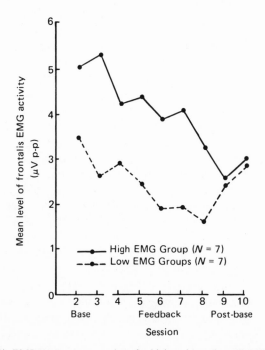

Figure 4. Frontalis EMB levels across sessions for high and low (baseline) EMG subjects. All subjects trained with frontalis EMG feedback.

Effects on Other Bodily Systems

One of the questions raised earlier was whether muscle relaxation would affect other bodily systems. Would it act to dampen autonomic or cortical activity?

Cortical Changes. A study by Budzynski (1969) demonstrated that the consequences of profound muscle relaxation are not limited to a particular muscle but are manifested in cortical changes as well. This experiment drew on the work of Venables and Wing (1962), Maley (1967), and Rose (1966), which showed that the fusion threshold for paired flashes of light may be used to determine cortical activation level. In general, individuals who are anxious or hyperalert are usually able to discriminate smaller differences in the time interval between the pairs of successive light flashes than are individuals with more normal activation levels; i.e., the anxious subjects have lower thresholds.

In Budzynski's (1969) experiment, two-flash thresholds were used to assess the cortical effects of profound muscle relaxation. Twelve normal subjects were trained (feedback training on the frontalis and a neck muscle) to produce thorough muscle relaxation by means of the EMG feedback technique. Each of the 12 subjects showed an increased two-flash threshold (their discrimination interval was longer) in the relaxation condition. Similarly, each subject showed a decreased heart rate and, generally, a decreased respiration rate during profound relaxation (as compared to an isometric, muscle-tensing condition). Thus, when EMG activity diminished, other indicators of activation level such as heart rate and two-flash threshold also changed in the direction of lowered arousal.

Experiential Correlates. Verbal reports from subjects also indicate that the effects of thorough relaxation are not confined to the particular muscle for which feedback is being provided. Adjective checklists completed after EMG feedback training sessions have shown that sensations of heaviness and tingling of the limbs are common, as are certain body image changes such as experiences of floating, lightness, or turning. Also common are phenomena linked to autonomic changes—sensations of warmth, and increased salivation. Drowsiness and hypnagogic (sleep-onset) imagery are also reported frequently. Subjects generally reported the relaxation to be a mildly pleasurable experience, much like waking up from a refreshing nap. These descriptions are in good agreement with those reported in the autogenic training literature (see Luthe, 1965), and although the same pattern of sensations is not reported by every individual, the categories mentioned above occur frequently enough to be of predictive value, when group results are considered.

The Shaping of Low Arousal

An earlier study (Sittenfield, Budzynski, & Stoyva, 1972) bears on the question of whether muscle relaxation affects other bodily systems. This experiment supports the concept that muscle, autonomic, and cortical systems (at least in a relaxed, presleep condition) are likely to move in the same direction—although perhaps at different speeds. It further supports the theoretically and practically important idea that muscle relaxation may be an important first step in the biofeedback training of certain autonomic and cortical responses, particularly those responses associated with a low arousal condition of the organism.

In this experiment we asked whether subjects would acquire some degree of voluntary control over the production of theta. Since we were particularly interested in exploring the use of feedback techniques in cases of sleep-onset insomnia, we sought to determine whether normal subjects could learn to increase theta EEG frequencies above resting baseline levels.

The theta rhythm, 4-7 Hz, is strongly associated with drowsiness, and is recognized as the dominant electroencephalographic (EEG) frequency in Stage 1 of sleep (the sleep-onset stage; see Rechtschaffen and Kales, 1968). It is well known, particularly through the work of Foulkes (1966), that the theta rhythms of sleep onset are closely associated with hypnagogic or sleep-onset imagery. This material typically consists of a flow of fleeting, disconnected visual images, and typically has little or no effect. Recall of specific imagery is reported to occur in over 80% of awakenings (Foulkes, 1966).

Pilot observations soon showed that producing and maintaining a predominantly theta EEG is a very subtle task. Typically, base operant levels of this rhythm are very low, so there is little or nothing to feedback to the subject—a feature which can make learning very frustrating. Also, verbal reports strongly indicate that theta vanishes with the slightest striving on the part of the subject; he must learn to do the opposite, to "let go." Further, when theta is dominant, the subject seems to slip into a dissociated state. And the imagery that occurs is likely to assume a "real" or hallucinatory quality—a feature we were afraid might interfere with learning since attention would probably wander away from the feedback signal.

Because learning to modify theta levels was obviously a demanding and subtle task for most subjects, we hypothesized that a phased training (involving steps of graduated difficulty) might be a more effective approach than using only theta feedback for the entire training period. As Jacobson (1938) had already noted in his extensive work with progressive relaxation—and we had similarly observed—profound muscle relaxation is frequently associated with reports of drowsiness. We therefore decided to test out a two-phase training for the induction of theta. Experimental subjects were first given four sessions of EMG feedback training—to begin the shift toward low arousal. This was followed by four sessions of theta feedback training. Control subjects received theta feedback for each of their eight training sessions.

The 10 experimental subjects were divided into 5 subjects with high baseline EMG levels and 5 subjects with low baseline EMG levels. Similarly, the 10 control subjects were divided into a high-EMG group and a low-EMG group. Each of the 20 subjects was run for 13 half-hour sessions—3 baseline sessions, 8 feedback training sessions, and 2 postbaseline sessions (without feedback). In every session the following parameters were continuously measured: theta EEG (filtered output), alpha EEG (filtered output), fontalis EMG, forearm EMG, and heart rate. By means of resetting (Drohocki) integrators, information on each parameter was transformed into a train of digital pulses. These pulses were continuously summed by means of digital counters and totaled on a minute-by-minute basis (see Figure 5 for digital readout and quantification system).

For the subjects as a whole ($N = 20$), postbaseline values for theta were over 50% higher than baseline values, in terms of digital counts produced by the theta resetting integrator (see Figure 6). One of the four groups, however, did *not* succeed in increasing theta levels. This was the high-EMG group in the single-step training condition (eight sessions of strictly theta feedback). These results indicate that *before high EMG subjects are able to increase their theta levels, they must first learn to reduce their EMG activity.* However, in the case of subjects with low-baseline EMG values, either technique (theta feedback for all eight training sessions, or the two-step procedure) can be used for increasing theta level.

Also of interest was that for the group as a whole ($N = 20$), baseline heart rate and frontalis EMG levels showed a correlation of +.83 (rank-order). In the case of the 10 high-EMG subjects, there was a decline of over seven beats per minute in heart rate (comparing pre- with postbaseline values). Low-EMG subjects showed little or no change. Thus high-EMG subjects showed a combination of decreased EMG activity, decreased heart rate, and increased theta levels—an observation that supports the idea of a shaping technique to produce low arousal.

Another intriguing observation was the evidence of a reciprocal relationship between frontalis EMG levels and abundance of theta. This relationship was particularly strong at sleep onset—where Stage 2 "spindling" sleep begins. At

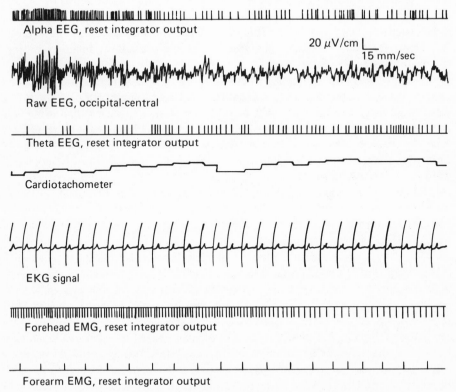

Figure 5. Quantification system and digital readout for EMG and EEG.

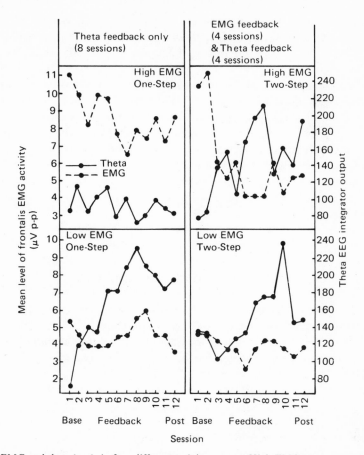

Figure 6. EMG and theta levels in four different training groups. High-EMG one-step group (N = 5) received eight sessions of theta feedback only. Low-EMG one-step group (N = 5) received eight sessions of theta feedback only. High-EMG two-step group (N = 5) received four sessions of EMG feedback, followed by four sessions of theta feedback. Low-EMG two-step group (N = 5) received four sessions of EMG feedback, followed by four sessions of theta feedback.

this point, and just prior to it, frontalis EMG regularly showed a sharp drop and theta rhythms displayed a strong increase. Interestingly, this observation is consistent with the previously mentioned statement of Jacobson (1970, p. 41) that when EMG activity in the facial and laryngeal muscles falls to zero (or close to zero) levels, then the subject is asleep.

An Adaptation Effect? But cannot an objection frequently leveled at the alpha control studies also be raised against this one? Were the increased theta levels merely the result of some nonspecific effect, such as adapting to the laboratory? This interpretation is improbable since, although high-EMG subjects given the two-step training showed increased theta levels, high-EMG subjects given only the one-step training (theta feedback only) did not, despite 13 sessions in the laboratory. The theta curve for the latter subjects remained flat (see Figure 6). It should also be noted that alpha levels remained on a plateau for the 13 sessions. This was true for each of the four groups.

These results indicate that, with appropriate feedback training, subjects can learn to increase their levels of theta—an observation in keeping with the commonplace notion that it is difficult to fall asleep if one remains muscularly tense. The study also shows that there is nothing automatic about increasing theta—some techniques work, some do not; the training must be tailored to fit the characteristics of the subject.

Further, the results support the concept of shaping a low arousal condition. In such an approach, subjects would begin their training with the comparatively easy response of learning muscular relaxation—a task that begins a shift toward parasympathetic activity. Subsequently, they would be trained on the more subtle task of changing some specific response such as lowering heart rate or blood pressure, or increasing theta—all associated with low arousal (see last section for further discussion).

Summary of Validation Studies

In a series of interlocking experiments with EMG feedback we have established the following:

Frontalis Study. EMG feedback proved superior to no-feedback and to irrelevant feedback in the production of low frontalis EMG levels (Budzynski & Stoyva, 1969). This superiority was apparent not only during training, but also on a postexperimental session without feedback (see Figure 2).

Masseter Study. In an experiment with masseter relaxation, it was found that the superiority of EMG feedback over the two control conditions was apparent even within a single training session (Budzynski & Stoyva, 1973a; see Table 1).

Frontalis versus Forearm Relaxation. Some muscles are better than others for relaxation training purposes. Thus subjects who received frontalis feedback training showed substantial decreases *both* on this muscle and on the forearm extensor (which was not receiving feedback). However, the converse relationship was not true. Subjects receiving forearm EMG feedback showed a substantial decline in forearm EMG levels but little change in frontalis EMG activity. This observation supports the notion that the frontalis is a very useful muscle for relaxation training purposes (see Table 2; Ball et al., unpublished observations).

High versus Low EMG Subjects. The individuals who showed the most dramatic drop in EMG levels were those whose muscle tension levels were compara-

Table 1

Comparisons among All Four Groups

Group	Analog– auditory (E)	Digital– visual (L)	Irrelevant (LT)	Silent (S)
Mean EMG (mV)	3.04	3.28	5.33	6.80
SD	1.40	1.19	3.47	4.89

Table 2
Frontalis Feedback versus Forearm Feedback in
Producing Relaxation

Group A:	Frontalis feedback, pre–post declines	
	$N = 7$	
	Frontalis decline	31%
	Forearm decline	45%
Group B:	Forearm feedback, pre–post declines	
	$N = 7$	
	Frontalis decline	2%
	Forearm decline	41%
Group C:	Control subjects	
	$N = 7$	
	Frontalis decline	9%
	Forearm decline	39%

tively high at the beginning of training. Those whose EMG levels were already low at the beginning of training showed only a moderate decline in EMG activity with feedback training—a result in keeping with the law of initial values (see Figure 4; Ball et al., unpublished observations).

Cortical Changes. Evidence for cortical changes produced by profound muscle relaxation was noted in an experiment by Budzynski (1969). Subjects were less able to detect paired flashes of light in the relaxed condition (i.e., whether a paired flash of lights looked like one light or two). Moreover, verbal reports of thoroughly relaxed subjects indicate that sensations of heaviness, warmth, and drowsiness are common—an observation supporting the idea that muscular relaxation has widespread effects on the organism.

Shaping of Theta EEG. Subjects whose baseline EMG levels were high (these are likely to be older subjects, or those in demanding jobs) did better at increasing their theta levels if they were given a two-step feedback training—first, EMG feedback training, then, theta feedback training (Sittenfeld et al., 1972). But subjects with high-baseline EMG levels who received only theta feedback training failed to augment their theta levels (see Figure 6).

On the other hand, subjects whose starting EMG levels were low did well at increasing theta with either type of training. That is, with low-EMG subjects, those who were given simply the one-step training (theta feedback for all training sessions) learned to produce just as much theta as those who were given a two-step training (EMG feedback for first half of training, followed by theta feedback for second half of training).

In addition to increased theta, the (high-EMG) subjects showed a decline in heart rate, which appeared to be closely associated with decreasing frontalis EMG levels. Also evident was a clear reciprocal relationship between frontalis EMG activity and theta levels at the moment of sleep onset. At this point, or shortly prior to it, there was a sharp drop in frontalis EMG activity and a large increase in EEG theta rhythms.

THEORETICAL BACKGROUND

As already indicated, our basic *working hypothesis* has been that the response to stress can be modified. We regard systematic training in muscle relaxation, and its associated low arousal condition, as a first step in this endeavor.

Our working hypothesis is in turn linked to the idea that in many instances modern man's response to a stress is maladaptive—he reacts excessively, or for too long a time. The individual who repeatedly manifests such responding may eventually begin to develop problems, particularly in his most reactive bodily system (e.g., essential hypertensives show large blood pressure increases under stress; see Engel & Bickford, 1961; Wolff, 1968). Fortunately, there is a substantial body of theoretical support that can be marshaled for the foregoing position.

Characteristically, the writers about to be cited point to evidence of hyper-reactivity and sustained arousal in the stress-linked disorders. Coupled with such hyperreactivity is an inability to return to baseline or resting values after stimulation has occurred.

Charvat, Dell, and Folkow. For example, Charvat, Dell, and Folkow (1964) speak of the "defense-alarm" reaction, maintaining that under the conditions of civilized living, the somatomotor component of the defense-alarm reaction is suppressed. However, the visceral and endocrine components of this reaction continue to linger, a phenomenon that may have adverse long-term consequences.

Working under the aegis of the World Health Organization and charged with the task of studying *Mental Factors and Cardiovascular Diseases*, Charvat et al. (1964, p. 130–131) arrived at the following general conclusions:

> Phylogenetically ancient defense mechanisms—originally intended to meet concrete physical dangers in primitive life—have been gradually transferred to the more subtle threat inherent in complex social relations and competitive situations. . . .
>
> Therefore, it is important to realize that civilized man differs from animals and, from very primitive man, in two respects. Firstly, the situations in which mental stress—and its appropriate efferent expressions—is produced, have become far more complex, subtle and manifold insofar as socio-economic relationships rather than immediate physical danger provide the most commonly occurring afferent stimuli. Secondly, when in civilized man "defense-alarm" reactions are produced, the soma-tomotor component is usually more or less effectively suppressed; in other words, *the originally well coordinated somatomotor, visceromotor and hormonal discharge pattern becomes dissociated.*
>
> There are, however, good reasons to assume that the visceromotor and hormonal changes, induced in connection with emotional stress and the defense-alarm reaction, will remain essentially the same. This implies that the mobilization of the cardiovascular and metabolic resources, intended to support a violent physical exertion will not be utilized in the natural way. For such reasons the hormonally produced changes of the blood and the chemical environment of the heart and blood-vessels can be expected to be more long-lasting than when a violent muscular exertion ensues.*

---

* It should be noted that even though modern man may effectively suppress *overt* somatomotor behavior under stress, it is probable that the tension in his skeletal musculature increases.

Charvat et al. are careful to emphasize, however, that the cardiofascular consequences of the dissociation of the originally well-coordinated somatomotor, visceromotor, and hormonal discharge pattern have yet to be thoroughly documented. The critical question still to be clearly demonstrated is whether stressful psychological stimuli lasting for long periods contribute substantially to disorders such as the hypertensive states and other cardiovascular disorders.

Cannon. Also pertinent is the well-known work of Cannon (1932), who described the *fight-or-flight* or *defense-alarm* reaction. The aroused sympathetic nervous system mobilizes a set of physiological responses marked by increases in blood pressure, heart rate, blood flow to the muscles, and oxygen consumption.

Wallace and Benson (1972, p. 90), writing in the context of the Cannon tradition, have recently voiced sentiments similar to those expressed by Charvat et al. (1964). In their view, modern man retains an easily triggered fight-or-flight reaction (well suited to meet the hazards of Neolithic living).

> During man's early history the defense-alarm reaction may well have had high survival value and thus have become strongly established in his genetic makeup. It continues to be aroused in all its visceral aspects when the individual feels threatened. Yet in the environment of our time the reaction is often an anachronism. Although the defense-alarm reaction is generally no longer appropriate, the visceral response is evoked with considerable frequency by the rapid and unsettling changes that are buffeting modern society. There is good reason to believe the changing environment's incessant stimulations of the sympathetic nervous system are largely responsible for the high incidence of hypertension and similar serious diseases that are prevalent in our society.*

Wolff. Again, in the extensive researches of Wolff (1968), ample evidence was found indicating the hyperreactivity of frequently stressed individuals. Such hyperreactivity was especially pronounced in the pathologically disturbed organ system; e.g., hypertensives showed large excursions of blood pressure during a stress interview. (The latter was the major experimental manipulation that Wolff employed in his far-ranging series of studies.) This pattern of hyperreactivity in the affected organ system was noted in a variety of stress-related disorders such as cardiac problems, hypercholesterolemia, vascular headaches, and duodenal ulcers.

Wenger. Another pertinent line of theory is Wenger's (1966) concept of autonomic balance. This refers to whether sympathetic or parasympathetic activity seems to be dominant in an individual. The estimate of autonomic balance ($\bar{A}$) for an individual is a composite of the values obtained by him on each of seven autonomic variables. Low scores reflect sympathetic dominance; high scores indicate parasympathetic dominance.

Wenger (1966) carried out a prospective study on over 1,000 healthy aviation cadets. In his follow-up 20 years later, Wenger found that the formerly healthy

---

* Wallace and Benson (1972), who have investigated the physiological effects of regular transcendental meditation, postulate that this practice produces an integrated hypometabolic pattern mediated by the central nervous system. This hypometabolic pattern has effects *opposite* to those seen in the fight-or-flight reaction—decreased oxygen consumption, decreased respiratory and heart rate, diminished blood lactate levels, and increased peripheral blood flow.

cadets who had shown lower Ā scores (sympathetic dominance) now displayed a higher incidence of high blood pressure, persistent anxiety, and heart trouble.

Wenger's observation of sympathetic dominance in so many disorders is generally compatible with Charvat et al.'s (1964) theory of the deleterious effects of the *defense-alarm* reaction under the conditions of civilized living, and with Malmo's concept of a deficit in the regulation of the autonomic nervous system.

Malmo. Malmo (1966) hypothesizes that a deficiency of the autonomic nervous system regulatory mechanism may be characteristic of many anxiety and psychotic states. For example, Malmo (1966) noted that in anxiety neurotics, forearm EMG levels in response to a startle stimulus took considerably longer to return to prestimulation values than was the case for normals.

In another experiment, comparing blood pressures in normals against those of neurotic patients during a mirror-drawing task, Malmo and Shagass (1952) found that for the neurotics, systolic pressures continued to rise during the task, in contrast to the normal group whose pressures tended to level off.

Observations of this nature led Malmo (1966) to conclude that in anxiety neurotics—and perhaps in acute schizophrenics—there is evidence of defective regulatory mechanisms of both the skeletal musculature and the autonomic nervous system. Malmo speculates that it may be defective inhibitory components of reticular and limbic systems that are involved in the physiological overreaction to stressful stimulation.

Lader and Mathews. Another theoretical position that postulates defective regulatory mechanisms is that of Lader and Mathews (1968). Lader and Mathews, who suggest that anxiety and physiological arousal are related, developed a model in which they proposed that systematic desensitization can be best thought of as a habituation phenomenon, and that habituation occurs most readily in a low arousal condition. Thus desensitization works best when the patient maintains as low an arousal level as possible (while at the same time clearly visualizing the anxiety stimulus).

Lader and Mathews further postulate a critical level of arousal beyond which repeated presentation of an anxiety stimulus is not accompanied by any habituation. Instead, the level of arousal becomes higher with each successive stimulus, thus producing a *positive feedback loop*—leading to undamped oscillations experienced as a panic attack of anxiety.*

Sternbach. A formulation combining many of the previously noted ideas is that of Sternbach (1966, p. 156), who envisages stress-linked disorders as involving a sequence of interlocked events.

---

* Lader and Mathews (1968) have presented evidence that patients with generalized or pervasive anxiety are at higher arousal levels than patients with specific phobias—their pervasive anxiety patients produced a larger number of spontaneous GSR fluctuations than did their normals, or patients with specific phobias. Pervasive-anxiety patients are also much more difficult to desensitize than are persons with circumscribed phobias. For example, in our work with several dozen cases over the past 5 years, we have noted that pervasive-anxiety patients typically required over twice as many relaxation training sessions as patients with specific phobias (21 vs. 9). They also required twice as many desensitization sessions (10 vs. 5).

We begin with a person who has response-stereotypy to the extent that whatever the nature of the activating stimulus, one response system always or usually shows the greatest magnitudes of change as compared to his other response systems. This person also has a *deficiency in feedback control* so that either in initial responsiveness, or in rebound, some limit is exceeded by this maximally reactive system which results in some tissue damage or symptom appearance. This event will occur either when a stressful situation arises which is specifically stimulating to the responsive system in which the individual is also maximally reactive, or when any stressful situation occurs which is of sufficient intensity and/or frequency to result in maximum and/or frequent reactivity. In the absence of objective real-life stressors, this condition may be met by the individual whose set is such that he perceives ordinary events as if they were those stressors. . . . [italics ours].

Some Difficulties with the Working Hypothesis

To many readers, the gap between the experimental data so far presented and the theoretical objective of modifying the response to stress may seem rather large. In the hopes of diminishing this gap, and of rendering our argument more plausible, several related questions will now be examined.

Response Specificity. An issue likely to be raised by psychophysiologists concerns response specificity. Are the physiological response patterns of particular subjects stable enough over time to warrant the assumption that excessive activation of some bodily system leads to a stress-related disorder?

Within psychophysiology, the question of response specificity has been a leading area of investigation for the past two decades. In part, this research has been a justifiable reaction against an oversimplified interpretation of Cannon's conceptualization of the fight-or-flight response—in particular, the idea that there is a *uniform* physiological reaction pattern to stress. As a result of psychophysiological research (see Sternbach, 1966), evidence mounted that the individual's profile of activation under stress was no means identical with every stressor (response specificity). However, Sternbach (1966, p. 144) notes that though normal subjects show a low degree of response stereotypy, psychosomatic patients, on the other hand, display a high degree of response stereotypy—i.e., a great variety of stress situations trigger the "favored" response. For instance, it has been documented that hypertensives, in a variety of stress situations, show strong pressor episodes (Engel & Bickford, 1961; Wolff, 1968).

Transfer to Everyday Life. Another important issue is whether a cultivated low arousal response, accquired in the laboratory, will later transfer to those everyday life situations in which the individual feels tense, anxious, or under pressure. In othe words, can the patient maintain the low arousal response outside the laboratory? Though this transfer question has been insufficiently explored by feedback researchers, the older self-regulation disciplines of progressive relaxation and autogenic training offer some valuable leads.

Probably the most important factor is the need for frequent practice. The autogenic exercises, for example, are carried out several times each day for several months. Finally, the low arousal shift becomes a highly overlearned response, and the individual's excessive reactivity to stress situations is said to diminish (see Luthe, 1969, Vol. IV). Some other promising maneuvers could probably be drawn from autogenic training. (1) The use of brief training episodes. With extended practice the trainee is said to become proficient at producing a low arousal condition quickly (Luthe, 1969, Vol. I). (2) Practicing in several different bodily postures. (3) The use of training phrases (e.g., "My arms and legs are heavy and warm"). These phrases are repeated silently during the exercises and not only serve to help the patient recapture the sensations appropriate to low arousal but assist in the dampening of conceptual activity—reports from subjects indicate that active, goal-directed thinking acts to prevent a shift into a relaxed, low arousal condition (as, for example, when one is trying to fall asleep).

Other techniques to assist in the transfer problem are currently being explored in this laboratory on a case-by-case basis: (1) the use of a portable home EMG feedback units, (2) cassette tape-recorded relaxation instructions for home use, (3) the use of fading procedures in the laboratory in which the subject learns to perform the response even as information feedback is gradually withdrawn.

It may also be noted that both progressive relaxation and autogenic training were mainly developed prior to World War II. Advances since that time—in electronics, cybernetics, psychophysiology, the principles of learning, and stress research—should permit the evolution of more powerful versions of these pioneering self-regulation techniques.

Autogenic training and progressive relaxation are both valuable in pointing to clinical applications of systematic training in cultivated low arousal. Both of these independently developed techniques have been applied to a variety of stress-related disorders—sleep-onset insomnia, tachycardia, anxiety neuroses, gastrointestinal disturbances, and essential hypertension (all of which are frequently associated with hyperarousal or hyperreactivity).

The clinical approach we are beginning to explore in this laboratory is to employ the technique of shaping low arousal to certain stress disorders frequently associated with hyperactivation. Patients are first taught the comparatively easy (whole-body) response of muscle relaxation. Subsequent training depends on the physiological *stress profile* of the individual. Thus a trainee who shows large heart rate increases under stress receives mainly heart rate feedback for his later phase of training. Insomniacs are later trained in producing theta rhythms.

In a subsequent phase it may be possible for a trainee to learn to control two or three bodily systems simultaneously through multiple feedback. After he proves able to control these systems, even under laboratory stress conditions, systematic desensitization could be added. The trainee could be asked to imagine real-life stressful situations while he maintains a low arousal condition. In this fashion, transfer to *in vivo* situations could be aided. The latter technique has already been used with a number of generalized anxiety patients (Budzynski & Stoyva, 1973b).

Potential Application to Essential Hypertension

Various sources of evidence suggest that the technique of cultivated low arousal may sometimes be useful in the treatment of essential hypertension.

Though the precise causes of this disorder are still a matter of controversy, the reaction to stress is generally thought to play a prominent part in its etiology. Thus two leading cardiovascular physiologists, Folkow and Neil (1971), maintain that essential hypertension results when the *defense-alarm* reaction is too frequently activated. If the individual, under threats of one kind and another, is *constantly mobilizing* his defense-alarm reaction (and its attendant elevated blood pressure) for extended periods, then blood pressures finally become reset at permanently higher levels. What begins as an adaptive, normal reaction designed to meet stresses of short duration becomes a pathological one in its consequences when the hypertensive response is extended for too long.

But perhaps the hypertensive's defense-alarm reaction can be modified. A combination of techniques might be attempted, proceeding from a general response to a more specific one—in keeping with the concept of systematically shaping a low arousal condition. If practiced often enough, the low arousal response may become part of the individual's new, and more moderate, reaction to a variety of stressors.

Particularly if the disorder were in its early, labile phase—prior to any permanent renal or vascular changes—the following combination of techniques might be attempted. First, systematic training in general muscle relaxation could be used in training patients to lower their arousal levels. Sources in the autogenic training literature report that the autogenic exercises often produce a reduction in blood pressure levels. For example, Klumbies and Eberhardt, at the University of Jena, applied autogenic training to 26 young adult hypertensives (see Luthe, 1969, Vol. II, pp. 70–72). It should be emphasized that frequent home practice was involved—brief episodes eight to ten times per day. After 4 months of training, systolic pressures showed an average decrease of 35 mm Hg; diastolic pressures showed an average decrease of 18 mm Hg—most of which took place during the first month. It may be noted that Jacobson (1938, p. 423) also has reported pressure decreases when progressive relaxation was applied in cases of moderate essential hypertension.

In a feedback training program, patients could first be trained in readily attaining muscular relaxation. Next, patients could be trained with specific feedback of blood pressure to help them to produce lower pressures, as in the work of Shapiro, Tursky, Gershon, and Stern (1969). Finally, if these patients are afflicted by various anxieties, which aggravate their disorders, then systematic desensitization could be used to help them moderate their anxieties.

If the biofeedback techniques are able to prove their mettle in stress-related disorders, then the practical consequences are considerable. These techniques may evolve into a means of modifying man's defense-alarm reaction. Methods of modifying the reaction to stress, such as those suggested by biofeedback techniques, could have widespread applications.

ACKNOWLEDGMENTS. The material in this chapter was originally presented in abridged form as a presidential address by the first author at the Fourth Annual Meeting of the Biofeedback Research Society, Boston, Massachusetts, November

1972. This research was supported by the Advanced Research Projects Agency of the Department of Defense and was monitored by the Office of Naval Research under Contract N00014-70-C-0350 to the San Diego State College Foundation, by National Institute of Mental Health Grant Number MH-15596, and Research Scientist Development Award Number K01-MH-43361-01.

REFERENCES

Balshan, I. D. Muscle tension and personality in women. *Archives of General Psychiatry*, 1962, *7*, 436.

Budzynski, T. H. Feedback-induced muscle relaxation and activation level. Unpublished doctoral dissertation, University of Colorado, 1969.

Budzynski, T. H., & Stoyva, J. M. An instrument for producing deep muscle relaxation by means of analog information feedback. *Journal of Applied Behavior Analysis*, 1969, *2*, 231.

Budzynski, T. H., & Stoyva, J. M. A biofeedback technique for teaching voluntary relaxation of the masseter. *Journal of Dental Research*, 1973, *52*, 116. (a)

Budzynski, T. H., & Stoyva, J. M. Biofeedback techniques in behavior therapy. In N. Birbaumer (Ed.), *Neuropsychologie der Angst*, Reihe Fortschritte der klinischen Psychologie, Bd. 3. München, Wien: Verlag Urban and Schwarzenberg. 1973, Pp. 248–270. (b)

Budzynski, T. H., Stoyva, J. M., & Adler, C. S. Feedback-induced relaxation: Application to tension headache. *Journal of Behavior Therapy and Experimental Psychiatry*, 1970, *1*, 205.

Cannon, J. *The wisdom of the body*. New York: Norton, 1932.

Charvat, J., Dell, P., & Folkow, B. Mental factors and cardiovascular disorders. *Cardiologia*, 1964, *44*, 124.

Davis, J. F. *Manual of surface electromyography*. WADC Technical Report, No. 59–184, 1959.

Engel, B. T., & Bickford, A. F. Response specificity. *Archives of General Psychiatry*, 1961, *5*, 82.

Folkow, B., & Neil, E. *Circulation*. New York: Oxford University Press, 1971.

Foulkes, D. *The psychology of sleep*. New York: Scribner, 1966.

Green, E., Green, A., & Walters, D. Voluntary control of internal states: Psychological and physiological. *Journal of Transpersonal Psychology*, 1970, *1*, 1.

Jacobson, E. *Progressive relaxation*. Chicago: University of Chicago Press, 1938.

Jacobson, E. *Modern treatment of tense patients*. Springfield, Illinois: Charles C Thomas, 1970.

Lader, M. H., & Mathews, A. M. A physiological model of phobic anxiety and desensitization. *Behaviour Research and Therapy*, 1968, *6*, 411.

Luthe, W. Autogenic training: Method, research, and application in medicine. *American Journal of Psychotherapy*, 1963, *17*, 174.

Luthe, W. (Ed.). *Autogenic training: Correlationes psychosomaticae*. New York: Grune and Stratton, 1965.

Luthe, W. (Ed.). *Autogenic therapy* (Vols. 1–4). New York: Grune and Stratton, 1969.

Maley, M. J. Two-flash threshold, skin conductance and skin potential. *Psychonomic Science*, 1967, *9*, 361.

Malmo, R. B. Studies of anxiety: Some clinical origins of the activation concept. In C. D. Spielberger (Ed.), *Anxiety and behavior*. New York: Academic Press, 1966. Pp. 157–177.

Malmo, R. B., & Shagass, C. Studies of blood pressure in psychiatric patients under stress. *Psychosomatic Medicine*, 1952, *14*, 81.

Rechtschaffen, A., & Kales, A. *A manual of standardized terminology, techniques, and scoring systems for sleep stages of human subjects*. Bethesda, Maryland: U.S. Department of Health, Education and Welfare, 1968.

Rose, R. J. Anxiety and arousal: A study of two-flash fusion and skin conductance. *Psychonomic Science*, 1966, *6*, 81.

Sainsbury, P., & Gibson, J. F. Symptoms of anxiety and tension and the accompanying physiological changes in the muscular system. *Journal of Neurology, Neurosurgery, and Psychology*, 1954, *17*, 216.

Shagass, C., & Malmo, R. B. Psychodynamic themes and localized muscular tension during psychotherapy. *Psychosomatic Medicine*, 1954, *16*, 295.

Shapiro, D., Tursky, B., Gerson, E., & Stern, M. Effects of feedback and reinforcement on the control of human systolic blood pressure. *Science*, 1969, *163*, 588.

Sittenfeld, P., Budzynski, T. H., & Stoyva, J. M. *Feedback control of the EEG theta rhythm*. Paper presented at the American Psychological Association meeting, Honolulu, Hawaii, 1972.

Sternbach, R. A. *Principles of psychophysiology: An introductory text and readings*. New York: Academic Press, 1966.

Venables, P. H., & Wing, J. K. Level of arousal and the subclassification of schizophrenia. *Archives of General Psychiatry*, 1962, *7*, 114.

Wallace, R. K., & Benson, H. The physiology of meditation. *Scientific American*, 1972, *226*, 84.

Wenger, M. A. Studies of autonomic balance: A summary. *Psychophysiology*, 1966, *2*, 173.

Wolff, H. G. *Headache and other head pain*. New York: Oxford University Press, 1963.

Wolff, H. G. *Harold G. Wolff's "Stress and disease."* S. Wolf (Ed.). Springfield, Illinois: Charles C Thomas, 1968.

Wolpe, J. *Psychotherapy by reciprocal inhibition*. Standford: Standord University Press, 1958.

Wolpe, J., & Lazarus, A. A. *Behavior therapy techniques*. New York: Pergamon Press, 1966.

35

EMG Training and Headache Reduction: Some Methodological Issues

Leon S. Otis, David Low, and Ann Turner

We've been running experiments on voluntary control of tension headaches since 1971, and our results have done nothing but cause problems for us. They simply are not orthodox. More specifically, they raise questions about the relationship of head and neck muscle tension to the etiology, onset, and control of tension headaches. And what is learned by our subjects does not appear to fit either the operant learning model or the skills learning model—not, at least, in any obvious way. This is, perhaps, not quite correct. Some skills *are* being learned and reinforcement of operant behavior *does* occur. The skills being learned, however, do not appear to be the ones we think we are training, and the reinforcement we are paying attention to does not appear to be the one that is responsible for making the subject headache-free.

I'd like to briefly review that we've been doing and solicit your assistance in trying to make some sense out of our data. We have a theory, but it is a theory born out of mild desperation. Maybe you've got a better one that requires fewer epicycles.

All in all, we've run 80 medically defined tension headache subjects in six experiments. I'll briefly review the main findings of the first four experiments and present some data from the fifth; the sixth is in progress.

In our first experiment feedback was not provided during lower tension commands (that is, when the subject was told to decrease his trapezius neck muscle tension he did not receive feedback) but only during 1-minute raise tension commands. Ten sets of 1-minute raise, rest, and lower commands were given in sequence for 10 sessions over two 5-day periods. The results were little short of amazing: Nine of 11 feedback subjects reported significant decreases in headaches after the 2nd week of training and 7 of these subjects were headache-free. Six of 8 that responded to a 1-year follow-up continued to have a significantly lower headache score than their pretraining score.

We faced a dilemma in trying to explain these results. The classic assumption, based on a reasonable amount of respectable research, is that tension headaches arise from the sustained maintenance of high levels of head and neck

Leon S. Otis and David Low • Stanford Research Institute, Menlo Park, California 94025. Ann Turner • Psychiatrist, Palo Alto, California 94301.

muscle tension. In this experiment we trained our subjects to become more tense and yet their headaches disappeared.

We claim no brilliance for this design. Our findings resulted from serendipity. The subjects were *supposed* to get feedback for both the raise *and* lower tension conditions. A fluke in the computer, however, withheld feedback during lower commands. The subjects, of course, complained that they experienced great difficulty in responding to the lower-tension commands; but knowing that lowering tension is a difficult task, we simply encouraged them to keep trying.

After a good deal of puzzlement our results finally made sense. The Jacobsen Progressive Relaxation Technique trains muscle relaxation by having subjects increase tension and then letting go. This is similar to our increase-tension condition followed by the rest period (i.e., return-to-baseline condition). Unlike the progressive relaxation technique, however, we were showing the subjects, by feedback, how well they were doing.

The reinforcement, of course, was the relief of tension upon reachieving the baseline condition following each raise command. This would appear to be a much more powerful reinforcing state of affairs than one would expect from that achieved by lowering tension from baseline and returning to baseline. It also had the advantage of training subjects to sense the difference between high and relatively lower (i.e., baseline) levels of muscle tension. Accordingly, away from the laboratory, they might have become more adept at sensing muscle tension buildup and immediately relaxing—thereby aborting an incipient headache.

This first experiment makes the point that "face validity" doesn't necessarily make things so. Others have trained tension headache subjects with feedback to reduce muscle tension levels below baseline. This approach has a great deal of face validity and it also works. But it takes a long time to teach the average subjects to accomplish this rather difficult task; it's much easier and requires a much shorter time to train subjects to tense and let go. What our results told us is that it seems much more important to train people to sense (by experiencing) voluntarily induced high and low levels of tension than it is to train them directly to lower tension. This point has been made before for cardiac patients by Bernie Engle; he found it beneficial to have his patients learn to increase, as well as decrease, their cardiac arrythmias. We also had the terrible thought that you may not even have to provide external feedback to achieve this goal. We chose not to follow up on this traumatic thought and proceded to continue our feedback experiments. Lately, however, we've been forced to reconsider this possibility. But before I go into that issue, let me briefly tell you what else we've found.

First, subjects appear to learn to raise or lower on command (as tested without feedback) fairly quickly, or they don't learn at all. In our second experiment, additional training was without effect in learning better muscle tension control or in further reducing headache density.

Second, sitting quietly for an equivalent number of sessions has no effect on achieving better muscle tension control, or on headache density. Neither does noncontingent feedback.

Third, contrary to expectation, in two replications we could find no correlation between EMG muscle tension levels and alpha, beta, or theta EEG frequencies. Alpha and theta are thought to reflect a relaxed state of affairs.

Fourth, trapezius EMG levels during headache episodes *do not*, in our experience, differ from resting levels during nonheadache periods. In fact, in a few cases we have found *lower* EMG levels during headache episodes than during nonheadache periods. However, resting EMG levels after feedback training appear to be reliably lower during both headache and nonheadache periods.

Fifth, feedback training of any one of the muscle groups of the head and neck seems to generalize to other muscle groups in the cephalic region but not to muscles of the appendages. And finally, we found that the Rotter's I-E Scale successfully predicted in 11 of 13 cases who would complete and who would drop out of an experiment. We are currently checking this important finding in another experiment; the waste in time and lost data that can be saved by identifying potential dropouts during subject selection is, obviously, of considerable importance. Other personality evaluation procedures are also being looked at.

Now to return to the two questions we put aside earlier. The first is: How important is external feedback, per se—at least for learning voluntary control of tension headaches? The second is: What are subjects learning during feedback?

In our most recently completed experiment we found that three of four control subjects that simply performed tense–relax exercises for 10 1-hour sessions without feedback had a significant reduction in headache scores whereas only two of six feedback subjects experienced headache relief. This is not altogether surprising since three of the feedback subjects also had migraine problems (we were exploring the efficacy of our techniques for tension headache subjects who also suffered from migraine). The results of this experiment suggest that external feedback may be of limited utility when, as in our procedure, internal feedback is sufficiently discriminable for subjects to learn to sense differences in the state of some internal processes.

The experiment now in process raises some fundamental questions regarding what the subjects are learning during feedback training. The critical learning may not be what the researcher is trying to teach them.

In an effort to sharpen our headache-reporting procedures, we issued 2-hour pocket timers with an alarm and daily logs to our subjects. They were instructed to set the timer for 2 hours on awakening and, when the alarm sounded, to record (on the log) the presence or absence of a headache at that moment and its intensity. They were also asked to recall the previous 2 hours and estimate headache density for that period. The timer was then reset for the next 2 hours, and so on throughout the working day. Subjects were relieved from this schedule after working hours and during weekends.

The design called for six pretraining recordings of EMG resting level—three during headache episodes and three during nonheadache episodes. All 16 subjects had completed their 3 days of nonheadache EMG recordings within the first 2 weeks. Six weeks later we gave up trying to complete the 3 days of EMG recordings during headache episodes. Only five subjects had completed these data: Two

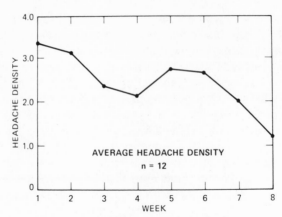

Figure 1. Average drop in headache density.

had come in twice, and three once. Telephone follow-ups and review of the daily logs indicated that our subjects were becoming headache-free. Remember that they had received no training of any sort and were simply recording headache density whenever the timer went off and turning in daily logs! The average drop in headache density for the group is shown in Figure 1. Of considerable interest is the fact that even though there was a considerable drop in headache density, there was no change in pre- and postbaseline EMG levels. Half of these subjects are currently receiving raise-tension feedback training and the remainder are receiving no training; all are continuing with the timers.

These preexperimental results, coupled with our findings that tension levels of muscles of the cephalic region are not correlated with presence or absence of a headache has led us to the following hypothesis.

We believe that what subjects learn—whether in a feedback session or when they are forced to stop whatever they are doing when the timer sounds—is to "get in touch with themselves." Admittedly, this is a fuzzy concept, and we can offer no operational definition. However, biofeedback clinicians and behavioral therapists have reported similar findings for patients asked to chart their own behavior. For example, in obesity control, the act of charting has resulted in considerable weight loss within the first few weeks of the program in the absence of deliberate diet control. The concept we are trying to put across is reminiscent of Don Juan's admonition that to become a man of power (that is, to be fully in control), one must learn to "stop the internal dialogue." Perhaps, this is what we're teaching our subjects—to gain control by stopping their internal dialogue.

In this regard, we pose this question: Is it possible that this is the critical learning in feedback training whether we train our subjects in EEG, heart, blood pressure, or muscle tension control? We'd appreciate your views.

NOTE. The material in this chapter was originally presented at a meeting of the Biofeedback Research Society, Monterey, California, February 5, 1975.

36

Paraprofessional Relaxation Training Technicians in a Biofeedback Clinic

Carol Schneider and Dona Culver

The word *patient* has connotations of someone passively waiting for the doctor, listening while being told what is wrong, taking medicine, and "patiently" waiting until the drug takes effect. Something is being done to the patient rather than his doing something. The role of the patient seldom includes being an active participant in understanding and doing something himself about what is wrong. Our biofeedback program seeks to change the treatment role of the patient so that he becomes an aware, understanding observer of what is happening to his physiology. With this awreness, control or change often becomes possible. With his continued efforts at voluntarily doing something to change the information he is receiving about his physiology, potential change can become a reality. Biofeedback is any process that detects a specific aspect of the body's physiological functioning, converts these data into signals that can be heard, seen, or felt by the person himself, and feeds those signals back to him.

For the person to make proper use of the biofeedback information to change his physiology, several weeks of training are needed. Certain aspects of the training are routine (e.g., instructions about relaxation procedures, explaining the machines and how to use them, collecting data, giving information about progress in training, and charting symptoms to teach the changes). Other aspects of the training are far from routine. The trainer observes in the training sessions the aspects of the patient's emotional functioning that get him into trouble with his world and his physiology. There are often blocks to learning, distorted expectations from the program, and a host of other problems that make successful training complex. Some therapists have reacted to the complexity by doing all the training themselves in sessions that combine the routine aspects and therapy. In our clinic, we have chosen to train paraprofessional technicians to do the actual biofeedback and tension-control training. The professionally trained clinicians supervise the technicians and see the patients once each week while they are in need of stress management psychotherapy. The therapist deals with aspects of the patient's maladaptive functioning that come up in the biofeedback sessions (as

Carol Schneider and Dona Culver • Biofeedback Clinic, University of Colorado Student Health Service, Boulder, Colorado 80309. CS is also affiliated with the Department of Psychiatry, University of Colorado Medical School, Denver, Colorado 80362.

reported by the technicians) and in life outside the biofeedback setting. Technicians well trained as both instrument handlers and observers of patient response are a must in this type of program.

TRANSFERENCE OF TRAINING

Transferring responses that are developed in a clinical situation with biofeedback equipment to other life situations is often seen as an important, but difficult, part of biofeedback training. In some ways, this is the last phase or stage of biofeedback training, something to work on after the patient has mastered the training and perhaps has gained some degree of increased self-confidence. In other ways, however, the transference of training begins at the first training session and becomes increasingly important as the program continues.

Certain basic attitudes and assumptions on the part of the patient are important to develop. From the beginning day, the technician must emphasize the significance of daily practice of relaxation skills or other responses at home, *away from the biofeedback facilities*. Such practice must include both tape sessions and self-instruction. The transfer of training to the home, work, or school situation must be acknowledged as the major goal or purpose of using biofeedback to learn. The technician can explain that, to some extent, stress responses involve conditioned responses or learned harmful habits. Relaxation requires a type of learning that is new to the patient. However, it is still a form of learned response, and, therefore, must be *practiced* more than one or two times during the week in a clinic setting. Having a set of tape recordings at home (tapes that guide a person through stages of relaxation practice) reinforces practice away from the clinic. Asking the patient to keep daily records of symptoms and practice sessions also reinforces home practice, especially if the technician places a great deal of importance on these records and shows an interest in looking at them.

Secondly, the technician and the patient should devote some time to discussing the patient's pace of life and the situations where he experiences the most tensions and symptoms. For example, is the patient extremely tense during classes at school or during working hours, or does he become tense and anxious when he interacts with a spouse, when he begins to do homework or cook dinner? Such questions are important for the technician to ask the patient. The technician needs to ask the patient when it would be most beneficial for him to take 30 minutes of "time-out" to practice relaxation, or when it is possible for the patient to find time to practice. If a patient complains that regular home practice is impossible, due to a lack of time, the technician should slowly go through the patient's schedule with him in more detail to find time when the patient could take at least a 20-minute break. For example, the technician could ask the patient when his longest uninterrupted work session occurs, and how long it lasts; when the person's classes or job seem to be the most challenging; when he could arrange to be alone for a brief period of time, or when the children take naps. In other words, the technician could have the patient "map" on paper his typical day in hours, from waking up to going to sleep, in order to locate optimal times to devote to practicing. This scheduling problem may be factual, it may be resistance, or it may be an indication of the patient's neurotic style. The technician should treat it as factual but should also make a note to tell the therapist. Then the therapist can explore the problem as possible resistance or make the necessary therapeutic intervention.

Besides this ever-present focus or emphasis on practicing away from the biofeedback facilities, some specific strategies can be used to enhance this transfer of training. If the technician remains seated quietly in the same room with the patient during the biofeedback session, the patient will become accustomed to relaxing in the presence of another individual. This situation is far from being the same as remaining relaxed in a department store or classroom, but it seems to be a step in the right direction. The patient is learning to perform in a situation that he may view as evaluative. Also, the patient can practice relaxation with the biofeedback equipment in a reclining position and in other positions where he usually finds himself being tense. For example, when he is in an upright sitting position in job or school situations, he could try to train himself to achieve lower levels of relaxation in that position. The ability of the patient to verbalize or discuss relaxation strategies may enhance this transfer of training. In order to verbalize strategies, the patient would have to think about how he relaxes, and how he *doesn't* relax, and formulate a plan for, or definition of, his relaxation and how to initiate it. If a person can verbally express how he brings about the desired response, he may be able to respond in this way more easily and automatically in various circumstances. Technicians could encourage patients to talk about their individual strategies and to describe any accompanying sensations. Likewise, the use of key phrases or significant images may serve as cues to initiate a desired response, such as relaxation. Words, sounds, phrases, or images that feel relaxing or seem to induce relaxation for a person can be recalled by the client when he is attempting to relax in any situation. For example, the word *hot* is a cue word for temperature training. Another person might use the word *calm* as a cue word or the phrase "I am calm now" as a phrase on which to focus his attention. A person may find the image of ocean waves to be relaxing and peaceful. A person may visualize hands rubbing across the forehead relaxing the muscles involved in tension headaches. In a job setting, when he knows he needs to relax, the person could recall the relaxing image as part of his strategy to ease away tension.

After the patient has achieved initial success in relaxation training (the ability to lower tension levels quickly and keep the tension away), the use of fantasy or imagery may be a powerful aid to the transfer of training for some people. During biofeedback sessions, the patient might be able to imagine himself in a situation that is usually quite stressful for him. Once he has fantasized himself to be in this particular place, he may be able to train himself to relax and manage the stress in that imaginary setting. Relaxation training in fantasy circumstances could generalize to the actual stressful situation. Teaching this is the primary function of the desensitization tape, but some patients begin doing this job of coupling stressful fantasy and relaxation on their own much earlier in the program.

Written reminders to "relax" attached to notebooks, and pieces of brightly colored stick-on tape placed on watch faces, are two examples of physical means to aid in reminding to check for tension. Placing a small band of tape on the watch is especially useful because people are usually in a rush when they check their watch. The tape needs changing every week, so that adaptation to the color does not occur. A note or a small sign to "be calm" placed in a location that is visible to the patient could remind the person to check himself for tension at various points throughout the day. Repeating a relaxation phrase before each class begins, before answering a phone, or while waiting for anything (e.g., traffic lights) may be useful. An unlimited variety of strategies of this nature can be devised by patients to help themselves center their attention or focus on the need to relax periodically until this type of awareness becomes more automatic or spontaneous.

As the patient becomes more capable of relaxing, with respect to achieving lower levels of tension *and* integrating this response into his regular life-style, the frequency of biofeedback sessions should decline to complete the transfer of training. (See later section on termination of training.)

FAILURE IN THE BIOFEEDBACK PROGRAM (TROUBLE-SHOOTING GUIDELINES)

Certain patients seem to be particularly *failure-prone* from the beginning of biofeedback training. These people seem to be bound to fail, and this is often as much of a frustrating experience for the technician as it is for the patient. The technician observes the patient's failure, but it is sometimes difficult to discuss this with the patient and to delineate the factors or reasons contributing to this lack of progress. The following circumstances seem to accompany failure to benefit from this type of relaxation training. Recognizing the basis for the problem may at least help relieve the technician's frustration and confusion. An awareness of these circumstances may also suggest to the technician ways of reducing the high probability of failure in some cases.

Inadequate Development of an Awareness of Muscle Tension

The initial task in relaxation training is to learn (from biofeedback) to discriminate tension. The patient must become familiar with what it feels like *to him* to be tense; he must become aware of when he is tense before he can attempt an opposite response. One biofeedback session, where a person is asked to tense and relax the major muscle groups, *may* be enough to develop this type of awareness. However, some people seem to require more practice at this first task (perhaps two sessions devoted to this, or some brief discrimination exercises at the beginning of each session). If the technician does not allow enough time for a patient to achieve this initial step, the patient may fail to make significant progress. This failure experience is an additional barrier and the patient may drop out of this treatment modality. With each individual, a technician must assess whether or not the patient is able to discriminate tension. If the patient can verbalize what his tension feels like, make a comparison of relaxation and tension, or somehow comment on the two different states, it is a good indication that he is aware of tension. If he is not, see the section on special training for problem areas.

Lack of Motivation to Succeed in Biofeedback Training

Some patients may not be motivated to succeed for various reasons. These people almost certainly fail at the training and drop out at some point, *or* they fail continually and remain in training for an extended length of time. In some cases it doesn't seem important to succeed. A person may not experience the symptoms as painful enough to work at eliminating them. Some people may not understand the role of tension in creating and maintaining a physiological disorder; they will not be motivated to participate in a program that seems unrelated to the disorder. A symptom may "work for" the patient, e.g., by being ill, he may avoid some type of responsibility, some significant person may care for him only when he is ill, or coming into the clinic may be the only place where he can communicate his feelings. Such secondary gain aspects of the symptom need to be worked with in therapy. A patient's motivation may be changed during the course of therapy sessions, or he might gain a more adequate understanding of the psychological stress-related nature of the problem. However, failure is almost inevitable if the motivation remains the same. If a technician sees that a patient is in some way unmotivated to succeed, he should talk to the patient's therapist as soon as possible to consider changing the motivation or reconsider biofeedback training.

Viewing the Biofeedback Situation as an Evaluation Circumstance

If a patient feels that he is being tested or evaluated in the biofeedback session, he defeats himself. He may strive so hard to relax that tension is increased. The patient might become defensive about being evaluated and resist relaxation. A person could also become involved in a competitive relationship with the biofeedback equipment or with the technician (e.g., asking how he compares with other patients). He could place himself in a win/lose situation, which is incompatible with the passive type of concentration necessary for deep relaxation (letting go, allowing it to happen). These kinds of circumstances almost always ensure failure experience and increase the possibility of an overall failure to progress. Technicians should avoid judgmental, evaluative comments. With some people, a direct discussion of these problems may be all that is necessary. Explaining directly to the patient that he is not being evaluated may dissolve the misconception. In many cases, a less direct message may be necessary: Point out something *successful* about each biofeedback session and reinforce this aspect of it. (This is unusual and unexpected in evaluative or "test" situations.) The perfectionistic character of these patients often causes them to define themselves as failures if they don't learn immediately. Working with them about realistic expectations and progress is crucial to their treatment.

Interference at Times of Crisis

If a patient is experiencing some type of a crisis situation, it may be necessary for him to *first* deal with this situation in therapy (e.g., resolve a problem in a marital crisis). It may be impossible to succeed at relaxation training before the patient has made a major decision, or calmed down enough to even think about relaxation. If a person seems to be failing, this possibility should be discussed with the patient's therapist. Sometimes, patients will need a session of talking and thus they can begin to relax again. This is often useful, but care must be taken to avoid biofeedback sessions becoming therapy sessions themselves, for if that happens, the goal of learning to relax becomes subverted. It is often better in those cases to refer a patient back to the therapist and do biofeedback training later.

Inability to Shut Out Intruding Thoughts

"Intruding thoughts" (distracting, upsetting, or obsessive thoughts during a relaxation period) may occur frequently and impede success at relaxation training. This type of problem may be dealt with by the technician's *not* paying attention to these thoughts. The technician may tell the patient that these thoughts occur frequently at first and that the patient should just try to focus on his muscles and allow the thoughts to fade at their own pace. This strategy reduces a common tendency for the client to "drive out" the thoughts (thereby defeating relaxation). A second strategy is to substitute a relaxation thought or image in place of intruding thoughts. Provide the client with something he can think about during relaxation, if he must think about something. This thought should be conducive to relaxation or something that will not oppose relaxation. A variant of Fehmi's open focus training has been used for this problem with some success. A third suggestion is to discuss the intruding thought with the patient. The obsessive personality is very likely to have difficulty controlling thoughts, as rumination is a way of life. Likewise, intruding thoughts can be a form of resistance to learning. This resistance may be related to fears about giving up the symptoms.

Viewing Biofeedback as an Instant Cure-All or Mystical Therapy (Electronic Yoga)

If a client thinks of biofeedback as an instant "cure-all"—a situation where he will not have to take responsibility for practicing and making progress—he will fail at training. At the time of the diagnostic session, each client must be given some type of adequate introduction to dispel myths (see section on myths and misconceptions). Clients who are looking for an instant, effortless change will be inclined to drop out of treatment after the diagnostic session. It may be helpful in some cases for the technician to explain that most lasting achievements have never been effortless or instant. Perhaps the technician could persuade clients to give relaxation a "trial run" to see if the necessary effort is too demanding of their time and energy. When a person actually begins relaxation training, he may see that the effort involved is a new and different type of effort from what he is used to making. (It is more a matter of taking the responsibility to practice and *making* time to relax than of striving or working.)

MYTHS, DEFENSIVE POSTURES, AND MISCONCEPTIONS THAT INTERFERE WITH RELAXATION

The following are some common statements or beliefs that patients hold about relaxing. The statements are written in the words we hear and the discussions are written as if the technician is actually talking to the patient.

1. *Relaxation is a natural process and doesn't take any practice.*

Right and wrong. Right, that relaxation is a natural process, as natural as walking, talking and whistling. Wrong, that it doesn't take any practice. Watch a small child who hasn't yet mastered the skills of walking, talking, or whistling, and it becomes obvious that "natural processes" take a lot of practice. Relaxation is a skill that we must learn, in the same way that we learn any other skills, by practice and experience.

2. *If I ever let myself get completely relaxed, I may never be able to "come out of it."*

Wrong. There is absolutely no way you can get "stuck" in relaxation. Each of us has considerable experience in moving between the states of relaxation and alertness. We do it each time we fall asleep and again when we wake up. If someone expresses the fear that if he lets himself go he won't be able to "come out of it," there might be other fears for which this is a cover. Gently explore what he thinks might happen if he gets really relaxed. Sometimes this fear covers a fear of dying or of losing control.

3. *If I can just learn to relax, all my problems will disappear.*

Unfortunately, not true. Relaxation is not magic, it won't make you a "different person." Unrealistically high expectations of the biofeedback program can be just as detrimental to the learning of relaxation as unyielding skepticism. The best approach to this attitude is to objectively discuss what can realistically be expected from participation in the biofeedback program.

4. *If I let down and relax, something terrible might happen.*

This is a more general statement of #2. The "something terrible" might be as concrete as "my headache will get worse" or as vague as "I might lose control." Most of the fears are unrealistic ones and can usually be put to rest by a frank, open discussion about the kinds of feelings and sensations that one could realistically expect from relaxation. Sometimes, however, this fear represents an inability to give up the symptom because it is so much a part of the person he cannot imagine life without it. The terrible thing may be that he will no longer be himself. The therapist needs to be notified of the "something terrible" reaction.

5. *Learning to relax is like learning to do anything else, it takes work and effort.*

This almost sounds right, but a person who believes this will never learn to relax. Relaxation doesn't take work and effort but rather practice and experience. This is more than a mere quibble about words; it means a difference in how you approach the task. Work and effort requires you to be active and expend energy. Relaxation is just the opposite. When you relax you are quiet and passive. Relaxation doesn't take work, but it does take time and practice. This practice involves "allowing" yourself to relax and experience the feelings and benefits of relaxation. Allowing oneself to let go, to let down, and to disengage has been called a "passive concentration" phenomenon by many people. Some people are so competitive and striving that it is very hard to learn to let go of that orientation.

6. *I don't have enough time, as it is, to do everything I have to do. Relaxation is basically a waste of time that could be more productively spent.*

Production is a function of both time and efficiency. While it is true that learning to relax takes some time, in the long run it needn't hurt anyone's productivity. If anything, it might help, because a rested, relaxed person is often more efficient in his work. Although this is true, it may not be the best approach to take with a person who has this type of feeling. They are often in the biofeedback program because this dedication to the work ethic has started to take its toll. These people often need help in seeing that relaxation is a permissible, enjoyable, beneficial, and healthy way to spend some time. It is important that the negative attitude toward relaxation as a waste of time be dealt with, since no one can relax in time given grudgingly and halfheartedly.

7. *If I learn to relax, I can't deal effectively in places where I need to be angry.*

This misconception is based on the conception that relaxation equals passivity. If you are relaxed, you are not necessarily passive at all. Ideally, you will be more able to do the things you really want to do when you relax because:

a. You will have more energy. Tension burns energy wastefully. Conserve your energy for the really big things in life.
b. You will not be so physically sick or so paralyzed by anxiety that you can't think straight or act appropriately. You can calmly consider the alternatives and select the one that fits you and the situation best.

8. *I am learning to relax if I fall asleep during the practice sessions.*

Right and wrong. If you are in the stage of borderline sleep called "theta," or "hypnogogic," and you have enough repetitions of the material you are trying to learn, you will learn the *words*. If you are in deep sleep you won't ever do that. Even in theta, you will not learn the accompanying sensations (heaviness, warmth, relaxed feelings) that accompany the words. Try to stay awake during your practice. If you fall asleep, you may need to change the time of your sessions, practice more often by giving yourself the instructions, or move on to the next tape. Sleeping is very refreshing and relaxing, but it is not the same as learning to relax *voluntarily*. If you want to use the tapes to get to sleep faster or to take a nap with, be sure to schedule extra learning sessions for yourself.

COMMON QUESTIONS ASKED BY PATIENTS

1. *Am I normal?* (in regard to the readings from the feedback machines).

There are no "normals"—each person's physiology is unique—with their own cycles and baselines. What is important in biofeedback relaxation training is for the individual person to lower his or her present baseline.

2. *Are the machines safe?*

Yes, all models of biofeedback equipment are entirely safe. Both the GSR and EMG machines run solely on batteries. The temperature machine only reads the temperature of the skin, not passing any current through the skin.

3. *How long will this take?*

The answer to this question depends on several factors: (a) How much the person puts into practicing with the relaxation tapes at home; (2) how much the person practices with the relaxation tapes and biofeedback combined; and (3) how much the individual *generalizes* using the relaxation procedures to other situations.

4. *Why use the biofeedback at all, since I get relaxed enough with the tapes?*

The real use of the biofeedback procedure is for the person to discover how relaxed they *actually* are, by seeing the tension indications visually or by hearing them. Often one can feel relaxed and believe oneself to be relaxed. However, by using an objective measure one can discover if one is really as relaxed as possible. Eventually you will be able to relax and monitor tension without the machine so well that tension control is automatic. The machine can be a real help in getting to that desirable end.

5. *Can I get too relaxed?*

When I get relaxed, all I seem to do is fall asleep.

When I relax, I feel strange sensations—is this normal?

All of the above questions are centered around the actual feelings one has when one becomes extremely relaxed. For many people, relaxation is such a new and different state of consciousness for them, that it is a strange experience. Many feelings can and do go along with this experience for them, such as those reflected by the above questions. What is important is for the person practicing the biofeedback relaxation procedure to become aware of how his body feels when it is relaxed, i.e., when the EMG reading is less than 3.3 microvolts. It is normal to feel strange when one relaxes to this level. Many people describe such things as the disappearance of body boundaries, tingly feelings, rushes of warmth, or floating sensations. The technician should try to encourage the person who wonders about these sensations to enjoy them and to learn to expect them when he is relaxed.

THE ROLE OF THE TECHNICIAN AND THE RELATIONSHIP WITH THE PATIENT

The one-to-one interaction between the patient and the biofeedback technician is, in several ways, essentially a type of helping and educative relationship. The technician initially introduces the patient to a form of training with biofeedback (such as relaxation training) by explaining the basic concept of biofeedback. This explanation should be in terms that make sense to the patient, often using examples of different types of biofeedback training. The technician can supplement this verbal explanation with some brief literature or an article about biofeedback.

The technician illustrates the specific biofeedback program being offered to the patient by outlining the progressive steps or stages involved in the training, specifying the procedure of feedback sessions, and explaining the biofeedback equipment in a functional, nontechnical manner. This is usually done as the patient is being hooked up to the biofeedback equipment and actually begins to monitor a given aspect of his or her physiology.

In general, the technician guides the client into the program by teaching the patient about the precise nature of biofeedback training (often dispelling myths and misconceptions as this is done) and by demonstrating the procedure involved. From the beginning, the patient is a knowledgeable, active participant in this aspect of treatment, instead of being a passive receiver of something he does not understand.

The technician is an informative source in piecing together information (such as the nature of the patient's symptoms, his motivation to practice and succeed with the training, and his life situation or pace). This information is necessary in order to help the patient establish realistic expectations about the time necessary to learn and the amount of practice needed to succeed. After gathering such information, the technician is in a position to help the patient design an individual relaxation schedule or practice plan, and to advise the patient on how to achieve a transfer of training from the clinic setting to other life situations.

The patient views the biofeedback technician as someone who is there to reliably and accurately answer questions, if possible. If not, the technician is someone who will seek out the answers to those questions that he cannot answer, often by consulting with a psychologist or a physician. Keeping records of the patient's progress in the clinic by monitoring biofeedback equipment, reviewing symptom charts, and keeping track of the client's problems (such as in finding practice time or in dealing with intruding thoughts during relaxation) are also part of the technician's job. By maintaining these records, in the form of organized written data, the technician offers another type of important feedback to show the client how he is doing in his training, how he is being effective in relaxing, and what areas or aspects of training will require the most attention.

Equally important in the technician–patient relationship is the technician's presence as an accepting, understanding human being. The technician needs to convey empathy or to communicate to the patient that he understands the patient's symptoms and is aware of how painful or distressing these symptoms are. Such empathy can be communicated if the technician pays close attention to the patient (in listening and responding, and by facing the person and maintaining eye contact) as the patient talks about his experiences with this training. The technician can then tell the patient how it makes sense to him that the symptoms are disturbing and that learning a new response is frustrating at times. This conveys the message that the technician is truly interested in, and respects, the other person, and is ready to work along with the patient to achieve some degree of mastery over the symptoms. The biofeedback technician can be seen as a human contact in a program that might seem "mechanical" in nature. The patient makes contact with more than the biofeedback equipment.

The technician's behavior, such as maintaining a relaxed attitude in front of the patient, even in facing problems and irritations, serves as an example or model to the patient. For instance, the technician should remain calm in talking to a patient, despite the fact that the patient is becoming anxious about his inability to achieve a greater degree of success with the training program. Technician self-disclosure, instances when the technician shares his own sometimes frustrating experiences in handling stress and learning relaxation, can likewise be a vital part of the technician–patient relationship. Self-disclosure is helpful to the extent that it keeps the focus of discussion on the patient's potential alternative solutions to his own problems, and doesn't cause the patient to worry or be concerned with the technician's problems.

The technician is also a source of support for the patient, if the technician expresses pleasure to the person following successful experience and indications that the patient is trying to practice at home. Such reinforcement prompts the patient to repeat his attempts to cooperate in the training. The technician needs to point out all indications of progress to the patient, no matter how small. The technician should turn most of the patient's experiences into successes of some kind, if possible. For example, even if the patient is unable at first to decrease his EMG tension level, his frustration at his inability shows that he is at least *aware* or concerned about the tension. The technician could help the patient to see that an awareness of tension is the first step in a process and that this awareness is, indeed, a form of progress. That which the patient may view as failure can potentially be converted into a reinforcing successful experience. This is especially important when the patient is as demanding and perfectionistic about himself as a psychosomatic patient usually is.

Listening, communicating an understanding of the patient's feelings, being knowledgeable in answering questions, and setting a positive example behaviorally all help to establish a relationship where the patient sees the technician as a type of teacher or helper. The technician is seen as a "helper" in the sense that he knows the subject of biofeedback training; he is someone who is reliable, someone who is living effectively, someone who is capable of helping another person with a certain aspect of living. This type of relationship puts the technician in a position where he can offer suggestions and constructive criticism without insulting or offending the patient.

POTENTIAL PROBLEMS IN PATIENT–TECHNICIAN RELATIONSHIPS

As the treatment progresses and the alliance with the patient in the task of learning tension control becomes stronger, technicians may experience phenomena in the area that the Freudians call transference and countertransference. The angry client may try to provoke a fight with the technician. Refusing to argue or be defensive is the proper way to deal with provocation. Focusing on the positive alliance between yourself and the patient can help avoid the struggle that angry patients face in so many other areas of their lives.

Make sure also that the patient doesn't attribute his success solely to you and your marvelous job of telling him what to do.

TERMINATION

If the patient indicates to the technician that he wishes to make no further appointments, he should be encouraged to return one more time so that his progress can be discussed with him and some questions can be asked about what changes have occurred and what aspects of the program have been either helpful or not as helpful as he'd hoped they would be. If he does not keep the appointment, or if he stops coming without warning, a phone call should be made and the patient asked if he would prefer to answer some questions about the program over the phone rather than in person.

QUESTIONNAIRE

The two-page termination questionnaire should be administered either in person or by phone to every patient with whom a technician has had at least one training session, and who indicates he is not returning.

The technician can certainly chat informally before and/or after the formal questionnaire and write any pertinent comments on the questionnaire. Particularly if he has worked over an extended time and has formed a relationship that is meaningful to him and the patient, the technician should inquire about feelings related to the termination of the contact with him. Sometimes this can be done by sharing the fact that he has found this person a real pleasure to work with and has some feelings about saying good-bye, and then inviting the patient to share his feelings. At other times, sharing the regret that not as much was accomplished as the technician and patient had hoped for will give them a chance to share some negative feelings. At any rate, the technician should recognize there may be significant, and appropriate, feelings from the patient regarding termination with him as well as the machines. If the technician is leaving and the patient will continue on with someone else, always ask for the patient's feelings and/or reservations about having to transfer to another trainer. Remember that the technician has given much more than instructions and a hookup to an electronic instrument or two. He has advised, encouraged, listened to problems, been interested and sometimes frustrated, and has shared a significant experience (ideally positive but occasionally negative). Expressing his feelings has been a problem for the patient or he wouldn't have been there. So help him to say whatever is on his mind at termination.

FOLLOW-UP

Before the patient leaves, inquire whether he would have any objections to answering a few questions about the frequency of his physical symptoms in six months. If he has none, ask him for his permanent address or an address from which he is sure mail will always be forwarded. This is usually a parent's address, but it could be a best friend who will always know where he is living. File that address in the biofeedback card file with a date of termination.

At this final session, it is particularly important to talk of the necessity for continuation of home practice in order to maintain mastery of relaxation or temperature control. Biofeedback has not "cured" the patient of the symptom, only helped him control it. A new and useful skill has been learned, but it must be regularly utilized in order for it to remain a successful way for him to control his symptoms.

37

EMG Biofeedback in Physical Therapy

C. K. Fernando

CLINICAL APPLICATION OF BIOFEEDBACK TECHNIQUES IN NEUROMUSCULAR CONDITIONS

The use of biofeedback is becoming increasingly valuable in the field of physical therapy. It has been proven effective in muscular reeducation and muscular relaxation. Audiovisual muscular reeducation techniques make use of electromyographic devices and amplify internal physiological processes in the body that are normally not seen or perceived by the therapist or the patient. Making use of auditory and visual feedback, the patient is given two information inputs other than those normally available to him with which to process information concerning physiological events.

Audiovisual neuromuscular techniques are an adjunct to all the other therapies commonly used. To use this technique, one should be well versed in many other applied sciences like electromyography, pathology, neurology, kinesiology, and muscle reeducation techniques. In this chapter, we shall discuss the clinical application of the following audiovisual neuromuscular techniques: inhibition of spasticity, recruitment of motor unit activity, muscle reeducation of tendon transfers, muscle relaxation, and the use of the techniques as an evaluation tool with incomplete spinal cord lesions. These techniques can be used alone or sometimes in combination. I shall illustrate how they are used in different patients with different conditions and I shall give you some case illustrations. The types of patients we are familiar with present the following:

1. Upper motor neuron lesions, e.g., cerebrovascular accidents, incomplete lesions of spinal cord injuries.
2. Lower motor neuron lesions, e.g., peripheral nerve injury, Bell's palsy.
3. Hysterical paralysis.
4. Muscle spasms of unknown etiology causing pain.
5. Spasmodic torticollis.

Cerebrovascular Accidents

The residual paralysis of CVAs is normally treated by physical therapists whether it is spasticity, flaccidity, or other problems associated with this syn-

C. K. Fernando • Physical Therapy Department, Schwab Rehabilitation Hospital, and Mt. Sinai Medical Center, Chicago, Illinois 60608.

drome. Normally, in the early stages, the physical therapy management is instituted to prevent deformity, to bring about movement, and to improve functional
activities and activities of daily living. However, in many patients, we are all
aware that either flaccidity continues to exist for more than a few days due to
spinal shock or, as spasticity is exhibited, the patient is in synergy and unable to
perform normal functional activities due to lack of isolated movement. In many
others, ambulation becomes a serious problem due to the presence of clonus.
These three problems, flaccidity, spasticity, and clonus, seem to be tenable to
treatment by audiovisual neuromuscular reeducation, in conjunction with standard therapeutic modalities.

Flaccidity. Patients who are flaccid after a CVA for more than a week or
two weeks should be started on this technique of treatment—specifically, recruitment of motor unit activity. The patient is first prepared physically and
psychologically. Then the equipment is prepared and applied to the patient. Having
explained to the patient what is expected of him and having applied the electrode on
the muscle or muscle groups that are to be treated, the therapist instructs the
patient to make as much noise as possible on the audio and to bring about on the
scope activity that he and the therapist can see. Obviously, before treatment begins,
the patient should be evaluated as to the amplitude of the activity seen on those
muscles at rest and on passive movements and active motions. One should note not
only the amplitude but also the interference pattern as to whether it is complete,
incomplete, or nonexistent. As I pointed out earlier, the patient is asked to make as
much noise as possible and to make sure that there is some activity seen on the
scope. If nothing is seen, then the therapist starts passively moving the joint or
joints in question and tells the patient to attempt to do what the therapist is doing.
If there is no success with this, then the patient is asked to do the required action
with the good limb, at the same time trying to do the same motion with the affected
one. This is cross-facilitation. If this is not effective, gross motions are begun with
the effective limb while at the same time the patient is working with the ineffective
limb. All of these strategies are used until something is seen on the scope and heard
on the audio. Tapping, stretching, and vibration could also be added to the adjuncts
used. Tapping on the muscle, stretching the effective muscle, or vibrating the effective muscle with the electrodes in place are the three strategies used, so that the
patient can bring about one little activity in that group of muscles which can be
picked up by the audio and the oscilloscope. The moment either the therapist or the
patient hears the first signs, then the patient is asked to continue to do whatever he
did to bring about that noise.

Sometimes this strategy might be continued for a couple of days with no success; other times it might be rewarded within a few minutes of instituting the
technique. If the technique is started in the lying position and results are negative,
then it is worthwhile trying the treatment in other positions. If the technique
becomes effective in the lying position, then the position is changed to the sitting
position, and later to the standing position.

Now I shall give you a case illustration of a patient. Mr. B came to Mount
Sinai with a monoparesis of the right lower extremity. The normal physical
therapeutic procedures were tried on him for 2½ weeks with no success. A

program of audiovisual neuromuscular reeducation was instituted. What we were trying to do and what was expected of him were explained to the patient. His problem was a drop foot with no dorsiflexion and eversion. With the patient lying down, surface electrodes were placed on the tibialis anterior with a ground electrode placed next to it. The machine was on. The patient was instructed to do anything he could to make a noise on the audio. For a few minutes this was tried, and as he could not make any response on the machine, the therapist stretched the dorsiflexors. This brought a few rumbles of activity, which were heard on the audio and seen on the scope. The patient now built upon this, and within minutes he was firing a few motor units although he could not dorsiflex or evert the foot. The initial amplitude of motor unit activity was about 10 mV and the interference pattern was incomplete. The patient continued to recruit motor unit activity. The therapist instructed the patient to dorsiflex the good foot. Then it was noted that there was an increment in motor activity and more noise was heard. The patient continued to come to physical therapy daily. A temporary short leg brace was given to the patient and the audio-visual techniques were continued. His motor unit activity continued to improve, and his amplitude and interference pattern became near normal. At the end of three weeks, he had complete dorsiflexion and he was discharged from the hospital with a normal gait. It should be mentioned here that when the tibialis anterior began to show a trace of motion, and later range of motion, we still continued him on the audiovisual techniques in addition to the normal therapeutic techniques of muscle reeducation. It could be said that because of audiovisual neuromuscular reeducation we were able to reeducate the paralyzed muscles in a shorter time. In short, I would go so far as to say that all patients who show flaccidity for more than a few days—7 to 10 days—should be begun on audiovisual neuromuscular reeducation in addition to other techniques. The moment something is seen and heard that could not previously be perceived by the patient or the therapist, that activity is picked up and then the patient can continue to build on that minute amount of activity. It is the difference between flying with radar and flying without radar. In one instance, the pilot is flying blindly, but with radar he is flying with equipment that tells him his height, his position, and his location. It is the same thing here. If a therapist treats his patient without seeing or hearing, it is as if he is flying without instruments, and so is the patient. But the moment the two additional inputs are given, the patient and the therapist can see and hear, which is a great help to the reeducation process. It helps both the therapist and the patient physiologically and psychologically as they feel that something is returning that would not have been seen or heard if not for this type of instrumentation. The ideal treatment protocol for this type of patient would be a half hour of therapy every day using audiovisual neuromuscular technique, with the patient given a minitrainer or a portable EMG biofeedback unit to practice this strategy on his floor or at home two or three times a day for a half hour each time.

Spasticity. For patients who are in synergy and whose muscles are in spasticity with no isolated motions present, this technique could be instituted to break the synergy and bring about isolated motions, thereby helping the activities of daily living. To bring about inhibition of spasticity and help the return of isolated motions, one first has to inhibit spasticity of his agonists and then recruit motor unit activity of the antagonists. Finally, general relaxation techniques are used to bring about general relaxation of the whole body. So it is a question of judiciously using several techniques to bring about the desired motions. Let us take an example where the patient is in flexor synergy, where the biceps of the patient are in spasm and the upper limb is in abduction at the shoulder, with flexion of the elbow and flexion of the wrist. First, as before, the patient is evaluated to determine the amount of spasticity of the biceps at rest, on passive motion, and on voluntary motion. This is noted. The interference pattern is also noted as to whether it is complete, partial, or incomplete. As before, the patient is prepared and the treatment begins. When the electrodes are placed on the biceps, one will see and hear activity even at rest. Now the patient is instructed to lower this sound level and to bring about silence. If the patient is unable to do this, then the therapist will instruct him to increase that activity by trying to do a motion in synergy. The moment he does this he will be able to hear the rumblings on the audio and see the activity on the scope. Now, the therapist will instruct the patient to lower that. This is done a few times until the patient understands what is expected of him.

Sometimes the therapist might even stretch the elbow and the biceps, and the patient will try to relax it and thereby lower the noise. This is repeated a few times. The electrodes are now placed on the antagonists or the triceps group. The patient is now asked to bring about more sound by extending the elbow. These two procedures are executed: first, inhibition of the biceps, and second, motor unit recruitment of the triceps. Again, it should be pointed out that this type of therapy is not begun on day 1 or day 2. If no results are seen with the standard techniques available, only then do we recommend the use of these techniques. Some of the patients may have a functional return without this treatment modality.

It is interesting that there are many documented reports of this technique used in the literature. Sometimes the technique might be used differently. Electrodes are placed on the biceps and the patient is asked to extend the elbow and at the same time is told to lower the noise and the activity seen on the scope. This should be done gradually, meaning a few degrees of motion at a time while lowering the noise. Once he learns to extend the elbow a few degrees each time, lowering the noise, then he can move to the next stage. Sometimes, because of spasticity in the biceps, the patient is unable to extend at all. Then the electrodes are placed on the triceps and the patient is asked to bring about motor unit activity. When he hears and sees the activity of the triceps, he is able to overcome his spasticity, or in spite of the spasticity he'll be able to get more range in extension. In this type of patient, recruitment of motor unit activity is done first and then inhibition of spasticity is performed as a second technique. As I said before, this strategy is used depending on the patient and his problem and the expertise of the therapist himself. As with all other techniques of therapy, one has to grasp the problem and tailor the therapeutic strategies depending on the patient's needs. Here I have to again mention the scientific truism that even normal people are unable to bring about inhibition of motor unit activity and learn to fire a single motor unit. Dr. Basmajian calls them motor unit morons, and according to him about 10% of the population are motor unit morons. It is possible that among patients you also might see many who will not be able to learn this technique. Maybe they fall into this category of motor unit morons. As I said, all patients do not learn to inhibit their spasticity by this technique. It is worthwhile trying this technique on patients because nobody knows all the answers of inhibiting spasticity. Now I shall give you an illustration of a patient.

Mr. K, a 39-year-old male, was referred to us with a diagnosis of left infantile spastic hemiplegia. The date of onset was from age 5. He was on a program of physical therapy and outpatient therapy. In addition to the standard physical therapy procedures, he was also on a program of biofeedback techniques for inhibition of spasticity of the left biceps. On his initial evaluation, he had a 50-degree inhibition in extension at his left elbow and the upper extremity was in flexor synergy. At discharge, after 6 weeks, he was out of this synergy pattern and his extension improved by 20 degrees. The techniques used were inhibition of spasticity of his biceps and recruitment of motor unit activity of his biceps. He received half-hour sessions daily for 6 weeks.

Clonus. Many CVAs and other lesions of the pyramidal system result in clonus, which causes difficulty in ambulation. The moment the effective foot is placed on the ground, a rhythmical tremor of the agonists and antagonists of the ankle results. Audiovisual neuromuscular reeducation techniques seem to be amenable for treatment of this problem.

The patient is prepared physically and psychologically. The electrodes are first taped to the tibialis anterior and then the foot is dorsiflexed by the therapist with the patient in the lying position. The moment clonus is evoked, the patient will see activity of the tibialis anterior on the scope and hear it on the audio. The patient is instructed to lower the noise level. This is repeated a few times, and soon the patient learns to lower the activity. Once the patient learns this technique in the lying position, the technique is prepared in a dynamic situation. We use the Kinetron when the patient is sitting down and walking on the Kinetron. The moment the patient sees clonus, he tries to inhibit it. This process is repeated for a half hour each day.

Incomplete Lesions of the Spinal Cord

The patient should be evaluated to find out whether there are any muscles or groups of muscles below the lesion that are innervated and to study the amplitude of these potentials and the interference pattern. Audiovisual neuromuscular reeducation techniques could also be used in those incomplete lesions where there is spasticity in muscles that could cause difficulty in ambulation. This spasticity could be inhibited using audiovisual neuromuscular reeducation techniques in addition to other therapeutic techniques.

Evaluation of Patients with Incomplete Lesions of the Spinal Cord

We are all aware of cases in which the spinal cord is not completely severed by gunshot injuries and other traumatic lesions of the cord. Therefore, there is a possibility of many groups of muscles below the level of injury being viable. But due to the fact that in the acute stage of treatment the patient is immobilized, the chances of these viable muscles being atrophied is great. When a patient is brought to a rehabilitation center, it is only correct to test for all those areas below the level of the lesion to find out the size and the nature of potentials, if there are any. This is determined by placing electrodes below the level of the lesion and studying the amplitude and the duration of these motor unit potentials. Of course, this is a painstaking and time-consuming process, but it is well worth-while, because if there are any muscles that are viable, then the therapeutic process can begin immediately. Those groups of muscles that are still innervated should be started on a therapeutic regime right away. The technique of motor unit recruitment should be commenced and therapeutic exercises should be initiated for those muscles below the level of the lesion. For those patients whose lower limbs are in spasm, the technique of inhibition of spasticity is begun. Here it should be mentioned that the technique of inhibition should commence in the lying position, then in the sitting, and finally in the standing position, and even in ambulation.

I shall give case illustration of two patients. Mr. P. was a 26-year-old male who came to us with a T-6 lesion due to a gunshot injury. In the early stages of his hospitalization, he had decubitus ulcers, atrophy of both lower limb muscles, and contractures of both feet. However, when we started his evaluation we found much motor unit activity below T-6 level in the abdominal musculature, and we started working on those areas using the motor unit recruitment technique to increase the activity of the muscles in question. Before long, the amplitude of the potentials was near normal and so was the interference pattern of the abdominal musculature below the lesion. The patient continued to receive treatment with audiovisual neuromuscular reeducation techniques and normal therapeutic techniques for these muscles. Finally, when he left us, his lesion was like a T-11, L-1 lesion. He left us with long leg braces and a pelvic band, having good sitting balance and good uppers (which, of course, were normal) and able to do much more than if he were treated in the normal way as a T-6 lesion.

The second patient, Mr. B, was a quadriparesis due to a neurofibroma at C-6 level. After surgery of the neurofibroma, he was gaining strength and power on all muscles, although his rehabilitation period took as long as 6–8 months. But due to the early immobilization in a Minerva corset after the laminectomy, and complete bed rest, there was much atrophy of all muscles of the body and severe spasms of his adductors and his quadricep groups of the lower limbs. As I mentioned, when we started his rehabilitation program and were able to start ambulation, his main difficulty was adductor spasm, which caused much difficulty in ambulation even in the parallel bars. Then we started the technique of inhibition of spasticity using biofeedback techniques of the adductors. The patient was treated lying down, and we found he was able to overcome his adductor spasticity in this position. But the moment he sat down, he again had spasms. So we continued to treat in the sitting position and later there was a carry-over in the sitting position. But when he again commenced walking, he continued to have spasms. Then in simulated walking in the lying position, we taught him inhibition of spasticity while the motions were done in this position by a therapist. Using this technique, we were able to inhibit spasticity completely, and he left the rehabilitation center using a walker with no spasticity of the lowers. It should be mentioned that not only biofeedback but also normal therapeutic exercises were employed as a part of his rehabilitation program.

Lower Motor Neuron Lesions

In lower motor neuron lesions, the technique of motor recruitment begins early in the therapeutic program. I think this is one technique that should be used with all peripheral nerve injuries the moment the first signs of innervation are seen by electrodiagnostic techniques, either EMG techniques or strength duration curves. We perform strength duration curves with these patients every 2 weeks. The moment we see signs of partial regeneration, then we begin the motor unit recruitment technique.

In patients where there are signs of partial regeneration and yet no active muscle movement is apparent, this technique is very effective. This type of patient responds better to therapy as the therapist and the patient can see the activity, although it is not seen or perceived without instrumentation.

I shall give you some case illustrations. Mr. H. is a 36-year-old male. In 1974 he sustained a gunshot injury to the lateral aspect of his left knee. He presented a drop foot due to paralysis of the tibialis anterior and peronei and was unable to dorsiflex and evert the foot. Marked atrophy of the tibialis anterior was seen.

The patient was referred to physical therapy for nearly nine months. He was treated using the standard techniques of therapy—electrical stimulation, passive motions to joints, and active exercises—and was given a dorsiassist. In addition to this, strength duration curves were done every 3 weeks. On the first sign of regeneration, the patient was started on a program of audiovisual neuromuscular reeducation. Surface electrodes were placed on the tibialis anterior with the ground electrodes next to it. The motor unit recruitment technique was utilized for the treatment of the patient. Treatment was begun when the patient had been physically and psychologically prepared. On the first evaluation, the patient was able to evoke a few motor unit potentials whose amplitutde was about 20–30 MV with an incomplete interference pattern. The technique of motor unit recruitment was done three times a week for half-hour sessions with cross-facilitation techniques, and gross motion patterns for the paralyzed limb. Before long, the patient was evoking near-normal motor unit potentials with a near-normal interference pattern. The atrophy of the tibialis anterior was minimized and the patient began to dorsiflex his foot.

Mr. S. was a patient with Bell's Palsy who was referred to us. He had facial paralysis on the right side when we saw him the first week after the onset. A strength duration curve was done and it was found to be normal. He was started on biofeedback techniques using the recruitment of motor unit activity. The electrodes were first placed on the obicularis oris, then the buccinator, and finally the frontalis muscles, and the patient was instructed to evoke as much motor unit activity as possible. He continued to increase the size of the motor unit potentials and the interference pattern became normal within 2 to 3 weeks, whereupon this patient was discharged.

It should be mentioned here that it's easy for the patient as well as the therapist to determine whether the patient is exercising the muscles in question when he is hooked onto EMG equipment.

Hysterical Paralysis

Patients with hysterical paralysis show many signs and symptoms. Some are seen with spasticity and yet others are completely flaccid. Once a determination is made of hysterical paralysis and the treatment plan is designed, then biofeedback techniques have a very valuable place in the treatment of this problem. It should be mentioned that biofeedback techniques are used in combination with psychotherapy, psychological counseling, and other modalities of therapy. I shall give two case illustrations of patients—one with flaccidity and one with spasticity.

Miss W. came to us with a foot problem. This patient was a 27-year-old air hostess who had met with an auto accident and had complete eversion of the foot with spasticity of the peronei. The foot was everted about 50 degrees from the normal, and she was ambulating while holding the foot in this position. The initial diagnosis was contusion of S-1, S-2, low back pain, and spasticity of the peronei with eversion of the foot. She had had this problem for 7 months and, after consulting many physicians all over the country, had been advised to undergo laminectory and orthopedic surgery for the foot. However, she refused this type of surgery and came to our institution for rehabilitation. When I evaluated this patient, I saw motor unit activity on the peronei at rest and noted that this group of muscles were in severe spasms. I explained to the patient what was expected of her and what would be seen on the scope when she completely relaxed. The electrodes were placed on the peronei and when the technique of inhibition of spasticity was begun, the patient was able to completely relax the peronei and even bring the foot to the mid-position, actively, although she was in severe pain. The pain was due to the fact that the foot was held in that position and the joint capsules were in contracture. The patient was able to bring the foot to the neutral position using biofeedback techniques on her own volition. However, at the end of treatment, the foot went back to the valgus position as before. We continued to use this technique every day, sometimes twice a day, for 3 weeks. In addition to that, she had whirlpool baths, therapeutic exercises, ambulation training, and isokinetics. Before long, she was able, even without biofeedback techniques, to hold the foot in the neutral position and even to do dorsiflexion and plantar flexion. She was discharged 4 weeks after admission with a portable unit on which to practice relaxation techniques of the peronei. We can now report that she is normal and able to ambulate and that she is back at work.

The second patient was a 31-year-old female with a past history of recurrent CVAs. Her admission diagnosis was right hemiparesis secondary to CVA with flaccidity of both extremities of the right side. During the first episode of the CVA when she was referred to us, she spent 6 weeks in the rehabilitation process with us and was discharged with a long leg brace and with a muscle power of trace to poor in the lower extremity. However, at the end of 6 months, she completely recovered. The second time, she was again diagnosed as CVA and referred to our institution. Within 3 to 4 days, there was a complete return of all power and motion of the right upper extremity, but the right lower extremity continued to be in complete flaccidity with no motion at all. We commenced biofeedback techniques for this patient using the motor unit recruitment technique. Electrodes were placed on the quadriceps and the therapist explained to the patient what was expected of her. The technique we used was motor recruitment. The patient was in the sitting position with both feet hanging over the side of the bed. The therapist extended her extremity and told the patient that he would let go his hand so that the leg would fall down if the patient did not contract those muscles. This was done a few times and as the patient could not contract her quadriceps, she was not able to hold that position. Eventually, the patient began to tighten the quadriceps and when she did this, one could see a few motor unit potentials on the scope and hear the noise on the audio. This reinforced the patient, and within minutes she was firing huge motor units with near-normal interference patterns. This technique was continued with all the other muscles of the lower extremity—the dorsiflexors, the plantar flexors, the evertors—and within a half hour she was able to fire all motor units in all the musculature of that limb. We then started ambulating her, and she was able to hold the knee in place. However, she continued to ambulate with a drop foot for a few days. Biofeedback techniques were continued for a few more days and the patient thereafter continued to do only therapeutic exercises.

If we had not instituted biofeedback training at that time, I am sure she would have just continued to be in the rehabilitation institute like the first time, and her return would have been much slower. It should be mentioned here that biofeedback techniques in patients with hysterical paralysis are only a vehicle to get to the point where the patient accepts her problem and goes along with the therapist to get better.

Muscle Spasms of Unknown Etiology

These patients are in severe pain due to the vicious cycle of muscle spasm, pain, and more muscle spasm. Sometimes, this type of patient does not respond to drugs and continues to be in this vicious cycle. We had a few patients referred to us because of this problem and we found biofeedback techniques were effective in alleviating this problem.

The first patient, Mrs. S, was a female who was a paraplegic 5 years ago. Her problem was severe muscle spasm of both sternocleidomastoid muscles, causing pain that did not respond to any of the drugs the physicians prescribed. She was referred to us for biofeedback techniques. In addition to the biofeedback techniques, we also gave her hot packs to help relaxation. The technique was one of general relaxation. The electrodes were applied first on one sternocleidomastoid muscle and then on the other. When the patient was evaluated, we could see huge motor unit activity in her sternocleidomastoid muscle even while at rest. The patient was prepared physically and psychologically and the treatment procedure was explained to her. First the electrodes were applied on the right sternocleido-mastoid muscle, and the patient was instructed to move her neck to the left. One could now see more activity on the scope and hear it on the audio. The patient was then instructed to bring the neck to the mid-position and lower the noise completely. Soon she learned to do this. The same procedure was done with the left sternocleidomastoid muscle. She learned to relax both muscles in the mid-position with the help of the equipment. This procedure was also tried without the equipment. She was in therapy for a few days, and at each therapy session, in addition to this techique, she was also taught breathing exercises and general relaxation techniques. Within 5 days she was able to control her spasms and was discharged from the hospital. However, this patient was readmitted within a few months for the same problem. This time, in addition to treating her in the hospital as before, she was given a portable unit to take home with her. She practices this technique twice daily at home for a half hour each time. She has not returned to the hospital with this problem ever since.

The second patient was a patient with osteogenita imperfecta. Her problem was severe muscle spasms in the paraspinal muscles of the back, causing her severe pain. She was not responding to analgesics and the physicians referred her for general relaxation techniques. When she came to us, we evaluated her and found the paraspinal muscles in severe spasm even at rest. The patient was begun on therapy in the prone position with electrodes on one paraspinal group and then on the other. The technique used was relaxation of her spasms. The electrodes were on one paraspinal group with the ground close to it, and the patient was in a prone position, able to see and hear the audiovisual results. She was instructed to raise her head and shoulders and come back to the neutral position and then lower the noise completely. Within minutes the patient learned the technique. The carry-over was slow, but within a couple of days the patient learned to reduce her spasms and even control her pain.

These patients were referred to us because they could not control the spasms and hence the pain. The ideal protocol of treatment for these patients as inpatients is to see them twice a day for 30 minutes of training each time. In addition to this, both these patients were taught Jacobson's relaxation techniques and general relaxation of all muscle groups.

Spasmodic Torticollis

Spasmodic torticollis is a problem of unknown etiology. For many years it was thought of as a problem in the basal ganglia. However, this theory has now been discarded. We have seen about 10 or 11 patients with spasmodic torticollis. Our experience shows that every patient is different and, therefore, the strategy to be used on every patient depends on his own particular problem. In general, each patient should be evaluated not only for the activity of the sternocleidomastoid muscles but also for that of the upper trapezius and the paraspinal muscles. They should be evaluated during all the motions for each muscle. Once a patient has been evaluated, then a program is designed. Our success rate so far is not as good as what is reported elsewhere in the country. But we see a 20–30% success rate with our group. Some of the patients, in addition to receiving biofeedback techniques, are also in psychological counseling.

We see a few types of movement disorders with these patients.

1. The patient whose sternocleidomastoid muscle on one side is hypertrophied and in spasm with the head turning to the opposite side is called the classical type.
2. There are patients who, in addition to problem 1, also have atrophy of the sternocleidomastoid muscle on the other side. Most patients will present both these problems.
3. Some patients will present hypertrophy and spasm of one sternocleidomastoid muscle with head turning to the opposite side. In addition to this, the sternocleidomastoid muscle on the other side will be cocontracting. That is when the head turns to the side opposite the hypertrophied side, and the sternocleidomastoid muscle on the atrophied side will also work with the hypertrophied side to rotate the neck.
4. Some patients, in addition to the classical picture, will also have spasms of the trapezius and the paraspinal muscles.

All patients in spite of spasmodic torticollis, could continue to work in their chosen field if they were able to release their spasms and bring the neck back to the mid-position. All these patients, in an anxiety-producing environment, are unable to bring the neck back to the mid-position smoothly but do that only in two or three stages in a jerky fashion. Although many of the patients we treated continued to have their problems all who had no structural involvement learned to release their spasms and bring the neck back to the midline in a smooth movement.

Let us discuss the problems of a patient we treated and the strategies used to treat him. Each patient is initially evaluated and a treatment plan designed to suit the individual needs.

Mr. O, a 56-year-old salesman, had spasmodic torticollis for 2 years. He had been treated by many other physicians and therapists before seeing us. His main difficulty was that he was unable to drive his car as his neck turned to the side while he was driving. He had left spasmodic torticollis with spasm of the right sternocleidomastoid muscle, with the neck turning to the left.

On evaluation we found that (1) the right sternocleidomastoid muscle was hypertrophied and the neck rotated to the left; (2) the right sternocleidomastoid muscle was in severe spasm; (3) the left sternocleidomastoid muscle was atrophied; (4) the left sternolceidomastoid muscle was cocontracting with the right to turn the neck to the left; (5) when the patient turned the neck to the right, the left sternocleidomastoid muscle was firing a few motor units of very small amplitude; and (6) when the neck was turned to the left, he was unable to bring the neck back to the midline smoothly; instead he brought it to the mid-position in a jerky manner.

The treatment consisted of:

1. Inhibition of spasms in the right sternocleidomastoid muscle.
2. Recruitment of motor unit activity of left sternocleidomastoid muscle.
3. Isometric exercises for left sternocleidomastoid muscle.
4. Reeducation of the left sternocleidomastoid muscle to rotate the neck to the right side.
5. Inhibition of the left sternocleidomastoid while the neck turned to the left side.
6. Teaching the patient recruitment of motor unit activity while turning the right sternocleidomastoid muscle to the left and inhibition when he brought the neck back to midline.
7. Jacobson's relaxation techniques to practice at home.

Within 12 treatments, he was able to bring the neck back to midline smoothly. His atrophy of the left sternocleidomastoid muscle was normal and the left sternocleidomastoid muscle learned its normal motion. When he stopped his treatment, he was able to drive his car although his condition was not entirely resolved.

NOTE. The material in this chapter was originally presented at the Training Workshop for Professionals: Neuromuscular Reeducation, sponsored by the Biofeedback Society of America, Orlando, Florida, March 1977.

CARDIOVASCULAR BIOFEEDBACK I—
TEMPERATURE

Peripheral temperature change is a response to sympathetic activity and the thermoregulatory homeostatic process of the body. It is an indirect measure of blood flow in tissues, with changes in temperature indicating corresponding changes in blood flow. (A more direct measure of changes in blood flow is with photoplethysmographic methods; however, most studies have used temperature training as the preferred biofeedback modality.) There are multiple factors that will affect the rate of blood flow. At the arterial level, blood flow is affected by changes in the diameter of the arterial walls. Contraction of the smooth muscles in the arterial walls, caused by increased sympathetic activity, causes vasoconstriction. This in turn decreases blood flow and tends to lower skin temperature. Vasodilation occurs when there is a decrease in sympathetic activation of the smooth muscle followed by a corresponding increase in blood flow, and thus in skin temperature.

The thermoregulatory process is crucial in the homeostatic state of man. If there is a decrease in core temperature, vasoconstriction of the periphery will occur to prevent or reduce further heat loss. Artificial changes that interfere with this process could be dangerous. As an extreme example, during decreases in core temperature, ingestion of alcohol will enhance peripheral vasodilation, fighting against the innate homeostatic balance and thereby further increasing heat loss. This could, upon further exposure to cold, lead to hypothermia and death. Homeostatic balance mechanisms affect the whole organism and within this framework, the optimum temperature is contingent on internal as well as external factors.

Major increases in sympathetic activity are usually associated with the fight/flight response, otherwise known as the alarm reaction or startle response. During the activation of the fight or flight response, vascular responses occur in conjunction with muscular bracing. This prepares the body for action by shifting blood away from the periphery and GI tract and into the muscles and head (Cannon, 1963). Experientially, the components of this response are felt as cold hands and feet. This stress response can be triggered by an external stimulus (near accident while driving) or by an internal event (feeling angry at your boss). Even a simple cognitive task such as subtracting serial 7s inside one's head (i.e., 100, 93, 86 . . .) is associated with increased sympathetic activity.

This response to stressors is our basic natural reaction to stimuli. There is nothing wrong with this response; however, after the stressor disappears, the system should return to baseline. Pathology tends to occur when the system reacts chronically instead of transiently and thus increases the baseline.

This chronic stress response is a component in 80% of all illness. These illnesses are psychosomatic—the chronic response to stress that, initially, manifests itself in muscular bracing and/or vasoconstriction. (Extreme vasodilation, such as blushing, can also lead to psychosomatic problems.) The vascular system is the mainstay of all cellular life, with the bloodstream transporting the nutrients to and the waste products away from the cells. Any part of the body can be affected, since change in one system affects all other parts and systems.

This philosophy is in agreement with the suggestion made by Charles F. Stroebel (director of research at the Institute of Living, Hartford, Connecticut) that many illnesses are vasoconstrictive in origin. For example, migraine is caused by local biochemically induced vasodilation in response to excessive sympathetic vasoconstriction, which decreases blood flow to the brain; Raynaud's disease is associated with decreased blood flow in the periphery; ulcers may be local responses to decreases in blood flow in the stomach lining; heart attacks in young people, where there is no evidence of arterial sclerotic plaques, may be the result of local vasomotor spasms, which deprive the cardiac tissue of oxygen. Similarly, angina is a vaso-occlusive cardiac problem. Even congestive dysmenorrhea may be conceived of as decreased blood flow, while allergies may often involve local vasodilation.

Temperature training is the major technique used to increase peripheral blood flow. Temperature, like all other physiological measures, is subject to the Law of Initial Values (LIV) and the corresponding biological limits. The LIV states "that an ANS response to stimulation is a function of the prestimulus level. . . . The higher the prestimulus level of functioning, the smaller the response to a function-increasing stimulus. And at more extreme prestimulus levels there is more tendency for no response to stimulation, and even for "paradoxical" responses—those which reverse the typical directions of responses" (Sternbach, 1966, p. 44. For a further description and implications of the LIV, see Sternbach, 1966, Chapter 4).

Temperature training was originally initiated by Elmer Green and associates at The Menninger Foundation (Green & Green, 1977). Following their initial findings, experimental and clinical applications of temperature biofeedback have grown at a surprisingly rapid rate. Two of the researchers who have contributed to this growth are Taub and Emurian (Chapter 38), who demonstrate some of the research techniques of temperature biofeedback. Yet even in the research setting, Taub is sensitive to the interpersonal dynamics associated with temperature self-regulation. He has reported that, for unknown reasons, some laboratory assistants are highly successful in teaching trainees to alter their hand temperature (8 out of 9) while others are highly unsuccessful (1 out of 10) (Taub, personal communication, 1977).

Why some trainers are more successful than others has not been systematically explored. Peper's article (Chapter 4) graphically illustrates in the urination example that "set-setting" is critical for autonomic self-regulation. A similar process, known as the "Rosenthal effect," in which experimenters' expectancy affects the outcome, often operates in psychology.

The interaction of belief, knowing, and experience permeates Chapter 39, in which Peper and Grossman show the exciting possibility and application of autogenic temperature self-regulation in children with migraine. Their experience indicates that cooperative children learn much more rapidly than motivated adults. What is exciting in the work with children is that the disease pattern appears to be permanently changed. In allopathic medicine, palleation and cure are difficult to separate. Upon a four-year follow-up, the children had very few headaches and were easily able to control those they had. Learning autogenic feedback training possibly allowed the children to change their illness-producing physiological pattern and learn alternative ways of reducing stress responses.

Finally, Sargent, Walters, and Green (Chapter 40) report on the pioneering autogenic temperature feedback training approach for migraines. Although there is a lack of controlled studies, temperature biofeedback training for classical migraine (i.e., the patient has a physiological warning that a headache is coming on) has had a success rate of about 80% for the basic reason that the patient can practice his skills before the onset of the headache. Common migraine, on the other hand, only has a success rate of about 30–40% since there is no warning of headache ahead of time. it is extremely difficult to inhibit a migraine once it has begun. The failure and dropout rate of the latter group, therefore, is much higher and is mainly due to the lack of immediate success. In order to decrease the intensity and occurrence of common migraine, it is imperative to practice the relaxation exercises and hand-warming techniques multiple times during the day, until they have become part of the daily life pattern. A similar approach appears to be successful in the treatment of Raynaud's disease (Stroebel, personal communication, 1977; Surwit, Pilon, & Fenton, 1977).

Temperature training is usually embedded in an autogenic training matrix (see Chapter 11 for the detailed discussion of AT). AT suggests numerous guidelines that the biofeedback practitioner might adapt for temperature training. The major distinction between AT and pure temperature training is that AT is based upon a homeostatic model while temperature feedback training is purely localized training. Autogenic feedback training integrates AT with feedback. Heaviness in AT is associated with EMG feedback training and warmth in AT is associated with temperature feedback training. The overall strategy in AT, and one that should be considered when doing temperature biofeedback training, is to account for the homeostatic system. To allow the biological system to gently readjust during the AT process, the tendency is to train slowly, thus avoiding feedback oscillations during the adaption phase, especially if there are indications of other vasomotor instabilities. For example, if a trainee shows increased vasomotor reactivity, such as blushing, the conservative guideline would be to reduce the intensity of the training. Similarly, when working with trainees who have had recent strokes or heart attacks, the trainer may find the cardiovascular system too fragile to initiate any temperature training. Finally, warming of the head is contraindicated since trainees may experience headaches. These observations do not imply contraindications, but only that, as in other modalities, one must always be aware of the possible dangers and biological limitations.

Temperature self-regulation is an exciting area and its limits are only now being explored. Within an autogenic training framework, the warmth and cooling phrasing has been applied to numerous pathologies, ranging from asthma to hemorrhoids. The excitement stems from the fact that temperature regulation can be used for general stress reduction as well as locally to enhance or reduce blood flow.

To date, there have been numerous unique applications of temperature training. Although most of these studies have not been replicated, they suggest promising new areas of thermal self-regulation. French, Leeb, Fahrion, Law, & Jecht (1973) trained male college students to increase their scrotum temperature as a possible means of male birth control. Their subjects demonstrated a significantly long-lasting reduction in sperm count. When a follow-up was done, there appeared to be no negative side effects of this training. The question that needs to be raised, however, is what is optimal scrotum temperature, since increased and prolonged warmth may be associated with increased pathology (e.g., testicular tumors in undescended testes). Sedlacek and Heczey (1977) taught women to increase vaginal temperature as a means of decreasing the symptoms of dysmenorrhea, while Bradley (personal communications, 1977) taught women to increase vaginal temperature to enhance the ease of natural childbirth and to shorten time in labor.

There are many cases in which one cannot easily measure temperature changes. To overcome this problem, Peper developed a transfer procedure in which the person first overlearns the peripheral warming, thereby learning (knowing) the feeling of warmth. The person, through the use of imagination, then transfers the sensations of warmth to the appropriate area. For example, after temperature training, one trainee learned to feel a "blanket of warmth" around her spastic colon, which decreased the symptomatology (see Chapter 10).

It is our experience that temperature training is easy to learn through passive volition and with appropriate feedback and guidance. Often a simple sensory feedback exercise of feeling one's pulse in the periphery is followed by an increase in temperature in that area. Although much of this discussion focused on the use of temperature training to reverse pathogenic vascular responses, such training can also be applied for health maintenance as well as being used as an exciting research tool to investigate the parameters of vascular self-regulation.

REFERENCES

Cannon, W. *The wisdom of the body*. New York: Norton, 1963.

French, D., Leeb, C., Fahrion, S. L., Law, O. T., & Jecht, E. W. Self-induced scrotal hyperthermia in man followed by a decrease in sperm output: A preliminary report. *Andrologie*, 1973, *5*(4), 311–316.

Green, E. E., & Green, A. M. *Beyond biofeedback*. New York: Delacorte, 1977.

Sedlacek, K., & Heczey, M. A specific biofeedback treatment for dysmenorrhea. *Proceedings of the Biofeedback Society of America*, 1977, 26.

Sternbach, R. *Principles of psychophysiology*. New York: Academic Press, 1966.

Surwit, R. W., Pilon, R. N., & Fenton, C. H. *Behavioral treatment of Raynaud's disease*. Paper presented at the Association for Advancement of Behavior Therapy, December 1977.

38

Feedback-Aided Self-Regulation of Skin Temperature with a Single Feedback Locus

Acquisition and Reversal Training

Edward Taub and Cleeve S. Emurian

A technique has been developed that enables most humans to establish rapid self-regulatory control of their own skin temperature when provided with immediate visual feedback information concerning variations in local skin temperature. Training took place during 15-min periods within 45-min sessions. Clear evidence of learning was usually manifested within four sessions. After acquisition occurred, mean change per session was approximately 2.2°F, ranging up to 6.5°F. Training was continued with some subjects who were taught to alter temperature in opposite directions during successive periods on the same day. After practice, these subjects routinely displayed ranges of 9–14°F within 15 min.

A technique for enabling most humans to establish rapid self-regulatory control of their skin temperature has been developed in this laboratory over the course of the last 5 years (Emurian & Taub, 1972; Taub & Emurian, 1971, 1973; Taub, Emurian, & Howell, 1974). It involves operant shaping of small variations in skin temperature by means of changes in a visual information display. The practical significance of this work is that the temperature of tissue is directly related to the volume of blood flowing through it. Thus, it appeared that the monitoring and feeding back of temperature information might constitute a means of controlling volume blood flow in peripheral vascular beds—a means that would be sufficiently rapid and inexpensive to have potential use for clinical purposes.

The feasibility of enabling human beings to self-regulate skin temperature was originally suggested by work in which curarized rats were trained in single sessions to differentially constrict the vasculature of one ear while dilating that of the other ear (DiCara & Miller, 1968a). In two other studies, curarized rats were trained to change urine output greatly by altering blood flow through the kidneys (Miller & DiCara, 1968), and to change blood flow in the vessels of the tail (DiCara & Miller, 1968b).

Classical conditioning of vasomotor responses in human subjects has been performed for some time, especially in the USSR (for a summary of the Soviet work, see Razran, 1961). Some of the more recent experiments carried out in the

Edward Taub and Cleeve S. Emurian • Institute for Behavioral Research, Silver Spring, Maryland 20910. CSE is presently at the Department of Psychiatry and Behavioral Sciences, The Johns Hopkins School of Medicine, Baltimore, Maryland 21205.

United States include those by Baer and Fuhrer (1970), Shmavonian (1959), and Teichner and Levine (1968). The operant training of vasomotor responses in humans appears to have been first carried out successfully by a Russian investigator, Lisina (1965). Her training technique, which may be termed *operant— respondent overlap*, involved first eliciting vasomotor responses reflexly, and then obtaining operant control of them through the use of "additional afferentation" or biofeedback. Snyder and Noble (1968) were able to increase the frequency of transient vasoconstrictive events by wholly operant methods involving presentation of a light when finger pulse-volume amplitude fell below a criterion value. The objective of the work reported herein was to produce both increases and decreases in blood flow that could be sustained over substantial periods of time.

METHOD

Subjects

The subjects were 21 young adults (8 males and 13 females) who were obtained for the study through advertisements on university bulletin boards. Applicants were accepted as they presented themselves, without reference to sex or age. The age range of the subjects was from 18 to 27 years, except for 3 women who were in their mid-30s. The blood pressure of all subjects was measured prior to the first session, and they were screened for previous history of cardiovascular disease or abnormality, but none had to be eliminated on these grounds.

Experimental Setup

Each subject was seated in a semirecumbent position in a reclining chair positioned along the short dimension of an experimental room, 2.7 × 5 m. To promote an atmosphere of relaxation, the floor of the room was carpeted, and illumination was kept low. The subject's hands were placed in a relaxed position in pronation on a board resting on the arms of the chair. One thermistor probe was secured with paper tape to the web dorsum of the subject's dominant hand, approximately 3 cm behind the metacarpophalangeal joint of the index finger; another was placed at another location, usually the web dorsum of the other hand. A white, variable-intensity feedback light was located on the wall in front of the subject, slightly above eye level. When the light was operating, the intensity was directly proportional to skin temperature on the dominant hand. About 50 cm above the variable-intensity light was a green light of constant intensity, which signaled the times when the experimental task was to be performed. After placement of the thermistor probes, the subject was usually left alone in the room for the duration of the session. The experimenter stayed in a separate room containing the programming and recording equipment.

Ambient temperature in the experimental chamber, which was usually 74°F, and relative humidity were recorded from a location close to the subject at the beginning and end of each session. It was found to be rare for temperature to vary more than 1°F, or relative humidity more than 1%.

Apparatus

The feedback light was a frosted, 24-V lamp (2.8 mean spherical candle-power), the intensity of which was voltage-dependent and varied in proportion to the difference between a measured web-dorsum temperature and a preset reference temperature. The reference temperature was adjustable over a 15°F span (83–98°F). The system was so constructed that when the measured temperature was equal to the reference temperature, the light intensity was at a pre-selected, fixed value. The sensitivity of the system was such that voltage changes representing less than .01°F resulted in discriminable light-intensity changes, provided the changes were not too slow. However, the physical characteristics of the thermistors rendered .02°F the smallest valid unit of temperature change. For any given reference-temperature setting, the temperature range covered by the variation in feedback light intensity, from light-off to maximum, was .3°F, but the difficulty of discriminating intensity changes at the higher intensities probably reduced the effective feedback range to .25°F. The intensity of the feedback light was monitored remotely by a slave light and by a meter reading the potential used to drive the feedback light. The absolute accuracy of the system, as contrasted to its moment-to-moment resolving power, was ± .5°F. In terms of the purpose of this experiment, however, the moment-to-moment resolving power was the more important design consideration, since it is with respect to this characteristic that feedback is meaningful.

The time constant of the thermistors was approximately 3 sec. The thermistors and the remainder of the system were calibrated with a reference thermometer calibrated by the National Bureau of Standards. Programming equipment was used to control automatically the length of the trials and of the intertrial intervals.

Procedure

In general, the experimental approach was exploratory. In view of the absence of previously published reports as to the feasibility of our specific objectives, the primary purpose was to determine whether this type of conditioning was possible, and, if so, how the largest effects could be obtained in the shortest time. Consequently, no attempt was made to adhere to a specific experimental design. Subjects were run different numbers of days, and not all subgroups had the same number of subjects. In this initial work, effort was expended along a given avenue only if it appeared to give promise of increasing the power of the technique. However, the basic experimental setup, the apparatus, and many aspects of the procedure were the same for all subjects.

Each subject was first given a baseline session, during which he simply sat quietly while his skin temperature was monitored over a period of approximately 45 min (the approximate length of training sessions). Operation of the feedback light was introduced on the second day. Before the session began, the relation between skin temperature and the intensity of the feedback light was explained, and the subject was told either to increase skin temperature and light intensity (9 subjects) or to decrease them (12 subjects). The direction of original training for each subject was always opposite to the general trend in temperature change on the subject's baseline day.

The training sessions consisted of 3 periods: a stabilization period, a self-regulation period, and a rest period. These periods were divided into 65-sec intervals, which, in the self-regulation period, consisted of a 60-sec trial and a 5-sec intertrial interval.

In the stabilization period, the subject sat quietly for a minimum of 10 intervals, or until the skin temperature of his dominant hand reached a stability criterion of no greater variation than .25°F in 4 consecutive 65-sec intervals. If the stability criterion was not achieved in 30 such intervals, the self-regulation period was nevertheless initiated. However, this occurred only infrequently.

The self-regulation period consisted of 15 trials. At the beginning of the first trial, the green, fixed-intensity lamp was lit, indicating that work should begin on the assigned task. The white feedback light was activated at the beginning of the third trial, and thereafter the two lights were turned on concurrently during the trials and off during the intertrial intervals.

At the conclusion of the self-regulation period, the subject was asked to relax during an additional 10-interval rest period, while his skin temperature continued to be monitored. Except when a subject objected, music of a self-chosen type was played softly during the initial stabilization period and the final rest period on training days, and during the equivalent periods on baseline days, in order to reduce boredom and somnolence.

Session length, including all three periods, varied from approximately 38 min to 1 hr, depending on the time required to meet the initial stability criterion. The average length of the stabilization was fifteen 65-sec intervals; the average session length was 43 min. The measured temperatures were recorded at 65-sec intervals at beginning of the intertrial intervals or their equivalent.

During the intertrial interval before each feedback trial in the self-regulation period, the potential used to drive the output stage of the feedback lamp driver was adjusted so that the feedback light, when first illuminated, was always at one of two standard intensities—bright if the subject's task was to decrease temperature, dim if it was to increase it. The initial intensity of the light, whether dim or bright, always represented the subject's skin temperature at the end of the intertrial interval. Thus the procedure involved an adjustment of the set point of the feedback system at the beginning of each trial with respect to the subject's current skin temperature. The "dim" initial intensity was 1 log mL above light-off (determination by Macbeth illuminometer). This brightness range corresponded to .1°F; since the smallest meaningful unit of feedback was .02°F, the subject probably had little difficulty in discriminating the smallest amount of temperature change detectable by the system at low feedback-light intensity levels, even if that change was somewhat slow. However, this type of analog feedback obviously introduced a component of brightness discrimination into the task, and this component increased as the rate of temperature change decreased and the brightness of the lamp increased.

When the task was to increase temperature, the temperature range covered by the feedback light was .15–.2°F in the desired upward direction, the amount depending on whether temperature change in the range corresponding to the higher light intensities was slow or fast, and .1°F in the wrong direction. When the task was to decrease temperature, the standard initial setting of the light was at an intensity such that the subject would continue receiving feedback from temperature changes of .05–.1°F in the wrong direction, depending on speed of change, and .2°F in the desired downward direction.

Before the beginning of the baseline session and the initial training session, subjects were given sets of instructions to read. The instructions for the baseline day consisted of a general description of the procedure for the entire period of the subject's involvement, as well as specific instructions for the baseline day. The instructions for the initial training session indicated for the first time the directionality of the subject's task assignment and described details of the procedure. The most important points in the instructions are given below:

> When a green light comes on, please try to decrease (increase) the temperature of your [dominant] hand. You will be able to do this without moving. In fact, it has been found that tensing the muscles interferes with the ability to do this. Simply stay relaxed and think of your hand as being cooler (warmer).
> After a couple of minutes, a white light will come on. This light will change in brightness as your hand temperature changes; the cooler (warmer) your hand, the dimmer (brighter) the light. This light will stay on for a minute, then go off for a few seconds; and this cycle will be repeated a number of times. During the blackout periods, the light may automatically reset to a different intensity. When it is on, try to make the light as dim (bright) as possible.
> When the green and white lights go off, please stop trying to control your hand temperature.

The detailed instructions are available from the authors on request.

Subjects were asked to relax, whether their task was to take temperature up or down. Care was taken to assure that all aspects of the task and situation were fully understood. If a subject had no questions after reading the instructions, the experimenter would initiate an informal discussion to ascertain whether some unsuspected area of misapprehension existed. During these discussions, and at all other times during the experiment, an attempt was made to keep the subject–experimenter interaction as relaxed and friendly as possible. In addition, the experimenter mentioned that virtually everyone could perform the task and expressed confidence in the subject's ability to do so. The use of thermal imagery was encouraged; the nature of the imagery was left largely up to each individual.

All subjects received a flat fee for participating in the experiment. In addition, nine subjects (reinforcement group) were reinforced for changes in skin temperature in the assigned direction at the rate of $.25 for each .25°F change. These subjects were also shown a graph of their performance at the end of each session, and the day's performance was discussed. This was another source of feedback and of verbal reward from the experimenter when the subject had done well.

Table 1

Distribution of Subjects in Subgroups

| | Reinforcement group | | | | Nonreinforcement group | | | | |
| | Increase | | Decrease | | Increase | | Decrease | | |
Day	M	F	M	F	M	F	M	F	Total
4	0	3	3	3	2	4	3	3	21
5	0	3	2	2	2	3	3	2	17
6	0	2	2	2	1	3	2	1	13

All 21 subjects were trained for a minimum of 4 days, and some were given additional training. The choice of subjects to receive additional training was determined solely by their availability; no other selection factor was involved. As shown in Table 1, there were data from 21, 17, and 13 subjects on days 4, 5, and 6, respectively, and the reductions on days 5 and 6 were distributed almost evenly among subgroups. Moreover, the mean performance on day 4 of the 4 subjects not run on day 5 was .9°F greater than the mean of the whole group, while the mean performance on day 5 for the 4 subjects not run on day 6 was .9°F lower than the mean of the whole group.

RESULTS

Figure 1 presents the data for the first six training sessions. The ordinate represents a relative measure of change in skin temperature, comparing change on a training day with change on the baseline day. In effect, each subject's performance was ipsitized with respect to temperature change on his baseline day. The reported values were calculated by (1) determining, for the baseline day, the change in skin temperature from the initial stability point (the mean of the last four 65-sec intervals of the stabilization period) to the peak trial in the direction of greatest change during the next fifteen 65-sec intervals, which during training sessions would be the self-regulation period; this is the baseline-day change for the subject concerned; (2) determining the equivalent training-day change; and (3) algebraically subtracting the baseline-day change from the equivalent training-day change. The value of the training-day change—step (2)—depended on the direction and nature of the temperature change on a given day. If this change was monotonic in either the instructed or the wrong direction, the initial stability point was subtracted from the peak trial value. If it was not monotonic, the trial used in calculating the training-day change was the peak trial in the instructed direction (whether this was above or below the initial stability point).

An analysis of variance (2 × 4) was performed comparing the 9 subjects instructed to raise their temperature (the *up* group) to the 12 subjects instructed to lower their temperature (the *down* group) as a function of training day, for the first 4 days. The difference between the groups was significant beyond the .001 level. The growth in the temperature effect over days approached, but did not reach, significance ($p < .091$). Similarly, the interaction of instructed direction by days approached, but did not reach, significance ($p < .092$).

A similar analysis of variance (2×6) was performed on the 13 subjects who completed all 6 days of training. As in the preceding analysis, the groups effect was significant beyond the .001 level. The growth of the effect over days was not significant ($p < .189$); however, the interaction was significant ($p < .02$). The lack of a significant days effect may be due to a reduction in the sample size in this analysis (from 21 to 13).

While the analyses of variance indicated that the temperature changes of the *up* and *down* groups differed significantly, they did not address the question whether the temperature changes of the groups differed significantly from baseline-day measurements. To resolve this question, the magnitudes of the changes from baseline for the *up* and *down* groups were combined, disregarding the direction of the change, and separate *t* tests were performed for each of the 3 days in the second half of the training series (days 4–6). The results of each test were significant beyond the .001 level.

The mean change per 15-trial self-regulation period on training days 4, 5, and 6 was 2.2°F, ranging up to 6.5°F; larger changes were recorded later in training. Of the 21 individual sessions on day 4, 19 involved temperature changes in

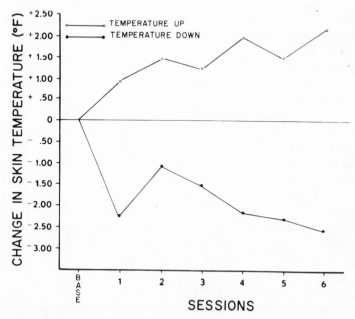

Figure 1. Course of learning self-regulatory control of skin temperature with feedback given from a single location on the dorsum of the dominant hand, for the first 21 consecutive subjects.

the instructed direction; 15 of the 17 individual sessions on day 5, and all 13 of the individual sessions on day 6, were in the instructed direction. The directionality of the results was evaluated by separate sign tests for each day and was, in each case, significant beyond the .001 level. Of the four temperature changes in the wrong direction, two were produced by the same subject, who could not be considered as having learned control, and one was produced by a subject whose control must be considered equivocal. The remaining 19 subjects, including the other subject with a single negative score, were able to learn what appeared to be unequivocal control of skin temperature. In those cases where learning occurred, it was always apparent by the fourth training session.

The temperature change for *down* subjects on training day 1 was 2.3°F. The reason for this unusually large value so early in training is unknown, but it was not the result of a few deviant scores, since 10 out of the 12 *down* subjects performed better on the 1st than on the 2nd training day. Neither does it seem to be related to performance anxiety (which does lower hand temperature), since the phenomenon did not appear in the results for the *up* subjects, either in the grouped data, which may be seen in Figure 1, or in the first few minutes of the individual session graphs, where it should be most pronounced. Inspection of Figure 1 indicates that there is an orderly growth in the magnitude of the effect from training day 1 to training day 6 for *up* subjects and from training day 2 to training day 6 for *down* subjects. In both cases, the magnitude of the effect more than doubles within the times indicated. However, the data for *down* subjects on day 1 preclude any clear conclusion concerning whether the temperature change is progressive in nature over training days. The perturbation in the growth of the temperature effect for the *down* subjects probably accounts for the marginal significance of the days effects and the days-by-groups interactions in the analyses of variance.

Inspection of the individual curves indicates that those for 7 subjects (5 *down* and 2 *up*) are clearly growth functions; each of 9 other subjects exhibited abrupt achievement of a level of self-regulatory ability that was close to maximum for his series. This occurred on day 1 for 6 subjects (3 *down*, 3 *up*), on day 2 for 1 subject (*up*), and on day 4 for 2 subjects (1 *up*, 1 *down*). The records of 5 subjects cannot be assigned to either category, either because there was no apparent learning (1 *up*, 1 *down*) or because the curves are ambiguous with respect to the classification (1 *up*, 2 *down*).

The initial stability point did not change significantly during training. The mean initial stability point for all subjects on the baseline day was 89.7°F; for the 6 training days, it was 89.9°F. Moreover, the initial stability point did not tend to shift in the instructed direction across training days for either *up* or *down* subjects.

Subjects were able to decrease their skin temperature .4°F more than they were able to increase it; they did .7°F better when given money reward contingent on performance than when given only a flat rate for participating in the experiment; and females performed better than males by .8°F. However, these differences were not significant (*t* tests).

Bidirectional Training

After original training, two subjects, selected on the basis of their good initial performance, were asked to reverse the direction of their self-regulatory control. After mastery, their next task was to alternate the direction of control on 3 successive days, and then to go in opposite directions during successive periods on the same day. The self-regulation periods were shortened from 15 to 10 min and were separated by rest intervals of 5 min. The 2-min no-feedback period previously occurring at the beginning of the self-regulation periods was eliminated. At the end of bidirectional training, the subjects routinely displayed temperature ranges of 10–14°F within 15 min. The largest single change observed was 9°F within a span of 1 min.

Table 2 presents, for the two bidirectional subjects, the number of training sessions in the early phases of training, the mean temperature change on the last 3 days of both the initial and the reversal series, and the temperature change on each of 3 successive days on which the desired direction of change was reversed each day.

Subject B.I.'s performance during a bidirectional session is shown in Figure 2. As may be seen, her stimulus control was excellent. She proceeded in the instructed direction immediately, and there was excellent recovery to the initial stability value during rest periods. From minutes 12–25 in the session, there was a measurable change of almost 14°F. The dashed line indicates that the subject went off the measurement scale of the apparatus at minute 5 and stayed there for 7 min. Thus, the temperature change was at least 14°F and may have been greater. Similar considerations concerning off-scale performance also apply to the last training period. In Figure 3, which shows comparable data for subject L.P., the temperature change is just as great and the stimulus control is just as good as in Figure 2.

Table 2

Summary of Direction–Reversal Training Data

Subject	Item	Original training series	Reversal series	Reversal on successive days		
L.P.	Direction	*Up*	*Down*	*Up*	*Down*	*Up*
	Number of sessions	22[a]	8	1	1	1
	Temperature change (°F)	3.6[b]	4.1[b]	6.2	3.9	4.5
B.I.	Direction	*Down*	*Up*	*Down*	*Up*	*Down*
	Number of sessions	7	13	1	1	1
	Temperature change (°F)	6.3[b]	3.5[b]	4.8	5.2	8.2

[a] There was a 4-month hiatus between sessions 13 and 14.
[b] Values are the means of the last 3 days of the series.

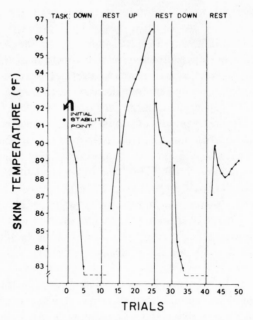

Figure 2. Self-regulatory control of skin temperature on the dorsum of the dominant hand in opposite directions during successive periods in bidirectional training session 2 for subject B.I.

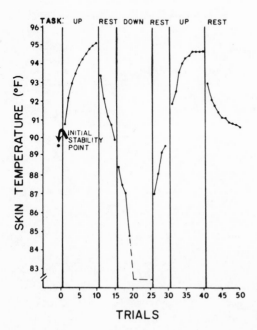

Figure 3. Self-regulatory control of skin temperature on the dorsum of the dominant hand in opposite directions during successive periods in bidirectional training session 8 for subject L.P.

Figure 4 summarizes all bidirectional sessions for the two subjects. The "steady-state" mean range of temperature change for a session was 13+ °F for one subject and 12+ °F for the other. Comparison of the data summarized in Table 2 and Figure 4 indicates that the amount of temperature change exhibited in either direction increased when rapid reversals of temperature direction were required. The improvement occurred during the 3 successive temperature-reversal days for subject B.I., and was then maintained during bidirectional sessions. For subject L.P., temperature change on the successive reversal days was similar to that exhibited at the end of the initial and reversal series. On the first bidirectional day, there was a decline in her temperature range; thereafter, however, improvement was rapid, and by the fourth bidirectional day, her control exceeded that displayed earlier in training.

In previous work, two pilot subjects had shown temperature-change ranges of 10°F and 9°F when bidirectional testing was terminated at sessions 6 and 4, respectively.

Controls for "Cheating"

All subjects were requested to sit quietly throughout the training sessions, moving as little as possible. In pilot work, however, 13 subjects were asked, prior to training, to make certain gross movements and sustain them for 20 sec, in order to determine the effect that this type of forbidden maneuver could have on hand temperature. The data are summarized in Table 3. As may be seen, most of

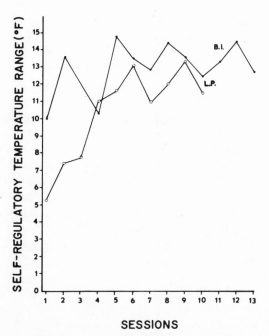

SESSIONS

Figure 4. Range of self-regulatory temperature change in all bidirectional sessions for subjects B.I. and L.P.

Table 3

Temperature Changes with Gross Maneuvers of the Arms and Hands[a]

Maneuvers	Temperature Changes (°F)		
	$\bar{X}$	σ	Median
Self-Regulating Arm			
Raise arm	.8	1.4	.5
Lower arm	.2	.2	.2
Make fist with hand	.7	.8	.5
Tense hand and arm	.4	.5	.2
Flex arm	.6	.8	.2
Total maneuvers	.5		
Contralateral Arm			
Raise arm	.1	.1	.1
Lower arm	.1	.1	.1
Make fist with hand	.1	.1	.2
Tense hand and arm	.2	.2	.1
Flex arm	.1	.1	.1
Total maneuvers	.1		

[a] For calculation, temperature values were considered independently of the direction of change.

the values were comparatively small, especially considering that the maneuvers involved maximal limb excursions and muscular contractions. Of particular interest was one pilot subject who eventually became excellent in self-regulatory ability in both the upward and downward directions, frequently exhibiting temperature ranges of more than 8°F during bidirectional sessions in the experimental series and more than 13°F in later testing. Yet, in her control-movement/muscle-tension data, she showed no temperature change greater than .2°F.

During approximately one-third of the bidirectional runs of the two bidirectional subjects whose data are reported here, a large, transparent Plexiglas box was placed over the self-regulating hand (with a drop cloth to seal the opening for the wrist) to rule out the possibility that subjects could be effecting temperature changes by blowing on the thermistor. The box was also placed over the self-regulating hand of other subjects in selected sessions. This procedure made no difference in the extent of control exhibited by the subjects. When the contralateral, non-self-regulating hand was cupped closely over the thermistor without touching it for 1 min, the maximum temperature increase observed was .7°F.

Verbal Report

In debriefing interviews after each training session, subjects described the techniques that they had used in trying to achieve self-regulation. Early in the training, these included imagery, relaxation, self-suggestion, direct commands to the hand, and direct commands to the feedback light. In general, the reports indicated that it was subjectively easier to decrease than to increase hand temperature, but, as reported above, this greater ease was not reflected in a significantly greater ability in *down* subjects.

Although there was wide variation in the verbal reports with respect to use of different strategies, there was little relation between the strategies employed and the degree of self-regulatory ability demonstrated. The only theme that had any commonality was that when subjects tried too hard, the results were counterproductive, but when they relaxed and tried to accomplish the goal easily, success could often be achieved. A relaxed attitude was found to be just as important for subjects attempting to decrease temperature as for those attempting to increase it. In general, the greater the determination and focusing of attention, the less the control. The successful attitude has been called one of *passive volition* (Green, Green, & Walters, 1970; Sargent, Green, & Walters, 1972). This term is probably as descriptive as any for this difficult-to-describe attentional state. The foregoing applies primarily to the early stages of learning. When subjects had been trained for an extended period and had achieved a high level of performance, they found it difficult to specify exactly what they did, They simply performed the task—i.e., attempted to make the hand warmer or cooler, as requested.

Other Factors

Well-trained subjects were able to perform the task even when subjected to a variety of stressors, such as cold and pain (Taub et al., 1974). The performance of female subjects did not appear to be affected by the menses during any stage of training.

All subjects were given the MMPI at the end of the last session of their initial training period. It was found that the ability to self-regulate skin temperature did not correlate highly with any of the standard MMPI scales.

DISCUSSION

The results demonstrated that it is possible to train most humans, in a relatively short span of time, to either increase or decrease skin temperature on the hand dorsum through the use of augmented feedback. The magnitude of the effect obtained in the experiments varied with sex, direction of instructed temperature change, and use or nonuse of performance-contingent money reward, but the differences were not significant. However, the experimenters felt that money reward was a useful adjunct to training; at minimum, it maintained interest in the task and willingness to participate in further testing. Consequently, this practice has been retained in later experiments.

When individual subjects were trained to take temperature in opposite directions, they reported, after mastery had been achieved, that the self-regulatory task in either direction became easier. Subject B.I. increased the magnitude of her control during the 3-day period when the instructed direction of temperature change was reversed on a daily basis. Subject L.P. exhibited a similar improvement, but somewhat later, after several days of bidirectional training. However, the data do not permit determination of whether the improvement was a function of the bidirectional performance, as the subjects reported, or simply a result of the additional training days.

The most striking feature of the verbal reports of subjects early in training is their diversity and their apparent irrelevance to excellence of performance, except with respect to the clear value of relaxing and adopting an attitude of "passive volition." However, due to the lack of sufficient EMG data at present, it is not possible to tell whether the report of relaxation is actually accompanied by a low level of muscular tension.

As subjects become increasingly proficient at the self-regulatory task, they tend to use fewer strategies of which they are aware. Bidirectional subjects in particular were unable to explain how they achieved their results. In fact, they reported that thinking about the task too much interfered with performance. People are equally unable to explain how they accomplish motor tasks, even such simple ones as raising and lowering an arm—and thinking too much about the task is commonly held to interfere with the performance of such complex motor skills as typing, playing the piano, or singing a difficult passage.

In conclusion, subjects vary widely in their ability to achieve self-regulatory control of skin temperature, and some appear capable of only slight or moderate control. However, at least one-third of the population tested demonstrated self-regulated temperature changes of sufficient magnitude to have potential use in clinical and other practical situations.

Since the purpose of the work reported herein was primarily methodological, some comments on the purpose and value of the different procedures employed are presented in the Appendix. It also contains a discussion of the question whether cheating or somatic mediation could have contributed to the results.

APPENDIX

Comment on Procedures

The baseline day and the initial stabilization period were essential to permit discrimination between learning effects and other, more general effects. In an ambient environmental temperature in the low to mid-70s, as was the case here, the normal temperature values for a subject at rest range from 85° to 93°F (Hardy & DuBois, 1938; Mendelson, 1926; Newburgh, 1949; Woods, Griffith, Page, & Rodier, 1967; Woodworth & Schlosberg, 1955). Under the conditions of the described experiment, the temperature on the web dorsum of the dominant hand was found to stabilize at approximately 90°F. If a subject's temperature had deviated too greatly from the normal values at the time when he was asked to self-regulate temperature, then it would have been difficult to determine whether subsequent temperature changes were self-regulatory in nature or merely represented a drift toward the norm.

On baseline days, the hand temperature of the subjects had a somewhat greater tendency to increase (12 subjects) than to decrease (9 subjects). In subsequent work, the direction of baseline-day temperature change has been up and down with approximately equal frequency. In pilot work, however, each of 12 subjects displayed a marked tendency for temperature to increase on baseline days and in stabilization periods. This tendency may have been related to a relaxation procedure, followed in the pilot work but not thereafter, that required the subjects to first tense and then relax the muscles of their arms several times before the beginning of each session (Jacobson, 1929). Whatever the reason in this particular case, it is clear that, in general, too large a proportion of subjects having a tendency for hand-temperature shifts in a given direction when not self-regulating probably indicates that some unrecognized aspect of the experimental situation was not under adequate control.

Hand temperature tended to fluctuate widely at the beginning of sessions, and when the changes were large, they were usually upward. Hand temperature is influenced by a variety of factors, including prior ambient temperature, level of physical activity, and—most important of all in the present context—emotional state. A laboratory situation is a tense one for most naive subjects, and anxiety tends to decrease the temperature of the extremities. Our subjects were first "wired up" and then asked to perform a task that to many of them appeared bizarre and infeasible. When allowed some time to adjust to the situation, the subjects who were tense began to relax, and their hand temperature consequently increased. Because we were interested in obtaining precise control over blood flow in as specific an area as possible, we did not want to confuse the effects of general relaxation with those of specific training; we therefore decided not to introduce the experimental task until the initial relaxation process was completed.

Since the time required for hand temperature to stabilize varied from subject to subject and from day to day in the same subject, the initial stabilization period could not be specified in terms of any set temporal interval. Consequently, the method used to define temperature stabilization (4 consecutive minutes with no greater variation than .25°F) was a measure that actually reflected this parameter.

The rest period in unidirectional sessions had no specific function in the training of subjects, but the temperature record during this interval did provide a good indication of how well the experimental task had been learned. In the early phases of training, subjects tended either to stay at the level attained during the self-regulation period or to continue progressing in the same direction. After additional training, however, there was a tendency for skin temperature to change direction rapidly during the rest period and return toward baseline values. The purpose of introducing two 5-min rest periods between the three 10-min self-regulation periods in the bidirectional sessions was to relieve possible fatigue and thus provide optimal conditions for performance.

The 5-sec time-out intervals between trials were introduced initially to provide time to reset the feedback light to a constant intensity. It was felt that the resetting would be confusing to the subject if he were observing the light at the time it occurred. In later work (Taub et al., 1974) the time-out interval was eliminated when a new apparatus was used that permitted rapid ($<$ .5-sec) resetting of the information display. However, many subjects complained that 15 min was too long to focus attention on the task, especially before mastery had been achieved. A 10-sec time-out interval was therefore introduced (between 50-sec trials). Most subjects expressed a preference for this arrangement.

The purpose of the 2-min no-feedback interval at the beginning of the self-regulation period was to provide an index of the extent to which the augmented feedback was important for the subject's performance, but it was not found to be of any value for this purpose. In the early stages of learning, temperature changes tended to be too slow and small to be manifest by comparison of the no-feedback interval and the rest of the self-regulation period. Later in training, when the response was under better stimulus control, feedback was found to be no longer necessary to support self-regulation (Taub et al., 1974). Consequently, in later work, the no-feedback interval was eliminated.

During pilot work, subjects were required to adhere to a strictly standardized testing schedule. It was emphasized that they must come to the laboratory on consecutive days, at approximately the same time each day, and that approximately the same amount of time should be allowed to elapse each day between their last meal and the testing session. They were also asked to refrain from smoking for at least ½ hour before coming to the laboratory. It was found, however, that variations in these factors did not importantly affect results. Consequently, no attempt was made to control them rigorously in later work.

The data from baseline days indicate that the hand temperature of some subjects has a natural tendency to drift consistently in a given direction during the interval equivalent to the self-regulation period on training days. This tendency introduces a constant bias, onto which the temperature self-regulation effect must be imposed. It is important to take this factor into account in estimating the magnitude of the self-regulatory effect; it was taken into account here by ipsitizing the data in the manner described at the beginning of the Results section. In addition, subjects in initial training were always required to self-regulate temperature in the direction opposite to that recorded in the baseline sessions, in order to increase the probability that observed effects would be an expression of learning rather than the sensitization of a preexisting tendency.

Feedback Presentation Mode

Two deficiencies were noted in the present feedback system: First, since the rate of temperature change controlled the rate of light-intensity change, very slow temperature changes resulted in such slow brightness changes that subjects had difficulty in discriminating them, especially when the feedback light was in the higher intensity range. Second, the light could not register large changes in temperature. Although it was reset to a standard intensity at the end of every 1-min trial, it could not indicate changes larger than .25—.3°F within a given trial. Subjects at the beginning of training, when still heavily dependent on feedback, would often self-regulate skin temperature considerably more than this feedback-limited value, and would then not uncommonly fall back. It appeared that these temperature reversals following large spurts in the correct direction resulted from the lack of temperature feedback information to support the new, high level. These two negative features were corrected in an apparatus built for subsequent work (Taub et al., 1974).

One advantageous feature built into the analog light-intensity feedback system without explicit awareness of its potential value was the relatively small display capacity of the system for temperature change in the wrong direction. In later work, it was found that when subjects were able to discriminate that large temperature changes had taken place in the wrong direction, their motivation and subsequent performance were adversely affected.

Cheating and Somatic Mediation

In studies in which subjects acquire an ability not shared by the general population, it is important to assess the possibility that the subjects are—whether deliberately or inadvertently—"cheating" in some way, that is, achieving the required effect by some trivial means or "trick" unknown to the experimenter. We believe that this possibility has been rendered unlikely in our temperature self-regulation work, both through the use of a number of control procedures and by certain internal indications in the data. These procedures and indications are the following.

1. Measurements taken prior to training (when subjects were still ignorant of the specific nature of the task) indicated that the temperature changes resulting from gross maneuvers of the arms and hands (see Table 3) were small in comparison to those later demonstrated during training sessions.

2. The Plexiglas box placed over some subjects' self-regulating hand effectually ruled out the possibility that the temperature-sensing elements could be affected by the subject's expiration.

3. On several occasions, the experimenter remained in the experimental chamber with subjects, and these subjects, though under direct observation, were nevertheless able to demonstrate clear self-regulatory control over skin temperature.

4. The requirement that subjects self-regulate temperature in first one, then the other, direction is a useful procedure in determining whether the results are due to some artifact. Our bidirectional subjects were able to vary their skin temperature equally well in either direction. If they had devised some "trick" to make it appear that they had self-regulatory control of this parameter, it would have had to be a trick that worked equally well in either direction, or else two separate tricks of equal effectiveness.

Other aspects of the data from later work in this series of experiments are relevant to the issue of cheating (Taub et al., 1974). While none of these points is conclusive, they are suggestive.

5. In the early stages of training, there is, typically, "following" by the untrained hand of temperature changes in the self-regulating hand. Subsequently, after the task has been well learned, following by the untrained hand drops out completely. Moreover, as training progresses, the response gradually tends to develop considerable anatomical specificity on the self-regulating hand itself. The maximum temperature control is exhibited primarily around the feedback locus

and decreases with distance from that location; in some cases, there was little correlation in temperature change between points separated by as little as 2 cm on the dorsum of the hand. These phenomena appear to be typical of the "sharpening of response" or response-differentiation process that normally occurs as training proceeds in other learning situations.

6. In the session after learning was first demonstrated, feedback was still necessary for performance of the task in the two cases tested. Four sessions later, however, both subjects could perform as well without feedback as with it.

7. EMG was recorded from the lateral aspect of the forearm of the self-regulating hand in seven sessions with two bidirectional subjects. In two of these sessions with one subject, there was a moderate correlation between EMG amplitude and skin-temperature variation. In the remaining three sessions with that subject, and in two sessions with the other subject, there was no correlation whatever between EMG and temperature change.

Much of the data just cited not only bears on the issue of cheating but also suggests that the observed self-regulatory changes in skin temperature were not mediated by somatic muscular activity. Of particular relevance are the EMG data (point 7 above), the ability of subjects to perform the task while under direct observation by the experimenter (point 3), the control-movement/muscle-tension data (point 1), and the evidence relating to the gradual development of anatomical precision in the response (point 5). It is also of interest that those subjects performing best in either the upward or the downward direction usually reported being physically relaxed. Again, these phenomena are indicative rather than conclusive. For example, the EMG data, which address the issue most directly, are from only one set of muscles. Even though these are the muscles that are most directly involved in the movements of the hand, the possibility of somatic mediation cannot be excluded in the absence of EMG records from all portions of the body.

ACKNOWLEDGMENTS. This research was supported by ARPA of DOD under ONR Contract N00014-70-C-0350 to the San Diego State College Foundation.

Portions of this chapter were presented at meetings of the Biofeedback Research Society, St. Louis, October 1971, and Boston, November 1972, and the Eastern Psychological Association, New York, April 1972.

We thank Dr. Joseph Rothberg for the design and construction of the feedback system, Maurice Swinnen for the design and construction of the thermistor probes and thermistor bridges, Susan N. Rice for testing the pilot subjects, Dr. Leonard T. Fielding for evaluation of the MMPI, Dr. Solomon S. Steiner and Dr. Donald W. Stilson for their comments, and Jean Swauger for technical assistance.

REFERENCES

Baer, P. E., & Fuhrer, M. J. Cognitive processes in the differential trace conditioning of electrodermal and vasomotor activity. *Journal of Experimental Psychology*, 1970, *84*, 176–178.

DiCara, L. V., & Miller, N. E. Instrumental learning of vasomotor responses by rats: Learning to respond differentially in the two ears. *Science*, 1968, *159*, 1485–1486. (a)

DiCara, L. V., & Miller, N. E. Instrumental learning of peripheral vasomotor responses by the curarized rat. *Communications in Behavioral Biology*, 1968, *1*, 209–212. (b)

Emurian, C. S., & Taub, E. *Self-regulation of skin temperature using a variable intensity light*. Paper presented at Eastern Psychological Association Meeting, New York, April 1972.

Green, E. E., Green, A. M., & Walters, E. D. Voluntary control of internal states: Psychological and physiological. *Journal of Transpersonal Psychology*, 1970, *11*, 1–26.

Hardy, J. D., & DuBois, E. F. Basal metabolism, radiation, convection and evaporization at temperatures of 22° to 35°C. *Journal of Nutrition*, 1938, *15*, 477.

Jacobson, E. *Progressive relaxation*. Chicago: University of Chicago Press, 1929.

Lisina, M. I. The role of orientation in the transformation of involuntary reactions into voluntary ones. In L. G. Voronin, A. N. Leontiev, A. R. Luria, E. N. Sokolov, & O. S. Vinogradova (Eds.), *Orienting reflex and exploratory behavior*. Washington, D. C.: American Institute of Biological Sciences, 1965.

Mendelson, E. S. Measurement of the superficial temperature gradient in man. *American Journal of Physiology*, 1926, *114*, 642–647.

Miller, N. E., & DiCara, L. V. Instrumental learning of urine formation by rats; changes in renal blood flow. *American Journal of Physiology*, 1968, *215*, 677–683.

Newburgh, L. H. (Ed.). *Physiology of heat regulation and the science of clothing*. New York: Hafner Publishing Company, 1949.

Razran, G. The observable unconscious and the inferrable conscious in current Soviet psychophysiology: Interoceptive conditioning, semantic conditioning and the orienting reflex. *Psychological Review*, 1961, *68*, 81–147.

Sargent, J. D., Green, E. E., & Walters, E. D. The use of autogenic feedback training in a pilot study of migraine headaches. *Headache*, 1972, *12*, 120–124.

Shmavonian, B. M. Methodological study of vasomotor conditioning in human subjects. *Journal of Comparative and Physiological Psychology*, 1959, *52*, 315–321.

Snyder, C., & Noble, M. E. Operant conditioning of vasoconstriction. *Journal of Experimental Psychology*, 1968, *77*, 263–268.

Taub, E., & Emurian, C. S. *Operant control of skin temperature*. Paper presented at the meeting of the Biofeedback Research Society, St. Louis, 1971.

Taub, E., & Emurian, C. S. Self-regulation of skin temperature using a variable intensity light. In J. Stoyva, T. Barber, L. V. DiCara, J. Kamiya, N. E. Miller, & B. Shapiro (Eds.), *Biofeedback and self-control: 1972*. Chicago: Aldine-Atherton, 1973. P. 504 (abstract).

Taub, E., Emurian, C. S., & Howell, P. *Further progress in training self-regulation of skin temperature*. Paper presented at the meeting of the Biofeedback Research Society, Colorado Springs, 1974.

Teichner, W. H., & Levine, I. M. Digital vasomotor conditioning and body heat regulation. *Psychophysiology*, 1968, *5*, 67–76.

Woods, P. J., Griffith, B. A., Page, R. P., & Rodier, P. M. Human responses to various conditions of water temperature. *Perception and Psychophysics*, 1967, *2*, 157–160.

Woodworth, R. S., & Schlosberg, H. *Experimental psychology* (Rev. ed.). New York: Henry Holt, 1955. Chap. 10.

39

Thermal Biofeedback Training in Children with Headache

Erik Peper and Elmer Grossman

Two young girls with a history of headaches were trained with autogenic training phrases and with thermal biofeedback training. Subject L.S. (age 9) had suffered serious spells of vertigo complicated with nausea since the age of 3, which by the age of 5 increasingly transformed itself into a typical migraine. Subject J.C. (age 13) had had recurrent headaches since the age of 5; they were often bilateral and included nausea and vomiting (not a typical childhood migraine). Both girls rapidly learned to control their peripheral temperature in two training sessions while practicing for 3 weeks at home and at school with and without equipment; both have been symptom-free (without medication) for the last 6 months. Unlike adults, in whom training must first remove the accumulated self-destructive patterns, both girls learned very rapidly and accepted this as a natural process. This learning process may foster a shift in health attitudes from helplessness to self-responsibility.

So far as we know, autogenic biofeedback training as a preventive for headaches in children has not been attempted before. We would like to report some findings with two young girls which suggest that training children to learn new antistress techniques and preventive health habits may actually be teaching them a different attitude toward health: health is one's own responsibility.

Headaches and especially migraines are still a medical enigma, and the exact cause is unknown even though the symptoms are clearly mediated through the autonomic nervous system. Stress often precipitates a headache episode. Although there have been many attempts at classification of headaches, it appears in all cases observed by photographic thermography that there is an imbalance of temperature, and therefore of blood flow, in the head.[1,2] By regulating the blood flow, or controlling muscle tension by voluntary control of the autonomic nervous system, headaches may be ameliorated.

Recently thermal and electromyographic feedback programs, supplemented with variations of autogenic training or Jacobson progressive relaxation, have been used as a treatment paradigm for headaches. Budzynski, Stoyva, and Adler[3] found that there was a significant reduction in headache activity when they trained adults tension-headache patients with electromyographic feedback. For 8 weeks the subjects learned to decrease their frontalis muscle tension. The reduc-

Erik Peper • Center for Interdisciplinary Science, San Francisco State University, San Francisco, California 94134.   Elmer Grossman • Private Practice, Berkeley Pediatric Medical Group, Berkeley, California 94709.

tion in headache activity held for both the 8-week training period and the 12-week follow-up period. Sargent, Green, and Walters[4] have used autogenic training phrases and thermal feedback with 90 adults who had migraine to achieve an 80% reduction in migraine activity in a 3-month training period. Autogenic feedback training paradigms are partially derived from Luthe and Schultz,[5] who report that with autogenic training a majority of patients respond with lessening of frequency and intensity of headaches. Learning low muscle activity as well as increasing hand warming (generalized vascular dilation) is the opposite physiological response to those brought on by stress. To learn this voluntary control, the person attempts to carry the more relaxed state within him in all phases of his life, which implies that he subtly changes his life-style and attitude.

THERMAL FEEDBACK TRAINING WITH TWO YOUNG GIRLS WHO HAD A HISTORY OF HEADACHES

Subject L.S., age 9, at age 4 was having episodes of vertigo, pallor, and vomiting, often followed by sleep. She had a number of the episodes, and finally a neurologist made the diagnosis of benign aural vertigo, otherwise known as Basser's disease. At age 5 she began having some episodes with headaches, which were typical migraine with vomiting followed by sleep. The episodes of vertigo became less frequent while the episodes of migraine became much clearer. The migraine became somewhat milder around age 7, but the episodes became longer. By age 8, she was having no more episodes of vertigo but was having migraines very regularly, probably several times a month.

Training. Initial autogenic training was started on May 17, 1973, when she had a severe headache. Her father taught her the autogenic phrases that evening during the migraine and she cured herself of the migraine within the hour. Since that time, she has been essentially headache-free. In September, in order to authenticate the temperature warming and autogenic training, she was given two thermal biofeedback training sessions. She took a temperature unit home for 2½ months to continue the practice. By the second biofeedback training session she was able consistently to warm her hands as much as 10 degrees. She reported that she warmed her hands by thinking and feeling: "I was swimming in spaghetti and meatballs"; "I felt gooey and warm, I kept saying warm, warm, warm"; or "I felt chicken soup flowing down my arm."

Although she has had no headaches, just recently she has had one severe dizziness spell, which may mean that although she has learned to warm her hands, she has not practiced faithfully. We feel that in order to be successful, the subject has to adopt a slightly different attitude toward life or, in her case, to carry the relaxed feeling with her all the time. This has currently been reemphasized, with instructions to feel a warm cocoon around herself throughout the day.

Subject J.C., age 13, at age 5 had severe headaches with frequent vomiting, often followed by sleep. She had a sense that the headache was coming, although she reported no specific sensations. Her headache was either frontal or occipital, like a tight band. The severity of the headache, sleep, the vomiting, and the prodrome are classical migraine symptoms. The headaches tended to be on Thursday, Friday, and Saturday and were erratic in frequency.

Training. She was first seen in September 1973 for thermal biofeedback training and rapidly learned to increase her hand temperature. Both with her and with L.S., during the training session, the classic technique of autogenic training was not used, but analogies were made to self-control and Houdini; we emphasized that she could totally control her own body and need not be at the mercy of others. After a 2-week interval she was seen again and could increase her hand temperature from 87° to 96° F. and reported that her hands and feet were glowing. She practiced off and on with the machine for about 2 months.

In addition, each girl was encouraged to practice without the feedback unit at home and in school, and to keep a daily log.

Subject J.C. reported that she warmed her hands in the following manner: "(1) I though to myself that I was in control of everything. (2) Fingers get warm. (3) Fingers, I feel them warming. (4) Warm toast, lobsters, ovens, summer. (5) I would look at the meter. (6) I would be proud of myself because I had succeeded." The training has been successful till now and she has been headache-free since the training was started.

The preliminary report gives encouragement that biofeedback training may be extremely useful in children especially if the process is designed as one of play—self-exploration and self-responsibility. Both subjects learned temperature training in one session and practiced the skill willingly at home with the feedback unit. There appeared to be no previous constraints in their attitudes that said "you cannot do it." In fact, the experimenters assumed that the child could do it. The very quick skill acquisition, unlike the experience with adults,[3,4] was rapid and was accepted as something very natural. Possibly there are no accumulated self-destructive habit patterns, since life habits were not yet well established and autonomic learning processes are not marked by the belief structure that questions, "Is it possible?" of our rational thinking, which says, "I have to understand it before doing it."

Moreover, J.C. spontaneously generalized the learning process to other body systems that she apparently could feel. She reported that with a similar technique, but not with actual feedback, she moved her teeth faster so that her orthodontic headgear could come off sooner. As she says, it worked. In her six-step process, in step 2 she says, "Teeth move"; in step 3, "I can feel them moving"; so that "instead of having to wear my headgear for two years all day long, and then move onto nighttime, I only had to wear my headgear for four months. Now I'm on nighttime wear."

Whether or not she actually moved her teeth more rapidly is not the issue; however, it does imply a different concept of reality in which one can be responsible for one's own health and growth. What may be possible is inevitably limited by the boundaries of one's own belief.

Biofeedback training, used wisely, and if the subject generalizes the skills, may teach an attitude toward health that can buffer him against stress and encourage his own sense of self-esteem. We are encouraged that biofeedback training for children may be useful in numberous childhood symptoms. The newly learned experiences may prevent the child from becoming a drug-dependent patient in his adult life.

EPILOGUE

At a 5-year follow-up, both girls are found to be headache-free.

REFERENCES

1. Ruegsegger, P. Refective headaches. *Headache*, 1970, *9*, 201–206.
2. Ruegsegger, P. Man and his headaches. *Headache*, 1970, *10*, 126–130.
3. Budzynski, T. H., Stoyva, J. M., & Adler, C. S. Feedback induced muscle relaxation: Application to tension headache. *Behavior Therapy and Experimental Psychiatry*, 1970, *1*, 205–211.
4. Sargent, J. D., Green, E. E., & Walters, E. D. Preliminary report on the use of autogenic feedback techniques in the treatment of migraine and tension headaches. Topeka. The Menninger Foundation, 1971.
5. Luthe, W., & Schultz, J. H. *Autogenic therapy: Medical applications*. New York: Grune and Stratton, 1970.

40

Psychosomatic Self-Regulation of Migraine Headaches

Joseph D. Sargent, E. Dale Walters, and Elmer E. Green

A historical perspective regarding research and treatment of the migraine syndrome and the studies in animals and humans relating to control of the autonomic nervous system is given. Pilot experience with 75 subjects is presented, and a detailed clinical account of one successful subject with pertinent research records in given. Reference is made to the implications of this clinical research to psychosomatic medicine.

Migraine headaches have been described in the literature for the past 2000 years, but it has been only in the past three to four decades that this affliction has been subjected to scientific scrutiny, beginning with Wolff and his colleagues. Since then many investigators have intensely studied this disorder; however, its pathophysiology still remains poorly understood.

It is estimated that as much as 5–10% of the U.S. population suffers from migrine attacks. As yet, no effective treatment has been developed that does not have significant side effects and risks that seriously affect patients' acceptance. The plethora of recommended treatment methods is evidence of the lack of a truly successful treatment for migraine.

For the most part, migraine attacks, although intensely disabling at times, are a benign disorder for which patients are often overly medicated and are frequently given potentially addicting drugs. Because this type of headache poses such a difficult problem, any possible approach that can safely answer this enigma merits study, and such an approach is the use of autogenic feedback training to control blood flow dysfunction in migraine.

BACKGROUND

Possible Mechanisms for Migraine Attacks

Graham and Wolff were the first to show that the pulsation of the temporal artery during the headache phase was increased.[8] Their work was based on observations of ergotamine tartrate effects on extracranial vessels in relief of

Joseph D. Sargent • Department of Neurology, Neurosurgery and Internal Medicine, The Menninger Foundation, Topeka, Kansas 66601. E. Dale Walters and Elmer E. Green • Biofeedback Center, Research Department, The Menninger Foundation, Topeka, Kansas 66601.

migraine attacks. Ergotamine tartrate diminished the increased amplitude of the arterial pulsation with corresponding relief of the headache. These results seemed reasonable in view of the previous work with histamine, which had clearly shown that stretched extracranial arteries were capable of producing pain.[3,19]

Schumacher and Wolff, working further with methods to increase intracranial pressure and the administration of amyl nitrite, reached the following conclusions: "The essential migraine phenomena result from dysfunction of cranial arteries and represent contrasts in vascular mechanisms and vascular beds. Preheadache disturbances follow occlusive vasoconstriction of cerebral arteries, where the headache results from dilation and distension chiefly of branches of external carotide arteries."[26] Thus the vascular theory of migraine was born.

A chance cerebral angiogram done on a patient while in a classic migraine attack showed a diminution in the size of the internal carotid system with reflux into the vertebral vessels during the prodromal phase. At the beginning of the headache phase, blood flow returned to normal.[4] O'Brien has shown a profound reduction in blood flow in the cerebral cortex with the changes lasting much longer than the aura. This change may even occur without symptoms and is generalized and bilateral in distribution. From this evidence it can be concluded that each attack of migraine is biphasic with the occurrence of the aura being "an accidental expression of a more generalized process."[14]

Wolff proposed in his neurogenic theory of migraine headache that vasodilation of the cerebral circulation occurred whenever adequate blood supply to the brain is endangered. If cerebrovascular dilation is great enough, the extracranial arteries will dilate and release a number of chemical factors with production of edema and a lowering of pain threshold. What initiates vasoconstriction is not clearly delineated.[30]

In recent years, investigators have postulated that an agent (or agents) causing vasoconstriction may be released to start the headache sequence. Sicuteri has proposed that such liberated chemical substances are amines such as norepinephrine, epinephrine, or serotonin, all powerful vasoconstrictors.[28] Other biochemical agents implicated in the headache sequence are acetylcholine, adenosine, triphosphate, bradykinin, and histamine.[15] Of these, serotonin may be the most important one, since under some circumstances it can also be a vasodilator substance.[16] In the migraine attack, some migrainous subjects have excreted increased amounts of catecholamine end products, particularly, 5HIAA from serotonin and VMA from norepinephrine and epinephrine.[28] Lance, Anthony, and Hintenberger have shown a corresponding reduction in blood serotonin levels.[12]

According to Friedman and Elkind, "Methysergide maleate (Sansert) has proven to be the most useful prophylactic agent in migraine."[6] Interestingly, this medicine is an antiserotonin agent and has two actions—inhibition of central vasomotor reflex effects and accentuation of peripheral vasoconstriction produced by catecholamines. Also ergotamine tartrate has significant central effects, in addition to its well-known peripheral vasoconstrictor effect, as demonstrated in man and animals.[8,21,22,30] Thus Friedman concludes that the "traditional view that migraine consists of phases of vasoconstriction and vasodilation is far too simplified, and it is apparent that migraine is a complex vasomotor disturbance."[7]

Because the migraine syndrome is a multifaceted clinical disorder, some investigators have postulated a dysfunction in the hypothalamus as the provoking element in the attack. Thus Graham has suggested that the hypothalamus can profoundly influence the autonomic control of the peripheral vasculature and has postulated a periodic central disturbance of hypothalamic activity or labile threshold accounting for the periodicity of the migraine attack and providing a mechanism whereby emotional disturbances could be mediated by pathways from the limbic system to the hypothalamus.[18] From three groups of clinical observations, Herburg has proposed an etiologic role in migraine headaches for the variation of hypothalamic activity. These groups of clinical observations are as follows: (1) the peripheral vasomotor involvement as seen in the temporal arteries, conjunctiva, and skin; (2) metabolic and vegetative disturbance, such as variations in water balance, food intake, mood, and sleep; and (3) the "accentuated secondary drives" of the migraine personality, which have been related to hypothalamic activity.[11] Rao and Pearce failed to demonstrate in migraine subjects a disturbance in the hypothalamic-pituitary-adrenal axis using metyrapone and insulin hypoglycemia tests. However, a consistently observed pattern of "hypoglycemia unresponsiveness" suggested a possible hypothalamic dysfunction.[20]

Treatment of Migraine

Friedman, commenting on drug therapy in migraine, found "that the results of drug prophylaxis were remarkably similar, irrespective of the drug, and only a few drugs were more effective than a placebo."[7] Ergotamine tartrate is still the drug of choice for the migraine attack and methysergide maleate has proved to be the most useful prophylactic agent in migraine.[7] However, both of these medications have significant adverse side effects that may decrease patient acceptance. "In general, the surgical therapy of migraine is not effective and should be discouraged."[7] In a small, selected number of cases, psychotherapy and treatment of allergic factors precipitating migraine headaches can be beneficial.

In the United States there is a sizable segment of poorly controlled migraine sufferers who might welcome a totally new approach to the treatment of migraine.

Research Experience Leading to Pilot Study

Neal Miller recently performed research that challenges the concept that "learning" in the autonomic nervous system is a reflection of skeletal muscle activity. He has shown that heart rate, gastrointestinal contractions, blood pressure, and the rate of saliva and urine formation in animals can be directly controlled through "operant conditioning techniques" via the autonomic nervous system.[13] In humans, there is scientific evidence for voluntary control of the autonomic nervous system through the training techniques of yoga, biofeedback training,[5,10,23,24,27,29] and the work of Schultz and Luthe on "autogenic training."[25]

Autogenic training, according to Luthe, is a basic therapeutic method of a series of psychophysiologically oriented approaches that are in contrast to other medical or psychologic forms of treatment. It involves the simultaneous regulation of mental and somatic functions. The desired somatic responses are brought about by passive concentration upon phrases of preselected words. The first two specific somatic responses in preliminary training brought under voluntary control are heaviness in the limbs and warmth in the extremities.

In treating migraines, Schultz and Luthe reported that the majority of their patients responsed with lessened frequency and intensity of headaches with autogenic training exercises. A number of patients reported a cure after several months of practice and learned to interrupt the onset of an attack by starting autogenic exercises as soon as prodromal symptoms appeared.[25]

Biofeedback training, a recently developed technique, holds promise of accelerating psychosomatic self-regulation. This technique, when combined with autogenic phrases, is called autogenic feedback training and uses visual and auditory devices to show the subject what is happening to normally unconscious bodily functions as he attempts to influence them by his use of mental, emotional, and somatic visualizations. Work in our laboratory has shown that skin temperature in the hands is directly related to blood flow in the hands,[23] and an increase in skin temperature of the hand is used as an index of voluntary control of the sympathetic section of the autonomic nervous system.

The possibility of using autogenic feedback training for migraine patients was suggested by the experience of a research subject who, during the spontaneous recovery from a migraine attack, demonstrated considerable flushing in her hands with an accompanying 10° F rise in 2 minutes. Knowledge of this event quickly spread throughout the laboratory and prompted two individuals with migraine to volunteer for training in hand temperature control. One was wholly successful and learned to eliminate migraine for the most part. The other had a partially beneficial result, and she was able to somewhat alleviate headache intensity and reduce frequency of headache. On the basis of this prepilot experience, it seemed useful to conduct further study with a number of headache patients in a clinical setting.

RATIONALE

Although considerable research must be conducted before we are certain about the neural mechanisms involved in "voluntary controls" training programs, it seems quite clear that the limbic-hypothalamic axis is an essential part. The classic paper of Papez,[17] "A Proposed Mechanism of Emotion," has laid the groundwork for an understanding of bioemotional factors, and additional work has elaborated Papez's position.[1] It seems clear beyond reasonable doubt that the limbic system, the "visceral" or "emotional" brain, is the major responder to psychologic stress and that psychosomatic problems become chronic in somatic processes through numerous interconnections between the limbic system and autonomic control centers in hypothalamic sections of the midbrain. The chain of

events might be hypothesized as follows: psychologic response (p
stimuli)→limbic response→hypothalamic response→autonomic respon..
response.

In the case of migraine, which seems to be a part of a stress-related syndrome, the somatic response is dysfunction of vascular behavior in the head,
related to intense sympathetic dysfunction, if other parts of the syndrome (such as
cold hands, due to vasoconstriction) can be used as indicators. Vasoconstriction
in the hands is a function only of sympathetic activation and vasodilation is a
one-variable indication of decrease of sympathetic outflow. There peripheral
vascular structure does not have significant parasympathetic innervation.

With these concepts and facts in mind, it seems reasonable to hypothesize
that autogenic-feedback training for hand warming is effective in amelioration of
migraine, because patients are learning to "turn off" excessive sympathetic outflow. Since the sympathetic control centers for vascular behavior are located in
subcortical structures, it seems that the attack on vascular dysfunction in the head
is linked to a general relaxation of sympathetic outflow, rather than through
hydraulic maneuvering of blood in various portions of the body. This hypothesis
of sympathetic relaxation rather than blood volume changes per se, as the effective agent in migraine amelioration, is supported by the fact that patients who put
their hands in warm water in order to increase the blood volume in the hands
usually do not obtain migraine relief. A couple of patients who have obtained a
measure of relief in this way have, according to the sympathetic-control
hypothesis, merely taught themselves to relax with the conditioned stimulus of
warm water.

The limbic system is certainly brought into action by the interaction of
patient and machine. Considerable emotion is involved in learning to control the
temperature machine, and if this involvement increases the sympathetic activation, then the resultant vasoconstriction causes the hands to cool. In order to
"make" the hands get warm, it is literally necessary to lean "passive volition."
This includes a condition of relaxed detachment, in which the body is told what to
do through autogenic imagery and then is allowed to do it without anxious
introspection. Only under this condition, which seems to be opposite to the
normal state preceding migraine attack, can the hands be made to become
warmer at will. In other words, learning to control hand temperature is a good
indicator of learning to control central processes that are associated with vascular
dysfunction. It is voluntary control of this functional relationship, in the authors'
opinion, that is responsible for migraine relief. It includes normalization of
homeostatis balance in hypothalamic control centers.

METHODS

The initial 75 subjects out of a total of approximately 150 in the pilot study
have been either self-referred or referred by physicians in the community. Each
patient, before participating in the project, had a detailed history, complete
physical examination, and laboratory studies (EEG, skull X rays, echoencephalo-

gram, chest X ray, serology, CBC, and urinalysis). Subjects with severe psychologic and/or physical disorders were eliminated from the study. There were 2 with cluster headaches, 5 with combined headache, 11 with tension headaches, and 57 migraine sufferers.

Each patient received instructions in the use of a "temperature trainer," which indicated the differential temperature between the midforehead and the right index finger. He was also given a typewritten sheet containing autogenic phrases. The first group of phrases helped the subject achieve passive concentration and relaxation of the whole body. The second group of phrases focused on the achievement of warmth in the hands. After learning the phrases, the participant dispensed with the typewritten sheet and visualized the changes while watching the temperature trainer. A positive warmth response, as indicated by the trainer, was accomplished by increasing temperature of the hands in comparison to the forehead and helped the subject to learn to observe the change of feeling that occurred in his hands while practicing. Since absolute temperatures were not measured at either site, it was impossible to know whether a positive response indicated an actual increase in hand warmth or a decrease in forehead temperature. However, results from our laboratory with absolute temperature feedback have indicated that the specific change in temperature occurs in the hands rather than in the forehead. Also, most subjects reported that a positive response with the trainer was associated chiefly with the feeling of change in the hands rather than change in the forehead. The coordination between mind and body or psychosomatic responses is an important aspect of the training exercises, because it allows the subject to overcome his initial doubt with respect to the control of basic physiologic processes. A positive response on the trainer reinforces the patient's confidence in doing his exercises.

One month prior to training, a subject charted daily the type of headache, and if a headache was present, he rated headache severity, presence or absence of associated symptoms, degree of disability from the headache, and duration of headache. Also the type, strength, and total number of units taken in 24 hours for each medication used for headache and its associated symptoms were recorded (see Figure 1).

After instruction in the use of the temperature trainer and hand temperature control each participant practiced daily at home and recorded presence of absence of relaxation and warmth in the hands, readings from the trainer at the start and end of each practice session, and the interval of time to detect warmth in the hands from the beginning of the session. Later in the training period, the subject tried to control his headache by warming his hands and estimated his success at doing it. The meticulous recording of all data was expected of each participant while in the study.

At first the subject was seen at weekly intervals until he had a consistent, positive response on the meter and an associated change of feeling in the hands. After mastering the hand-warming technique, he practiced on alternate days without the trainer and usually the trainer could be withdrawn within a month after starting. Subsequently, he was expected to continue daily practice sessions and was encouraged to use hand warming to help control headache. After the

1. Date							
2. Type of Headache (check one or more) If headache is present check items 3 thru 6	☐ Migraine ☐ Tension ☐ Sinus ☐ None	☐ Migraine ☐ Tension ☐ Sinus ☐ None	☐ Migraine ☐ Tension ☐ Sinus ☐ None	☐ Migraine ☐ Tension ☐ Sinus ☐ None	☐ Migraine ☐ Tension ☐ Sinus ☐ None	☐ Migraine ☐ Tension ☐ Sinus ☐ None	☐ Migraine ☐ Tension ☐ Sinus ☐ None
3. Intensity of headache *a (circle one)	1 2 3 4	1 2 3 4	1 2 3 4	1 2 3 4	1 2 3 4	1 2 3 4	1 2 3 4
4. Presence of associated symptoms (circle one)	YES NO	YES NO	YES NO	YES NO	YES NO	YES NO	YES NO
5. Rate degree of disability from headaches *b (circle one)	0 1 2 3 4	0 1 2 3 4	0 1 2 3 4	0 1 2 3 4	0 1 2 3 4	0 1 2 3 4	0 1 2 3 4
6. Length of headache (in hours)							
7. Strength of Tab., Cap. or Shot / No. in 24 hrs / Name 1. 2. 3. 4. 5.	1. 2. 3. 4. 5.	1. 2. 3. 4. 5.	1. 2. 3. 4. 5.	1. 2. 3. 4. 5.	1. 2. 3. 4. 5.	1. 2. 3. 4. 5.	1. 2. 3. 4. 5.
8. Rate presence of warmth in hand *c (circle one)	0 1 2	0 1 2	0 1 2	0 1 2	0 1 2	0 1 2	0 1 2
9. Rate ability to bring warmth to hands *d (circle one)	0 1 2 3 4	0 1 2 3 4	0 1 2 3 4	0 1 2 3 4	0 1 2 3 4	0 1 2 3 4	0 1 2 3 4
10. Rate degree of relaxation *e	0 1 2	0 1 2	0 1 2	0 1 2	0 1 2	0 1 2	0 1 2
11. Change of temperature registered on meter							
12. Rate ability to control headaches with exercise *f (circle one)	0 1 2	0 1 2	0 1 2	0 1 2	0 1 2	0 1 2	0 1 2

Figure 1. Headache project data collection sheet. (*a) 1—Slight, 2—moderate, 3—moderately severe, 4—severe; (*b) 0—no interference with activities, 1—interferance with activities, 2—had to go to bed, 3—go to emergency room of doctor's office for treatment, 4—need to be hospitalized; (*c) 0—none, 1—questionable, 2—present; (*d) 0—absent, 1—more than 5 minutes, 2—between 3 and 5 minutes, 3—between 1 and 3 minutes, 4—less than 1 minute; (*e) 0—none, 1—questionable, 2—present; (*f) 0—none, 1—partially successful, 2—successful.

trainer was withdrawn, the participant returned to the clinic every 1–3 months. During the return visits, pertinent data that may have influenced the patient's headache and his response to the exercises were recorded, and he practiced voluntary relaxation on the warmth trainer. The expected follow-up period was a minimum of a year, preferably for 2–3 years.

As the data were collected, it was scored, and graphs were plotted so that the subject's progress over 1 year could be viewed at a glance. The variables evaluated to date are (1) headache intensity, (2) the total of individual analgesics used, and (3) total potency of analgesics used. The subjects rated on a 5-point scale the severity of the most intense period of its activity in each 24-hour period. Each analgesic was assigned a number, representing its potency, the extremes of which were aspirin[1] and morphine,[7] and the potency scale represented the sum of strengths of analgesics used in 24 hours.

Each patient's progress was evaluated as to degree of improvement, based on the senior author's global clinical judgment with benefit of the plotted data.

As an outgrowth of this work, it seemed necessary to determine the behavior of skin temperature in the forehead and hands as the patient tried to warm his hands. The Biomedical Electronics Laboratory of The Menninger Foundation built a temperature scanner, which measures in rapid sequence skin temperatures from four sites. A number of subjects were evaluated using this temperature scanner.

RESULTS

Work in the headache project, begun almost 4 years ago, was initially reported after accumulating data on 28 subjects, of whom 19 were afflicted with migraine.[23] A later report was based on the data from 33 migrainous individuals. Of the 33, 32 had migraine attacks and 68%–90% of the patients were considered to be improved in the judgment of three raters.[24]

Of the initial 75 subjects in the headache project, approximately 81% of the migraine patients followed for over 150 days were helped to a significant extent. The degree of improvement ranged from slight to very good (see Table 1).

Since the initial study with 75 patients, we have worked with approximately 75 additional patients using absolute temperature feedback. Those data have not been completely scored to date. To understand fully what we have done in this study, we feel that it will be particularly helpful to follow one participant from entrance into until voluntary withdrawal from the project.

Illustrative Case

Mrs. L. O. was first seen by me in consultion in January 1971 in a community hospital for a long, complex illness. As a result of this encounter, the patient was started on Tofranil at 10 mg t.i.d. for endogenous depression. Interestingly, the symptom of headache assumed little importance of its own at that time in the midst of other complaints. Evenually her personal physician increased the Tofranil to 100 mg daily with considerable improvement of her depression, but the headache problem continued unabated to the time of my next consultation in October 1971.

At the time of the second consultation the patient was 58 years old and now complained principally of headaches that seemed typical of migraine and were located always on the right side of the head. A complete physical examination with emphasis on the nervous system and laboratory work-up including an EEG, echoencephalogram, and skull X-rays revealed no other causes for headache except for an "abnormal EEG with photic sensitivity and a spike focus in the left temporal region." A repeat EEG in August 1972 was normal.

Table 1

Classification of Degree and Type of Improvement and Evaluation of Treatment for the Initial 75 Headache Patients[a]

Degree of improvement	Type of improvement	Number of migraine patients	
None	Headache activity continued at the same levels with little or no reduction in medication	8	19% not improved
Slight	Shortened headache duration, for instance, from 24 hours to 12 hours, reduced severity of headache, for instance, from severe to moderate, and reduced frequency of headache, for instance, from 20 headache days/month to 15/month.	9	
Moderate	All in the slight category and, in addition, aborting headache after its onset by voluntarily relaxing, and some reduction of drug use.	9	
Good	All in the slight and moderate categories and, in addition, detection of *preheadache* symptoms and voluntarily relaxing to avoid headache, and considerable reduction of drug use.	10	81% improved
Very good	All in the slight, moderate, and good categories and, in addition, almost complete elimination of drug use for headache relief except for a few brief, isolated episodes.	6	
	Total	42	

[a] The data of the following groups of patients are not included in this table. (1) 15 migraine patients, 8 with tension headache, and 1 with cluster headache who did not participate in the project for a criterion of 150 days and (2) 5 patients with mixed headache (vascular and tension components), 1 with cluster, and 3 with tension headache who participated for over 150 days, but represented too few cases for evaluation.

She was accepted for participation in the headache project in October 1971 and concluded her participation in January 1973. Data were collected on this patient for just over 1 hour. Figure 2 shows the patient's progress as indicated by (1) ratings of headache severity, (2) number of analgesic drugs used, and (3) sum of the potency of analgesic drugs used. Baseline data for 1 month prior to training are also shown. On visual inspection, it can be seen that steady improvement occurred in the control of headache. By the 20th week, mean severity of headache was reported as slight to none and remained at that level except for several slight episodes.

Figure 3 shows the skin temperature behavior of Mrs. L. O. from four body locations over time in a practice session "without headache" during a follow-up office visit. A similar record is shown in Figure 4 of Mrs. L. O. during another follow-up session with a moderately severe frontotemporal migraine, which was partially relieved by hand warming. Comparison of the headache and nonheadache sessions of Mrs. L. O. indicates some differences in skin temperature behavior: (1) During nonheadache, right-hand skin temperature is warmer throughout the session than left-hand skin temperature, but during headache, right-hand skin temperature is cooler through the session than left-hand skin

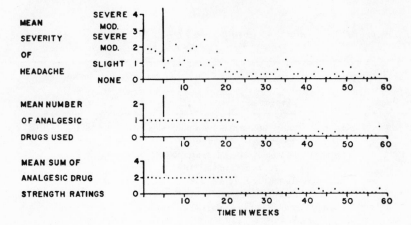

Figure 2. Clinical progress for 1 year of Mrs. L. O. in the reduction of severity of headache and analgesic drug use during baseline, training, and follow-up.

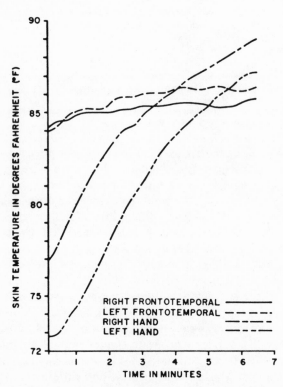

Figure 3. Skin temperature behavior of Mrs. L. O. from four body locations over time in a practice session "without headache" during a follow-up office visit.

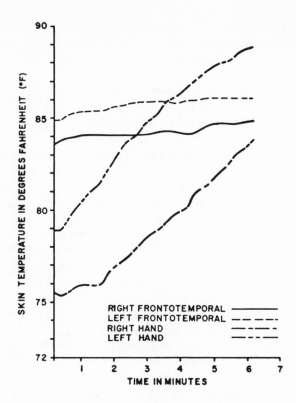

Figure 4. Skin temperature behavior of Mrs. L. O. from four body locations over time in a practice session with right frontotemporal migraine during a follow-up office visit.

temperature; (2) zero-time or starting right-hand skin temperature for the headache and nonheadache sessions are approximately the same, i.e., within 1½° F; and (3) zero-time or starting left-hand skin temperature is warmer by 6° F during headache than during nonheadache. What these observations may mean in terms of vascular behavior in migraine headache is, at present, not certain; however, they will be the subject of continuing research.

DISCUSSION

The results of the initial 75 patients, some of whom were discussed in a previous paper, were reevaluated according to degree of improvement defined by behavioral criteria. It is of interest that a significant degree of improvement was seen in 81% of the 42 migraine patients who were followed for more than 150 days. Furthermore, some individuals do not seem to be helped by using hand warming to control migraine headache. Nineteen percent of the migraine patients received little or no reduction of headache activity and drug use in relief of headache.

Many patients who develop voluntary control of migraine headache progress through a hierarchial series of behaviors. Patients who exemplify headache control at the "good" level, for instance, demonstrate relatively consistent behaviors of detection of preheadache symptoms and voluntary relaxation to avoid migraine attacks; however, this does not exclude, at certain times, headaches that may become temporarily beyond an individual's immediate control, such as awakening from a sound sleep with a moderately severe headache.

From our clinical experience, it seems all normal individuals have the physiologic capability to produce warmth in their hands. Psychologic factors seem to be important in determining sucess or failure in learning to increase blood flow into hands. Persons who were comfortable with the hypothesis that thoughts and feelings have an influence over bodily processes seemed to learn much faster. Also it seems as though psychologic-mindedness is helpful in learning psychosomatic self-regulation of migraine headache. Younger persons seem to respond quicker to the training than older individuals. A possible explanation for this finding may be that a person's life values increase in rigidity with increasing age; a person may then ajust less readily to new situations. The issue of being in command of situations seems important in patients who could not give up their headache; symptoms substitution was found in only one person out of approximately 150 that we have seen. Although the above psychologic factors may be important in learning hand blood flow control in management of migraine attacks, we have no systematic data to support these claims. This is an area in which we plan to do further research.

In our opinion, most of the clinical studies in headache research are carried out for too brief a period of time. In our project, we have a number of subjects who have been followed for 1–3 years. These extensive follow-ups will help provide hypotheses concerning whether successful subjects can sustain their improvement over a long period of time and whether initially unsuccessful subjects can improve if followed long enough.

The absolute skin temperature scanner has given us flexibility by monitoring four different skin sites at a time and recording these on a paper strip. These permanent tracings are now obtained on all new patients accepted into the project, and therefore, data are available on skin temperature behavior in subjects while voluntarily relaxing.

Since many migraine patients also have tension headache at times, the work of Budzynski, Stoyva, and Adler should be cited here. They report that "in general the results seemed to indicate that chronic tension headache sufferers can be trained to voluntarily lower their striate muscle tension in the face of daily life stresses and to reduce the incidence of tension headaches."[2] In their program, tension headache patients were given a thorough medical examination to confirm the diagnosis of tension headache. Then, patients received feedback for muscle action potentials or electromyographic activity (EMG) generated in the forehead area. Patients generally received two or three 30-minute feedback training sessions per week from 4 to 8 weeks and worked at a reducing frontalis EMG to low levels. Patients were encouraged to practice relaxation training at home at least once a day. It was found that (1) both headache activity and EMG levels declined as training progressed and (2) patients reported changes in their day-to-day lives outside the laboratory such as a heightened awareness of maladaptive rising tension, an increasing ability to reduce such tension, and a decreasing tendency to overreact to stress.

Because headache poses such a difficult problem, any possible approach that can safely answer the headache problem merits study. Such an approach is the use of autogenic feedback training to increase hand blood flow for treatment of migraine and the use of frontalis EMG feedback training for tension headaches.

Biofeedback and voluntary control may have usefulness in the treatment of a great number of psychosomatic disorders and may provide new tools to explore the mind/body interface.

The authors think that an important trend is beginning to take place in the areas of psychosomatic disorders and medicine. This is the increasing involvement of the patient in his own treatment. The traditional doctor–patient relationship is giving way slowly to a shared responsibility in which the patient is helped to become aware of his problems, both physical and emotional, and can therefore become a responsible partner in going toward psychosomatic and physical health.

In summary, (1) most migraine patients, aided by autogenic feedback training, learn to voluntarily regulate their headaches; (2) patients develop psychosomatic self-regulation of migraine headache by voluntarily relaxing the sympathetic section of the autonomic nervous system in the hand, thereby increasing the blood flow to that area; (3) the degree of improvement varies across migraine patients, as some patients' improvement is better than others; (4) there seems to be a hierarchy of behaviors through which the migraine patients progress toward regulating their headaches; and (5) during training sessions in the clinic, it has been observed that significant increases occur in hand skin temperatures, while only small changes occur in frontotemporal skin temperatures.

REFERENCES

1. Brady, J. V. The paleocortex and behavioral motivation. In H. F. Harlow & C. N. Woolsey (Eds), *Biological and biochemical bases of behavior*. Madison: University of Wisconsin Press, 1958.
2. Budzynski, T., Stoyva, J., & Adler, C. Feedback-induced muscle relaxation: Application to tension headache. In T. X. Barber et al. (Eds.), *Biofeedback and self-control*. Chicago: Aldine-Atherton, 1971.
3. Clark, D., Hough, M., & Wolff, H. G. Experimental studies on headache observations on histamine headaches. *Archives of Neurology and Psychiatry*, 1932, *140*, 23.
4. Dukes, H. T., & Vieth, R. G. Cerebral arteriography during migraine prodrome and headache. *Neurology*, 1964, *14*, 636.
5. Engle, B. T., & Melmon, K. R. Operant conditioning of heart rate in patients with cardiac arrhythmias. *Conditional Reflex*, 1968, *8*, 130.
6. Friedman, A. P., & Elkind, A. H. Appraisal of methysergide in the treatment of vascular headaches of the migraine type. *Journal of the American Medical Association*, 1963, *184*, 125–128.
7. Friedman, A. P. Migraine headaches. *Journal of the American Medical Association*, 1972, *223*, 1399–1402.

8. Graham, J. R., & Wolff, H. G. The mechanism of the migraine headache and the action of ergotamine tartrate. *Archives of Neurology and Psychiatry*, 1938, *39*, 737.

9. Green, E. E., Ferguson, D. W., Green, A. M., et al. Preliminary report on Voluntary Controls Project: Swami Rama. Research Department, The Menninger Foundation, June 1970.

10. Green, E. E., Green, A. M. & Walters, E. D. Voluntary control of internal states: Psychological and physiological. In T. X. Barber et al. (Eds.), *Biofeedback and self-control*. Chicago: Aldine-Atherton, 1971.

11. Herburg, I. J. The hypothalamus and the aetiology of migraine. In R. Smith (Ed.), *Background to migraine*. London: Heinemann, 1967.

12. Lance, J. W., Anthony, M. & Hintenberger, H. The control of cranial arteries by humoral mechanism and its relation to the migraine syndrome. *Headache*, 1967, *7*, 93–102.

13. Miller, N. E. Learning of visceral and glandular responses. *Science*, 1969, *163*, 434–445.

14. O'Brien, M. D. The relationship between aura symptoms and cerebral blood flow changes in the prodrome of migraine. In D. J. Dalessio, T. Dalsgaard-Nielsen, S. Diamond (Eds.), *Proceedings of the International Headache Symposium. May 16–18, 1971, Elsinore, Denmark*. Basle, Switzerland: Sandoz, Ltd. 1971.

15. Ostfield, A. M. Migraine headache, its physiology and biochemistry. *Journal of the American Medical Association*, 1960, *174*, 110–112.

16. Page, J. H. Serotonin (5 hydroxy tryptamine). *Psychological Review*, 1954, *34*, 536–588.

17. Papez, J. W. A proposed mechanism of emotion. *Archives of Neurology and Psychiatry*, 1937, *38*, 725–743.

18. Pearce, J. *Migraine: Clinical features, mechanisms and management*. Springfield, Illinois: Charles C Thomas, 1969.

19. Pickering, G. W. & Hess, W. Observations on the mechanism of headache produced by histamine. *Clinical Science*, 1933, *57*, 77.

20. Rao, L. W. & Pearce, J. Hypothalamic-pituitary-adrenal axis studies in migraine with special reference to insulin sensitivity. *Brain*, 1971, *94*, 289–298.

21. Rothlin, E. Recherches experimentales sur l'ergotamine, alcaloi de specifique de l'ergot de seigle. *Archives of International Pharmacodynamic Therapy*, 1923, *27*, 459.

22. Rothlin, E. & Cerlitti, A. Untersuchmumgere über die kreislauf wirkung des ergotamine. *Helvetica Physiologioa et Pharmacologica Acta*, 1949, *7*, 333.

23. Sargent, J. D., Green, E. E., & Walters, E. D. The use of autogenic feedback training in a pilot study of migraine and tension headaches. *Headache*, 1972, *12*, 120–124.

24. Sargent, J. D., Green, E. E., & Walters, E. D. Preliminary report on the use of autogenic feedback training in the treatment of migraine and tension headaches. *Psychosomatic Medicine*, 1973, *35*, 129–135.

25. Schultz, J. H., & Luthe, W. *Autogenic therapy* (Vol. 1), New York: Grune and Stratton, 1969.

26. Schumacher, G. A., & Wolff, H. G. Experimental studies of headache. *Archives of Neurology and Psychiatry*, 1941, *45*, 199.

27. Schwartz, G. E., Shapiro, D., & Trusky B. Learned control of cardiovascular integration in man through operatn conditioning. *Psychosomatic Medicine*, 1971, *33*, 57–62.

28. Sicuteri F. Vasoneuroreactive substances and their implications in vascular pain. In A. P. Friedman (Ed.), *Research and clinical studies of headache*. Baltimore: Williams & Wilkins, 1967.

29. Weiss, T., & Engel, B. T. Operant conditioning of heart rate in patients with premature ventricular contractions. *Psychosomatic Medicine*, 1971, *38*, 301. 321, 1971.

30. Wolff, G. H. *Headache and other head pain* (2nd ed.). New York: Oxford University Press, 1963.

Section VII

ELECTRODERMAL BIOFEEDBACK

The skin is the body's largest organ, protecting us from exposure and forming our contact with the external world. It is highly reactive, with changes noted in texture, color, temperature, moistness, etc., in response to internal and external stimuli. Consequently, when a person has an emotional experience or reacts to stimuli, the characteristics of the skin change.

It is surprising that, despite the measure of electrodermal activity being one of the earliest to be recorded in physiology and psychophysiology (see Chapter 1), little systematic biofeedback work has been done with changes in skin quality. The two most common measures used are the galvanic skin response (GSR) and the skin potential response (SPR). Both tend to measure an orienting response (see Sokolov, 1963, for a good definition of the orienting reflex). The importance of the measure of EDR is both the base level and the response. GSR has at least two components, "the base level, which may be indicative of diffuse, non-directed activation or the response amplitude, which may perhaps be interpreted as effective responsibility" (Edelberg, 1972, p. 373). This becomes one of the major problems in studying electrodermal activity, for the GSR tends to be an idiosyncratic response. In a field where data are looked at in terms of averages and group data, idiosyncratic responses are washed out and lost. (This phenomenon is illustrated by the story of the statistician whose head was in the oven and whose feet were in the freezer—and whose average temperature was normal.) This is precisely the major difference between passive recording (psychophysiology) and biofeedback. What is important here is exactly that idiosyncratic mind/body activity.

Thus one of the major contributions of biofeedback is the exploration of this idiosyncratic response. Each time the feedback signal occurs, one asks what was happening inside the person. The biological measure (e.g., GSR) can be used to enhance the appropriate integration of mind and body. For example, one would expect an increase in GSR when a person smiles. If the response, however, occurs some of the time and not at other times, the question arises as to what is different emotionally between the conditions of the smiling that caused one to elicit a certain GSR and the other not.

In this area, too, patterns of response must be considered. Very little work has been done exploring differential responding between the right and left sides of the body (Myslobodsky & Rattok, 1975, is one of the few) or foot versus hand responding. It is worth noting here that Wilhelm Reich (Zuckerman, 1971) has been the only researcher who explored the GSR of erotic body surfaces.

Another application of GSR is mentioned in the section dealing with hypertension (Section VIII). As will be seen, GSR was successfully used in the holistic treatment of hypertension (Patel, Chapters 44 and 45).

   The two articles in this section describe the electrodermal response. Strong (Chapter 41) gives a short discussion of the physiological basis of the GSR. The absolute measure is difficult to monitor since it varies somewhat with room temperature, ingested medication, skin preparation, electrode stability, and other factors. However, as mentioned previously, what may be more important is *not* the absolute measures but the responsivity of the system. Chapter 42 by Toomim and Toomim deals with this responsivity within a framework of psychotherapy.

   It is our hope that future research in biofeedback will examine more closely the relationship between electrodermal activity and emotional responsivity.

   For additional information on electrodermal response, we suggest Prokasy and Raskin (1973).

REFERENCES

Edelberg, R. Electrical activity of the skin. In N. S. Greenfield & R. A. Sternbach (Eds.), *Handbook of psychophysiology*. New York: Holt Rinehart & Winston, 1972.

Myslobodsky, M. S., & Rattok, J. A symmetry of electrodermal activity in man. *Bulletin of the Psychonomic Society*, 1975, *6*(5), 501–502.

Prokasy, W. S., & Raskin, D. *Electrodermal activity in psychological research*. New York: Academic Press, 1973.

Sokolov, E. N. Higher nervous function: The orienting reflex. *Annual Review of Physiology*, 1963, *25*, 545–580.

Zuckerman, M. Physiological measures of sexual arousal in the human. *Psychological Bulletin*, 1971, *75*, 297–329.

41

Galvanic Skin Reflex

P. Strong

THE AUTONOMIC NERVOUS SYSTEM

The human autonomic nervous system is the system within the body that regulates body functions such as temperature, respiration, and glandular activity. When a subject is psychologically excited or is in some other elevated state of psychological activity, the subject perspires or "sweats." This is due to an emotional stimulus initiating a response in the autonomic nervous system, which in turn produces a response in the subject's sweat glands. Detection of this sweat gland activity is thus an indication of the subject's psychological state or state of arousal.

Activity of the sweat glands is referred to by one or more of the following terms: *electrical skin resistance* (ESR), *galvanic skin reflex* (GSR), *electrodermal response* (EDR), and *psychogalvanic reflex* (PGR). Occasionally, the term *GSR* is referred to as the galvanic skin resistance. These terms all relate to one or both of the following physiological changes associated with sweat gland activity: a change in resistance and the generation of a potential between areas containing many sweat glands and areas almost devoid of them. The change in resistance is referred to as the Fere effect on the exosomatic response of the GSR. A decrease in the subject's resistance indicates arousal. Relaxation is indicated by an increase in resistance. The generation of a potential difference is referred to as the Tarchanoff effect or the endosomatic response of the GSR. This resistance change and potential generation is represented by δR and E in Figure 1.

GSR MEASUREMENT BY RESISTANCE CHANGE

GSR measurement by this technique involves the detection of an impedance between two electrodes on the subject. The GSR primarily changes the resistive component of this impedance; it is thus important that the measurement technique used be insensitive to reactive component changes. The simplest technique would appear to be the passage of a DC current via the electrodes and the detection of the voltage drop produced between the electrodes due to this current flow. Since, however, the GSR is usually recorded for prolonged periods, the electrodes

P. Strong • Tektronix, Inc., Beaverton, Oregon 97077.

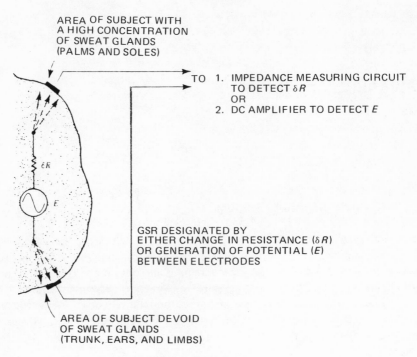

AREA OF SUBJECT WITH
A HIGH CONCENTRATION
OF SWEAT GLANDS
(PALMS AND SOLES)

TO   1.   IMPEDANCE MEASURING CIRCUIT
           TO DETECT δR
           OR
      2.   DC AMPLIFIER TO DETECT E

GSR DESIGNATED BY
EITHER CHANGE IN RESISTANCE (δR)
OR GENERATION OF POTENTIAL (E)
BETWEEN ELECTRODES

AREA OF SUBJECT DEVOID
OF SWEAT GLANDS
(TRUNK, EARS, AND LIMBS)

Figure 1. GSR measurement.

used cannot be relied upon as these electrodes will undoubtedly produce a DC offset potential of several hundred millivolts due to the passage of current for a prolonged period. This offset potential could not be differentiated from a potential produced by a change in the subject's resistance. For this reason, DC techniques have been found to be unsatisfactory.

Since it is desirable to employ a measurement technique sensitive primarily to resistance change, and since it is undesirable to use DC measurement techniques, very low frequency AC techniques are invariably used. These measurement techniques involve the passage of an AC current of perhaps 10 microamperes peak at a frequency of 2 or 3 Hz. The resulting voltage drop between the electrodes can then be detected as an AC signal that will be independent of any DC offset potentials generated at the electrodes; such a technique is shown in Figure 2. Referring to Figure 2, a constant-current pulse generator adapter, used in conjunction with a Type 561B or 564B oscilloscope's calibrator, provides pulses of 10 microamperes, with a duration of 40 milliseconds. Since this pulse wave form has only a 10% duty cycle, a change in subject resistance, when using an AC-coupled amplifier, will primarily alter the displayed pulse amplitude and will cause almost no shift in the oscilloscope zero level or baseline.

Since, when recording the GSR, we are recording resistance changes due to action of the sweat glands at the surface of the skin, electrodes should be used that make direct contact with the skin as the use of any conductive electrode paste would interfere with the action of the sweat glands. The electrodes used should also have no chemical effect on the action of the sweat glands. Thin lead plates are preferred for GSR electrodes as they meet the above requirements and they are also malleable and can be molded to suit the subject's contour. Lead plate electrodes are used in the photograph shown in Figure 2; one electrode is placed on the palm of the hand in a region of high sweat gland concentration and the other electrode is placed on the back of the hand in a region almost completely devoid of sweat glands.

The range of resistances encountered in normal subjects when recording between two electrodes on the hand is from 20,000 ohms to perhaps 0.2 megohms. In some instances, particularly if the autonomic nervous system is

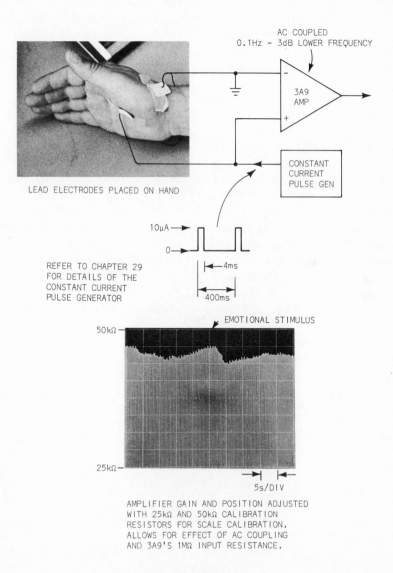

Fig. 13-2. GSR measurement.

malfunctioning and the sweat glands are effectively denervated, the resistance between the electrodes will exceed 1 megohm.

GSR MEASUREMENT BY POTENTIAL DETECTION

GSR measurement by this technique involves the detection of a DC potential between two electrodes on the subject. This DC potential will normally be less than 1 millivolt. An electrode offset potential in excess of 1 millivolt may be produced at the electrode–subject interface, and any unbalance in this offset potential between the two electrodes cannot be differentiated from the GSR potential. Although solid silver electrodes, or perhaps silver plate electrodes, are used, this offset potential unbalance is difficult to control and will invariably contribute a considerable DC potential to the GSR potential. For this reason, GSR measurement by this technique is rarely attempted.

ELECTRICAL SKIN RESISTANCE

The electrical skin resistance (ESR) is basically the same as the GSR. The term *ESR* is, however, usually reserved for measurement of the distribution of sweat glands on the human body rather than the actual change in the activity of these sweat glands. The ESR is measured in the same way as the GSR; however, the ground electrode is applied by means of a silver clip attached to the ear and the active or exploring electrode consists of a noncorroding silver or lead disc or a small roller wheel. Sweat gland distribution is detected by moving the position of this exploring electrode. The change in resistance between a sweating and a non-sweating area is distinct and a small movement of the exploring electrode can result in a resistance change in excess of 100%. Instruments specifically designed for measurement of the electrical skin resistance are referred to as dermometers.

42

GSR Biofeedback in Psychotherapy:
Some Clinical Observations

Marjorie K. Toomim and Hershel Toomim

The traditional function of the psychotherapist has been to help the patient move from conflict and anxiety toward free and effective functioning. In order to do this the therapist has relied largely on (1) the client's subjective report as to what is and is not relevant material; (2) the client's sensitivity to, perception of, and readiness to report sensations associated with changing emotions; (3) the therapist's theoretical orientation, his value system, and his sensitivity to, perception of, and interpretation of both verbal and body language. If the therapist and patient disagree on the importance of a particular word, concept, or body movement, the therapist often blames the patient for "resisting." The subjective nature of the therapeutic process has perhaps correctly left it vulnerable to attack from more experimentally oriented psychologists. The process may often be likened to one "black box" relating to another "black box."

Another problem in psychotherapy has been that of attempting to alter a psychophysicological system such as emotional responsivity with purely psychological means (verbal interaction). Some efforts have been made to make changes in these systems by addressing the physiology primarily, as in Reichian therapies. Psychophysiologists have attempted to correlate specific emotions with specific physiological responses but have found the human organism too complex for such codification. Some autonomic organ systems are stimulated in a sympathetic direction, some in the parasympathetic direction with arousal (Lacey, 1967); there are marked differences among individuals as to which organs are activated with stress and the effects of various stressors on any one organ system (Ax, 1953, 1969); and dynamic processes of inhibition and excitation create variation in organ function so that any one visceral response does not necessarily reflect a single behavioral dimension (Gellhorn, 1967). As noted below, individuals may respond to the experience of helplessness or severe conflict with a paradoxical drop in skin conductance (Toomim & Toomim, 1975), though such a drop is usually associated with relaxation.

While no instrumentation has been developed that quantifies and identifies specific emotions, most people respond to emotional arousal with at least one

Marjorie K. Toomim • Biofeedback Institute of Los Angeles, Los Angeles, California 90048. Hershel Toomim • Biofeedback Research Institute, Los Angeles, California 90048.

peripheral organ system. Inexpensive, battery-powered biofeedback instruments now make it possible to monitor one or more of these systems continuously during psychotherapy sessions so that body/mind relationships may be clearly and immediately established. The therapist may then use his knowledge of the client, his therapeutic skills, instrumental readings, and changing client responses to vary content and therapeutic process so as to increase or decrease affective states. Continuous monitoring of otherwise subliminal physiological changes allow the therapist to recognize significant content during the session.

While interindividual variance in psychophysiological response systems is large, the therapist soon learns the organic response pattern of individuals and attends, then, to intraindividual variation in effecting therapeutic change.

Both EMG and GSR instrumentation have been used successfully in systematic desensitization therapy. Wolpe (1967) reports using the GSR in creating hierarchies where patients can not clearly define their subjective experience for the correct ordering of anxiety-provoking stimuli. Budzynski and Stoyva (1969) used continuous monitoring with EMG in a biofeedback paradigm. Here, the patient gains continuous awareness of the physiological process being measured—in this case, the frontalis muscle—so that he may learn voluntary control of the function. The control involves changing both body tension and mental set.

The following chapter reports the use of GSR feedback as an integral part of a dynamic psychotherapy process. The therapeutic process was eclectic, with emphasis on emotional flooding (Hogan, 1967). Peaks in reactivity or paradoxical response patterns were emphasized in order to intensify the client's experience and facilitate emotional release. Desensitization techniques call for manipulations that reduce organic arousal (Jacobson, 1938; Wolpe, 1958).

PHYSIOLOGY OF SKIN RESISTANCE AND THE GSR

The reader is referred to Martin (1961), Lang (1971), and Prokasky and Raskin (1973) for comprehensive reviews of GSR research relevant to use in psychotherapy. Briefly, the galvanic skin response is a measure of sweat gland activity. While sweat glands are innervated by only the sympathetic branch of the autonomic nervous system, their reactivity is mediated by cholinergic transmission at the end organ. Darrow (1943) notes that conditions that alter cholinergic activity may limit the magnitude of the GSR response to stimulation. These conditions include the amount of available acetylcholine, the concentration of cholinesterase, the presence of adrenalin, and antidiuretic hormone.

Changes in skin resistance form part of the emergency reaction of the sympathetic nervous system and may thus be used as a rough measure of an individual's physiological stress pattern. This measure has also been used to indicate general arousal, activation level (Schlosberg, 1954), and energy mobilization (Duffy, 1951).

Several investigators have found various aspects of the GSR within subjects reliable over time. Freeman and Griffin (1939), Lacey and Lacey (1962), and

Block (1965) find its magnitude reliable; Bull and Gale (1971) find its latency, magnitude, and recovery reliable. Hughes and Shean (1971) find the interaction of feedback and awareness an effective means of modifying ongoing GSR reactivity in both high and low neurotic Ss.

The GSR has been criticized as a monitor of internal change because it so readily responds to such psychologically irrelevant functions as coughing, deep breathing, and body and hand movements. However, the GSR feedback technique described below makes use of these functions that confound the experimentalist. They are included in computing the individual's baseline measure. They contribute to an understanding of the general GSR activation pattern of each individual. GSR responses defined as therapeutically relevant must cause a change in the GSR that is both greater than and more persistent than that created by these extraneous factors. In addition, the therapeutically relevant GSR response may be manipulated by further exploration of the anxiety-provoking or conflictual material that accompanies the skin-conductance rise or suppression. Thus, if the individual laughs or breathes deeply while talking about, for example, his mother, and the GSR feedback tone rises (skin conductance increases), it will soon return to baseline if the *material* is not emotionally arousing. If it is emotionally arousing, the GSR will continue to respond as long as the relevant content is foreground and emotionally stimulating. Or it may "flatten"—stop responding and then respond again when the disturbing material is no longer foreground.

The skin conductance instrument used for this work (Biofeedback Research Institute Model 505) accurately quantifies the skin conductance level in micromhos. It has a psychotherapy scale in which amplified rate of change of conductance is added to the ongoing conductance level. This provides the necessary sensitivity to relevant small changes and maintains the indications within the usable dynamic range of the instrument. With this technique the therapist is free to attend to relevant psychological material without being distracted by necessary instrument adjustments for under- or overrange activity.

METHOD

The GSR is introduced to the client in the following way. He is shown the instrument, and its function as a monitor of general nervous system activation is briefly explained. If the client is willing to use this device, electrode cream is placed on the electrodes and they are connected to the palmar surface of the dominant hand. The client is then instructed that he may move his hands at will. As he moves, he notices a rise in the GSR feedback tone, which signifies a rise in skin conductance. This familiarizes him with the sound of the instrument and the effect of movement on the GSR. He is then asked to take a deep breath. Again, there is usually a rise in the GSR feedback tone. The intensity of this response, as well as the length of time it takes for the GSR to decrease, are observed. A few minutes of relatively light conversation ensues while the client adapts to the new situation. The conversation also includes teaching about the instrument, exploration of feelings about its use, and evoking fantasies about what it might reveal about his inner or "secret" being. The client's attention is directed to changes in the feedback tone and he is asked to describe any physical sensations that correlate with large changes in the tone. This process forms a basis for interpreting the GSR response of each individual. It also establishes a baseline for that session.

Both the client and the therapist hear the feedback tone. This allows the client as well as the therapist to maximize understanding of the ways the individual responds to both external and internal stimuli. Also, the client becomes more involved in directing the content of the therapeutic hour to areas that are potentially most difficult for him to deal with. His own internal responsivity is the measure of significance. Therapist and client together are guided by the GSR feedback in focusing their efforts. Defensive maneuvers are reduced. Questions of "who is right" about the importance of certain data are eliminated. The GSR serves as an impartial third party in the therapist–client relationship. For example, a large increase in GSR conductance was found to accompany a client's habitual pattern of placing his right hand on his left biceps. He thought this irrelevant. However, no skin conductance rise accompanied his touching any other part of his body. He then willingly explored the factors that might be related to this particular body posture. It was found that he always sat at the dining table with his father at his left. Further, he always felt uncomfortable about the people who sat at his left in classes and meetings. He expected them to be critical of him. Without the GSR feedback this "body language" would not have been "decoded."

GSR REACTIVITY PATTERNS

According to observations made in this study, most individuals may be described along three GSR reactivity dimensions. They may be seen as overreactors, underreactors, and variable reactors. When attempting to place individuals in one of these categories, it is important to observe them in a number of circumstances. For example, a person whose GSR freely varies (a variable reactor) in ordinary circumstances may become an under- or paradoxical reactor when very tired or hungry, or when stressed in a particular manner. The following description reflects reactivity patterns in an ordinary conversation condition.

Overreactors. These are people who respond to stimuli excessively. A deep breath results in a marked rise in skin conductance, which persists for a minute or more. A change from a neutral to a mildly exciting or emotionally charged stimulus results in a sharp rise in skin conductance, which persists beyond the time that the subject matter is under consideration. The rise from a baseline of 10 micromhos might be as much as three micromhos. The overeactor may not be able to lower his skin conductance (the GSR feedback tone) at will. This individual feels uncomfortable when he lowers his skin conductance level below baseline through ordinary relaxation procedures (being quiet for a few minutes, attending to breathing, etc.). He may describe the subjective state that accompanies lowered skin conductance as "a feeling of deadness," or "This is how I feel when I am depressed." A typical overreactor may be described as follows:

> Clara, a 24-year-old wife and mother, was unable to feel satisfied with anything. She fought constantly with her husband; she could not concentrate more than a few minutes on any subject; she felt anxious most of the time. GSR levels fluctuated in wide swings of 3 micromhos or more in general conversation, 10 or more when dealing with emotional material. Using the GSR feedback tone, she learned to differentiate her feelings when skin conductance was relatively high and relatively low. She was quite uncomfortable at first at the low level, but soon was able to tolerate relaxation as measured by a low, relatively stable GSR. She would not practice quieting procedures at home, for they made her feel depressed. It appeared that much of her angry, fear-inducing, erratic behavior was designed to maintain a high level of arousal. It was as if she were addicted to her own high arousal state. At first she was encouraged to explore activation behavior that was less damaging to her interpersonal relationships. She began to substitute shopping, telephoning, etc., for fighting and complaining as a way of staying "high." Her husband, who reacted to her hyperactivity by withdrawing, was encouraged to accept "constructive" activity and to *do* more with her. She thus felt less frustrated and rejected. Gradually, along with the ordinary psychotherapeutic process, which relieved some of her internal psychodynamic stress, she learned to tolerate being quiet for longer and longer periods of time. She found she could feel alive with less sympathetic nervous system activation. When she left therapy, she was still highly responsive, but was able to channel her activity into areas that were constructive; she could be comfortably quiet when she wanted to be.

Underreactors. These are people whose skin conductance changes very little with changes in attention, body movement, or emotional stimulation. A deep breath may result in little more than a rise of 1 micromho from a baseline of 10 micromhos. Even laughter, clapping the hands sharply in front of the individual's face, or the gentle touch of a hand may leave the GSR relatively unaffected. These individuals tend to have little awareness of the subjective feelings which accompany internal body processes and emotions.

> Alan, a 35-year-old business executive, came to therapy because he felt that he was missing out on things. His wife complained he was not sufficiently responsive to her. He did not feel she was justified in her complaint, for he believed he was very much in tune with her. His GSR level varied no more than .3 micromhos during the greater part of the first interview, rising only briefly when he mentioned sex. He began to understand what he was missing, namely his own body responsivity. He now understood and accepted his wife's complaint. He began to break up his compulsive work pattern and to focus more on his feelings. Therapy centered on his fear of losing control, and gradually his GSR activity level increased. He is now finding ways to allow himself to feel emotionally alive, rather than pushing himself to feel alive through constant intellectualization and compulsive working.

> Dick, a 27-year-old student, appeared extremely active and alive. He was almost manic in his rapid speech, ready laugh, and optimistic, positive view of life. He felt, however, that he was out of touch with people somehow. The GSR baseline was high, about 15 micromhos, but changed little, even when he laughed. When he was asked to be quiet for a few minutes, to speak more slowly and go beneath surface thoughts and feelings, the GSR became more reactive and he began to feel sad. Using the GSR feedback, he soon learned the difference between defensive and meaningful laughter. His activity and his laughter activated the GSR only when it was genuine. As Dick quieted, the GSR baseline lowered to around 2.5 micromhos and he felt comfortable over a wide range of GSR levels.

Variable Reactors. These people's GSR reactivity pattern moves up and down in an undulating manner that clearly reflects changes in attention, excitation, and emotional involvement. A deep breath results in a marked increase in skin conductance, which returns to baseline rather quickly. Changes of 2 or more micromhos are common. These individuals easily learn to recognize changes in internal states that accompany emotion.

Awareness of GSR reactivity patterns adds an important dimension to psychotherapy—the immediate awareness of subliminal psychophysiological processes. Such phrases as "I feel turned off," "I seldom get angry," "I have to keep active," "I feel funny inside when I think of . . . ," "I freeze under stress" become clear at an objective, physical level. Both therapist and client become more accepting of the individual's quality of being and the extent to which his sympathetic nervous system reactivity patterns limit his range of overt behavioral patterns in relationships with himself and others.

GSR BIOFEEDBACK TRAINING

The immediate awareness of sympathetic nervous system reactivity through GSR feedback allows for retraining of maladaptive patterns. (Crider, Shapiro, & Tursky, 1966; Hughes & Shean, 1971; Johnson & Schwartz, 1971; Shapiro, Crider, & Tursky, 1971; Shapiro & Crider, 1971). The individual decides what levels or patterns of activation he deems positive and negative. The feedback tone then serves as the reinforcer that moves him to alter thoughts, attitudes, and body mechanisms so as to increase the likelihood that he will respond—at least at the electrodermal level—in a way he positively values.

A paradoxical GSR response proved extremely valuable in the case of a 35-year-old man who was unable to maintain an erection. Four years of conventional psychotherapy had resolved most other problems but made no impact on this one. He claimed his sex drive was quite high and reported often feeling sexually aroused. When GSR feedback was introduced, we found however, the feedback tone *dropped* with every mention of sex, despite a high level of muscular tension, particularly in his legs. He defined this physiological state as "sexual arousal." The GSR was then used to train a new and more usual definition of the sexually aroused state with increase in skin conductance.

GSR FEEDBACK AS GUIDE TO RELEVANT CONTENT

There are two GSR patterns that indicate that the therapeutic material at hand is important: (1) a sharp *rise* in conductance level beyond that which is usual for the individual indicates that emotionally meaningful material is at or near the conscious level and is ready to be dealt with; (2) a *paradoxical flatness* or *drop* in skin conductance, especially in the context of obvious emotional distress, indicates deeply repressed material is coming to awareness and that the individual is strongly resisting. An essential condition of relevance is that the GSR reactivity pattern closely follows the material at hand. So long as the emotionally arousing material is foreground, the tone continues to stay high or go higher, or it maintains its paradoxical flatness until a breakthrough in awareness occurs, at which point it rises precipitously.

An example of the first instance, where material is close to the surface, is that of a 42-year-old man who has spent some years in therapy and who is a variable reactor.

> Jim has blamed much of his present difficulty with women on his mother, who indeed did contribute a great deal to his poor life adjustment. However, the gently undulating tone of the GSR during mother-blaming stories and mother-destruction fantasies indicated that this material was now relatively comfortable for him. His apparent anger was an "acting" of feeling, rather than true feeling. A reference to his sister, however, was accompanied by a 3.5 micromho rise. Motivated by his understanding that such a rise in the GSR feedback tone indicated important material was at hand, he explored his feelings for his sister and found them important in his relationships with women. He had previously felt this relationship was not relevant to his present problem and resisted dealing with it since his relationship with his sister was now satisfactory.

The following is an example of the paradoxical GSR response in which the skin conductance level remains flat or decreases when the individual is obviously distressed:

> Susan woke in panic every morning at 4:30–5:00, and the anxiety did not subside until after breakfast. In a hypnotherapy session, she remembered being 8 years old and hearing the screams of a neighbor dying of cancer. Tears came to her eyes and she reported feeling fear and tension, but the GSR was flat. When she was asked to be quiet and go deeper into the hypnotic state, the GSR tone suddenly rose precipitously. Questioned, she stated that the lullaby from *Hänsel and Gretel* was running through her head. She thought it unimportant. The words to the remembered portion are "14 angels guard my rest." Further exploration revealed a repressed childhood fantasy that she must be very bad to need 14 angels to guard her rest every night, and that death was in the closet waiting to get her when she masturbated. Yet she was in conflict. She could not stop masturbating. Further exploration revealed an elaborate fantasy of which only a few elements had previously surfaced in dreams. After working through this material, she was able to sleep and wake normally.

The GSR feedback tone represents a guide to both therapist and client as to the value of the content in a therapeutic transaction. The therapist is less likely to be led into blind alleys and trapped by defensive maneuvers. Most clients appreciate this objective evidence of relevance. It cuts down their time in therapy and deepens the level at which they work. The client's resistance to threatening material is reduced, thus smoothing the flow of the therapeutic experience for both therapist and client.

CONCLUSION

GSR biofeedback is a useful aid in dynamic psychotherapy. It increases the effectiveness of the therapist through providing immediate awareness of body/mind relationships and sympathetic nervous system reactivity patterns. It further provides the client with a fuller awareness of himself, encourages the cooperation of the client, and reduces the hit-or-miss quality of the therapeutic process. It increases the likelihood that relevant content will be dealt with and accompanying emotions elicited. It adds a new dimension to the practice of psychotherapy—the direct training of dysfunctional sympathetic nervous system reactivity patterns and some of the attitudes that maintain the stress response.

The introduction of continuous monitoring of internal processes within the therapeutic setting reduces the body/mind dichotomy. It is particularly valuable to the primarily verbal therapist who wants direct access to the body.

REFERENCES

Ax, A. F. The physiological differentiation between fear and anger in humans. *Psychosomatic Medicine*, 1953, *15*, 433–442.

Ax, A. F. Autonomic response patterning of chronic schizophrenics. *Psychosomatic Medicine*, 1969, *31*, 353–364.

Block, J. D. Stimulus discrimination among autonomic measures: Individual and group characteristics. *Psychosomatic Medicine*, 1965, *27*, 212–228.

Budzynski, T. H., & Stoyva, J. M. An instrument for producing deep muscle relaxation by means of analog information feedback. *Journal of Applied Behavior Analysis*, 1969, *2*, 231–237.

Bull, R. H. C., & Gale, A. The relationships between some measures of the Galvanic Skin Response. *Psychoneurological Science*, 1971, *25*, 293–294.

Crider, A., Shapiro, D., & Tursky, B. Reinforcement of spontaneous electrodermal activity. *Journal of Comparative and Physiological Psychology*, 1966, *61*, 20–27.

Darrow, C. W. Physiological and clinical tests of autonomic functions and autonomic balance. *Physiological Review*, 1943, *23*, 1–36.

Duffy, E. The concept of energy mobilization, *Psychological Review*, 1951, *58*, 30–40.

Freeman, G. L., & Griffin, L. L. The measurement of general reactivity under basal conditions. *Journal of General Psychology*, 1939, *21*, 63–72.

Gellhorn, E. Motion and emotion: The role of proprioception in the physiology and pathology of the emotions. *Psychological Review*, 1964, *71*, 457–472.

Gellhorn, E, *Principles of autonomic-somatic integration; physiological and clinical implications*. Minneapolis: University of Minnesota Press, 1967.

Hogan, R. A. Implosive therapy in short term treatment of psychotics. In H. Greenwald (Ed.), *Active psychotherapy*. New York: Atherton Press, 1967.

Hughes, W. G., & Shean, G. D. Ability to control GSR amplitude. *Psychoneurological Science*, 1971, *23*, 309–311.

Jacobson, E. *Progressive relaxation*. Chicago: University of Chicago Press, 1938.

Johnson, H. J., & Schwartz, G. E. Suppression of GSR activity through operant reinforcement. In T. X. Barber et al. (Eds.), *Biofeedback and self control*. New York: Aldine-Atherton, 1971.

Lacey, J. I. Somatic response patterning and stress: Some revisions of activation theory. In M. H. Appley & R. Trumbull (Eds.), *Psychological stress: Issues in research*. New York: Appleton-Century-Crofts, 1967.

Lacey, J. I., & Lacey, B. E. The law of initial value in the longitudinal study of autonomic constitution: Reproducibility of autonomic response patterns over a four year interval. *Annals of the New York Academy of Sciences*, 1962, *98*, 1257–1290.

Lang, P. The application of psychophysiological methods to the study of psychotherapy and behavior modification. In A. E. Bergin & S. L. Garfield (Eds.), *Handbook of psychotherapy and behavior change*. New York: Wiley, 1971.

Martin, I. Somatic reactivity. In H. J. Eysenck (Ed.), *Handbook of abnormal psychology*. New York: Basic Books, 1961.

Prokasky, W. F., & Raskin, D. C. *Electrodermal activity in psychological research*. New York: Academic Press, 1973.

Schlosberg, H. Three dimensions of emotions. *Psychological Review*, 1954, *61*, 81–88.

Shapiro, D., & Crider, A. B. Operant electrodermal conditioning under multiple schedules of reinforcement. In T. X. Barber et al. (Eds.), *Biofeedback and self control*. New York. Aldine-Atherton, 1971.

Shapiro, D., Crider, A. B.. & Tursky, B. Differentiation of an autonomic response through operant reinforcement. In T. X. Barber et al. (Eds.), *Biofeedback and self control*. New York: Aldine-Atherton, 1971.

Toomim, M. K., & Toomim, H. *Psychodynamic correlates of the paradoxically invariant GSR*. Paper read at the Biofeedback Research Society Convention, Monterey, California, February 1975.

Wolpe, J. *Psychotherapy by reciprocal inhibition*. Stanford, California: Stanford University Press, 1958.

Wolpe, J. Reciprocal inhibition as the main basis of psychotherapeutic effects. In H. Greenwald (Ed.), *Active psychotherapy*. New York. Aldine-Atherton, 1967.

CARDIOVASCULAR BIOFEEDBACK II—HYPERTENSION

There are two major approaches to self-control of blood pressure: (1) learning voluntary control of systolic and diastolic levels by having the blood pressure automatically fed back and (2) the general use of relaxation and stress management techiques as an indirect way to allow the blood pressure to return to a homeostatic level. The first approach, developed from research techniques, taught patients with essential hypertension to lower their blood pressure. For a comprehensive review of this biofeedback approach, the reader is referred back to Chapter 1.

The major problem to overcome was how to continuously monitor and feed back blood pressure. Up to that point, the only available method for recording blood pressure was the traditional stethoscope and sphygmomanometer, a technique described by Strong in Chapter 43. Since the stethoscope had to be used and the cuff manually inflated, this system was not adequate for feedback training.

This difficulty was partially solved when Shapiro, Tursky, Gershon, and Stern (1969) developed an automated constant cuff sphygmomanometer that monitored and periodically fed back blood pressure levels. However, this automated system still used the standard blood pressure cuff, which occludes blood flow. This makes continuous monitoring impossible since an inflated cuff inhibits normal blood flow to the arm and therefore cannot be left on for extended periods of time. Until recently, this was the only noninvasive method available for blood pressure biofeedback. In the last few years, however, a new noninvasive technique, which records pulse-wave velocity without a cuff, has been developed and seems promising as a relative on-line blood pressure feedback device (Steptoe, 1977).

Although Kristt and Engel (1975) were successful in feedback blood pressure, overall there has not been much clinical success with this method. However, clinical outcome studies that have used the second approach mentioned above, i.e., teaching relaxation and stress management, and that emphasized changing the life-style of the patient, have shown greater promise. Historically, this approach was derived from yoga, progressive relaxation, and autogenic training, procedures that have been demonstrated to be successful in helping hypertensives become normatensive individuals. The emphasis in these programs has been to encourage the transfer of the learned autonomic control from the clinical setting into the "real life" of the patient. In this process, the patients can start changing their illness-producing life pattern.

Most of these studies have used EMG- or GSR-assisted relaxation training. Chapters 44 and 45 by Patel review the hypertension studies she has done with GSR feedback, including a 12-month follow-up study. The success of these studies is extremely encouraging. Evidence strongly suggests that home practice of relaxation exercises is a critical aspect of this training. There appears to be a one-to-one correlation between long-term success and amount of home practice. This does not minimize the effectiveness of biofeedback training but rather emphasizes the importance of the integration of biofeedback with stress management training and other types of relaxation techniques (regardless of whether these are progressive relaxation, autogenic training, or yogic exercises). At present, the most promising biofeedback studies fuse the two approaches and encourage the patient to change his illness-producing life-style.

To repeat the critical issues, blood pressure training as a treatment for hypertensives must involve a change of illness-producing life-styles. A similar approach can also be used for most chronic illness, and again calls attention to the totality of mind/body synchrony. Health is not the absence of symptoms but synchronous, fully functioning mind/body activity, a flexible alternation of rest/activity, alertness/drowsiness, love/hate, controlling/letting go.

The following are critical issues to look for in feedback studies with hypertensives:

1. How much home practice was done?
2. How much emphasis was placed on transfer of learning?
3. Was voluntary control of blood pressure taught?
4. Was there any follow-up and how long did it last?*
5. How was success defined—decrease in blood pressure, decrease in medication, etc.?
6. Were subjects taught bidirectional (increase and decrease) control so that they could discriminate differences?

In this introduction we focused on biofeedback with essential hypertension. For additional reading on experimenta research, including animal work, we suggest Obrist, Black Brener, and DiCara (1974); and for cardiovascular physiology Berne and Levy (1972) and Rushmer (1972).

REFERENCES

Berne, R. M., & Levy, M. N. *Cardiovascular physiology.* St. Louis: C. V. Mosby, 1972.
Kristt, D. A., & Engel, B. T. Learned control of blood pressure in patients with high blood pressure. *Circulation,* 1975, *51,* 370–378.
Obrist, P. A., Black, A. M., Brener, J., & DiCara, L. V. (Eds.). *Cardiovascular psychophysiology.* Chicago: Aldine, 1974.

---

* Since there are no symptoms associated with increases in blood pressure, it is especially important to follow up and monitor those hypertensive patients who have successfully lowered their blood pressure and reduced their intake of antihypertension medication. This would uncover those patients whose blood pressure once again increased. Similiar rules of long-term follow-up would apply to any pathology not accompanied by symptoms (e.g., glaucoma).

Rushmer, R. F. *Structure and function of the cardiovascular system.* Philadelphia: W. B. Saunders, 1972.

Shapiro, D., Tursky, B., Gershon, E., & Stern, M. Effects of feedback and reinforcement on the control of human systolic blood pressure. *Science,* 1969, *163,* 588–589.

Steptoe, A. Blood pressure control with pulse wave velocity feedback: Methods of analysis and training. In J. Beatty & H. Legewie (Eds.), *Biofeedback and behavior.* New York: Plenum, 1977.

43

Blood Pressure

P. Strong

INDIRECT BLOOD PRESSURE MEASUREMENT

By far the most common form of blood pressure measurement is the indirect measurement using the familiar pressure cuff, hand pump, and pressure dial device, used by all physicians, referred to as a sphygmomanometer. The sphygmomanometer, as shown in Figure 1, incorporates a pneumatic cuff encircling the upper arm. An inflatable section of this cuff is inflated by a small hand pump and the pressure in the system is indicated by a mechanical pressure gage or, in some models, a mercury manometer. The cuff is inflated to a pressure greater than the blood pressure in the large brachial artery of the arm. This

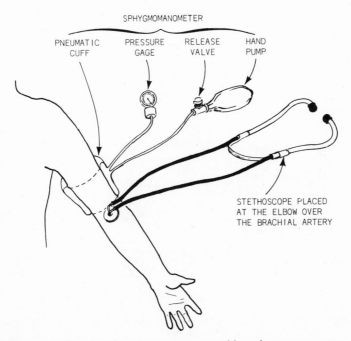

Figure 1. Indirect blood pressure measurement with a sphygmomanometer.

P. Strong • Tektronix, Inc., Beaverton, Oregon 97077.

pressure thus collapses the artery and occludes (cuts off) blood flow to the arm. As the pressure in the cuff is gradually released, using a release valve built into the hand pump, a point is reached where the cuff pressure and the peak or systolic arterial pressure are the same. At a pressure slightly below this level the peak arterial pressure slightly exceeds the cuff pressure and blood is able to squirt through the compressed segment of the brachial artery. This squirting blood results in turbulence within the artery creating sounds known as "Korotkoff" sounds. These sounds are usually detected with a stethoscope placed over the brachial artery. As the pressure in the cuff is further decreased, Korotkoff sounds continue until a point is reached where no further turbulence is produced as no constriction exists in the brachial artery. This point represents the diastolic blood pressure. As it is somewhat difficult to detect the pressure where the Korotkoff sounds begin and cease, this sphygmomanometer technique cannot be relied upon to produce an accuracy of much better than about 10 millimeters of mercury. While the technique is inaccurate, it is simple to perform and very little discomfort is felt by the patient. In the hands of a skilled operator highly repeatable results are obtained and, since the clinician is usually more interested in trends than exact numbers, the technique is entirely appropriate.

44

12-Month Follow-Up of Yoga and Biofeedback in the Management of Hypertension

Chandra Patel

Twenty hypertensive patients treated by psychophysical relaxation exercises were followed up monthly for 12 months. Age- and sex-matched hypertensive controls were similarly followed up for 9 months. Statistically significant reductions in blood-pressure (B.P.) and antihypertensive drug requirements were satisfactorily maintained in the treatment group. Mere repetition of B.P. measurements and increased medical attention did not in themselves reduce B.P. significantly in control patients.

INTRODUCTION

After a preliminary investigation had established that psychophysical relaxation based on yogic priniciples and reinforced by biofeedback instruments could produce a statistically significant reduction in high B.P.[1], a further trial was set up with age- and sex-matched controls, so that the effect of increased medical attention and repeated B.P. measurements could be eliminated. I report a 12-month follow-up in the treatment and control groups.

PATIENTS

Twenty hypertensive patients treated by the new therapy were compared with 20 age- and sex-matched hypertensive controls from the same general practice. To eliminate any bias in selection, patients of the same age and sex whose names began with the same or nearest alphabetical letter were chosen as controls. If a patient of the same age was not found, then a patient born in the following or preceding year was sought. Details of the patients and controls are given in Table 1.

Chandra Patel • General Practitioner, Croyden, Surrey, England. Present affiliation: Senior Research Fellow, Department of Epidemiology and Medical Statistics, London School of Hygiene and Tropical Medicine, University of London, London WC1, England.

Table 1

Trial Patients and Controls

	Trial	Controls
Total	20	20
Males	9	9
Females	11	11
Average age (yr)	57.35	57.2
Average duration of hypertension (yr)	6.8	7.05
No. on antihypertensive drugs	19	18
Original systolic B.P. before drug treatment [mm Hg (mean ± *SD*)]	201.5 ± 24.2	197 ± 31.8
Original diastolic B.P. before drug treatment [mm Hg (mean ± *SD*)]	121.8 ± 12.4	115 ± 17.8

METHODS

Patients were asked if they would cooperate in research on high B.P. that would involve coming to the surgery over a period of 3 months three times a week for half an hour of relaxation training. Appointments were given to suit individual circumstances, but once an appointment time was fixed it was kept for all the sessions. History taking, investigations, number of attendances, time spent at each session, and procedure for B.P. measurements were kept the same in the controls as in the treatment group, but instead of being trained in relaxation the control patients were asked to rest on the couch.

The treatment patients were followed up monthly for 12 months. The control group patients were followed up similarly for 9 months after the initial 3 months of control study. Their B.P. was taken while standing, sitting, and supine on arrival only. No more training sessions were given during the follow-up period, although patients in the treatment group were encouraged to continue practice in relaxation and meditation. Drug dosage was only adjusted to keep the B.P. within a satisfactory range.

RESULTS

The results in the control patients were analyzed and those of the treatment patients were reanalyzed by a statistician. To eliminate any unconscious bias in the previous analysis[1] the mean of 18 B.P. measurements taken during the first three sessions of the relaxation training was taken as a "pretrial" baseline B.P. and an average of 24 measurements taken during the last four sessions as the "end of trial" B.P. Similar criteria were applied in the analysis of data from the control group (Table 2).

In the treatment group the average systolic pressure at the end of the training period was reduced by 20.4 ± 11.4 mm Hg (mean difference ± SD), while the diastolic pressure was reduced by 14.2 ± 7.5 mm HG (P < 0.001). The total drug

Table 2

Alteration in B.P. over the 3 Months of Relaxation Training

	Treatment group	Control group
"Pretrial" B.P.[a]		
Mean systolic ± SD	159.1 ± 15.9	163.1 ± 20.9
Mean diastolic ± SD	100.1 ± 12.8	99.1 ± 12.8
"End of trial" B.P.[b]		
Mean systolic ± SD	138.7 ± 16.0	162.6 ± 24.4
Mean diastolic ± SD	85.9 ± 8.7	97.0 ± 12.0
Difference		
Systolic ± SD	20.4 ± 11.4	.5 ± 14.5
Diastolic ± SD	14.2 ± 7.5	2.1 ± 6.2
Paired t test		
Systolic	7.75	.15
Diastolic	8.50	1.52
P	<.001	>.1

[a] Mean of 18 B.P. measurements taken during the first 3 sessions of relaxation training.
[b] Mean of 24 B.P. measurements taken during the last 4 sessions of relaxation training.

requirement in 12 patients fell by an average of 41.9% (range 33–100%).[1] In the control group systolic B.P. was reduced by 0.5 ± 14.5 and diastolic B.P. by 2.1 ± 6.2 mm Hg. Their drug requirement remained unchanged.

During follow-up B.P.s were taken "on arrival" only. The patients did not have their half-hour of relaxation or rest as described in (Table 3). When these

Table 3

Follow-up Results

	Treatment group	Control group
End of trial arrival *B.P.*		
Systolic ± SD	144.6 ± 11.0	167.7 ± 9.73
Diastolic ± SD	86.0 ± 5.74	97.1 ± 6.54
3-mo follow-up		
Systolic ± SD	143.9 ± 13.38	167.6 ± 8.08
Diastolic ± SD	84.0 ± 3.84	97.4 ± 7.73
6-mo follow-up		
Systolic ± SD	146.7 ± 10.72	164.1 ± 15.0
Diastolic ± SD	88.3 ± 6.84	97.3 ± 8.02
12-[a] and 9-[b] mo follow-up		
Systolic ± SD	144.4 ± 9.83	163.6 ± 9.42
Diastolic ± SD	86.7 ± 3.33	98.1 ± 7.83
P	>.01	>.1

[a] Treatment group.
[b] Control group.

follow-up B.P.s are compared with average "end of trial" pressures found on arrival at the surgery, the maintenance of the reduction in B.P. is very satisfactory.

In the first 3 months the drugs in one patient in the treatment group were further reduced (clonidine was reduced to 0.3 mg. in patient 10), making the total drug reduction 42.9%. In the second 3 months, however, another patient's drug requirement increased, making the total drug reduction 40.2% (methyldopa was increased to 250 mg daily in patient 11). In the control group the drug requirement increased by 5.5% in the first 3 months of the follow-up period.

DISCUSSION

The results in control patients show that merely repeating B.P. measurements and increasing medical attention does not reduce B.P. in long-established cases of hypertension, although there is often some initial reduction in B.P. in new cases of hypertension because of emotional desensitization—i.e., patients get used to the physician and the procedure.

Although the program worked out during follow-up was quite effective in reducing B.P., some patients found it difficult to discipline themselves to 20 minutes of regular relaxation and mediation twice or even once a day during the follow-up period. Since relief in terms of symptoms is almost nonexistent in hypertensive patients, the motivation to continue this time-consuming discipline is often not strong enough. Methods had to be found to incorporate relaxation and mediation in their daily activities—e.g., red traffic lights and ringing telephones and doorbells served as signals to quickly check for tension and relaxation. This has been found to be an effective substitute for regular practice.

Placebos can reduce high B.P.[2-6] In a double-blind study of patients whose initial B.P.s were more than 200/120 mm Hg, both guanethidine (average dose 60 mg per day) and oral placebo produced comparable and statistically significant reductions in B.P. over a 12-week period.[7] The average decreases in the placebo group were 25 and 12 mm Hg for the systolic and diastolic B.P.s, respectively. These results show that people can reduce their B.P. without the help of active drugs, and the higher the initial B.P. the bigger the drop.[7] The term *placebo* often implies that the beneficial effect is only transient and that it is possibly due to a favorable doctor–patient relationship. However, in my study, the beneficial effect in the treatment group has lasted for as long as 1 year and is still continuing. The doctor–patient relationship was exactly the same for both the groups and hence the mechanism of the therapeutic effect must be different.

If the patient can follow a suitable program of relaxation, it is not only possible to reduce the resting B.P. and antihypertensive-drug requirement but also the magnitude and duration of the rises in B.P. associated wth everyday emotional stresses.[8]

Evidence in laboratory animals suggests that reduction in proprioception lowers the sympathetic responsiveness of the hypothalamus and vice versa.[9-12] The rise in B.P. is a part of the sympathetic response. B.P. was reduced in hypertensive patients by profound relaxation of muscles with considerable reduction in electromyographic activity.[13,14] Meditation was associated with reduced oxygen consumption, carbon dioxide elimination, respiratory rate, and minute ventilation, without any change in the respiratory quotient.[15,16] Cardiac output and heart rate were also reduced and B.P. remained low throughout in normotensive people, whereas B.P. gradually decreased in hypertensive people.[17] There was a fourfold increase in the electrical resistance of the skin,[15] while alpha and theta waves predominated in the electroencephalogram (EEG).[18] It has been suggested[19] that EEG pattern of meditators demonstrates not only increased parasympathetic predominance but also concomitant relatively weak sympathetic discharge, which prevents the EEG pattern of alpha dominance from passing into a state of sleep. Wallace and Benson[15] described this as a "wakeful hypometabolic state." This relaxation response[20,21] seems to be the reverse of the "fight or flight" response, and regular elicitation of this relaxation response[20,21] may not only reduce the high B.P. but may also maintain the reduction. Brod[22] demonstrated that the hemodynamic pattern in patients with essential hypertension under resting conditions is similar to that found in normotensive people in response to emotional stress.

It is postulated that reduction in B.P. is brought about by a lower sympathetic tone, which is maintained by altered habitual interaction with the environment.

ACKNOWLEDGMENT. I thank Dr. Khosla for statistical help, Professor Pilkington for helpful suggestions in preparing this paper, and my partners and staff for their cooperation during this study. This work was supported by a grant from the South-West Thames Regional Health Authority.

REFERENCES

1. Patel, C. H. *Lancet*, 1973, *ii*, 1053.
2. Pickering, T. *Lancet*, 1973, *ii*, 1440.
3. Miller, N. E. In N. E. Miller, T. X., Barber, L. V. DiCara, J. Kamiya, D. Shapiro, & J. Stoyva, (eds.), *Biofeedback and self-control*. Chicago: Aldine Publishing Co., 1974.
4. Althausen, T. L., Kerr, W. J., & Burnett, T. C. *American Journal of Medical Science*, 1929, *177*, 398.
5. Althausen, T. L., Kerr, & W. J. *American Journal of Medical Science*, 1929, *177*, 470.
6. Ayman, D. F. *Journal of the American Medical Association*, 1930, *95*, 246.
7. Grenfell, R. F., Brigg, A. H., & Holland, W. C. *Southern Medical Journal, Nashville*, 1963, *56*, 1410.
8. Patel, C. H. *Clinical Science and Molecular Medicine*, 1975, *48* (Suppl. 2), 171–174.
9. Gellhorn, E. *Psychological Review*, 1964, *71*, 457.
10. Bernhaut, M., Gellhorn, E., & Rasmussen, A. T. *Journal Neurophysiology*, 1953, *16*, 21.
11. Gellhorn, E. *Electroencepholography and Clinical Neurophysiology*, 1958, *10*, 697.
12. Hodes, R. *Electroencephalography and Clinical Neurophysiology*, 1962, *14*, 220.
13. Jacobsen, E. *Progressive relaxation*. Chicago: 1938.
14. Love, W. A., Jr., Montgomery, D. D., & Moeller, T. A. Proceedings of the Biofeedback Research Society Meeting, Colorado Springs, 1974, p. 34.

15. Wallace, R. K., & Benson, H. *Scientific American* 1972, *226*, 84.
16. Allison, J. *Lancet*, 1970, *i*, 833.
17. Benson, H., Rosner, B. A., Marzetta, B., & Klemchuk, H. M. *Lancet*, 1974, *i*, 289.
18. Banquet, J. P. *Electroencepholography and Clinical Neurophysiology*, 1973, *35*, 143.
19. Gellhorn, E., & Kiely, W. F. *Journal of Nervous and Mental Disease*, 1972, *154*, 399.
20. Wolpe, J. *Psychotherapy by Reciprocal Inhibition*. Stanford: 1958.
21. Breary, J. F., Benson, H., & Klemchuk, H. P. *Psychosomatic Medicine*, 1974, *36*, 115.
22. Brod, J. *Lancet*, 1960, *ii*, 773.

45

Randomized Controlled Trial of Yoga and Biofeedback in Management of Hypertension

Chandra Patel and W. R. S. North

Thirty-four hypertensive patients were assigned at random either to 6 weeks' treatment by yoga relaxation methods with biofeedback or to placebo therapy (general relaxation). Both groups showed a reduction in blood pressure (from 168/100 to 141/84 mm Hg in the treated group and from 169/101 to 160/96 mm Hg in the control group). The difference was highly significant. The control group was then trained in yoga relaxation, and their blood pressure fell to that of the other group (now used as controls).

INTRODUCTION

Previous studies[1,2] using yoga and biofeedback have shown that modification of behavior designed to maintain a low level of arousal is effective in reducing resting blood pressure (B.P.) over a long period. The present study was designed to establish the efficacy of the treatment more formally by allocating patients at random to "yoga" or a placebo treatment. As the result of previous experience the total period of training was reduced to 6 weeks, with two sessions per week, and the training technique was improved by repeating the instructions at each session and by fuller explanation of the disease process and the treatment.

PATIENTS

All 43 known hypertensive patients under 75 years of age in a group practice who had not participated in the previous trials were asked to take part. "Hypertensives" were defined as those under pharmacological treatment for at least 6 months, with initial diastolic B.P. levels of at least 110 mm Hg on two separate days. They were invited to come to the surgery twice a week for half-hour sessions, at times convenient to themselves between 1 p.m. and 8 p.m., and they were urged to keep to the same time for each session. Thirty-seven patients

Chandra Patel • General Practitioner, Croyden, Surrey, England.   W. R. S. North • MRC Department of Epidemiology, Northwick Park Hospital, Harrow, Middlesex, England.

agreed to take part, but 1 woman was excluded before the trial began because her B.P. returned to normal. Two others were excluded after the trial had started—1 in the control group because of a change in therapy due to severe side effects from guanethidine, and 1 diabetic in the treatment group who developed renal complications and later died.

Characteristics of the remaining 34 patients, who completed the trial, are summarized in Table 1. Of the treatment group, 15 were on specific antihypertensive drugs, 1 was on tranquilizers, and 1 was untreated. All the control-group patients were on antihypertensive drugs.

METHOD

All patients attended on 3 separate days to provide baseline B.P. The patients were then assigned at random to yoga and biofeedback or general relaxation. Pressures were taken in the standing, sitting, and supine positions, and repeated after half an hour's rest. A random-zero sphygmomanometer was used.[3]

All blood pressures (fifth phase) were measured "blind" by the practice nurse. Patients were asked not to change their drug therapy during the trial. The first phase of the trial consisted of 12 sessions, 2 a week for 6 weeks, B.P. being again taken in the standing, sitting, and supine positions before and after the half-hour session. Active treatment consisted, first, of meetings during which the patients were shown films and slides about hypertension, the different ways in which emotion affects bodily processes, the physiology of relaxation, the concept of biofeedback, self-control, and so on. They discussed their queries and problems freely. The rapport created between doctor and patients as well as that between the patients themselves greatly helped to strengthen the program and ensure cooperation. Next, during individual training, patients lay on a couch or a reclining chair with legs apart and slightly rotated at the hip joint, arms by the side, shoulders flat, jaw limp, and eyes lightly closed; the head was raised to a comfortable position, but they were encouraged to lie as flat as possible. They were first asked to breathe slowly and rhythmically. Next, they were instructed to go over the different parts of the body mentally in a regular sequence, allowing each part to relax completely. Patients were instructed verbally on this methodical relaxation for 10 to 12 minutes and were then encouraged to remain relaxed for the rest of the session. Once the patient had mastered the method of relaxation, a

Table 1

B.P. (mm Hg) before Trial

Group	N	Age (yr)		Systolic B.P. (mm Hg)			Diastolic B.P. (mm Hg)		
		Mean	Range	Mean	SD	Range	Mean	SD	Range
Treated	17 (6 M, 11 F)	59.5	39–75	167.5	23.6	135–201	99.6	9.3	81–114
Control	17 (7 M, 10 F)	58.6	34–75	168.9	20.0	130–206	100.6	11.4	81–127

type of transcendental meditation was introduced. Throughout the session the patient was connected to one of two biofeedback instruments giving a continuous audio signal whose pitch fell as the patient relaxed. Generally, the instrument measuring electrical resistance of the skin (Relaxometer, Aleph One Ltd., Cambridge; G.S.R. 90, Biofeedback Systems Ltd., Manchester) was used for the first few sessions followed by an electromyograph (Myophone, Aleph One Ltd.). This confirmation of relaxation was intended to encourage further relaxation. Patients were also encouraged verbally and shown their B.P. records; they were also instructed to practice relaxation and meditation twice a day and gradually to try to incorporate these habits into routine activities, the methods depending on individual circumstances. For example, each patient had a red disc attached to his watch to remind him to relax whenever he looked at the time, and some were told to relax before answering the telephone. Patients in the control group attended for the same number of sessions and for the same length of time. However, they were asked to relax on the couch or the reclining chair without being given specific instruction, and they were not connected to biofeedback instruments.

At the end of the trial all patients were followed up every 2 weeks for 3 months.

In case the observed difference had been due to unknown factors not eliminated by randomization we then treated the control group with yoga and biofeedback therapy.

Phase 2 of the trial began 2 months after the end of the follow-up for phase 1. The previous control group, now the new treatment group, attended for 12 treatment sessions as in phase 1. One patient dropped out because he could not attend sessions regularly. The previously treated group were used as controls, but were seen only at the beginning and end of this phase to give B.P. readings for comparison. Only one initial and one follow-up reading was made in each group.

Two patients changed their drugs during the trial. One woman in the treated group had hydrallazine added to her propranolol therapy but remained on it for only 3 weeks in the middle of phase 1. Another woman in the control group was taken off guanethidine at the end of phase 1, and remained off treatment for phase 2.

RESULTS

Every B.P. used in the analysis is the mean of three readings taken with the patient standing, sitting, and lying. Although measurements were made at the beginning and end of each session, only those at the beginning of sessions have been used here (B.P. at the end of sessions was invariably lower). In addition, figures for "initial" pressures in phase 1 are the means of readings at the three preliminary sessions, and those for "final" pressures the means of the six follow-up sessions. (In phase 2 there was only one preliminary and follow-up session for both groups.) The results for the first phase of the trial are summarized in Table 2, showing only the average initial and final B.P.s in each group. Systolic B.P. fell by an average of 26.1 mm Hg in the treated group and by 8.9 mm Hg in the con-

Table 2

Change in B.P. (mm Hg) during Phase 1

Group	N	Mean initial B.P.		Mean final B.P.		Drop in systolic B.P.			Drop in diastolic B.P.		
		Systolic	Diastolic	Systolic	Diastolic	Mean	SD	Range	Mean	SD	Range
Treated	17	167.5	99.6	141.4	84.4	26.1	16.5	7 to 60	15.2	8.1	1 to 30
Control	17	168.9	100.6	160.0	96.4	8.9	14.5	−11 to 32	4.2	5.9	−10 to 13
Difference		—	—	—	—	17.77	($t = 3.23, p < .005$)		11.01	($t = 4.59, p < .001$)	

Table 3

Change in B.P. (mm Hg) during Phase 2

Group	N	Mean initial B.P.		Mean final B.P.		Fall in systolic B.P.			Fall in diastolic B.P.		
		Systolic	Diastolic	Systolic	Diastolic	Mean	SD	Range	Mean	SD	Range
Treated (formerly control)	16	176.6	104.3	148.6	89.3	28.1	15.9	3 to 67	15.0	9.4	0 to 32
Control (formerly treated)	17	148.8	87.8	146.2	86.2	2.6	7.2	−4 to 20	1.6	3.7	−2 to 9
Difference		—	—	—	—	25.5	—	—	13.4	—	—

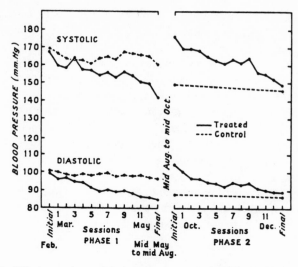

Figure 1. B.P. changes (means) during two phases of trial of yoga and biofeedback.

trols. The corresponding figures for diastolic pressures are 15.2 and 4.2 mm Hg. The differences between the groups are highly significant. In addition, there was a significant fall in both systolic and diastolic pressure in the control group, though this did not apply to all patients. Two controls showed a rise in both systolic and diastolic B.P., and another six had a rise in one of the two. No patients in the treated group showed a rise in pressure. The means of each group week by week in phase 1 are shown in the left-hand half of Figure 1.

At the beginning of phase 2 B.P. was higher in the new treatment group (formerly control) than at the beginning of the first phase; this could be partly because only one reading was taken. B.P. in the former treated group, however, was close to the level at the end of phase 1; this group was not seen again till the end of the trial. The results are shown in Table 3 and the second half of Figure 1. The results for the phase 2 treated group were similar to those in phase 1 (i.e., pressure fell significantly), while B.P. in the phase 2 control group changed very little. No significance tests were performed for this phase as their validity seems doubtful, but it is clear that there is again a large difference. No member of the treated group showed a rise in B.P.

DISCUSSION

In phase 1 the treated group showed a much larger reduction in B.P. than the control group. Evidence that this was due primarily to the relaxation technique they had learned is provided by the fact that at the start of phase 2 their B.P. remained at its lower level, while that in the control group had risen to at least the initial level.

Biofeedback therapy has two components. The first is objective and depends on showing changes in a physiological function as displayed by auditory or visual signals. The second is thought to be a subjective state that cannot be monitored.

A subject may evolve his own means of producing a desirable change in a biofeedback experiment, but to advance this from a simple demonstration of control over an autonomic function in an experimental situation into a meaningful therapeutic procedure in daily life it is necessary to evolve a technique that will produce predictable objective changes.

A subsidiary study on these patients[4] indicates that the treated patients showed a smaller rise in B.P. than the control patients after being subjected to experimental stress.

In view of the possible importance of this type of therapy and the absence of undesirable side effects, it seems desirable that further trials should be carried out in otherwise untreated patients under single-blind conditions, perhaps in hypertension clinics.

ACKNOWLEDGMENTS. We thank Prof. T. R. E. Pilkington for his encouragement to start this project; Dr. W. E. Miall for his help and criticism; Dr. Denis Craddock, Dr. Barbara Barnes, and Dr. Robert Cruthers for allowing their patients to participate; Mrs. M. Gould for taking all the B.P. measurements; and Mrs. A. Miller for helping with group discussions. This work was supported in part by a grant from the South-West Thames Regional Health Authority. Reprinted with kind permission from *Lancet*, 1975, *ii*, 93–95.

REFERENCES

1. Patel, C. *Lancet*, 1973, *ii*, 1053.
2. Patel, C. *Lancet*, 1975, *i*, 62.
3. Wright, B. M., & Dore, C. F. *Lancet*, 1970, *i*, 337.
4. Patel, C. *Clinical Science and Molecular Medicine*, 1975, *46*, suppl. p. 171.

OTHER APPLICATIONS

The book up until now has covered only the more commonly used biofeedback devices. In this section we hope to point out that in fact we need not be limited to traditional EEG, EMG, temperature, GSR, and blood pressure feedback. Any system that is capable of changing and can be measured can be used as a feedback device.

There are an infinite number of unexplored biofeedback applications. One important component of biofeedback is the monitoring and feeding back of biological information from the body in real time. The whole area of metabolic illnesses, therefore, could be explored through on-line feedback of the biological processes. Some types of diabetes could become amenable if one could feed back blood insulin and glucose levels. The major problem with present biomedical technology is not that one cannot monitor these biochemical processes but rather that the monitoring techniques are invasive and thereby not socially acceptable (i.e., there is a high trainee attrition rate when invasive and/or painful methods are used over repeated periods of time).

There is a real need for socially acceptable monitoring systems that are compact and that can easily be carried around outside the training office. One of the best examples of this was the mood ring, which monitored finger temperature. The changes in colors of the stone (liquid crystal) indicated the change in temperature. Another portable device now being used is an EMG device used for bruxism. Solberg and Rugh (Chapter 47) describe a study examining the use of EMG in bruxism. Applications of biofeedback in dentistry is one of the new and novel approaches and applications of biofeedback training (Rugh, Perlis, & Disraeli, 1977).

Feedback training needs to reinitiate the "normal" biological pattern. This is vividly demonstrated in Chapter 46, by Engel, Nikoomanesh, and Schuster, on the operant conditioning of rectosphincteric responses in the treatment of fecal incontinence. The successful training of the rectosphincteric response was dependent on the knowledge of the timing sequence of the internal and external anal sphincter as well as the inducement of pressure on the rectum wall. Although the approach of Engel et al. is highly symptom oriented, it is based on physiological knowledge. Their rapid success may have been due in part to the undesirable aspects of the illness and the absence of life patterns that encouraged the continuation of an illness-producing life-style.

In many cases, feedback allows verbal instruction to be translated into physiological signals. The feedback describes the appropriate direction of response or acts as an error signal for the subject. In this framework, anything can be used as a feedback device. Peper and Shambaugh's Chapter 48 pragmatically gives a number of useful suggestions of economical feedback devices.

It is hoped that the reader will reconsider common and/or biomedical devices from a cybernetic point of view. For example, in intensive care units in hospital, the EKG monitors should be used by the patients instead of being used just by the medical staff. The patients then become students and partners in the healing process by attempting to keep the appropriate EKG signal on and learning to suppress the pathological EKG signal. In this sense, the patients become active participants in the healing process instead of being depressed, overwhelmed, and passive victims of their diseases and social milieu.

As stated, almost anything can be used for feedback. Vachon and Rich (1976) have used pulsed air to feed back the air resistance during inhalation in asthmatics. More ingeniously, and with good clinical results, Tiep, Analiz, and Cordell (1977) have fed back the wheezing sounds of asthmatics recorded with a modified electronic stethoscope recording near the neck. The electronic stethoscope has also been used by Furman (1973) to teach patients with excessive diarrhea to control their bowel motility.

When considering the different systems usually trained for voluntary control, it is ironic that breath, a process under both voluntary and involuntary control, has been so little and so infrequently regarded as an important pattern in the study of physiological systems. Psychophysiology has been notoriously deficient in investigating breath patterns. Breath of life—or the gateway to consciousness, in yogic terms—has usually been investigated in terms of respiratory volumes or rates. The optimum breath for health and alteration of consciousness has not been systematically explored. Feedback techniques could help shed light on this area. Breath is a *pattern*. It, like any other biological process, does *not* operate in isolation but as part of a system. Within this system, the respiratory process is also a pattern. [Note that this relates back to Chapter 33, in which Whatmore and Kohli described dysponesis and stated that the frontalis should not be recorded alone but in combination with other muscles (i.e., pattern). This concept is also brought up by Schwartz in Chapter 3.] Within the complexity of respiration, each variation represents a psychosomatic pattern. Therefore, before considering respiratory feedback, one must decide which aspect is to be fed back: mouth and/or nose breathing, right and/or left nostril, abdominal and/or thoracic ratios, the slope of the inspiration and expiration curves, the pause times, or the additional bracing of other muscles. By using respiratory feedback, one may be able to explore the multiple dimensions of illness (hyperventilation syndrome), health (natural childbirth), and consciousness (pranayama and kundalini yoga).

Biofeedback has been applied in many novel areas. Some suggested areas are found in the following articles: Cornsweet and Crane (1973), Cowings, Billingham, and Toscano (1977), Danskin and Walters (1973), Johnston and Lee (1976), King (1972), Lanyon, Barrington, and Newman (1976), Peper and Robertson (1976), Rosen (1977), Tarchanoff (1973), Webb (1977), and Welgan (1974).

Hopefully, what we suggest in this section is to be bold in attempting to explore new experimental, clinical, and educational feedback techniques.

REFERENCES

Cornsweet, T. N., & Crane, H. D. Training the visual accommodative system. *Visual Research*, 1973, *13*, 713–715.

Cowings, P., Billingham, J., & Toscano, W. Learned control of multiple autonomic response to compensate for the debilitating effects of motion sickness. *Therapy in Psychosomatic Medicine*, 1977, *4*, 318–323.

Danskin, D. G., & Walters, D. E. Counseling and education. *Personnel and Guidance Journal*, 1973, *51*(9), 633–638.

Furman, S. Intestinal biofeedback in functional diarrhea. A preliminary report. *Journal of Behavior Therapy and Experimental Psychiatry*, 1973, *4*, 317–321.

Johnston, R., & Lee, K. Myofeedback: A new method of teaching breathing exercises in emphysematous patients. *Physical Therapy*, 1976, *56*(7), 826–831.

King, M. *Brainwave biofeedback as a science lesson*. Presented at the First Area Convention, National Science Teachers Association, San Diego, 1972.

Lanyon, R. I., Barrington, C. C., & Newman, A. C. Modification of stuttering through EMG biofeedback: A preliminary study. *Behavior Therapy*, 1976, *7*, 96–103.

Peper, E., & Robertson, J. A. Biofeedback use of common objects: The bathroom scale. *Biofeedback and Self-Regulation*, 1976, *1*, 237–240.

Rosen, R. Operant control of sexual responses in man. In G. Schwartz & J. Beatty (Eds.), *Biofeedback theory and research*. New York: Academic Press, 1977.

Rugh, J. D., Perlis, D. B., & Disraeli, R. I. (Eds.). *Biofeedback in dentistry: Research and clinical applications*. Phoenix: Semantodontics, 1977.

Tarchanoff, J. R. [Voluntary acceleration of the heart beat in man] (D. A. Blizard, Trans.). In D. Shapiro et al. (Eds.), *Biofeedback and self-control*. Chicago: Aldine, 1973.

Tiep, B. L., Analiz, J., & Cordell, J. Respiratory biofeedback: Two non-invasive approaches in the treatment of patients with chronic obstructive disease. *Proceedings of the San Diego Biomedical Symposium*, February 1977.

Vachon, L., & Rich, E. S. Visceral learning in asthma. *Psychosomatic Medicine*, 1976, *38*, 122–130.

Webb, N. C. The use of myoelectric feedback in teaching facial expression to the blind. *Biofeedback and Self-Regulation*, 1977, *2*(2), 147–160.

Welgan, P. Learned control of gastric acid secretion in ulcer patients. *Psychosomatic Medicine*, 1974, *36*, 411–419.

46

Operant Conditioning of Rectosphincteric Responses in the Treatment of Fecal Incontinence

Bernard T. Engel, Parviz Nikoomanesh, and Marvin M. Schuster

Six patients with severe fecal incontinence and manometric evidence of external-sphincter impairment were taught to produce external-sphincter contraction in synchrony with internal-sphincter relaxation. These responses were induced by rectal distention. During follow-up periods ranging from 6 months to 5 years, four of the patients remained completely continent, and the other two were definitely improved. One patient who was trained to relax her internal sphincter as well as to contract her external sphincter not only was continent but also regularly had normal bowel movements, which she had not had before. The training technic was relatively simple to apply, and learning occurred within four sessions or less. The findings highlight the importance of synchronized rectosphincteric responses in the maintenance of fecal continence, and they show that these responses can be brought under voluntary control in patients with chronic fecal incontinence, even when the incontinence is secondary to organic lesions.

Recent research has shown that a number of physiologic functions that are known to be autoregulated can also be brought under voluntary control with use of the technics of operant conditioning.[1-3] The degree of voluntary control that can be learned is sufficient to produce clinically important effects.[4] Patients with atrial fibrillation can learn to control their ventricular rates,[5] those with premature ventricular beats can learn the prevalence of this arrhythmia,[6] and a patient with intermittent Wolff–Parkinson–White disease was able to learn independent control of cardiac rate and cardiac conduction.[7] Patients with essential hypertension were able to lower their systolic blood pressures substantially in the laboratory.[8] Patients with ruminative vomiting were able to learn to inhibit that symptom.[9,10] The purpose of this report is to describe our findings in the application of operant conditioning procedures in the control of severe chronic fecal incontinence.

METHODS

We studied seven ambulatory patients with histories of chronic severe fecal incontinence (Table 1). The adult patients had daily incontinence of solid stool.

Bernard T. Engel • Laboratory of Behavioral Sciences, National Institute on Aging, Baltimore City Hospitals, Baltimore, Maryland 21224, and Johns Hopkins University School of Medicine, Baltimore, Maryland 21205. Parviz Nickoomanesh • Baltimore City Hospitals, Baltimore, Maryland 21224, and Johns Hopkins University School of Medicine, Baltimore, Maryland 21205. Marvin M. Schuster • Division of Digestive Diseases, Baltimore City Hospitals, Baltimore, Maryland 21224, and Departments of Medicine and Psychiatry, Johns Hopkins University School of Medicine, Baltimore, Maryland 21205.

Table 1

Patient Summaries

Case No.	Age (yr)	Sex	Incontinence			Follow up Period (yr)
			Frequency	Duration (yr)	Cause	
1	54	M	Daily	4	Laminectomy	5
2	40	F	Daily	5	Proctectomy for tumor	5
3	44	F	Daily	8	Unknown	1½
4	54	F	Daily	5	Hemorrhoidectomy	1
5	44	M	Daily	5	Diabetic neuropathy	1½
6	43	F	Daily	3	Fissurectomy; radiation proctitis; vesicorectocele repair	—[a]
7	6	F	Episodically[b]	Lifelong	Myelomeningocele	½

[a] Patient withdrew from study.
[b] Patient also unable to have regular bowel movements.

None had fecal impaction by history or by rectal examination. The child had required surgical construction of an ileal bladder because of severe urinary incontinence resulting from a neurogenic bladder. Since toilet training she had experienced episodic incontinence of solid stool occurring from twice a week to every 2 weeks. She also had a history of fecal impactions that had to be removed manually or with enemas.

All patients went through a series of three phases of study. Phase 1 was a diagnostic procedure during which the severity of impairment of rectosphincteric reflexes was objectively determined. During this procedure the patient was placed in the right lateral position, and a Miller–Abbott balloon with 50-ml capacity was inserted into the rectum. A double balloon tied around a hollow metal capsule was positioned at the internal and external sphincters respectively.[11] Polyethylene tubing from each balloon led to pressure transducers (Sanborn, 267B pressure transducers). Electrical outputs from these devices were subsequently amplified and recorded by a direct-writing polygraph (Sanborn, model 150, multichannel recorder). In normal subjects momentary inflation of the rectal balloon causes a reflex relaxation of the internal sphincter and reflex contraction of the external sphincter; these responses are quantitatively related to the volume of air used to distend the rectum.[12] In our patients the external-sphincter response was either diminished or absent as measured by our technics. After the diagnostic studies had been completed and before training studies were initiated, we explained in detail to each patient (except the 6-year-old child) the nature of the normal rectosphincteric reflex and the way in which his response differed from normal.

During phase 2, the initial stage of training, instantaneous feedback was provided to the patient by means of permitting him to watch the polygraph tracings of his sphincteric responses as they were being recorded. He was reminded of the differences between his responses and normal responses. He was encouraged to try to modify his responses to make them appear more normal. He was praised whenever he produced a normal-appearing response, and he was told whenever the response he produced was poor. This verbal reinforcement was gradually diminished as it became clear that the patient knew what was expected of him, and as it became clear that the patient was able to affect his sphincteric responses. Each patient was able to sense the rectal distention, and each patient knew that this stimulus was the cue to initiate sphincteric control.

Phase 3 was the final stage of laboratory training. This phase had two goals. In the first place, we attempted to train the patient to refine his sphincteric responses—i.e., to approximate the amplitude of a normal sphincteric response, and to synchronize sphincteric responses so that the external-sphincter contraction occurred simultaneously with internal-sphincter relaxation. This refinement of motor control was also accomplished through verbal reinforcement in conjunction with feedback (visual observation) of recorded sphincteric activity. The second goal of phase 3 training was to wean the patient from any dependency on the apparatus. In this stage of training we periodically withheld visual feedback by covering the polygraph so that the patient was unable to see the tracings. After a series of trials the patient was permitted to observe his performance.

Each laboratory session comprised about 2 hours. During a session the patient received about 50 training trials. Each session also included a 10-minute break about three-quarters of the way through the session. Usually, patients went through two phases of study within a single session. A period of about 3 weeks elapsed between sessions, during which the patient was encouraged to practice the technic that he had learned in the laboratory.

Results were analyzed in two ways. In the laboratory the manometric tracings obtained after rectal distention were evaluated for the presence of sphincteric responses, for the temporal relation between internal-sphincter relaxation and external-sphincter contraction, and for relative changes in amplitude of sphincteric responses. The stimulus used during these tests was a volume of air previously determined to be subthreshold (i.e., a volume of air that elicited no detectable sphincteric response to 10 consecutive distentions), or if the patient had no apparent response at any level of distention, we used 30 ml of air as the stimulus. The second way in which we evaluated our results was clinical. During the 3 weeks between sessions the patient was asked to assess the effectiveness of his previous training in terms of his ability to remain continent. This clinical assessment continued after training was completed. Each patient (parent in the case of the child) was interviewed at 3-month intervals until bowel control had been stable for 6 months. Patients were then interviewed yearly.

RESULTS

All patients completed their training within four sessions or less. Follow-up periods ranged from 6 months to 5 years. Four of the patients (Cases 1, 2, 3, and 7) have been completely continent since their last laboratory studies. Case 4 reports "rare" episodes of staining but no occasions of gross incontinence. Case

5, who has severe diabetes, is no longer incontinent at night but sometimes does soil during the waking hours. Case 6 withdrew from the study after the first session because she found the procedure too painful; she was the only patient who complained of pain and the only one who had an anal fissure. Case 3 misunderstood the instructions after the first session and practiced sphincteric control during bowel movements as well as at other times. She returned after the 3 weeks complaining of constipation. After her misunderstanding was clarified, constipation was no longer a problem.

All patients who completed the study also had objective evidence of learned sphincteric control. This effect is shown in Figure 1, which presents the manometric changes occurring in one patient during the various phases of training. Initially, this patient had no external-sphincter response to 25-ml distention of the rectal balloon (Figure 1A). In the course of training her responses to 20 ml became normal (Figure 1B). During a series of trials in phase 3 of training when she was being weaned from dependency on the equipment, she was allowed to view alternate responses only. Figure 1C shows her responses with and without feedback. Overresponse occurred when feedback was withheld. This tendency to

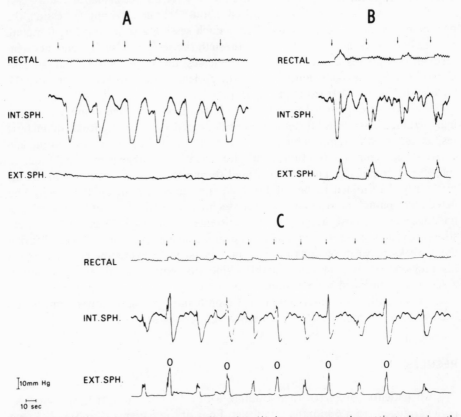

Figure 1. Sphincteric responses to rectal distention (↓) in a representative patient showing the response to 25-ml distention before training (A), responses to 20-ml distention during early training (B), and responses to 20-ml distention (C) with and without (O) feedback. Note the tendency to overrespond during trials when feedback is withheld.

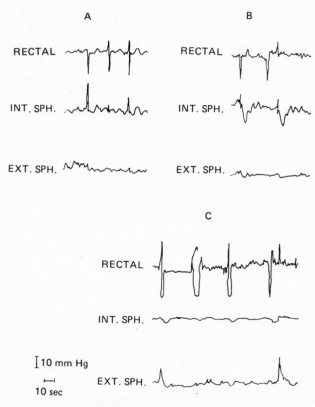

Figure 2. Sphincteric responses to rectal distention (↓) in a 6-year-old girl. A shows responses to 30-ml distention before training; note absent internal sphincteric response as well as absent external sphincteric response. B indicates responses to 30-ml distention during training to relax the internal sphincter, and C shows responses to 30-ml distention during training to contract the external sphincter. External-sphincter training followed internal-sphincter training.

overcontrol was also seen in other patients; however, it diminished with further training.

During the diagnostic testing period with the 6-year-old child we observed not only an absent external-sphincter response but also an absent internal-sphincter response (Figure 2A). During the first training session, therefore, we concentrated on teaching her to relax this sphincter, which she was able to do by the end of the session (Figure 2B). During the next training session we concentrated on training her to contract her external sphincter, which she also learned to do (Figure 2C). After the completion of training she not only was continent but also was able to have normal bowel movements regularly.

DISCUSSION

The operant conditioning technic used in this study permits one to train a subject to change the prevalence of a naturally occurring response. If the subject is rewarded immediately after he responds, he will increase his rate of responding; if he is punished immediately after he responds, he will decrease his response rate. This training technic does not cause the subject to develop new associations—it only affects the rate of occurrence of existing responses. Consequently, it is clear that all patients in this study must have had the capacity to produce sphincteric responses before we studied them. This capability was present even in those who, under the conditions of our study, had no manometric evidence of recto-sphincteris responses during the pretraining phase. This inference is buttressed by the observation that these patients had "anal reflexes" (sphincter contraction in response to perianal pinprick). It is possible that greater volumes of rectal distention than we tried might also have elicited some response.

So-called psychogenic overflow incontinence was ruled out in all patients. None of the adults had fecal impaction by history or on rectal examination. The child had neurologic deficits that are common in patients with myelomeningocele. She had a neurogenic urinary bladder, and she had an atonic colon. All the patients had markedly impaired external-sphincter reflexes to rectal distention. This type of manometric response is different from that seen in patients with psychogenic megacolon.[13]

It is possible to identify four factors that appear to be important in application of operant conditioning to pathophysiologic states such as fecal incontinence. One factor is the presence of a well-defined, readily measurable response—in this instance, synchronized sphincteric reflexes.[11] The second factor is a response that exhibits variability and is under nervous-system control, like sphincteric activity.[14] The third factor is the occurrence of a clearly recognizable cue that signals the patient to initiate sphincter control. In the laboratory the sensation induced by balloon distention served this function. This sensation was appreciated by all patients. The patients presumably were able to learn the meaning of this sensation, and when it occurred naturally, they could interpret this feedback appropriately. The fourth feature is the presence of strong motivation on the part of the patient to bring his response under control. In our adult patients the social disruptions caused by their disorders provided the necessary motivation. In the 6-year-old child we gave additional incentives during the training sessions to reward her performance and to maintain her attention. These incentives were inexpensive items (e.g., colored, felt-tipped pens), which were given to her after she achieved some goal (e.g., three consecutive correct responses). Other investigators have also used rewards to maintain patient performance.[8] In one study electric-shock avoidance was used to train a severely dehydrated, malnourished, 9-month-old boy to suppress ruminative vomiting.[9] In most clinical studies, however, the desire of the patient to "get well" is sufficient motivation.[4,6,7]

The findings with the patient who was trained to control her internal sphincter are notable for two reasons. The first is the fact that when this control developed, she became able to have regular voluntary bowel movements, which she had been unable to have before training. This finding underscores the role of the internal sphincter in defecation.[11] And second is the fact that the internal sphincter is under autonomic control and therefore, presumably, involuntary.[14] There is now considerable evidence that autonomically mediated responses can be made voluntary. It has been shown that curarized rats can be trained to bring a number of autonomically mediated responses under voluntary control. Such responses include heart rate, gastric motility, renal output, and even blood flow to one ear.[15] It has been shown that both the initiation and the interruption of urination in curarized man are under voluntary control.[16] The lower esophageal sphincter, an autonomically innervated smooth muscle, can also be brought under voluntary control.[17] These findings imply that there may be other important clinical applications of operant conditioning to the treatment of disorders affecting gastrointestinal smooth muscle.

REFERENCES

1. T. X. Barber, L. V. DiCara, J. Kamiya, et al. (Eds.). *Biofeedback and self-control 1970*. Chicago: Aldine-Atherton. 1971.
2. J. Stoyva, T. X. Barber, L. V. DiCara, et al. (Eds.). *Biofeedback and self-control 1971*. Chicago: Aldine-Atherton. 1972.
3. D. Shapiro, T. X. Barber, L. V. DiCara, et al. (Eds.). *Biofeedback and self-control 1972*. Chicago: Aldine-Atherton. 1973.
4. Shapiro, D., & Schwartz, G. E. Biofeedback and visceral learning: Clinical applications. *Seminars in Psychiatry*, 1972, *4*, 171–184.
5. Bleecker, E. R., & Engel, B. T. Learned control of ventricular rate in patients with atrial fibrillation. *Psychosomatic Medicine*, 1973, *35*, 161–175.
6. Weiss, T., & Engel, B. T. Operant conditioning of heart rate in patients with premature ventricular contractions. *Psychosomatic Medicine*, 1971, *33*, 301–321.
7. Bleecker, E. R., & Engel, B. T. Learned control of cardiac rate and cardiac conduction in the Wolff-Parkinson-White syndrome. *New England Journal of Medicine*, 1973, *288*, 560–562.
8. Benson, H., Shapiro, D., Tursky, B., et al. Decreased systolic blood pressure through operant conditioning techniques in patients with essential hypertension. *Science*, 1971, *173*, 740–742.
9. Lang, P. J., & Melamed, B. G. Case report: Avoidance conditioning therapy of an infant with chronic ruminative vomiting. *Journal of Abnormal Psychology*, 1969, *74*, 1–8.
10. White, J. D., & Taylor, D. Noxious conditioning as a treatment for rumination. *Mental Retardation*, 1967, *5*, 30–33.
11. Schuster, M. M. Motor action of rectum and anal sphincters in continence and defecation. In C. F. Code (Ed.), *Handbook of Physiology. Section 6. Alimentary Canal. Vol IV, Motility*. Washington, D.C.: American Physiological Society, 1968. Pp. 2121–2146.
12. Schuster, M. M., Hookman, P., Hendrix, T. R., et al: Simultaneous manometric recording of internal and external anal sphincteric reflexes. *Bulletin of the Johns Hopkins Hospital*, 1965, *116*, 79–88.
13. Tobon, F., Reid, N. C. R. W., Talbert, J. L., & Schuster, M. M. Nonsurgical test for the diagnosis of Hirschsprung's disease. *New England Journal of Medicine*, 1968, *278*, 188–194.
14. Christensen, J. The controls of gastrointestinal movements: Some old and new views. *New England Journal of Medicine*, 1971, *285*, 85–98.
15. Miller, N. E. Learning of visceral and glandular responses. *Science*, 1969, *163*, 434–445.
16. Lapides, J., Sweet, R. B., & Lewis, L. W. Role of striated muscle in urination. *Journal of Urology*, 1957, *77*, 247–250.
17. Nikoomanesh, P., Wells, D., & Schuster, M. M. Biofeedback control of lower esophageal sphincter contraction. *Clinical Research*, 1973, *21*, 521.

BACKGROUND READING

References 4 & 12.
Reynolds, G. S. *A primer of operant conditioning*. Glenview, Illinois: Scott Foresman, 1968.

47

The Use of Biofeedback Devices in the Treatment of Bruxism

William K. Solberg and John D. Rugh

The results of pilot investigations recently completed at the UCLA TMJ Clinic suggest that the treatment and investigation of self-destructive oral habits may be facilitated by the use of portable muscle hyperactivity devices worn by patients (Figure 1). The need for these devices is supported by considerable evidence suggesting that abnormal oral habits such as bruxism may cause or contribute to excessive tooth wear, trauma from occlusion, and TMJ pain and dysfunction.[1,2,3] Treatment and investigation of these problems has been difficult because the habits involved are usually performed unconsciously; thus patients are unable to report the occurrence, nature, or frequency of their habit. The present investigators have developed a portable muscle biofeedback unit that delivers an audible "warning" tone should the patient clench or grind his teeth (Figure 2).

Tape-recorded interviews have been conducted with 15 TMJ patients after wearing the biofeedback unit from 2 to 7 days. After this self-monitoring period, most patients reported clenching or grinding habits during stressful or emotionally arousing situations; however, some also reported clenching when physically exhausted after a "trying" day. The patients further reported that the biofeedback unit aroused an awareness of their oral habit behavior, thus allowing them to control the habit and to relax the muscles of mastication. The patients were generally surprised to find how frequently they engaged in clenching or grinding and they unanimously agreed that they had benefited by this insight. These results are similar to others[4] whereby the self-monitoring of other undesirable behaviors has been reported to decrease the behavior monitored (Figure 3). It is felt this results from the patient becoming aware of otherwise unconscious behavior patterns and by the identification of stressful situations that elicit this behavior. Patients may learn either to avoid stressful situations or to cope with them in other ways. In the present study, both of the above alternatives were often elected by the patient.

The patient's reports and clinical examinations revealed that 10 out of 15 patients' disorders had significantly improved during their "training" period with

William K. Solberg • School of Dentistry, University of California, Los Angeles, California 90024. John D. Rugh • Department of Restorative Dentistry, University of Texas Health Science Center, San Antonio, Texas 78284.

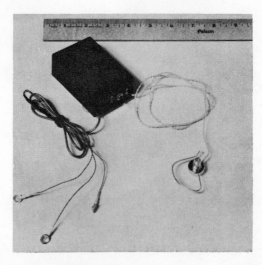

Figure 1. The biofeedback unit is no larger than a pack of cigarettes. Attached is the lead with three electrodes and a signal device.

Figure 2. The biofeedback unit is worn by the patient during everyday activities. The recording electrodes are seen attached over the masseter muscle area. The earpiece provides a tone that is preset to trigger upon tooth clenching.

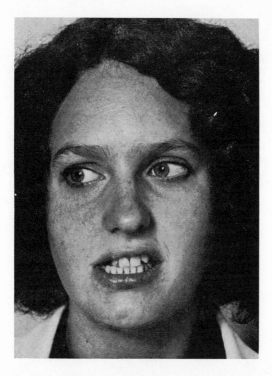

Figure 3. While wearing the biofeedback unit, this patient discovered that she habitually set her teeth on the "lock and key" position shown above. She quickly learned to avoid this as a result of biofeedback therapy.

the device. Moreover, the ability of the patient to report the exact tooth-to-tooth location of the bruxism implies that biofeedback therapy can be used to advantage as an adjunct in pinpointing the site where occlusal alteration is indicated. More detailed investigations examining the diagnostic and therapeutic value of the muscle biofeedback units are currently underway.

NOTE. The content of this chapter is a 6-months progress report from a research grant of the Southern California Dental Association titled, "The Use of Muscle Hyperactivity Detectors in the Diagnosis and Treatment of Self-Destructive Oral Habits."

REFERENCES

1. Vestergaard Christiansen, L. Facial pain from tooth clenching. A preliminary report. *Tandlaege-bladet*, 1970, *74*, 175–182.
2. Laskin, D. M. Etiology of the pain dysfunction syndrome. *Journal of the American Dental Association*, 1969, *79*, 148.

3. Moulton, R. D. Emotional factors in non-organic temporomandibular joint pain. *Dental Clinics of North America*, 1966, *609* (November).
4. Thomas, E. J., Adrams, K. F., & Johnson, J. B. Self monitoring and reciprocal inhibitions in the modification of multiple tics of Gillis De La Tourette's syndrome. *Journal of Behavioral Therapy and Experimental Psychiatry*, 1971, *2*, 159–171.

48

Economical Biofeedback Devices

Erik Peper and Stephen Shambaugh

Most people who have even heard of biofeedback think you need an enormous lab with expensive equipment to "do it." No so! Biofeedback has emerged in the last decade or so as a particular application of a much broader perspective called cybernetics. Cybernetics attempts to develop a theory of communication and control in machines and in living organisms (Weiner, 1954). The word is from the Greek *kybernetes*, meaning steersman. It was chosen to describe the basic concept of a feedback mechanism. Using this concept, the central nervous system no longer remains a self-contained organ receiving sensory information and contracting the muscles. In fact, some of its most characteristic activities are explainable only as circular processes traveling from the nervous system into the muscles and reentering the nervous system through the senses.

To demonstrate the concept, try the following simple experiment. Raise your arms until they point straight out from each side. Now, keeping your elbows straight, slowly swing your arms toward each other in a horizontal plane so when the arms come together in front of you they will touch only at the tips of the index fingers. Simple, isn't it? Try it again with your eyes closed; it is now more difficult. To perform the action successfully, there must be a report to the nervous system, conscious or unconscious, of the amount by which our fingers missed touching. The report may be visual, at least in part, but it is more generally kinesthetic, or proprioceptive. If the proprioceptive sensations are wanting, and we do not replace them by a visual or other substitute, we are unable to perform even simple motor acts. In the above example, the end result of insufficient feedback is ataxia (the inability to coordinate voluntary muscular movements). The opposite, excessive feedback, also creates difficulties as the muscles overshoot and go into uncontrollable oscillation known as purpose tremor.

To summarize thus far, feedback is the circular flow of information in a circuit or loop, which creates a relationship between various aspects of ourselves and our environment (social and physical). As a circular flow of information, feedback is essential to all learning processes. Conceptually, biofeedback is a special case of this broader feedback concept. Biofeedback applies only to the flow of information that creates a bridge between the level of conscious awareness and other levels of human physical functioning.

Erik Peper • Center for Interdisciplinary Science, San Francisco State University, San Francisco, California 94134. Stephen Shambaugh • Human Development and Aging Program, University of California San Francisco, Berkeley, California 94143.

Biofeedback extends our conscious awareness toward learning to detect and in some cases to control subtle changes in our psychophysiology. These changes usually occur beneath our customary level of awareness. That is, not until the cumulative magnitude of the change reaches a critical threshold does it come to our attention. Often the time lag between the occurrence of these small changes and our subsequent perception of them is far too long for meaningful learning to occur. Thus, for biofeedback to be useful, it must rapidly detect, amplify, and display the biological information. In this sense, biofeedback demonstrates and authenticates that a psychophysiological change has taken place. This is the function performed by the expensive clinical and laboratory biofeedback machines.

However, we can learn to detect extremely subtle biological changes proprioceptively without the use of an external device. For most of us, our proprioceptive sense is mainly used for coordinating rapid and gross motor movements. The process is usually performed unconsciously. Yet most of us can learn to sharpen the proprioceptive and other senses. A number of approaches such as relaxation training, meditation, and various forms of slow movements like T'ai Chi Chuan can enhance this awareness. The following technique demonstrates our ability to sense subtle changes in pressure, muscle movement, balance, and gravity if we are quiet enough. Through quiet movement and focused attention, we increase the signal-to-noise ratio.

> For the next ten minutes, walk as slowly as you can. Observe the slow movement of the leg, ankle, and feet, simultaneously being aware of the center of gravity in the lower abdomen. Each step is a movement of only inches. Observe carefully, feel the air moving past the arms and face. Feel the shifting of weight from one leg, one foot, to the other. Let your eyes be closed, and if your attention drifts, gently bring it back to the task. At the end of 10 minutes, note how you feel, how you have slowed down, and how your feelings have changed.

This exercise illustrates our capability for sensing subtle changes to the extent we can feel them like the gradual changes in pressure, the shifting of the weight, the tightening of the different muscles, and the sense of balance and gravity. These sensations are usually masked by our rapid movements and activities.

Thus feedback of one's own biological information may be accomplished in two ways:

1. By attending to the information displayed from an external feedback device, the trainee can learn self-regulation. The information loop is completed outside the individual's nervous system. The feedback signal reenters the body (nervous system) exteroceptively.
2. By sitting or moving gently in a quiet environment, a trainee can learn to heighten perceptual awareness interoceptively and respond to his or her biological state without external devices.

Both processes may be used in conjunction with one another to enhance clinical success. However, at home or at school we need not limit ourselves to the expensive commercial equipment (electromyograph, electrodermograph, temperature trainer, electroencephalograph, etc.) in order to obtain reliable information about our biological functioning. From a cybernetic perspective, any thought, speech, or other action involves the feedback of information creating circular flows. We are surrounded by potential sources for the feedback of information about ourselves. The range of potential applications for the concept is extremely broad, limited only by our imagination and ingenuity.

All biofeedback involves skill learning with or without the use of adjunctive devices. These devices may vary considerably in both complexity and level of sophistication and may include electronic, electrochemical, mechanical, and interpersonal components. Our hope is to foster an attitude in which the user may perceive anything as a feedback device if it provides information that enhances the learning of the task at hand. Often simple inexpensive household devices are most suitable.

Any device or technique to be used in a feedback modality should comply with these guidelines:

1. It must be electrically and mechanically safe.
2. It must be noninvasive.
3. It must detect and feed back the appropriate signal.
4. The feedback signal must occur in "real" time, so that there is little or no delay between the occurrence of the physiological event and the feedback signal.
5. The trainee must understand the task and the meaning of the feedback signal. (Obviously with appropriate reinforcers this may not be necessary, but we feel that feedback training should enhance an individual's autonomy.)

The cybernetic perspective, outlined above, broadens the biofeedback concept to include the following possibilities:

1. The use of human beings as sensitive feedback machines (either for oneself or another), such as in physical therapy or the Alexander technique.
2. The substitution of more economical alternatives for existing biofeedback machines.
3. The development of new and novel feedback machines to provide the appropriate signals for learning new tasks.
4. The translation of skills learned in the clinic or laboratory into the home environment.

THE USE OF HUMAN BEINGS AS FEEDBACK DEVICES

Human beings can be the most sensitive feedback devices; they simply need to be trained. This was illustrated in the slow walking exercise. In addition, another person can be a source of feedback information. For example, in a passive movement exercise, the person may sit quietly while someone else gently moves the first person's jaw around in a random pattern (up and down, sideways, etc.). The person whose jaw is moved neither helps nor hinders the movement but just lets go and allows the jaw to be moved. Any resistance is felt by the mover. Most people have difficulty in letting go of their muscles. If the person really lets the jaw loose, it can be moved in any direction without resistance. This is a good source of feedback because the people can feel their own jaws proprioceptively.

This exercise provides a physical demonstration of psychological styles. The person who helps the movement of the jaw demonstrates anticipation and compliance, whereas one who hinders the movement demonstrates resistance. In either instance, successful performance of the task will involve letting go of predispositions and living more flexibly in the present.

This exercise is one way to translate an EMG feedback exercise (to decrease dysponesis) into a form that does not require expensive equipment. When practiced at home, the exercise involves another person and thus provides feedback to the practitioner about the social environment of the trainee. For instance, if the trainee did not do the practice, this might indicate an absence of close relationships or a lack of assertiveness in asking for assistance, while the unwilling cooperation of another might indicate family discord. Hence this home exercise is a way to explore the dynamics of the individual's household.

As individuals become more sensitive to their psychophysiological processes, they are able to observe the correlations between these processes and the environmental cues that elicit a stress response. In this way, the individuals' proprioceptive awareness provides necessary information enabling them (1) to identify the irritant (stressor) that triggered the response and (2) to work on changing their response by continuing to breathe and letting the jaw go slack. This model may be applied to other stress-triggered behavioral patterns such as gasping or breath holding.

THE USE OF ECONOMICAL BIOFEEDBACK DEVICES AS SUBSTITUTES FOR EXPENSIVE ELECTRONIC HARDWARE

EMG Feedback Approaches

Habitual tensing of the jaw has been implicated in bruxism, tension headache, and temporal mandibular joint syndrome (Rugh and Solberg, 1975). There are many ways to train subjects to reduce jaw tension. With EMG biofeedback, monitored from the massiter, temporal, or frontalis muscles, subjects can become aware of their own reactivity. The person learns to recognize the absolute level of the muscle tension and to identify the minimum increase from that level. How can a person carry this awareness into his daily life? How can he be aware that he is tightening his jaw when engaged in other activities?

1. Love (personal communication, 1978) suggested placing a hard candy between the molars. When the individual is intensely involved in some activity like tennis, and clenches his jaw, the loud crunch refocuses awareness on his jaw activity.

2. Stroke patients who experience a loss of proprioceptive information often have difficulty becoming aware of excessive bracing in the somatic musculature. An economical form of visual feedback of excessive muscular bracing can be

created by placing a large bead of putty or soft clay on parallel bars or banisters. The tighter the person squeezes the rails, the deeper the hand sinks into the putty.

3. Writer's cramp due to excessive pressure on a pen may be corrected with the aid of a pressure alarm. A small metal clip attached to the pen band will close a circuit when squeezed, setting off a buzzer powered by a small battery. The total cost is under two dollars.

Temperature Feedback Approaches

1. Peripheral hand warming can often be encouraged and fed back in a number of ways. The subject can compare the temperature of his hands against his stomach to check for relative warmth or coolness. Or the person can observe subjective sensations associated with increase in temperature. The sensation of throbbing (pulse) usually occurs when the temperature is about 88°F or higher. These two examples are relatively inaccurate approaches, but they can be helpful as reinforcement in those cases where the subject has previously learned to increase peripheral temperature.

2. A more accurate device is a small thermometer that the person holds between two fingers.* A more interesting and economical tool is the "mood ring." It is a finger ring that in place of a large stone contains a thermal sensitive "liquid crystal." The crystal's color changes with temperature. By the color of the ring, the trainee knows the temperature of his hands. Liquid crystals also are available in dots and strips that the person can tape to his skin.

EEG Theta Feedback Approaches

A Japanese tea bell may be used to enhance theta EEG reverie (Muldoon & Carrington, 1958). Theta bursts (associated with hypnagogic and hypnapompic imagery) occur when muscle tonus suddenly decreases as the person starts to fall asleep. While lying down, the trainee holds the bell lightly, with the forearm in the air resting on the elbow. When the muscles become flaccid, the arm falls, and the person is roused. Another variation of this idea was developed by Aquarius Electronics. A small tilt platform with microswitches is placed under the head. Whenever the head moves, a white noise occurs, gently waking the person.

Other Feedback Devices

1. Two bathroom scales may be used to feed back weight distribution and train patients to develop a sense of balance. A person learns to become aware of microchanges associated with weight shifts if he places one foot on each bathroom scale (Peper & Robertson, 1976).

2. Mirrors make multipurpose feedback devices. A small mirror placed under the nose makes an excellent nasograph, showing relative air volume exhaled from each nostril. A mirror can also be used to promote awareness of

* Consciousness Living Foundation, P.O. Box 513, Manhattan, Kansas 66502.

body posture, habitual patterns of movement and misplaced efforts, and to give visual feedback for role playing. (Obviously tape and video feedback are alternatives.)

3. A modified electronic stethoscope was used by Tiep, Analiz, and Cadell (1977) to feed back wheezing to asthmatics.

4. Gogiometers (devices that measure joint angles) can be used to feed back joint movement, thereby demonstrating to patients with neuromuscular diseases that they have some joint movement in the affected area (Johnson, 1978).

5. A perineometer has been used in a pilot study by Peper and Meier (Peper, 1977) to train women to control the pubococcygeal muscle independently of abdominal tension, thereby shifting the quality of the orgasm. A finger inserted in the vaginal barrel can also be used as a pressure transducer.

6. A laboratory pH meter can be used to feed back vaginal pH.

7. A snore alarm has been made with a small microphone placed at the throat to trigger an alarm when the person snores

CONCLUSION

The cybernetic view of biofeedback involves a shift in perspective in which the feedback more accurately defines the movement toward the desired goal. With this point of view, we encourage the development and assessment of new, economical feedback devices to improve learning. For example, a pressure transducer in a skier's boots would enhance verbal instructions like "lean forward" or "place more weight on the tips of the skis." Similarly, a mercury switch mounted on top of a golfer's hat could indicate postural shifts while he swings at the ball. Thus feedback can enhance the learning of complicated motor skills. Once we perceive that learning can be enhanced with appropriate feedback, the future uses depend upon the creativity of the user.

REFERENCES

Green, E. E., & Green, A. *Beyond biofeedback*. New York: Delacorte, 1977.
Johnson, H. E. *Future possibilities for electromyographic and other biofeedback modalities in neuromuscular rehabilitation*. Paper presented at the Seminar on Biofeedback in Rehabilitation, Berkeley, 1978.
Muldoon, S., & Carrington, H. *The projection of the astral body*. London: Rider, 1958.
Peper, E. Presidental address. Biofeedback Society of America, Orlando, March 1977.
Peper, E., & Robertson, J. A. Biofeedback use of common objects: The bathroom scale in physical therapy. *Biofeedback and Self-Regulation*, 1976, *1*(2), 237–239.
Rugh, J. D., & Solberg, W. Electromyographic studies of bruxist behavior. *Journal of the California Dental Association*, 1975, *3*, 56–59.
Tiep, B. L. Analiz, J., & Cadell, J. Respiratory biofeedback: Two non-invasive approaches in the treatment of patients with chronic obstructive disease. *Proceedings of the San Diego Biomedical Symposium*, February 1977.
Weiner, N. *The human use of human beings*. New York: Anchor/Doubleday, 1954.

Conclusion

As stated throughout this book, biofeedback can be used in many different settings. As a medical tool, it is used to treat specific malfunctioning systems, as is vividly illustrated in Engel's study on fecal incontinence (Chapter 46); as a relaxation technique it is used to achieve a release from stress within a homeostatic balance, thereby attaining a state of wellness; while as a research tool, it can be used to investigate functional dynamics of an organism.

Biofeedback expands beyond medicine and psychology, into education and the arts. This interdisciplinary aspect of biofeedback is its intrinsic excitement. The merging and reintegration of disparate disciplines requires "renaissance people." Though its roots are in psychophysiology and biology, biofeedback's practitioners come from many areas ranging from the strict sciences to education to meditation and altered states of consciousness. The basic premise that connects these different people together is the ability, through biofeedback, to learn about oneself and become conscious of the process by which learning occurs.

In many ways, "becoming conscious" is what biofeedback is all about. It teaches us that we have the ability to control ourselves and brings into awarness the fact that our mind/body is a system, with changes at any level affecting the entire system. In short, to stay healthy, we learn to listen to our bodies, and therefore our minds.

In this process, feedback enhances the autonomy of the individual. Feedback points out that we are so often reacting instead of acting, responding instead of initiating. Now we can learn strategies to help us change our behavior. It changes our perception of ourselves. We are no longer automated machines that must adapt to the industrial setting with corresponding increases in stress-induced illness. Through enhanced feedback we can be aware that we are responding. Feedback allows us to become synchronous with our own biopsychological needs. In fact, health occurs when mind/body/spirit are in synchrony. One way to enhance this process is to adapt our environment to our needs instead of the other way around. This means we listen to our body/mind signals, and when we experience those signals, *we act*. This may mean that our normally fixed 9:00-to-5:00 industrial job needs to become a more flexible system in which the important commitment is to the individual and his wellness rather than to the mechanical structure of the organization.

We would like to reemphasize that biofeedback is experiential. Reading this book should be just an introduction. To be more fully understood, biofeedback must be experienced.

In many ways, biofeedback introduces a new style of thinking—the practitioner is a participant in the learning process. Psychology has gone through a transformation from group to individual data, from behaviorism back to introspection and, with introspection, to learning to integrate the mind/body.

In essence, feedback enhances the signal-to-noise ratio so the mind can listen to itself (and since the mind and body are integrated, this is equivalent to the mind listening to the body). Relaxation, autogenic therapy, meditation, and yoga reduce the noise levels, while electronic feedback signals increase the signal level. In each case, the signal-to-noise ratio is optimized and people are in closer contact with themselves.

We would like to end with a poem by the Japanese Haiku poet, Basho (Shapiro, 1978). What this poem suggests is an openness to experience. Biofeedback, like the poem, provides us with a way to open up the boundaries of our perceptions. Read the poem, then close your eyes and listen to the poem again in your mind/body.

> Over the darkened sea
> only the shrill voice of a flying duck is visible
> in soft white.

REFERENCE

Shapiro, D. *Precision nirvana*. Englewood Cliffs, New Jersey: Prentice-Hall, 1978.

Appendix

SELECTED READINGS

Books Published on Biofeedback

Basmajian, J. V. (Ed.). *Biofeedback: Principles and practice for clinicians.* Baltimore: Williams & Wilkins, 1979.

Beatty, J., & Legewie, H. (Eds.). *Biofeedback and behavior.* New York: Plenum, 1977.

Biofeedback and self-control annuals (1970–1977). Chicago: Aldine, 1971, 1972, 1973, 1974, 1975, 1976, 1977, 1978.

Birk, L. (Ed.). *Biofeedback: Behavioral medicine.* New York: Grune and Stratton, 1973.

Blanchard, E. B., & Epstein, L. H. *A biofeedback primer.* Reading, Massachusetts: Addison-Wesley, 1978.

Brown, B. B. *New mind, new body.* New York: Harper, 1974.

Brown, B. B. *Stress and the art of biofeedback.* New York: Harper, 1977.

Butler, F. *Biofeedback: A survey of the literature.* New York: Plenum, 1978.

Fuller, G. D. *Biofeedback: Methods and procedures in clinical practice.* San Francisco: Biofeedback Institute, 1977.

Gaarder, K., & Montgomery, P. *Clinical biofeedback: A procedural manual.* Baltimore: Williams & Wilkins, 1977.

Green, E. E., & Green, A. M. *Beyond biofeedback.* New York: Delacorte, 1977.

Hume, W. I. *Biofeedback: Research and therapy.* Montreal: Eden Press, 1976.

Jones, G. *Visceral learning.* New York: Cornerstone Library, 1974.

Karlins, M., & Andrews, L. *Biofeedback: Turning on the power of your mind.* Philadelphia: Lippincott, 1972.

Owen, S., Toomim, H., & Taylor, L. P. *Biofeedback in neuromuscular reeducation.* Los Angeles: Biofeedback Research Institute, 1975.

Rugh, J. D., Perlis, D. B., & Disraeli, R. I. *Biofeedback in dentistry: Research and clinical applications.* Phoenix: Semantodentics, 1977.

Schwartz, G., & Beatty, J. *Biofeedback theory and research.* New York: Academic Press, 1977.

Stern, R., & Ray, W. J. *Biofeedback.* Homewood, Illinois: Dow Jones-Irwin, 1977.

Whatmore, G., & Kohli, D. R. *The psychophysiology and treatment of functional disorders.* New York: Grune and Stratton, 1974.

Wickramasekera, I. *Biofeedback, behavior therapy, and hypnosis.* Chicago: Nelson-Hall, 1976.

Journals

Many articles are published in a variety of journals, and some of these have been reprinted in the Aldine Annuals (see section above). The two journals that published the majority of the biofeedback work are *Biofeedback and Self-Regulation* and *Psychophysiology*.

Newsletters

Biofeedback Network
Dub Rakestraw, Editor
103 South Grove
Greensburg, Kansas 67054

Brain/Mind Bulletin
M. Ferguson, Editor
PO Box 42211
Los Angeles, California 90004

Books Published in Related Areas

Stress

Cannon, W. *The wisdom of the body*. New York: Norton, 1963.
Lazarus, R. S. *Patterns of adjustment*. New York: McGraw-Hill, 1976.
Levi, L. *Society, stress and disease*. New York: Oxford, 1971.
McQuade, W., & Aikman, A. *Stress*. New York: E. P. Dutton, 1974.
Monat, A., & Lazarus, R. S. (Eds.). *Stress and coping, an anthology*. New York: Columbia University Press, 1977.
Pelletier, K. *Mind as healer, mind as slayer*. New York: Delta, 1977.
Selye, H. *The stress of life*. New York: McGraw-Hill, 1956.
Simeons, A. T. W. *Man's presumptuous brain*. New York: Dutton, 1961.

Behavior Therapy

Franks, C. M., & Wilson, G. T. *Annual review of behavior therapy*. New York: Brunner/Mazel, 1973.
Lazarus, A. A. *Behavior therapy and beyond*. New York: McGraw-Hill, 1971.
Leitenberg, H. (Ed.). *Handbook of behavior modification and behavior therapy*. Englewood Cliffs, New Jersey: Prentice-Hall, 1977.
Paul, G. I. *Insight vs. desensitization in psychotherapy*. Stanford: Stanford University Press, 1966.
Smith, M. J. *When I say no, I feel guilty*. New York: Bantam Books, 1975.
Wolpe, J. *The practice of behavior therapy*. New York: Pergamon, 1969.

Hypnosis

Erickson, M. H., Rossi, E. L., & Rossi, S. I. *Hypnotic realities*. New York: Irvington Publishers, 1976.
Fromm, E., & Shor, R. E. *Hypnosis: Research developments and perspectives*. Chicago: Aldine, 1972.
Hilgard, E. R., & Hilgard, J. R. *Hypnosis in the relief of pain*. Los Altos, California: William Kaufmann, 1975.
Kroger, W. S. *Clinical and experimental hypnosis*. Philadelphia: Lippincott, 1963.
Weitzenhoffer, A. M. *General techniques of hypnotism*. New York: Grune and Stratton, 1957.

Body Techniques

Alexander, F. M. *The resurrection of the body*. New York: Dell, 1971.
Barlow, W. *The Alexander technique*. New York: Knopf, 1973.
Dychtwald, K. *Bodymind*. New York: Pantheon, 1977.
Feldenkrais, M. *The case of Nora*. New York: Harper, 1977.
Garfield, C. A. (Ed.). *Rediscovery of the body*. New York: Dell, 1977.
Shealy, C. N. *Ninety days to self-health*. New York: Dial, 1977.

Visualization

Assagioli, R. *Psychosynthesis*. New York: Viking, 1965.
Masters, R., & Houston, J. *Mind games*. New York: Dell, 1972.

Samuels, M., & Samuels, N. *Seeing with the mind's eye*. New York: Random House/Bookworks, 1975.

Meditation and Altered States

Benson, H. *The relaxation response*. New York: William Morrow, 1975.
Mishlove, J. *The roots of consciousness*. New York: Random House/Bookworks, 1975.
Tart, C. (Ed.). *Altered states of consciousness*. New York: Wiley, 1969.
Tart, C. (Ed.). *Transpersonal psychologies*. New York: Harper, 1975.
Tulku, T. *Gesture of balance: A guide to awareness, self-healing and meditation*. Berkeley: Dharma Publishing, 1977.

SOURCES OF INFORMATION ON BIOFEEDBACK AND RELATED AREAS

Biofeedback Society of America

The Biofeedback Society of America has been in existence since 1969 and in 1977 changed its name from the Biofeedback Research Society. There are two Society divisions, applied and experimental, and state societies may be recognized as chapters of the national organization.

Membership in the Biofeedback Society is open to professionals interested in the investigation and applications of the biofeedback approach, and in the scientific and professional advancement of biofeedback. Membership in the divisions, experimental and applied, is open to those who satisfy the divisional requirements. Membership in the Society includes a subscription to *Biofeedback and Self-Regulation* (optional to students), the official journal of the Society. Members also receive a subscription to *Biofeedback*, a quarterly newsletter that serves as an informal medium for information exchange for the Society.

The Society regularly fosters an annual scientific meeting emphasizing both basic research and clinical applications. The Society also sponsors a 4-day Biofeedback Workshop for Professionals in the fall of the year. The program aims to cover the general area of applied biofeedback, emphasizing the most current information on the use of biofeedback and its potential in the treatment of psychophysiological problems and related disorders. The practical and clinical uses of biofeedback therapy are demonstrated and its application to psychiatry and general medical practice are discussed in depth by an outstanding faculty engaged in biofeedback research and its current clinical applications. The program includes participants working with instruments in small groups under the guidance of professionals.

A number of publications are available through the Society.

For more information, contact:

Francine Butler, Ph.D., Executive Director
Biofeedback Society of America
University of Colorado Medical Center, C268
4200 East Ninth Avenue
Denver, Colorado 80262
(303) 394-7054

State Societies

Many state societies have been formed and many are still forming. For information regarding any of these, write Francine Butler at the address above.

Related Sources

American Association for the
  Advancement of Tension Control
PO Box 8005
Louisville, Kentucky 40208

International Committee on
  Autogenic Training
Medical Center
5300 Côte des Neiges
Montreal H3T 1Y3
Quebec, Canada
(514) 713-3100

Society for Psychophysiological Research
Stephen W. Porges, Ph.D., Secretary-Treasurer
Department of Psychology
University of Illinois
Champaign, Illinois 61820

BIOFEEDBACK EQUIPMENT MANUFACTURERS AND RELATED INFORMATION

Biofeedback companies, as in any developing industry, are in an exciting growth phase, with a number of companies appearing and disappearing. The ones listed here have been checked as of March 1978. The following section listing biofeedback companies is divided into these parts:

- Those companies that are members of the biofeedback manufacturing association and as a group have worked diligently to improve the quality of biofeedback instrumentation.
- Those additional companies whose instruments we have generally found to be of high quality. This does not imply that the other companies are *not* of high quality, just that we have not tried them.
- Additional companies.
- Other relevant equipment sources that trainees could use for finding home biofeedback devices.
- Sources of cassette tapes relating to biofeedback.
- Sources of films on biofeedback.

Members of the Biofeedback Manufacturing Association

Autogenic Systems Inc.
809 Allston Way
Berkeley, California 94710
(415) 548-6056

Cyborg Company
342 Western Avenue
Boston, Massachusetts 02134
(617) 782-9820

Biofeedback Research Institute
6325 Wilshire Boulevard
Los Angeles, California 90048

Other Companies of High Quality

American Biofeedback Corporation
Hunter Brook Road
Yorktown Heights, New York 10598
(914) 962-4694

Biofeedback Electronics, Inc.
PO Box 1491
Monterey, California 93940
(408) 373-2486

Biofeedback Systems, Inc.
2736 47th Street
Boulder, Colorado 80301
(303) 444-1411

Lafayette Instrument Co.
Box 1279
North 9th Street Road and
    Sagamore Parkway
Lafayette, Indiana 47902
(317) 423-1505

Coulbourn Instruments, Inc.
Box 2551
Lehigh Valley, Pennsylvania 18001
(215) 395-3771

J&J Enterprises
22797 Holgar Court NE
Poulsbo, Washington 98370
(206) 779-3853

Systec, Inc.
500 Locust Street
Lawrence, Kansas 66044
(913) 843-8844

Narco Bio-Systems, Inc.
7651 Airport Boulevard
PO Box 12511
Houston, Texas 77017
(713) 544-7521

Additional Companies

Advanced Electro Labs, Inc.
PO Box 2386
Pomona, California 91766
(714) 624-0393

Advanced Health Systems, Inc.
54 East South Temple
Salt Lake City, Utah 84111
(801) 531-1213

Aleph One Limited
61 Beechwood Avenue
Bottisham, Cambridge CB5 9BG
England

Biocybernetic Institute
1052 Rhode Island
San Francisco, California 94107

Biofeedback International, Inc.
PO Box 38537
Presidio Station
San Francisco, California 94129
(415) 922-4200

Biofeedback Instrument Company
255 West 98th Street
New York, New York 10025
(212) 850-2156

Biofeedback Training Institute
1800 North Highland Avenue
Suite 500
Hollywood, California 90028
(213) 462-1319

BioMedical Instruments
PO Box 248
Warren, Michigan 48090
(313) 756-5070

Bio-My Products
390 Oak Avenue
Carlsbad, California 92008
(714) 729-6345

Coherent Communications
13733 Glen Oaks Boulevard
Sylmar, California 91342
(213) 362-2566

Edmund Scientific Co.
EDSCORP Building
Barrington, New Jersey 08007
(609) 547-3488

Electronic Developments
Unit 37/E Platts Eyot
Lower Sunbury Road
Hampton, Middlesex TW12 2HF
England

Electronic Aids, Inc.
PO Box 125
Kings Park, New York 11754
(516) 269-6868

Enting Instruments and Systems
Vijftig Bunderweg 1
Dorst (n.b.)
Netherlands

Extended Digital Concepts
PO Box 9161
Berkeley, California 94709
(415) 848-5100

Ferrall Instruments
PO Box 1037
Grand Island, Nebraska 68801
(308) 384-1530

G & W Applied Science Laboratories
335 Bear Hill Road
Waltham, Massachusetts 02154
(617) 890-5100

Marietta Apparatus Company
118 Maple Street
Marietta, Ohio 45750
(614) 373-5763

Med Associates, Inc.
Box 47
East Fairfield, Vermont 05448
(802) 827-3848

Medical Device Co.
1555 Bellefontaine Street, N.Dr.
Indianapolis, Indiana 46202

Motion Control Inc.
1005 South 300 West
Salt Lake City, Utah 84101
(801) 364-1958

Neuronics
104 East Oak
Chicago, Illinois 60611
(312) 649-1400

Royer-Anderson
763 La Para Avenue
Palo Alto, California 94306
(415) 493-3330

Self-Control Systems
PO Box 6462
San Diego, California 92106

Somatronics, Inc.
399 Buena Vista East
Suite 323
San Francisco, California 94117
(415) 626-3120

Staodynamics
601 South Bowen
Longmont, Colorado 80501
(303) 772-3531

Stoelting Co.
1350 South Kostner Avenue
Chicago, Illinois 60623

Thought Technology, Ltd.
NDG Postal Station
PO Box 431
Montreal, Quebec H4A 3P8
Canada
(514) 484-0305

World Energy Corporation
Biofeedback Products Division
1555 Lakeside Drive
Oakland, California 94612
(415) 839-6900

Other Relevant Equipment Sources

Bio-Temp Products, Inc.
3266 North Meridian
Suite 705
Indianapolis, Indiana 46209
(317) 924-0111
    (Portable wrist and finger
    temperature bands)

John Chaney Instrument Co.
965 Wells Street
PO Box 72
Lake Geneva, Wisconsin 53417
(414) 248-4449
    (Hand-held thermometers)

Conscious Living Foundation
PO Box 513
Manhattan, Kansas 66502
    (Hand-held thermometers)

Medical Device Corporation
1555 Bellefontaine Street, N.Dr.
Indianapolis, Indiana 46202
    (Temperature-sensitive dots)

Cassette Tapes

Affective House
PO Box 35321
Tulsa, Oklahoma 74135

Biofeedback Computers, Inc.
6218 Brookline Drive
Indianapolis, Indiana 46220
(317) 255-2195

Biofeedback Recordings, Inc.
PO Box 1501
Monterey, California 93940
(408) 373-2486

Biogenic Cassette Tapes
Pain and Health Rehabilitation Center
Route 2, Welsh Coulee
LaCrosse, Wisconsin 54601

Biomonitoring Applications
270 Madison Avenue
Suite 1506
New York, New York 10016

National Book Co.
1019 SW Tenth Avenue
Portland, Oregon 97205

Film Sources

Biofeedback: Yoga of the West
Hartley Productions
Catwalk Road
Cos Cob, Connecticut 06807

Involuntary Control
Wiley Films
605 3rd Avenue
New York, New York

Dialogue on Biofeedback
USDA
Motion Picture Division
Room 1614, South Building
Washington, D.C. 20250

(Film on biofeedback)
Veterans Administration
810 Vermont Avenue, NW
Washington, D.C. 20420

Name Index

Key: Numbers joined by a hyphen (e.g., 1-10) indicate pages of a chapter of which the named person is an author. The other numbers, separated by commas (e.g., 11, 12), indicate pages on which the named person is mentioned or cited.

Aarons, L., 83
Abe, T., 178, 179
Adler, C., 52, 85, 88, 188, 209, 224, 364, 413, 489, 504
Adrian, E. D., 49, 326, 330, 331
Agnew, H. W., 331
Ajzen, I., 201, 202, 203
Akutsu, K., 330
Alexander, A. B., 29
Alexander, F., 7
Allers, R., 382
Allison, T., 347, 358, 359, 360
Amadeo, M., 382
Analiz, J., 542, 562
Anand, B. K., 141
Ancoli, S., 1-4, 6, 141-149, 230, 276, 341-346
Anderson, P., 281, 327
Andersson, S. A., 281, 327
Andrews, J. M., 79, 80, 82
Andrews, L. M., 77
Angers, P., 169, 179
Anthony, M., 494
Armington, J. C., 331
Aserinsky, E., 382
Ashby, W. R., 48
Assagioli, R., 138
Austin, M., 330
Ax, A. F., 513

Babb, M. I., 347
Bacon, J., 25
Baer, P. E., 470
Bagchi, B. K., 141, 300, 330, 331, 333
Bahler, W. W., 347, 359
Baker, L. E., 230, 235, 243, 257
Ballard, P., 105

Balshan, I. D., 415
Bancaud, J., 299
Bancroft, J., 31
Bandura, A., 7
Banquet, J. P., 65, 141, 147
Banuazizi, A., 12
Barber, T. X., 12, 29, 69, 210
Bard, P. B., 327
Barlow, D. H., 78, 107, 287
Barlow, W., 390, 397
Barrick, J. E., 223
Barrington, C.C., 542
Basmajian, J. V., 11, 52, 234, 363, 364, 365, 371-375, 377-378, 398, 456
Batenchuck, C., 12
Beary, J. F., 20
Beatty, J., 6, 11
Beck, A. T., 393
Beck, R., 229, 237-240
Beecher, H. A., 164, 208
Bender, L., 390
Benson, F., 275, 299-312
Benson, H., 11, 13, 14, 18, 19, 20, 21, 33, 37, 59, 97, 98, 100, 172, 178, 427
Berger, H., 280, 326, 330, 331
Bergman, J., 100
Berne, R., 524
Bernhaut, M., 388, 389, 390
Bernstein, D. A., 164, 172, 176, 178, 179, 188, 189, 190, 192, 193, 196, 197
Berntsen, I., 360
Bibring, G. L., 208
Bickford, A. F., 426, 429
Bickford, R., 327
Billingham, J., 179, 542
Bilodeau, F., 169, 179
Birk, L., 6, 7, 10, 38, 250

Bjerner, B., 338
Black, A. H., 12, 69, 524
Blackwood, G. L., 29
Blake, H., 331
Blanchard, E. B., 5, 13, 77-110, 91, 94, 97, 348
Bleecker, E. R., 22, 23, 25, 35, 92, 93, 94, 95, 96
Block, J. D., 515
Bloor, P., 327
Blowers, G. H., 327
Blum, R. H., 299
Blumberger, S. R., 169, 174
Bobroff, A., 394
Bogen, G. M., 167, 176
Bogen, J. E., 167, 176
Booker, H. E., 81, 82, 154
Borkovec, T. D., 164, 172, 176, 178, 179, 188, 189, 190, 192, 193, 196, 197
Bouchard, C., 169, 179
Bouyer, J. J., 347
Bowersox, S., 359
Bradley, P. B., 212
Brady, J. P., 20
Brady, J. V., 11, 14, 33, 496, 500
Bram Amar, P., 195
Brazier, M. A., 327, 392
Brener, J., 12, 13, 14, 15, 16, 53, 69, 524
Brown, B. B., 6, 49, 51, 52, 101, 210, 275, 276, 294, 325, 333
Brown, C., 230, 235, 243
Bruno, L. J. J., 34
Bubnoff, N., 389
Buckhout, R., 202, 205
Budzynski, T., 11, 20, 52, 53, 75, 81, 85, 88, 90, 94, 155, 157, 187, 188, 189,

573

Subject Index